THE NEW WEALTH MANAGEMENT

CFA Institute is the premier association for investment professionals around the world, with over 101,000 members in 134 countries. Since 1963 the organization has developed and administered the renowned Chartered Financial Analyst® Program. With a rich history of leading the investment profession, CFA Institute has set the highest standards in ethics, education, and professional excellence within the global investment community and is the foremost authority on investment profession conduct and practice.

Each book in the CFA Institute Investment Series is geared toward industry practitioners along with graduate-level finance students and covers the most important topics in the industry. The authors of these cutting-edge books are themselves industry professionals and academics and bring their wealth of knowledge and expertise to this series.

THE NEW WEALTH MANAGEMENT

The Financial Advisor's Guide to Managing and Investing Client Assets

Harold Evensky, CFP

Stephen M. Horan, CFA

Thomas R. Robinson, CFA, CFP

WILEY

John Wiley & Sons, Inc.

Published by John Wiley & Sons, Inc., Hoboken, New Jersey.
Published simultaneously in Canada.

For general information on our other products and services or for technical support, please contact our Customer Care Department within the United States at (800) 762-2974, outside the United States at (317) 572-3993 or fax (317) 572-4002.

Wiley also publishes its books in a variety of electronic formats. Some content that appears in print may not be available in electronic formats. For more information about Wiley products, visit our web site at www.wiley.com.

Library of Congress Cataloging-in-Publication Data:

Evensky, Harold.
    The new wealth management : the financial advisor's guide to managing and investing client assets / Harold Evensky, Stephen M. Horan, Thomas R. Robinson.
        p. cm. — (CFA Institute investment series ; 28)
    Rev. ed. of: Wealth management. ©1997.
    Includes bibliographical references and index.
    ISBN 978-0-470-62400-5 (cloth); ISBN 978-1-118-03689-1 (ebk); ISBN 978-1-118-03690-7 (ebk); ISBN 978-1-118-03691-4 (ebk)
        1. Portfolio management. 2. Financial planners. 3. Investment advisors. I. Horan, Stephen Michael. II. Robinson, Thomas R. III. Evensky, Harold. Wealth management. IV. Title.
    HG4529.5.E955 2011
    332.6—dc22   2010053526

Printed in the United States of America

10 9 8 7 6 5 4 3 2 1

Harold:
To all my wonderful associates at E&K, my two amazing co-authors,
and to Deena, who makes it all worthwhile

Stephen:
To Connie and Cayse

Thomas:
To Linda

CONTENTS

ACKNOWLEDGMENTS

We would like to thank the many individuals who played important roles in producing this book.

The CFA Institute Investment Series was developed under the leadership and guidance of Robert R. Johnson, CFA, now senior managing director of CFA Institute. Most of the titles in the series are developed out of the CFA Program curriculum. The CFA Program is a generalist program in investment analysis and portfolio management and emphasizes the highest ethical and professional standards for the investment profession. Over time, the number of CFA Program candidates and CFA Institute members who practice in the private wealth area has increased, calling for additional educational content in this important area. The private wealth content in the CFA Program has increased as well, and this new edition of Harold Evensky's *Wealth Management* is designed to be a practical guide to implementing many of the concepts found in the CFA Program to private wealth practice.

Christopher Wiese managed the process of acquiring the rights to the earlier edition and guided the manuscript through all stages of production. Tina Sapsara kept the authors on task and edited the manuscripts to a uniform style. We also appreciate Deena Katz adding her expertise for our capstone chapter.

FOREWORD

The New Wealth Management is a new edition of the book *Wealth Management*, originally written by Harold Evensky. Fourteen years may be a long time to wait between editions, but the new edition is more of an overhaul than a mere update. Two co-authors have also been added to the mix, Stephen Horan and Thomas Robinson; both are accomplished authors in their own right. The current book builds on the strong foundation of the earlier edition while encapsulating the many advances and examples of rethinking that have been accomplished during the intervening time.

CFA Institute has participated in the financial revolution in many of its publications. *The New Wealth Management* is a part of the CFA Institute Investment Series. Most readers are probably familiar with Stephen Horan, because he has been the manager of the education and private wealth management content for the series. He is a professor, frequently published author, and the editor of the CFA Institute book *Private Wealth: Wealth Management in Practice*. He brings extensive knowledge and an ability to implement it. Thomas Robinson is managing director of the CFA Institute Education Division. He is also a regularly published author in the fields of accounting and financial planning, as well as an accomplished professor. He has had extensive speaking and consulting experience relating to the issues that come up in this book. CFA Institute is fortunate to have these two very active contributors who are so well-versed in the issues that financial practitioners face.

The combination of the renowned Harold Evensky with CFA Institute support makes for a great book. The writers are not only excellent expositors, but also at the forefront of the field. In this book, they include the latest advancements but still make the book practical for the financial advisor. Advisors need to know not only the latest techniques, but also how to communicate with their clients.

Of course, I am partial to some of the discoveries that I have been involved in. The first edition certainly took the holistic approach to investing, in which each individual client's specific circumstances are considered and asset allocation portfolios are customized to the client's needs. But now we have a life-cycle approach to use to determine the appropriate asset allocation for each individual. The approach makes use of a "life balance sheet" that uses human capital theory to consider both the net employment capital and the financial assets as two separate but related sources to fund the lifetime retirement and other expenditure needs.

Now that the life-cycle approach is more developed, we can start with the readily valuable data from a family's earnings, financial wealth, age, cash flow needs, retirement plans, and so on. These data are then supplemented with information about the nature of the client's employment, risk questionnaires, and capital market assumptions. The theoretical framework of the life cycle approach was barely available at the time the initial edition was published. Now, we really can take a holistic approach to investing that considers not only the nature of capital markets, but also the client's circumstances and needs, as well as the personality characteristics that make each client unique.

The importance of the asset allocation decision has also been further clarified in the intervening time between the editions. No longer do we merely think that asset allocation policy explains more than 90 percent of performance. We know now that asset allocation policy usually explains 100 percent of the typical *return level* because most active management does not actually add any alpha. This is particularly true on average, by definition, because in aggregate all money managed can only sum to a broad market return.

The differences among various manager returns are also only partially explained by asset allocation policy manager differences. Roughly half of the differences in the variation of returns among money managers comes from asset allocation policy differences, whereas the remaining half of the variation of returns among managers is explained by differences in asset allocation timing, security selection, and fees.

Even the time-series variation of returns has three parts: participation in the overall market movement (instead of just holding cash), each portfolio manager's asset allocation policy differences from the overall market or peer group, and the variation in returns caused by the active management of each portfolio manager's specific timing, security selection, and fee level. It is the first two parts that explain about 90 percent of the variation in time-series returns of a typical portfolio. But the major part of portfolio variation comes from the market movement, in which most funds participate. Most of us performed well in the bull market of 2009, whereas most of us performed poorly in the bear market of 2008.

I have only touched on a few of the ideas in the book. I hope, though, that this Foreword has whetted your appetite for all the ideas that are inside. These include discussions on risk and taxes, as well as such implementation topics as goal setting, client education, and manager selection. Harold Evensky, Stephen Horan, and Thomas Robinson have done a great service for the financial advisor.

Roger Ibbotson
Chairman and CIO, Zebra Capital Management
Professor in Practice, Yale School of Management

PREFACE

Short-term clients look for gurus. Long-term clients want sages. There are no gurus.
—Harold Evensky

Welcome to *The New Wealth Management*. What you are about to read is a blend of a textbook, an investment process road map, lessons, opinions (lots of opinions), and recommendations based on the experience of practitioners and recent research.

It is easy for a professional, interested in portfolio or asset management, to find and accumulate a library appropriate to the subject (references to the best will be provided throughout this book). There is a continuing stream of books published on the evaluation, selection, and management of individual stocks and bonds. However, for the holistic practitioner managing private wealth and responsible for orchestrating a portfolio of multiple managers, the selection is limited. The only guidance has been to attend professional conferences and network with like-minded professionals. *The New Wealth Management*, first published as *Wealth Management* in 1997, was written to address this need. This edition captures the recent advances and thinking that have evolved since the first edition. And there has been quite a bit.

Perhaps a brief profile of the practitioners envisioned as the audience for this book will assist you in determining if this book is for you.

- Those whose clients are individuals, pensions, or trusts with significant investable assets whose primary goal is to earn reasonable returns for the risk they are prepared to take.
- Those who advise clients on the development and implementation of an investment policy.
- Those who assist clients in the selection of multiple managers, exchange-traded funds (ETFs), or mutual funds.
- Those who monitor and manage multiple asset class investments for client portfolios.
- Those who call themselves financial planners or provide financial planning services.

If you are involved in advising clients regarding investing or managing multiple asset class portfolios for clients, this book has been written for you even if your primary profession is as a comprehensive financial planner, investment advisor, accountant, insurance specialist, securities broker, trustee, or lawyer.

WEALTH MANAGERS AND MONEY MANAGERS

One of the most confusing issues for the public (and many professionals) is distinguishing between the profession of money management oriented toward managing assets for institutions or others that may have already determined an appropriate asset allocation and the profession of wealth management geared toward individuals who need assistance in both asset allocation and asset selection. In order to proceed without further semantic confusion, we will define these terms as they are used in this book.

Wealth managers bear little resemblance to money managers for institutions, such as mutual funds or pension funds. Wealth management is more comprehensive, customized, and complex. Appreciating the differences is particularly important for practitioners, especially for those who hope to transition their careers from an institutional setting.

Exhibit P.1 summarizes some of the more striking differences. Money managers are professionals responsible for making decisions regarding the selection of individual bonds and stocks for a portfolio. The money manager offers the client an expertise, a philosophy, and a style of management.

EXHIBIT P.1   Wealth Management versus Money Management

	Wealth Management	Money Management
Scope	Comprehensive	Focused
	Life balance sheet	Financial assets
Management approach	Customized	Standardized
	Orientation toward client goals	Orientation toward relative returns
	After-tax wealth accumulation	Periodic pretax returns
Client profile	Complexity of the individual	Few constraints
	Diversity of client goals	Homogeneous
	Limited investment sophistication	High investment sophistication
	Psychological/behavioral profile	Psychology neutral
Investment constraints	Dynamic	Static
	Finite or multistage	Infinite
	Tax aware	Tax neutral

Wealth management is more comprehensive because the scope of advisement extends far beyond the management of a fixed sum of financial assets. The wealth manager incorporates a client's implied assets, such as expected retirement benefits and the value and character of the earnings stream, into the analysis. The portfolios of a government employee and an investment banker will probably look very different. Moreover, the nature of their financial goals (such as retirement, a vacation home, or travel) is likely to differ. These elements combine to form what can be thought of as a life balance sheet that calls for unique solutions.

How then does the customization required of the wealth manager differ from that of the money manager? The difference relates not to the resources or the demographics of the clients but rather the differences in their goals. Wealth management clients' goals vary over a wide spectrum, whereas money manager clients' goals typically do not. If money managers present themselves to the market as experts in the investment of large-cap domestic equities, they may well define their goal as providing a risk-adjusted return superior to the S&P 500 index. Hence, all investors selecting that money manager should have, by definition, the same goal at least with respect to their use of that manager.

Money managers inform the public of their expertise and philosophy and invite investors to trust them with investment dollars. It is the investor's responsibility to determine how much of the portfolio to allocate to a particular asset class (e.g., intermediate-term corporate bonds) and the money manager's responsibility to do a competent job of managing the funds in that class.

For example, the money manager might have expertise in intermediate-term corporate bond management and a philosophy that value can be added by the manager's unique analytical ability to discover value through the analysis of underlying but unappreciated credit qualities. Money managers' focus is on the asset class of their expertise. Their efforts are devoted to the process of successfully implementing their philosophy. In the case of the corporate bond manager, it may be through a detailed study of bond indentures, corporate earnings statements, and corporate earnings prospects.

The practice of a money manager is focused and institutional. Money managers are focused on the implementation of their philosophy, called an investment mandate. Their goal is to maximize return. They are an institution in that they expect to be measured against other institutional managers in their asset class. The money manager is also more likely to be managing assets for other institutions, whereas the wealth manager is usually managing wealth for individuals.

Much of the confusion in separating these two professions results from the fact that many practitioners perform elements of both roles (e.g., asset allocation and individual security selection). Nevertheless, each is a separate responsibility and requires different areas and levels of expertise.

As a result, the wealth management approach is entirely different. It requires customized solutions to address clients' unique needs. The approach also requires a change in mind-set. Mutual funds compete for business by advertising their return—usually relative to competitors or an index. Investors may chase these historical returns when left to their own devices. Ironically, this is not what individual investors are most concerned about. Their primary concern is their ability to accumulate, after taxes, adequate assets to meet their financial goals. Achieving this requires a unique solution for each client.

Wealth managers address the complexity of individuals with diverse goals and often limited investment sophistication. They understand that individuals tend to react to risk in ways that traditional institutional models fail to recognize. The bottom line is that the client defines the practice, and dealing with individuals requires a very different analysis than dealing with a pension fund investment committee.

After all, individuals are unique. Their life circumstances and tolerance for risk tend to change over time. It's a rare individual who does not reevaluate his or her appetite for risk after a portfolio drops in value by 30 percent. Unlike a mutual fund or pension fund with an infinite time horizon, individuals and families have multiple time horizons. Retirement planning, for example, can be divided into two distinct phases of accumulation and distribution.

It is also important to incorporate the influence of taxes. Taxes affect not only the types of assets that might be appropriate for clients but also the types of accounts or taxable entities that are best used.

As a fundamentally unique profession, wealth management requires a broad skill set of the practitioner.

WEALTH MANAGERS AND ASSET MANAGERS

These are new marketing titles that have blossomed as a result of the media hype associated with the popularization of the research of Brinson, Hood, and Beebower and others regarding the importance of asset class diversification. Along with the proliferation of inexpensive optimizers and packaged model portfolios, the marketing appeal of becoming an asset manager has been overwhelming for many practitioners. In theory, an asset manager differs from a money manager in that the former is focused on multiple asset class portfolios, whereas the latter concentrates on individual securities in a single asset class.

Unfortunately, in reality, many self-proclaimed asset managers are neither competent to implement recommendations based on optimizers nor trained to intelligently evaluate and select from the multitude of predesigned models offered to practitioners by the middleman packagers. Many self-proclaimed asset managers are not professionally educated to adequately integrate the unique needs of the client with the portfolio design. The title "asset manager" suggests a professional, but it may mask an untrained salesperson.

A typical recruiting ad touts "By automating this tedious and recurring process, advisors can spend less time on back-office tasks and more time building their businesses" or "Complete Turnkey System Allows Your Brokers to Be Totally Dedicated to Marketing and Sales!" Practitioners falling into this classification should either read further and strive to become wealth managers or return to the field of their primary expertise.

WEALTH MANAGER—A NEW PROFESSION

Most professionals whose practices have evolved into what we call "wealth management" or "private wealth management" are experienced financial planners or investment advisors focused on serving individuals.

The wealth manager's efforts are devoted to assisting clients in achieving life goals through the proper management of their financial resources. While the money manager may not necessarily know if a client is male or female, single or married, a doctor, lawyer, or candlestick maker, the wealth manager must know all of this, as well as the client's dreams, goals, and fears. The wealth manager designs a client-specific plan. In doing so, the wealth manager is concerned with data gathering, goal setting, identification of financial (and nonfinancial) issues, preparation of alternatives, recommendations, implementation, and periodic reviews and revisions of the client's plan.

The practice of the wealth manager is holistic and individually customized. It is holistic because there is very little about the client's global fiscal life that is not important information. It is customized because success is measured not by performance relative to other managers (the wealth manager does not try to maximize returns) but rather by the client's success in meeting life goals.

INVESTMENT PLANNING TODAY

Client needs come in an almost endless array of combinations. There is no generic client for the wealth manager. Much of the popular literature offers two forms of modeling guidance for investors—multiple-choice and aged-based investing. Both are carried over from the institutional concept of a model portfolio.

A major function of the wealth manager is to advise clients on the allocation of their investments across different asset classes and across different taxable entities. In order to place the contents of this book in perspective, consider the simplistic advice that is currently proffered to the investing public.

Multiple-Choice Investing

One form of asset allocation advice is based on scoring the results of a simple investor questionnaire. The process may be so basic that investors simply have to select, from among a series of descriptions, the single phrase that most closely represents their goal. The following is an example from a simple questionnaire:

- My objective is to have minimal downside risk.
- My objective is long-term growth of capital and an income stream.

Other more sophisticated questionnaires may have from 5 to 25 questions. The following are questions taken from a nine-question quiz offered by a multiple-fund company:

- I have funds equal to at least six months of my pay that I can draw upon in case of an emergency. "Yes" scores 1 point; "No" scores 0.
- Does the following statement accurately describe one of your views about investing? "The only way to get ahead is to take some risks." "Yes" scores 1 point; "No" scores 0.

All too often these multiple-choice questions are a perfunctory attempt to satisfy an advisor's legal requirement to "know your client." That said, questionnaires can be a useful tool to collect data about a client's fiscal life and even personality type that may provide insights regarding his or her risk tolerance. Even so, simplistic questionnaires fall short of being able to provide a reliable, replicable process on which to base an investor's asset allocation.

Age-Based Investing

An increasingly popular offering is to relate the portfolio allocation decision to the client's stage of life: age-based investing. As we will frequently remind the reader, this is a useful concept for a sociologist but dangerous if applied to the unique needs of individual clients. The age-based concept tends to institutionalize the belief that age is the paramount, if not the sole, criterion to be considered when designing an investment portfolio.

One of the most popular formulas, designed to provide a stage-of-life allocation:

$$\text{Investment in Stocks} = 100 - \text{Current Age of Investor}$$

$$\text{Investment in Bonds} = \text{Balance of Investor's Assets}$$

This is certainly an easy technique:

Age	Stock	Bonds
40	60%	40%
55	45	55
80	20	80

In fact, this is such an easy rule of thumb that it has become one of the most often-quoted suggestions in the popular media and was once equated with the concept of life-cycle investing. Since then, the field of life-cycle investing has matured to take a more holistic view of the client, incorporating an understanding of the client's earning potential, investment goals, risk tolerances, and risk exposures.

Unfortunately, the popular press is not the only supporter of age as the simplistic default solution. The examples that follow, from a college investment text, reflect a similar academic institutionalization of age as the major portfolio allocation criterion. Although the text refers to investors as "preferring" and "favoring" or being "principally concerned with" certain goals, most readers are likely to conclude that an investor's age should be the primary determinant of portfolio allocations.

Middle-aged clients (middle 40s) are seen as transitioning their portfolios to higher-quality securities, including "low-risk growth and income, preferred stocks, convertibles, high-grade bonds, and mutual funds."

Investors moving into their retirement age are described as having portfolios that are "*highly conservative* [emphasis in original], consisting of low-risk income stock, high-yielding government bonds, quality corporate bonds, bank certificates of deposit (CDs), and other money market investments."

We will reserve for later a discussion about the wealth manager's concepts of "higher-quality," "low-risk," and "conservative." They differ significantly from the usage here. Suffice it to say, these canned approaches for planning the financial welfare of our clients are woefully inadequate.

The following example of two demographically and sociologically similar families will set the stage for the balance of the book and place in perspective the positive difference professional guidance can make for our clients.

EXAMPLE P.1   The Browns and the Boones

The Browns, husband and wife, live in Denver, are working professionals, are both 57 years old, are in good health, and expect to retire together when they reach 62. Our other married couple, the Boones, also live in Denver, are working professionals, are 57 years old, are in good health, and expect to retire together when they reach 62. Both couples consider themselves moderately conservative. Neither the Browns nor the Boones have any desire to leave an estate.

With this information about demographically twin couples, let's see how successfully multiple-choice and life-cycle solutions would serve the Browns and the Boones.

First, we must determine the recommended investment allocations. For this example, we have used the published recommendations of a large investment advisory firm, a large accounting firm, and a major trust company, along with the recommendation determined by the "100" formula for clients meeting the profile of the Browns and Boones. Exhibit P.2 summarizes these recommendations.

EXHIBIT P.2 Asset Allocation Recommendations for the Browns and the Boones, Multiple-Choice and Age-Based Models

	Stocks	Bonds
Investment advisory firm	30%	70%
Large accounting firm	80	20
Trust company	50	50
100 − Age	43	57

Note that the recommendations are significantly different between sources but are the same for the Browns and the Boones, as they have similar ages and planned retirement dates.

Now envision personal circumstances that would lead a wealth manager to recommend radically different allocations for the Browns and the Boones. Mr. Brown has a defined-benefit pension, while his wife and the Boones have defined-contribution plans. Mrs. Boone is very comfortable with risk, but her husband is a bit more cautious, as are the Browns. Their goals may be subject to differing inflation rates: the Browns plan to retire to a small house in a planned retirement community, while the Boones want to travel extensively. Standardized solutions fail miserably to provide useful guidance for such variations. Multiple-choice solutions are simplistic and unprofessional, making them a poor way to plan for a client's future. As noted earlier, age-based investing, as a concept, may work well for a sociologist dealing with large populations. However, translated to the micro level of individual clients, it results in families consisting of 2.3 children and 1.8 parents.

WHAT COMES NEXT

The balance of *The New Wealth Management* discusses issues of importance to the wealth manager. The depth and nature of coverage of these issues will vary significantly.

Some areas assume an existing familiarity with the subject and only highlight specific issues (e.g., client goals and constraints). Other discussions assume a familiarity but also assume that a review may be helpful (e.g., the mathematics of investing). When there are existing references readily available on the subject, *The New Wealth Management* provides an overview and will guide you to appropriate references (e.g., development of an investment policy). Some issues are well covered by other texts; however, there are particular aspects that deserve special attention. In these instances, in addition to referencing other work, *The New Wealth Management* focuses on these special issues (e.g., asset allocation and sensitivity analysis). For issues that are not covered by traditional texts, this book covers the subject in more depth (e.g., behavioral finance). In all areas, we have provided additional resources so that you may read further on a subject you find of interest.

We have attended innumerable professional meetings and read uncounted articles and books on subjects related to the practice of wealth management. All too often, we've been left with the thought "That's nice; now what do I do with it?" If there has been one overriding goal in the preparation of this book, it has been to avoid leaving you, the reader, with that thought. *The New Wealth Management* provides immediate and practical assistance for the practitioner. It includes far more than theory and philosophy. At the practice management level, we include detailed examples of risk tolerance questionnaires and data gathering guides. For use in investment implementation and management, we include specific recommendations for fund selection criteria and asset class rebalancing criteria. Throughout are examples and vignettes that practitioners should find helpful in client presentations and meetings. At a professional level, *The New Wealth Management* includes many recommendations regarding what we consider investment myths (e.g., tax management, income portfolios, and intuitive optimization). Our conclusions may contradict the strong convictions of many readers, but we don't intend to pick a fight. You may take our recommendations for what they are worth to you. The purpose is to assist the reader in developing a clear philosophy and process that will work in your practice.

As you can see, *The New Wealth Management* is eclectic. It is neither an academic textbook nor a comprehensive practitioner manual. It is some of both, and more. It most closely resembles a series of essays on the most important issues for a wealth manager. These essays are integrated, by general subject matter, into a series of chapters. The chapters generally follow the wealth management process. Our goal is to assist the reader in becoming a better and more profitable (emotionally and financially) wealth manager. So, make the book work for you. Skip, jump, or plow straight on through; there are no rules, only what works for you.

CHAPTER 1

THE WEALTH MANAGEMENT PROCESS

The responsibility of advisors revolves around both helping families to keep doing the "right" thing and providing them with as much comfort as possible in doing so.
—Jean Brunel

We discussed in the Preface that wealth management geared toward individuals is fundamentally different from money management for institutions. Money managers are focused on the portfolio, whereas wealth managers are focused on the client; therefore, wealth management is a more comprehensive, customized, and complex approach that captures a broad array of issues and interactions that asset managers can often safely ignore. Exhibit 1.1 presents a series of important elements of the wealth management investment process. This chapter provides an overview of that process and is a road map for the rest of this book, which establishes a framework for an effective wealth management practice. We provide a brief introduction of these ideas in this chapter to give an overall perspective, and leave more detailed treatment for the relevant chapters that follow.

The wealth management investment process can be organized into four general, interrelated categories.

1. *Client relationship.* The start of any wealth management process is establishing a solid client relationship built on communication, education, and trust. These elements are represented in the bottom-left part of Exhibit 1.1.
2. *Client profile.* As alluded to earlier, understanding your client in a private wealth management context is complex and based on many factors, some of which are represented by the parallelograms across the top of the chart.
3. *Wealth management investment policy.* Using the relationship and profile factors as inputs, developing a wealth management investment policy is at the heart of the wealth management process.
4. *Portfolio management, monitoring, and market review.* Represented by the systems to the right, implementation, monitoring, and review processes are iterative in nature. That is, they are recurring processes that rely on ever-changing information—such as changes in performance, client circumstances, and market conditions. Many behavioral tendencies exhibit themselves in this part of the process, especially in response to volatile market conditions.

EXHIBIT 1.1   The Wealth Management Investment Process

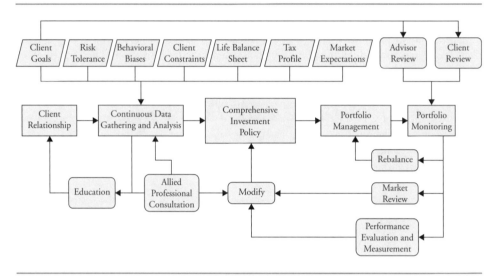

It is important to recognize that this process is independent of a client's wealth level. Although the relevant issues and optimal solutions are often related to net worth (e.g., the use of trusts, the management of estate taxes, philanthropy), the fundamental process remains unchanged.

THE CLIENT RELATIONSHIP

Because everything is client driven, developing a strong relationship with the client is critical to gathering the appropriate data and helping the client understand what the plan is intended to accomplish. Let's begin on the left side at the bottom-left section of Exhibit 1.1. You may have already noticed from the schematic that the overall wealth management investment process is recursive and ongoing. Developing a client relationship is also iterative, because the wealth manager is continually collecting data from the client and working with other allied professionals, such as attorneys and accountants. The wealth manager uses this information to educate the client about the process in general, possible investment alternatives, and the purpose of chosen investment strategies.

Education is important for developing a strong relationship and ensuring that the advisor and client are speaking the same language. For example, does the client understand what the advisor means when the advisor discusses the concept of risk? Education is performed in cooperation with other investment professionals involved in the client's financial affairs. Expert professional consultation requires effective and active collaboration among the advisory team members. Typically, the catalyst for this collaboration is the wealth manager, and it requires communication and interpersonal skills. It also involves incorporating accountability into the process, which we discuss more fully later.

The educational process is tailored to the individual, evolves over time, and adapts to a client's changing levels of familiarity and comfort. For example, as a client becomes more familiar with different asset classes and notions of risks, the wealth manager may introduce and suggest different investment strategies that might have been avoided earlier in the relationship because their complexity might have potentially compromised the rapport between advisor and client. We discuss client education more thoroughly in Chapter 6.

There are as many data-gathering and educational techniques as there are wealth managers. However, successfully building the relationship depends, in part, on understanding the unique characteristics of each individual. Some clients may be reserved, withholding valuable information from their advisors. Other clients, such as successful self-made entrepreneurs, may have little tolerance for exchanging information and want to jump directly to the implementation stage of an investment strategy. Many people (investors and noninvestors alike) exhibit behavioral biases that shape the way they approach decisions and react to investment outcomes. A deft wealth manager identifies these traits and biases and develops tactics to address them. We address these techniques in Chapter 4.

THE CLIENT PROFILE

Determining the client's profile is a detailed endeavor and is the area in which the differences between private wealth management and institutional investment management are most pronounced. The parallelograms across the top of Exhibit 1.1 list some of the primary elements of a client profile.

Client Goals

An investment strategy starts with identifying an investor's goals. Asset managers often think of client goals in terms of return requirements, which can come in many forms. They may be expressed as nominal returns or real returns. They may also be expressed in absolute terms or relative to a predetermined benchmark, such as a market index. In any case, goals and objectives must be consistent with an investor's risk tolerance. That is, an investment objective or agreed-upon investment goal should not require more risk than an investor can reasonably bear. For example, a 10 percent real return investment objective is not congruent with a moderately conservative risk tolerance.

In a wealth management context, a client's goals can be broader than simply identifying return requirements. They can include planning for wealth transfers; managing risks (e.g., property, longevity); managing family dynamics; and preparing for charitable donations. They do not stand in isolation, but are related to each other, forming part of an integrated whole. Moreover, clients tend to express their goals not in quantitative terms (like percentage return) but in qualitative terms. They often wish to maintain their current standard of living through retirement, pay for a child's college education, or leave some kind of legacy after their passing. The wealth manager's job is to help clients quantify these goals with time and dollar specificity and to prioritize them.

Risk Tolerance

Many methods exist for determining a client's risk tolerance, from the objective to the subjective. Wealth managers often review past investment behavior. Many wealth managers refine their understanding with questionnaires and interviews, while others form opinions based on their holistic experience with the client and an understanding of the client's lifestyles and habits. In any case, although risk tolerance commonly refers to an investor's emotional tolerance for volatility or suffering a loss, it is also important to understand a client's risk capacity (i.e., the financial capacity to withstand market losses).[1] They need not be the same. When an investor's risk tolerance exceeds his or her risk capacity, the lower risk capacity should prevail and the wealth manager needs to educate the client on that client's financial capacity to withstand losses. If risk capacity exceeds risk tolerance, resolution is also needed. When market losses exceed a client's risk tolerance level, a nervous client is likely to bail out of the market independent of his or her risk capacity. As a result, the decision should generally be resolved in favor of the more conservative risk tolerance. This discrepancy is illustrated in Exhibit 1.2. We discuss a client's risk tolerance more fully in Chapters 4 and 5.

EXHIBIT 1.2   Risk Tolerance versus Risk Capacity

	Risk Capacity	
Risk Tolerance	*Below Average*	*Above Average*
Below Average	Below-average risk tolerance	Resolution needed
Above Average	Resolution needed	Above-average risk tolerance

Source: Adapted from John L. Maginn, Donald L. Tuttle, Dennis W. McLeavey, and Jerald E. Pinto, "The Portfolio Management Process and the Investment Policy Statement," and James W. Bronson, Matthew H. Scanlan, and Jan R. Squires, "Managing Individual Investor Portfolios," both in *Managing Investment Portfolios*, 3rd edition (Hoboken, NJ: John Wiley & Sons, 2007): 12, 36–38.

Behavioral Biases

Behavioral biases also affect the way investors approach investment decisions and experience outcomes. Standard finance theory suggests investors prefer certain gains to uncertain gains, all else being equal. In other words, investors are risk-averse, which is borne out empirically. However, when it comes to losses, experiments suggest that most people prefer uncertain losses to certain losses. For example, when individuals are presented with the choice of losing $500 for certain or going double-or-nothing (i.e., losing either nothing or $1,000) with equal probabilities, most go double-or-nothing. This phenomenon is called loss aversion—investors are reluctant to take risk for gain but will take risk to avoid loss. It is a behavioral bias that affects investors' reactions to risk and hence can affect asset allocation. It can manifest itself as the negative emotional impact of realizing an investment loss, thereby making it difficult for an investor to cut losses. We discuss the loss aversion phenomenon and the psychology of risk more fully in Chapter 4.

Client Constraints

Constraints establish the parameters within which the wealth manager must work. They can be categorized into time horizon, priority, liquidity requirements, legal considerations, taxes, and unique circumstances. Here, too, wealth management presents unique challenges. Private clients typically have multistage investment horizons. They may, for example, have a period of anticipated wealth accumulation, concurrent with or followed by a series of large cash needs

---

[1]In other contexts, risk tolerance is understood as the *willingness* to accept risk, and risk capacity as the *ability* to accept risk.

(e.g., funding college education or starting a business), followed by a retirement phase. Some clients may also wish to transfer wealth after death to subsequent generations or charity that extends the time horizon further. Although the succession of these stages may result in a nearly infinite time horizon, it should not be treated as a generic infinite time horizon, because the intermittent stages are significant. A schedule of anticipated funding requirements will help the wealth manager design a plan to meet interim liquidity needs without interrupting the balance of the portfolio.

Legal considerations are potentially vast. Clients with plans to transfer wealth through an estate plan or charitable giving may encounter complex legal issues around estate taxes, trusts, and perhaps establishing endowments. While the wealth manager must be familiar with the tax and legal issues of these different strategies, this is an area for collaboration and coordination with other professionals, such as attorneys or accountants. Effective coordination ensures that achieving goals in one part of the overall wealth management plan does not unduly infringe on other parts of the plan.

Potential client-specific circumstances are many and varied—ranging from managing concentrated stock positions that either are illiquid or have very low cost basis to managing family dynamics. Although it may not fit everything neatly into standard categories, an effective plan incorporates these unique circumstances. Chapter 3 discusses client constraints in more detail.

Life Balance Sheet

No chief executive officer (CEO) can effectively run a business without understanding its financial position. Similarly, wealth managers need a framework to assess their clients' overall financial status. A "life balance sheet" is one such framework that provides a comprehensive accounting of a client's assets, liabilities, and net worth.

The left side of the balance sheet lists a client's assets. It certainly includes traditional financial assets, such as stocks, bonds, alternative assets, and the like. The listing of assets would also include tangible assets such as real estate, gold, and collectibles. (We discuss how to treat a client's primary residence more fully later.) The left side of the balance sheet must necessarily include implied assets, as well. Implied assets are nonliquid assets, often nontradable, that nonetheless accrue value to the client. Human capital, for example (sometimes called net employment capital), represents the present value of the investor's expected earnings stream. (Again, more on this in a later chapter.) Similarly, expected pension benefits represent implied assets that can be valued in present value terms based on expected cash flows.

Liabilities on the right-hand side of the balance sheet can be viewed similarly. Mortgages, car loans, and other debt secured by tangible property are explicit liabilities to be considered in weighing one's assets against one's liabilities. But investors' implied liabilities are determined by their investment goals. For example, a client wishing to maintain a certain standard of living through retirement is expressing an implied liability to be funded by the assets on the left side of the balance sheet. Aspirations to fund a child's college education, purchase a vacation home, start a business, or fulfill a charitable bequest represent implied liabilities in a similar fashion.

Exhibit 1.3 presents a simple life balance sheet with a few explicit and implied assets as well as implied liabilities. In addition to the traditional investment portfolio, assets include the value of the investor's personal residence, holdings of company stock, and company stock options. In this example, assets total $2.8 million. Liabilities include the capitalized expenses associated with funding children's college education and retirement in present value terms. In this case, liabilities total $1.8 million, which represents the amount of capital necessary to fund these core requirements. Therefore, this amount is sometimes referred to as "core capital." These figures imply that assets are sufficient to meet these core obligations, leaving $1 million of excess capital, or discretionary wealth. Investors with insufficient assets to meet core capital needs must accumulate more assets, reduce the obligations they wish to fund, or risk leaving these needs unsatisfied.

EXHIBIT 1.3   Hypothetical Example of a Life Balance Sheet

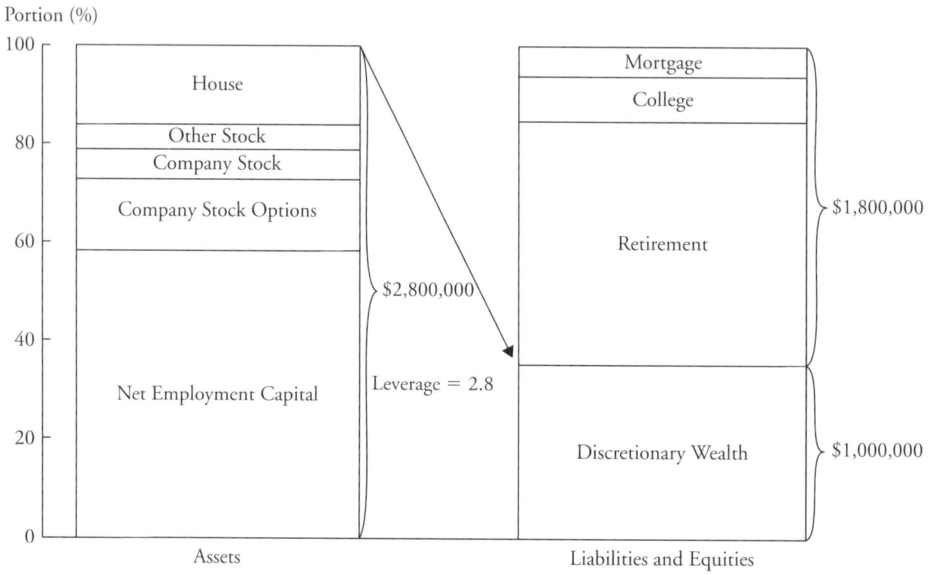

Source: Adapted from Wilcox, Horvitz, and diBartolomeo (2006, 18).

An alternative, and more traditional, approach is to prepare a balance sheet without the implied assets and liabilities. In this case a separate analysis is performed to determine future cash needs such as college and retirement and to determine how much additional periodic investment is needed such that when combined with the client's current portfolio there are sufficient future funds to meet cash needs. In either case the wealth manager has information to determine whether the current investment plan and assets are sufficient to meet future objectives.

As you can see from this example, investors' human capital can represent the bulk of their assets. The present value of their expected earnings stream can exceed the value of their financial assets by quite a bit. This situation is common for young investors who have many years in the workforce ahead of them, but have yet to accumulate a large amount of financial capital. Typically, financial capital and human capital follow opposite patterns over one's lifetime, with financial capital replacing human capital over time as shown in Exhibit 1.4. The value of human capital relies heavily on its nature, depending not only on an investor's current and expected wages, but also on the volatility of the earnings stream. For example, a tenured university professor faces far less human capital risk than an investment banker does.

EXHIBIT 1.4   Stylistic Depiction of Financial Capital and Human Capital

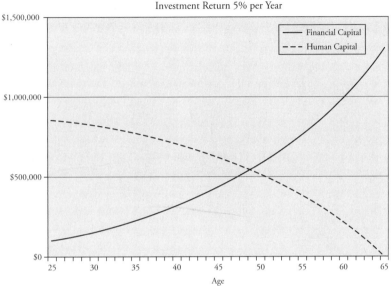

Age 25, Income $50,000, Income Increases with Inflation, Real Discount Rate for
Future Income and Mortality 5% Initial Protfolio Amount $100,000; Real
Investment Return 5% per Year

Tax Profile

The intersection of taxes and investments is one of the most daunting of challenges for the wealth manager. Even determining an investor's marginal tax rate is complicated by varying tax brackets, alternative tax structures, phaseouts, taxation of retirement benefits, and more. Similarly, a seemingly simple task of determining an investor's current asset allocation is complicated by the notion that assets held in tax-deferred accounts have a different after-tax value than those held in taxable accounts. Moreover, a portfolio's tax drag is jointly determined by its asset class composition, the types of accounts, and the level of taxable turnover.

There are also opportunities to optimize a client's after-tax returns by placing certain types of assets into certain types of accounts—a practice called "asset location" (not to be confused with asset allocation). For example, it is often beneficial to hold bonds in tax-deferred accounts and to hold equity (particularly if it is passively managed) in taxable accounts.

Many high-net-worth individuals have large holdings in low-cost-basis stock. These positions may have been handed down from previous generations, accrued from executive stock options, or secured through a public stock offering of an entrepreneur's business. Various strategies for managing these low-basis positions exist, and the best choice depends heavily on the nature of the position and the specific circumstances.

The world of estate taxes adds another layer of complexity to the wealth management process. Trust structures are often useful ways to achieve wealth transfer goals. Wealth managers are typically not estate planners, but a familiarity with estate planning issues allows the wealth manager to work with estate planners and accountants to develop and implement a solid estate plan. The situation becomes even more complex when a client or family has multijurisdictional accounts or residences. We discuss wealth management in the taxable environment fully in Chapter 11.

Market Expectations

The astute reader may notice that capital market expectations for the macroeconomy and various asset classes are not part of a client's profile. Rather, they are determined outside and independent of the client's unique circumstances, and in that sense deserve to be categorized separately. Although this is certainly true, establishing expectations of the capital markets is an important input to establishing investment policy.

WEALTH MANAGEMENT INVESTMENT POLICY

Once a wealth manager establishes a client's profile and capital market expectations, the wealth manager's next task is to develop an investment policy statement (IPS). The IPS serves as the governing document for all investment decision making. It sets out the investment objectives (risk and return) and the constraints (liquidity, time horizon, tax considerations, legal and regulatory factors, and unique circumstances) for managing the portfolio. Some wealth managers include the planned asset allocation in the IPS, as well. Exhibit 1.5 presents an outline for a typical investment policy statement.

EXHIBIT 1.5   Investment Policy Statement

___

   a. Brief client description
   b. Client goals
   c. Investment objectives
       i. Return objective
      ii. Risk objective
   d. Investment constraints
       i. Time horizon
      ii. Tax considerations
     iii. Liquidity needs (e.g., cash flow management)
     iv. Legal and regulatory concerns
      v. Unique circumstances
   e. Strategic asset allocation
       i. Asset class constraints
      ii. Investment constraints (e.g., margin restrictions)
     iii. Investment strategies
     iv. Investment styles
   f. Implementation, monitoring, and review
       i. Responsibilities of client, manager, custodian, and other parties involved
      ii. Performance measures, evaluation, and benchmarks
     iii. Review schedule
     iv. Rebalancing guidelines

Investment risk management should be a focus of attention for the wealth manager. The first step, of course, is identifying the series of risk exposures. Clients with little excess capital or discretionary wealth, as described in the previous section, typically face longevity risk. That is the risk that their assets will be insufficient to fund their retirement needs due to unexpectedly poor investment performance, inflation erosion, and/or an unexpectedly long life span. Yes, living too long is a risk, but it can be managed in a number of ways, including the use of immediate annuities. Alternatively, one may not live long enough to convert one's human capital into financial capital and therefore face disability and mortality risk (the risk of dying too soon). The concentration of assets allocated toward human capital in the life balance sheet is typically significant for younger clients, and life/disability insurance is commonly used to manage this risk.

For wealthy investors or families with plenty of assets to fund their spending needs and hence plenty of excess capital, longevity risk and mortality risk may be inconsequential. However, they face other investment risks in connection with executive stock options, restricted stock, deferred compensation plans, or other concentrated stock positions. Protecting assets and income against the dilutive effects of inflation is also a common concern for all investors, including affluent and high-net-worth investors.

The three basic investment risk management strategies are diversification, hedging, and insurance. The financial advisor has different tools from which to choose to implement each of them. For example, an investor wanting downside protection in the stock market can purchase a structured product, such as an annuity that provides a minimum cash flow but also allows the investor to participate in some market appreciation or use an options-based strategy. The wealth manager chooses the proper tool based not just on the size of the client's assets and liabilities, but also on the risk profile of those assets and liabilities. Examples of investment policy statement excerpts are presented in Chapter 13.

Some wealth managers also become actively involved in aspects of planning beyond investments. For example, it may be appropriate to incorporate estate planning and charitable giving plans, ensuring that strategies in one area are consistent with the other. For entrepreneurs, a broader wealth management policy would also consider business succession plans or plans to liquidate or sell a business. Like many tax, estate planning, and legal issues, these require the expertise of other investment professionals, such as investment bankers. Consideration might be given to creation of a broader wealth management policy statement that could become the center of the wealth management process and govern wealth management decisions.[2] Such a statement would incorporate the investment policy statement as well as other concepts, such as risk management and wealth transfer goals, as outlined in Exhibit 1.6.

PORTFOLIO MANAGEMENT, MONITORING, AND MARKET REVIEW

How investment policy is executed is represented by the system in the right-most part of Exhibit 1.1. It requires that the parties involved (e.g., client, manager, custodian, allied professionals) have an understanding of each other's responsibilities as well as their own. One way of implementing investment policy is to construct portfolios by selecting individual

---

[2]Most advisors simply refer to this as an investment policy statement even when it includes non-investment-related goals.

EXHIBIT 1.6   Wealth Management Policy Statement

1. Investment policy statement
   a. Brief client description
   b. Client goals
   c. Investment objectives
      i. Return objective
      ii. Risk objective
   d. Investment constraints
      i. Time horizon
      ii. Tax considerations
      iii. Liquidity needs (e.g., cash flow management)
      iv. Legal and regulatory concerns
      v. Unique circumstances
   e. Strategic asset allocation
      i. Asset class constraints
      ii. Investment constraints (e.g., margin restrictions)
      iii. Investment strategies
      iv. Investment styles
   f. Implementation, monitoring, and review
      i. Responsibilities of client, manager, custodian, and other parties involved
      ii. Performance measures, evaluation, and benchmarks
      iii. Review schedule
      iv. Rebalancing guidelines
2. Risk management and insurance
   a. Longevity risk (i.e., the risk of living too long)
   b. Mortality risk (i.e., the risk of dying too soon)
   c. Medical, disability, and long-term care (i.e., the risk of living with costly illness)
      i. Living wills
      ii. Health care proxies
   d. Property risk (e.g., asset protection from creditor claims)
   e. Business risk
   f. Political risk
   g. Legal risk
3. Wealth transfer goals
   a. Estate planning (e.g., transfers to heirs)
   b. Philanthropy
   c. Business succession

assets. Alternatively, the wealth manager may select mutual funds, exchange-traded funds (ETFs), or asset managers who are responsible for picking individual assets. These issues are discussed in Chapters 14, 15, and 16. In either case, the wealth management investment process is never complete. After initial plans are implemented, the portfolio and policy are monitored periodically by both advisor and client. In addition to measuring performance, the wealth manager needs to measure and monitor a portfolio manager's investment style, portfolio manager changes, asset size, and other factors that can affect the consistency of expected investment performance.

Accountability requires performance measures and benchmarks that are agreed on at the beginning of the process. Measuring and evaluating investment performance is its own field of study and is what naturally comes to mind when one thinks of investment performance measurement. For the wealth manager, performance is measured by whether the client is able to meet his or her life goals.

Performance can and should, however, include other factors such as the receipt of agreed-upon information, the delivery of statements, and the completion of scheduled reviews. This review process is informed by updates and changes to the client's profile as well as developments in the marketplace. Sometimes the review process requires only that the portfolio be rebalanced. Other times, depending on the extent of changes and developments, the investment policy statement may need revision, perhaps in consultation with other investment professionals.

Part of this review involves examining how the whole process functions, ensuring that it is effective and that accountability is built into the system—a process that involves coordination with other professional advisors as in the beginning. The review process often triggers the need for ongoing education for the client as circumstances change and new issues need to be addressed. Armed with this information, as well as a review of the market and portfolio performance, the wealth manager can modify the process as needed. In any case, the wealth management investment process is nonlinear and recursive.

PARTING COMMENTS

This process has clear implications for how wealth management is practiced. It is a client-centric endeavor rather than a product- or sales-oriented activity. The implications for the business of wealth management and the practice philosophy are outlined in Chapter 17. One should recognize, however, that the framework for sound wealth management is inextricably tied to the way in which the advisor practices. In the following pages, we provide the analytical framework around which you can build a practice and provide enduring value to the clients you serve.

RESOURCES

Ellis, Charles D. 1998. "Why Policy Matters." Chapter 9 in *Winning the Loser's Game: Timeless Strategies for Successful Investing*, 3rd edition. New York: McGraw-Hill.

Horan, Stephen M., ed. 2009. *Private Wealth: Wealth Management in Practice*. CFA Institute Perspectives Series. Hoboken, NJ: John Wiley & Sons.

Maginn, John L., Donald L. Tuttle, Dennis W. McLeavey, and Jerald E. Pinto. 2007. "Asset Allocation." In *Managing Investment Portfolios: A Dynamic Process*, 3rd edition. John L. Maginn, Donald L. Tuttle, Jerald E. Pinto, and Dennis W. McLeavey, eds. CFA Institute Investment Series. Hoboken, NJ: John Wiley & Sons.

Wilcox, Jarrod, Jeffrey E. Horvitz, and Dan diBartolomeo. 2006. *Investment Management for Taxable Private Investors*. Charlottesville, VA: Research Foundation of CFA Institute.

CHAPTER 2

FIDUCIARY AND PROFESSIONAL STANDARDS

The most treasured asset in investment management is a steady hand at the tiller.
—Robert Arnott

With the career opportunities that a wealth manager can expect to receive come great responsibilities. Managing wealth for others has evolved over time into a profession that carries with it legal, ethical, and other standards, often, but certainly not exclusively, within the context of trusts. In this chapter we first review the historical context of what it means to be a fiduciary and what duties apply. Next we present professional standards that are applicable to wealth managers. We then provide guidance for the management of client accounts in accordance with these standards.

FIDUCIARY DUTY

The highest standard that applies when a wealth manager is making investment decisions for others is that of a fiduciary. A fiduciary duty is a legal concept that can be imposed when someone (a fiduciary) is making decisions for another's benefit (a principal or beneficiary). The level of personal liability a fiduciary assumes is significant. Investing as a fiduciary was once a rather simple process of defaulting to a conservative portfolio of high-quality bonds with an occasional sprinkling of blue-chip stocks. Today this simple investment solution no longer suffices. There has been a shift in the standards applied to investing as a fiduciary. For anyone serving as an investment fiduciary or advising clients who are fiduciaries, knowledge of these changes is imperative. With a primary focus on the requirements for private fiduciaries, the following discussion provides a history of the concept from its beginning in England.

Early History

The concept of trusts dates back to twelfth-century England and was frequently related to endowments of land. In the simple world of these early trusts, land rents provided a consistent and increasing income stream and the land itself provided for capital preservation and growth. As society progressed and the economy became more complex, there was an evolutionary development leading to the creation of securities, such as bonds, and a shifting of trust investments from real property to financial securities. While the earlier focus had been the preservation of real wealth, the focus now became the preservation of capital. Based on the premise that the only security appropriately safe for trust investments was government bonds (and, as some commentators suggest, the government's desire to assure a market for government bonds), English law mandated government bonds as the sole investment acceptable for most trusts. This was also the legal heritage in the United States until *Harvard College v. Amory* in 1830.

Harvard College v. Amory

Francis Amory had been appointed the trustee of his friend John McLean's estate upon McLean's death. The estate consisted of approximately $50,000 in bank, insurance, and industrial stock. Mrs. McLean was the income beneficiary until her death and Harvard College one of the remainderman beneficiaries. By the time of Mrs. McLean's death the estate had shrunk to $40,000 and Harvard sued Amory claiming that he, as trustee, had incurred the $10,000 shortfall as a result of his improper investments in equities. Under existing English common law it seemed clear that Harvard would succeed in its claim.

The final ruling of the Massachusetts court, however, was a relaxing of the English common law standard regarding investments. In what has been called the single most profound state court decision, the court developed what has become known as the "prudent man" standard, a clear and flexible guideline for fiduciaries based on conduct and not results.

In rejecting the claim of Harvard College, the court recognized that all investments have risk—"Do what you will, the capital is at hazard." The court also specifically addressed the myth of the safety of government bonds. The court queried: "[W]hat becomes of the capital when the credit of the government shall be so much impaired as it was at the close of the last war?"

In what has become a well-known statement of prudence, the court ruled that trustees should "observe how men of prudence, discretion and intelligence manage *their own* affairs, not in regard to *speculation*, but in regard to the *permanent disposition* of their funds, considering the probable income as well as the probable *safety of the capital* to be invested." (Italics added) As the balance of this chapter discusses, the words in italics highlight the major issues that have plagued fiduciaries and the courts ever since.[1]

It is important to note that the decision did not explicitly approve of common stocks as appropriate investments for fiduciaries. Rather, as noted earlier, it established the prudent man rule with two definitive but flexible standards:[2]

---

[1] The complexity of investment markets, the overwhelming influence of institutional investors, the continuing evolution in investment theory, and the enforcement of new laws governing investment fiduciaries provide wealth managers both an opportunity and a responsibility. The opportunity is to become a professional advisor to nonprofessional fiduciaries, and the responsibility is to provide competent and legally defensible advice to those fiduciaries. For all clients the wealth manager should follow appropriate professional standards (whether required or voluntary). These standards are what separate professionals from other participants in the market. The italic notation throughout is authors' emphasis.

[2] Jeffrey N. Gordon, "The Puzzling Persistence of the Constrained Prudent Man Rule," *New York University Law Review*, 1987, 1–52.

1. A process standard based on "how men of prudence . . . manage their own affairs." The court recognized that investing funds is a continual and implicitly risky process. It also recognized that there is no rational basis for setting strict and arbitrary standards for fiduciary investing. Decisions must constantly be made, and the results monitored and, if appropriate, revised. The court's solution for establishing a viable and living standard against which to measure the actions of a trustee was the prudent man standard.

2. A standard for judging the appropriateness of a fiduciary investment, namely, one appropriate for the "permanent disposition" of the trustee's "own funds." The court also recognized that generally the funds placed under the control of a trustee have a long investment horizon. In the terminology familiar to modern wealth managers, permanent disposition equates to the "long term." They also recognized that beneficiaries of trusts do not become a unique form of humanity by act of law. Beneficiaries are likely to have generally the same general goals as the balance of humanity. No unique constraints on the trustee's investment authority were appropriate, hence the reference to "own funds."

The new freedom provided by the flexible "prudent man" standard of *Harvard College v. Amory* was limited (for the next 110 years only eight other U.S. states adopted the rule). In fact, following a case in the late 1800s, the New York legislature passed a statute limiting trust investments to bonds and mortgages unless otherwise provided in the trust documents. Led by New York's action, by 1900 most states had enacted "legal list"[3] laws, and Massachusetts was almost alone in adhering to the original "prudent man" standard.

Restatement of Trusts

Little change came to the law of fiduciary investing until 1935 with the issuing of the *Restatement of Trusts*[4] by the American Law Institute (ALI)[5] and the first publication of *The Law of Trusts* by Professor Austin Wakeman Scott, the father of American trust law. The *Restatement of Trusts*, for which Scott drafted the report, and *The Law of Trusts* formulated the drafters' interpretation of the *Harvard College v. Amory* prudent man rule. Unfortunately, the result was a "constrained" prudent man standard. The three constraints were:

1. A standard of safety described as "having primarily in view *the preservation of the estate*" versus *Harvard College v. Amory*'s "*permanent disposition* of their funds." In this difference you will recognize the conflict between the preservation of principal and the preservation of real value. Although today the term *preservation* might include the concept of purchasing power, at the time of the ruling it clearly referred to the original principal. This restriction severely restricted a trustee from considering any form of equity investment. Permanent disposition, however, is a less restrictive criterion. As noted

---

[3]A legal list was an actual published list of legally approved forms of investments.

[4]The *Restatements of the Law* are treatises on U.S. legal topics published by the American Law Institute, an organization of legal academics and practitioners, as scholarly refinements of black-letter law.

[5]The American Law Institute is the leading independent organization in the United States producing scholarly work to clarify, modernize, and otherwise improve the law. The Institute (made up of 4,000 lawyers, judges, and law professors of the highest qualifications) drafts, discusses, revises, and publishes *Restatements of the Law*, model statutes, and principles of law that are enormously influential in the courts and legislatures, as well as in legal scholarship and education.

earlier, it suggests a long-term investment horizon. Under these circumstances, the preservation of purchasing power is a legitimate factor to be considered.

2. Support for the prudent trustee standard over the prudent man rule as reflected in Scott's commentary in *The Law* regarding "men who are safeguarding property for others."

3. An attempt to separate speculation from prudence by setting specific rules that had the effect of significantly limiting investment flexibility as investment knowledge grew and as new investment vehicles and strategies were developed.

Model Prudent Investor Act

Whether in response to the changes in the economy or in response to the migration of trust business to Massachusetts (where trust company portfolios operating under the Massachusetts prudent man rule were outperforming "legal list"–governed trust companies by 100 percent), the American Bar Association (ABA) developed a model prudent investor act modeled after *Harvard College v. Amory*.

The bad news was that the influence of Scott and the old paradigm remained, as reflected in the description of "speculative" investments by one of the central participants in the development of the ABA model: "all purchases of even high-grade securities for the purpose of resale at a profit" and "all programs not mandated by the trust instrument that are undertaken to increase the number of dollars to compensate for loss of purchasing power."

The good news was that by 1950, following the release of the ABA model, most states had adopted some form of the prudent man standard eliminating the legal list and allowing at least some allocation to common stock. By 1990, only three states had any form of legal list. Scott was also the author of the *Second Restatement of Trusts*, and there was little substantive change.

Endowments and Pension Funds

Following World War II, while noninstitutional investment trustees were having trouble balancing the demands of beneficiaries with the resources of trusts invested largely in fixed income securities under existing laws, institutional trustees were truly between a rock and a hard place. By the late 1960s, few institutions had adopted a total return policy, and little was invested in common stock. Inflation ravaged the real value of their endowment bond portfolios. Funding from major foundations became a critical source of income. This dependence was of concern to the foundations, and the largest, the Ford Foundation, commissioned a study of the investment practices of endowments. Known as the *Barber Report* after its chief author and published in 1969, the study found that endowment returns were poor compared to returns of large general growth funds. The reason for the poor performance was attributed to the institutions' erroneous adherence to what the report considered to be an outdated investment paradigm.

Institutions, for the most part, managed their investments under the belief that they were governed by trust law. Therefore, they felt constrained by the legal standard that capital gains belonged to corpus and only interest income and dividends could be spent. The result was a traditional trust policy of preserving capital and maximizing current income.

The *Barker Report* concluded that endowments did not have beneficiaries as construed under trust law. Hence, there were no parties with conflicting interests. In fact, endowments were not subject to trust law but were subject to corporate law. Institutions could therefore consider total return and long-term real growth.

Although there was no immediate rush by institutions to test the new nontrust theory, the report led to the adoption in 1972 by the National Conference of Commissioners on

Uniform State Laws of the Uniform Management of Institutional Funds Act (UMIFA). Concerned with the long-term as well as short-term needs of institutions, the Act explicitly provides for:

- The prudent use of appreciation (a total return policy).
- Investment authority to invest in stock.
- The board's right to delegate investment authority.

Compared to the restrictions faced by those controlled by traditional trust law, this was an extraordinary change. By September 1995, 38 states had adopted, in whole or in part, the UMIFA. Still, many institutions continued to manage their assets under the old paradigm. As late as 1993, the Council on Foundations lamented, "The sad truth is that too many foundation endowments (of whatever kind) are currently managed in a way that is woefully behind the times."[6]

In 2006, the National Conference of Commissioners on Uniform State Laws adopted the Uniform Prudent Management of Institutional Funds Act (UPMIA), replacing the UMIFA and updating the rules on investment decision making, permitting charitable organizations to use modern investment techniques.

ERISA—A Special Case

The most significant act regarding fiduciary investing since *Harvard College v. Amory* was the enactment in the United States of the Employee Retirement Income Security Act (ERISA) of 1974. It would be difficult to overemphasize the fundamental changes that ERISA brings to legal mandates regarding investment fiduciary responsibility. Suffice it to say that ERISA, at least in the realm of its influence, was the first act to bring fiduciary investment law into the twentieth century. While the subsequent work of the *Restatement of the Law Third, Trusts* and the Uniform Prudent Investor Act may ultimately prove more important due to their wider influence, ERISA in a real sense paved the way for their acceptance.

Section 404(a)(1)(b) of ERISA requires a fiduciary to act "with the care, skill, prudence, and diligence *under the circumstances then prevailing* that a prudent man acting in a like capacity and *familiar with such matters* would use in the conduct of *an enterprise of a like character and with like aims.*" (Emphasis added)

Some commentators have suggested that the ERISA qualification "familiar with such matters" set a "prudent expert" standard. Although we believe that this may overstate the intention of the law, ERISA clearly introduces the requirement that fiduciaries consider the concepts of modern investment theory and manage in accordance with the unique nature of the plan.

Recent History

In the early 1980s, Columbia, Harvard, Princeton, and Stanford universities commissioned a study of fiduciary investing. The universities selected Bevis Longstreath, a former Securities and Exchange Commission (SEC) commissioner, to lead the project. The results of Longstreath's work were published in 1986 as *Modern Investment Management and the Prudent*

---

[6]John A. Edie and Lowell S. Smith, "Investing: What Every Foundation Trustee Should Know," *Foundation News*, November/December 1993, 26.

Man Rule. In his conclusions, Longstreath recommended that the American Law Institute (ALI) undertake a new *Restatement of Trusts.*

Restatement Third of Trusts

Whether or not a direct result of this recommendation, on May 18, 1990, the ALI adopted the *Restatement of the Law Third, Trusts, Prudent Investor.* It was published in 1992. This *Restatement* reflects statutory trends (e.g., ERISA and UMIFA), as well as the efficacy of the significant empirical and theoretical research in investment management. It provides for a dynamic model of trust investment management unique to the needs of the trust. For experienced financial planners, it is a familiar and comfortable model.

The Foreword by Geoffrey Hazard, director of the American Law Institute, places the *Third Restatement* in perspective:

- ". . . the revised *rule focuses on the trust's portfolio as a whole* and the investment strategy on which it is based, rather than viewing a specific investment in isolation."
- "Reflecting modern investment concepts and practices, the prudent investor rule *recognizes that return on investment is related to risk, that risk includes deterioration of real return owing to inflation, and that the relationship between risk and return may be taken into account* in managing the trust assets. Correlatively, the formulation *requires the trustee to take account of the relationship between return and risk in light of the purposes and circumstances of the trust.*" (Emphasis added)

In the Introduction, Professor Edward C. Halbach Jr. concisely and specifically summarizes the heart of the *Restatement* in terms of "principles of prudence":

> *In addition to the fundamental proposition that no investments or techniques are imprudent per se, there are a few principles of prudence set out in the sections that follow. These principles instruct trustees and the courts that:*

> 1. *Sound diversification is fundamental* to risk management and is therefore ordinarily required of trustees.
> 2. Risk and return are so directly related that *trustees have a duty to analyze and make conscious decisions concerning the levels of risk appropriate* to the purposes, distribution requirements, and *other circumstances of the trusts* they administer.
> 3. Trustees have a *duty to avoid* fees, transaction costs and other *expenses that are not justified by needs and realistic objectives* of the trust's investment program.
> 4. The fiduciary duty of *impartiality requires a balancing* of the elements between production of *current income* and the *protection of purchasing power.*
> 5. Trustees *may have a duty as well as having the authority to delegate* as prudent investors would. (Emphasis added)

Uniform Prudent Investor Act

Although the *Third Restatement* is a very influential document, by the date of its publication only six U.S. states (California, Delaware, Georgia, Minnesota, Tennessee, and Washington) had modified their rules regarding prudent investing to allow much of the flexibility reflected in the *Restatement.* Illinois, having developed a new law based on a draft of the work of the ALI, was noted in the *Restatement* as the first "prudent investor" statute based on the *Restatement.*

Still, at the time most states had "constrained" prudent investor legislation dating back to the 1950s. The next step in this now rapid evolutionary process was the introduction of the Uniform Prudent Investor Act (UPIA) in 1994.

The UPIA was approved and recommended for enactment in all states in August 1994 and approved by the American Bar Association in February 1995. The UPIA was not just an academic exercise, but a draft of specific legislation issued by commissioners representing all of the 50 states. At last, U.S. fiduciaries, after a history dating back over 90 years, have the opportunity (as well as the obligation) to invest in a flexible and intelligent manner, based on objective standards. Since the UPIA serves as the framework for most state prudent investor legislation, the most significant changes enacted by the Act are set forth here.

The UPIA recognizes the significant changes in investment practice in the past 30+ years and the development of modern portfolio theory. It draws heavily on the *Restatement of the Law Third, Trusts*. The sections of the Act generally mandate the same kinds of actions noted earlier in the discussion of the *Restatement*. The primary objective of the Act is to make fundamental changes in five criteria for prudent investing. As noted in the Act's prefatory note:

- The standard of prudence is applied to any investment as part of the total portfolio, rather than to individual investments. In the trust setting the term *portfolio* embraces all of the trust's assets.
- The trade-off in all investing between risk and return is identified as the fiduciary's central consideration.
- All categorical restrictions on types of investments have been abrogated; the trustee can invest in anything that plays an appropriate role in achieving the risk/return objective of the trust and that meets the other requirements of prudent investing.
- The long-familiar requirement that fiduciaries diversify their investments has been integrated into the definition of prudent investing.
- The much-criticized former rule of trust law forbidding the trustee to delegate investment and management functions has been reversed. Delegation is now permitted, subject to safeguards.

International Considerations

The history highlighted in this chapter charts the evolution in the United States from legal lists to the modern concept of the prudent investor. There has been a similar trend in other countries, and similar prudent investor concepts have replaced legal lists in, for example, the United Kingdom, New Zealand, and Canada. Wealth managers need to determine what legal concepts are currently in effect in the jurisdictions in which they practice.

PROFESSIONAL STANDARDS

Beyond local legal standards, professional bodies establish standards and best practices that wealth managers should follow. This section presents standards for those holding the Chartered Financial Analyst (CFA) and Certified Financial Planner (CFP®) certificates, two of the most widely recognized professional designations. These organizations require that members or holders of their professional designations abide by their standards. If a professional is found to have violated these standards, he or she is subject to disciplinary action, which often involves loss of the professional designation. Many of these standards can be voluntarily adopted by investment advisors and their firms even if they do not hold the specific professional designation. Other organizations of investment professionals have similar standards to those described here.

CFA Institute

CFA Institute is a global, not-for-profit association of investment professionals that awards the CFA[R] and Certificate in Investment Performance Measurement (CIPM[R]) designations. The CFA Program is a study and examination program on investment analysis and portfolio management leading to the CFA designation. Those pursuing this program are referred to as CFA Program candidates. CFA Institute also promotes high ethical standards for the investment profession and offers a range of educational opportunities online and around the world through over 100 local societies.

CFA Institute requires that members (who do not need to be CFA charterholders) and candidates working toward the CFA designation abide by the CFA Institute Code of Ethics and Standards of Professional Conduct (SOPC).[7] These standards have also been adopted for use by investment firms and other organizations. For example, the Chartered Alternative Investment Analyst (CAIA) Association has adopted these standards and tests candidates for the CAIA designation on these standards. CFA Institute also puts forward other standards and testifies before regulatory bodies around the world regarding high standards and improvements that can be made to capital markets. CFA Institute also publishes other standards and guidelines such as the recently released Asset Manager Code of Professional Conduct, which outlines ethical and professional responsibilities for firms that manage assets for clients.

CFA Institute Code of Ethics

The Code of Ethics, first created in the 1960s, is the ethical cornerstone of CFA Institute and provides a benchmark for investment professionals around the world. CFA Institute members and CFA Program candidates must adhere to the Code as well as to local law, and are therefore required to abide by the stronger of the two. The Code requires that these investment professionals place clients' interests first, act with integrity, and maintain their professional competence. The Code states that members and candidates must:

- Act with integrity, competence, diligence, respect, and in an ethical manner with the public, clients, prospective clients, employers, employees, colleagues in the investment profession, and other participants in the global capital markets.
- Place the integrity of the investment profession and the interests of clients above their own personal interests.
- Use reasonable care and exercise independent professional judgment when conducting investment analysis, making investment recommendations, taking investment actions, and engaging in other professional activities.

---

[7]CFA Institute codes and standards can be downloaded on a complimentary basis in full text from www .cfainstitute.org.

- Practice and encourage others to practice in a professional and ethical manner that will reflect credit on themselves and the profession.
- Promote the integrity of, and uphold the rules governing, capital markets.
- Maintain and improve their professional competence and strive to maintain and improve the competence of other investment professionals.

CFA Institute Standards of Professional Conduct

Whereas the Code outlines principles of ethical professional behavior, the Standards of Professional Conduct provide specific applications of those principles in seven areas:

1. Professionalism.
2. Integrity of capital markets.
3. Duties to clients.
4. Duties to employers.
5. Investment analysis, recommendations, and action.
6. Conflicts of interest.
7. Responsibilities as a CFA Institute member or CFA Program candidate.

In order to comply with the standards, investment professionals must, among other requirements, maintain independence and objectivity, exercise diligence in making investment recommendations, disclose any potential conflicts of interest, not act on material nonpublic information, and not engage in any conduct that would compromise the reputation of CFA Institute and the CFA designation.

Further, adherents to the standards owe a duty of loyalty, prudence, and care to clients—always placing clients' interests above their own. In particular, they "must determine applicable fiduciary duty and must comply with such duty to persons and interests to whom it is owed."

Adherents must deal fairly and objectively with all clients and preserve the confidentiality of information about current, former, or prospective clients. When providing advisory services, these professionals must look into a client's situation, including risk and return objectives, and determine the suitability of particular investments for that client.

Asset Manager Code of Professional Conduct

While the Standards of Professional Conduct (SOPC) apply to individuals, the Asset Manager Code of Professional Conduct is designed to be adopted by firms. The asset manager principles are very similar to those in the SOPC and provide that asset managers have the following responsibilities to their clients:

- Act in a professional and ethical manner at all times.
- Act for the benefit of clients.
- Act with independence and objectivity.
- Act with skill, competence, and diligence.
- Communicate with clients in a timely and accurate manner.
- Uphold the rules governing capital markets.

Pension Trustee Code of Conduct

The Pension Trustee Code of Conduct was the output of a coalition of organizations including the Council of Institutional Investors, Organization for Economic Cooperation and Development, and pension organizations from several countries. The code can be adopted by governing bodies of pension funds. It establishes an ethical framework for members of the governing body and shows a commitment to serving the interests of pension participants and beneficiaries. The code sets forth the following ethical principles:

- Act in good faith and in the best interests of the pension scheme participants and beneficiaries.
- Act with prudence and reasonable care.
- Act with skill, competence, and diligence.
- Maintain independence and objectivity by, among other actions, avoiding conflicts of interest, refraining from self-dealing, and refusing any gift that could reasonably be expected to affect loyalty.
- Abide by all applicable laws, rules, and regulations, including the terms of the scheme documents.
- Deal fairly, objectively, and impartially with all participants and beneficiaries.
- Take actions that are consistent with the established mission of the scheme and the policies that support that mission.
- Review on a regular basis the efficiency and effectiveness of the scheme's success in meeting its goals, including assessing the performance and actions of scheme service providers, such as investment managers, consultants, and actuaries.
- Maintain confidentiality of scheme, participant, and beneficiary information.
- Communicate with participants, beneficiaries, and supervisory authorities in a timely, accurate, and transparent manner.

Global Investment Performance Standards

The Global Investment Performance Standards (GIPS®) are a set of ethical principles that provide investment firms with guidance on how to calculate and report their investment results to prospective clients. CFA Institute created and administers the GIPS partnering with 30 local country sponsors around the world. The standards are designed to provide full and fair disclosure to prospective clients, including requiring certain calculation methods.[8]

Other Standards and Guidelines

CFA Institute provides additional standards and guidance in a number of areas, including research objectivity standards, soft dollar standards, guidelines for relationships between corporate issuers and analysts, and guidelines on processing trades. The common theme in these standards is to ensure a fair marketplace that puts client/investor interests above the interests of other parties.

---

[8]For full standards see www.gipsstandards.org.

Certified Financial Planner Certificants

In the United States, the Certified Financial Planner Board of Standards, Inc., has responsibility for granting the CFP® certification and setting related standards. In 2004, the Financial Planning Standards Board (FPSB) was established to manage the international use of the CFP® marks. Today the CFP® designation is offered in over 20 countries. The organizations in each of these countries serve on an advisory group to the FPSB board of directors in setting standards. Each country organization incorporates these standards into territory-specific standards. These can be more or less restrictive than those of the international organization and may have been embedded in local regulations.

In this section we discuss the FPSB standards.[9] Individuals should determine what additional local standards may apply to them.

Financial Planner Code of Ethics and Professional Responsibility

The FPSB Financial Planner Code of Ethics and Professional Responsibility is designed to reflect financial planners' duties to clients, first and foremost, but also to the public, colleagues, and employers. The Code expresses eight principles:

Principle 1—Client first: Place the client's interests first.
Principle 2—Integrity: Provide professional services with integrity.
Principle 3—Objectivity: Provide professional services objectively.
Principle 4—Fairness: Be fair and reasonable in all professional relationships. Disclose and manage conflicts of interest.
Principle 5—Professionalism: Act in a manner that demonstrates exemplary professional conduct.
Principle 6—Competence: Maintain the abilities, skills, and knowledge necessary to provide professional services competently.
Principle 7—Confidentiality: Protect the confidentiality of all client information.
Principle 8—Diligence: Provide professional services diligently.

Financial Planning Practice Standards

The FPSB Financial Planning Practice Standards provide guidelines for financial planners to use when working through the financial planning process with clients.[10] This includes establishment of the initial relationship with the client; collection of client information; analysis of the client's situation; development, presentation, and implementation of recommendations; and review and reevaluation. The financial planner must inform the client about the process, the planner's competencies, and what services can be provided. Planners must work with the client to identify objectives, needs, and priorities, and to collect sufficient qualitative and quantitative information before making recommendations. The planner then analyzes the information and compares the client's current situation to the objectives, needs, and priorities. Based on the analysis, the planner develops recommendations and strategies and presents them to the client so the client can make an informed decision. Once client decisions are made, implementation responsibilities should be determined as well as a plan for periodically reviewing and reevaluating the client's situation.

---

[9]For full standards see www.fpsb.org.
[10]We will continue to refer to the wealth management process, rather than the financial planning process, except where a different term is used in professional standards or regulations.

PROVIDING WEALTH MANAGEMENT SERVICES

In the real world, what does this all mean in terms of prudent wealth management? What specific actions are required if you are considered to be a fiduciary under the *Third Restatement* or UPIA? In practice, the term *fiduciary* is often used loosely to mean that the client's interests are placed first even though a legal fiduciary relationship (such as with a trust) may not exist. More specifically, a fiduciary owes the client a duty of loyalty that is manifested in the care, skill, and prudence that the advisor brings to the investment management process. Although fiduciary duty is not specifically stated in the Investment Advisors Act of 1940,[11] which governs most independent financial advisors, it is widely recognized that fiduciary duty still applies due to the relationship of trust that exists between the advisor and client.[12]

The following discussion relates the actions that can be taken by wealth managers to make sure they are putting the client's interests first and fulfilling their duty of loyalty, prudence, and care. It specifically references fiduciary requirements from the *Restatement* and the UPIA for those situations in which a legal fiduciary relationship exists.

Follow a Portfolio Management Process and Consider the Uniqueness of the Client

The preceding fiduciary discussion and professional standards remind wealth managers that they must adhere to the cardinal rule of financial planning—attention to the unique goals of the client:

> [A] *trustee shall invest and manage trust assets . . . by considering the purposes, terms, distribution requirements, and other circumstances of the trust.*

The danger of ignoring this requirement is illustrated in the following hypothetical illustration from the *Restatement*:

> *T is trustee of a trust that pays its income to L for life, with remainder thereafter to pass to R or R's issue. T has adopted a continuous long-term strategy of investing the trust estate in short-term bank and federal obligations. Although in a sense cautious, this investment program would ordinarily be viewed as failing to take adequate account of the fiduciary duty of caution as it applies to safeguarding the real value of capital.* [Restatement]

---

[11]However, in the U.S. Supreme Court case *SEC v. Capital Gains Research Bureau, Inc.*, 375 U.S. 180 (1963), the court ruled, "Congress intended the Investment Advisers Act of 1940 to be construed, like other securities legislation 'enacted for the purpose of avoiding frauds,' not technically and restrictively, but flexibly to effectuate its remedial purposes. . . . In light of this, and in light of the evident purpose of the Investment Advisers Act of 1940 to substitute a philosophy of disclosure for the philosophy of caveat emptor . . . Nor is it necessary in a suit against a fiduciary, which Congress recognized the investment adviser to be, to establish all the elements required in a suit against a party to an arm's-length transaction. Courts have imposed on a fiduciary an affirmative duty of 'utmost good faith, and full and fair disclosure of all material facts,' as well as an affirmative obligation 'to employ reasonable care to avoid misleading' his clients."

[12]The Fiduciary Obligation for Investment Advisers to Apply Prudent Processes—Perspectives of The Committee for the Fiduciary Standard, January 31, 2010.

The UPIA and the *Restatement* constantly reiterate that the measure of prudence is adherence to a prudent process:

The test of prudence is one of conduct, not one of performance. [Restatement *and UPIA*]

It is important for the wealth manager to follow an appropriate wealth management process (such as that described in this book) or a financial planning process as defined in professional standards in which the unique characteristics of the client are considered.

Develop an Investment Policy Statement

Most wealth managers are familiar with the importance of a written investment policy. Having a formal investment or wealth management policy/strategy is a best practice for anyone providing investment management services.

The trustee must give reasonably careful consideration to both the formulation and the implementation of an investment strategy, with investments to be selected and reviewed in a manner reasonably appropriate to that strategy. [Restatement]

 A trustee's investment and management decisions . . . must be evaluated as part of an overall investment strategy. [UPIA]

Design the Policy for Total Return

The archaic concept of separating income and capital appreciation has been discarded. Fiduciaries are now required to use the more rational criterion of total return.

Among circumstances that a trustee shall consider in investing and managing trust . . . [is] expected total return. [UPIA]

 In the absence of contrary provisions in the terms of the trust, this requirement of caution requires the trustee to invest with a view both to safety of the capital and to securing a reasonable return. [Restatement]

The *Restatement* continues in its commentary:

Reasonable "return" refers to total return, including capital appreciation and gain as well as trust accounting income. . . . The capital growth element of these return objectives, however, is not necessarily confined to the preservation of purchasing power, but may extend to growth in the real value of principal in appropriate cases. [Restatement]

Included in the discussion of total return is a more modern concept of safety that includes purchasing power, interest rate, and reinvestment risk, as well as market risk. Particular attention is devoted to the preservation of real value.

"Safety" of capital includes not only the objective of protecting the trust property from the risk of loss of nominal value but, ordinarily, also a goal of preserving its real value—that is, seeking to avoid or reduce loss of the trust estate's purchasing power as a result of inflation. . . . The trustee is also under a duty to the remainder beneficiaries to exercise reasonable care in an effort to preserve the trust property, and this duty ordinarily

includes a goal of protecting the property's purchasing power. . . . Thus, a trustee has a duty to seek to balance the income and principal elements of total investment return.
[Restatement]

Manage Risk

Modern fiduciary law now recognizes the seminal work of Harry Markowitz. Risk management, rather than risk avoidance, is the standard.

These changes have occurred under the influence of a large and broadly accepted body of empirical and theoretical knowledge about the behavior of capital markets, often described as "modern portfolio theory." . . . Subsection (b) also sounds the theme of modern investment practice, sensitivity to the risk/return curve. . . . The Act impliedly disavows the emphasis in older law on avoiding "speculative" or "risky" investments. Low levels of risk may be appropriate in some trust settings but inappropriate in others. It is the trustee's task to invest at a risk that is suitable to the purpose of the trust. [UPIA]
. . . the duty of caution does not call for avoidance of risk by trustees but for their prudent management of risk. For these purposes, risk management is concerned with more than failure of collection and loss of dollar value. It takes account of all hazards that may follow from inflation, volatility of price and yield, lack of liquidity, and the like.
[Restatement]

Should there be any lingering doubt that risk management no longer suggests implementing a traditionally conservative portfolio, the notes to the *Restatement* warn, "Beneficiaries can be disserved by undue conservatism as well as by excessive risk taking."

Minimize Diversifiable Risk

The conclusion of William Sharpe and others that unsystematic risk is unrewarded risk is an integral part of the investment mandates required by the *Restatement* and the UPIA. Unsystematic risk (i.e., diversifiable risk) is referred to as uncompensated risk. For fiduciaries, unwarranted acceptance of diversifiable risk is irresponsible. This serves as a strong warning to any trustee who contemplates concentrating the trust investment portfolio:

In the absence of contrary statute or trust provision, the requirement of caution ordinarily imposes a duty to use reasonable care and skill in an effort to minimize or at least reduce diversifiable risks. . . . minimization of the latter [diversifiable risk] becomes a significant goal of prudent investing. [Restatement]

The UPIA clearly delineates between these risks:

Modern portfolio theory divides risk into the categories of "compensated" and "uncompensated" risk . . . compensated risk—the firm pays the investor for bearing the risk. By contrast, nobody pays the investor for owning [uncompensated risk]. . . . Risk that can be eliminated by adding different stocks (or bonds) is uncompensated risk. The object of diversification is to minimize this uncompensated risk. [UPIA]

Determine the Risk Tolerance of the Client

As noted earlier, each client is unique. The wealth manager must obtain information on the risk tolerance of every client. In the case of trusts, fiduciaries must not only *consider the purposes, terms, distribution requirements, and other circumstances of the trust*, but they must also consider the risk tolerance of their client (i.e., the trust). Thus, an investment fiduciary must not only be able to manage risk, but must also have an understanding of cognitive psychology and know how to evaluate risk tolerance.

> [R]*isk management by a trustee requires that careful attention be given to the particular trust's risk tolerance, that is, to its tolerance for volatility.* [Restatement]
>   . . . *the trustee can invest in anything that plays an appropriate role in achieving the risk/return objectives of the trust. . . . Returns correlate strongly with risk, but tolerance for risk varies greatly with the financial and other circumstances of the investor, or in this case of a trust. . . . It is the trustee's task to invest at a risk that is suitable to the purpose of the trust.* [*UPIA*]

Diversify across Poorly Correlated Asset Classes

Although the courts have long recognized the importance of diversification, until the *Second Restatement* the legal mandate for diversification was limited. The *Second Restatement* provided for "reasonable diversification." However, without an awareness of the concept of correlation, diversification simply referred to the number of investments. Harry Markowitz's seminal work *Portfolio Selection: Efficient Diversification of Investments* was not published until 1959. Now that Dr. Markowitz has been awarded the Nobel Prize (1990) for his work in this area and 50 years of new portfolio theory has accumulated, fiduciary investment law incorporates this concept in the definition of diversification.

> *These changes have occurred under the influence of a large and broadly accepted body of empirical and theoretical knowledge about the behavior of capital markets, often described as "modern portfolio theory."* [*UPIA*]

Should a fiduciary contemplate falling back on the traditional default of government bonds, the *Restatement's* reporter's notes include an ERISA case example:

> *The court does not question that United States Treasury bonds are among the most liquid of all investments and that they carry essentially no risk of default. However, the issue is not whether government bonds are, as a general rule, a sound investment; nor is the issue whether the court approves of Trevor Stewart's [the defendant] philosophy of investing heavily in long-term United States government bonds. Trevor Stewart in essence argues that the risk of loss through default is the only risk of loss contemplated by ERISA. . . . This argument is without merit.*

The *Restatement* provides clear guidelines for asset classes to be considered.

> *Basic asset classifications might begin with cash equivalents, bonds, asset-backed securities, real estate, and corporate stocks, with both debt and equity categories further divided by their general risk-reward or income/growth characteristics, by the domestic, foreign, tax-exempt, or other characteristics of the issuers, and the like.*

It may come as a surprise to many sophisticated fiduciaries, however, that the commentary goes even further on this subject to suggest:

> *Foreign Investments. The amount of assets held in trust in the United States and looking for favorable investment and diversification opportunities is so large today as to make a rule proscribing or even looking askance at offshore investments both unworkable and unwise.*

Develop an Appropriate Asset Allocation and Consider the Use of Pooled Investment Vehicles

Expanding beyond the broader definition of diversification, the *Third Restatement* unequivocally adopts the concept of asset allocation as an integral part of the prudent investment process:

> *Asset allocation decisions are a fundamental aspect of an investment strategy and a starting point in formulating a plan of diversification.*

In order to assist in diversification and control costs, the modern investment fiduciary may consider pooled investment vehicles such as ETFs and mutual funds as means for diversification.

> *[F]or a trust of moderate size . . . the alternative of purchasing suitable mutual funds might be more inviting to the trustee because it offers a means of obtaining much greater diversification for what will usually be a lower cost.* [Restatement]
> *Trusts can also achieve diversification by investing in mutual funds.* [UPIA]

Liquidate Inappropriate Investments

In the past, trustees have frequently maintained positions transferred into the trust. Often little or no thought was given to the appropriateness of the assets in light of the needs of the trust beneficiaries. Frequently, the trustee took comfort in the language of the trust document. Standard boilerplate frequently had a clause allowing the trustee to maintain inherited assets. In the future, such a naive defense will no longer serve as a safe harbor for fiduciaries. Modern trust standards mandate that, in most circumstances, the trustee must diversify.

> *In making and implementing investment decisions, the trustee has a duty to diversify the investments of the trust unless, under the circumstances, it is prudent not to do so.* [UPIA]

Regarding inherited assets, the *Restatement* and UPIA make it clear that unsuitable inherited assets remain unsuitable, even if the assets were suitable when purchased and even if the trustee is given authority to continue to hold inherited assets.

The UPIA requires that "within a reasonable time after accepting a trusteeship or receiving assets, a trustee shall review the trust assets and make and implement decisions concerning the retention and disposition of assets, in order to bring the trust portfolio into compliance with the purposes, terms, distribution requirements, and other circumstances of the trust and . . . to dispose of unsuitable assets within a reasonable time . . . [and that] extends as well to investments that were proper when purchased but subsequently became improper."

The *Restatement* echoes this requirement. If by the terms of the trust or an applicable statute the trustee is permitted but not directed

> *to retain investments originally transferred to the trust, the trustee is not liable for retaining them when there is no abuse of discretion in doing so. The authorization to retain, however, ordinarily does not justify the trustee in retaining such assets if, under the circumstances, retention would be imprudent.*
>
> *This may require the trustee to convert investments received as part of the trust estate even though those assets are not otherwise either improper investments for the trustee or of a type unsuitable to the trust's investment objective. Thus, if the trustee receives a testator's residuary estate in trust and half of the trust estate consists of the shares of a particular corporation, the trustee is ordinarily under a duty to sell some or all of the shares to invest the proceeds in other assets so that the trust portfolio will not, without some special justification, include an excessive amount of the securities of a single corporation or carry an unwarranted degree of uncompensated risk.*

Delegate Where Appropriate

As noted earlier, one of the most significant changes is the authority to delegate active investment responsibility. Because the issues of modern investment management are varied and complex, there is a recognition that the trustee may not have the requisite knowledge and that professional advice will be in the best interest of the trust. In addition, for trustees who intelligently select competent and qualified advisors, the law provides a safe harbor that will insulate the trustee from the actions of the advisor.

> *As a start, it is important that a trustee be reasonably knowledgeable or have professional advice in order to achieve the informed diversification normally required of trustees.* [Restatement]
>
> *A trustee who meets the duties of care, skill, and caution in the selection of an investment advisor . . . is not liable to the beneficiaries or the trust for the decisions or actions of the agent to whom the function was delegated.* [UPIA]

Consider the Use of Both Passive and Active Managers

Both the *Restatement* and the UPIA emphasize the trustee's responsibility to control costs. This mandate requires the trustee to consider the cost efficiencies of passive investing and mutual funds. Trustees should be able to justify the additional costs incurred for active management.

> *Current assessments of the degree of efficiency support the adoption of various forms of passive strategies by trustees. . . . On the other hand, these assessments do not bar the prudent inclusion of active management strategies as well in the investment programs of trustees. . . . The greater the trustee's departure from one of the passive strategies, the greater is likely to be the burden of justification and also of continuous monitoring.* [Restatement]

Charitable Trusts

Although both the *Restatement* and the UPIA apply to private trusts, they make abundantly clear that the standards are expected to apply to all fiduciaries, including those of charitable trusts.

The Uniform Prudent Investor Act regulates the investment responsibilities of trustees. Other fiduciaries—such as executors, conservators, and guardians of the property— sometimes have responsibilities over assets that are governed by the standards of prudent investment. It will often be appropriate for states to adapt the law governing investment by trustees under this Act to these other fiduciary regimes. [Restatement]

Although the Uniform Prudent Investor Act by its terms applies to trusts and not charitable corporations, the standards of the Act can be expected to inform the investment responsibilities of directors and officers of charitable corporations. . . . In making decisions and taking actions with respect to the investment of trust funds, the trustee of a charitable trust is under a duty similar to that of a private trust. [*UPIA*]

Reasonable and Adequate Basis

In addition to sound processes for portfolio management, the Committee for the Fiduciary Standard states that fiduciaries have duties with respect to the due diligence applied to security selection and monitoring. In other words, wealth managers must have a reasonable and adequate basis for making investment recommendations that are suitable to a client's financial situation.

Practice Management Processes

In addition to sound processes for investment and portfolio management, the Committee for the Fiduciary Standard also points out that fiduciaries must ensure that their practice management systems and procedures are prudent. The CFA Institute Asset Manager Code of Conduct highlights these responsibilities, which include establishing a business model that avoids conflicts of interests and putting in place processes to disclose conflicts that are not avoided.

The wealth manager must also have systems to preserve the confidentiality of current, former, and prospective clients. For example, portable electronic devices with client contact information would require password protection to preserve confidentiality. Wealth managers must have trading policies that treat their clients fairly and equitably. They must also maintain records, properly document their investment decisions to ensure that recommendations have been made with reasonable and adequate basis, and establish a business-continuity plan to address disaster recovery or financial market disturbances.

Know Your Legal Duties

As of this writing, the regulatory landscape is quite fluid. Brokers are sometimes governed by one regulator while investment advisors are governed by another. Some regulators and market pundits have advocated for a convergence of standards so that professionals who look similar to an unsuspecting investing public are held to a similar standard. A possible outcome is that convergence might happen under a standard of care that is weaker than the fiduciary standard established by trust law but nonetheless carries the same name.

Whatever the outcome, wealth managers must have a clear understanding of their legal duties as well as their professional duties. If they abide by the CFA Institute Code and Standards, the CFP Board of Standards, FPSB, or other professional standards, then they are bound by the more rigorous of either the legal standards or the professional standards.

PARTING COMMENTS

In addition to these new laws, there are numerous other circumstances that will serve to increase the potential liabilities of fiduciaries:[13]

- The expectations of beneficiaries, molded by the historically extraordinary returns of the past decade, are frequently unrealistic. Even during periods of more realistic returns, beneficiaries are likely to become disappointed and angry. This may well provide fertile ground for litigation.
- Popularization of investment issues by the public media (e.g., *Money*, *Worth*, and *Kiplinger*) means a more knowledgeable client. If the client's own evaluation of the markets contradicts the investment results of the fiduciary, the client may no longer meekly accept the benefits offered.
- Government enforcement has increased at both state and national levels to protect investors.
- If a portfolio has been managed by an independent fiduciary, the significant transfer of wealth over the next decade will, in many cases, trigger a review by the children of the past investment management of their parents' funds.
- Boards and participants of endowments and charitable trusts are demanding a higher level of accountability than in the past.

RESOURCES

CFA Institute Standards of Practice Handbook, 9th edition. 2005. Charlottesville, VA: CFA Institute. www.cfaj.org/publications/Advocacy_English_code.pdf.

Financial Planning Standards Board. 2009a. Financial Planner Code of Ethics and Professional Responsibility. www.cfp.net/learn/codeofethics.asp; www.cfp.net/learn/standards.asp.

Financial Planning Standards Board. 2009b. Financial Planning Practice Standards. www.fpsb.org/site_docs/081125_CodeofEthics_LR.pdf; www.fpsb.org/site_docs/090800-FPSB-082_Practice Standards.pdf.

Restatement of the Law Third, Trusts. 2003, 2007. Reported by Edward C. Halbach Jr. Philadelphia, PA: American Law Institute.

Uniform Prudent Investor Act. 1994. Drafted by the National Conference of Commissioners of Uniform State Laws. www.law.upenn.edu/bll/archives/ulc/fnact99/1990s/upia94.pdf.

---

[13]Donald B. Trone, "Fiduciary Responsibility," IAFP, 1995 Success Forum; Donald B. Trone, "Fiduciary Responsibility: The Third Restatement of Trusts and the Prudent Man Rule," *Track VII/ Special Issues*, Monday, September 11, 1995, 407–418.

CHAPTER 3

CLIENT GOALS
AND CONSTRAINTS

Change is the investors' only certainty.

—T. Rowe Price Jr.

Everything is client driven. The process begins with the formal establishment of the client relationship. Even at this early stage, the wealth manager must customize his or her approach to reflect the client's unique needs, circumstances, and experience. This would include not only obvious factors, such as the client's investment experience, but also significant personal issues, such as marital status and circumstances (e.g., recent divorce, impending retirement, and fiduciary considerations).

GOAL SETTING

Individuals, if they think about goals at all, tend to think of goals as very generalized. For example, a typical client, when asked about goals, might respond as follows: "Well, I really would like to be able to pay for my children's education, retire, and enjoy my retirement."

This rather simplistic response misses all of the major attributes necessary for an advisor to begin the planning process, namely the attributes of specificity and priority. Goals must be time and dollar specific and prioritized. The first step in the process of wealth management is for the client to define goals with specificity. It is the responsibility of the wealth manager to educate the client in this process.

Goal setting is an integral part of the wealth management process; it is, in fact, the foundation on which all subsequent work depends. The following discussion addresses in great detail the issues involved, examples of various types of goals, problems related to recognizing and quantifying goals, and suggestions for assisting clients in resolving these issues.

Hidden Goals

When asked about their goals, clients not only fail to provide specificity, but they frequently also neglect to include many critical issues—aspects we refer to as the "hidden goal." In particular, issues related to risk management seem so obvious they are rarely consciously considered as explicit goals. Certainly, if clients were asked directly, they would agree that they have the goal of avoiding financial devastation as a result of being found at fault in an auto accident. Similarly, most would agree that they would like to replace their home should it burn down in a fire, without having to devastate their investment portfolio.

Even though not stated, it is a primary goal of all individuals to cover risks that might destroy their fiscal lives, so it is important that investors address these issues at the beginning of the investment planning process. Good planning requires that these hidden goals be clearly defined as well as quantified in order to ensure that adequate reserves are available to pay the cost of risk management. Although it may not be the wealth manager's responsibility to determine the total extent and cost of risk management, he or she might consider referring clients to other appropriate professionals.

Perhaps the most obvious of these goals would be the funds required to maintain a family's standard of living in the event of the incapacity of a primary breadwinner until such time as the more formalized risk management (e.g., disability insurance) begins to provide a supplemental income stream for the family. Other less depressing examples would include funds to help a child take advantage of a new business opportunity, or to supplement the tuition cost for a favored daughter unexpectedly accepted by a prestigious medical school.

Another hidden goal is the rainy-day reserve. Once a determination has been made as to the extent and cost of formal risk management (i.e., cost of insurance), there is still an exposure to uninsured risks and unexpected emergencies or opportunities.

For the client, the hidden goals are first priority. The resources needed to fund appropriate insurance coverage and emergency reserves must be quantified and set aside in appropriate liquid investments.

Noninvestment (Short-Term) Goals

As market volatility may result in periods of losses for both bond and stock investments, one of the fundamental beliefs in Harold's practice is that no investments should be considered unless the time horizon for the funds in question is at least five years (i.e., roughly an economic cycle). For funds needed in less than five years, the key criterion is liquidity. In order to help clients distinguish between saving for short-term liquidity needs and long-term investing, Harold has captured the belief in a mantra that he repeatedly drums into his clients' subconscious: "Five years, five years, five years." This constraint should overlay all investment decisions. Hence we refer to these short-term goals as noninvestment goals.

Intermediate Goals

Only after determining and quantifying the cost of the hidden goals and carving out liquid reserves for noninvestment (short-term) goals can the wealth manager assist the client in moving to the next category, the intermediate goals.

A client's intermediate goals are those that are consciously anticipated, are finite in time, and need to be paid for out of savings. These may include college education, weddings, second homes, boats, and trips around the world.

These are goals that a client can typically describe (e.g., the statement in the earlier example that "I really would like to be able to pay for my children's education"). However, the descriptions usually lack the three criteria necessary for goal setting and wealth management: time specificity, dollar specificity, and priority.

For example, to plan for funding the cost of a college education, it is necessary to determine the number of years prior to the beginning of funding, the length of the funding, and the amount of the funding. The funds required for a college education goal may vary by orders of magnitude depending on any one of these specific attributes.

Lifetime (Retirement) Goal

The fourth of five goal categories is generic for all investors—the lifetime goal of financial independence. Retirement planning is unique in its lack of uniqueness. Clients have different hidden goals. Some clients may need three months' cash flow reserves, others 12 months. Some clients may need disability insurance, whereas others may not; some may need life insurance, whereas others may not. Intermediate goals are also unique to each client. Most individuals, however, wish to reach financial independence. At that point, their investment portfolio should provide the supplemental real cash flow needed to maintain their standard of living.

The commonness of the goal, however, does not eliminate the need for time and dollar specificity and prioritization. The client who says "I want to retire and keep on enjoying the quality of my life after retirement" has at least elucidated the retirement goal. Still, the wealth manager remains in a quagmire of uncertainty as to how long that retiree may need funds and what "quality of my life" means to that client. Quantification of time for the retirement goal includes not only the age at which an individual wishes to retire but for a married couple, if both were working, the retirement age of each, as well as each of their life expectancies. Quantifying a retirement goal in numbers is far more complex than simply stating, "I need $40,000 a year to live on." The following is a discussion of some of the major factors.

Living Expense Classes

The dollar amount of living expenses may be separated into four possible classes.

Ongoing Increasing Expenses (Basic Living Expenses)
These living expenses are expected to increase annually with inflation. In some cases it may be appropriate for the wealth manager to break this class down into subclasses. For example, subclasses representing those expenses expected to increase in parallel with the consumer price index (CPI) or a similar index of inflation, a subclass for those expenses expected to increase at a much higher rate (e.g., medical costs), and a subclass for those expected to increase less than the CPI.

Limited-Duration Level Expenses (Fixed and Terminal)
This class includes retirement living expenses that do not inflate with inflation, and, in fact, terminate prior to the client's expected mortality. The most obvious example is a home mortgage. One of the most dangerous errors made in retirement planning is the application of a simple single inflation factor to a client's projected required retirement living expenses. This is a simplifying assumption endemic to most retail retirement planning software and much of the professional software.

Consider a client whose preinflation retirement goal is $60,000 per year. Using an inflation assumption of 4 percent, a future value calculation shows that this individual would need almost $90,000 to maintain the same standard of living after 10 years. Would the conclusion be different if the $60,000 requirement comprised $40,000 inflatable living expenses and $20,000 for three more years of home mortgage (principal and interest) payments? Of course it would; in fact, in 10 years, the client would require less than $60,000 to maintain the same standard of living. Obviously, the consequences of simplifying assumptions can lead to worthless conclusions.[1]

Ongoing Level Expenses (Permanent/Noninflatable) and Limited-Duration Increasing Expenses (Terminal/Inflatable)

These last two categories of expenses, although encountered less often, still arise occasionally. When they do, they need to be treated appropriately. The first class includes expenses that are likely to be permanent but will not be subject to inflation. An example is a principal and interest payment on a mortgage that is likely to extend beyond the client's life span. The last class includes expenses that are expected to terminate prior to expected mortality but will inflate prior to their termination. Examples include adjustable-rate mortgages, college tuition, parent care, travel, and even weddings.

Mortality

Harold once had a client who balked at extending his certificate of deposit (CD) maturities to five years. His excuse was that "I'll never live that long." Well, as a professional wealth manager, Harold perfected his response to clients who threaten him with dying early. His answer is "Go ahead, make my day!" The purpose of this answer, in addition to trying to make light of a difficult subject, is to emphasize that the client's real risk is not dying, but living "too long." Harold explains that his clients become like family and the thought of losing any of them is painful; however, what keeps him awake at night—and ought to keep clients awake, too—is the fear that they will outlive all the planning. This may seem like a silly conversation, but it serves as one of these rare "Aha!" times when the clients' eyes light up and they say, "I understand." Long-term planning for a 70- or 80-year-old client now makes sense to them.

Because of the importance of incorporating a time frame into the planning process, the last item of specificity necessary is an estimation of mortality. Bruce Temkin, a highly respected consulting actuary, has made a mini-crusade out of educating advisors on the importance of considering heredity in the retirement planning process. As he has so frequently and eloquently pointed out, the use of a standard actuarial table is a poor way of setting specificity for a client's expected mortality. The dominant factor is the client's unique gene pool. To address this aspect of estimating a client's mortality, it is important to query the client regarding the mortality of his or her closest blood relatives.

The silliness of the traditional mortality table approach was best pointed out by a story told by Lynn Hopewell, one of the profession's early thought leaders. Lynn had worked long and hard in the preparation of a plan for a client who was an engineer. Lynn anticipated that the engineer would be both interested and capable of evaluating the details of the plan itself. As Lynn was also trained as an engineer, he felt quite comfortable with the detailed mathematics involved in completing his work. Indeed, he was quite proud of the result and looked forward to making a presentation to his client. During that presentation, Lynn felt pleased with the client's questions and his own ability to answer those questions with confidence. The engineer clearly appreciated the quality and mathematical rigor of the plan that

---

[1]Technically, payments on the last few years of a conventional home mortgage comprise mostly principal repayment and relatively little interest expense. In consequence, we use the term *living expense* here loosely to mean fixed and terminal cash flows. The implications for the client's retirement goal and living standard remain unaffected.

Lynn had prepared. Once Lynn had completed his full presentation, he and his client sat back for a wrap-up discussion. Lynn was looking forward to the praise he believed he deserved for a job well done.

Indeed, the client did begin by complimenting Lynn on his work and the quality and depth of the calculations and presentation. He then added that he did have one little question that was disturbing him. With continued confidence in his ability to answer any question his client might have, Lynn invited the engineer to ask his question. The client said, "I think I understand this. If I do, it seems to me that this plan is designed to assure that I have adequate funds for the balance of my life." Lynn answered, "Yes, that's true." The client then said, "And if I understand how you arrived at how long I'll need those funds, you used a mortality table." Lynn said, "Yes, that's true. In fact I used the most widely respected and most current of all mortality tables." The client then said, "I appreciate that, and if I understand the way those mortality tables work, they are based on the general population, and what the table means is that, on average, a man my age will die by the chart's mortality age." Lynn said, "Absolutely correct." The client then said, "What confuses me is that it seems that you've designed a plan that I have a 50 percent chance of outliving."

Lynn said that with the last question he was absolutely floored, but in keeping with the honest and professional person that he was, he answered, "That's right."[2]

The point of the story is certainly not to pick on Lynn Hopewell, who was undeniably one of the finest wealth managers in the country. In fact, it is primarily due to Lynn's personal efforts that advisors today (including our firm) no longer make that mistake. We now know that setting retirement goals with specificity requires the most thoughtful efforts of both the advisor and the client. In terms of mortality, it is well to consider that not only will using a standard mortality figure lead to a 50 percent probability of the client outliving the plan, but in addition, most individuals who have the resources to pay for the advice of a wealth manager also have the resources to pay for better health care and nutrition than had been enjoyed by the population used to develop the mortality tables. Exhibit 3.1 presents a mortality table currently used in Harold's practice. It reflects the belief that, at a minimum, one should use an age that reflects a mortality projection in which we can be at least 70 percent confident. Depending on a client's family health history, you might use an 80 percent or 90 percent level of confidence, or in rare occasions (e.g., the client's grandfather just got married in a shotgun wedding) you might use a 95 percent standard.

EXHIBIT 3.1   Mortality Table: Retirement Planning Longevity Projections

Current Age	Sex	IRS Unisex	Cumulative Probability			
			70%	80%	90%	95%
50	M	83	88	91	95	98
	F	83	92	95	98	101
55	M	84	89	92	96	99
	F	84	92	95	98	101

(Continued)

[2]Lynn Hopewell, "Decision Making under Conditions of Uncertainty: A Wakeup Call for the Financial Planning Profession," *Journal of Financial Planning* (April 2004). This is a reprint of Lynn's classic article first published in the *Journal* in October 1997.

EXHIBIT 3.1 (Continued)

			Cumulative Probability			
Current Age	Sex	IRS Unisex	70%	80%	90%	95%
65	M	85.5	89	92	96	99
	F	85.5	93	95	99	101
70	M	86	90	93	96	99
	F	86	93	95	99	101
75	M	87.5	91	93	97	100
	F	87.5	93	96	99	101
80	M	89.5	92	95	98	100
	F	90.5	94	97	100	102
85	M	91.9	94	95	99	102
	F	91.9	95	98	101	103

EXAMPLE 3.1   Time Horizon

For example, according to Exhibit 3.1, a 50-year-old male named Theodore has a 70 percent chance of passing away before age 88. So, we could use 38 years as Theodore's maximum time horizon with 70 percent confidence. If we want to know his longest possible time horizon with more certainty, we can say with 95 percent confidence that Theodore will not live past age 98. Although we have more certainty about his maximum longevity, we also have a time horizon that is 10 years longer.

As if the time horizons we are dealing with are not long enough, they actually underestimate time horizons for couples. Exhibit 3.1 lists mortality projections for individuals. Suppose Theodore is married to Margaret, who is also 50 years of age. Margaret has a 70 percent chance of passing away before age 92. Not only does Margaret extend the planning horizon due to her gender, but one of them is very likely to live past age 92 even if the other passes on. In other words, although Theodore and Margaret have only a 30 percent chance of living past the ages of 88 and 92, respectively, there is a 51 percent chance that one of them will live past these respective ages even if the other does not.[3] This combined survival probability lengthens the time horizon and makes the challenge of sustaining withdrawals over a retirement horizon even more difficult.

Squaring the Curve
One last important mortality-related issue to consider is a concept introduced by Professor Neil Cutler. It is not uncommon to find retirement projections incorporating the assumption that, as the client grows older, the need for income will diminish. This assumption is based on

---

[3]The combined probability of their survival past ages associated with 70 percent cumulative probability equals $0.30 + 0.30 - (0.30)(0.30) = 0.51$, assuming their survival is independent of each other.

the belief that health will deteriorate with age and, as a result, spending needs will also drop. Professor Cutler warns that this assumption may have been appropriate a generation ago; however, it is likely to be dangerously misleading for baby boomer and Generation X retirees. As shown in Exhibit 3.2, in the future, rather than deteriorating over time, an individual's health is likely to remain relatively stable until just before death—thus a squaring of the curve. The financial result of this phenomenon is that income needs in retirement are not likely to fall with age. Our clients will likely maintain their spending habits until their deaths.

This reality hit home for Harold on a long and gracious cruise from the United States to Hong Kong. Given that he is at an age to qualify for Social Security benefits, it was the first time in a very long while that he could remember being with a large group of people where, along with his wife, he was one of the youngest of the group. There were many on that cruise in their 70s, 80s, and even 90s, often with canes or walkers, having a good time and, from a practitioner's perspective, freely spending money. It was squaring of the curve in action.

EXHIBIT 3.2   Squaring of the Curve

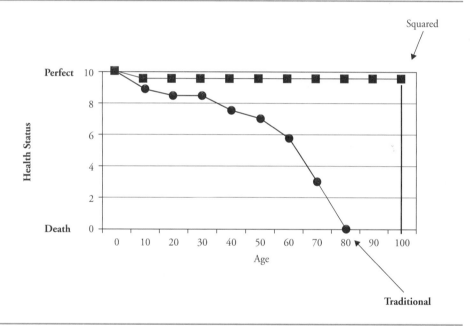

Generally the wealth manager will not be involved in the determination and resolution of the hidden goals, and may or may not be involved in the determination and resolution of the interim goals. In most cases, however, the retirement goal will be the primary guide in the wealth management process. For this reason, a major component of a wealth manager's analytical toolbox must be a detailed and competent knowledge of capital needs analysis as well as appropriate analytical software.

Wealth Transfer Goals

The amount of resources (or assets) one needs to meet clients' highly prioritized hidden, noninvestment, intermediate, and retirement goals is sometimes called *core capital*. The clients' goals represent liabilities in the context of their life balance sheets. Ideally, the clients' assets are sufficient to achieve their goals. In some cases, the assets may fall short and the life balance sheet provides a useful way to communicate that unpleasant reality and initiate the difficult discussion of reevaluating goals.

In contrast, assets may be more than sufficient to fund these goals, in which case a client has *excess capital* that can be safely transferred to children, grandchildren, or charities without jeopardizing the other goals. In fact, for some clients, transferring wealth to a particular cause may have higher priority than the goals we've just discussed. The eccentric billionaire who lives frugally but anonymously and generously donates to worthy causes is an extreme example. If wealth transfer goals are a priority, they too need articulation with respect to timing specificity (e.g., gift versus bequest, income beneficiary versus remainderman) and dollar specificity (e.g., determining how much can be safely transferred).

Goal Priority

Once the client has determined time and dollar specificity for his or her hidden, non-investment, intermediate, and retirement goals, it then becomes necessary to prioritize those goals. Frequently, the client's list of goals includes funding for college education and paying for a child's wedding. These are in addition to the goals of risk management and retirement. Although the cash flow planning software used by many professionals assumes that the average client will prioritize goals chronologically, with the hidden goals first, noninvestment goals second, intermediate goals third, and the retirement goal last, advisors do not deal with average clients. They deal with unique individuals (who are frequently anything but average or even reasonable), and they also deal with clients who lack an understanding of the entire process of goal setting, risk management, and retirement planning.

For example, simply due to lack of knowledge, many clients misprioritize their risk management. They carefully provide for adequate life insurance and ignore their need for disability coverage and long-term care insurance. Others will attempt to use a bucket approach for the frequently impossible task of independently funding a multitude of goals without having any reason to believe that they will have the resources required. Consider the following misprioritizing examples.

Common goals include special travel and college funding. An example of the danger of chronological prioritization would be scrapping a long-planned vacation because funding for that goal has come up short, only to find, a few years later, that the clients had overfunded for college tuition. Unfortunately, clients can't go back in time and take the vacation that, in hindsight, they now realize they could have afforded. In some cases, clients will misprioritize their goal planning as a result of a lack of understanding of the rules and regulations of investments and their related tax consequences.

A simple but common error found with younger investors is confusion between the prioritization of their college funding goal for their children and their own retirement goal. Consider a young couple with their first child and a desire to plan for college funding. Assume that although both parents are working, the most they can save on a yearly basis is $4,000. Both the husband and the wife qualify for fully deductible individual retirement accounts (IRAs).

It is likely that in this scenario, the family would begin saving funds for their child's education either in their own names or in a uniform transfer to minors account for their child. If an advisor were to suggest that they consider making contributions to their retirement account, it is likely that they would respond that they couldn't do that because they plan on using the funds for their child's education. If asked why they could not utilize their retirement account to fund their child's education, they are likely to respond that it is a retirement account and can't be used for education. Even if they are aware that the funds are available to them but subject to a 10 percent tax penalty, they are unlikely to have considered the long-term implications. The reality is that by the time their child reaches college age, they may well be able to pay the cost from personal savings without having to invade their IRA accounts. Should it turn out that they need the IRA funds to pay for college, the deferred-tax compounding for 18 years might well offset the tax penalty.

Aside from the tax consequence of using retirement money to pay for a child's education, money is fungible. By that we mean that how you label the saved and invested funds is independent of how you actually use them. For example, our young couple may save $4,000 per year and accumulate $100,000 for their retirement. If the same amount of money had been invested in a similar way for college, it would grow to the same amount. But savings in the IRAs would maintain flexibility. The $100,000 can be used for either purpose, except for a possible tax penalty for a nonqualified withdrawal.

So far, the example has focused on the possible flexibility of using a retirement account for potential college funding needs. Still to be addressed is the question of the prioritization of the goals. Suppose that, with the assistance of the wealth manager, it is determined the couple will be unable to fully fund both the college education and their retirement goals. The chronological default assumption is that the college funding should be accomplished first and the retirement funding second. Certainly, an argument can be made for this prioritization. The number of years between college funding and retirement is frequently of such length that it is difficult to make reasonable projections. Thus, there is a significant likelihood that during the period savings could be increased. In fact, it's likely that the couple will have enough saved independently to pay for college and will also have a well-funded retirement account. If the decision is made early to reduce funding of the college education in order to fully fund retirement, after the fact it may be too late to reverse that decision.

In spite of the compelling logic of prioritizing college before retirement funding, it is important to keep in mind that clients are unique. There are clients who believe that it is appropriate for their children to take responsibility for their college costs. These parents would rather err on the side of overfunding their retirement goal.

Prioritization is the client's responsibility. It is the wealth manager's responsibility to assist the client in understanding the consequences of these choices.

RISK OBJECTIVE

It is generally easier for private clients to think about investment objectives in terms of outcomes—the goals they would like to achieve. These outcomes are of course determined by investment returns. Integral, however, in the goal-setting process is the identification of risk objectives, because risk and return are so inextricably linked.

A common measure of investment risk is the standard deviation of returns. Most clients, however, have great difficulty internalizing risk expressed in this manner. They have little interest in learning enough statistics, studying enough return distributions, and learning about Chebyshev's theorem[4] to make good sense of what that means to them. Rather, most clients think about wealth in dollar terms, not percentage terms. If you ask your million-dollar clients

---

[4]In probability theory, Chebyshev's inequality states that more than $1/k^2$ of a distribution's values lie within k standard deviations of the mean regardless of the shape of the probability distribution.

if they can tolerate a 25 percent loss, you may get a different reaction than if you asked them how they would feel if their portfolio were worth $750,000 instead of a million dollars. Moreover, their answer to the question will likely change depending on whether they have recently experienced a significant gain or loss in their portfolio.

For individual investors, risk is more often defined as the chance of not realizing their goals, particularly their high-priority goals. Therefore, risk is typically measured in absolute and real (inflation-adjusted) terms rather than relative to a market index or a group of peers.

Once risk is defined, the wealth manager must estimate an investor's risk profile. It is composed of at least two elements—risk tolerance and risk capacity. An investor's risk tolerance is determined largely by internal factors, like attitudes and personality, while risk capacity is determined largely by external factors, like financial situation.

One way to gauge an investor's risk tolerance is through personality typing. (See Exhibit 3.3.) At the risk of overgeneralizing, investors who base decisions primarily on reasoning and other cognitive factors tend to be either methodological investors or individualist investors. Methodological investors look for concrete external data on which to base decisions and are almost Zen-like in their ability to stick to a proposed investment plan. They tend to be less willing to accept risk (i.e., more risk averse) than individualist investors, who are more inclined to process data in an independent manner even if it yields a contrarian result.

Cautious and spontaneous investors tend to base decisions on emotional factors. Cautious investors tend to place high importance on financial security and react very negatively to losses, even small ones. They therefore tend to exhibit little willingness to accept risk compared to spontaneous investors, who are more likely to trade frequently, rebalance their portfolios, and distrust investment advisors.

The way in which investor psychology interacts with risk is an extremely important, yet sometimes subtle, factor in estimating an investor's willingness to accept risk. It has spawned an entire field of study called behavioral finance.

EXHIBIT 3.3   Personality Types

	Decisions based primarily on thinking	Decisions based primarily on feeling
More risk averse	Methodical	Cautious
Less risk averse	Individualist	Spontaneous

Source: Bronson, Scanlan, and Squires (2007).

Risk capacity is based more on external, situational factors, and analyzing a client's situational profile can provide clues. For example, consider a typical entrepreneur who has built a small private business from the ground up. Most of his wealth may be tied up in an illiquid interest in the company. Moreover, depending on the nature of the industry, the value of the business and his earnings from it may be highly volatile. These changes in value and cash flow are also likely to be correlated with changes in the equity markets. All else being equal, these factors point to a reduced ability to accept risk in his investment portfolio because most of his other wealth is illiquid, risky, and highly correlated with the market. (Note that this situation might stand in stark contrast to the personality type and penchant for risk taking of a typical entrepreneur.)

By contrast, consider an investor who is the primary income beneficiary of a well-managed trust and who works as a government employee in defense contracting, both of which are more than sufficient to meet her ongoing living expenses, emergency reserves, and even some liquidity needs. These sources of cash flow are very stable and increase her capacity to accept risk in her investment portfolio because the consequences of experiencing below-average performance, though not pleasant, are manageable.

Investors' ability to accept risk also increases with their wealth level, all else being equal. If a person's wealth is more than sufficient to meet her future needs, she has more ability to accept risk with what is left over. This idea must be accompanied by an important caveat. Sufficiency is highly dependent on one's lifestyle and needs. A portfolio that is sufficient to maintain a modest lifestyle and provide financial security in relatively predictable circumstances may be insufficient for a more glamorous lifestyle in less predictable circumstances. See, for example, Michael Jackson, Evander Holyfield, Ed McMahon, or Michael Vick—all of whom have experienced severe financial problems. Sports figures are notorious for adopting unsustainable lifestyles. In fact, 60 percent of former National Basketball Association (NBA) players are broke within five years of retirement from the sport.[5] The point is that wealth by itself does not indicate an investor's capacity to accept risk. This ability needs to be viewed in light of financial goals. The life balance sheet we introduced in Chapter 1 is an instrumental tool to help make this evaluation.

Often, an investor's risk tolerance and risk capacity are in conflict, as in the case of the entrepreneur described earlier. If tolerance exceeds capacity or capacity exceeds tolerance, the wealth manager should try to educate the investor to help align the two. Barring that reconciliation, the more conservative of the two should prevail.

CONSTRAINTS

Having completed the education of the client relative to the time and dollar specificity of goals as well as their prioritization, and having evaluated the client's risk objectives, the wealth manager can then begin to educate that client with respect to his or her unique constraints.

For each of the goals, the constraints include the client's time horizons, the goal's liquidity and marketability requirements, the client's personal tax environment, his or her risk tolerance and capacity, and legal and regulatory considerations. The balance of this chapter discusses time horizon, liquidity, and marketability. The next two constraints, taxes and risks, are so complex that they have been allotted their own chapters. Legal considerations, such as the use of trusts or early withdrawal penalties from qualified plans, are often related to taxes but can also involve the proper management of trust structures, which often constrains investment and spending decisions.

---

[5]Pablo S. Torre, "How (and Why) Athletes Go Broke," *Sports Illustrated*, March 23, 2009.

Time Horizon

The time horizon will have been established by the goal-setting process. Having learned the necessity of determining time specificity for each goal, including the mortality determination for retirement planning, the client will have not only an understanding but an ownership of the time horizon for goals.

This process usually results in a multistage time horizon that will likely comprise various intermittent liquidity needs, like an emergency reserve or a child's college education. These shorter-term liquidity needs have implications for the liquidity and marketability of the securities in the portfolio. The shorter the time horizon for a major liquidity need, the greater the liquidity constraint on the portfolio (discussed next).

Generally, the longer an investor's time horizon, the greater the ability to accept risk, because the investor may have the benefit of time to adjust and adapt if investments perform below expectations.[6] Investors may be able to adjust to poor returns if they are in the accumulation phase, adding to their financial capital, and they have the ability to alter their capital accumulation plans. Basically, time may buy them flexibility, which in turn can increase their ability to accept risk. It need not always be the case, though.

Liquidity

Once clients have completed the process of prioritizing and defining their goals with time and dollar specificity, they can then intelligently determine the levels of liquidity and marketability necessary for each of those goals. For example, the goal of an adequate emergency reserve requires the attribute of liquidity. An investor should not place emergency reserves in the equity market or in an intermediate-term bond fund. Their moderate liquidity is an inappropriate attribute for the time horizon of an emergency reserve.

Liquidity generally refers to the ease with which a portfolio can satisfy an investor's needs, and it has at least two components—marketability and price volatility—that are all too frequently confused by investors, media, and advisors. In order to avoid semantic confusion, for purposes of this discussion, these two terms will be defined to describe very specific attributes of investments.

1. *Marketability.* Marketability is an attribute that measures an investor's ability to readily convert an investment to cash at *prevailing* market prices. In the equity market, it is a function of brokerage fees, trading volume, and bid-ask spreads. The greater the costs of finding a willing buyer, the less liquid an asset is and the less appropriate it is for funding an investor's liquidity needs. Liquid investments would include money market funds, Treasury bills, and cash.
2. *Price volatility.* An asset may be very easy to sell in all market conditions, but if its market price is inherently volatile (like stock prices), then liquidity is compromised. Consider Carlita, who had a million-dollar portfolio at the beginning of 2008. One of her goals was to purchase a half-million-dollar boat in one year. Her investment advisor told her that her portfolio was invested in a diversified and easily traded Standard & Poor's 500 index fund that had sufficient liquidity to meet her needs. By the end of 2008, however, her S&P 500 portfolio was worth only $630,000. Yes, she could easily liquidate

---

[6]This is not a comment on the debate about whether equity investments become less risky in the long run. Rather, it is simply an evaluation of an investor's ability to absorb investment risk.

$500,000 of her index fund and had the money to do it. However, price volatility would leave her with only $130,000 after the boat purchase! She had probably had her sights set on four times that amount. Her advisor had failed to consider her liquidity need as a short-term liability to the portfolio. By investing the entire million dollars in equities, the advisor was effectively leveraging her up two times and accepting enormous price risk.

The experience of many years on a call-in investment radio program in Miami taught Harold, all too clearly, the dangers of misunderstanding the attributes of liquidity, price volatility, and marketability as defined earlier.[7] During periods of falling interest rates, he frequently had conversations that resembled the following:

"Hello, Mr. Talk Show Host. I just bought a Ginnie Mae. What is it?" The caller (we'll name her Mrs. Hampton) was usually a widow living on Miami Beach who had recently received the proceeds of a maturing jumbo (i.e., $100,000) certificate of deposit. She was very unhappy when quoted the new lower CD renewal rate. As a result, she had responded to one of the many brokerage firm ads that tend to crop up during periods of low interest rates (i.e., advertising safe investments with much higher returns).

Once in the salesman's office, Mrs. Hampton was presented with a recommendation to purchase a Ginnie Mae (Government National Mortgage Association or GNMA). The marketing material and the salesman's pitch addressed all of her concerns. She was assured that not only was the interest rate being paid on the GNMA much higher than the current rate on CDs, but the GNMA, like the CD, was government guaranteed. For a widow from Miami Beach, there is nothing so musical to the ear as the phrase "government guaranteed." Lest a potential client miss the point, the marketing material typically had a full-color American flag on one side, a picture of apple pie on the other side, and the phrase "government guaranteed" printed in 80-point type. Generally, the sale was consummated at this point. In those rare instances when a Mrs. Hampton might ask, "What happens if I want to sell?" the salesman would frequently employ the "arm around the shoulder" close. This required him to get up from behind his desk, walk over, put his arm comfortingly around the client, and say, "Don't worry, Mrs. Hampton, if you ever want to sell, just give me a call and we will sell it that very instant." If she had not been convinced before, she was convinced now.

A few days later, while listening to a call-in investment talk show on her radio, Mrs. Hampton, realizing she really doesn't know what a Ginnie Mae is, calls a total stranger (Harold), and asks him what she just bought with her $100,000. He proceeds to explain the nature of a Ginnie Mae: Although the principal at maturity may be effectively guaranteed by the U.S. federal government, the investment is subject to interest rate risk prior to maturity. This means that if interest rates rise over the next few years and she wishes to sell prior to maturity, she might receive less than her original investment. If interest rates fall over the next few years, borrowers of the underlying mortgages may prepay more quickly than anticipated, returning money to Mrs. Hampton in a low interest rate environment.

At this point, Mrs. Hampton very confidently informs Harold and 250,000 other listeners that although it might be true of other people's Ginnie Maes, it is not true of hers. Upon asking her why, she patiently explains that the salesman said she could sell whenever she wanted to. Mrs. Hampton heard "liquid"; the salesman meant "marketable." The sequel to

---

[7]Harold's partner at the time, Jeff Kassower, was the show host. He invited Harold to join him and thus provided him the opportunity to spend many years attending the best school for learning about client psychology that exists—talk radio.

that story (and many, many similar calls) is that interest rates subsequently rose significantly. As a result, there were many Ginnie Mae investors who were unpleasantly surprised at the precipitous drop in value of their government-guaranteed investments.

The emotional trauma suffered by these investors was a direct result of not understanding the difference between liquidity and marketability. While the statements of the salesman describing the investment—namely, that it was guaranteed and that the client could sell whenever she wished—were quite true, for the average investor it was very misleading. Most individuals equate the ability to sell when they want (marketability) with the ability to get their original investment back. They are not considering the other aspect that makes an investment liquid (lack of price volatility).

Another example, familiar to advisors who have been in business for many years, is the case of a retiree, who we'll call Mr. Trujillo, who sat down with Harold and asked what to do with the funds from a maturing CD. It seems he had been rolling over his one-year CDs, and as rates had continued dropping, his income had also continued dropping. He made it quite clear to Harold that he was extremely concerned about risk. Harold suggested that he might want to consider a five-year CD. Mr. Trujillo turned so pale that Harold was concerned for his health, and the retiree said, quite seriously, "Sonny, at my age, long term is a green banana." Harold explained that if his comfort level for an investment horizon was only one year, there was really no good alternative to the one-year CD that he currently owned. Mr. Trujillo looked at Harold as if he had claimed that the world was actually square and not round. He then suggested that Harold had no idea what he was talking about. It seems his neighbor had just recently purchased a preferred utility stock that was paying almost twice what the one-year CD was paying. He had expected Harold to make a similar recommendation. Harold started explaining that if Mr. Trujillo was uncomfortable with a five-year maturity, he might be significantly less comfortable with a five-million-year maturity. Harold thought his use of the words "five-million-year maturity," in lieu of trying to explain an infinite maturity on a preferred stock, was an effective way of emphasizing the point. He was wrong. Mr. Trujillo was not persuaded. He responded that Harold really did not seem to understand the investment market. Everyone knew that the company issuing the preferred stock that he wished to buy was a big, well-known utility. Its shares traded every day on the New York Stock Exchange. He could sell whenever he wished. Once again, it was a tragic mistake of assuming that marketability is all that is necessary for liquidity.

The final confusion that relates to the attributes of liquidity is investors' common practice of assigning moral judgment to the attributes themselves.

The thought process is that marketable investments are good, and poorly marketable investments are bad. It is common to hear these moral adjectives applied to the spectrum of investments. It is imperative, as part of the education process, for the wealth manager to clarify for the client that liquidity and marketability are different attributes of investments. They carry no moral connotations. Wealth managers must guide their clients to evaluate investment attributes in terms of "appropriate" and "inappropriate" instead of "good" or "bad."

Once a client has a solid understanding of the constraints of liquidity and marketability, he or she will be an infinitely better investor as well as an infinitely better client.

Income Portfolios: The Myth of Dividends and Interest

The myth of the income portfolio is so closely related to the concepts of price volatility and marketability that a short divergence at this stage seems useful. One of the most insidious and erroneous paradigms adversely affecting portfolios of individual and institutional investors is that of the income portfolio (the myth). The term *myth* is used here and in later discussions to describe what we believe to be an unfounded and false belief. The myth, rooted in a historical heritage dating back to twelfth-century English land rents, is that investors must construct portfolios that generate dividends and interest (i.e., they must not touch principal) in order to receive cash flow.

The myth is also frequently exacerbated by the myth that retirees are on a fixed income. Wealth managers should disabuse clients of this notion. To the extent retirees depend on Social Security benefits, that portion of their income stream usually is adjusted annually for inflation; it is generally not fixed. To the extent that their income is dependent on their investment portfolios, the danger is that they might buy into the myth and construct a so-called income portfolio. The problem is that the myth is wrong! An income portfolio is fixed by design—inappropriate design. An income policy enforces an inappropriate constraint on portfolio design that, in almost all cases, will result in an inferior portfolio. In many instances, it will lead to the design of a portfolio that is not only inefficient, but also one that will not allow the client to accomplish his or her goals.

Plainly, any investment's return is comprised of two components: income (in the form of interest or dividends) and capital gains. Therefore,

$$\text{Total Return} = \text{Income} + \text{Capital Gains}$$

Having an income portfolio does not increase total return. It simply decreases the amount of return delivered in the form of capital gain. Focusing on only the income portion is an artificial constraint on the type of eligible securities for the portfolio and can limit the ability to diversify.

A *total return* approach translates an individual's goals and investment constraints into a return requirement. The wealth manager then constructs a portfolio with a total return to satisfy these needs. With the notable exception of taxes, which we will address in Chapter 11, it is relatively unimportant whether the return comes in the form of income or capital gain.

Consider a very simple world in which there are only three investment alternatives: money market, bonds, and stock. These investments have the following expected returns, and the projected inflation rate is 4 percent:

Investment	Interest	Dividends	Capital Gains	Total Return
Money market	3%	0%	0%	3%
Bonds	5	0	0	5
Stock	0	2	7	9

In this world, as in our world, there are likely to be investors with many different cash flow requirements.

Consider Ms. Salter, who has no cash reserve requirement but who needs a 3.5 percent cash flow per year. What are her investment choices if she is constrained by the myth?

As reflected in Exhibit 3.4, if Ms. Salter's cash flow has to be generated solely from dividends and interest, the maximum allocation to stock that will accomplish that goal is 50 percent. Any allocation to stock in excess of 50 percent will result in a cash flow of less than her 3.5 percent requirement.

EXHIBIT 3.4   Allocation Alternatives for Ms. Salter

Bond Allocation	Cash Flow from Bonds	Stock Allocation	Cash Flow from Stocks	Total Cash Flow
100%	5.0%	0%	0.0%	5.0%
90	4.5	10	0.2	4.7
80	4.0	20	0.4	4.4
70	3.5	30	0.6	4.1
60	3.0	40	0.8	3.8
50	2.5	50	1.0	3.5
40	2.0	60	1.2	3.2

Exhibit 3.5 considers a number of possible constraints that might face a client such as Ms. Salter. For example, Scenario 1 corresponds to the need reflected in Exhibit 3.4. Scenario 4 assumes a need for a 3.5 percent cash flow, but also a need for a 15 percent cash reserve. The column labeled "Maximum Equity Allocation" is the maximum percentage that could be invested in equities and still result in the portfolio dividend and interest amounts meeting the client's needs. The last column is the wealth manager's recommendation for equity allocation based not just on Ms. Salter's cash flow and reserve, but also on her long-term goals.

EXHIBIT 3.5   Allocations for Ms. Salter According to the Myth

Scenario	Cash Reserve Requirements	Cash Flow Required	Maximum Equity Allocation	Wealth Manager's Allocation
Scenario 1	0%	3.5%	50%	60%
Scenario 2	0	4.0	30	60
Scenario 3	0	4.5	10	60
Scenario 4	15	3.5	40	65
Scenario 5	15	4.0	20	65
Scenario 6	15	4.5	0	65

Exhibit 3.5 dramatically demonstrates the fallacy of constraining a portfolio to meet the requirements of the myth. For all of the scenarios without a reserve, the wealth manager has determined that, taking into consideration the client's needs for current *real* income *and* long-term goals, the portfolio should be 40 percent bonds and 60 percent stocks. Where there is a need for a reserve, the advisor has determined that the equity portion of the investment portfolio should be increased to 65 percent because the cash allocation results in opportunity cost but increases Ms. Salter's ability to accept risk elsewhere in her portfolio. A client, heeding the advice of the person designing the portfolio to meet the cash flow requirement by matching it to dividends and interest, would always have a significantly lower allocation to equities. Of course, the consequence of ignoring the recommendations of the wealth manager is likely to be that the investor will run out of financial resources long before she runs out of the need for those resources. In other words, myopically following the myth is likely to render the investor destitute long before death.

Step away from the paradigm of dividends and interest. Focus instead on total *real* return. Without the constraint of the myth, it is possible to balance the need for real cash flow with the need for long-term growth. First design the portfolio for the required total real return. Then design a strategy to provide for the necessary cash flow from the portfolio's dividends, interest, and *capital gains*. A simple solution is to intermittently sell a portion of the portfolio equal to the amount necessary to meet cash flow needs. In Ms. Salter's case, if she follows the wealth manager's advice and invests in a portfolio of 40 percent bonds and 60 percent stock, her portfolio will have an expected total return of approximately 7.4 percent. As necessary, she will liquidate adequate resources to provide herself with a real cash flow of 3.5 percent per year. In addition to meeting her cash flow requirements, the remaining 3.9 percent of portfolio growth will meet her long-term need of maintaining purchasing power over time by growing the nominal value of her portfolio by the expected inflation rate.

The two major arguments against moving from an income portfolio to a total return portfolio are that the income portfolio is more transaction-cost and tax efficient, and that the total return portfolio is subject to market volatility. However, these arguments do not hold up under any historically reasonable scenario.

Regarding taxes, there are strategies—one example is discussed next—that can reduce unnecessary trading. Perhaps more important, an income portfolio is an inherently tax-inefficient strategy for generating cash flow in some jurisdictions. Cash flow from dividends and interest can be subject to higher income tax rates.[8] In the total return portfolio, cash flow from capital gains can be taxed at a lower capital gains rate. The bigger the difference between these two rates, the bigger the relative tax drag on the income portfolio.

Market volatility is a serious concern when designing a strategy to obtain cash flow from a total return portfolio. However, if the portfolio is properly designed, the risk is more psychological than financial. If any portion of a portfolio is invested for growth, there is a real likelihood that the client will at some point be dipping into principal. Psychologically, this can be a disturbing event. It is, unfortunately, a reality of investing. Part of the solution is client education. In addition, there are strategies that may minimize the client's concern. One used at Harold's firm is discussed next. The financial risk is likely to be temporary. Over the planning horizon, if the cash flow demand is reasonable relative to the targeted total return, the portfolio value will likely recover and continue to grow.

EVENSKY & KATZ CASH FLOW STRATEGY

Although we have discussed this concept with our client during the educational session, prior to beginning the risk coaching process we once again emphasize our firm mantra: "Five years, five years, five years!"

We believe in the concept of time diversification at least in the sense that time provides flexibility for investors to respond to changing market conditions.[9] Further, as a general rule, we believe that five years is a good minimum standard to use as a criterion for investment time diversification. It is important to note that this is a rolling, not a fixed, standard. If a client informs us that the investment funds will be needed in exactly five years, the portfolio would not meet our standard one day later when the holding period will have dropped to four years and 364 days.

Although we know that our clients' real time horizon is typically 20+ years and their psychological time horizon is 10 seconds, our clients would balk if we started off discussing a 20-year period. Their initial orientation is short term (remember the green banana).

---

[8]Obviously, municipal bonds will generally provide tax-free returns; however, the income will be lower.
[9]This is a controversial issue, and it is discussed in some detail in Chapter 8, "Investment Theory."

The art of data gathering (which is one element of managing client expectations) includes obtaining commitment as well as information from clients with 10-second psychological time horizons and 20-year real horizons. We find that the five-year mantra is an effective tool.

The mantra is not a bluff. Unless clients can swear (or affirm) upon penalty of dire consequences that there is no expectation (even remote) of needing the corpus of the portfolio for a period of five years, we do not consider the funds investment funds. We will neither develop an investment plan nor assume the responsibility of investing the assets. We do not make the clients sign in blood, but we do have them acknowledge, in writing, at the end of the questionnaire their affirmation of the answers they have provided.

Our firm's five-year mantra serves as the basis for our cash flow strategy.[10] Namely, we want to have a significant time window (preferably five years) prior to having to sell a potentially volatile investment. If we simply sold investments quarterly or annually to meet our client's cash flow needs, there would be little flexibility. We might be forced to liquidate positions when their value was down. In addition, in order to keep the portfolio in balance, we would have to sell very small percentages of many investments, resulting in significant transaction costs.

To address the liquidity criteria embodied by our five-year mantra, we set up, for our clients, a second account that we title the "cash flow reserve account," depicted in Exhibit 3.6. It is designed to hold liquid funds for short-term needs. For any lump-sum goals (e.g., college funding, purchase of a second home), we set aside a sum equal to any anticipated need during the next five years. With respect to a client's regular, but more modest, supplemental annual cash flow needs (e.g., additional funds for living expenses in retirement, set at a maximum of 5 percent), we concluded that setting aside five years' worth of cash flow in money market funds resulted in too large an opportunity cost. After modeling and testing a number of alternatives, we concluded that a two-year cash flow reserve carve-out was both economically and behaviorally optimal. We found that having two years' worth of grocery money set aside during stressful market cycles provides adequate comfort for our clients to weather the market's not-infrequent bumpy ride. Recognizing that there are periods that place a strain on investment portfolios well beyond two years, the strategy incorporates what we refer to as a second-tier emergency liquidity reserve. This second tier is composed of the fixed income allocation at the short end of our fixed income ladder.

Every portfolio we design has at least a 20 percent fixed income allocation, and that allocation is laddered such that within the investment portfolio we have at least an additional three years' worth of living expenses invested in high-quality, short-duration positions. We consider this our secondary liquidity reserve. Since implementing this strategy in the early 1980s, we've never had to tap that second-tier liquidity, but it's comforting to us and our clients to know it's in place. We, not the market, remain in control.

For example, if you were to open an investment account for a client requiring a 5 percent annual real cash flow from a $1 million investment account, you would open two accounts:

Cash flow reserve account	$100,000
Investment account	$900,000

---

[10]This strategy, introduced in Harold's *Wealth Management* (McGraw-Hill, 1997), is now popularly referred to as a "bucket" strategy. A detailed discussion of this strategy may be found in "Withdrawal Strategies: A Cash Flow Solution," in *Retirement Income Redesigned: Master Plans for Distribution*, Harold Evensky and Deena B. Katz, eds. (New York: Bloomberg Press, 2006), 185–202.

Having set aside this cash flow reserve, you can discuss with your clients the likely t
of their drawdown needs and design a simple investment plan for the cash flow account. Ir
where clients are very unsure of their needs, you may recommend starting with 100 perc... ...
money market funds. For most clients, the funds will be laddered using money markets and
Treasury bills and/or short- and limited-term, high-quality, low-volatility bond funds.

Evensky & Katz formally reviews investment accounts at least quarterly. At that time they
also review the status of the client's cash flow account. If, in the normal course of events,
they find a need to trade in the investment account, they use this opportunity to transfer

EXHIBIT 3.6   Cash Flow Strategy

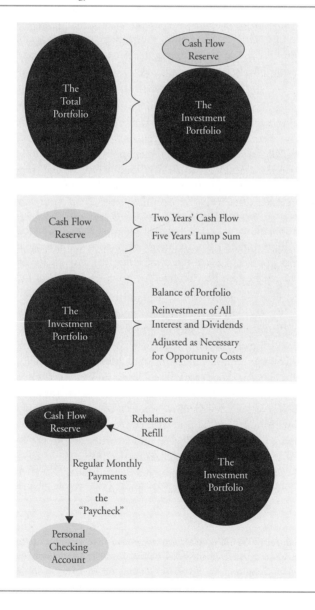

funds from the investment account to the cash flow account, bringing the cash flow account back up to the two-year reserve. If they see no need to adjust the investment account and the cash flow account has at least six months' worth of reserves, they will generally not make any transfers. In the normal course of rebalancing, changing managers, adding asset classes, adjusting for new client funds, and so on, there should not be a significant problem in maintaining the client's cash flow reserve between six months and two years.

Is the Strategy Successful?

Unequivocally, yes. The Evensky & Katz strategy has been successful for many years, helping clients weather the 1987 crash, the 2000–2001 tech stock bust, and the 2008–2009 recession. More specifically, it accomplishes the following goals:

- The single most important contribution of the strategy is its management of the volatility risk associated with distribution. Short-term market volatility has a profound effect on the sustainability of withdrawals. As a consequence, for investors drawing funds from savings to provide for daily living expenses, market volatility is one of the most significant financial risks. Utilizing the proposed cash flow strategy largely eliminates the forced sale of investment assets to meet anticipated cash flow needs by placing the timing of the sale of investment assets in the hands of the investor.
- Clients need real, not nominal, cash flow; hence a major goal of cash flow planning is to ensure that the client's income keeps pace with inflation. As the reserve requirement is reviewed regularly (in our practice the review is quarterly), it's quite easy to increase the payout to the client to adjust for any inflation erosion.
- As there is no need to independently consider the specific dividend and interest attributes of the investment portfolio, it can be designed for total return. This enables the allocation design of the portfolio to reflect the unique risk tolerance and return needs of the client. It also allows the practitioner to make the most efficient use of sheltered accounts.[11]
- The presence of an ample cash flow reserve also provides significant flexibility in the event of unanticipated needs and insulates the investment portfolio from being impacted by the need for short-term distributions. As a result, in managing the long-term investment portfolio, the wealth manager can focus on tax and expense efficiency.
- The strategy incorporates many lessons from behavioral finance, most significantly the power of framing. By providing a visible source of liquid funds, it frames the accounts in a manner consistent with an investor's separate-pocket mentality, and the scheduled monthly payments frame the income consistent with our clients' paycheck mentality.
- Clients are not affected by the following problems typically associated with the paradigm of interest and dividends:
  - Myth investors are psychologically locked into an artificial cash flow straitjacket. They let the volatility of interest rates and the markets determine their standard of living.
  - They are likely to constrain their current standard of living rather that dip into capital, even during periods of exceptional market growth.

---

[11]In an income portfolio, in order to generate the required annual cash flow, fixed income investments would generally have to be a significant portion of the assets in a taxable account. In a total return portfolio an advisor might use available sheltered accounts for investments in tax-inefficient Treasury inflation-protected securities (TIPS).

- They feel rich and spend all of the cash flow during periods of high interest rates (when their bond investments are losing value) and find it extraordinarily difficult to adjust their standard of living downward when rates cycle down (and their bond investments are gaining value).

- Clients are less likely to be enticed by the marketing hype that often seduces the income portfolio investor into products offering high current returns at the expense of total returns (e.g., high current payments generated by premium bonds or preferred stock) and into products offering high returns generated either by aggressive investing (e.g., high-yield bonds, emerging market debt, and leverage) or by aggressive strategies (e.g., a heavy concentration in volatile derivatives).

These cash flow reserve clients sleep well, they do not press us to chase after unrealistic cash flow products, they do not monitor interest rate changes on a daily basis, and they take market volatility in stride. Their mental security comes from being able to see, on their statements and in our reports, many years of available cash flow, reserved for that purpose and invested in liquid securities that are effectively immune to the short-term ravages of stock or bond market volatility. They don't panic during bear markets, because they know their grocery money is sitting in cash.

Although we believe that the effort is worth the results, the strategy we employ obviously adds time and cost to our handling of the client's account. A far simpler implementation strategy would be to simply set up an automatic percentage payment from the funds to the client. Although less tax efficient, it is still a superior solution to that of the myth of the income portfolio.

PARTING COMMENTS

Getting to know your clients and assisting them with establishing goals is a critical part of the wealth management process. If the goals, including hidden goals, are not identified, specified, and prioritized, it is doubtful any investment plan will achieve the client's goals other than by chance. Wealth managers should devote a significant amount of their time to this part of the process.

RESOURCES

Bronson, James W., Matthew H. Scanlan, and Jan R. Squires. 2007. "Managing Individual Investor Portfolios." In *Managing Investment Portfolios: A Dynamic Process*, 3rd edition. John L. Maginn and Donald L. Tuttle, eds. CFA Institute Investment Series. Hoboken, NJ: John Wiley & Sons.

Evensky, Harold, and Deena B. Katz. 2006. *Retirement Income Redesigned: Master Plans for Distribution—An Adviser's Guide for Funding Boomers' Best Years*. New York: Bloomberg Press.

Horan, Stephen M. 2004. "Breakeven Holding Periods for Tax Advantaged Savings Accounts with Early Withdrawal Penalties," *Financial Services Review*, Vol. 13, No. 3: 233–247.

Horan, Stephen M. 2005. *Tax-Advantaged Savings Accounts and Tax-Efficient Wealth Accumulation*. Charlottesville, VA: Research Foundation of CFA Institute.

CHAPTER 4

RISK IS A
FOUR-LETTER WORD

Security is mostly a superstition: it doesn't exist in nature.

—Helen Keller

The interaction between investor psychology and the uncertainties of both capital markets and individual cash flow needs mandates a new set of investment solutions.

—Jean Brunel

Fear of risk is probably a client's most restrictive investment constraint. One of the unique contributions of the wealth manager is the ability to assist clients in effectively dealing with the frightening specter of risk. It is the one constraint that most often prevents clients from achieving their life goals. This chapter provides the wealth manager with information, insights, and techniques to assist in better communicating with and educating clients about risk.

Prior to the development of probability theory, the issue of investment risk was moot. After all, the gods (or God) either did or did not provide rain for the crops. The concept of risk implies an ability to assume or avoid risk. For our ancestors, things (e.g., rain) either happened or did not happen. With the development of the concept of probability came the modern concept of risk.

For the modern wealth manager, the seminal event was the 1952 revelation of Harry Markowitz: "I was struck with the notion that you should be interested in risk as well as return." In hindsight, this seems a fairly obvious observation, but Dr. Markowitz was awarded the Nobel Prize in 1990 for his work that evolved from this simple notion.

Charles Ellis admonishes that risk management is the responsibility of the advisor, and Peter Bernstein provides the sobering reminder that risk is in the "eyes of the beholder and the eyes may be myopic."

Clearly, if risk is such an important concept and its management is the responsibility of the wealth manager, but its meaning varies for our clients, it is imperative that a wealth manager understand the psychology of risk. Behavioral finance, the field of study at the intersection of economics and psychology, is traced back to the late 1970s when Daniel Kahneman and Amos Tversky, and academics such as Hersh Shefrin, Richard Thaler, and Meir Statman, started researching investor decision making in a robust manner. As far back as 1934, however, Benjamin Graham and David Dodd spoke of "market quotations ... distorted by psychological excesses."[1] Therefore, the psychology of risk is well established in field investment and portfolio analysis. This chapter provides the wealth manager with a framework for communicating with clients regarding risks and evaluating clients' risk tolerance.

RISK TOLERANCE

As the simplified efficient frontier graph (risk versus return for available investments) in Exhibit 4.1 indicates, in developing a portfolio allocation for a client there are two fundamental factors that the advisor needs to balance: the return required to provide the growth necessary for the client to achieve his or her goals, and the risk associated with a specific portfolio allocation. The goal is to design, to the extent possible, a portfolio that provides the client with the necessary return at the lowest possible risk. We refer to this as "anchoring on the efficient frontier." This chapter addresses the risk anchor.

EXHIBIT 4.1   Efficient Frontier

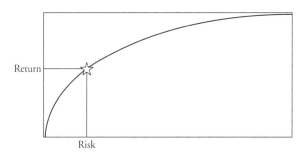

In order to determine the risk anchor, a practitioner must determine what, from the client's perspective, constitutes risk. This is not quite as simple as it may sound, because the issue is not one of risk measurement (e.g., standard deviation) but risk threshold (i.e., the limit of acceptable risk). The common terminology for this threshold is *risk tolerance*. Unfortunately, although a commonly used term, it is also often used in different ways. We believe that the key issue is a client's tolerance for risk when everything is going wrong. Therefore, we believe the most useful definition of risk tolerance to be that threshold of pain just before your client calls and says, "I can't stand it anymore; sell me out."

Risk Tolerance versus Risk Capacity

Confusing these two concepts is the potential fatal flaw of many risk tolerance questionnaires. While tolerance relates to an individual's *emotional* limit of acceptable risk, capacity refers to the *financial* capacity to withstand market losses. These two factors are not necessarily positively correlated. For example, it is not uncommon to find an investor with significant assets and modest demands on those assets such that a significant market loss would not affect

---

[1]The *Security Analysis* classic by Graham and Dodd was reprinted in its sixth edition in 2009 with updates and commentaries.

the ability to maintain the individual's desired quality of life (i.e., high risk capacity). However, that same investor might be unwilling to invest any significant portion of the portfolio in stock and might well bail out of whatever stock allocation there was in a significant bear market (i.e., low risk tolerance). As a consequence, questions regarding capacity are important for general planning purposes but are not relevant for evaluating tolerance. Examples of capacity questions would include:

- What is the term of the investment—short or long term? The typical question: "What is your age?" The portfolio of a long-term (e.g., young) investor may have significant risk capacity, as the probability of positive return increases over time.
- Financial resources well in excess of the amount needed to support the client's expected withdrawals. Typical questions addressing this issue: "What is your current income?" "Your savings are equal to how many months' salary?"

In many cases a client might sustain a significant short-term financial loss without expectation that the loss would result in being unable to meet his or her goals. As a consequence, based on capacity, a relatively high equity allocation might be quite appropriate. However, in the midst of a serious bear market, in spite of high capacity, as noted earlier, a client with a low risk tolerance might well panic and wish to sell out of stocks.

The important point to remember is that the goal of establishing a client's risk tolerance is to determine the likelihood of the client's sticking with an investment plan when the markets are in free fall. Although risk capacity is an important factor to be considered in the planning process, it should not be a factor in evaluating a client's risk tolerance.

Risk Tolerance versus Risk Behavior

There are many observers who believe that Risk Tolerance $= f$(Memory). This is formally stated as: "When risk becomes a reality, memory becomes short-term." For the typical client, the formula for this relationship is:

$$\text{Current Risk Tolerance} = \text{Normal} - \text{State Risk Tolerance} \times \text{Memory}$$

where Normal − State Risk Tolerance = 50 (i.e., a balanced portfolio of 50 percent fixed income and 50 percent equities), and Memory = a number between 0 and 2.

When equity market returns are high, memory becomes long term, approaching 2. When market returns turn negative, memory becomes short term, approaching 0.

Thus the normal client has a tolerance for 100 percent equities when the markets are up and 0 percent equities when market returns are down!

Geoff Davey, one of the profession's most knowledgeable individuals on the subject of risk tolerance and the founder of FinaMetrica, the leading risk profile questionnaire, suggests that our definition of risk tolerance is in fact a definition of risk behavior. He argues that if investors become so nervous in a down market that they sell everything, the action is more likely to be a result of risk behavior than risk tolerance. He explains that risk behavior is dependent on multiple factors, only one of which is risk tolerance. Those other factors include risk capacity, the relative importance of the goal(s), and perceived risk. He suggests that perception is most likely to be the dominant influence on behavioral change.

From a practitioner's perspective, the fundamental question in portfolio design would seem to be, in Geoff's terms, risk behavior; specifically, what is the maximum exposure to market risk that a client will accept without liquidating when faced with a serious decline such as that experienced from late 2007 to early 2008? As noted earlier, whatever terminology you use, the basic question facing the practitioner is how much of an exposure to stock is appropriate for clients such that it is unlikely that market panic will result in their calling and saying, "I can't stand it anymore; sell everything!"

Other Manifestations of Risk

It would seem that having to consider the many different aspects of risk discussed so far would be an adequate foundation to begin the construction of a risk tolerance questionnaire. It is not. The wealth manager must also consider other manifestations of risk.

Perceived versus Actual

A classic example is improper tax management resulting from confusion of tax reduction and after-tax maximization. The perceived risk is paying excess taxes. The real risk is the failure to maximize after-tax returns. We discuss this more fully in Chapter 11, "Taxes."

Loss of Principal versus Loss of Lifestyle

This relates to the public's ongoing confusion regarding the need for inflation-adjusted returns versus the need for principal guarantees. Nick Murray[2] cautions that risk is not implicit in the market but rather in clients and their emotions. One of Nick's many vignettes best tells this story:

EXAMPLE 4.1

When a client balks at making a risky investment in the stock market, Nick asks, "Whose side are you going to be on in the next Civil War?" The client is obviously confused by what seems to be such an insane question, but Nick explains that since it happened once it certainly can happen again, and since it's been so long already without repeating, it's likely to happen soon.

When the client responds that Nick is talking nonsense, he says, "Of course, and so are you." He then launches into his discussion of the "great anomaly."

Most investors who fear the market and idolize the safety of guaranteed returns (e.g., U.S. Treasuries and certificates of deposit) are driven by the great anomaly. This is a result of confusing certainty with safety.

As Nick points out, certainty of the return of principal is a measure of investment safety in only one economic environment—deflation. In any other economic scenario, the risk of investing is the erosion of purchasing power. Thus the cost of concentrating investments in so-called safe investments is likely to be very modest real returns. For most investors, a lifetime of modest real returns will translate to the necessity of reducing their living standard—not a very safe plan.

The wealth manager must clarify the importance of "loss of lifestyle" over "loss of principal." As addressed in more detail later in this chapter, a wealth manager's

---

[2]Nick Murray is the profession's preeminent writer/speaker on practical client psychology. Whenever you have an opportunity to read Nick's articles or hear him speak, do so. Your time will be well spent.

recommendation to buy equities is not solely for higher return; for long-term retirement planning, equities may be one of an investor's *safest* assets.

Unfortunately, there is no magic test available to the practitioner to establish this tolerance/behavior threshold. The solution is the use of professional tools such as FinaMetrica combined with guidance and education based on an understanding of our clients' behavioral characteristics. The field of study that addresses this issue and offers practitioners insights that will assist them in guiding their clients toward optimal solutions is behavioral finance. As Daniel Kahneman (who along with Amos Tversky is considered the founder of behavioral finance) wrote, "To advise effectively, advisors must be guided by an accurate picture of the cognitive and emotional weaknesses of investors that relate to making investment decisions."[3] That is the subject of the following discussion.

BEHAVIORAL FINANCE AND RELATED ISSUES OF BEHAVIORAL PSYCHOLOGY

People are strange. There is no more apparent example than the psychology of risk. People in general, and clients in particular, have difficulty distinguishing between knowledge-based risk and foolhardy speculation. As an example, investors grossly overestimate their knowledge and, even when provided with good data, they are poor mathematicians of probability.

Investors also have difficulty estimating the risks of future events. They are much more comfortable with short-term events in which they have more intuitive confidence in their knowledge. This results in a tendency to overstate their personal risk-taking propensity.

HEURISTICS AND BIASES

The client's unique bounds form the psychological structure from which his or her decision making emanates. Even within this decision-making framework, individuals have very limited ability to process large amounts of information. In order to manage quantity and complexity of information, the technique employed in decision making is the use of judgmental heuristics. In the language of cognitive psychology, heuristics are cognitive rules of thumb that simplify the decision-making process. More simply, they are mental shortcuts.

As the reader will learn from the following, many common heuristics are modified to become investing heuristics that guide the client's perception of investment risk and investment decision making. By understanding the nature of heuristics, a wealth manager will be able to better understand the underlying issues influencing a client's risk tolerance (e.g., confusion about certainty and safety). Also, the wealth manager will be more effective in assisting the client to modify misleading heuristics, as well as becoming a better educator and guide for clients in the useful application of these mental shortcuts.[4]

Although heuristics are often valuable and frequently enable an individual to make quick and sound decisions, they can be dangerously misleading as investors frequently misuse heuristics. For example, the quantity, quality, speed, and immediacy of information provided

---

[3]Daniel Kahneman and Mark Riepe, "Aspects of Investor Psychology," *Journal of Portfolio Management* (Summer 1998): 52–65.

[4]Shefrin (2002) discusses heuristics as one of the three themes of behavioral finance.

through the Internet, television, and print publications, like the *Wall Street Journal* and CNBC, often overwhelms other information in memory and results in an unwarranted extrapolation of the immediate information into the future.

In a sense, heuristics are analogous to mathematical optimizers in that they may maximize error. We tend to overweight information that is minimally relevant while minimizing important information. We overestimate our skill and knowledge, overestimate predictability, and believe we use far more data to make our decisions than we really do. By using shortcuts in the decision-making process, we magnify the impact of these errors.

As you read the following, consider how you can use the information to revise the tools you currently use to educate your clients (e.g., new graphics); to gather information (e.g., reframe questions in your risk tolerance questionnaire); and to confirm or modify your own personal investment strategy (e.g., rebalancing parameters, passive investing).

We discuss some of the most common heuristics that may negatively impact clients' (and our own) investment decisions.

Representativeness

$$\text{Estimated Future Probability} = f(\text{similarity to past events})$$

This is an easily recognized and easily applied shortcut. It assumes the probability of a future event is directly related to its similarity to past events (i.e., predicting the future from the past).

The risks of blindly following representativeness include:

- Similarities are often superficial and do not successfully extrapolate over time. Assuming it won't rain tomorrow because it didn't rain last week is a good way to get soaked.[5] Assuming a hot stock won't go down tomorrow because it did not go down last week is also a good way to get soaked.
- Similarities may be significant but short term. This can lead to confusing short-term trends within long-term cycles. Hot stocks may be exciting, but not profitable.

A related risk is known as the *gambler's fallacy*. This is the belief that, in a fair toss, a coin landing on heads is more likely after a long run of tails. Representativeness is poor protection against the laws of chance. In spite of these problems, our clients, without our guidance, will use representativeness as an investment guide.

The following are examples that the wealth manager may find useful in educating clients regarding the danger of a naive dependence on the representative heuristic.

EXAMPLE 4.2

Suppose you present to your client the following coin toss and ask him to estimate whether the next coin toss is more likely to be a head (H) or a tail (T).

H, H, H, H, H, H, H, H, H, H

---

[5]Zarowin (1987).

Many people fall victim to the gambler's fallacy and think that the coin is due for a tail. Other clients, knowing that coin tosses are random events and that each toss is independent of the previous one, will feel sophisticated in answering that the next toss is equally likely to be a head or a tail.

Having established the independence of one coin toss from another, now ask your client to choose between two stocks having the following historical returns:

	2005	2006	2007	2008	2009
Stock A	10%	8%	3%	7%	12%
Stock B	−8	3	0	−5	−11

Most clients will choose Stock A. But if stock returns from one year to the next are random events, like coin tosses (and they basically are), then, without additional information, your client should be indifferent between Stock A and Stock B.

As fundamental as this concept is, it is often a revelation to clients. It may require time for a client to resolve the cognitive dissonance created by drawing a parallel between the coin toss and stock selection. Having done so, however, you have laid the foundation to stick with a prudent investment plan when markets do not behave as expected.

Other examples of falling victim to this faulty heuristic include buying only Morningstar 5-Star funds, abandoning an asset class (e.g., emerging markets) after it has sustained a loss, or following the advice of the currently successful gurus.

Another example of representativeness among investors was the fund flow into mutual funds, especially technology funds, during the buildup of the Internet bubble. Outflows were greatest after the market had nearly bottomed out. More generally, Frazzini and Lamont (2008) show that investors tend to allocate money to funds that subsequently perform poorly.

People also tend to treat highly emotional experiences as being representative. According to Peterson (2007):

> *People preferentially remember events that have a strong emotional association. . . . As a result, they overweight the significance of these events when referencing the past to make forecasts about the future.*

EXAMPLE 4.3

Now that your clients feel like they understand representativeness, you can ask them which series of coin flips is more likely:

Series A: HHTHTTTHTH
Series B: HHHHHTTTTT

Even after having discussed the prior example and pointing out to the client that a coin toss is a random event, the representativeness heuristic may result in misinterpreting that knowledge. Feeling very sophisticated with their new insight that a coin toss is a random event, the client's representative heuristic interprets Series A as random and hence more likely than Series B. In fact, they are equally likely because each series is one of the 1,024 unique possible outcomes associated with 10 tosses. The series with the apparent pattern is no more or less unique that the more seemingly random series. Obviously, using common sense as represented by the use of the representative heuristic may get an investor into trouble.

EXAMPLE 4.4

Sylvia, 31, is single, outspoken, and bright. She majored in philosophy. As a student, she was concerned about issues of social justice and frequently participated in protest demonstrations. Which is more likely?

A. Sylvia is a bank teller.
B. Sylvia is a bank teller and active in the feminist movement.

If your client is like the majority of the respondents in a psychological study using a similar question, they will choose B. Their mental shortcut will tell them that the similarity of Sylvia's background to the description in B is so strong that it most clearly describes her current status. Mathematically, however, choice B is a subset of A and cannot be more probable.[6]

The examples just given highlight the tendency to emphasize case data over base data. *Base data* is the underlying reality (i.e., the statistical data of the universe under consideration) and *case data* is the story overlay. Many psychologists believe that our information processing system is more attuned to vivid and emotional case data than to cold, statistical base data; hence we tend to overemphasize case data.

EXAMPLE 4.5

A panel of psychologists interviewed a sample of 30 engineers and 70 lawyers. They summarized their impressions in short notes about each of these individuals. The following description was selected at random from the sample:

[6]This example was derived from Kahneman, Slovic, and Tversky (1982).

> *Herbert is 39 years old. He is married with no children. His father and grand-father were practicing engineers and his hobby is building miniature villages.*
>
> Is he more likely to be an attorney or an engineer? Psychologically, once again, the most persuasive information is the case data, and the majority of clients asked this question would answer, "An engineer." However, the controlling factor is the base data. Out of a total sample of 100, 70 percent are lawyers; therefore, there is a much greater probability that Herbert is an attorney.[7]

How do these examples relate to investment errors and the management of risk?

EXAMPLE 4.6

Consider how investors relate to new stock issues.

Fact A: A nightly business show anchor reports that the new issue of Techno Industries is highly recommended for purchase by a number of brokerage firms (case data).
Fact B: A research study reports that 70 percent of new technology issues are lower in price 12 months after their first issue (base data).

Guess which report is likely to be more impressive to the average investor. The belief that they will profit from the purchase of a new issue is driven by the story (case data), not the reality or relative success of new issues (base data). Emphasizing case data over base data typically results in buying high and selling low.

Shefrin and Statman (1995), for example, show that investors tend to believe that companies that have been profiled well in *Fortune* will be good investments. In fact, these companies perform no better and often perform worse moving forward.

Investment professionals, such as Warren Buffett, have certainly learned to avoid this trap. High-technology companies are visibly successful and garner much media spread, especially compared to more boring businesses. Guess which type Buffett buys.

Availability

Estimated Future Probability $= f$(information in memory)

This mental shortcut is based on using what comes to mind. It is much easier and faster to make a decision based on what we can easily recall, as opposed to taking the time to research and analyze the history we may not accurately remember. As a result, there is a tendency to

---

[7]Ibid.

overemphasize recent information. A good story often based on case data also plays a role in availability. After all, everyone remembers a good story far longer than a boring story.

EXAMPLE 4.7

This useful example can illustrate how the availability heuristic can trump reality. Ask your client if the letter *k* is more likely as the first or the third letter in a word in the English language. Most people searching their memory will find it easier to think of words like *know* and *king* that begin with the letter *k*, rather than *acknowledge*, and will choose the first letter as being more common. Actually, the letter *k* is three times more likely to be the third letter than the first.[8]

The availability heuristic is a partial explanation of why investors are often attracted to risky investments. For example, a stock that has recently reported extraordinary earnings will likely garner significant positive media attention regarding both the firm's high return and the fine management credited with that return. Extrapolating that top-of-mind news (i.e., availability) may lead many investors to believe that purchase of a significant position in the stock is a low-risk opportunity, ignoring the fundamentals of the firm and the potential risk of concentration in a single position.

The availability heuristic also manifests itself in a retirement plan setting. S. Benartzi (2001) finds that retirement plan participants frequently purchase their employer's stock voluntarily. This behavior further concentrates employees' risk exposure to their employer beyond their most valuable asset (i.e., the present value of their earnings stream). Why do they do this? Because the information available to them about their employer is abundant.

Thaler and Sunstein (2008) argue that "choice architecture" can help people make better decisions by defining a default choice that is likely to be in an individual's best interest. The default choice becomes readily available information that the investor will use to make decisions. As a wealth manager, you can frame a set of options available to a client by defining the most beneficial one as the default option—for example, a 40 percent bond/60 percent equity default option for 401(k) contributions. This anchors clients' frame of reference and allows their potentially harmful heuristics to work to their benefit.

Overconfidence

One of the archenemies to any investor is overconfidence, and heuristics tend to exacerbate this effect. According to Jason Zweig (2007), who reported on studies of the neurology of investor responses to risk and return, human beings are susceptible to the illusion of control and are more comfortable when they believe they have control. Ironically, ignorance can create this illusion of control and hence promote confidence when it is least warranted.

---

[8] *The AAII Journal*, Vol. 5, Maria Crawford Scott, ed. (Chicago: American Association of Individual Investing, 1983).

According to Michael Pompian (2006, 2009), who outlines almost 20 common behavioral biases among clients:

Recognizing and curtailing overconfidence is a key step in establishing the basics of a real financial plan.

Men, for example, tend to be more risk tolerant and more confident than women. Women, in turn, tend to be more susceptible to the gambler's fallacy. Also, inexperienced investors tend to underestimate risk and chase trends. As a result, they may invest in growth stocks as they rise, shortly before their prices start to fall.

Panic

Neuroeconomics is the study of how the brain reacts neurologically to economic stimuli, such as the experience of risk or return. Authors such as Jason Zweig (2007) and Richard Peterson (2007) present convincing evidence that panic reduces the brain's ability to process information clearly, encouraging decision makers to rely on flawed heuristics.

They recommend calming techniques for investors, such as taking deep breaths and thinking about something else to calm reflexes. As a wealth manager, you will find such techniques useful for calming not only your own nerves, but also those of your clients.

For example, when a client attacks you because his or her portfolio has precipitously dropped in value—a common experience for wealth managers in 2009—the natural response (often born of panic) is to defend one's positions and offer remedies to the current situation. Instead, the deft advisor calmly solicits more information from the client, like what specific emotion or concern the client is experiencing. Is it vulnerability, lack of control, the inability to send a child to college? The wealth manager can then craft a response that speaks more directly to these fundamental motivators.

Contagious Enthusiasm

This is the twin brother of bandwagon jumping and the first cousin to the greater fool theory. When an investment story is hot, the simplest mental shortcut is to follow the crowd. Success at this stage depends on simple luck. When the froth gets so crazy as to become a mania, luck is no longer adequate. Future profits depend on finding a greater fool to sell to when you want out. According to Shefrin (2002):

There are two aspects to the bandwagon effect. First, there is belief that the crowd must know something. Second, misery loves company. Because of the potential for regret, there is safety in numbers.

The first decade of the twenty-first century has two examples of this in a very short period of time. In the late 1990s, excitement about the so-called new economy created by the Internet had contributed to the frenzied buying of technology stocks until their price peaked in March 2000. Then the luster wore off and stocks entered a three-year bear market.

This story repeated itself in real estate to cause the subprime crisis that precipitated a market collapse in 2008.

The role of the wealth manager is to protect clients from making decisions based on these guides. In this case, in addition to general education, try framing the consequences in a personal way.

For the advisor, attempting to talk a client out of investing in a hot tip is likely to be a frustrating experience. No matter how lucid and sound the advisor's argument, the client is unlikely to be listening too attentively and, to the extent he pays attention, he will be discounting the advisor's objections as coming from someone who just doesn't understand the magnitude of the opportunity.

Turn the tables. Tell your client, "I'm not too familiar with that area, but from what you have told me, it sounds like a very exciting opportunity. Of course, any investment may have some risks. What might go wrong?" Guiding your clients to do their own reality checks will take the focus off of the blind acceptance of the positive, forcing them to consider other less favorable outcomes.

Usually, clients' investing is based on contagious enthusiasm and they have not stopped long enough to consider any risks. Frequently the question of what might go wrong is all one needs to bring them back to reality.

As an alternative (or in addition), frame the consequences of potential outcomes in a very personal way:

- If you are right, you will make a handsome profit.
- If you are wrong, you will have to work an extra three years.

These and the following behavioral-based strategies are powerful tools available to the advisor in guiding clients to better decision making.

Confirmation Bias

The trouble with managing money is that everyone once made a successful investment.
—*Gary Helms*

Confirmation bias is a set of blinders an investor may wear after making an investment. It ensures that the investor will see only information confirming his or her original judgment. The wealth manager has two responsibilities regarding this bias. First, assume the responsibility of removing the client's blinders. Second, and even more important, wealth managers must assiduously guard against wearing their own blinders.

Regret, Pride, and Shame

Investors frequently endow their investments with personal characteristics and empower their investment decisions with social commentary.

The mental imperatives of good and bad are frequently applied to investments. It may be as global as "I don't invest in stock; it's risky (i.e., bad)," or more specifically, "I don't want to buy that stock; it's a dog!"

The result is an avoidance of investments that, in the broad sense of a total, diversified portfolio, are appropriate. Instead, the investor ends up with an inappropriate concentration of "good" investments (e.g., CDs and high-quality municipals).

Investment decisions are empowered with social commentary when investors avoid actions in order to avoid looking dumb. Consider the investor who buys a "dog" stock (possibly a well-priced value stock) while a friend buys a hot and highly touted growth stock (an overpriced story). If they both lose money, the value investor thinks he or she is unlucky and the friend is stupid.

Anticipatory Regret

A related symptom is anticipatory regret. If an important decision can have a negative consequence (e.g., losing money), then to avoid the pain and shame of loss, the best solution may seem to be to do nothing.

This aspect of a client's investment psychology is often the most difficult with which to deal. It reflects an individual's core beliefs about his or her own personality. There are no simple solutions. During the ongoing education process from first meeting to last meeting, the wealth manager needs to help the client to continually air these issues.

MENTAL MATH

This can be thought of as mathematics for the brain. Like the math we learned in school, mental math has its own form of adding, subtracting, and estimating. It can make a maze look logical. A wealth manager must be adept at its intricacies in order to provide guidance to clients.

Adding and Subtracting

Subtracting costs more than adding. Investors place higher psychological value on losses than on gains. This results in a reluctance to cut losses (i.e., realize losses). Such an action requires an emotionally charged negative entry into the mental account.[9] It also tends to focus the investor on the individual security and away from the total portfolio.

Techniques for dealing with this include:

- For a client still holding a loss position, reframe the question: "What would you do with the cash rather than the stock?" The obvious question is "Would you buy the stock?" Often the answer is "No, it's a dog." With that acknowledgment, the client may have a new and more flexible perspective.
- For a client who has agreed to sell, albeit reluctantly, focus the client on the benefits of the trade and the value of the asset purchased with the sale proceeds. The tax savings generated by a bond swap is a classic example of this strategy.

Estimation

The less likely the long-term payoff, the more likely mental math will overestimate its probability. Mentally we tend to construct our future estimates on the basis of a series of shorter-term estimates. It is safer and more accurate to evaluate the probability of individual events than an entire series.

The following example demonstrates the conflict between this form of mental math and probability theory.

---

[9]See, for example, Kahneman and Tversky (1979).

EXAMPLE 4.8

Bella Julias, your client, is considering investing in Hot Tech, a company that has a new product under review. If Hot Tech can get government approval, it will develop a prototype. Ms. Julias thinks approval is a no-brainer and assigns it a 90 percent probability of success.

Once Hot Tech starts to build the prototype, Ms. Julias estimates the probability of success to be 90 percent. Hot Tech then proposes to build a plant to test-market regionally. Ms. Julias estimates a 90 percent chance of success for the regional test.

Once successfully marketed regionally, Hot Tech plans on rolling it out nationally. Your client remains optimistic, and once again estimates a 90 percent chance of success. In order to make an investment in Hot Tech, she needs to feel confident that the company has a good chance of a successful national launch of its new product (i.e., at least a 75 percent chance). Does she invest?

Most clients' mental arithmetic results in their concluding that the investment has a 90 percent chance of success. They would not only invest, but also brag to friends about their astute analysis.

Assuming Ms. Julias correctly estimated success for each step in the process, the actual overall estimate of success is: $0.9 \times 0.9 \times 0.9 \times 0.9 = 65.5$ percent!

If there are only three more steps in the chain, each with a 90 percent probability of success, the overall probability of success falls to *less than 50 percent!* Detail in the analysis may make the chance of ultimate success seem real, but it is not necessarily reality.

Multiple Accounts

A final interesting twist to mental math is mental accounting (i.e., creating multiple independent mental accounts). The result is that clients often think of their investments as being allocated to separate pockets. Examples would include classifications based on how the client obtained the funds (e.g., an inheritance) or the nature of the account (e.g., retirement).

Unless there are legal restrictions relative to ownership interest (e.g., Uniform Transfers to Minors Act accounts or irrevocable trusts), this form of mental accounting places arbitrary and potentially counterproductive restrictions on the development of an investment policy.

As an example, suppose you recommend a modest investment for your client with an aggressive, high-turnover active equity manager. Due to the potential for significant short-term gains, you prudently propose that the investment be made in the client's tax-deferred retirement account. Many investors might balk at this suggestion, responding that they can't take such a risk with their retirement funds; those dollars need to be in safe investments. In this case, as a professional, you recognize that planning holistically for your clients means viewing all of their assets in total and designing the implementation process to use their sheltered dollars most efficiently. Unfortunately, as in this example, many clients' separate account mentality hampers their ability to see the bigger picture. Our role is to help our clients avoid inefficient decisions based on separate pocket thinking and educate them regarding the importance of viewing *all* of their investable assets as a part of their *total portfolio.*

Small versus Large Samples

Investors tend to place significant but inappropriate faith in small samples. For example, the success one friend has investing in gold may lead to an assumption that gold is the place to be. Extrapolating continued success from a short run of extraordinary performance is the same math that results in an investor moving funds to the hot manager of the week.

EXAMPLE 4.9

Try the following test to assist your client to understand the danger of small sample math:

Coin 1 was tossed 10 times and landed on heads 7 times.
Coin 2 was tossed 100 times and landed on heads 65 times.

Which coin is likely to be more honest?

Coin 1 is 55 times more likely to be honest. Although it landed on heads as a percentage of tosses more frequently than coin 2 did, the sample was so small that the results are not as statistically meaningful as those for coin 2, which was tossed enough times to suggest that the probability of its being an honest coin is remote. In fact, coin 2 has only a 0.1 percent chance of being a fair coin.

Relative versus Absolute

This is a kissing cousin to the dangerous misuse of statistics. Here are a few useful examples to use with your clients.[10]

EXAMPLE 4.10

You are participating in a game of chance and are offered the following choices:

A. Win $1,000 without rolling a pair of dice.
B. Roll the dice and win $1,000 per spot on the rolled pair of dice.

If we use standard deviation as our relative measure of risk, choice A is clearly less risky. After all, choice A has a standard deviation of zero. If we are a little less myopic and look at absolute risk, B is clearly superior. If we roll the dice there is no likelihood of underperforming A.

---

[10]This example is derived from Kahneman, Slovic, and Tversky (1982).

> Suppose the choice is:
>
> A. Win $3,000 without rolling the pair of dice.
> B. Roll the dice and win $1,000 per spot on the rolled pair of dice.
>
> We've now added an element of uncertainty regarding B's superiority. However, the probability of B being at least as good as A is still 97 percent.[11]

If those examples don't clinch your clients' understanding, ask if crossing the street twice in one day instead of once really doubled their risk.

Relative versus Relative

Obviously a member of the same family as "relative versus absolute," this is the basis for the controversy between proponents of mean variance and semivariance.

Mean variance is the traditional financial model for estimating risk, and standard deviation is the most common measure. Semivariance proponents argue that it is nonsense to worry about "good" variance (e.g., doing better than you expect). All the client and wealth manager should be concerned about is doing worse. Further, if the distribution of an investment return is not normal, the recommendations arrived at based on downside loss (e.g., semivariance) will differ from those based on total variance (e.g., normal standard deviation).

Even if we resolve this dispute in favor of semivariance, there are additional questions to consider. What are we going to select as the criterion for loss: negative return, not keeping up with inflation, or not meeting a benchmark return?

FRAMING

In 1979, Kahneman and Tversky published their second groundbreaking paper, "Prospect Theory: An Analysis of Decisions under Risk." In this paper they argue that framing (i.e., changing the way options are presented) may result in dramatic changes in preferences. A few simple examples highlight this reality. For example, if offered a choice of candy bars, would you prefer the one that's 10 percent fat or the one that's 90 percent fat free? How about a choice between an order of prunes and an order of dried plums?

The concept of framing is one of the most powerful tools in practitioners' repertoire for managing clients' expectations and managing their understanding and response to risk. The following are a few examples of how framing may be applied in wealth management.

Quarterly Reports

Most practitioners provide comprehensive quarterly performance reports. In these reports it is common to include performance data for the recent month, the past quarter, and

---

[11]There are 36 possible outcomes for the total number of spots on a pair of dice (6 × 6). Only one outcome has less than three dots, so 35 of them are at least as good as choice A.

year-to-date. This focus on short-term returns contradicts our efforts to focus our clients' attention on long-term investing. Modifying the quarterly reports (i.e., reframing) to provide only performance for periods in excess of one year assists our clients to focus on longer-term performance.

It is also traditional to include as performance benchmarks the returns of the Standard & Poor's (S&P) 500 index and other similar market metrics. However, our relationship with our clients is as a wealth manager, not a money manager. Wealth management portfolios are not based solely on the equity market. Furthermore, our goal for our clients is not beating the market but rather achieving a real return that will enable them to meet their life goals. Replacing the market benchmarks with the consumer price index and measuring the real returns of clients' portfolios reframes the performance in a manner consistent with their goals.[12]

Loss Averse versus Risk Averse

Prospect theory teaches that investors are more loss averse than risk averse and many investors fail to achieve financial independence due to confusion over the difference. Harold helps educate his clients by reframing their understanding through a simple two-part test:

Question #1: You walk into a big Vegas casino and are told you are the millionth visitor and you win a prize. You're naturally very happy; however, as it's Vegas, the casino offers you a choice: either $800,000 cash or a chance to pick a ping-pong ball from a bag holding 10 balls—eight white and two black. If you pick a white one you win $1 million. If you pick a black one, you win nothing. Which one do you choose?

Question #2: It turns out you're not in Vegas; you're in Hades, surrounded by fire and brimstone. The Devil walks up to you and says, "Let me tell you how it works down here. You lost but—no surprise—I'm a gambler so I'll offer you a choice. Either pay me $800,000 or pick a ping-pong ball from this bag I'm holding. It contains 10 balls—eight white and two black. If you pick a white one you owe me $1 million. If you pick a black one, owe me nothing. Which one do you choose?"

After decades of asking this question of new clients, Harold has found that over 90 percent select the guaranteed return in the casino but take a chance with the Devil's offer. These results help demonstrate to clients that they do not want to take a chance to get rich but they are prepared to take a chance to avoid becoming poor. He then goes on to explain why his recommendation for equity exposure might be the same as what the clients rejected when it was presented by their broker, but his reason for the recommendation would be quite different.

For example, Mr. and Mrs. Conservative Client, if you were to go to a traditional broker with a portfolio of certificates of deposit (CDs), the broker might say, "You'll never get ahead with those CDs; I'd recommend we move half of those funds to stocks to make you some money." Your reaction would probably be "No, thanks."

---

[12]Reframing the time period and benchmarks for the client's quarterly portfolio review is not to suggest that shorter-period performance and market metrics are not appropriate benchmarks; they obviously are. However, they should be used to evaluate and monitor the managers selected to implement the various asset class and style allocations of the client's portfolio, not the entire portfolio.

After the planning process, Harold may end up making exactly the same recommendation (i.e., move half your money to stocks), but for a totally different reason. His rationale will be to avoid losing your standard of living. Based on his planning and accounting for inflation, he believes you need to include equities in your portfolio to maintain your lifestyle. After this reframing, he has had traditional CD investors say, "That makes sense. I'm ready to listen."

Harold says that this simple question has converted many longtime CD enthusiasts into very patient and successful long-term investors.

PARTING COMMENTS

Is behavioral finance an oxymoron? We conclude with the wise words of Richard Thaler:

> [I]n the not-too-distant future, the term "behavioral finance" will be correctly viewed as a redundant phrase. What other kind of finance is there? Enlightened economists [and wealth management practitioners] will routinely incorporate as much behavior into their models as they observe in the real world. After all, to do otherwise would be irrational.[13]

RESOURCES

Adler, David E. 2009. *Snap Judgment.* Upper Saddle River, NJ: FT Press.

Benartzi, Shlomo. 2001. "Excessive Extrapolation and the Allocation of 401(k) Accounts to Company Stock." *Journal of Finance,* Vol. 56, No. 5 (October): 1747–1764.

Brunel, Jean L. P. 2006. *Integrated Wealth Management: The New Direction for Portfolio Managers.* London: Euromoney Books.

Byrne, Alistair, and Mike Brooks. 2008. *Behavioral Finance: Theories and Evidence.* Charlottesville, VA: Research Foundation of CFA Institute.

Frazzini, Andrea, and Owen A. Lamont. 2008. "Dumb Money: Mutual Fund Flows and the Cross-Section of Stock Returns." *Journal of Financial Economics,* Vol. 88, No. 2: 299–322.

Graham, Benjamin, and David L. Dodd. 1934. *Security Analysis.* New York: McGraw-Hill.

Kahneman, Daniel, Paul Slovic, and Amos Tversky, eds. 1982. *Judgment under Uncertainty.* New York: Cambridge University Press.

Kahneman, Daniel, and Amos Tversky. 1979. "Prospect Theory: An Analysis of Decisions under Risk." *Econometrica,* Vol. 47, No. 2 (March): 263–291.

Peterson, Richard. 2007. *Inside the Investor's Brain: The Power of Mind over Money.* Hoboken, NJ: John Wiley & Sons.

Pompian, Michael. 2006. *Behavioral Finance and Wealth Management: How to Build Optimal Portfolios That Account for Investor Biases.* Hoboken, NJ: John Wiley & Sons.

Pompian, Michael. 2009. *Advising Ultra-Affluent Clients and Family Offices.* Hoboken, NJ: John Wiley & Sons.

Shefrin, Hersh. 2002. *Beyond Greed and Fear.* New York: Oxford University Press.

Shefrin, Hersh, and Meir Statman. 1995. "Making Sense of Beta, Size, and Book-to-Market." *Journal of Portfolio Management,* Vol. 21, No. 2 (Winter): 26–34.

---

[13]Richard Thaler, "The End of Behavioral Finance," *Financial Analysts Journal* (November/December 1999): 16.

Shiller, Robert J., and George A. Akerlof. 2009. *Animal Spirits: How Human Psychology Drives the Economy, and Why It Matters for Global Capitalism.* Princeton, NJ: Princeton University Press.

Thaler, Richard H., and Cass R. Sunstein. 2008. *Nudge: Improving Decisions about Health, Wealth, and Happiness.* New Haven, CT: Yale University Press.

Wood, Arnie, ed. 1995. *Behavioral Finance and Decision Theory in Investment Management.* Charlottesville, VA: CFA Institute.

Zarowin, Stanley. 1987. "Investing Psychology Winners and Losers." *Sylvia Porter's Personal Finance, July–August,* 50–55.

Zweig, Jason. 2007. *Your Money and Your Brain.* New York: Simon & Schuster.

CHAPTER 5

DATA GATHERING
AND ANALYSIS

Garbage in, garbage out.

—Unknown

In order to establish an investment policy for a client, the wealth manager must have a clear understanding of the client's level of risk tolerance and investment goals/objectives. In combination, this data will enable the wealth manager to design an asset allocation that is intended to provide sufficient return to meet the client's objectives while respecting the client's level of risk tolerance—enabling the client to sleep at night. This chapter discusses methods of measuring a client's level of risk tolerance and computing the capital needed to meet client objectives.

MEASURING RISK TOLERANCE

Risk tolerance is one of the most important factors in portfolio design. Unfortunately, it is also the most difficult to evaluate. The difficulty often begins with a fuzzy definition of risk tolerance in the minds of the wealth manager and the client. Even worse, these fuzzy definitions may differ between client and wealth manager. Consequently, the first step is to define the concept in terms that are clear and consistent for both the client and the wealth manager. We propose the following discussion with your clients:

> *Mr. and Mrs. Client, in order to help design a portfolio allocation that balances your need for returns to achieve your goals and your risk tolerance, we need for you to understand what we mean by "risk tolerance." We all know that investment markets have good periods, but they also have bad periods and those bad periods can be very scary. We define your risk tolerance as that threshold of emotional pain that you will be willing to accept when your investment portfolio seems to be hemorrhaging value and the news headlines scream bad news in 50-point type. That is the point at which you may feel miserable when you look at your statement but will not feel compelled to throw in the towel, liquate all of your investments, and go to cash. Selling out in panic almost guarantees long-term failure.*

In summary, we define your risk tolerance as that level of market volatility that you may find most uncomfortable but you will not call us saying, "I can't stand it anymore—sell me out!"

Unfortunately, even after mutually agreeing on a definition of risk tolerance, risk remains a four-letter word describing a concept that looks like a reflection in a mirror maze. So how can a wealth manager possibly evaluate a client's risk tolerance? The answer is by becoming a great artist with the palette of behavioral psychology, by using a variety of techniques, and by evaluating clients' current financial position in relation to their goals.

Know the two basic principles of assessing risk tolerance:

1. Be aware of the potential conflicts between your objective view of risk and the client's emotional view. This is a major danger when the wealth manager is communicating on an intellectual frequency and the client is receiving on an emotional frequency. Nick Murray notes that a wealth manager "cannot plan around or through someone's definition of risk . . . it must be shared." He goes on to warn that if clients have "a diseased concept of risk [they] will have a diseased concept of safety."
2. Do not assume client knowledge. Even the most successful and sophisticated business or professional client is likely to have at best a rudimentary knowledge of modern investment theory. Most will certainly be subject to the misuse of heuristics.

A primary purpose of a formal risk tolerance questionnaire is to facilitate a dialogue in order to assist the client in developing a healthy concept of risk and reaching informed decisions. Wealth managers need to be vigilant in avoiding the imposition of their own psychological biases.

Risk versus Uncertainty

An important concept practitioners need to keep in mind when applying the technology of risk management to their client's circumstances is the difference between risk and uncertainty. As first addressed by Frank Knight in his 1921 book *Risk, Uncertainty and Profit*, risk represents a quantifiable concept whereas uncertainty describes circumstances where there is no possibility of developing a quantitative determination of true probability. The danger for practitioners is placing too much reliance on financial technology (e.g., Monte Carlo simulations) when evaluating issues that have significant elements of uncertainty.

Willingness versus Ability

A fundamental element of assessing clients' risk tolerance is distinguishing clearly between their willingness to accept risk and their capacity to accept risk. In Chapter 1, we introduced the distinction between willingness and ability to accept risk.

Observing their behavior in other parts of life can offer insights into clients' willingness to accept risk (e.g., propensity to gamble, to be spontaneous, or to engage in extreme sports), but one must be careful not to place too much weight on these observations because taking risks driving a race car does not necessarily equate to investment risk taking.

Ability to accept risk is determined by more objective factors. It need not correspond to willingness and is based on answers to questions like these six:

1. How volatile/risky is your employment?
2. How correlated are your job prospects with stock market returns?
3. What is your time horizon?
4. What are your liquidity constraints?
5. What are financial resources?
6. How do your financial resources relate to your investment goals?

When an investor's willingness to take risk exceeds his or her ability, the wealth manager assumes an educational mandate to resolve the difference.

EXAMPLE 5.1

Robin Thompson is a successful, self-made entrepreneur. He is a bachelor with no children and has more than sufficient wealth through his publishing company to fund his life's goals and objectives. As we will demonstrate more clearly later in this chapter, his well-funded status generally suggests he has a large capacity to accept risk because possible poor investment outcomes will not affect his primary goals.

Mr. Thompson, however, is someone comforted by having control over the risks he assumes. It was one of the traits that contributed to his business success. Consequently, he is highly uncomfortable accepting risk he cannot control, and he views investment risk in a similar manner. As a result, Mr. Thompson has high capacity but low willingness to accept risk. The wealth manager should not impose his or her understanding of risk on Mr. Thompson (first basic principle discussed earlier).

Spectrum of Risk Analysis Questions

Exhibit 5.1 reflects the interplay between a client's emotional orientation and a wealth manager's desire to quantify risk tolerance. Depending on the location in this spectrum, questions may be based on behavioral psychology, finance, investment theory, or decision science (e.g., probability). This section outlines each of them in turn, starting with the lower right.

EXHIBIT 5.1   Spectrum of Risk Analysis

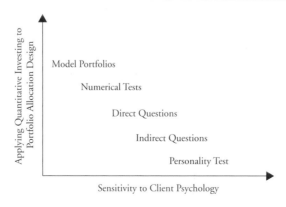

Personality Tests

A number of proprietary tests are available on the market. Unfortunately there is little or no research supporting the validity of these tests for use as a risk tolerance questionnaire.

Indirect Questions

These quasi-psychological questions, while not directly related to a client's core personality (hence "quasi"), may assist in validating the consistency of the client's answers with more direct and numerical questions. For example:

Which of the following comes closest to your ideal employment compensation structure involving some mix of salary and commissions?

1. Entirely salary
2. Partially salary
3. Equal mix of salary and commissions
4. Primarily commissions
5. Entirely commissions

Direct and Numerical Questions

Direct and numerical questions are similar in that they address issues directly related to portfolio design. Direct questions require qualitative responses, and numerical questions require quantitative responses. Examples include:

After making an investment, do you typically feel thrilled, satisfied, confused, or regretful?

You invest $10,000 in a stock that drops 10 percent in value the following day. Do you invest an additional $10,000, sit tight, sell, or wait for it to get back even and then sell?

By how much could the total value of all your investments go down before you would begin to feel uncomfortable?

These questionnaires typically provide a numerical score that is intended to guide the test-taker with a recommended bond/stock allocation based on scoring the response to the questions. The best known and most well-established questionnaire of this type is FinaMetrica, a risk profile system launched in Australia in 1998.[1] As with any system, the practitioner needs to carefully review client responses for potentially contradictory answers so that the contradictions in those responses can be fully discussed with the client.

EXAMPLE 5.2   Conflicting Client Responses

A client questionnaire poses the following query:
    "Investments can go up or down in value, and experts often say you should be prepared to weather a downturn. By how much could the total value of all your investments go down before you would begin to feel uncomfortable?"

---

[1]www.riskprofiling.com.

The client responds:

"Down 33 percent."

A subsequent question asks:

"You are considering placing one-quarter of your investment funds into a single investment. This investment is expected to earn about twice the certificate of deposit (CD) rate. However, unlike a CD, this investment is not protected against loss of the money invested. How low would the chance of a loss have to be for you to make the investment?"

The client answers:

"Very little chance of loss."

Without discussing this seeming conflict, the advisor would not know if the client can really live with a volatile portfolio as described in the first response.

Model Portfolios

Model portfolios allow clients an opportunity to select their own allocations from a variety of choices. Although it can be effective as part of a comprehensive evaluation process, model portfolio selection should never be relied on by the practitioner as a single criterion when making a recommendation. The client's stand-alone answer to a question of this nature is very likely to violate the two principles of risk assessment:

1. Be aware of the potential conflicts between your objective view of risk and the client's emotional view.
2. Do not assume client knowledge.

Risk Assessment Framework: A Practical Example

The following questionnaire, based on the principles of behavioral finance, has been developed over a number of years. Although the ultimate goal of this questionnaire is to establish a bond/stock allocation that advisor and client mutually agree will meet the client's risk tolerance, we refer to this as a "risk coaching" process. The point is to emphasize the interactive and consultative nature of the process. The questionnaire currently used by Evensky & Katz has continually evolved, beginning at the yellow pad stage and developing into its current format. We supplement the Risk Tolerance Questionnaire (RTQ) with FinaMetrica and a more traditional financial planning data gathering guide. This RTQ is used both to capture specific information regarding risk tolerance and, equally important, to provide a springboard for conversation and client education.

We believe that any risk tolerance process should facilitate a discussion about risk and help manage client expectations. Consequently, this questionnaire is completed during a discussion between the client and the advisor; it is not given to the client to take home and complete. Once we have completed an education program and feel reasonably confident that we have answered all of our clients' questions as well as provided them with a solid foundation regarding important investment issues, we sit with clients to complete our RTQ. The following is a detailed discussion of our questionnaire and the issues we raise with our clients.

Frequently, we are concerned with all of a client's investment assets. Occasionally, however, our advice may be requested regarding a specific investment portfolio that represents only a portion of the client's investments (e.g., a pension plan or trust fund). For that reason, the first question we ask is directed at placing into perspective those investments about which we are being asked to advise.

Question 1
- What is the approximate value of this investment portfolio?
- What percentage of your total investments is represented by this portfolio?

We begin the process with a framing question that may seem rather obvious, that is, the approximate value of the investment portfolio. Unfortunately, like so many other aspects of wealth management, the answer to this question is often not simple. There are two factors that the question is designed to parse. First, it distinguishes between investment and non-investment resources (i.e., funds that need to be liquid). Second, it is intended to determine how this particular investment portfolio fits in the universe of the client's total investment universe.

The first factor relates to the Evensky & Katz mantra: five years, five years, five years. Namely, the value entered in answer to question 1 should include only funds that clients are reasonably confident that they can leave invested for a minimum of five years.

The second goal is to place this number in the perspective of the client's total financial plan. To do so we follow up with a request for the percentage of the client's total investments that the investment portfolio represents. This question supplements the more detailed traditional data gathering guide in order to determine whether this particular investment portfolio is part of a much larger portfolio. If it is only part of a larger portfolio (e.g., a client's pension), it is necessary to determine how it should be integrated with the client's other assets.

Question 2
- Is there an immediate or near-term (i.e., within five years) need for income from this portfolio?
- If "yes," when will the income be needed?

At the beginning of this dialogue we warn our clients that there are a number of trick questions. This is the first of those questions, because there is only one right answer and that answer is "no." Remember, at the beginning of the planning process we have discussed with our client the need for short-term cash flow and, to the extent the client has such a need, we have carved that amount out of the investment portfolio. Should the client answer yes to this question, it provides an opportunity for the practitioner to determine if there are additional cash flow needs not yet accounted for. If that proves to be the case, the original entry in "value of investment portfolio" can be further reduced in order to allow the client to answer no.

The purpose of this question and question 3, in conjunction with our mantra, is to frame in the client's mind the long-term nature of the investment portfolio.

Question 3
- Will significant cash withdrawals of principal and/or contributions be made over the next five years?

This is the second purposely redundant question. Having asked about the need for income, question 3 addresses the need for any significant principal withdrawals within our five-year period. This is a second opportunity to query for unique short-term cash flow needs.

EXAMPLE 5.3   Investment Portfolio

Evan and Rebecca Schramm have a current portfolio of $1 million in investable assets. Through the planning process, you learn they need $200,000 available in three years for a down payment on a second home at retirement. You explain to Mr. and Mrs. Schramm that the investment portfolio is really $800,000 and therefore the $200,000 for the second home will be invested in relatively liquid assets in a separate portfolio (referred to as "liquidity reserves" or the "cash flow reserve account").

Mr. and Mrs. Shramm go on to indicate that they have a need of $50,000/year from investments to supplement their pension income. You therefore carve out an additional $100,000 (two years' worth of cash flow), leaving an investment portfolio of $700,000. Now they can answer no to questions 2 and 3.

Question 4
- What is the portfolio's investment time horizon?

Investment time horizon refers to the number of years you expect the portfolio to be invested before you must dip into principal. Alternatively, how long will the objectives stated for this portfolio continue without substantial modification?

a. Three years
b. Five years
c. Ten years
d. Over 10 years

(If you have indicated less than 10 years, please explain when the funds will be needed.)

Questions 1 through 3 set the framework for the dollar amounts to be invested or withdrawn from the portfolio and initiate our emphasis on the importance of the holding period. Question 4 continues the process of educating the client relative to the realities of risk and volatility.

Presumably the client has already answered question 4 by responding to questions 2 and 3. We find, however, that when translated into actual holding periods measured in years, the client's 10-second horizon may move front and center. It is not unusual to find someone answering question 2 with a no and question 3 with a no only to answer question 4 with a choice of "three years." Such contradictory responses bring the client's concerns out into the open.

In order to force the discussion, we add an additional statement requesting if anything "less than 10 years" is selected that the client explain when the funds will be needed.

As wealth managers, we know that most clients have a very long investment horizon. Even those clients consulting us for retirement planning and postretirement planning in reality have their life expectancy as an investment horizon. Question 4 allows us the opportunity to discuss this reality in depth. For example, it forces our 70-year-old retired widow (with an 18-plus-year life expectancy) to acknowledge that she really does not plan on spending much of her principal in the next three to five years. Once we have had an opportunity to discuss the concept of a planning horizon based on life expectancy, most clients understand that the bulk of their corpus must remain intact in order for them to continue to maintain their lifestyle for the balance of their life.

Question 5

- Optional: My (our) goal for this portfolio is an annual return of _____ percent
  - This is based on an expected inflation rate of _____ percent.
  - A page of long-term historical data is provided for reference.

This might be an optional question that experience suggests has been neglected. During the third or fourth year of a roaring bull market, Harold delivered to a client what he believed to be a superior investment policy proposal. "Mr. Client," he said, "after a great deal of analysis, we recommend that you reposition your portfolio from 60 percent bonds to 40 percent bonds and increase your stock allocation from 40 percent to 60 percent. We believe that this will provide you with a long-term real return of approximately 6 percent over the inflation rate." To Harold's astonishment, the client jumped up, slammed his fist down on our conference room table, and screamed, "My barber can do better than that!" And he then stormed out of the room.

Obviously, Harold had lost sight of the basic rule to *really* know the client. He performed a great deal of work for naught. He failed to uncover his client's unrealistic but, for him, hidden agenda. Harold subsequently added Question 5 to uncover any expectations regarding returns that the client may have.

In asking about the goal, we emphasize that we're not asking what return clients would like to have but rather whether they have in mind a return that they think they might reasonably expect on their portfolio.

If the client provides an answer (it is optional, and most of our clients skip this part) with an unrealistic goal, we may find ourselves on the defensive. After all, the client may ask, "Why couldn't you deliver my request?" By adding a space for the client to provide the inflation assumption that underlies the return goal, we shift the burden. The second part of the question tends to serve as a stumbling block. The table of historical real returns at the end of the questionnaire places the burden on the client to defend an expectation significantly in excess of what has been achieved in the past.

Question 6

- For each of the following attributes of an investment, circle the number that most correctly reflects your level of concern. The more important, the higher the number. You may use each number more than once.

	Most					Least
Capital preservation	6	5	4	3	2	1
Growth	6	5	4	3	2	1
Low volatility	6	5	4	3	2	1
Inflation protection	6	5	4	3	2	1
Current cash flow	6	5	4	3	2	1
Aggressive growth	6	5	4	3	2	1

This is our ultimate integration of the art and science of wealth management. The question resembles a myriad of similar matrix questions that have been used by other planners over the years. It has, however, been designed to be a much more structured and comprehensive data gathering question than is reflected on its surface.

We introduce this table with the explanation that it lists various attributes of an investment; they are neither good nor bad, simply attributes. We explain that what we would like to know is how important each of these attributes is for our clients. In order to frame their responses, we tell them that they should assume that over the life of their plan (i.e., until their death or the death of the surviving spouse) they can accomplish their goals. What we are asking in this question is how they feel about these attributes over the next five years. If we are working with a couple, we emphasize that we're looking for each person to provide his or her own ranking, as we recognize that there may be significant differences between individuals.

Our clients are not constrained in prioritizing the six different attributes. They may rate each one as strongly or as weakly as they desire. For example, they may rank all "most important" or all as "least important." By not forcing clients to prioritize, we find that it lets them focus on each attribute individually. They are not restricted by the impact a choice for one attribute may have on their ability to weight the remaining attributes.

The next component of the structure is the order in which the attributes are listed. The order is an important element in the educational process.

"Capital preservation" is very purposefully placed first. We ask, "Ms. Client, again assuming that over the long run your plan works out fine, how important is it to you—assuming you neither add nor withdraw funds from your investment portfolio—that when you pick up your statement five years from now it reflects a value at least equal to today's value?" It is very rare for a client not to instantly circle 6 (most important). Figuratively, and frequently in reality, the client circles 6, looks at the planner, slams her fist on the table, and says, "There! I'm conservative! I told you so!" Basically, it is an opportunity for the conservative client to clearly and emphatically demonstrate that she is *really* conservative and that capital preservation is of paramount importance. She has placed her conservatism on the table and now feels much better about the process.

"Growth" follows "capital preservation." This question is presented as "Mr. Client, how important is growth of your portfolio? That is, how important is it to you that over the next five years you would like to see some growth in the value of your portfolio?" Conservative investors like to have some growth in their portfolios. In fact, it's very common for conservative investors to circle a 5 or 6. This is the first "gotcha" built into the matrix. Even our most conservative investor is aware that safe investments such as money market funds and Treasury bills do not have the attribute of growth. At this point, they begin to realize that they may, in fact, have some contradictory goals. We use the conflicting goals of capital preservation and growth as an opportunity to continue our ongoing discussion about multiple forms of risk.

Volatility is frequently a confusing concept to the client. Listing "low volatility" provides us an opportunity to discuss risk measurement and to distinguish between volatility and capital loss. We introduce this question as follows: "Ms. Client, you indicated in response to the first attribute that capital preservation is very important. Now we're asking about volatility; that is, how do you feel about the ride between now and five years from now? For example, if an investor put $100,000 in the market on January 1, 2002, five years later she would have almost $150,000. However, nine months after making her initial investment, she would have lost almost 30 percent. The five-year gain would not have had much meaning if she bailed out in September 2002. So our question is, how important, or unimportant, do you consider interim volatility?"

We add, "If you believe you'd throw in the towel if your portfolio was underwater after a year, then you might select 6, but if you think you could hang on for three years, then pick 4."

"Inflation protection" is the ultimate "gotcha." Almost all clients rank this a 5 or 6. This is particularly true of retirement and postretirement clients. If we have not previously done so, this is the occasion we use, without fail, to address the conflict between inflation protection and capital preservation. Even the most naive of investors knows that no single kind of investment will satisfy both of these goals. Very few clients rate inflation protection much below a 5 as their level of concern. In most cases, the ranking of inflation protection is the same as that for capital preservation. Occasionally it is even higher.

"Current cash flow" is our opportunity to call the bluff of many of our clients. From the earlier questions, particularly questions 2 and 3, as well as our general data gathering and other questions, we ensure that there is no need for cash flow from the investment portfolio for at least five years. However, in spite of the client's earlier answers confirming no need to tap into the investment portfolio, many clients when answering this question automatically default to the assumption that they require some cash flow from the investment portfolio. It is not at all uncommon for a client to say something to the effect of "Well, I need at least 4 percent or 5 percent." If they provide any response other than "1" (i.e., not important), we say, "Mr. Client, I'm sorry—I must have made a mistake. Let me get it corrected. What will you need that 5 percent for?" The client may say, "Well, I think I need about $XX to cover living expenses" or "I may need $XX for my daughter's wedding." This is when we revisit our original discussion regarding our five-year mantra. If we have accurately captured our client's needs, we have already carved out of the investment portfolio the $XX needed for expenses and the $XX for the wedding. Those funds are not in the investment portfolio but rather in the side cash flow reserve account. If the client raises a need for funds that we neglected to consider, we simply go back to question 1 and reduce the entry accordingly. For example, if we had originally entered $1 million as the value of the investment portfolio and in question 6 the client indicates a need for $50,000 for a wedding in three years that we had not considered, we would change the original entry to $950,000 and then ask the client how he or she would answer question 6. We would keep up this process until the client is comfortable answering "1."

The final choice, "aggressive growth," is very purposefully included as the last attribute. We started out question 6 by allowing our clients to emphasize their desire to protect principal.[2] We end the discussion of question 6 by discussing aggressive growth with our clients. We define the term as it is used in the mutual fund industry. We explain that we are not talking about high growth, but rather aggressive strategies, such as short sales and margin, or highly volatile investments such as commodities. This gives our client the opportunity to once again slam his fist on the table, look us straight in the eye, and say, "Absolutely not," as he circles "1." He now feels terrific! In our practice, we have a policy of avoiding managers who implement aggressive strategies, so the rejection of aggressive growth has little or no effect on our recommendations other than to provide a level of comfort to our clients.

---

[2]Asking about capital preservation may seem like a silly question because few clients have a desire to lose principal. However, as experienced expert witnesses, we recognize that a desire for capital preservation is always an element of a claim, so practitioners may as well lean into it and document this goal in a context that recognizes other conflicting goals.

Question 7

- Optional: Do you have any asset class constraints (limitations)?

	Minimum	Maximum
T-bills, CDs, money market	_____	_____
Intermediate government bonds	_____	_____
Intermediate corporate bonds	_____	_____
Intermediate municipal bonds	_____	_____
Long-term government bonds	_____	_____
Long-term corporate bonds	_____	_____
Long-term municipal bonds	_____	_____
High-yield bonds	_____	_____
Foreign bonds	_____	_____
Domestic equities (e.g., S&P 500)	_____	_____
Domestic equities, over the counter	_____	_____
Foreign equities	_____	_____
Real estate investment trusts	_____	_____
Commodities	_____	_____
Hedge funds	_____	_____
Private equity	_____	_____

"Asset class constraints" is the second of the two optional questions in the questionnaire. Very much like previous questions, this one is designed to address any potential hidden agenda that we may otherwise miss in discussions with our clients. We explain that the question is not asking if the clients like or are even familiar with a particular investment. Rather, we simply wish to know if they will at least consider a recommendation rather than rejecting it out of hand. On occasion, it provides the opportunity to increase the client's willingness to consider an investment class that might otherwise be rejected, by offering to put a maximum cap on an asset class. For example, clients unfamiliar or uncomfortable with the possibility of foreign investing may be willing to consider such an investment if they know that our recommendations will be limited to a maximum allocation, such as 15 percent. In our practice we find that setting specific caps is rarely problematic in our ability to design what we believe to be a functionally efficient portfolio.

Question 8

- What percentage of your investments are you likely to need within five years?

You will note great similarities between questions 2, 3, 4, and 8. There is no mistake in this. We are adamant in our insistence that the investment portfolio must have a minimum of a five-year horizon. Once again we discuss our firm mantra: five years, five years, five years. The only acceptable answer to question 8 is "0 percent."

Question 9

- Up to what percentage of this portfolio can be invested in long-term investments (i.e., over five years)?

This is simply another way of asking the same question we posed in questions 2, 3, 4, and 8. The only acceptable answer is "100 percent." Now that the client has entered "0 percent" in question 8 and "100 percent" in question 9, that client is under no illusions regarding the fact that these funds have a long-term investment horizon.

In question 9 we explain to our clients that the redundancy is included not only to educate, alert, warn, and prepare them for intermediate-term volatility. It is also designed to serve as a comforting reminder in the future. When the markets have turned nasty, we will remind them that the world did not actually come to an end. We knew the downturn would happen, just not when it would happen.

We tell them that when the market does take a big plunge and they become nervous, we will pull out this old questionnaire and flip it open to the questions they have just answered. We will then remind them that they need not panic. With our cash flow reserve account we have anticipated this type of market turmoil. Their portfolio was designed with the knowledge that they would not be forced to liquidate at the bottom. It works. Our experience after Black Monday 1987 was a surprise even to us. We called all of our clients, anticipating that many would be very concerned. *All* of our clients dutifully repeated back to us, "We know: five years, five years, five years." They knew that the world had not come to an end. They also knew that they had no immediate need for their investment funds—their grocery money was sitting in a money market in their cash flow reserve account. Black Monday served as interesting cocktail party patter, but was a nonevent in our clients' lives. We had a similar reaction during the tech crash of 2000 and the bear market of 2009.

During all of these painful market periods, to drive the point home I would say, "By the way, we are on the phone." After a few seconds of confused silence, my client would say, "Of course we are—you called me. So what?" to which I would respond, "I guess that means AT&T is in business today, and I bet families are drinking Coca-Cola at Disney as we speak. I have no idea what happened to the market, but you own AT&T, Coca-Cola, Disney, and thousands of other fine companies around the world. I think they are just as good as yesterday, so relax and enjoy your life." Our clients slept well while others fretted.

Question 10

- Investment risk means different things to different people. Please rank the following statements from 1 (the statement that would worry you the most) to 4 (the statement that would worry you the least).

    _____I would be very concerned if I did not achieve the return on my portfolio that I expected (i.e., my target rate of return).

    _____I would be very concerned if my portfolio was worth less in real dollars because of inflation erosion.

    _____I would be very concerned with short-term volatility (i.e., if my portfolio dropped substantially in value over one year).

    _____I would be very concerned with long-term volatility (i.e., if my portfolio dropped in value over a long period of time—five years or longer).

This is an attempt to educate our clients regarding the many manifestations of risk, including the risk of losing their standard of living, the risk of not meeting their goals, and the risk of not sleeping well (i.e., market volatility). The first two concerns listed address the issue of returns. We emphasize that their goals are accomplished by earning an appropriate real rate of return (ROR), not by earning an arbitrary fixed target return. The next item helps clarify for clients that short-term volatility is a reality that they have to live with.

Question 11

- Except for the Great Depression and the bursting of the Internet bubble, the stock market recovered its previous high level in no more than four years. During the Great Depression, the market almost recaptured its highs in nominal terms in about eight years, but fell again and ultimately regained August 1929 levels after 15 years. During the early 2000s, the dividend-adjusted value of the S&P 500 took about seven years to regain the nominal highs of the Internet bubble. Bond investments tend to rebound in two years. Knowing this and that it is impossible to protect yourself from an occasional loss, answer the following question:

    If my portfolio produces a long-term return that allows me to accomplish my goals, I am prepared to live with a time of recovery of:
    a. Less than one year
    b. Between one and two years
    c. Between two and three years
    d. Between three and four years
    e. More than four years
        If you select less than "between three and four years," are you prepared to substantially reduce your goals?

This question goes straight to the heart of market volatility and its emotional power. The description emphasizes that even investors in the bond market have gone through periods in which their portfolios would have had to wait a few years for positive returns. Stock markets have had bear markets lasting for more than four years. With the historical warning that there is no way of protecting against bear markets, we then ask how long they will be able to maintain their wits if their portfolio has an extended loss. We explain that we are talking in terms of 12-month periods and not the day after Black Monday. For example, if they invested their money on January 1, 1997, a two-year down market would mean that the portfolio value would be less on January 1, 1999.

    We then allow the client to choose among "less than one year," "between one and two years," "between two and three years," "between three and four years," and "more than four years." Note that if anything less than "between three and four years" is checked, we ask the question, "Are you prepared to substantially reduce your goals?" We explain that if they check anything less than two years, our recommendation would have to be that their funds be placed in fixed income investments with maturities of less than three years. Clearly, if historically the markets have required as long as two years for bonds and four-plus years for stocks to recover, any investment in either of those asset classes, or a combination thereof, is likely to exceed the client's risk tolerance.

Question 12

- Please check the statement that reflects your preference:
    - ☐ I would rather be out of the stock market when it goes down than in the market when it goes up (i.e., I cannot live with the volatility of the stock market).
    - ☐ I would rather be in the stock market when it goes down than out of the market when it goes up (i.e., I may not like the idea, but I can live with the volatility of the stock market in order to earn market returns).

Question 12 is perhaps my personal favorite and my clients' least favorite of all our questions. We do not believe in market timing, and we require our clients to acknowledge that they are prepared to accept the reality that they cannot market-time. This question simply points out that if the client wishes to participate in the positive periods of the market, he or she must be prepared to accept the down periods as well. Should a client ever indicate that he cannot live with the volatility of the stock market, we explain that the only alternative is an all-bond portfolio, which, in all likelihood, will not provide a return adequate to meet the client's long-term goals.

Question 13

- Several portfolio performance projections are listed here. Assuming that inflation averages 3 percent, check the portfolio that most nearly reflects your goal for your portfolio.

		Hypothetical Risk Exposure	
Overall Risk Level	Projected Total Return (Inflation = 3%)	"Worst Case"* (12 months)	Bear Market[†] (10/07–2/09)
Low/low	6.0%	− 4.0%	− 10.6%
Low/low	6.8	− 7.0	− 14.5
Mod/low	7.2	− 9.0	− 16.2
Mod/low	7.4	− 10.0	− 20.1
Mod/low	7.6	− 11.0	− 22.9
Mod/mod	7.8	− 13.0	− 25.7
High/mod	8.0	− 14.0	− 29.1
High/mod	8.3	− 16.0	− 32.4
High/high	8.6	− 20.0	− 35.2
High/high	8.8	− 22.0	− 40.8
High/high	9.0	− 24.0	− 45.9
High/high	9.4	− 27.0	− 50.9

*We use the term *worst case* to describe the worst annual return that a portfolio is likely to experience 90 percent of the time. Remember—these are hypothetical projections and they represent the change over a 12-month period, *not* a day or week just after a market crash.

[†]Obviously 90 percent of the time leaves the possibility that 10 percent of the time returns can be worse. For example, in early 2009 the *New York Times* published an article titled "Off the Charts," noting that although there had been many bear markets during the previous 82 years, there had never been a 10-year stretch as bad as the one that ended in January 2009. With the economy suffering its worst recession in over five decades, the bear market period from October 2007 to February 2009 was the worst market environment since the Great Depression and the magnitude of the losses were significant. The hypothetical losses in this table are based on unrebalanced allocations to the S&P 500 and intermediate-term high-quality bonds. During a bear market, rebalancing a portfolio would potentially increase losses.

This was added a number of years ago and recently updated to reflect the recent bear market to provide some way for our clients to select, on the investment spectrum, a risk/ return intersection that best represents the balance between their goal for returns and their tolerance for risk. For the "Overall Risk Level" column, we have divided the risk level into two time frames: short term (one to five years) and long term (over five years). We then ask clients to select, in qualitative terms, their risk tolerance. For example, if a client indicated he was very conservative and his risk tolerance was very low, he would check "low/low." We believe that, most of the time, during a 12-month period his return is likely to be at break-even or better. During a bear market, we believe the portfolio would drop in value less than 5 percent. We also explain that assuming a long-run inflation rate of 3 percent, we believe that a realistic total return expectation is 6 percent. The point of providing a "low/low" alternative is to demonstrate to the client that we can design a conservative portfolio, but we believe it will provide a very low total return.

The second column is based on our current projections determined from our optimization work. The numbers are adjusted to take the fund expenses and our management fee into account. Note that we anchor the projections with a specific estimate for inflation. When we develop a policy, our target is a real rate of return (ROR), not a nominal return. For example, if we designed a policy to meet the return expectation of 8 percent from the table, the target return would be 5 percent real ROR, not 8 percent nominal.

The last columns titled "Hypothetical Risk Exposure," include a "Worst Case," based on two standard deviations. As noted in the footnote, we tell our clients that this is the worst return that we believe they are likely to see 1 out of 10 years, or 10 out of 100 years, based on 12-month intervals.[3] It also includes hypothetical returns during the 10/07 to 2/09 bear market.

Question 14
Now you have a test to take. There are two parts to the test.

Question #1. Choose (a) or (b):

(a) You win $80,000.	☐
(b) You have an 80 percent chance of winning $100,000 (or a 20 percent chance of winning nothing).	☐

Question #2. Choose (a) or (b):

(a) You lose $80,000.	☐
(b) You have an 80 percent chance of losing $100,000 (or a 20 percent chance of losing nothing).	☐

Modified from the work of Kahneman and Tversky, this is another "aha" question and perhaps the most effective question in the Risk Tolerance Questionnaire (RTQ). The following is how we present it.

---

[3]For any mathematicians reading this, we are aware that two standard deviations does not translate to our "1 in 10 years"; however, for purposes of framing our client's expectations, we believe that the simplicity of the approximation is appropriate. In fact, this more conservative presentation helps accommodate the fact that historical returns have not followed a normal distribution, which has a tendency to underestimate the frequency of extreme events for distribution with more than normal kurtosis. Here, too, we rely on simplicity to frame client expectations.

Mr. and Mrs. Client, instead of asking you to answer this question directly, I'm going to give it to you in a two-part test. Ready? Okay, Part 1: You've just walked into a huge Las Vegas casino, and as you enter, you see hundreds of people standing around staring at you, balloons and confetti drop from the ceiling, a band strikes up, and a gentleman in a magnificent tux walks up to you. In his left hand he's holding a brown paper bag and his right arm is outstretched, and on it he's balancing packets of cash that seem to reach to the ceiling. As he reaches you he says, "Welcome! You're our millionth visitor, and *you win*! But naturally, as you're in Vegas, you get a choice. If you point to my right arm where I'm holding $80,000, it's yours! Your other choice is to put your hand in this brown paper bag and pull out one ping-pong ball. In the bag there are 10 balls, eight white and two black. If you pull out a white ball, you win $100,000! If you pull out a black ball, you win *nothing*!"

It is very rare indeed that the choice is not (a).

Next we tell the client it's time for the second part of the test.

Mr. and Mrs. Client, I made a mistake. You're not in Vegas; you're in Hell, and the Devil walks up to you. He says, "Well, given that you're here, it's no surprise that you lost; but the good news is that you have a choice." He then throws out his right arm and says, "If you point to that arm, you will owe me $80,000. Or you can put your hand into this brown paper bag and pull out one ping-pong ball. In the bag there are 10 balls, eight white and two black. If you pull out a white ball you owe me $100,000. If you pull out a black ball, you owe me *nothing*!

For question #2, it is very rare that the choice is not (b).

We use this as an opportunity to explain the difference between risk averse and loss averse. We tell our clients that we understand their concern with risk. But we believe by answering (a) in question #1 and (b) in question #2 that they have, in fact, demonstrated that they are not risk averse, but they are loss averse. We show them that choosing to win $80,000 is a very clear demonstration that they do not wish to take a risk in order to earn more money. However, in choosing (b) in question #2, they have obviously elected to take a risk. They have elected to take this risk in order to avoid losing money. We explain that this is in keeping with research by behavioral economists and our philosophy. When we recommend investments that our clients might perceive as uncomfortable—for example, a higher proportion of investments in equities, or a portion of their investments in international and small company stock—we do so not to make them richer, but rather to assist them in maintaining their standard of living.

After going through this discussion, we find that clients who, for perhaps 60 or 70 years of their lives, have considered themselves very conservative CD investors, all of a sudden light up and say, "Aha, I understand. I may not be comfortable making the investments that you suggest, but I am prepared to make those investments now that I understand the reason why. It makes sense to me."

We point out the difference between our recommendation and that of a traditional stockbroker. Brokers recommend the purchase of equities because they will make money; we recommend the purchase of equities so that our clients can maintain their standard of living.

Historical Returns

The last page of our questionnaire is a table of summary statistics for long-term returns. It serves as a reality anchor for our clients. Throughout the process we explain to them that our investment philosophy is based on the belief that, over the long term, at best they can expect historical real rates of return. These historical returns are presented in Exhibit 5.2.

EXHIBIT 5.2   Summary Statistics of Annual Returns, 1926 to 2009

Asset Class	Compounded Return	Standard Deviation
Large stocks	9.8%	20.5%
Small stocks	11.9	32.8
Government bonds	5.4	9.6
Treasury bills	3.7	3.1
Inflation	3.0	4.2

Source: Ibbotson SBBI 2010 Classic Yearbook, 28. © Morningstar.

Finally, we ask our clients to sign an acknowledgment that they have participated in the process and that they are committed to the answers they have given.

By completing and signing this questionnaire, you agree that its contents were discussed and explained to you and that you agree your answers are correct to the best of your knowledge. You also understand that this questionnaire does not make or imply any guarantee regarding the attainment of your investment objective. Please make us aware of any changes in your personal or financial circumstances.

X _____   *Date:* _____

While their acknowledgment may serve as a defense for us in the event of disagreement with our clients, that is not its purpose. We tell our clients that the completed questionnaire will be their psychological lifesaver when the market drops.

When they start to panic, we can remind them that they saw it coming. We anticipated volatility. They are simply suffering through the unpleasant portion of normal market cycles. We know they do not like to worry, and we will assure them that we know they are worried. Still, they made a commitment a long time ago to persevere—not to get rich, but to maintain their quality of life. We have been doing this long enough and have enough experience to know that it is very comforting for our clients to see proof that they had anticipated a bear cycle. They will not be happy, but they will go about their business, confident that the world has not come to an end and that tomorrow will be a brighter day.

MEASURING CAPITAL NEEDS

As noted in the previous sections, funds are carved out of the investment portfolio for the spending or capital needs of the client over the short term. The client may need to make additional investments or modify investment policy in order to meet long-term goals, such as college funding or retirement. Capital needs analysis (CNA) or capital accumulation planning is a time-value calculation, based on explicit assumptions. The analysis is a present value calculation that factors in the client's unique investments, risk tolerance, tax status, income, and expense factors. By determining the return requirement necessary to balance the client's current portfolio with future needs (subject to the client's unique constraints), CNA is the analytical tool used to quantify the return requirement for investment planning.

An effective CNA is a comprehensive approach to evaluating the client's retirement goals. Specifically, it should incorporate an evaluation of the unique composition of the client's portfolio. As an example:

- *Unique asset classes.* The client's investments need to be subdivided into economically unique asset classes. A quasi-class, such as "limited partnerships" or "hedge funds," is useless, as it describes an investment's legal structure, not its economic exposure (such as a long investment in large-capitalization stocks).
- *Tax environment.* Investments must also be classified according to their tax consequences. For example, an investment in the tax-sheltered environment of a pension will have a significantly different long-term after-tax return than a similar investment held in a personal account. A CNA should account for the tax benefit of shelters.
- *Distributions.* Some investments may have required distributions independent of a client's cash flow needs (e.g., pensions and IRAs for clients reaching age 70½). The required distribution may have tax consequences and reinvestment constraints resulting in lower future return expectations. A CNA should account for these events.
- *Interim expenses.* Many clients will have to make demands on their investment portfolios prior to retirement (e.g., subsidize current standard of living, college expenses, weddings). A CNA must account for the timing of these expenses and the impact of inflation.
- *Savings.* This is the flip side of distributions. The CNA must account for the timing, magnitude, and changes in additional contributions to investment accounts.
- *Postretirement income and expenses.* As discussed earlier, these cash flow streams must be delineated in detail with respect to timing, magnitude, changes, and tax consequences.

Capital needs analysis, like our clients' lives, is not a simple process and, if successfully applied, is a mathematically holistic view of our clients' resources and needs.

Assumptions

Capital needs analysis involves making a number of assumptions, such as whether to assume income from governmental Social Security systems. Often the client will have an inclination to request that we, the wealth managers, use *conservative* assumptions. Unfortunately, the concept of conservative assumptions in a CNA is illusionary. The consequences of using conservative assumptions are *aggressive* investment recommendations.

Consider the client who requests that the analysis not allow for invasion of principal. You are certainly familiar with the lament, "I don't ever want to dip into capital!" As conservative as the requests may seem to the client, the result is that it may require a much larger allocation to growth investments (which clients think of as risky) in order for the client to accomplish this financial goal. Example 5.4 may be useful in explaining the problem of erroneously equating "conservative" with "preserving capital."

Other assumptions that may be illusionary-conservative and result in inappropriate, aggressive portfolios include: "I don't trust Social Security, so let's be conservative and leave it out" or "Well, let's be conservative and ignore that inheritance," and the perennial favorite, "Well, taxes always go up, so let's increase my tax bracket."

The common default to safe investments confuses safety with certainty. Investors may be certain that an investment in a high-quality bond or CD will be returned to them at maturity, but they can also be reasonably sure that if their goal is to maintain their standard of living, after factoring in inflation, it will not be the safe alternative for their entire nest egg.

EXAMPLE 5.4   Retirement Income Needs

Ms. Moore has a portfolio of $200,000 currently invested in money market funds. After accounting for other sources of income during retirement (e.g., Social Security), she has determined that she will require a living expense supplement for 20 years of $7,000 per year, or 3.5 percent of her portfolio. In addition, she agrees that an inflation factor of 4 percent per year seems reasonable. Her choices are limited to safe fixed income investments that are expected to return an after-tax, real rate of return of 1 percent, and equities that are expected to provide an after-tax real rate of return of 6 percent. By investing in a balanced portfolio (i.e., 50 percent fixed income and 50 percent equity), Ms. Moore can expect to meet her goals if she uses about half of her portfolio principal throughout retirement. In contrast, if she chooses to be *conservative* and attempts to preserve her corpus all through retirement, she would have to invest 100 percent in equities. Even then, she would eventually be forced to use 40 percent of the original investment to continue to fund her income needs.

Conservative CNA is based on utilizing the best available information. It is the responsibility of the wealth manager to use his or her utmost professional judgment in determining when to include or exclude certain assumptions. Such decisions should not be made based on a simplistic belief that an assumption of lower income is inherently conservative. It is not. The estimation of the probability of the future income stream should be based on the wealth manager's informed judgment.

Mortality

As discussed earlier, even if the wealth manager avoids all of the problems just mentioned, the conclusions of a CNA will be nonsense unless the manager heeds the guidance of Lynn Hopewell and Bruce Temkin and uses reasonable mortality assumptions in the process. Our questionnaire includes a section requesting the age of death (if they died of natural causes) of our client's siblings, parents, and grandparents, or, if those relatives are still living, an evaluation of their general health. The goal is to accumulate enough data to make an educated judgment regarding how long lived our clients are likely to be. At a minimum, we use a 70 percent mortality standard. For clients from very long-lived families, we may use a 90 percent standard.[4]

Data Gathering Guide

Exhibit 5.3 outlines a simplified version of a data gathering form used to capture the information needed to complete a CNA. It will serve as a guide for the following discussion.

---

[4]For example, a 70 percent standard means that we would use, as our estimate for the client's mortality, an age by which 70 percent of the population the same age as our client will have died.

EXHIBIT 5.3   CNA Data Gathering Guide

Basic Data

Each Spouse

Current Age

Retirement Age

Mortality Age

Pre and Post Retirement

Inflation

Pre and Post Marginal Tax Bracket

Assets

Type	*Taxes*
Fixed	After Tax
Short	Taxable
Short/Inter	*Liquidation Constraints*
Intermediate	Partial
Equity	Lump Sum
Real Estate	Age
Other	Payout Required
	Sequence

Pre Retirement

Contributions	*Distributions*
Amount	Amount
Growth	Growth
Begin/End	Begin/End

Post Retirement Income

Annual Amount

Growth

Begin

End

Taxes

Expenses

Source

Amount

Growth

Begin

End

CNA Software

The first use of this data gathering guide is as a tool to judge the analytical software the wealth manager plans on using to perform the calculations. Don't spend days, or even hours, constructing massive spreadsheets to evaluate various software vendors' products. Instead use Evensky's Screening Process. Originally conceived for the evaluation of comprehensive financial planning software, it has proven to be a simple and invaluable technique for selecting mutual fund software, asset allocation software, and CNA software. The idea is simple. Do not bother looking in detail at software that will not meet your minimum requirements. Suppose that you were looking for a new car and saw a beauty that you thought you might like to own. What would be your reaction if you discovered that, inexplicably, the manufacturer had omitted a speedometer and there was no way to add one? Would you really spend time inquiring about city and highway mileage and choice of colors? Of course not. If a CNA program will not let you enter data in the detail you consider necessary, do you really care how beautifully it can produce colored charts and graphs? Again, of course not! Reject software that will not accept data in the detail you deem necessary. Then, eliminate any software that will not meet your practice-specific criteria (e.g., color graphics or Windows based). Finally, select the best from the survivors of the prior screens. When you consider that the results of a CNA drive the investment portfolio allocation and determine the future quality of life for the client, it should be obvious that shortcut or simplistic analysis not only is inadequate, it's unprofessional.

Unrealistic Client Expectations

Before even beginning the CNA, there is one client issue that must be addressed. It can potentially torpedo all of the wealth manager's future work. Determine whether your client has unrealistic expectations regarding assets in the current investment portfolio. We have all had clients who believe that their heavy concentration in their very favorite stock will grow at an unrealistic rate ("I work for the company—I know a good thing when I see it"), or own an apartment that they believe will have returns exceeding all other real estate ("This apartment is in the best neighborhood in the city—it can't go wrong!"). In these cases, you have two alternatives. One is to run a CNA using the clients' estimates and then rerun it with your more realistic estimates. Show the clients their risk of a reduced standard of living if unsystematic risk catches up with them or if their optimism turns out to be wrong. The second alternative is to do a simple economic analysis and demonstrate to your clients how much more return they are projecting than the experts have historically been able to achieve.

Data Gathering—Step by Step

First, start with the determination of the client's current personal status. In addition to the obvious questions, such as current age, spouse's age, and expected retirement dates, the wealth manager needs to capture information helpful in determining a mortality age.

Existing Portfolio

Next, we need to consider the client's existing portfolio. As discussed earlier, the investments need to be separated by function. Most software provides for a single investment class. This simplified approach is woefully inadequate. Among other things, a single portfolio with a blended return cannot account for additional investments in or withdrawals from an asset class. It cannot account for different tax consequences or varying liquidation priorities. Some software solutions purport to separate investments but use pseudo classes: pensions, mutual funds, and partnerships. As investments in each of these pseudo classes could be in almost any true economic class (such as short-term bonds, long bonds, domestic stock, international stock, gold), pseudo classes are useless. Exhibit 5.4 presents a taxonomy of asset classes that will be discussed further in later chapters.

EXHIBIT 5.4   Taxonomy of Asset Classes/Styles

    I. Cash Equivalents
   II. Fixed Income
        a. Short term
              i. Corporate
             ii. Government
            iii. Municipal
             iv. International
        b. Short/intermediate term
              i. Corporate
                    1. Investment grade
                    2. Below investment grade
             ii. Municipal
                    1. Investment grade
                    2. Below investment grade
        c. Intermediate
              i. Corporate
                    1. Investment grade
                    2. Below investment grade
             ii. Municipal
                    1. Investment grade
                    2. Below investment grade
            iii. International
                    1. Developed nations
                    2. Emerging markets
        d. Long-term
              i. Corporate
                    1. Investment grade
                    2. Below investment grade
             ii. Municipal
                    1. Investment grade
                    2. Below investment grade
            iii. International
                    1. Developed nations
                    2. Emerging markets
  III. Equities
        a. Stock
              i. Large capitalization domestic
                    1. Growth
                    2. Value
                    3. Yield[a]

EXHIBIT 5.4   (Continued)

---

       ii. Small-capitalization domestic
          1. Growth
          2. Value
          3. Microcap[a]
      iii. International
          1. Developed countries
             a. Top down
             b. Bottom up
             c. Small company
          2. Emerging markets
  IV. Alternative Investments
      a. Real estate (really another type of equity)
      b. Natural resources
      c. Hedge funds (may be considered a "pseudo" asset class)
      d. Private equity (equity)
      e. Venture capital
      f. Structured products (equity)
      g. Other

---

[a]We include this in "value."

Return Assumptions

Having separated the investments into true economic classes, the wealth manager needs to make assumptions regarding the returns for each class and next must determine the tax status of those returns. Investments in a client's personal account will be currently taxed at some mix of the ordinary rate and the capital gains rate, whereas investments in individual retirement accounts (IRAs), pensions, or annuities, will grow tax-deferred and be subject to ordinary taxes on future distributions. This requires a careful review of each investment. The wealth manager cannot simply assume that taxable gains are correlated with turnover. This will be discussed at length in Chapter 11 on wealth management in a taxable environment. For example, investments in actively traded equity accounts may generate less taxable income than a low-turnover mutual fund. In fact, some tax-aware investment strategies, such as tax-loss harvesting, require some amount of turnover to harvest valuable tax opportunities.

Reinvestment Risk

In order to account for reinvestment risk, each investment must be considered in terms of its marketability. For example, suppose your client has a half million dollars invested in a floating-rate real estate mortgage. The mortgage was placed at a rate quite favorable for the client. It is paying a real rate of return (ROR) of 6 percent. Ten years from now, when the mortgage matures, the proceeds are likely to be invested at a much lower rate.

Generally speaking, mortgaged-backed securities (MBSs) tend to have significant reinvestment rate risk for a somewhat different reason. That is, mortgagors tend to refinance their mortgages when rates are low, which returns principal to the MBS holders at a time when reinvestment rates for similar securities are also low.

Savings and Liquidations

Clients do not take savings and invest them in their portfolios as a whole. That is, the savings are not reinvested pro rata over the existing portfolio but are, in fact, invested in specific accounts. If funds are withdrawn prior to retirement for interim goals (such as college funding or paying for a child's wedding), the funds are also drawn from specific accounts, not pro rata across the portfolio.

Preretirement additions to the portfolio may come from numerous sources, such as savings, lump sums (e.g., gifts and inheritances), and sales of businesses. Hence, the wealth manager needs to factor in any expected changes (such as a gradual increase in savings).

Withdrawals are the mirror image of investments. We need to account for preretirement withdrawals for such interim goals as supplementing preretirement living conditions or college funding. As with investments, we need to determine when and from which accounts the withdrawals are likely to be made.

Postretirement Assumptions

These can be divided into two categories:

1. *Income sources independent of the investment portfolio.* The primary factors are the source and amount (e.g., pensions), changes in that amount (e.g., pension payment with a cost of living adjustment), the timing, and the tax consequences (e.g., Social Security taxation).
2. *Postretirement expenses.* The necessity to classify postretirement expenses into at least four classes was discussed at length in the earlier section on client goals.

Given this multiplicity of postretirement income classes, perhaps one day the media will stop recommending such worthless rules of thumb as: "You need 70 percent of preretirement income."

The following examples may be helpful in evaluating a software package's ability to handle these issues. The question in all cases is: "Can the software handle the client's unique circumstances?"

- Clients may have significant personal investments in fixed and variable annuities.
- A client estimates that he will receive an inheritance in 10 years. As it is a portion of a family business, it will pay an increasing amount yearly. He plans to sell his interest three years after the inheritance.

Analysis

Once the number crunching has been completed, the wealth manager will have determined the ability of the client's current portfolio to meet her retirement goals. Basically, the CNA will lead to one of four conclusions: the client can, with her existing portfolio allocation, just achieve her goals; she will fall short of the goals; she needs to change the allocation to reflect a higher percentage of growth assets in order to meet the goals; or her goals are so modest compared to her resources that she may increase the fixed income allocation and still achieve the goals.

In our practice, the results of the CNA are a major component in the next stage of the wealth management process—the asset allocation. We will revisit this idea a little later.

CNA Caveats—Sustainable Withdrawal Rates

We are firm believers in the use of a detailed and comprehensive CNA to assist our clients to quantify their retirement planning goals. William P. Bengen, however, published a series of articles showing that a reliance on average returns to estimate the sustainability of a retirement portfolio is dangerous.[5] Many other authors have joined in this work, as well.[6]

These articles are wake-up calls and reminders that our use of long-term conservative real rates of return in our CNA will not protect our client from becoming a "black hole" investor. The "black hole" investors are the ones who had the misfortune to begin the drawdown of their retirement funds just at the beginning of a major market correction (e.g., 1937, 1946, 1969, 1973, 1974, 2000, 2008). For those unfortunate souls, an early erosion of corpus may make it impossible for the portfolio to recover sufficiently to maintain their standard of living. This is also referred to as "sequence of return" risk. After reading these articles, we realized that we had fallen into the trap of believing that using long-term average returns implied we were being conservative. We forgot that averages can be dangerous. A man with his head in the oven and his body in a freezer may have a temperature of 98.6 degrees on average, but he is not comfortable.

EXAMPLE 5.5   Sustainable Withdrawals

Let's assume that we believe the long-term average return from equities will be 9 percent and inflation will be about 3 percent. How much could clients with a $1 million portfolio safely withdraw each year (pretax), maintain their future purchasing power, and be reasonably assured not to run out of money over the next 30 years?

One might do a simple calculation and determine that a 6 percent withdrawal rate would be safe. The flaw in this computation is that a withdrawal rate of that magnitude would be safe only if the return were exactly 6 percent each and every year. If returns are at all variable, the maximum safe withdrawal rate is considerably less. In fact, the research of Bengen and others shows that the maximum safe withdrawal rate would be in the 3 to 4 percent range, with a probability of success (i.e., not running out of money) of about 95 percent.

If one considers the life balance sheet discussed in Chapter 1, the present value of a client's retirement needs and other spending goals are essentially liabilities that would be similar to the obligations that a pension fund owes to pensioners. The assets on the left side are intended to fund those liabilities.

In the context of pension fund management, Robert Merton (2008) points out that defined-benefit pension plans have traditionally discounted their liabilities using the expected rate of return on the investments used to fund them. This approach makes the liabilities' size appear much smaller.[7] A plan sponsor cannot change the size of its pension liabilities by changing the risk of the assets used to fund them.

By implication, the wealth manager does not make a client's retirement more attainable by simply investing in riskier assets with a higher average return. Although the average return makes a retirement goal appear more attainable, the additional risk increases the possibility of

---

[5]See Bengen (1994, 1996, 1997, 2001, 2006) in the Resources list.
[6]See, for example, Cooley, Hubbard, and Walz (2001, 2003a, 2003b).
[7]See also Merton (2003, 2006a, 2006b).

a shortfall.[8] This is not to suggest that a balanced portfolio of different asset classes is undesirable. It highlights that relying solely on the average return, particularly of risky asset classes, to perform a CNA can lead to excessive risk taking.

We found Bengen's papers to be an important influence on our implementation of our CNA and an effective way of communicating the issues to our clients. Research on sustainable retirement withdrawals is discussed further in later chapters once we have addressed the limitations of statistics in this context. Based on these papers, the conclusion our investment committee reached was that we would continue to use CNA as our primary analytical tool; however, we would constrain our recommendations based on the conclusions of the articles. Also, we would add to our client education program a special discussion to address the differences between historical averages and historical reality.

PARTING COMMENTS

As noted in the previous chapter, it is critical to get to know your clients. This includes having a shared understanding of their risk tolerance and collecting sufficient information to develop a sound investment policy to help them achieve their goals.

RESOURCES

Bengen, William P. 1994. "Determining Withdrawal Rates Using Historical Data." *Journal of Financial Planning*, Vol. 7, No. 4 (October): 171–180.

Bengen, William P. 1996. "Asset Allocation for a Lifetime." *Journal of Financial Planning*, August 1996: 58–67.

Bengen, William P. 1997. "Conserving Client Portfolios during Retirement, Part III." *Journal of Financial Planning* (December): 84–97.

Bengen, William P. 2001. "Conserving Client Portfolios during Retirement, Part IV." *Journal of Financial Planning* (May).

Bengen, William P. 2006. "Baking a Withdrawal Plan 'Layer Cake' for Your Retirement Clients." *Journal of Financial Planning* (August).

Blayney, Eleanor. 1995. "Assessing Your Client's Tolerance for Risk." IAFP Advanced Planners Conference.

Bodie, Zvi. 1991. "Shortfall Risk and Pension Fund Asset Management." *Financial Analysts Journal*, Vol. 47, No. 3 (May/June): 57–61.

Bodie, Zvi. 1996. "Pensions for an Aging World." *Benefits Quarterly*, Vol. 12, No. 1 (First Quarter): 17–22.

Bodie, Zvi, and Dwight Crane. 1999. "The Design and Production of New Retirement Savings Products." *Journal of Portfolio Management*, Vol. 99, No. 25 (Winter): 77–82.

Cooley, Philip L., Carl M. Hubbard, and Daniel T. Walz. 1999. "Sustainable Withdrawals from Your Retirement Portfolio." *Financial Counseling and Planning*, Vol. 10, No. 1: 39–47.

---

[8]Bodie (1991) makes a similar argument from a slightly different perspective. He shows that a defined-benefit pension plan's shortfall risk increases substantially as the portfolio's exposure to equities increases. According to Bodie, the present value of the benefits equals the cost of the pension fund to immunize the pension obligation, which implies discounting the pension liabilities using a zero-coupon risk-free yield curve. See also Bodie (1996), Bodie and Crane (1999), and Love, Smith, and Wilcox (2007).

Cooley, Philip L., Carl M. Hubbard, and Daniel T. Walz. 2001. "Withdrawing Money from Your Retirement Portfolio without Going Broke." *Journal of Retirement Planning*, Vol. 4, No. 4: 35–42.

Cooley, Philip L., Carl M. Hubbard, and Daniel T. Walz. 2003a. "A Comparative Analysis of Retirement Portfolio Success Rates: Simulation versus Overlapping Periods." *Financial Services Review*, Vol. 12, No. 2 (Summer): 115–138.

Cooley, Philip L., Carl M. Hubbard, and Daniel T. Walz. 2003b. "Does International Diversification Increase the Sustainable Withdrawal Rates from Retirement Portfolios?" *Journal of Financial Planning*, Vol. 16, No. 1 (January): 74–80.

Guyton, Jonathan T. 2004. "Decision Rules and Portfolio Management for Retirees: Is the 'Safe' Initial Withdrawal Rate Too Safe?" *Journal of Financial Planning*, Vol. 17, No. 10 (October): 54–62.

Guyton, Jonathan T., and William J. Klinger. 2006. "Decision Rules and Maximum Initial Withdrawal Rates." *Journal of Financial Planning*, Vol. 19, No. 3 (March): 48–58.

Kahneman, Daniel, Paul Slovic, and Amos Tversky, eds. 1982. *Judgment under Uncertainty*. New York: Cambridge University Press.

Kahneman, Daniel, and Amos Tversky. 1979. "Prospect Theory: An Analysis of Decisions under Risk." *Econometrica*, Vol. 47, No. 2 (March): 263–291.

Love, David, Paul A. Smith, and David Wilcox. 2007. "Why Do Firms Offer Risky Defined Benefit Pension Plans?" *National Tax Journal*, Vol. 60, No. 3 (September): 507–519.

Merton, Robert C. 2003. "Thoughts on the Future: Theory and Practice in Investment Management." *Financial Analysts Journal*, Vol. 9, No. 1 (January/February): 17–23.

Merton, Robert C. 2006a. "Allocating Shareholder Capital to Pension Plans." *Journal of Applied Corporate Finance*, Vol. 18, No. 1 (Winter): 15–24.

Merton, Robert C. 2006b. "Observations on Innovation in Pension Fund Management in the Impending Future." *PREA Quarterly* (Winter): 61–67.

Merton, Robert C. 2008. "The Future of Retirement Planning." In *The Future Lifecycle Saving and Investing*, 2nd edition. Charlottesville, VA: Research Foundation of CFA Institute, 5–14.

Milevsky, Moshe A., and Chris Robinson. 2005. "A Sustainable Withdrawal Rate without Simulation." *Financial Analysts Journal*, Vol. 61, No. 6 (November/December): 89–100.

Spitzer, John J. 2008. "Retirement Withdrawals: An Analysis of the Benefits of Periodic 'Midcourse' Adjustments." *Financial Services Review*, Vol. 17, No. 1 (Spring): 17–29.

Stout, R. Gene, and John B. Mitchell. 2006. "Dynamic Retirement Withdrawal Planning." *Financial Services Review*, Vol. 15, No. 2 (Summer): 117–131.

CHAPTER 6

CLIENT EDUCATION

You have to pick what you're going to be worried about. Markets are volatile, but retirement is certain.

—Nick Murray

The ultimate success of any client relationship begins with the appropriate education of the client. No matter how astute or sophisticated the client may be in his or her own profession, without prior education by the advisor, the client will rarely, if ever, have an understanding of the issues necessary to become a successful participant in the wealth management process. Clients, without this preparation, will not understand the terminology of the wealth manager. If the advisor begins the goal setting and data gathering process prior to the education process, the advisor may think he or she is speaking English, but to the client it may sound like Sanskrit. There is a significant probability that either the necessary information will not be captured or the client will not accept the wealth manager's final recommendations.

MINI-EDUCATIONAL PROGRAM

Prior to beginning the process of having the client complete a risk tolerance questionnaire, Harold provides the client with a mini-educational program. Depending on the client's questions and any tangents that the conversation may follow, this program typically takes between a half hour and one-and-a-half hours. He has it prepared to be presented either by flip chart or computer display.

The purpose of the program is fourfold:

1. To introduce the client to the basic concept of modern investment theory (for example: asset allocation, types of risk, manager style).
2. To provide a basic vocabulary framework (for example: volatility, style, risk).
3. To make the client aware of the firm's philosophy and biases (for example: belief in the critical importance of asset allocation and a total rejection of traditional market timing).
4. To help the client obtain an overview and understanding of the planning process that will guide any recommendations.

What follows is a description of how Harold guides a client through that initial educational process from his point of view. The examples are certainly not exhaustive and there are other examples throughout this book; however, these include samples and explanations of the types of tables, illustrations, and presentations Harold has found useful in practice.

THE INVESTMENT PROCESS

After a few slides that introduce the firm, we begin the education process with the flowchart of the investment process shown in Exhibit 6.1 (a simplified version of Exhibit 1.1 in Chapter 1). Modeled after one developed by Don Trone,[1] it is an effective introduction to our philosophy.

EXHIBIT 6.1   The Investment Process

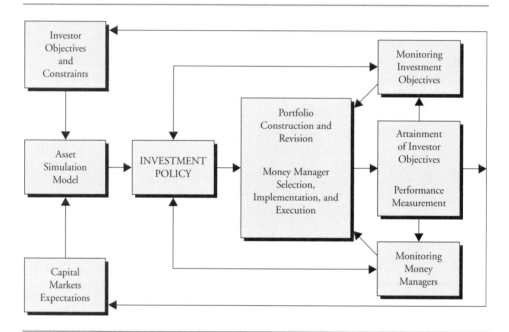

We begin with a description of the top left-hand box, "Investor Objectives and Constraints." This is an opportunity to discuss the need to define each of the client's objectives with time and dollar specificity and to rank them in order of priority. We explain to our student-client that "constraints" can include any restrictions on the investment process that the client may desire. Examples might include keeping the stock inherited from grandma, setting aside $20,000 for mad money, or restricting any allocation to international stock to no more than 15 percent of the portfolio. The point we wish to make is that our clients drive the investment process. Our job is to educate and assist them to achieve their goals, not to tell them what their goals should be.

Included in the discussion at this stage is an introduction to our data gathering process. We want our clients to understand that we follow a very structured process. This enables us to

---

[1]Donald Trone, William Allbright, and Philip Taylor, *The Management of Investment Decisions*, Irwin, 1996; the earlier work of Donald Trone, William Allbright, and William Madden, *Procedural Prudence* (SEI, 1991).

obtain the information necessary to adequately and accurately reflect their objectives and constraints. We want them to know that planning is a joint effort and how important it is for them to thoughtfully and actively assist us in completing the data gathering forms. Equally important, we want them to be proactive and bring to our attention anything they believe we may have neglected to ask.

Over and over (probably ad nauseam) we emphasize that planning the client's future is the sole reason for this process, and this first step is the most important.

"Asset Simulation Model" and "Capital Market Expectations" are usually discussed together. After a brief description of the concept of portfolio diversification, we explain that we use a sophisticated mathematical model that provides guidance for the most efficient combinations of investments. As the model requires a number of assumptions, we explain that it is our job to develop these assumptions. We'll begin by determining what asset classes our client will consider. We explain that the more flexibility we have in selecting investments, the better job we believe we can do. Once we've made that determination, for each of the asset classes we're going to consider in our optimization process, we make three estimates. The first is what return we believe each investment is likely to earn over the next three to five years (i.e., an economic cycle). Our second estimate is a measure of how confident we are of that first estimate. For example, although we might expect large-cap domestic stocks to *average* 9 percent per year, we would not expect 9 percent per year like clockwork. There will be good and bad years. We might estimate a risk factor of 20 percent, which means that we would expect the stock returns to range from –11 percent to +29 percent most of the time; however, we expect that when we look back after many years, the average return would have been about 9 percent.

Third, we point out that investments do not all go up and down together (this is usually accompanied by moving your hands in opposite directions—the action helps to wake the client up). To account for this, we estimate each asset class movement relative to all of the others we've considered.

Although we do not go into great detail regarding our capital market projections, we do discuss the basis for our estimates. We explain that although we consider historical data, we do not believe in using historical projections. Instead, we develop our own forward-looking estimates based on historical relationships and trends and our expectations regarding the economy over the next five years.

Once we have all of our estimates, we feed them into our computer optimizer and, after lots of thinking and fiddling, we arrive at portfolio allocations that allow for the most efficient combinations of risks and returns. In discussing the asset simulation model, I liken it to playing the piano. I tell the client that while we are exceptionally good technicians and scientists and we use the most sophisticated computer hardware and software, 90 percent of the process is art. I add that we are also exceptionally fine artists. The end result is not an answer from a black box. It is a recommendation from our brains and hearts, based on historical data, our experience, estimates of other professionals, and information developed by a mathematical model[2] that we have selected and understand.

With the results of this analysis in hand, combined with our client's unique return requirements and risk tolerance, we determine what we believe will be the most efficient portfolio for their needs and then prepare an "investment policy" statement, a comprehensive and detailed investment road map. This is a unique document customized for our client.

---

[2]As discussed later, we use a constrained Markowitz mean-variance optimizer.

It not only will tell the client where to invest, but it also will provide investment selection and rebalancing criteria, and standards to measure the performance of the policy.

We explain that with the road map in hand, we can then select the best managers for each piece of the portfolio. After all, we know what asset classes and styles we wish to invest in and the policy tells us how much to place in each. We also know what kinds of returns we expect of the manager of each class and how much risk we expect that manager to take, as those assumptions were used to construct the policy.

Once we have implemented the policy, we monitor the process. We monitor the overall goal of the policy, we monitor the assumptions underlying the policy against our updated market expectations, and we monitor the policy against the client's current objectives and constraints.

A manager who fails to meet the standards set for performance is fired and a new manager is hired. If the portfolio fails to meet the goals of the policy, it is modified. If the client's goals and/or constraints change, the policy is reviewed and possibly revised. If our forward-looking expectations change, the policy is modified. The process is ongoing, and it begins and ends with our client.

ASSET ALLOCATION

There has been so much nonsense written about modern portfolio theory and strategic asset allocation that it is important to emphasize that the policy allocation process is not "buy and hold," but rather "buy and monitor." Although strategic in nature, our forward-looking expectations and our policies undergo review at least annually. We consider current and future valuations and adjust as we deem necessary.

As practitioner research on the impact of asset allocation is so important to the core of wealth management, we spend time describing the nature of this work using results from the Brinson, Hood, and Beebower (BHB) (1986) study depicted in Exhibit 6.2 (examined further in a later chapter). Depending on the client, we may even review with him or her the tables from the original studies. If the client is really interested, we'll discuss Jahnke's[3] warning regarding the misinterpretation of the BHB study and Ibbotson and Kaplan's[4] analysis of the sources of portfolio performance.

We emphasize that we are experts in portfolio allocation. We explain that we understand that the real excitement is in selecting managers, and we believe we are also experts in manager evaluation and selection, but we want our clients to always keep in mind the importance of the allocation decision.

Frequently we will use this chart as an opportunity to discuss buying low and selling high. Everyone agrees that there is no better way to success in the market. We point out that's the purpose of the investment policy rebalancing parameters; unfortunately, when we actually trigger the rebalancing, it may not feel like the best system. We use the following example to help our clients understand.

In August 1987, when the stock market was reaching a peak, we were selling stock and buying bonds. We were not doing this because we were market timers. We did not anticipate

---

[3]William W. Jahnke, "The Asset Allocation Hoax," *Journal of Financial Planning* (February 1997).
[4]Roger G. Ibbotson and Paul D. Kaplan, "Does Asset Allocation Policy Explain 40, 90, or 100 Percent of Performance?" *Financial Analysts Journal* (January/February 2000); Roger G. Ibbotson, "The Importance of Asset Allocation," *Financial Analysts Journal*, Vol. 66, No. 2 (March/April 2010): 18–20.

EXHIBIT 6.2   Percentage of Total Return Variation Explained by Investment Activity

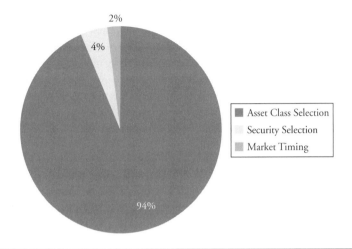

Based on 91 pension plans 1973 to 1985.

a crash; we had no idea the market was going to take a dive. We were only rebalancing. If a client had started with a portfolio split 50 percent bonds and 50 percent stocks, by August 1987 the portfolio might have become 40 percent bonds and 60 percent stocks, simply as a result of the run-up in stock prices. As our policy said 50/50, we sold stock and bought bonds to bring the portfolio back in balance. Occasionally, the question arose: "Are you nuts? Selling stocks and buying bonds in one of the best bull markets?" The answer was: "No, we're not crazy; we're just doing what we do—very unemotionally rebalancing back to the policy."

Well, in October 1987 when the market tanked almost overnight, some 50/50 portfolios were closer to 60/40—not because of any action we had taken but because stocks were worth less. Naturally, we started buying stocks to rebalance back to 50/50. This time the question was: "Are you nuts? Buying stocks when the world's coming to an end?" The answer again was: "No, we're not crazy; we're just doing what we do—very unemotionally rebalancing back to the policy." We made similar equity sales in January 2000 and in the summer of 2007 prior to similar, but more protracted, market corrections. We similarly replenished stock allocations during these corrections.

After this vignette, we invite the student-client to tell us if we sold high or low (obviously high) and if we had purchased high or low (obviously low). Aha! We sold high and bought low: just what we wanted to do. It just did not feel so good at the time.

Generally, this is an interesting discussion and a new perspective for clients. They begin to understand the power of an investment policy, the reason for rebalancing, and the benefits of being an intelligent contrarian. They also understand that there is no free lunch. Good long-term performance is paid with the coin of fear and worry. Also, diversification almost always guarantees that a client will have some investment that is doing poorly. That's the one we'll be buying.

Frequently, the discussion about selling high and buying low leads to the question of why not just avoid the market lows by getting out of the market. The next three illustrations all relate to market timing. These illustrations are part of our answer. Before going further, however, a note to any timer fan. You may want to skip to the next discussion, as we are timing skeptics.

We usually begin the discussion of market timing by relating it to a Ouija board (we have one in the office). We place far more faith in the Ouija board.

We tell our clients that we have the following objections to market timing:

- Almost all studies—academic and practitioner—conclude that, over time and after transaction costs and taxes, market timing does not add value. The few studies in support of timing are primarily based on hypothetical back-testing, are prepared by marketers of timing services, and/or ignore transaction costs and taxes.
- Market returns, both positive and negative, frequently occur in short spurts. Successful market timing requires not one but two correct calls—getting out of the market before it goes down *and* getting in before it goes back up.
- We ask our clients to name the top 10 market timers of all time. Obviously they can't name one. We suggest that if anyone had ever consistently successfully timed the market, not only would we know their names, but they also would have been listed in the *Forbes* richest lists. Finally, if anyone ever did develop a system for successful market timing, it stretches credulity to believe that they would share it.

EXHIBIT 6.3   Why Market Timing Doesn't Work

2009 Market Performance

	S&P 500 Appreciation	# of Trading Days
Entire year	27.8%	252 days
Feb. 9–Mar. 6	−21.4	18
Mar. 6–Apr. 24	26.8	34
Jul. 13–Aug. 7	14.94	200

Exhibit 6.3 demonstrates the difficulty of catching market spurts. In 2009, almost all of the year's positive return occurred during 34 of the 252 trading days. Almost 96 percent was attributable to a 34-day market run-up from March 6 to April 24. This phenomenon has been examined over many years and in many markets with the same results. For example, a recent study, "Black Swans and Market Timing: How Not to Generate Alpha," found that these results held over a long period of time in 15 of the major international capital markets. The author, Javier Estrada, concludes:

> *The evidence, based on more than 160,000 daily returns from 15 international equity markets, is clear: Outliers have a massive impact on long-term performance. On average across all 15 markets, missing the best 10 days resulted in portfolios 50.8 percent less valuable than a passive investment; and avoiding the worst 10 days resulted in portfolios 150.4 percent more valuable than a passive investment. Given that 10 days represent, in the average market, less than 0.1 percent of the days considered, the odds against successful market timing are staggering.*[5]

---

[5]Javier Estrada, "Black Swans and Market Timing: How Not to Generate Alpha," *Journal of Investing* (Fall 2008): 20–34.

EXHIBIT 6.4   Market Timing Is Risky: S&P 500 Index, January 1988–December 2004

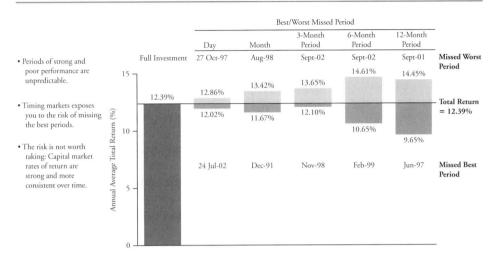

Note: Time periods greater than one month are based on monthly rolling periods, and dates indicated are end of period. The S&P data are provided by Standard & Poor's Index Services Group. Indexes are not available for direct investment. Their performance does not reflect the expenses associated with the management of an actual portfolio. *Source:* Dimensional Fund Advisors Inc.

Exhibit 6.4 demonstrates the same problem over a 17-year period. As we point out during the discussion, there is a real likelihood that a timer will miss many of these short periods of rapid upswings, as they frequently occur when the market is bouncing back from a low and the timer is awaiting a confirmation. This is when timers often stay on the sidelines waiting for a trend to be established. For anyone old enough to remember Joe Granville, his poor performance after successfully calling the 1987 crash is a particularly powerful example.[6]

---

[6]From Harold Evensky, "Maybe MPT Isn't Dead," *Financial Advisor*, August 2009:

> What, you haven't heard of Joe Granville? Until the late 80's he was THE market guru, with typical guru modesty. According to Robert Shiller in his book *Irrational Exuberance*, Granville was quoted by *Time* magazine as saying "I don't think that I will ever make a serious mistake in the stock market for the rest of my life," and he predicted that he would win the Nobel Prize in economics. In 1981, when he was grossing $6 million a year for his newsletter advice, his two word "sell everything" warning to his subscribers triggered a massive market selloff with a record number of shares trading. Just prior to the 1987 crash, Mr. Granville again warned of a market disaster. He was obviously correct on that call and his picture was on the cover of major magazines and papers around the world.
>
> Maybe you've not heard of Mr. Granville because, as with all other timers, his crystal ball had flaws. A few years ago, the *Hulbert Financial Digest* reported that *The Granville Market Letter* "is at the bottom of the rankings for performance over the past 25 years—having produced average losses of more than 20 percent per year on an annualized basis."

EXHIBIT 6.5   Market Timing Should Be Avoided as an Investment Strategy

For the 88-Year Period from 1901 to 1988

Buy-and-Hold Stock Return	9.4%
Perfect Forecasting of All Bear/Bull Markets	15.8%
Correct Forecasting 50% of the Time	6.6%
Correct Forecasting of Bear Markets, 50% Bull Markets	8.7%
Correct Forecasting of 71% of Bear/Bull Markets	9.4%

Exhibit 6.5 presents the results of a long-term study that debunks the statement "I only have to be right 51 percent of the time." In fact, to match the performance of a buy-and-hold portfolio, you would have needed to be correct 71 percent of the time.

MODERN PORTFOLIO THEORY

Having made clear our position regarding market timing, we once again return to a discussion of asset allocation. This illustration more formally lists the steps we go through to arrive at the client's policy. The commentary about Sharpe and Markowitz presented in Exhibit 6.6 provides an opportunity for us to discuss some of the history behind the theory and to introduce our client to the personalities involved and their impressive credentials. We find that this background adds an element of comfort for our clients.

EXHIBIT 6.6   Modern Portfolio Theory and the Capital Asset Pricing Model (CAPM)

How Do We Decide Which Asset Classes to Utilize and in What Combination?	
Since 1952, major institutions have been using a money management concept known as Modern Portfolio Theory. It was developed at the University of Chicago by Harry Markowitz and later expanded by Stanford University Professor William Sharpe. Markowitz and Sharpe won the Nobel Prize in economics for their investment methodology. Although the process is mathematical in nature, it is important to note that math is nothing more than the expression of logic. As you examine their process, you can readily see the commonsense approach that they have taken.	The Five Steps of Developing a Strategic Plan Using Modern Portfolio Theory
	• Risk Tolerance • Expected Return • Standard Deviation • Correlation Coefficients • Efficient Frontier

Source: John Bowen.

We follow up this discussion with the next two illustrations.

EXHIBIT 6.7   Standard Deviation as a Measure of Risk

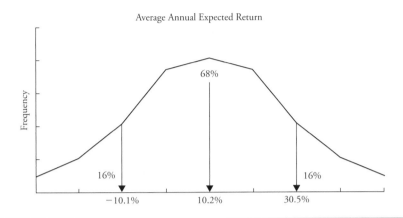

Exhibit 6.7 is a picture of a standard bell curve showing the mean return and returns for one standard deviation above and below the mean. We find it helps us explain the difference between capital loss and market volatility. We refer to one standard deviation as "most of the time." If we talk about returns two standard deviations below the mean, we refer to them as "worst case." The quotation marks are important, as clearly we've seen markets beyond two standard deviations and far more often than the normal distribution would suggest.

From this discussion, we want our clients to understand that volatility does not necessarily equate with permanent loss. We want them to begin to distinguish between volatility and disaster.

EXHIBIT 6.8   Correlation Coefficient at Work

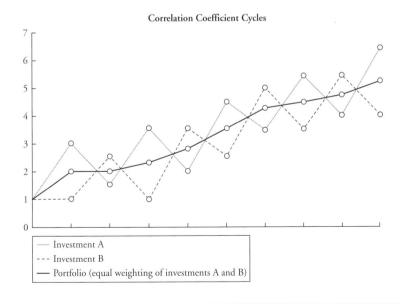

Exhibit 6.8 is used to describe correlation. We show clients that if they bought either investment A or B, over time the investment would grow in value, but the ride would be unpleasant. If instead they made an equal allocation to each investment, then the out-of-sync ups and downs would cancel out. The clients' blended portfolio return would almost match the return of A or B but with much less volatility. We remind them, however, that reduced volatility has a price. If they own both A and B, they give up the opportunity to make a killing. If A is up, B is down. They can never be at the top. Of course, they also give up the opportunity to get killed. Frequently we use the following story to expand on the concept.

Suppose you need a 10 percent return to maintain your lifestyle and you have only three investment choices: a CD paying 8 percent and two stocks. One stock is Snap's Swimwear and the other is Boone's Bumbershoots. If the weather is sunny all year, you earn 20 percent in Snap's. Of course, you'd better hope it doesn't rain. When it rains, Snap's earns zero.

If you think it will rain, you should buy Boone's! The bumbershoot company will earn 20 percent when it rains (and zero when the sun shines).

You have consulted a professional money manager who has hired the world's best meteorologists and statisticians to help design a portfolio. The recommendation is a portfolio of 65 percent Snap's and 35 percent Boone's. With that combination, the manager believes that you will have a 70 percent chance of earning 14 percent. The small print at the end of his recommendation points out that there is a 30 percent probability of a 5 percent return.

At this point, most clients react with the question: "Where do I find the CD?" A wealth manager would recommend a 50/50 split for a no-risk 10 percent return.

We find this story to be a very effective way to explain correlation and Markowitz's discovery of the safety provided by diversifying assets. It is also useful in demonstrating the difference between a money manager's goal of maximizing return and a wealth manager's goal of assisting clients to achieve their own personal goals.[7]

INVESTMENT RISK

Risk is a concept we never stop discussing with our clients. We discuss it during our data gathering, when we meet for quarterly reviews, and in our newsletters. The pie chart in Exhibit 6.9 is simply an introduction to risks and the fact that there is *no* risk-free investment.

We point out that the investment risk pie is sliced into many wedges to show that risk has many faces. The pie also shows that there are two major categories of risk. We explain that most investors worry about only one type of risk, which we have labeled "unsystematic risk," composed of business risk and financial risk. This is the familiar "I'm not worried about the return *on* my investment. I'm worried about the return *of* my investment."

We point out that there are two general reasons a business might default on its obligations to an investor. The business might go broke due to bad management: The company was in the typewriter business and failed to move into word processors. Alternatively, the company might be well managed and reasonably leveraged, but unfortunately the sales price of its product might fall at the same time its borrowing ability disappears (e.g., real estate developers during the housing bust; the resulting financial squeeze put many of them out of

---

[7]For an excellent detailed example of the benefit of diversification, turn to Chapter 9, "The Rewards of Multiple-Asset-Class Investing" in Roger Gibson's *Asset Allocation* (2007), a must reference book on the subject.

EXHIBIT 6.9   Investment Risk

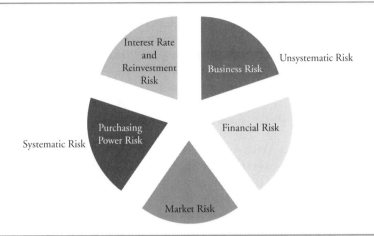

business). Even if the company does not file for bankruptcy, the stock price may drop like a rock. The first scenario is business risk and the second is financial risk.

It's not just some fly-by-night company that's subject to unsystematic risk, and keeping an eye on it is not a successful risk management strategy. Unsystematic risk can blindside you. At one point AT&T and IBM were considered so-called widow and orphan stocks (i.e., the ultimate blue chips). Unfortunately unsystematic risk doesn't play favorites, as investors in IBM learned when it dropped more than 60 percent from February 1991 to August 1993, and AT&T investors suffered a similar loss from October 2000 to September 2002. There is no shortage of examples to provide your client—Union Carbide and Bhopal, a crazy person putting poison in Tylenol bottles, Merck and Vioxx, or BP and the Deepwater Horizon. We know that our clients wouldn't care why the investment failed, only that it did. We explain that both of these risks are unique to the specific investment and represent unsystematic risk. We continue our explanation to include a discussion of the elimination of unsystematic risk through diversification.

To convey the concept of the safety obtained by diversification, we use a myriad of examples. One we've found particularly useful is comparing the risk of a vacancy if they owned a single-family home versus a 10-unit apartment building. Harold's most effective example, and a story he often tells clients, was the result of a stroke of luck. Harold read an article in the *Wall Street Journal* about toxic waste dumps just before his clients arrived. The clients, a husband and wife, held a large position of inherited stock in a single company. Harold recommended they sell in order to diversify and eliminate the unsystematic risk. They believed that their stock was in a really good company and were reluctant to sell. Remembering the article, Harold used as an example an investment in a company that had built a major manufacturing plant on an undiscovered toxic waste dump. The error was discovered after completion of the plant and, due to the excessive costs of any remedial solution, the plant had to be abandoned and the company went bankrupt. Harold's clients blushed, turned to each other, nodded, turned back to him, and said, "Okay, we'll sell." It seems that a number of years before, the husband had been a senior executive for a major manufacturer, and he was scheduled to run their latest and largest facility. That is, until it was discovered that the facility had been constructed on a toxic waste dump. The plant was abandoned. The company didn't fold, but cut back substantially, and he was out of a job.

Because we believe so strongly in the dangers of unsystematic risk, we typically spend a good deal of time discussing the concept of diversification. Just like the five-year mantra, we believe that quantifying the risk helps our clients relate to and remember the lesson of diversification, so we suggest that 10 is a good standard to remember. We tell them that if they get a good stock tip, don't buy until they get nine more good tips. The point we emphasize is that a portfolio of less than 10 diversified investments is likely to expose them to unnecessary loss due to excessive unsystematic risk.

Having made such a big deal about the safety provided by diversification, we tell our clients they may wonder why they should worry if they follow our advice and diversify.

We ask them to picture a diversified portfolio, not of 10 stocks but of 500 of the largest U.S. companies. In October 1987, that portfolio lost 20.4 percent in one day and over 50 percent from October 2007 to March 2009. The portfolio was the S&P 500. Obviously there was a risk other than lack of diversification. This risk is represented by the "market risk" wedge of the risk pie, namely, the risk that all investments in the market might fall in tandem.

We point out that it is just this type of risk that scares many investors away from the stock market. Instead, they invest in safe investments (i.e., bonds). Unfortunately, this move simply throws them into the slice labeled "interest rate and reinvestment risk" in Exhibit 6.9. Depending on the client, we may use historical charts, but usually we simply remind them that investors who purchased AAA, long-term bonds when rates were low did not feel so safe a few years later when rates were much higher. And their even more conservative friends, who continually rolled over one-year CDs, did not feel so safe when rates dropped and their income stream was significantly impaired.

Finally, we turn to "purchasing power risk." We tell our clients that this is likely to be their biggest risk and it is certainly the most insidious. Purchasing power erosion is like soil erosion. It works quietly and almost invisibly. Twenty-four hours a day, slowly but steadily, it can convert mountains of value into molehills.

We offer graphic supplements to the purchasing power risk wedge of Exhibit 6.9. Using Exhibit 6.10, we point out that over a one-year period, investors are just as likely to beat inflation no matter which investment they choose. However, over a lifetime, the risk of losing real dollars disappears for stock investors whereas it remains for other asset classes.

EXHIBIT 6.10   Percentage of Time Asset Classes Have Exceeded Inflation, 1926–2009

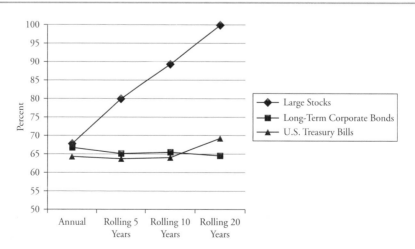

When we have finished discussing these illustrations and related vignettes, we want our clients to understand the many aspects of risk. We want them to know that there is no such thing as a safe investment; there are only investments with different types of risk. Not wanting to depress them, we tell them the good news is that there are relatively safe portfolios. And, as wealth managers, our expertise is in combining risky investments to design custom-tailored safe portfolios for our clients.

EXHIBIT 6.11   Equity Styles

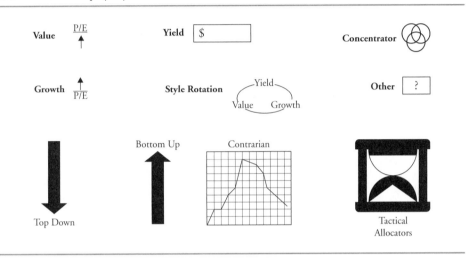

Our firm's investment philosophy places a heavy emphasis on diversification, including diversification of manager styles and strategies. As most prospective clients are not familiar with manager styles and strategies, we introduce them to the concepts at this stage. The first illustration we use is Exhibit 6.11, which depicts typical styles and strategies. As our asset class taxonomy includes growth and value as major classifications, we primarily focus on these two styles.

We use Exhibit 6.12 to emphasize the importance of style diversification. This table shows returns based on Fama-French's classification of growth versus value stocks, with the winner highlighted each period. We direct the client's attention to the constant flip-flopping of value and growth style returns. We ask clients how they would have felt from 2003 to 2006 if, as their criterion, they had selected the 2002 performance winner—large growth stocks. Then we ask how they would have felt in 2007 and 2008 if in late 2006 they'd switched to the four-year performance winner—large value stocks.

Clearly, picking the best in advance would have been tough (we believe impossible). A simple strategy of investing equally in each would have provided a much less volatile return series. This is just one more opportunity to emphasize the risk of following hot trends and the safety derived from diversification.

For many years, Harold used the illustration of the efficient frontier in Exhibit 6.13 to explain the concept of the efficient frontier. He eventually realized that the presentation was both too formal and too intimidating for many clients, and as a result he failed to get the point across. The way he approaches it now is far more casual, but he's found it very effective. If you find yourself more comfortable with the more professionally prepared presentation, that's not a problem; the following story is the same.

EXHIBIT 6.12   Comparison of Investment Styles

	1980	1981	1982	1983	1984	1985	1986	1987	1988	1989
Large Growth	35.2%	−7.1%	21.5%	14.7%	−0.7%	32.6%	14.4%	7.4%	12.5%	36.1%
Large Value	16.5%	12.8%	27.7%	26.9%	16.2%	31.8%	21.8%	−2.8%	26.0%	29.7%

	1990	1991	1992	1993	1994	1995	1996	1997	1998	1999
Large Growth	1.1%	43.3%	6.4%	2.4%	2.0%	37.2%	21.3%	31.6%	34.6%	29.4%
Large Value	−12.8%	27.4%	23.6%	19.5%	−5.8%	37.7%	13.4%	31.9%	16.2%	−0.2%

	2000	2001	2002	2003	2004	2005	2006	2007	2008	2009
Large Growth	−13.6%	−15.6%	−21.5%	26.3%	6.5%	2.8%	8.9%	14.1%	−33.7%	27.9%
Large Value	5.8%	−1.2%	−32.5%	35.1%	18.9%	12.2%	22.6%	−6.5%	−49.0%	39.2%

Source: Ibbotson SBBI 2010 Classic Yearbook. © Morningstar.

EXHIBIT 6.13   The Efficient Frontier

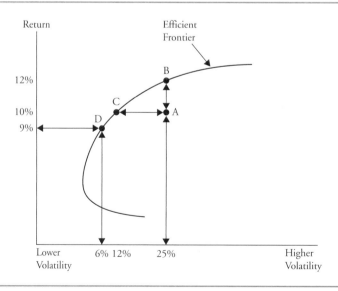

He introduces the discussion by saying, "Now I'm going to give you a quick lesson in the modern portfolio theory (MPT)." Harold will then tear off a piece of scratch paper from a pad or grab a napkin if he's been having a lunch meeting (the examples in the illustration are on a napkin). He will then draw the simple graph in Exhibit 6.14, panel A, placing three dots on the graph. He explains that the first point represents cash or money market investments (i.e., little return, little risk). The middle dot represents bonds, and the one on the right is all stock. He then points out that even with only three choices there is an almost infinite number of portfolios we might construct. For example, a portfolio might be 99 percent cash/1 percent bonds/0 percent stocks (or 99/1/0), or 99/0/1, or 0/99/1, or 1/99/0, or 2/98/0, and so on, and Harold adds a number of dots for additional possible portfolios on the graph (panel B). The client quickly gets the point. Harold then draws a curve (panel C) and explains that it represents the boundary where all of the dots fade out. He tells the client he knows everyone would love a portfolio up at the top left of the graph (i.e., high return, no risk) but that the real world lies on and below the curve. He explains that the curve is called the "efficient frontier," and its significance is that there is not one best portfolio but many possible best portfolios, and they all lie on the curve. "The question we need to determine is what the 'best' is for you, Mr. and Mrs. Client." That leads to the next stage of the discussion.

The discussion goes something like this:

"Mr. and Mrs. Client, in order to determine what's best for you, we need to estimate two things: what return you need to meet all of your goals, and how much risk you can live with in order to earn that return. To determine the return requirement, we're going to gather a great deal of information from you regarding your goals—for example, how much each one will cost, how frequently, and what's the goal's priority. We'll also factor in your taxes, inflation, Social Security, and any other financial elements necessary to model your financial life in detail. Using a process called a capital needs analysis, we'll crunch all of that data and arrive at an estimated return requirement. If I now draw a line across the graph at your required return level (Exhibit 6.14, panel D), I find that there are many portfolios to the right of where the line crosses the curve that would provide the return you need, but they're all riskier than the one where the line meets the curve. Why would you want them? The best is obviously the portfolio where the line and curve meet. Unfortunately, that's only half of the answer. Suppose that when we look to see what that portfolio looks like, we discover it's an 80 percent stock portfolio, and you can't possibly live with that kind of allocation. Obviously, we need to also consider how much risk you *can* live with.

"We define your risk tolerance as that point of misery you can stand when the markets are collapsing and the media are screaming 'Run for the hills' without calling us up and saying, 'I can't stand it anymore—sell me out!' We're going to work with you to make our best guess at determining that threshold." Panel E shows one possibility. Again there are innumerable portfolios at your risk level, but the one on the efficient frontier is obviously the best as it's the one with the highest return for the same risk. We now have two 'best' portfolios for you. Assuming you are comfortable with the goals you selected, our recommendation is for the lower-risk, lower-return 'best' portfolio. Why take more risk to make more money if you don't need it?[8]

---

[8]This is obviously not an issue of right or wrong; both portfolios are theoretically equally efficient, and without plotting a client's utility function against the efficient frontier, one cannot tell which one is more theoretically optimal for the client. Based on the research of behavioral finance that suggests investors are more loss averse than risk averse, along with my lack of confidence in how accurate any risk tolerance evaluation will be when markets collapse, I opt for the lower-risk, lower-return alternative. Some advisors may prefer to recommend the portfolio with the highest expected return that is within the client's risk tolerance. You need to determine your own policy.

"Suppose, however, that your risk tolerance plots like the left vertical line (in Exhibit 6.14, panel F). Now we have a problem. Our analysis suggests that you cannot achieve the return you require at a risk you can live with. You have a decision to make: Do you want to eat less well or sleep less well? Our recommendation is that you consider adjusting your goals, because saying you're willing to accept greater risk may be an easy decision today, but if markets turn really vicious, you're likely to forget your current resolve and may well bail out."

Having now, for many years, used this more informal MPT discussion, we've found it both a user friendly and an effective process for providing our clients with a substantive understanding of the planning process we will be working on together.

EXHIBIT 6.14   Efficient Frontier Possibilities

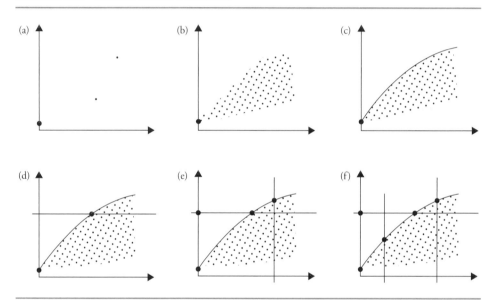

PARTING COMMENTS

A critical component of any client relationship is educating the client. A better-educated client is a better client. The concepts presented in this chapter enable the wealth manager to communicate key concepts and terms to clients in an easily understood manner. The examples are also useful for the inevitable reeducation that must occur occasionally—for example, when the client calls up and wants to invest in the previous period's best-performing stock or mutual fund.

RESOURCES

Brinson, Gary P., L. Randolph Hood, and Gilbert Beebower. 1986. "Determinants of Portfolio Performance," *Financial Analysts Journal* (July/August; reprinted January/February 1995): 133–138.

Gibson, Roger. 2007. *Asset Allocation: Balancing Financial Risk*, 4th edition. New York: McGraw-Hill.

Ibbotson, Roger G. 2010. "The Importance of Asset Allocation." *Financial Analysts Journal*, Vol. 6, No. 2 (March/April): 18–20.

Ibbotson, Roger G., and Paul D. Kaplan. 2000. "Does Asset Allocation Policy Explain 40, 90, or 100 Percent of Performance?" *Financial Analysts Journal* (January/February): 26–33.

Jahnke, William W. 1997. "The Asset Allocation Hoax." *Journal of Financial Planning* (February): 109–113.

Xiong, James X., Roger G. Ibbotson, Thomas M. Idzorek, and Peng Chen. 2010. "The Equal Importance of Asset Allocation and Active Management," *Financial Analysts Journal* (March/April): 22–30.

MATHEMATICS OF INVESTING

Two things cause a stock to move—the expected and the unexpected.

—Gary Helms[1]

The incredible pace of both academic and practitioner research in investment theory over the past 30-plus years can be attributed to four forces—theoretical breakthroughs, the development of comprehensive and accurate market databases, the refinement of analytical tools, and the availability of high-powered personal computers.

While wealth managers need not become expert in all of these areas, there are many analytical concepts they should understand and numerous academic theories they should be familiar with. A sound knowledge of these issues is one of the attributes that distinguishes a professional wealth manager from the nonprofessional.

The ultimate responsibility of the wealth manager is to integrate these issues, concepts, theories, and models into an investment philosophy to use as a guide in designing plans and providing recommendations for clients.

For example, does the wealth manager accept Eugene Fama's weak or perhaps the semistrong efficient market hypothesis? Do you agree with William Sharpe's capital asset pricing model (CAPM) and other asset pricing theories that unsystematic risk should be avoided? Should you follow the conclusions of Harry Markowitz's modern portfolio theory (MPT)? Is the market leptokurtic? Will the wealth manager determine allocation recommendations by using a parametric quadratic optimizer, optimizing for semivariance? Is multiple regression factor analysis a useful tool in manager evaluation? Should you supplement capital needs analysis with Monte Carlo simulation?

The following section provides a strong foundation for the theory that follows in later chapters. After completing this chapter, you will be familiar with many of the mathematical and analytical issues of importance for the wealth manager. You also will know the historical underpinnings of our profession, and will have met many of the pioneers who brought us to where we are today. You will have been introduced to the major research and become familiar with the significant terminology. Enough said; let's start.

---

[1] I discovered a treasure trove of pithy quotes by Gary Helms from the 1978 January/February *Financial Analysts Journal*, reprinted in *Classics* by Charles Ellis (Dow Jones-Irwin, 1989).

RETURN MEASURES

Market returns do not occur in a simple, orderly, and consistent manner. Although we might expect the annual return on a particular asset to be approximately 12 percent over the next five years, we would not expect it to grow by 1 percent per month. The general default assumption in investment theory is that returns will be normally distributed (a traditional bell-shaped curve). This assumption provides for simplification in the analytical process, but, as we will see from the actual data in this chapter, actual market returns have not exhibited a normal distribution. You will need to be able to understand what impact this has on your interpretation of models.

Exhibit 7.1 presents long-term average returns for the most commonly used asset classes.

EXHIBIT 7.1   Long-Term Historical Annual Returns, 1926–2009

	Geometric	Arithmetic
	Mean	Mean
Large company stocks	9.8%	11.8%
Small company stocks	11.9	16.6
Long-term corporate bonds	5.9	6.2
Long-term government bonds	5.4	5.8
Intermediate-term government bonds	5.3	5.5
U.S. Treasury bills	3.7	3.7
Inflation	3.0	3.1

Source: Ibbotson SBBI 2010 Classic Yearbook. © Morningstar.

Compounding

At face value, compounding seems like a trivial concept to include amid a forthcoming discussion of kurtosis and multiple linear regression. Still, the seemingly simple decision of when to use arithmetic compounding or geometric compounding is not so simple. Most wealth managers are trained ad nauseum in the use of the HP 12C and other time value calculators. We tend to scoff at the concept of arithmetic returns as being prekindergarten-level math. Real wealth managers talk in terms of internal rates of return and dollar-weighted returns. Unfortunately, finance experts tell us that in many instances, for predicting future values, correct estimating is arithmetic, not geometric.

Mark Kritzman, author of a once-regular column in the *Financial Analysts Journal* titled "What Practitioners Need to Know . . . ,"[2] best described the confusion in his May/June 1994 column, ". . . About Future Value."

> *Some analysts argue that the best guide for estimating future value is the arithmetic average of past returns. Others claim that the geometric average provides a better estimate of future value. The correct answer depends on what it is about future value that we want to estimate.*

---

[2]Earlier columns have been collected in a volume published by Irwin in 1995 (2nd edition, John Wiley & Sons, 2003): *The Portable Financial Analyst*, by Mark Kritzman.

Geometric versus Arithmetic

The arithmetic return is the simple average of returns over a number of periods, whereas the geometric return is the compound return realized over time based on a series of observed returns. Consider a very simple two-period example for a $1,000 investment:

Period	Return	Portfolio Balance
1	100%	$2,000
2	−50%	$1,000

The arithmetic average return is simply the average of the two annual returns, or 25 percent. The geometric return is 0 percent, because the ending portfolio value is equal to the beginning portfolio value. If we use the geometric future return as our guide, it suggests that the future expected return in any given year is zero. That does not seem logical given this manager's record. In fact, it's not zero; it is 25 percent. It is the arithmetic return that is the best estimate of the expected future return for the following year (in the absence of other forward-looking information). The geometric return is a better measure of expected return over many periods.

Consider a somewhat more detailed 10-period example. In this example the manager has a record that demonstrates he has just as much chance of gaining as losing. Starting with an investment of $1,000:

Period	Return	Portfolio Balance
1	−50%	$500
2	50	750
3	−10	675
4	10	743
5	−30	520
6	30	676
7	−20	541
8	20	649
9	−40	390
10	40	545

Arithmetic average return = 0%
Geometric return based on portfolio balance[3] = −5.9%

If, in the future, as in the past, it is just as likely that the portfolio will go up in value as it will drop in value, it seems reasonable that the expected return would equal the arithmetic return of 0 percent. However, with a history of a 6 percent compounded loss, it just does not

---

[3]Note these computations are for portfolios with no additions or withdrawals.

seem reasonable to expect that the investor has a 50/50 chance of a positive return. As in the prior example, this discrepancy is real.

One reason for the discrepancy relates to the asymmetric distribution of compounded returns (or ending wealth) noted earlier. The result of this skew is that geometric compounding will yield a future value that is less than the expected future value.

The arithmetic return is an unbiased estimate of a portfolio's expected future return for a particular period. Therefore, if the goal is to estimate future value for the next period, the arithmetic return is correct. The geometric return represents the fixed return required to achieve a specific return over a given period of time. It is, therefore, the best measure of past performance and a measure of expected returns over long periods of time based on the annual arithmetic return expected and the volatility of returns.[4]

Variance Drain

If there is any variance in the return series, the geometric return will always be less than the arithmetic return. Tom Messmore wrote a useful paper in the Summer 1995 *Journal of Portfolio Management* titled "Variance Drain."[5] The descriptive term *drain* was selected to draw attention to the fact that an active manager will usually generate a variance in excess of a passive alternative. In order to add value, the active manager must not only cover fees and transaction costs but must also cover the cost of the drain attributable to variance. The following approximation formula for calculating the variance drain is a useful addition to the mathematical tool kit of the wealth manager:

$$r_g \cong r_a - \frac{\sigma^2}{2}$$

or

$$\text{Variance Drain} = \frac{\sigma^2}{2} = r_a - r_g$$

where r_g = geometric return and r_a = arithmetic return.

Example 7.1 demonstrates this concept. We address it further later in the discussion of risk measures.

EXAMPLE 7.1   Geometric and Arithmetic Returns

The following are geometric and arithmetic returns for two hypothetical mutual funds for a five-year period:

Fund	Geometric Return	Arithmetic Return
Ultra Fund	21.6%	28.7%
Alpha Fund	21.0%	23.4%

---

[4]See Chapter 2, "Return Concepts," in *Equity Asset Valuation*, by Jerald E. Pinto, Elaine Henry, Thomas R. Robinson, and John D. Stowe, CFA Institute Investment Series, John Wiley & Sons, 2010.
[5]Tom Messmore, "Variance Drain," *Journal of Portfolio Management* (Summer 1995): 104–110.

The approximate variance drain for the Ultra Fund was 7.1 percent, compared to Alpha's 2.4 percent. In order to achieve approximately the same compounded return (and hence ending value) as Alpha, Ultra had to achieve a much better arithmetic average return.

RISK MEASURES

Returns, returns, and returns … it often seems that this is the only measure that counts when evaluating the performance of a manager or a portfolio. Advisors may argue over the return measure to use—for example, CFA Institute Global Investment Performance Standards (GIPS), time-weighted, dollar-weighted, average, compounded, and so on, but always "returns." Unfortunately, focusing solely on returns is akin to ordering gumbo and forgetting the Tabasco—nice but not enough. The necessary missing ingredient is a measure of risk.

Suppose we offered our clients a choice between two mutual funds (or individual managers). Manager A has a five-year arithmetic average annual return of 12 percent, and manager B's return has been 14 percent. Is there any doubt which manager would garner the bulk of the investment dollars? Now suppose we added the information that manager A has been investing in a portfolio of diversified, large-cap domestic equities and manager B has invested in a highly leveraged portfolio of small-cap emerging market securities. For many if not most investors, manager A now looks to be the more attractive. As simple as this example may seem, in the real world investment decisions are far too frequently made in favor of the manager Bs of the world. The element of risk is not factored into the decision process.

Put differently, let's use the concept of variance drain discussed earlier to discuss the importance of risk. Suppose manager A's average return was a constant 12 percent with no variance, while manager B's 14 percent return had a 25 percent standard deviation. Let's compare their geometric returns:

$$\text{Geometric Return for Manager A} = 0.12 - \frac{(0.00)^2}{2} = 12.0\%$$

$$\text{Geometric Return for Manager B} = 0.14 - \frac{(0.25)^2}{2} = 10.875\%$$

You would have accumulated 5 percent more wealth with manager A than with manager B over the historical five-year period because manager B's returns were riskier.[6]

Consequently, it is necessary to recognize that risk is not one-dimensional. Risk is multidimensional. Academics continue to argue over those dimensions (e.g., Fama and French's explanation of the risk associated with high book-to-market investing; we'll discuss that later). For now this section will focus on total investment risk and its components: systematic and unsystematic risks.

As actual returns are likely to be higher or lower than the expected return, a variation will exist around the expected return. For reasons we just discussed, it is useful to measure the risk

---

[6]$1.12^5/1.10875^5 - 1 = 5.18\%$. If manager A had returns with a 5 percent standard deviation, the two managers would have accumulated the same amount of wealth in the five-year period. Can you demonstrate why?

of annual returns by looking at how much they vary from year to year. Consider the following observed returns:

Year	Return
1	11%
2	12
3	9
4	9
5	8
6	11
7	10
Average	10%

While the arithmetic average return is 10 percent, the returns for each individual year deviate from that average in all but one year, as would be expected in a market environment.

Variance

If we simply measured the deviation between the average return and the measured annual returns in the preceding list and added up the results, the solution would equal zero. There are an equally distributed number of positive returns and negative returns around the average; hence they will cancel out.

The solution is to square the deviations. When squaring, all quantities become positive and this eliminates the self-canceling effect. The result of the average of the squares of the deviation is known as the variance. Mathematically, the variance is expressed as the average of the sum of the squared deviations from the arithmetic average return (using the number of observations minus 1 to compute the average).[7]

Exhibit 7.2 presents the computation of deviations from the average return from the data presented earlier. The variance would be 12 percent divided by 6 (7 observations minus 1) or 2 percent. Unfortunately, by solving one problem we've created a second. Squaring the deviation eliminated the negative values, but our new measure, variance, represents the average of the squared deviations. No useful information is conveyed by knowing that a portfolio has an expected return of 10 percent and 2 percent average squared deviation.

Standard Deviation

We can fix this new problem by simply reversing the process. If squaring the deviation caused the problem, what will happen if we now take the square root of the variance?

---

[7]For computations of variances and standard deviation for a population of values, the number of observations is used as the divisor. For computations for a sample of a population, the number of observations minus 1 is used. For this chapter we assume a sample of values in all computations of variance and standard deviation.

EXHIBIT 7.2   Average Returns and Deviations

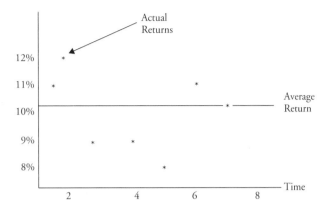

Time	Actual Return	Average Return	Deviation	Deviation Squared
1	11%	10%	1	1
2	12	10	2	4
3	9	10	−1	1
4	9	10	−1	1
5	8	10	−2	4
6	11	10	1	1
7	10	10	0	0
			0%	12%

$$\sqrt{\text{Variance}} = \sqrt{2\%} = 1.41\% = \text{Standard Deviation or } \sigma$$

The square root of 2 percent is 1.41 percent. At least we've eliminated the bothersome percentage squared units and now have a number in percentage units. Does the 1.41 percent convey any information?

Actually, quite a bit. The square root of variance is the familiar measure—standard deviation (σ)—and is calculated as the square root of the average of the sum of the squared deviations from the arithmetic average return.

We can now interpret the results as an average return of 10 percent with a standard deviation of 1.41 percent.

Now that the measure of volatility has been converted to standard deviation, the real power of the assumption of a normal distribution comes into play. We know from statistics that returns will fall within a range of ±1 standard deviation of the expected return 67 percent of the time, and ±2 standard deviations about 95 percent of the time. Therefore, in the example, we would expect that 67 percent of the time, the portfolio return would fall between 8.6 percent and 11.4 percent, and 95 percent of the time, we would expect returns between 7.2 percent and 12.8 percent if distributions are normal.

As we will see later in this chapter, market returns over time have not exhibited all of the characteristics of a normal distribution. Fortunately, a mathematician by the name of Chebyshev developed a general formula $(1 - 1/k^2)$ that estimates the proportion of values within k deviations from the mean for any distribution for k values greater than 1. So, for example, at least 75 percent of the values would be expected to occur within ± 2 standard deviations whether or not the distribution is normal. We will see how well both of these estimates hold with real data later.

In summary, standard deviation is a measure of the variability of returns of an asset compared to its average or expected return. Thus, it serves as a measure of total risk. Standard deviation may be a misleading measure if the evaluation period is not long enough to cover a manager's risk exposure (e.g., the standard deviation of many of the bond funds that were aggressively using derivatives prior to January 1992). Its use has also been criticized for rewarding poor and mediocre performance and penalizing upside volatility. The counterargument to this latter objection is that a significant upside standard deviation may be a warning of downside risk (e.g., junk bonds, Japanese stocks, high-tech stock funds, real estate).

Geometric Returns Revisited

Now that we have discussed variance and standard deviation, let's explore further the impact on variability on realized returns. Consider the series of annual returns for two investments presented in Exhibit 7.3.

EXHIBIT 7.3   Hypothetical Investments

	Investment X	Investment Y
Year 1	9%	8%
Year 2	10	10
Year 3	12	14
Year 4	10	10
Year 5	9	8
Arithmetic average	10%	10%
Standard deviation	1.22%	2.45%

Note that clearly the average arithmetic return was 10 percent for each, but the variability of investment Y is twice that of investment X. If you had invested $100,000 in each at the beginning of year 1 and liquidated the investments at the end of year 5, which one would have resulted in better realized compound performance?

Investment X would have resulted in an ending value of $161,011 for a realized annual geometric return of 9.995 percent, fairly close to the arithmetic average. Investment Y would have resulted in an ending value of $160,893 for a realized annual geometric return of 9.978 percent, a little bit less. The geometric return can be computed using a financial calculator or in Excel by solving for the internal rate of return based on the series of cash flows or values resulting from the investment. This is known as a dollar-weighted geometric return. A time-weighted geometric return can be computed by using the following formula:

$$r_g = \sqrt[T]{(1 + r_1)(1 + r_2)\ldots(1 + r_T)}$$

The dollar-weighted geometric return is a good measure for determining how an investor's account fared over time but includes the impact of investor contributions and withdrawals on returns. If we are looking to measure the performance of only the wealth manager's decisions, we should use the time-weighted return, which removes the impact of contributions and withdrawals. For investments such as A and B, where there are no additions or withdrawals during the interim periods, the dollar-weighted and time-weighted geometric returns are equivalent. Note that the order of the returns doesn't matter for this analysis when there are no contributions or withdrawals.

This difference between arithmetic and geometric returns will compound over time to have a significant impact on portfolios. The higher the variability of returns (variance and standard deviation), the greater the difference between the geometric and arithmetic returns, resulting in the variance drain discussed earlier. Only when there is no variability will the arithmetic and geometric returns be the same.

Semivariance

When Markowitz wrote his paper on modern portfolio theory (MPT), he noted that a measure of distribution known as semivariance would, theoretically, be the best measure of risk. At the time, most computers did not have the computational power to handle semivariance. Consequently, Markowitz opted for the more practical measure of mean variance. Today, with orders of magnitude greater computational power available at very low cost, there is an increasing interest in considering more complex solutions to investment issues, including the use of semivariance.

Earlier, variance was defined as the square of the deviation of distributions from the mean. The reason given for squaring the deviations was that otherwise those below the mean would cancel those above the mean. A sum of the deviations would be zero. In other words, we were concerned with *all* of the deviations from the mean.

As many academics and practitioners point out, variance resulting from upside deviations (i.e., making a lot more than anyone expects) should not result in branding a manager as a

EXHIBIT 7.4   Semivariance

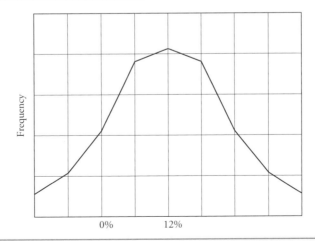

high risk taker. They argue that portfolio design should be concerned only with unwanted deviations, not all deviations.

One of the definitions of the word *semi* is "partial." So the easy way to think of semivariance is as partial variance (i.e., the bad part).

Exhibit 7.4 represents a hypothetical normal distribution for a market's expected return. Traditional risk analysis would concern itself with deviations both above and below the 12 percent mean return. In reality, your clients might be much more concerned with losses. Their focus of attention would be on those returns below 0 percent. A risk analysis based on this standard is an example of downside deviation (a variation on semivariance) with a target return of 0.

COVARIANCE AND CORRELATION

Harry Markowitz demonstrated that, although the return on a combination of assets is equal to their weighted returns, the risk of a portfolio is usually less than the weighted average of each asset's risk. This reduction in risk is due to diversification. The magnitude of the risk reduction is dependent on the degree of similarity in movement between the returns of the portfolio's assets. Let's take a look at Exhibit 7.5, which presents two investments that have exhibited the historical annual returns shown, as well as a portfolio consisting of equal investments in both.

EXHIBIT 7.5   Risk of Individual Investments versus a Portfolio

Year	Investment A	Investment B	Portfolio 50% A + 50% B
1	11%	9%	10%
2	12	8	10
3	9	11	10
4	9	11	10
5	8	12	10
6	11	9	10
7	10	10	10
Average	10.00%	10.00%	10.00%
Standard deviation	1.41%	1.41%	0.00%

Covariance

While each investment individually is risky, the combined portfolio is not. In this case the investments do not move in the same direction; when one performs above average the other performs below average. The measure of this comovement is the covariance.

Covariance is calculated by computing the product of the deviations from the average for each of the investments, summing these products, and then dividing by the number of observations, as shown in Exhibit 7.6.

EXHIBIT 7.6   Computation of Covariance

Year	Investment A	Deviation from Average	Investment B	Deviation from Average	Product of Deviations
1	11%	1.00	9%	−1.00	−1.00
2	12	2.00	8	−2.00	−4.00
3	9	−1.00	11	1.00	−1.00
4	9	−1.00	11	1.00	−1.00
5	8	−2.00	12	2.00	−4.00
6	11	1.00	9	−1.00	−1.00
7	10	0.00	10	0.00	0.00
				Sum/($N-1$) = Covariance	−2.00

The formula for the covariance of returns (x and y) on two securities (X and Y) is:

$$Cov_{xy} = \sum_{i=1}^{N} \frac{(x_i - \bar{x})(y_i - \bar{y})}{N - 1}$$

where i is each period, N is the number of periods, $\bar{x}$ is the average value of x, and $\bar{y}$ is the average value of y. For our sample data, the covariance is −2, which seems small.

Suppose we were interested in two stocks, Snap's Swimwear and Boone's Bumbershoots. We are interested in determining how the prices of these two stocks are likely to perform relative to each other. Therefore, we use the formula and calculate the covariance to be −15.1. Unfortunately, we're facing a familiar problem: a mighty fine number that conveys very little information. We cannot tell from the value −15.1 if this is high or low. Is the common movement between Snap's and Boone's significant or insignificant? All we know is that, because the number is negative, the two stocks are negatively related (i.e., their prices are likely to move in opposite directions). That's interesting but not very surprising given the nature of their products. What we would like to know is the strength of that relationship.

Correlation

In order to garner more useful information about the relationship between the price movements of securities X and Y, we need to use a technique mathematicians refer to as normalizing. This process will result in a measure that can range only between a value of +1 and a value of −1.

To develop this solution, consider the case of two assets, A and B, with prices that move in exactly the same pattern. In effect, what is the covariance of an asset with itself? The calculation would be:

$$Cov_{x,x} = \sum_{i=1}^{N} \frac{(x_i - \bar{x})(x_i - \bar{x})}{N - 1}$$

If that looks familiar, it should. It is simply the formula for calculating the variance of X—the sum of the squared deviations! In other words, the covariance of a variable with itself is its variance.

We also know that variance = standard deviation squared, so for two identical assets:

$$\text{Cov}_{x,x} = \text{Var}_{xx} = \sigma_x \sigma_x$$

Now, suppose we created a new measure calculated by dividing the covariance of two assets by the product of their standard deviations. The measure would be calculated as follows:

$$\frac{\text{Cov}_{x,y}}{\sigma_x \sigma_y}$$

If we applied this formula to the example for two identical assets, the result would be the following:

$$\frac{\text{Cov}_{x,x}}{\sigma_x \sigma_x} = \frac{\text{Var}_{xx}}{\sigma_x \sigma_x} = \frac{\sigma_x \sigma_x}{\sigma_x \sigma_x} = 1$$

Pretty clever. We've demonstrated that if we use this new measure, the result is exactly what we desire—a maximum value of 1 for two assets that move exactly together. Following the same process, we would find that if the assets moved exactly opposite each other, the division would result in −1. All other patterns of movement will result in a value between +1 and −1.

The name given to this standardized measure is the *correlation coefficient*. As shown earlier, it is calculated as:

$$\text{Cor}_{x,y} = \frac{\text{Cov}(X, Y)}{\sigma_x \sigma_y}$$

The correlation coefficient for our investments A and B would be −1 (or −100 percent), indicating that they move in perfectly opposite directions.

For many analytical purposes, the correlation coefficient provides a more meaningful measure than covariance. Covariance, however, remains important. Correlation measures only direction and degree of association. Unlike covariance, it provides no information regarding magnitude. For portfolio optimization analysis, information regarding magnitude is critical and covariance is an important tool.

R^2—the Coefficient of Determination

Harry Markowitz, William Sharpe, and others focused attention on the concepts of systematic and unsystematic risk. As discussed earlier, the laws on fiduciary investing are beginning to direct the courts' attention to the importance of minimizing nonmarket (i.e., unsystematic) risk. Obviously, it would be convenient to have a method of separating and measuring these two components of risk.

One approach to determining these two components of risk is based on Sharpe's capital asset pricing model (CAPM). According to CAPM, the systematic component of total risk can be determined by multiplying the market variance by the square of a factor known as beta (beta and CAPM are discussed in more detail in the next chapter). The unsystematic component of total risk is simply the difference between the total portfolio risk and the systematic risk. These relationships are shown in the following formulas:

$$\text{Total Portfolio Risk} = \text{Systematic Risk} + \text{Unsystematic Risk}$$

$$\text{Total Portfolio Variance} = \text{Market Variance} + \text{Nonmarket Variance}$$

or
$$\sigma_p^2 = \beta^2 \sigma_m^2 + \text{Nonmarket Variance}$$

where σ_m^2 is the variance of the market.

Unfortunately, the answer is in terms of variance. As we've seen earlier, variance conveys limited information. However, the solution is quite simple. Divide the market variance by the total portfolio to determine the percentage of variance from the impact of overall market movements. The result is a number ranging from 0 to 1. This is normally expressed as a percentage (0 to 100 percent) and provides a clear measure of the variability (or risk) of an asset explained by the market.

This measure is known as the coefficient of determination or, more commonly, the R^2 or R-squared. It can also be calculated by simply squaring an asset's correlation coefficient with the market. Let's take a look at the data in Exhibit 7.7.

EXHIBIT 7.7   Correlation and R^2

Asset	Market	Correlation	R^2
S&P 500 index fund	S&P 500	100%	100%
Blue-chip mutual fund	S&P 500	92	85
Large mutual fund XYZ	S&P 500	78	61
Investment grade bond fund	Barclays Bond Index	97	95

It's comforting to see that all of the risk associated with the S&P 500 index fund can be explained by the risk of the S&P index. Presumably, that's why someone would invest in a market index. Nor is it surprising to find that a blue-chip, top-down fund also has a risk exposure largely explained by the S&P 500. However, for some investors, it would probably come as a surprise that their investment in the behemoth mutual fund XYZ has a significant risk exposure *not* explained by the S&P 500. Finally, it's probably not surprising to find that the investment grade bond fund's variability can be explained by the Barclays Bond Index. The reason for including this last example is to remind the reader not to fall into the trap of always equating the market with the S&P 500. The analytical tools available to wealth managers are not restricted to one market. They allow us to focus on the market or markets of interest.

Regression

You might recall from a statistics class that R^2 is also an output of a regression model. In fact, that is how R^2 is generally computed—one return series is regressed against another to measure how closely they are associated. A simple regression model for two variables is presented as:

$$Y_i = b_0 + b_1 X_i + \varepsilon$$

Y represents the dependent variable and X represents the independent variable. The regression coefficients b_0 (the intercept) and b_1 (the slope) are computed by the software based on observed values of Y and X. The error term is represented by ε. The R^2 determined by the regression is the same as that obtained by squaring the correlation coefficient between the variables. Note that the slope coefficient shown here is known as beta in the context of evaluating the variability of returns on a stock relative to some market index. In that context the regression equation regresses the returns on some market index (r_m) in excess of the risk-free rate (r_f) against the excess returns of the security of interest $(r - r_f)$:

$$(r - r_f) = \alpha + \beta(r_m - r_f) + \varepsilon$$

Fortunately, most data sources on securities provide us with a computation of beta (generally computed on the past 60 months of stock returns) so that we don't have to compute it ourselves. If beta is equal to 1, this would mean the excess returns on the security have tended to move in proportion with the market index after factoring out other random movements. A beta of greater than 1 indicates greater systematic risk than that of the market, and a beta of less than 1 indicates lower systematic risk.

EXAMPLE 7.2   Use of Beta

An investment manager is interested in evaluating the relative risk of the stocks of AT&T and Verizon. She obtains the following information from Yahoo! Finance as of July 4, 2010. How would you interpret this information?

	Beta
AT&T	0.65
Verizon	0.55

Interpretation: Over the past 60 months, the stocks of both AT&T and Verizon have experienced less systematic risk than the market as a whole. AT&T has been a little more risky than Verizon.

A multiple regression examines the relationship of more than one independent variable with the dependent variable and takes the form:

$$Y_i = b_0 + b_1 X_i + b_2 X_i + \cdots + b_k X_{ki} + \varepsilon$$

In a multiple regression, the R^2 is computed by the software used based on how much variation is explained by the equation.

Use of R^2

In discussions of performance measurement, it is common for advisors to toss around terms such as alpha and beta and compare a manager's performance relative to various indexes, such as the S&P 500. The terms and indexes are valid but frequently misused. It's of no value to

EXAMPLE 7.3 Interpretation of Mutual Fund Data

The following data was extracted from Morningstar mutual fund reports as of June 30, 2010.

Vanguard 500 Index Investor Fund

	Standard Index—S&P 500	Best Fit—S&P 500
Beta	1.00	1.00
R-squared	100	100
Standard deviation: 20.73		

Vanguard FTSE All-World ex-U.S. Index Investor Fund

	Standard Index—MSCI EAFE	Best Fit—MSCI ex-U.S.
Beta	1.09	1.03
R-squared	97	98
Standard deviation: 27.50		

If we didn't pay too much attention, we might be inclined to believe that the international fund is only slightly more risky than the S&P 500 fund given that the computed betas are only a bit higher at 1.09 and 1.03; however, these betas are not directly comparable. The only conclusion that can be drawn from betas and R-squareds presented here is that:

- The Vanguard 500 Index fund exactly matches its underlying index by having a beta of 1.00 and an R-squared of 100, as it should.
- The FTSE All-World ex-U.S. fund is more volatile than its standard index (beta = 1.09) and is very highly, but not perfectly, correlated with that index (R-squared = 97%).
- The MSCI ex-U.S. index is a better fit for the FTSE fund and the fund should track that index very closely.

If we want to make an overall assessment of volatility for the two funds, we could look at the standard deviation of returns, which indicates that the international fund is considerably more volatile (35 percent more volatile in terms of standard deviation).

measure the risk of a portfolio by its beta if the beta is based on an inappropriate market. Many assume that regressing against the S&P 500 represents the market, but this is valid only for large-capitalization U.S. stocks. In order to properly evaluate the international funds, we need to compare them to an appropriate market. Morningstar has addressed this issue. Its reports now include modern portfolio statistics based on more closely related markets (Morningstar refers to this as the "best fit" index).

Unlike the Sharpe and Treynor measures described later in this chapter, the coefficient of determination is neither good nor bad; it simply conveys useful information. Although there is no magic number, as the R^2 falls below 100 (i.e., totally diversified against the benchmark), measures based on a diversified portfolio become less and less significant. In our firm we use a minimum of 75. Whatever minimum you elect to set for your analysis, consider using additional measures based on total risk (e.g., standard deviation).

HIGHER MOMENTS

The following discussion introduces you to a new mathematical vocabulary. Although it is unlikely that the wealth manager will ever have to calculate these measures, it is important that you understand their meaning. Investment research continues to expand the knowledge base regarding market forces. Only wealth managers who read and understand this research will be able to apply it for their clients' benefit.

If market returns resemble the familiar bell shape of a normal distribution, the median value and the mean value will be identical and the balance of the data points will fall symmetrically about the mean.

Unfortunately, the handy assumption that distributions are normally distributed is frequently inaccurate.

Skewness

Skewness measures the asymmetry of the distribution of returns. For example, the uneven distribution shown in Exhibit 7.8 is positively skewed.

EXHIBIT 7.8   Distribution with Positive Skew

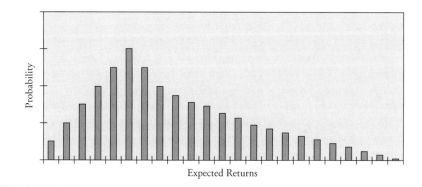

Divergence from the symmetrical bell shape of the normal distribution is called asymmetry. *Skewness* is the term used to describe a shift in the relationship between the median and mean and disproportionate distribution tails. If, as shown in Exhibit 7.8, there is a long tail to the right, the distribution has a positive skew. If, as Exhibit 7.9 illustrates, the long tail is to the left, it is negatively skewed.

EXHIBIT 7.9   Distribution with Negative Skew

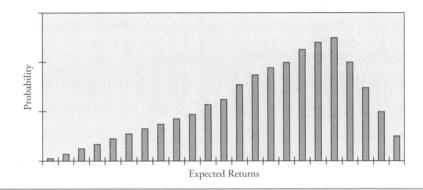

For a normal distribution, the only information necessary to completely describe the shape of the distribution curve is the mean and the standard deviation. As financial textbooks and journal articles frequently use statistical terms to refer to these measures, it's handy to know that the mean is referred to as the first moment of the distribution. Generally, as measurements are against the mean, the standard is to set the mean equal to 0. This is referred to as the first central moment. Standard deviation (i.e., the square of the deviations) is called the second central moment.

If the distribution is skewed, more information is required to determine the shape of the distribution curve. The measure containing this additional information (i.e., the skewness) is based on the cube of deviations from the mean. Skewness is hence called the third central moment.

Kurtosis

There remains one more aspect of the shape of distributions that it may be necessary to consider—the peakedness. All of the earlier illustrations, even if skewed, looked pretty much like the same mountains, some just pushed to the left, others to the right. As shown by the following distribution illustrations, there are other possibilities.

These distributions reflect different relationships between the peaks and the tails. The first illustration, with fat tails (more extreme observations) and an especially peaked peak is called leptokurtic (Exhibit 7.10). This distribution has more frequent extreme returns than a normal distribution would predict and has come to be known as tail risk.

The second illustration, without much tail and a relatively flat peak, is a platykurtic distribution (Exhibit 7.11). As the measure of this difference in peakedness involves raising deviations to the fourth power, it is not surprising that this measure, kurtosis, is called the fourth central moment.

EXHIBIT 7.10   Leptokurtic Distribution

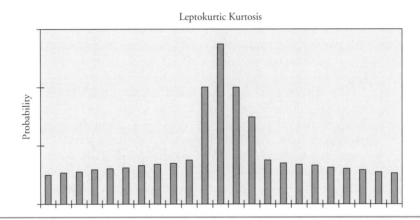

EXHIBIT 7.11   Platykurtic Distribution

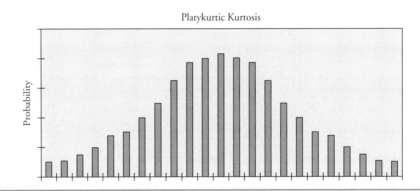

Market research suggests that market returns are negatively skewed and leptokurtic, so it is easy to see why there is so much criticism of the use of the simplified assumption of normal distributions. For example, Markowitz's selection of mean variance as a measure of risk requires not only restrictive assumptions regarding investor behavior (i.e., a measure of loss based on below-median performance), but also the restricted assumption of normal distributions. Let's take a look at some recent market data.

Black Monday and Black Swans

Nassim Taleb defined black swans as outliers beyond our regular expectations that have an extreme impact and that, in retrospect, we review as predictable.[8] Taleb has also frequently challenged the common assumption that returns are normally distributed. We must use caution

---

[8]Taleb (2007).

in applying standard statistics to market returns. Jack Bogle, writing in the *Financial Analysts Journal*, sums it up pretty well:

> [*T*]*he application of the laws of probability to our financial markets is badly misguided. If truth be told, the fact that an event has never before happened in the markets is no reason whatsoever that it cannot happen in the future.*[9]

An example of an extreme event occurred on October 19, 1987, when the Dow Jones Industrial Average (DJIA) dropped by 22.6 percent in a single day—still a record daily decline. Traditional statistics tell us that extreme events such as this should not occur very often. How often do they occur? Let's consider three-sigma events—events that are greater than or equal to three standard deviations away from the average. These should occur about 0.27 percent of the time (said another way, 99.73 percent of the time returns should be within three standard deviations either way from the average). If we examine the 20,215 daily returns for the DJIA from its inception on October 1, 1928, to April 3, 2009, we would expect 55 three-sigma events if daily DJIA were normally distributed. It turns out that there were 358 three-sigma events (1.8 percent of the days) during this period—more than six times the number expected for a normal distribution! Of those events, 196 were daily losses more than three standard deviations below the average, while 162 were daily gains more than three standard deviations above the average. Not only were daily DJIA returns not normally distributed, but they were negatively skewed.

Asset Class/Strategy Data

Let's take a look at some data for select asset classes and investment strategies to assess how normal their distributions are. Exhibit 7.12 shows the data based on monthly returns from June 1986 to December 2008 and includes the arithmetic mean monthly return, standard deviation of monthly returns, a measure of skewness where zero would mean no skew, and a measure of kurtosis (excess kurtosis) where zero would reflect a normal peaked distribution.

EXHIBIT 7.12   Monthly Returns, June 1986 to December 2008

	Mean	Standard Deviation	Skewness	Excess Kurtosis
S&P 500	0.77%	4.46%	−0.91	2.95
FTSE 100	0.79	4.63	−0.94	4.00
Small caps	0.87	5.83	−0.79	3.67
10-Year Treasuries	0.61	2.09	0.07	1.18
30-Year Treasuries	0.73	3.23	0.51	3.22
Equity REITs	0.80	4.69	−1.86	10.90
Commodities	0.78	5.94	−0.26	2.45

(Continued)

---

[9]John Bogle, "Black Monday and Black Swans," *Financial Analysts Journal* (March/April 2008): 30–40.

EXHIBIT 7.12 (Continued)

	Mean	Standard Deviation	Skewness	Excess Kurtosis
Buy write index	0.75	3.19	−1.89	7.24
Collar index	0.65	3.20	−0.05	0.24
Put write index	0.83	2.93	−2.66	12.14

Notice that the monthly returns for the S&P 500 were 0.77 percent with a standard deviation of 4.46 percent, were negative skewed, and exhibited kurtosis (more observations in the tails, or extreme events). The last two characteristics are not desirable when occurring together (we likely wouldn't mind extreme positive events). Let's examine this graphically. Exhibit 7.13 shows a histogram of monthly S&P 500 returns plotted with a normal distribution superimposed.

EXHIBIT 7.13   Histogram of S&P 500 Monthly Returns

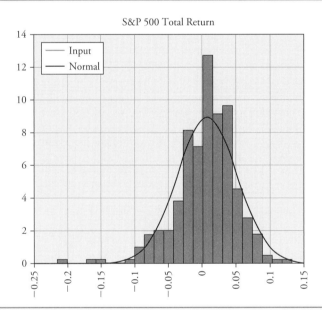

Notice the returns in the middle of the distribution exceeding those expected for a normal distribution and the extreme observations in the tails (particularly the negative observations). This distribution is clearly leptokurtic or, in more common parlance, it is a fat-tailed distribution.

Contrast the statistics for 10-year Treasury bond returns to those of the S&P 500. The Treasury bonds have lower average monthly returns and a lower standard deviation (risk). This is to be expected—the lower the risk of an investment, the lower the return it has to offer to attract investors. Notice also that the Treasury bonds have virtually no skew and very little kurtosis.

Now examine the statistics for small-cap stock returns relative to the S&P 500. Small-cap stocks have a slightly higher average monthly return and a higher standard deviation. Once again this is to be expected—the higher the risk of an investment, the higher the return it must offer to attract investors. Small-cap stocks exhibit a similar negative skew and higher kurtosis compared to the S&P 500.

Which asset class presented here has the most normal distribution of returns? The collar index has virtually no skew and no kurtosis. A collar strategy is one in which stocks are purchased and call options are written against them (selling some of the upside) while put options on them are purchased (protecting the downside). Not surprisingly, this cuts off the fat tails of the stock distribution but at high cost to returns (only 0.65 percent per month versus 0.77 percent per month for an unprotected strategy).

PERFORMANCE MEASURES—RETURN RELATIVE TO RISK

As noted in the previous section, when we compare investment alternatives we are concerned about both their return and their risk. If two otherwise similar potential investments offer the same return but differing levels of risk, we would prefer the one with the lower risk. In practice, however, investments will have different levels of expected return and expected risk. We therefore need to have a way to evaluate or rank these investments. This section discusses a number of metrics that allow us to measure return relative to risk for purposes of evaluating and ranking investment alternatives.

Sharpe Ratio

The Sharpe ratio belongs to a class of measurements known as "efficiency ratios." These are measures that indicate the amount of return earned per unit of risk (i.e., how efficiently the returns were earned). Focusing on the total portfolio risk, William Sharpe designed a ratio he termed the reward-to-volatility ratio,[10] now more commonly known as the Sharpe ratio. Based on his earlier work on the CAPM, Professor Sharpe suggested that an appropriate way to rank the risk-adjusted performance of various portfolios was by calculating their excess return per unit of risk. His ratio is simply:

$$\text{Sharpe Ratio}_i = \frac{r_p - r_f}{\sigma_p}$$

where

r_p = the portfolio return for the period
r_f = the risk-free rate of return for the period
σ_p = the standard deviation of the portfolio during the period

Thus, portfolios with higher Sharpe ratios provided superior excess returns per unit of risk over the period measured compared with portfolios with lower Sharpe ratios. Although the mathematics of calculating the Sharpe ratio are not particularly daunting, it is still comforting to know that it is available for most mutual funds from a number of sources.

Before we move on to the next measure, it's worth remembering that there are risks of misinterpreting the significance of all investment return and performance measures. The

---

[10]William Sharpe, "Mutual Fund Performance," *Journal of Business*, Vol. 39, No. 1, Part 2 (January 1966): 119–138.

Sharpe ratio is no exception. Efficiency ratios do not incorporate information related to correlation. Therefore, Sharpe ratios are most commonly used to compare similar asset classes and styles, such as to rank the performance of mutual fund managers.

Information Ratio

In a later article, Sharpe introduced a new version of his ratio that has become known as the information ratio. The information ratio is designed to adjust the return to reflect the risk of an appropriate portfolio benchmark. Numerically, it is the ratio of the portfolio's average differential return between a fund and its benchmark divided by the tracking error of the portfolio, or:

$$\text{Information Ratio} = \frac{r_p - r_b}{TE_p}$$

where r_b is the benchmark return.

The tracking error of the portfolio is the standard deviation of the differential return between the portfolio and the benchmark. The information ratio is useful for assessing how a manager, such as a mutual fund manager, is doing at generating a return in excess of the benchmark relative to the risk the manager is taking relative to the benchmark.

EXAMPLE 7.4   Use of Ratios

Sharpe ratios and information ratios should be used carefully. Assume that you currently use a passive manager in this asset class and you are considering replacing the passive manager with an active manager named Levine. The passive portfolio has an information ratio of 0.4. Levine's most recent performance is as follows:

Quarter	Excess Return over Benchmark
1	−1%
2	3
3	−1
4	3
5	−9
6	27
7	−9
8	27

Levine implemented a low-volatility policy for the first four quarters and, based on a conscious policy shift, a more aggressive strategy for the second year. The first year, Levine's average excess quarterly return was 1 percent, the standard deviation of the excess return was 2.3 percent, and the information ratio was 0.43. Thus, Levine's information ratio was better than the passive manager's 0.4 information ratio. In the second 52-week period, the portfolio's higher returns made up for its greater volatility and Levine once again achieved an information ratio of 0.43. This suggests that the active manager continued to outperform, on a risk-adjusted basis, the passive manager.

However, if we decided that a longer period would provide a better measure, Levine's information ratio calculated for the two-year period was only 0.35, slightly worse than that of the passive manager. How could Levine have superior performance each year but subperformance for the two-year period? Clearly, Levine cannot. What happened was that the shift in strategy was not reflected in the two one-year calculations. Combining the two years together results in a mathematically misleading conclusion that the portfolio had a greater volatility, resulting in a downward bias for the information ratio. What's the moral? Don't accept simple rules of thumb or measurements at face value, even if they are named after or created by a Nobel laureate.

Treynor Ratio

About the same time that Sharpe developed his ratio, Jack Treynor developed another measure of portfolio performance that combined both risk and returns[11] (actually, Treynor developed the first composite reward/volatility measure, but someone who has been awarded the Nobel Prize gets top billing). Building on capital market theory, Treynor developed a ratio similar to that later designed by Sharpe. The Treynor ratio, however, measures excess returns per unit of systematic risk (remember, the Sharpe ratio measures excess returns per unit of total risk).

$$\text{Treynor Index} = \frac{r_p - r_f}{\beta_p}$$

where

r_p = the portfolio return for the period
r_f = the risk-free rate of return for the period
β_p = the beta of the portfolio during the period

Beta is a measure of the variability of returns on an asset or portfolio relative to the variability of returns on the market. A beta of 1 would indicate similar variability to the market. As with the Sharpe ratio, the Treynor ratio is easily calculated, although it is less directly available from services such as Morningstar. This lack of availability is less troublesome than it might seem, for as you'll note in the next section, it's also less frequently applicable.

Alpha—Jensen's Differential Return Measure

Another ratio that utilizes beta is Jensen's differential return measure or, more popularly, the portfolio's alpha (α).[12] As with Treynor's index, the alpha is based on CAPM and its

[11]Jack Treynor, "How to Rate Management of Investment Funds," *Harvard Business Review*, Vol. 43, No. 1 (January–February 1965): 63–75.
[12]Michael Jensen, "The Performance of Mutual Funds in the Period 1945–1964," *Journal of Finance*, Vol. 23, No. 2 (May 1968): 389–416.

significance is related to the diversification of the portfolio. All assume that the relationship between risk and return remain linear throughout the entire range. Unlike the Sharpe and Treynor ratios, the return for each period, not averages, must be used.

$$\text{Alpha} = \alpha = (r_p - r_f) - \beta_p(r_m - r_f) - \varepsilon$$

where

r_p = the portfolio return for the period
r_f = the risk-free rate of return for the period
r_m = the market return for the period
β_p = the systematic risk of the portfolio for the period
ε = a random error term that is generally assumed to be zero, on average

Alpha is easily understood, as it measures, in terms of percent, the contribution of the portfolio manager. Stated more formally, it is a measure of the incremental rate of return per period measured in excess of the return attributable to the risk the portfolio has assumed. We discuss some limitations of Alpha in the next chapter.

Sortino Ratio

The ratios just discussed use measures of risk that include both downside variability and upside variability. Investors are most concerned with downside variability. As a result, Frank Sortino created the Sortino ratio, which measures excess returns relative to downside deviation:

$$\text{Sortino ratio} = \frac{r_p - MAR}{DD_p}$$

In the Sortino ratio, MAR is the minimal acceptable return that could be set at some absolute value by the investor, such as zero, the risk-free rate, or some target return. DD is the downside deviation measured similarly to standard deviation but using only returns below the MAR in the computation.

FIXED INCOME RISK MEASURES

Fixed income securities, or bonds, have some unique measures of risk for consideration. First let's review some fixed income basics. Fixed income securities typically have a promised interest rate (coupon rate) that is paid on specified dates, and a fixed maturity date. The value of such a security can be determined by discounting the expected future cash flows by the current market rate of interest for securities of similar risk and maturity. As a result there is an inverse relationship between market interest rates and bond values. As market interest rates rise, the value of bonds falls. Conversely, when market interest rates fall, the value of bonds rises. Exhibit 7.14 demonstrates this relationship for a 10-year $1,000 bond that pays a $30 coupon payment every six months and varying levels of semiannual market interest rates.

EXHIBIT 7.14   Relationship between Market Interest Rates and Bond Values

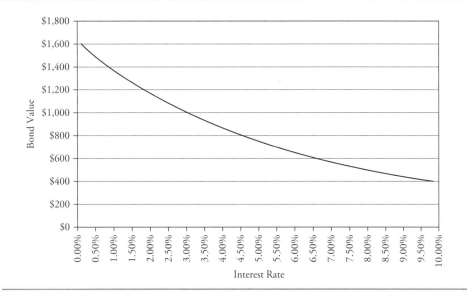

Duration

It is useful to assess the level of sensitivity of a bond to potential changes in interest rates.[13] Rather than creating graphs such as that in Exhibit 7.14 for each bond, there are metrics that are readily available to assess a bond's interest sensitivity. Generally speaking, the longer the time to maturity for the bond, the more sensitive it would be to changes in interest rates. However, maturity measures only the time until the principal is due and does not consider the coupon payments. Duration is a measure that incorporates both the magnitude of the interest and principal payments and the timing of those payments. It can be thought of as the weighted average time to receipt of both coupon and principal payments, where the weights are the present value of each cash flow. For the bond shown in Exhibit 7.14, the maturity is 10 years. Assuming the current level of interest rates is 3 percent semiannually, the duration (known as Macaulay duration) of that bond would be about 7.6 years. The Macaulay duration tends to over- or understate a bond's interest rate sensitivity. In order to reduce this error, today analysts use a modification of Macaulay's duration calculation, known as modified duration. The modified duration is computed by dividing the Macaulay duration by 1 plus the market interest rate per period. For our sample bond at a market rate of 3 percent, the modified duration would be 7.4.

This is the slope of the price-yield curve shown in Exhibit 7.14 at a given yield. Within a narrow range of interest rate change, modified duration serves as a reasonably accurate measure of interest rate sensitivity. Expected price changes can be calculated by the following formula:

$$\text{Price Change} = (\text{Modified Duration}) \times (-\text{Yield Change})$$

---

[13]Although limited, there has been work in developing the concept of duration for use in evaluating the interest rate sensitivity of nonbonds, such as stocks and REITs. Known as the implied duration, it is empirically derived as: Implied Duration = (–% Price Change)/(Yield Change).

So for a modified duration of 7.4, if market interest rose by 50 basis points per year the bond price would be expected to decline by about 3.7 percent; conversely, if market interest rates declined by 50 basis points per year the price would be expected to rise by about 3.7 percent. The higher the modified duration, the higher the price sensitivity of the bond, and hence the risk.

Modified duration has the following attributes:

- Positively related to maturity.
- Inversely related to coupon.
- Inversely related to yield.
- Significantly influenced by calls and sinking funds.

Modified duration has the following limitations:

- As noted in the following discussion of convexity, duration is useful over only a limited range of yield change.
- Price changes due to changing quality spreads and changing sector spreads are not considered.
- Duration assumes that the shape of yield curves (e.g., upwarding sloping versus downward sloping) will remain unchanged when, in fact, they do change.

Duration for a bond with embedded options, such as a callable bond, is more complicated. In such cases, an effective or option-adjusted duration must be used. The effective duration takes into consideration the impact of call and put options embedded within the bonds. If you are comparing ordinary bonds with no embedded options, modified duration can be used. If you are comparing bond funds that contain some bonds with embedded options, then effective duration, found in data services such as Morningstar, should be used.

EXAMPLE 7.5   Evaluation of Maturity and Duration

Levine is considering bond funds for inclusion in a portfolio and is interested in how the underlying fixed income securities would respond to an expected increase in interest rates. Levine obtains the following data from Morningstar. If annual market interest rates rise by 50 basis points, what is the expected impact on the price of each fund's bond portfolio?

Average Effective	Maturity	Duration
Vanguard Short-Term Bond Index Fund	2.8 years	2.6 years
Vanguard Intermediate-Term Bond Index Fund	7.5 years	6.4 years

The short-term fund would be expected to decline in value by 1.3 percent, whereas the intermediate-term bond fund would be expected to decline by about 3.2 percent.

Convexity

Although a handy measure, duration assumes a linear relationship between the change in yields and bond prices. This assumption is accurate only over small changes in interest rates (e.g., less than 100 basis points). If the change is greater, it is necessary to know something about the shape of the relationship. The measure of a bond's price sensitivity to change in yield is called convexity. Convexity describes the curvature of the price-yield curve for a given bond. Note that the bond price line in Exhibit 7.14 is curved and not a straight line. This particular shape is referred to as positive convexity. This attribute describes a relationship for most traditional bonds. Positive convexity is a desirable characteristic. As rates fall, the effective duration of a bond with positive convexity increases, thus increasing the rate of the bond's price appreciation. If, however, rates rise, the effective duration of a bond with positive convexity will fall, reducing the rate of the bond's price erosion. Negative convexity would be representative of a curvature in the other direction and is typical of mortgage-backed securities.

Market traders are aware of the benefits of positive convexity. The prices of bonds with this attribute include a premium. Purchasers of negatively convex bonds are generally compensated with higher yields. Although the basic risk/reward balance is accounted for by these market price adjustments, for active bond managers there is the potential opportunity to add value through yield curve strategies. By designing a portfolio with the convexity most likely to benefit from changes in the shape of the yield curves, managers can increase total return. Thus, convexity, as well as duration, is an issue of concern.

Yield to Maturity and Realized Compound Yield

As noted earlier, bonds typically sell at a price that is based on the current market rate of interest and its promised future payments. Investors can determine the market rate of interest by using the observed market price of the bond and solving for the internal rate of return, also known as the yield to maturity. This is the return the investor expects to receive over time based on the current price of future promised payments. If the investor holds the bond to maturity, receives all promised payments, and can reinvest coupon payments at the same return as the yield to maturity, then the ultimate realized return will be the yield to maturity. However, the assumption that coupon payments can be reinvested at that same rate is unlikely to hold, because the yield curve is rarely flat and the investor's actual yield, known as realized compound yield, is likely to differ.

The relationships among yield to maturity, reinvestment rate, and realized compound yield are as follows:

- If reinvestment rate $<$ yield to maturity, then realized compound yield $<$ yield to maturity.
- If reinvestment rate $=$ yield to maturity, then realized compound yield $=$ yield to maturity.
- If reinvestment rate $>$ yield to maturity, then realized compound yield $>$ yield to maturity.

PARTING COMMENTS

Successful investing requires a quantitative understanding of both return and risk. It is important to understand the limitations of each of these measures and to know which is most appropriate in a given circumstance. For example, the Treynor ratio would be an inappropriate measure for an undiversified portfolio, but the Sharpe ratio would be more appropriate in this situation. Or the information ratio would be more appropriate when risk is best measured relative to an index. These ideas are the building blocks on which modern finance and the wealth manager's work are founded.

RESOURCES

DeFusco, Richard A., Dennis W. McLeavey, Jerald E. Pinto, and David E. Runkle. 2007. *Quantitative Investment Analysis*, 2nd edition. CFA Institute Investment Series. Hoboken, NJ: John Wiley & Sons.

Fabozzi, Frank J. 2007. *Fixed Income Analysis*, 2nd edition. CFA Institute Investment Series. Hoboken, NJ: John Wiley & Sons.

Kritzman, Mark P. 2003. *The Portable Financial Analyst*, 2nd edition. Hoboken, NJ: John Wiley & Sons.

Lhabitant, Francois-Serge. 2007. *Hedge Funds: Quantitative Insights*. Hoboken, NJ: John Wiley & Sons.

Maginn, John L., Donald L. Tuttle, Jerald E. Pinto, and Dennis W. McLeavey, eds. 2007. *Managing Investment Portfolios: A Dynamic Process*, 3rd edition. CFA Institute Investment Series. Hoboken, NJ: John Wiley & Sons.

Pinto, Jerald E., Elaine Henry, Thomas R. Robinson, and John D. Stowe. 2010. *Equity Asset Valuation*, 2nd edition. CFA Institute Investment Series. Hoboken, NJ: John Wiley & Sons.

Taleb, Nassim. 2007. *The Black Swan: The Impact of the Highly Improbable*. New York: Random House.

CHAPTER 8

INVESTMENT THEORY

More people have read Sylvia Porter than Paul Samuelson.

—Gary Helms

In the professional media and at educational meetings of wealth managers, there are frequent debates about various approaches to investment management. These may range from heated arguments on the pros and cons of utilizing a mathematical optimizer to vituperative panel debates on the value (or lack thereof) of active versus passive managers. Generally, open discussion of these issues is healthy for a profession. Unfortunately, for wealth managers, there is frequently a problem. Perhaps because the profession is new, all too often these debates are joined by participants with no knowledge of the issues. Even worse, the audience frequently does not have the knowledge necessary to separate the wheat of the argument from the chaff of ignorant criticism.

After speaking at a prominent financial planning conference some years ago, Harold was teased (and occasionally cursed) for saying:

> [Peter] Bernstein concluded by saying: "Today, the classical capital ideas are suspected of suffering from kurtosis, skewness, and other less-familiar malignancies. They are under attack from non-linear hypotheses, overwhelmed by fears of discontinuities rather than pricing volatility." I submit to you that if you don't understand that paragraph in total and if you could not explain to your clients what that means, you should probably not be charging your clients money for managing their assets.[1]

The intention of this comment was not to belittle anyone unfamiliar with those esoteric terms. It was (and is) intended to be a wake-up call for those aspiring to be truly professional wealth managers. It is easy to reject an emphasis on academic theory as intellectual snobbishness and to suggest that use of sophisticated analytical tools is no more than an effort to market the cachet of a famous academic name. Unfortunately, these criticisms are often valid. The solution, however, is not to reject the lessons of academia and avoid the teachings of Nobel laureates. Rather, the wealth manager should develop

---

[1]This was quoted in the guest speaker column of the 50-year anniversary publication of the *Financial Analysts Journal*, January/February 1995. Be sure to add a copy of that issue to your library.

a familiarity with the very latest information and knowledge available from all appropriate professions, including finance, economics, investments, and psychology, and make decisions based on this knowledge and the wealth manager's own experience. The wealth manager assumes the responsibility of assisting real people to achieve their life goals through the intelligent management of their financial resources. That is an awesome responsibility. It cannot be met by advice based on common knowledge and rules of thumb.

The wealth manager does not have to agree with the conclusions of academic research, and may even reject the conclusions of Nobel laureates; however, the wealth manager should have a sound basis for acceptance or a sound basis for rejection.

Lynn Hopewell was perhaps the first to alert financial planners, practicing wealth management, to this problem. As editor of the *Journal of Financial Planning*, he wrote in his July 1995 editorial:

> *If, as I argued in the last issue's editorial, financial planning is becoming dominated by asset management services [wealth management], a question must be raised as to whence cometh asset-management education for planners. . . .*
>
> *[J]ust as financial planning is an amalgam of the technical matter from other disciplines such as insurance, tax, and estate planning, our asset-management knowledge base lies largely outside the financial planning profession.*
>
> *As asset management becomes more dominant in our business, asset-management education must likewise follow. If planners are to stay out of trouble by not being in "over their heads" in the asset-management game (a definite danger now), we need some concentrated offerings that focus on just this subject.*

Echoing Harold's conference comments, in the October issue of the *Journal*, Lynn wrote:

> *I will go even further—if you don't thoroughly understand the material in Padgette's article [a technical article on performance reporting], you may call yourself a financial planner, but you cannot call yourself an asset manager or investment professional. The essence of asset management is investment policy, portfolio design, and performance measurement. The technical tools are modern portfolio theory and statistics. If you don't master this material, you are like someone who claims to be a physician but who doesn't know about the body's circulatory or immune systems. We would not call that person a physician; we would call him a "quack."*

The following section is intended as an overview of the technical and academic background necessary for wealth managers. It places in historical perspective today's predominant and evolving theory. It provides a working knowledge of the key mathematical and analytical tools that should be a part of the wealth manager's repertoire.

EARLY HISTORY

Perhaps the earliest recorded work that can be said to relate the concepts of theory and investment markets was a doctoral dissertation in 1900 titled *The Theory of Speculation*, by the French mathematician Louis Bachelier. His conclusions seem incredibly contemporary.

Past, present, and even discounted future events are reflected in market price . . . the
determination of these fluctuations depends on an infinite number of factors; it is
therefore impossible to aspire to mathematical predictions of it. . . .
        The mathematical expectation of the speculation is zero.[2]

Unfortunately, at the time his work went unnoticed. It was not rediscovered until the
mid-1950s. Whether knowledge of Bachelier's work would have made any difference will
remain unknown. But by the 1920s, there were dozens of soothsayers marketing systems for
predicting the stock market.

In 1932, Alfred Cowles III, an early pioneer in the accumulation and measurement of
market data, established the Cowles Commission for Research in Economics. Since that date,
the Cowles Commission has been the home of many distinguished academics, including
Nobel laureates James Tobin and Harry Markowitz.

One of the Commission's first publications was Cowles's own research on the efficacy
of market forecasting. Based on a study of the predictive ability of leading subscription-
service market forecasters (including the still-touted Dow Theory), Cowles, unknowingly
echoing Bachelier, concluded, "It is doubtful." Cowles's research confirmed the conclusion
that the market outperformed forecasters. Many years later, Cowles made the following
sobering observations:

> *I had belittled the profession of investment advisors. I used to tell them that it isn't a*
> *profession and of course that got them even madder.*
>   *Market advice for a fee is a paradox. Anybody who really knew just wouldn't share*
> *his knowledge. Why should he? In five years, he could be the richest man in the world.*
> *Why pass the word on?*[3]

For the most part, however, the work of Cowles was as influential as that of Bachelier—it
was largely ignored.

FUNDAMENTALS—GRAHAM AND DODD

The publication in 1934 of *Security Analysis*, written by Benjamin Graham, a partner in a
Wall Street brokerage firm, and David Dodd, a Columbia University professor, heralded the
age of fundamental analysis. Graham was known as the "Dean of Wall Street" and was an
early proponent of a rating system for analysts, which came to be the CFA designation. This
classic book was recently republished with a new foreword by Warren Buffett and new
chapters by prominent value investors. Graham and Dodd focused attention on the evaluation of the intrinsic value of a stock. With a strong emphasis on balance sheet analysis (hence
"fundamentals"), they argued that a stock should be purchased only when its fundamentals
met or exceeded a series of specified criteria. The focus was the individual equity, not the
portfolio. Risk was subsumed in the concept of intrinsic value.

Many successful investment managers today remain strong adherents to the fundamental
concepts presented in *Security Analysis* over 60 years ago. The most famous and most

---

[2]Peter Bernstein, *Capital Ideas: The Improbable Origins of Modern Wall Street* (New York: Free
Press, 1992).
[3]Ibid.

successful is Warren Buffett. He very articulately presented this philosophy in 1984 in a speech he gave at the Columbia Business School in honor of the 50th anniversary of the book's publication. Responding to the statistical argument that in a normal distribution there will always be a few lucky managers with extraordinarily good records, he commented:

> *I think you will find a disproportionate number of coin-flippers in the investment world come from a very small intellectual village that could be called Graham-and-Doddsville. A concentration of winners that simply cannot be explained by chance can be traced to this particular intellectual village.*

He describes the common intellectual theme of investors from this village:

> *[They] search for discrepancies between the* value *of a business and the* price *of small pieces of that business in the market. Essentially, they exploit those discrepancies without the efficient market theorist's concern as to whether the stocks are bought on Monday or Thursday, or whether it is January or July. . . . Our Graham & Dodd investors, needless to say, do not discuss beta, the capital asset pricing model, or covariance in returns among securities. These are not subjects of any interest to them. In fact, most of them would have difficulty defining those terms. The investors simply focus on two variables: price and value.*
>
> *While they differ greatly in style, these investors are mentally always* buying the business, *not buying the stock.*

His personal observations on the work of academics may serve as a thoughtful introduction to the next section's discussion on modern investment theory:

> *Of course, the reason a lot of studies are made . . . is that now, in the age of computers, there are almost endless data available. . . . It isn't necessarily because such studies have any utility; it's simply that the data are there and academicians have worked hard to learn the mathematical skills necessary to manipulate them. Once these skills are acquired, it seems sinful not to use them, even if the usage has no utility or negative utility. As a friend said, to a man with a hammer, everything looks like a nail.*

Buffett's record and the commonsense philosophy of "buy value; buy the company, not the stock" is compelling. In developing a personal investment philosophy, the wealth manager must carefully consider the premise of the fundamentalists. However, there is more to the story than looking at individual securities, as became evident with modern portfolio theory.

MODERN PORTFOLIO THEORY

The spark that started the modern revolution in investment theory (what Peter Bernstein more colorfully calls the "Fourteen Pages to Fame") was the publication of a paper in the *Journal of Finance* of March 1952: "Portfolio Selection" by 25-year-old Harry Markowitz, a graduate student at the University of Chicago.

Markowitz's ultimate fame, including the 1990 Nobel Prize in economics, stemmed from his notion that "you should be interested in risk as well as return." That notion led to the insight that risk is central to investing and that the portfolio, not the position, is the fundamental entity for investment management.

Although today these insights seem less than revolutionary, consider the investment world in the 1950s. Evaluation of individual investment positions was paramount, and holding concentrated portfolios was common. Even John Maynard Keynes, the father of modern economics, and for many years manager of Kings College, Cambridge's endowment fund, had left a legacy consistent with a focus on the individual asset.

> *I am in favor of having as large a unit as market conditions allow . . . to suppose that safety first consists in having a small gamble in a large number of different [companies] where I have no information to reach a good judgment, as compared with a substantial stake in a company where one's information is adequate, strikes one as a travesty of investment policy.*[4]

Even when Markowitz defended his dissertation, Milton Friedman, then a professor at Chicago and a member of Markowitz's examining committee, challenged:

> *"Harry, I don't see anything wrong with the math here, but I have a problem. This isn't a dissertation in economics, and we can't give you a Ph.D. in economics for a dissertation that's not economics. It's not math, it's not economics, it's not even business administration."* [P.S. They did.][5]

With this academic and practitioner environment, it is not surprising that Markowitz's work was not an instant success. In 1966, a 20-year index of *Financial Analysts Journal* articles listed 41 articles on growth stocks, 24 on gold, and *only four* on security analysis.[6] There was *no* separate listing for portfolio management. Of course the same analysis today would show a preponderance of portfolio management articles.

Harry Markowitz's original article evolved into his thesis in 1955. The full evolution of his work was published in 1959 as *Portfolio Selection: Efficient Diversification*. It is now referred to as modern portfolio theory (MPT).

Covariance

As Harry Markowitz began to think through his notion that risk was important, he first considered the portfolio construction process of the fundamental investor.

An investor concentrating on fundamentals is primarily concerned with constructing a portfolio of stocks that maximizes his expected discounted earnings. Markowitz concluded that this approach would result in a concentration of stocks in a few hot economic sectors. The resulting portfolio would be nondiversified.

In the 1950s, it was well known that the expected return of a portfolio of assets was the simple weighted average of the expected returns of the individual assets in the portfolio. Harry Markowitz recognized that a similar calculation, simple weighted average of risk, would not result in a correct measure of the total portfolio risk. Total portfolio risk will always be less

---

[4]Ibid.
[5]Ibid.
[6]Ibid.

than or equal to (almost always less than) the simple weighted average. He determined that, in fact, total portfolio risk, as measured by standard deviation, is a function of covariance.

The mathematical statement of this relationship may be somewhat intimidating:

$$\sigma_{port} = \sqrt{\sum_{i=1}^{N} w_i^2 \sigma_i^2 + \sum_{i=1}^{N} \sum_{j=1}^{N} w_i w_j \text{Cov}_{ij}}$$

where

σ_{port} = the standard deviation of the portfolio
w_i or w_j = the weight of the individual assets i or j in the portfolio
σ_i = the standard deviation of each asset i
Cov_{ij} = the covariance between returns for assets i and j

where

$\text{Cov}_{ij} = \sigma_i \sigma_j \text{cor}_{ij}$
cor_{ij} = the correlation coefficient for assets i and j

While the wealth manager need not be able to derive Markowitz's formula, he or she should understand its import. Consider a portfolio equally divided (50 percent each) between stocks Orion and Pluto. For a two-asset portfolio, the equation for the standard deviation simplifies to:

$$\sigma_{port} = \sqrt{w_1^2 \sigma_1^2 + w_2^2 \sigma_2^2 + 2 w_1 w_2 \sigma_1 \sigma_2 \text{cor}_{1,2}}$$

We know the following about these stocks:

Stock	Expected Return	Standard Deviation
Orion	10%	10%
Pluto	10%	10%

With this information we can easily calculate the portfolios' expected return to be 10 percent, but what about the standard deviation? For that, we need to know the correlation of Orion and Pluto.

Suppose the two stocks are perfectly correlated; that is, the correlation coefficient = 1. Then the standard deviation of the portfolio is:

$$= \sqrt{(.5)^2(.1)^2 + (.5)^2(.1)^2 + 2(.5)(.5)(.1)(.1)(1.0)} = \mathbf{0.10} = \mathbf{10\%}$$

The solution is not too surprising. As both Orion and Pluto are totally correlated, mixing the two stocks in the portfolio has no impact on the portfolio's standard deviation. More generally, when investments are perfectly correlated, the portfolio standard deviation is a weighted average of the standard deviations of the individual securities.

Now consider the case where the correlation between Orion and Pluto = 0.5. The standard deviation of the portfolio is:

$$= \sqrt{(.5)^2(.1)^2 + (.5)^2(.1)^2 + 2(.5)(.5)(.1)(.1)(.5)} = \mathbf{0.087} = \mathbf{8.7\%}$$

Now we can see the power of diversification! The volatility of the two stocks did not change one iota. The only change in the calculation was the last number (i.e., the correlation). The standard deviation in each is still 10 percent, but the portfolio, at 8.7 percent, is less volatile than either Orion or Pluto alone! Notice, as well, that the stocks are not negatively correlated; they are simply not perfectly positively correlated.

EXAMPLE 8.1   Evaluation of Correlation Data

Mary Franklin currently holds investment A and is considering adding either investment B or investment C to her portfolio. Information on the three investments is as follows:

	Expected Return	Standard Deviation	Correlation with A
Investment A	8%	15%	
Investment B	6%	10%	0.3
Investment C	6%	8%	0.9

Assuming Mary would invest an equal amount in investment A and the second investment, which security would likely be preferable?

While investment C has the same expected return as B and a lower standard deviation, it is not necessarily preferable. Note it has a higher correlation with investment A. Computing the expected return of the possible portfolios yields the following information:

$$\sigma_{A+B} = \sqrt{(0.5)^2(0.15)^2 + (0.5)^2(0.10)^2 + 2(0.5)(0.5)(0.15)(0.10)(0.3)}$$
$$= 0.1019 = 10.19\%$$

$$\sigma_{A+C} = \sqrt{(0.5)^2(0.15)^2 + (0.5)^2(0.08)^2 + 2(0.5)(0.5)(0.15)(0.08)(0.9)}$$
$$= 0.1124 = 11.24\%$$

	Expected Return	Standard Deviation
Investment A + B	7%	10.19%
Investment A + C	7%	11.24%

Because of the much lower correlation, B, in spite of being riskier than C, is expected to provide a lower portfolio risk when combined with A as measured by expected standard deviation of the portfolio.

One of the key insights of Markowitz's work is that the risk of a portfolio is usually less than the weighted average risk of the individual assets. A little diversification provides a lot of risk reduction. As demonstrated by Exhibit 8.1 (useful for client education), 10 to 12 poorly correlated stock positions can significantly reduce portfolio risk. Unsystematic risk is also known as diversifiable risk—it can be diversified away by adding poorly correlated assets. Systematic risk is the overall risk of the market that cannot be diversified away, no matter how many individual securities are added.

EXHIBIT 8.1   Diversification

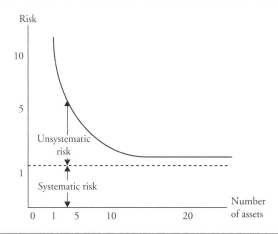

Risk versus Reward and MPT

Markowitz believed that there is trade-off that investors make between risk and reward. Investors either accept higher risk for greater returns or sacrifice returns in order to reduce risk. In addition, he believed that once investors determined their return goal and their risk tolerance, there was a single superior portfolio that would meet that return goal.

His interest in developing a rational solution to the problem of selecting this portfolio led to the development of a theoretical framework for portfolio design and diversification, modern portfolio theory (MPT). Included in his work was a formal methodology for determining the specific asset combination that was superior to all other alternatives.

MPT Assumptions

Modern portfolio theory is based on a theoretical mathematical model. A number of simplifying assumptions are necessary for such models to be developed. It is important that wealth managers understand these assumptions because reality often trumps theory. The wealth manager must understand that these models are only approximations of reality and must be used carefully. The following assumptions underlie MPT:

- Investors are rational and, hence, they want to maximize the expected utility of their investments.
- In order to accomplish this goal, they select investments solely according to their evaluation of their risks and returns.

- For a given return, rational investors prefer the lowest risk; and for a given risk, rational investors prefer the highest return.
- Return is measured as total return.
- Risk is defined as the uncertainty of the return and is measured by variance.
- Estimates of expected return, risk, and covariance are known to investors and fixed through time.
- Expected returns are normally distributed, or, alternatively, investors care only about total return and variance.
- Investors select their assets from a universe of risky assets.

The major criticisms of these assumptions are:

- Investors may not be rational as defined by economic theory. They may be either irrational or rational as defined by psychological theory.
- Market returns are not normally distributed.
- Investors have choices other than risky investments.
- Risk and return characteristics of a given security are not necessarily known in advance or fixed through time.
- Investors are more likely to care about downside risk than total risk (variance).
- There is no accepted "universe of risky assets."

Another limitation of such models is that in the real world, correlations between assets are not stable. In times of market crisis, correlations can rise and assets can fall in value simultaneously. This was evident in the most recent financial crisis when the only safe place to be was government bonds—other asset classes such as stocks, corporate bonds, real estate, and commodities saw an increase in their correlations with each other. In fact, this observation bolsters the importance and validity of the capital market line (CML) discussed in the "Capital Market Theory" section later in this chapter.

Despite these criticisms, MPT is powerful for understanding how portfolios can be developed to balance risk and return. Wealth managers need to consider the potential impact of market events (rising correlations) and plan accordingly (seeking downside protection or assets to include in the portfolio that are least likely to exhibit rising correlations with other assets in the portfolio). Academics and practitioners continue the search for improvements to existing models.

E-V Maxim

Based on these assumptions, Markowitz developed a rule for selecting investments that he called the "expected return–variance maxim" or E-V maxim. The rule is a mathematical formulation of the design of portfolios with the highest return for a given level of risk.

In the development of this rule, Markowitz considered a number of risk measures, including semivariance. He concluded, however, that the other alternatives were computationally unrealistic and selected variance as a measure that was fundamentally sound and practical for calculations.[7] This is a limitation to the model, as noted earlier.

---

[7]In addition to its computational complexity, semivariance also has some practical limitations. Fama and French note in an article entitled "Semi-Variance: A Better Risk Measure" on their Dimensional Advisors web site (www.dimensional.com) that investors may prefer a certain outcome to an uncertain gamble even on the upside. Investors may therefore be concerned with both upside and downside risk.

As variance is the measure of risk Markowitz selected, the solution is not linear, but rather quadratic. Further, the goal is to determine not one solution, but solutions for a series of risk levels. To accomplish this, a parametric quadratic program is used. This is the mathematical engine that drives the better of the oft-maligned so-called black box optimizers.

The output of a Markowitz optimizer is usually presented in graphic form. The curve in Exhibit 8.2 is called the efficient frontier and is plotted by connecting a series of positions representing the most efficient (highest return for a given level of risk) portfolio for each level of risk. The efficient frontier therefore represents the available combinations of assets in a portfolio to maximize the return for a given level of risk. While portfolios exist to the right of and below the efficient frontier, no portfolios are available to the left of and above the efficient frontier.

Using the generalized efficient frontier in Exhibit 8.2 as representative of the efficient frontier generated for a combination of real investment choices, the curve can be interpreted as follows:

EXHIBIT 8.2   Generalized Efficient Frontier

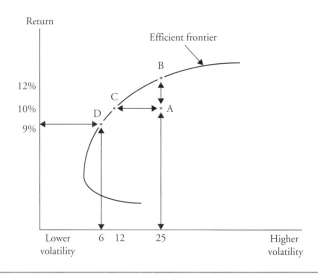

Point A represents a client's current portfolio. The expected return is 10 percent, with a risk of 25. As it lies below the efficient frontier, it is an inefficient portfolio for a rational investor. Remember the definition of a rational investor: For a given return, the investor will seek the lowest risk, and for a given risk, the investor will seek the highest return.

In this example, if the client is prepared to maintain the current risk level, he can reposition his assets to match portfolio B, increasing the return by 2 percent without increasing risk. If the client is happy with the return of the current portfolio, he can reallocate to match portfolio C and decrease risk while maintaining this return. Finally, if the client needs a return of only 9 percent, he could reallocate to portfolio D, the most efficient allocation for that specific return.

Markowitz's efficient frontier can be a very effective tool for educating clients. As discussed before, it demonstrates a number of important concepts:

- There is no single perfect portfolio. There is an infinite series of possible efficient portfolios.
- These efficient portfolios fall along the efficient frontier.
- A client's current portfolio (A) may be improved by rebalancing it to fall on the efficient frontier such that the client can maintain the expected return while reducing risk (C) or increase the expected return without increasing risk (B).
- Neither portfolio B nor C might be appropriate. If the client does not require the return expected by B or C and prefers less risk, it may be appropriate to design a portfolio with *less* return than the current one (e.g., portfolio D). Even though portfolio D is expected to underperform the current portfolio, it may be more appropriate if the client would like to reduce risk.

As a final note, it is important to remember that MPT is based on a number of debatable assumptions. Thus, the efficient frontier is a tool, not a guarantee. Empirical evidence, as well as academic research, suggests that it provides better guidance than alternative methods.

EXAMPLE 8.2   Return versus Volatility

Jane Chan is considering investments in three potential portfolios:

	Expected Return	Volatility
Portfolio X	8%	12%
Portfolio Y	8%	10%
Portfolio Z	6%	10%

Under the E-V maxim, what should Jane's preferences be among these portfolios?

- Comparing X and Y: X and Y have the same expected return while X has higher risk, so Jane should prefer Y over X.
- Comparing Y and Z: Y and Z have the same risk while Y offers a higher expected return, so Jane should prefer Y over Z.

In choosing one of these three portfolios, Jane should clearly prefer portfolio Y. Note that in the absence of portfolio Y, the choice between portfolios X and Z would not be clear—X offers a higher expected return than Z but with higher risk. The choice would depend on Jane's preferred levels of return and risk.

CAPITAL MARKET THEORY

The next major contribution to investment theory is generally credited to William Sharpe, a student of Markowitz and a corecipient with Markowitz of the 1990 Nobel Prize.[8]

---

[8]Independent work of a similar nature was concurrently developed by John Lintner and Jan Mossin. Their names are frequently linked in discussions on this subject.

Sharpe's work was an extension of Markowitz's portfolio theory to general market theory. The culmination was the publication in the September 1964 *Journal of Finance* of "Capital Asset Prices: A Theory of Market Equilibrium under Conditions of Risk."

Sharpe's theory provided a model for determining how financial assets are valued (i.e., priced) by the market. This model has become known as the capital asset pricing model (CAPM). Based on MPT, Sharpe utilized Markowitz's assumptions and added a number of significant new ones.

CAPM Assumptions

As with MPT, there are a number of assumptions underlying CAPM. Some of the most significant assumptions are:

- There is a risk-free asset—one with no uncertainty regarding the expected rate of return.
- Investors can borrow and lend at the risk-free rate of return.
- There are no taxes and no transaction costs.
- All investors have the same investment time horizon.
- All investors have identical expectations for asset returns.

In addition to the objections to the Markowitz assumptions, criticisms of Sharpe's new assumptions include:

- The inability of investors to borrow at the risk-free rate.
- The reality of taxes and transaction costs.
- Investors do not have uniform time horizons.
- Investors do not have identical expectations of returns.

Capital Asset Pricing Model

Sharpe concluded, based on the aforementioned assumptions, that risky portfolios on the efficient frontier could be combined with the risk-free asset to create opportunities above the efficient frontier. Sharpe constructed a capital market line (CML) as shown in Exhibit 8.3.

EXHIBIT 8.3   The Efficient Frontier and the Capital Market Line

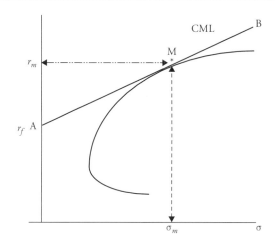

The point of tangency (M) of a line drawn from the return of the risk-free asset represents the single best portfolio for the world of homogeneous, Markowitz-efficient investors. By definition, the sum of all investor portfolios represents the market portfolio. Logically, if every investor holds portfolio M and if all investors hold the same portfolio, then the proportion of securities in each investor's portfolio must be the same as the proportion of securities in the market portfolio. Therefore, portfolio M is the market portfolio.

Taking the logic of the CAPM illustration one step further, all investors would obviously choose to own a portfolio of only two investments—the risk-free asset and the market portfolio. Doing so enables them to achieve a better risk/return relationship than most points on the efficient frontier. Under the assumptions of CAPM (i.e., the ability to lend or borrow at the risk-free rate at no cost), an investor could construct a portfolio anywhere along the line A–M by lending a portion of funds at the risk-free rate and investing the balance in the market portfolio. For an investor who wishes to ratchet up his returns above the average of the market portfolio, it is easily accomplished. The investor would simply leverage the investment by borrowing at the risk-free rate and investing the borrowed funds, along with all of his own assets, in the market portfolio. How much the investor borrows will determine where along the line M–B his leveraged portfolio will fall.

The line A–B is known as the "capital market line." In addition to showing that the efficient frontier can potentially be improved upon by borrowing or lending, the model can be extended to create a security market line (SML), which helps us understand the pricing of risky assets.

Security Market Line

In MPT, risk is a function of the covariance of one asset with the other portfolio assets. In Sharpe's world, there is only one market asset, the market portfolio. Thus, the only covariance of importance is the asset's covariance with the market portfolio, and this is the only measure of risk that matters. This covariance is effectively the systematic risk in Exhibit 8.1. Thus, according to CAPM, for diversified portfolios, total risk is irrelevant. Unsystematic risk is diversified away and all that remains is systematic risk—the risk of the market. CAPM can be extended to show that the rate of return on any security or portfolio depends on the risk-free rate of return, the expected rate of return on the market portfolio, the variance of the market portfolio, and the covariance of the security or portfolio with the market portfolio:

$$r = r_f + \left(\frac{\text{Cov}_{i,m}}{\sigma_m^2} \right) (r_m - r_f) + \varepsilon$$

Although this is a pretty simple description of the SML, CAPM takes it one step forward. As market risk is the primary exposure for a diversified portfolio, it would obviously be convenient to somehow have it serve as a standard against which the risk of other assets can be measured. The simple and elegant solution was the creation of a new term called beta (β), where:

$$\beta = \frac{\text{Cov}_{i,m}}{\sigma_m^2}$$

Now our formula can be rewritten as:

$$r = r_f + \beta(r_m - r_f) + \varepsilon$$

The beta (β) of the market is 1 since the covariance of an asset with itself is its variance.

EXHIBIT 8.4   Security Market Line

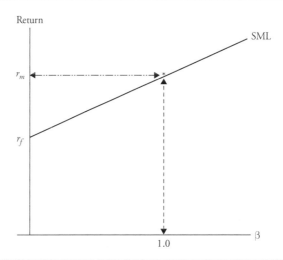

With this SML depicted in Exhibit 8.4, we can predict the relationship between beta (β) and expected return. A security or portfolio with a higher beta than the market (greater than 1) has higher risk and therefore should have a higher expected return than the market. Conversely, a security or portfolio with a beta of less than 1 has lower risk and should have a lower expected return than the market portfolio.

EXAMPLE 8.3   A Caution on the Use of β

Using the formula for the SML, we can now determine the expected return for an asset if we know the risk-free return, the expected market return, and the beta of the asset.

For example, assume that we expect:

$$r_f = 3\% \text{ and } r_m = 12\%$$

For stock A with $\beta_A = 1.2$ and stock B with $\beta_B = 0.7$ we can calculate the expected returns:

$$r_A = 0.03 + 1.2(0.12 - 0.03) = 13.8\%$$

$$r_B = 0.03 + 0.7(0.12 - 0.03) = 9.3\%$$

For some wealth managers, these results may come as a surprise. It is common to use beta as a single factor relating risk and return. Most investors would have calculated different expected returns:

	Common Use of Beta	CAPM Expectation
Stock A	12% × 1.2 = 14.4%	13.8%
Stock B	12% × 0.7 = 8.4%	9.3%

> Obviously the error is in not adjusting for the risk-free rate. As the differences may be significant, a wealth manager utilizing beta as a guide to risk must be sensitive to the possible misuse by others.

As noted in the preceding chapter, betas are determined by regressing excess returns on a security against excess returns of some market index in the following form:

$$(r - r_f) = \alpha + \beta(r_m - r_f) + \varepsilon$$

In this formula beta is the sensitivity of the security's excess returns relative to those of the market—the slope of the fitted curve. Alpha represents the intercept line. Rearranging this equation yields Jenson's alpha, which is a measure of the return in excess of that expected given the risk (beta) of a portfolio:[9]

$$\text{Alpha} = \alpha = (r_P - r_f) - \beta_P(r_m - r_f) - \varepsilon$$

A positive alpha means the investment generated higher returns than expected given the level of risk taken on. In strongly efficient markets, alpha is expected to be zero. A great deal of time is spent by many investors finding managers who are able to generate consistently positive alpha. Other investors are satisfied to get exposure to the broad markets (beta exposure) through index funds and similar investments.

Alphas are handy and available. They're included in most fund reports, including Morningstar, Value Line, and Wilson, and they're easy to explain to clients. Unfortunately they belong to the real world and naturally there are a few catches.

- The use of alpha implies that systematic risk is the proper measure of risk of the portfolio. Catch #1 is a warning that unless the portfolio is reasonably diversified, these measures are meaningless at best and potentially dangerously misleading.
- Catch #2 is more insidious. Even for a well-diversified portfolio (remember—a high R^2), the alpha value may be correct but statistically meaningless. Frequently the random error factor, noted in the alpha formula, is of such a magnitude that it renders the calculated alpha meaningless. As Maginn and Tuttle warn in the first edition of *Managing Investment Portfolios* (1990), "Statistical error is so large, because of large fluctuations observed in a limited sample of data, that statistically significant alphas seldom occur."
- Catch #3 is more obvious. These alphas assume that CAPM is valid. Put differently, alpha assumes that systematic risk is composed entirely of market risk. As we discuss later, Fama and French have shown us that there may be systematic risk factors related to size and value, as well.

Implications of CAPM

An investor should invest in a combination of only two investments—the risk-free asset and the market portfolio. Risk is composed of two components: systematic risk and unsystematic risk.

---

[9]The use of capital R versus lowercase r in these two formulas simply represents the use of expected returns versus observed returns. The math makes no distinction between the case.

Market or Systematic Risk

This is the risk associated with the market (i.e., economy) and cannot be diversified away. Hence market risk, a form of systematic risk, is also known as nondiversifiable risk. β is the measure of a security's market-related risk.

As market risk cannot be diversified away, some investors are prepared to pay a premium in order to avoid the risk. Those investors willing to accept the risk thus expect to be compensated.

Nonmarket or Unsystematic Risk

This is the risk unique to the security or portfolio. It can be eliminated through diversification. Hence, it is also referred to as diversifiable risk. As it can be eliminated by diversification, investors are not prepared to pay for assuming this risk.

Final Thought

By now the reader might enjoy a brief respite. So we will take this opportunity to place this theory in some perspective.

Because Markowitz and many of the other academics whose names are synonymous with modern investment theory were educated and/or teach at the University of Chicago's School of Economics, it may be useful to understand the Chicago perspective. The following illuminates one of the school's fundamental beliefs.

> *How many Chicago School economists does it take to change a lightbulb? None. If the bulb needed changing, the market would have done it already.*

OTHER ASSET PRICING MODELS

The goal of asset pricing models is to:

- Assist managers to understand the dynamics of asset pricing.
- Direct managers' efforts to those issues that can affect future returns.
- Help managers assess risk.
- Assist in the evaluation of portfolio performance.

To the extent that CAPM is seen to fail in meeting these goals, there have been alternate pricing models proposed.

Arbitrage Pricing Theory

In 1976, Stephen Ross published his arbitrage pricing theory (APT), a new asset pricing model that became a significant catalyst for new research.

Whereas CAPM is a single-factor model (the market portfolio), APT is a multifactor model. In addition to being more robust than CAPM by allowing for the influence of multiple factors, it does not require a number of the assumptions of CAPM. In fact, it has only three main assumptions: perfectly competitive capital markets, investor preference of more wealth to less wealth, and returns generated by a multiple-factor model (they need not be normally distributed). APT is a general model and is appealing because it does not use a single factor (variability relative to the market). However, the factors impacting returns in an APT model are not defined. Researchers have explored a variety of factors with mixed results, such as unexpected inflation, shifts in the yield curve, size factors (large versus small stocks), and value factors (low versus high price multiples).

The size and value factors are probably the most popular factors used among practitioners. Eugene Fama and Kenneth French have been most responsible for popularizing them (although R. W. Banz is largely credited with having discovered the size effect). They explain stock returns with the following three factors:

$$r = r_f + \beta(r_m - r_f) + sSMB + hHML + \varepsilon$$

The first factor is the market risk premium, much like we see in CAPM. SMB is a hypothetical portfolio that is long small stocks and short large stocks (i.e., small minus big). HML is a hypothetical portfolio that is long high book-to-value stocks and short low book-to-value stocks (e.g., high minus low).[10] The coefficients, s and h, measure a security's sensitivity to the extra return from small stocks and value stocks, respectively.

Like Stephen Ross's APT, there is little theoretical foundation for the size and value being the relevant factors beyond the market portfolio, but they have been found to explain returns quite well—so well, in fact, that beta has no statistically significant relationship to return once these factors are included.[11]

Final Thoughts on Asset Pricing Models

No model on theory has become the Rosetta stone of asset pricing. As with the efficient market hypothesis (EMH), research papers criticizing various asset pricing models have become a cottage industry. Objections include criticism of underlying assumptions and claims that empirical tests demonstrate their lack of predictive value.

Still, these models serve as a major catalyst for market research and an influence on market practice. They remain powerful theoretical concepts that continue to influence market theory and practice.

The wealth manager should neither accept pricing models as gospel nor reject them out of hand. With respect to individual asset selection, it is the role of portfolio managers to determine the influence of pricing models in their philosophy. The wealth manager's job is to intelligently evaluate the manager's philosophy.

Recognize that one of the key lessons of both CAPM and APT is that taking on unsystematic risk is not rewarded by the market. Unsystematic risk should be avoided by proper diversification. This important insight has sometimes been misunderstood to mean that diversification provides insurance against market downturns. It does not. It reduces idiosyncratic risk, but not market risk.

RANDOM WALK

Random walk, along with its close relation, the efficient market, is a phrase that tends to start active managers frothing at the mouth. Most investors believe that these terms describe a

---

[10]Note that Fama and French use the book-to-value ratio rather than the more familiar price-to-book ratio as a way to sensibly incorporate securities with negative (or zero) book value.

[11]In fact, the relationship between beta and return in Fama and French's original paper is negative in the presence of size and value.

market in which stock prices move in a totally random manner. Although some observers have suggested just such a conclusion, the concept does not depend on stock prices being statistically random; it says only that the arrival of new information is, by definition, random, so future price *changes* are random and the history of prices cannot be used to predict future prices.

The early work in this area by Bachelier (1900), Working (1934), and Cowles (1933) was largely ignored. The concept of market randomness was not revisited until the 1950s. Renewed interest in the 1950s started not in finance or economics but with statistician M. Kendall's "The Analysis of Economic Time Series," Harry Roberts's "Stock Market Patterns," and astrophysicist M. F. M. Osborne's "Brownian Motion in the Stock Market."[12] These studies suggested that market prices had no memory. Any information in the past sequence was reflected in the current price.

In the 1960s, economists picked up the gauntlet. In 1964, Paul Cootner published *The Random Character of Stock Prices*, and in 1965, Nobel laureate Paul Samuelson published "Proof That Properly Anticipated Prices Fluctuate Randomly." In this paper, Samuelson hypothesized an efficient market with normally distributed prices. He concluded that in such an environment market price changes would be random. The major synthesis of this evolving work is credited to Eugene Fama.

Fama, a newly minted PhD, began teaching at the University of Chicago in 1964. His doctoral thesis was concerned with the question of market efficiency. It was published in the January 1965 *Journal of Business* as "The Behavior of Stock Market Prices." The work was so persuasive that an abridged version was published in the *Financial Analysts Journal* as "Random Walks in Stock Market Prices," as well as in a 1968 issue of the trade journal *Institutional Investor*. At the end of 1969, Fama presented a paper to the American Finance Association and published "Efficient Capital Markets: A Review of Theory and Empirical Work" as the definitive synthesis on the subject in the May 1970 *Journal of Finance*.

EFFICIENT MARKET HYPOTHESIS

The efficient market hypothesis (EMH) is concerned with the relationship of stock prices with the actions of buyers and sellers. The premise of the EMH is that "security prices fully reflect all available information."

Fama suggested that this hypothesis could be more easily addressed if the test of its validity were divided into three subthemes (referred to as "forms"), with each form reflecting a different definition of *information* against which the hypothesis might be tested.

The most stringent test is the *strong form*. This tests whether all relevant information, public and nonpublic (including insider information), is reflected in security prices.

The *semistrong form* asserts that all useful publicly available information is immediately used by investors. Stock prices discount the information, and the market will instantaneously reach equilibrium.

The *weak form* assumes that current stock prices reflect all stock market information. It tests the hypothesis against information provided by historical market data (e.g., prices and trading volume). The weak form can be explained by the random walk theory. If price movements are in fact random, historical market information would obviously not provide

---

[12]Bernstein, *Capital Ideas*.

any useful information. However, the weak form may still be valid even if markets are not random. The question is *whether* historical data can provide useful information, not *why* it can or cannot.

If the weak form is correct, then adherents of traditional technical analysis cannot add value. The information utilized by technical analysis will have no predictive value. The weak form neither supports nor rejects the notion that other forms of information (e.g., good research) may be helpful in predicting future prices. A wealth manager who accepts the weak form will ignore managers who employ technical analysis, and will ignore the siren song of market timing. Regarding a wealth manager's use of active managers who use fundamental analysis, the weak form says, "You're on your own; this hypothesis has no opinion."

A wealth manager accepting the strong or semistrong hypothesis will not only avoid market timing and technically oriented managers, but will also avoid all active managers. As good as they may be, they simply cannot add value.

Thoughts on EMH

During the past 40-plus years, academics have empirically tested these hypotheses continually. Almost uniformly, the results support the weak market hypothesis and generally reject the strong hypothesis. There is no agreement on the results of the test of the semistrong hypothesis.

A wealth manager who employs managers utilizing only technical analysis, concentrates positions, or utilizes market timing may want to reconsider this philosophy. It may be legally safe to manage your own funds based on an unpopular theory. It is riskier to challenge generally accepted theory when advising others.[13]

For wealth managers who employ active managers who base their investment policy on fundamental research, there is better news. One of the major problems with the EMH is the interpretation of the word "information." The earlier discussion addressed only one aspect of information, namely the source. Left unresolved is the nature of "information." If it is simply data, it is available to all interested parties almost instantaneously. If "information" depends on interpretation, the role of an intermediary, such as a fundamental analyst, may be significant.

A wealth manager selecting active fundamental managers currently has significant academic support for that decision; however, research on the subject continues. There is just as much research supporting a more passive approach, and we discuss both bodies of work more thoroughly in Chapter 14. A wealth manager should stay apprised of the results of new studies, for one day the support for active management may disappear.

ASSET ALLOCATION

Harry Markowitz, with the development of MPT, refocused wealth managers' attention away from specific securities and onto the portfolio. Markowitz had demonstrated that asset

---

[13]Note that we do not mean to imply that examination of price charts is irrelevant. There is recent research that some aspects of technical analysis such as support and resistance levels are supported and there are behavioral implications why this may be so. See Andrew W. Lo, Harry Mamaysky, and Jiang Wang, "Foundations of Technical Analysis: Computational Algorithms, Statistical Inference and Empirical Implementation," *Journal of Finance*, Vol. 55 (2000).

allocation was important, but not how important. Many managers and investors continued to believe the advice given in the mid-1930s by Gerald Loeb: "The greater safety lies in putting all your eggs in one basket and watching that basket."[14]

The publication of "Determinants of Portfolio Performance" in the July/August 1986 issue of *Financial Analysts Journal*[15] was a seminal event in portfolio management. Largely as a result of that article, the concepts of investment policy and asset allocation have become part of the common investment lexicon for retail as well as institutional investors. We believe that the contribution of Gary Brinson, Randolph Hood, and Gilbert Beebower (BHB) is of such importance that every wealth manager should be familiar with their process and conclusions.[16] The next chapter discusses their work in detail and puts in it the context of more recent research.[17]

TIME DIVERSIFICATION

One of the truisms branded into the souls of most wealth managers is that "time diversifies risk." The original formulation of this belief is attributed to Peter Bernstein. His two basic premises were:

1. The longer the investment horizon, the larger the percentage of the portfolio that should be invested in stocks and other high-return assets.
2. In the long run, an investor can be reasonably sure that a higher-volatility portfolio will earn more than a lower-volatility portfolio.

Jeremy Siegel is also associated with this view by way of his book *Stocks for the Long Run*.[18] This belief has led wealth managers to preach to their clients that it is nonsense to say that the market is risky. It is risky in the short term and safe in the longer term. Time diversification is the basis for Harold's firm's mantra, "Five years, five years, five years." That is, no funds should be considered investment money unless the client believes he or she will have a five-year warning before needing to liquidate. Funds needed in less than five years should be placed in money market or short-term bond funds.

This faith in the salutary effect of time on risk was not created from naive optimism. Over time, it seems that above-average returns should offset below-average returns. Logically, the longer the time horizon, the more effective this dampening effect. Mathematically, for normally distributed returns, standard deviation of *total* return over a holding period increases with the square root of the time horizon, according to the following

---

[14]Gerald Loeb, "Is There an Ideal Investment?" in *Classics: An Investor's Anthology*, Charles Ellis, ed. (Dow-Jones Irwin, 1989), 266–276.
[15]Gary P. Brinson, L. Randolph Hood, and Gilbert L. Beebower, "Determinants of Portfolio Performance," *Financial Analysts Journal* (July/August 1986).
[16]Harold thinks it's so important that he named one of his cats Brinson. Of course, the other two are Sharpe and Markowitz.
[17]James X. Xiong, Roger G. Ibbotson, Thomas M. Idzorek, and Peng Chen, "The Equal Importance of Asset Allocation and Active Management," *Financial Analysts Journal*, Vol. 66, No. 2 (2010): 22–30.
[18]Siegel (2007).

expression, assuming that returns from one period to the next are not related (e.g., no mean reversion).

$$\sigma_{\text{Total Holding Period Return}} = \sigma_{\text{Periodic Compound Return}} \times \sqrt{(N)}$$

where N is the number of periods. Therefore, an equity fund with an annual standard deviation of 25 percent has a total return standard deviation over a four-year holding period of only 50 percent (i.e., 25% $\times$ $\sqrt{4}$) rather than 100 percent (i.e., 25% $\times$ 4). It can also be shown that the standard deviation of the annualized return over an N-year holding period is:

$$\sigma_{\text{Annualized Return over } N \text{ Periods}} = \frac{\sigma_{\text{Annual Return}}}{\sqrt{(N)}}$$

The volatility of the annualized return declines with the square root of time. For example, if an equity fund has a 25 percent annual standard deviation, the expected standard deviation of the annualized return over a four-year holding period is 12.5 percent (i.e., 25%/$\sqrt{4}$).[19] In other words, total holding period risk does not increase linearly with time. It increases less than that.

As comforting as it is to believe that time diversification is working in the client's favor, the wealth manager needs to be aware that some observers argue that this is another investment myth. It might be tempting to ignore these objections, but, as the list of critics includes Robert Merton, Paul Samuelson (Nobel laureate), and Zvi Bodie, it is wise to at least understand why they argue that time diversification is specious.

In 1969, publishing independently but reaching the same conclusions, Merton and Samuelson demonstrated that, although the standard deviation of average annual returns may decrease over time, the standard deviation of terminal values *increases*. And, although the likelihood of losing money may decrease over time, the size of a potential loss (should it occur) increases with the time horizon. More recently, Zvi Bodie[20] forcefully argued the same general conclusion. In other words, although the probability of loss decreases over time, the magnitude of potential losses increases. As a result, they argue that an investor's asset allocation decision should be independent of the time horizon. Mathematically, Merton's and Samuelson's conclusions are indisputable. How then does a wealth manager incorporate time diversification into his or her own personal philosophy?

Recognize that the rejection of time diversification rests on various assumptions, including the academic economists' favorite person, the rational investor. One of the attributes of a rational investor is a utility function that translates into a desire to maximize terminal wealth (actually the log of terminal wealth). Real clients of a wealth manager seldom have such simple goals. The academics' definition of a rational investor may be academic.

For most clients, their long-term goal is to earn a return adequate to maintain their standard of living. They have neither a reason nor a desire to take excess risks to earn returns in excess of their target. Any return significantly below the required return is likely to decimate the client's standard of living.

The significance of this in terms of time diversification is that the wealth manager's clients are far more sensitive to the probability of meeting their goal than the relative magnitude of a shortfall. For them, time diversification may work.

---

[19]Assuming its annual returns are not correlated from one year to the next.

[20]Zvi Bodie, "On the Risk of Stocks in the Long Run," *Financial Analysts Journal* (May/June 1995).

The following example[21] and tables[22] may be useful in demonstrating this concept to clients.

EXAMPLE 8.4   Ms. Kahn Time Diversifies

Ms. Kahn has $1,000 to invest for retirement. She has a choice between two investments:

1. A risk-free investment with an expected return of 4 percent and a standard deviation of 0 percent.
2. A risky investment with an expected return of 12 percent and a standard deviation of 16 percent.

EXHIBIT 8.5   Time Diversification—Risk-Free versus Risky Investments

Time Horizon in Years	Risk-Free Value[a]	Risky Value[a]			Probability of Underperformance
		Mean	10th Percentile	90th Percentile	
1	$1,000	$ 1,100	$ 900	$ 1,400	30.9%
5	1,200	2,000	1,200	2,900	13.2
10	1,500	3,800	1,700	6,400	5.7
20	2,200	14,200	4,400	27,600	1.3
40	5,000	202,800	33,200	444,500	0.1

[a]Rounded to the nearest $100.

Exhibit 8.5 compares the probability of terminal values for the risky and risk-free investments.

After 10 years, there is a 90 percent probability that the risky investment return will exceed the risk-free return by 13 percent. There is only a 5.7 percent probability that it will underperform the risk-free asset. After 20 years, the probability of underperformance drops to 1.3 percent. For a 40-year time horizon (common in retirement planning), the probability of underperformance drops to 0.1 percent!

---

[21]Steven R. Thorley, "The Time Diversification Controversy," *Financial Analysts Journal* (May/June 1995).

[22]William Reichenstein and Dovalee Dorsett, "Introduction," in *Time Diversification Revisited* (Charlottesville, VA: Research Foundation of CFA Institute, 1995), 1–8.

A common source of confusion in this debate revolves around the distinction between the effect of investors' time horizon on the risk of their investment versus the effect of their time horizon on their risk tolerance. Whether or not time diversifies risk in a mathematical sense, an investor's flexibility and ability to recoup investment losses by other means (e.g., working longer) tends to increase with their time horizon. That is, should they suffer an improbable large loss, a long time horizon gives them greater ability to adjust to that loss.

Mark Kritzman has an excellent presentation of the pros and cons of time diversification in a *Financial Analysts Journal* article.[23] In another *Financial Analysts Journal* article, Kritzman and his coauthor Don Rich note that investors are not exposed to risk simply at the end of the investment horizon.[24] They are exposed to risk throughout the investment term. Therefore, one should consider the risk of loss not just at the end of one's time horizon, but also consider within their horizon. Investors likely care about interim volatility for a number of reasons, but two of the most prevalent ones for the individual investor are the ability to stick with a predetermined and prudent investment plan during turbulent markets and unexpected changes in one's financial situation. Kritzman and Rich showed that the probability of incurring a loss at some point within the investment horizon necessarily *increases* with the length of that horizon.

Another reason to question whether time reduces risk is by observing the way put options are priced both in theory and in practice. Purchasing a put option is the equivalent of insuring the portfolio against losses below a certain level. The famous Black-Scholes option pricing model clearly shows that the price of put options (i.e., portfolio insurance) increases as the term of the option increases. This is, in fact, what we observe in practice, as well. If the cost of insuring the portfolio against loss increases with the time horizon, then time must not diversify risk.

Asset Allocation and Time Diversification

Combining the benefits of asset allocation and the benefits of time diversification can make a compelling story. Suppose that the client has the choice of investing in three portfolios—all bonds, all stock, or a diversified portfolio (see Exhibit 8.6).

EXHIBIT 8.6   Investor Portfolio Choices

	T-Bills	T-Notes	Bonds	S&P 500	Small Cap
Portfolio A	0.0%	0.0%	100.0%	0.0%	0.0%
Portfolio B	0.0	0.0	0.0	100.0	0.0
Portfolio C	5.0	12.5	22.5	50.0	10.0

If we wish to evaluate the risk the investor faces with these different investment choices, we can compare the expected portfolio returns to Treasury bill returns. Exhibit 8.7 shows the probability that the portfolio returns will exceed Treasury bill returns.[25]

---

[23]Kritzman (1994).

[24]Kritzman and Rich (2002).

[25]The table is based on an assumption of a mean-reversion model, but the results are essentially the same for the random walk model.

EXHIBIT 8.7   Probability of Exceeding Treasury Bill Returns—Asset Allocation Works!

Holding Period in Years	Portfolio A Stock[a]	Portfolio B Bonds[a]	Portfolio C Diversified[a]
1	61%	59%	66%
10	85	72	91
20	93	79	97
30	96	84	99

[a]Rounded to the nearest percentage.

As compelling as this presentation is, one must remember that although the probability of underperforming the risk-free asset decreases with the time horizon, the magnitude of the small-probability losses is much larger for the 30-year time horizon than for the one-year time horizon.

Time Diversification—A Caveat

Example 8.5 illustrates the hazards of relying on time diversification where a client's goal requires a specific terminal wealth value.

EXAMPLE 8.5   Time Diversification Caveat

Mr. Godchaux has funds set aside to fund his child's education in five years. He is considering investing in an equity fund with an expected annual return of 15 percent and an annual standard deviation of 30 percent. He is concerned with the high volatility of the fund. When Mr. Godchaux expresses his concerns to his advisor, the advisor explains that, as the portfolio is designed to be held for five years, the expected annual return for five years is still 15 percent, but the standard deviation of the annualized return is 13.4 percent (i.e., $30\%/\sqrt{5}$). Or, put differently, the standard deviation of the cumulative five-year return is only 67 percent (i.e., $30\% \times \sqrt{5}$) rather than 150 percent (i.e., $30\% \times 5$). The client is relieved. This is time diversification in action. But is his sense of security warranted?

Unfortunately, the answer is no! The problem is that although the standard deviation of the *annualized rate of return* is reduced to 13.4 percent, the volatility of the terminal value of the portfolio is not; it continues to grow with the square root of the time horizon. If the client's average return is off by just one standard deviation (a very real possibility), *his terminal wealth will be less than half the expected value*. Exhibit 8.8 demonstrates how significantly the terminal wealth can diverge over time.

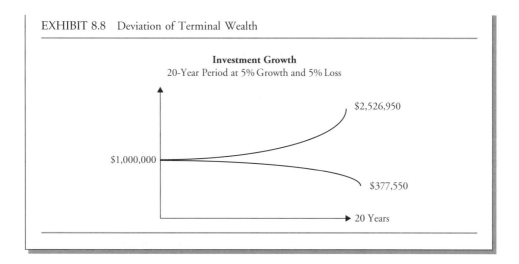

EXHIBIT 8.8   Deviation of Terminal Wealth

Investment Growth
20-Year Period at 5% Growth and 5% Loss

$2,526,950

$1,000,000

$377,550

20 Years

CHAOS THEORY

Merriam-Webster's dictionary defines *chaos* as "a state of things in which chance is supreme . . . a state of utter confusion." It would seem, then, that *chaos theory* is the ultimate oxymoron. How can there be a theory about chance and confusion? The answer is to redefine chaos. In mathematical terminology, chaos is a form of a deterministic nonlinear dynamic process.

Most of the science of the twentieth century is based on the work of ancient and classical scientists (e.g., Euclid, Galileo, and Newton). For the most part, the universe has been viewed as a smooth and continuously evolving process. This worldview also serves as the basis for modern capital market theory. Linearity is built into the concepts of efficient markets and rational investors. Information is readily reflected in security prices, and return distributions approximate normal distributions. Although there is increasing discussion of nonnormal distributions reflecting different levels of skewness and kurtosis, the analysis of these asymmetric models is still based on statistical concepts rooted in a linear universe.

In the 1970s, a number of respected scientists began to suggest that the classical foundation was built on an exception to the rules of nature. This new breed of scientist, the chaologist, believes that order, as we know it, is the exception, and that chaos, a new dynamic concept of order, is the rule. They believe that this new order, called chaos, has three major attributes:

1. First, nature is deterministic; that is, the past mechanically governs the future. There is an exact mathematical relationship between the future and the past. There is *no* randomness.
2. Second, the mathematical relationships relating the future to the past are *non*linear; that is, they are not related in a directly proportional way.
3. Finally, the process is dynamic and changes over time.

Chaotic systems can be recognized by a number of attributes. Although not random, they may appear random according to standard statistical tests. Chaotic systems have an extreme sensitivity to their initial conditions. As a result, specific future states are unpredictable.

The most familiar example of a chaotic system is the weather. While on a day-to-day basis the weather may seem random, it obviously has a certain predictability. No one is likely to get sunstroke in Syracuse in January. It is equally unlikely that it will snow in Miami in July. Thus, it is perhaps no surprise that the real impetus for current research in chaos theory began with the work of an MIT meteorologist, Edward Lorenz.

In the early 1960s, weather forecasting was considered guesswork. Computers were still big, slow, ungainly conglomerations of vacuum tubes.[26] As told in the book *Chaos*[27] by James Gleick, Lorenz was experimenting with a make-believe world and its weather system by programming his computer with 12 godlike rules regarding temperature, pressure, and wind speed. His program produced a graph of continually undulating lines representing the rise and fall of the temperature in his make-believe world. In the winter of 1961, Lorenz decided he would like to continue a study of a series he had begun earlier. Rather than starting over, he simply entered the data obtained from his last computer run and started once again crunching numbers. Having used exactly the same data as the earlier run, the graph should have generated a pattern similar to the original graph. But it didn't! The new graph rapidly diverged in shape from the original. After a few "months," his new world's weather pattern bore no resemblance to the weather pattern in his earlier analysis.

According to Gleick, Lorenz at first assumed that a vacuum tube had gone bad, but he soon realized that the cause of the dramatic changes was a tiny change in the data starting point. His computer calculated to an accuracy of six decimal places, but printed only three. If the ending point of the original run was 0.602193, it printed 0.602. When Lorenz entered the data for the second run, he typed 0.602 and the computer read it as 0.602000. Although the difference, one part in a thousand, seemed inconsequential, it had a profound effect. In other words, there was an extreme sensitivity to initial conditions.

A more colorful and useful (if explaining the concept to clients) description of extreme sensitivity is the butterfly effect: the notion that a butterfly flapping its wings today in Hong Kong can decide the difference between a beautiful weekend and a hurricane in Miami a month later.

Thirty years after Lorenz's original work, meteorologists' research facilities, with vast resources, including the latest supercomputers continuously crunching close to a million equations, can predict with useful accuracy up to only a week ahead. Even if the world's weather prognosticators could blanket the world at one-foot intervals with 100 percent accurate sensors measuring temperature, humidity, and any other desired input every 60 seconds, they couldn't accurately predict rain or sun in New Orleans one month later. The butterfly effect is too powerful. This is an important lesson to keep in mind as you read about chaos and the capital markets.

Chaos and the Capital Markets

Historically, investment theory has been based on the assumption that, for the most part, financial market relationships are linear. As an example, *Quantitative Techniques for Financial Analysts*, by Jerome L. Valentine and Edmund A. Mennis and published in 1980 by the Research Foundation of CFA Institute, in discussing regressions said, "A truly nonlinear regression is seldom encountered in actual practice." However, even then there were doubters.

---

[26] If you do not know what a vacuum tube is, you're disgustingly young, and I'm not going to tell you!
[27] J. Gleick, *Chaos: Making a New Science* (Viking, 1987; republished Penguin, 2008).

Benoit Mandelbrot, one of the original chaologists, suggested in the early 1960s that stock movements were chaotic. More recently, the publication of *Chaos and Order in the Capital Markets* by Edgar Peters focused increasing interest and research on the implications of chaos theory for investment professionals.[28]

Chaos World

Edgar E. Peters provides a simple and credible example to demonstrate how capital markets may very well function as a chaotic system.

Consider, he suggests, a penny stock (i.e., one selling for under $1). If the market was composed only of buyers, the price of the stock would rise only as a function of buyers entering the market. The price of the stock in the future could be calculated by the simple formula:

$$P_{(t+1)} = a * P_t$$

where

P_t = the price at time t

$P_{(t+1)}$ = the price at time $t + 1$

a = the rate the price would rise as a function of demand

To make the case more realistic, Peters adds sellers to the market. The actions of these sellers will tend to reduce the price as a function of P_t^2.

We can now develop a formula that mechanistically determines future stock prices:

$$P_{(t+1)} = a * P_t - a * P_t^2$$
$$= a * P_t^* (1 - P_t)$$

This seems to be a pretty simple world. Let's call it Penny World and investigate how the price of a stock, issued at 30 cents, might vary over time, depending on the single variable a. When $a = 2$:

Time	Price
0	30¢
1	= 2 * 0.3 * (1 − 0.3) = 42¢
2	49¢
3	50¢
4	50¢
5	50¢
100	50¢

Obviously, in this nice clean world, our stock reaches a fair price of 50 cents and stabilizes there.

---

[28]Peters (1996).

World in which $a = 3$:

Time	Price
0	30¢
1	63¢
2	70¢
3	63¢
4	70¢

At this higher growth rate, there is an oscillation between two fair values. When the price reaches 70 cents, the sellers begin to dump. The price drops until it reaches 63 cents, when the buyers jump back in and push it back up to 70 cents.

With very minor changes in the rate function a, the simple world can turn very strange. The equation we developed for Penny World is a form of what is known as the logistic equation. Exhibit 8.9, plotting all of the possible values for our stock for varying values of a, is called a bifurcation diagram.

EXHIBIT 8.9   Bifurcation Diagram for Penny World

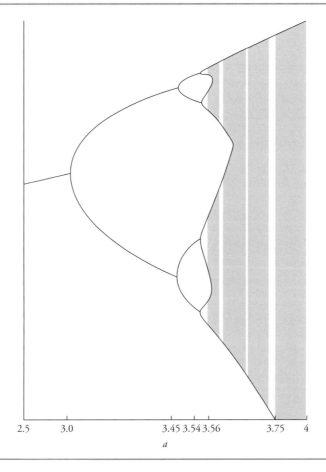

Peters's example demonstrates that it is easy to conceive of feedback mechanisms that would result in chaotic financial markets. The bifurcation diagram is a classic picture of a chaotic system. It is also a powerful demonstration of the impact minute changes in initial conditions may have on future events, even in a simple financial world. His work, along with that of other practitioners and academics, provides strong evidence of chaotic dynamics in the capital markets.

Implications of Chaos in the Capital Markets

Although it is far from an acknowledged fact that capital markets are chaotic systems, the implications of chaotic markets are so significant that the possibility should not be ignored. The implications include:[29]

- Chaotic markets appear to be the rule, not the exception. As demonstrated by Peters's example, complex markets may appear to be random when, in fact, they are following a few simple mathematical rules that incorporate an element of information feedback.
- It is not possible to accurately forecast, for anything but a very short horizon, expected returns and values. Even the most complex and sophisticated of econometric or timing models will fall prey to the same butterfly effect that cripples meteorologists' forecasts.
- Chaotic systems frequently seem to be highly structured and to have regular cycles, only to explode into unpredictable behavior (e.g., October 1987). This is the trap of quasi-periodicity that may lead to false faith in successfully back-tested trading systems.
- Traditional portfolio theory assumes no trends or cycles. However, as chaotic systems are not random, there are also positive implications for our ability to quantify reality:
  - Market return series may be bounded. For example, even if the specific temperature in New Orleans in the summer cannot be predicted, it can be predicted that it will be hot.
  - Previously inexplicable market behavior (i.e., leptokurtic distributions) may become explainable.
  - The array of linear-based analytical tools currently used by investment analysts may be successfully supplemented by nonlinear analytical systems, resulting in improved portfolio performance and/or a better ability to manage client expectations.
- The concepts of efficient markets, value investing, and tactical asset allocation may be consistent with chaos theory.

PARTING COMMENTS

What is a wealth manager to do with all of this theory? The following is from Michael Corning's review, in the July 1994 issue of the *Journal of Financial Planning*, of Edgar Peters's book, *Fractal Market Analysis: Applying Chaos Theory to Investments & Economics*. Michael did such a fine job of answering this question, we close this section with his "Final Thoughts":

> [W]e risk making two types of errors when faced with a new and provocative world view. Type I: We too quickly appropriate a new idea or theory. Type II: We too quickly dismiss a new idea or theory. With Type I errors, we agree without understanding; with

---

[29]James J. Angel, "Implications of Chaos for Portfolio Management," *Journal of Investing* (Summer 1994): 30–35.

Type II, we disagree without appreciating. The former is naive, the latter is insolent. With Type I errors, we are not fully utilizing our critical faculties; with Type II errors, we are forgetting our intuitive capacity. Ignorance is non-market risk. We have an obligation to our clients to diversify it away, and the best way to do that is with an open and critical mind.

RESOURCES

Banz, R. W. 1981. "The Relationship between Return and Market Value of Common Stocks." *Journal of Financial Economics,* Vol. 9, No. 1: 3–18.

Bernstein, Peter L. 2009. *Capital Ideas Evolving.* Hoboken, NJ: John Wiley & Sons.

Ellis, Charles, ed. 1988. *Classics: An Investor's Anthology.* Homewood, IL: Business One Irwin.

Graham, Benjamin, and David Dodd. 2010. *Security Analysis,* 6th edition. New York: McGraw-Hill.

Fama, Eugene, and Kenneth French. 1993. "Common Risk Factors in the Returns of Stocks and Bonds." *Journal of Financial Economics,* Vol. 33: 3–56.

Haugen, Robert. 1999. *The New Finance: The Case against Efficient Markets,* 2nd edition. Upper Saddle River, NJ: Prentice Hall.

Kritzman, Mark. 1994. "What Practitioners Need to Know . . . About Time Diversification." *Financial Analysts Journal,* Vol. 50, No. 1: 14–18.

Kritzman, Mark, and Don Rich. 2002. "The Mismeasurement of Risk." *Financial Analysts Journal,* Vol. 58, No. 3: 91–99.

Malkiel, Burton. 2007. *A Random Walk Down Wall Street: The Time-Tested Strategy for Successful Investing,* 9th edition. New York: W.W. Norton.

Peters, Edgar E. 1996. *Chaos and Order in the Capital Markets: A New View of Cycles, Prices, and Market Volatility,* 2nd edition. Wiley Finance. New York: John Wiley & Sons.

Reilly, Frank J., and Keith Brown. 2008. *Investment Analysis and Portfolio Management,* 9th edition. Cincinnati: South-Western College Publishing.

Siegel, Jeremy. 2007. *Stocks for the Long Run: The Definitive Guide to Financial Market Returns and Long-Term Investment Strategy,* 4th edition. New York: McGraw-Hill.

CHAPTER 9

ASSET ALLOCATION

Not to decide is to decide.

—Gary Helms

To set this chapter in perspective, we begin with a quote from the Introduction to *Global Asset Allocation*, one of the most technically rigorous and comprehensive texts on the subject of asset allocation:

> [A]sset allocation remains more art than science and will probably remain so as long as the models used are only approximations of a reality that is in a constant flux.[1]

Obviously the authors believe in the importance of technical competence, or else why write the book? However, once again the wealth manager is cautioned to become a competent artist.

WHY BOTHER? DETERMINANTS OF PORTFOLIO PERFORMANCE (BHB)

In "Determinants of Portfolio Performance," Brinson, Hood, and Beebower (BHB) (1995) set out to answer the question "What determines portfolio performance?" For their study, the authors used a database of large pension plans. The basic screen for a pension plan's inclusion in the study included:

- A corporate plan with the investment decisions resting solely with the corporation.
- A large asset base.
- Forty quarters of data available for 1974 to 1983.

The screen excluded public and multi-employer plans in order to eliminate plans that might be subject to legislative or legal constraints on the investment managers' activities.

The final data set used for the study included 91 plans ranging in size from $700 million to $3 billion in assets. The plan assets were separated into three asset classes: cash, bonds, and

---

[1]Scott L. Lummer, PhD, CFA, and Mark W. Riepe, "Introduction: The Role of Asset Allocation in Portfolio Management," *Global Asset Allocation* (New York: John Wiley & Sons, 1994), 1–6.

common stock. It was decided that the approximately 8.6 percent of plan assets not falling into these categories (i.e., real estate, venture capital, and private placements) were too small an allocation to be treated separately. They were prorated over the three major asset classes.

As a beginning premise, the authors determined that there were only three decisions that a portfolio manager could make that would have an impact on a portfolio's performance:

1. *Investment policy.* An investor cannot avoid implementing an investment policy. Either implicitly or explicitly there is a policy. Generally referred to as asset allocation, this includes the decision of what asset classes to include and the decision regarding the weights of each selected class.
2. *Timing.* This is the active decision to over- or underweight a specific asset class relative to the manager's long-term (i.e., normal or strategic) allocation. The decision to change weightings could be based on a desire either to increase returns or to decrease risk.
3. *Security selection.* This is the active selection of specific securities within an asset class, such as individual stocks, bonds, mutual funds, exchange-traded funds (ETFs), and so on.

Starting with the investment policy and the overlaying option of implementing timing and security selection strategies, the authors developed a graphic matrix of the decision process.

The authors (BHB) developed a framework for assessing the contribution to return variability of each of these decisions, as depicted in Exhibit 9.1.

EXHIBIT 9.1   Framework for Return Accountability

		Selection	
		Actual	Passive
Timing	Actual	IV. Actual Portfolio Return 9.01%	II. Policy and Timing Return 9.44%
	Passive	III. Policy and Security Selection Return 9.75%	I. Policy Return (Passive Portfolio Benchmark) 10.11%

- Quadrant I represents the impact of the portfolio based on the impact of policy alone computed as the weighted average benchmark return.
- Quadrant II represents the performance of the portfolio based on the impact of the policy and timing decisions. This is computed using the returns on each asset class benchmark weighted by the actual allocation for that time period.
- Quadrant III represents the performance of the portfolio based on the impact of the policy and security selection decisions. This is computed using the normal policy weights for each asset class times the actual return for the asset class each period.
- Quadrant IV represents the performance of the actual portfolio.

The analytical process employed was to run a regression analysis of each of the portfolios against the returns of Quadrants I, II, and III. The final reported results were for the 91 regression series.

The returns for the policy portfolio (I) were calculated assuming that the portfolio funds were invested at the original asset class percentage and passively invested in indexes. The

Shearson Lehman Government Corporate Index was used as the asset class return for bonds, the S&P 500 for stocks, and 30-day Treasury bills for cash. The result of these calculations was the return of the portfolio solely attributable to the policy decision.

The influence on return of the security selection strategy (portfolio III) was determined by running an analysis similar to the one for policy returns, but substituting the portfolio's actual asset class returns for the passive returns. By holding the policy allocations steady (i.e., ignoring the manager's actual timing decisions) the results provided a return measure attributable to the policy and security selection decisions. Subtracting from this result the returns solely attributable to policy yielded a remainder that was the return solely attributable to security selection.

The last calculation (portfolio II) used the index returns for the asset classes but adjusted the allocation percentages to reflect the timing decisions made by the portfolio manager. The result of this analysis was the returns attributable to timing and policy. The timing contribution was isolated by, once again, subtracting the policy contribution.

The results of this process, as shown in the Exhibit 9.1, were interesting. The mean average benchmark return (quadrant I) was 10.11 percent annually. The mean average actual return was 9.01 percent (quadrant IV). By applying the brains and talent of many of the best and brightest of the nation's portfolio managers to actively manage an investment portfolio, the returns were reduced! Active security selection reduced the returns below a passive portfolio by 0.36 percent (quadrant III versus quadrant I), active timing lost 0.67 percent (quadrant II versus quadrant I) and together, the underperformance was 1.03 percent per year. Although not the purpose of the study, these results (as well as those of most more recent studies) should certainly be considered by wealth managers when developing their own philosophy regarding the use of active and passive strategies.

In order to determine the importance of the policy decision, the final analysis was a regression of each portfolio's actual returns against the returns in quadrants I, II, and III in Exhibit 9.1. The R-squareds of the 91 regressions were averaged and the final results were reported as shown in Exhibit 9.2.

EXHIBIT 9.2   Percentage of Return Variation Explained

		Selection	
		Actual	Passive
Timing	Actual	IV. 100.0%	II. 95.3%
	Passive	III. 97.8%	I. 93.6%

As the authors observed, "the results are striking." "Startling" might have been even more descriptive. Over 93 percent of the variation in portfolio returns was attributable to policy (asset allocation). According to BHB, active security selection and timing played minor roles in determining portfolio performance for this group of pension plans incrementally adding only 4.2 percent and 1.7 percent respectively.

The conclusion of the study was:

> *Although [active] investment strategy can result in significant returns, these are dwarfed by the return contributions from investment policy—the selection of asset classes and their normal weights.*

In May/June 1991, Brinson, Singer, and Beebower published "Determinants of Portfolio Performance II: An Update" in the *Financial Analysts Journal*.[2] Based on a study of data from 82 large pension plans for a period between 1977 and 1987, they reconfirmed their earlier research. In the second study they concluded:

> *For our sample of pension plans, active investment decisions by plan sponsors and managers, both in terms of selection and timing, did little to improve performance over the 10-year period from December 1977 to December 1987.*

VALUE OF ASSET ALLOCATION DECISIONS (HEI)

Although no lesser authorities than William Sharpe and Fidelity Investments accept these conclusions,[3] the BHB study is not without its critics. The BHB study is often misquoted as stating that more than 90 percent of return is attributable to the asset allocation decision.[4] Further, the study was limited to a group of large pension funds, which are likely to have less variability in asset allocation than a broader sample of investors. The most cogent criticism was a Frank Russell Research commentary, *The Value of Asset Allocation Decisions*, by Chris R. Hensel, D. Don Ezra, and John H. Ilkiw (HEI), published in March 1990 and republished in the July/August 1991 *Financial Analysts Journal* as "The Importance of the Asset Allocation Decision."[5]

The Russell authors contend that the BHB study started with an inappropriate default portfolio (i.e., one not invested in any capital assets). If, however, a more realistic beginning (or naive) portfolio was selected for analysis, HEI conclude that the determinants of portfolio performance are quite different from BHB.

HEI argues that a reasonable choice for the naive portfolio is not an all-cash portfolio, but one resembling the average asset allocation held by large pension plans. This information is readily available, and it entails little cost or effort to design a policy based on what everyone else is doing. For purposes of HEI, this becomes the Russell naive portfolio.[6]

HEI concludes:

- If an investment in Treasury bills rather than the Russell naive portfolio was selected as a beginning point, the BHB position was correct.
- If the starting point is the Russell naive portfolio, the potential impact of security selection is almost equal to the influence of the specific policy allocation. Both have more influence than the potential attributable to timing.

---

[2]Gary P. Brinson, Brian D. Singer, and Gilbert L. Beebower, "Determinants of Portfolio Performance II: An Update," *Financial Analysts Journal* (May/June 1991).

[3]"It is widely agreed that asset allocation accounts for a large part of the variability in return on a typical investor portfolio."—William Sharpe; "we, like the rest of the industry, believe that 90% of return comes from the asset allocation decision."—Art Lutschaunig, VP, Fidelity Investments.

[4]It is important to note the qualification "variation." William Jahnke in "Asset Allocation Hoax," *Journal of Financial Planning*, February 1997, pointed out that the BHB study is often misinterpreted to state that asset allocation explains 90 percent of returns; it does not. As noted, BHB concludes that 93 percent of the variation in portfolio returns was attributable to policy (asset allocation).

[5]Hensel, Ezra, and Ilkiw (1991).

[6]In fact, the study notes that a simple policy of 60 percent stock and 40 percent bonds would achieve the same results.

- As a result, "Decisions regarding active management (market timing and security selection) can be just as worthy of a sponsor's attention [as the asset allocation decision]."

THE IMPORTANCE OF MANAGING ASSET ALLOCATION—THE PAST DECADE

Research on this important topic continues.[7] In 2000, Ibbotson and Kaplan performed a similar study on mutual funds and pension funds to extend the work of BHB. They asked three questions:

1. How much of the variation in returns across time is explained by asset allocation policy? (This is the same question posed by BHB.)
2. How much of the variation in returns among funds is explained by policy? (This is not posed or examined by BHB, but many have interpreted BHB in this manner.)
3. What portion of return level is explained by asset allocation policy return? (Similarly, this was not posed or examined by BHB, but many have interpreted BHB in this manner.)

Ibbotson and Kaplan concluded that about 90 percent of the variability of returns across time is attributed to policy, about 40 percent of the variability among funds is explained by policy, and about 100 percent of the level of returns is explained by policy.

More recently Xiong, Ibbotson, Idzorek, and Chen (2010) proposed a similar framework to that of HEI in that a portfolio's total return should be decomposed into three components:

1. The market return—essentially the first decision an investor makes is to be in the market (in this study an equally weighted investment in all available mutual funds in a broad mutual fund database was used as the market).
2. The asset allocation policy return in excess of the market return (the decision to make a specific asset allocation other than market weights).
3. The return from active portfolio management.

Using this framework, it is not surprising that Xiong et al. found, using a broad mutual fund database, that the first decision—to invest in the market—is the main driver of the variation in returns. For example, among balanced funds, market movement accounted for 88 percent of variability, asset allocation another 20 percent, and active management about 10 percent (the interaction of these decisions accounts for the fact that the percentages sum to great than 100 percent). The authors conclude that taken together, market movement and asset allocation (the first two decisions of investors) dominate the variation in returns. In a commentary on the results of this and other studies, Ibbotson observes:

> *What percentage of my return comes from my asset allocation policy? This question is very important, but has a fairly trivial answer. Asset allocation policy gives us the passive*

---

[7]In addition to the papers noted, other recent and relevant papers include: Joseph Davis, Francis Kiniary, and Glen Sheay, "The Asset Allocation Debate: Provocative Questions, Enduring Realities," Vanguard Investment Counseling & Research; Richard Ennis, "Parsimonious Asset Allocation," *Financial Analysts Journal* (2009); Yesim Tokat, Nelson Wicas, and Francis Kinniry, "The Asset Allocation Debate: A Review and Reconciliation," *Journal of Financial Planning* (October 2006); Mark Kritzman, "Are Optimizers Error Maximizers?" *Journal of Portfolio Management* (Summer 2006).

return (beta return), and the remainder of the return is the active return (alpha or excess return). The alpha sums to zero across all portfolios (before costs) because on average, managers do not beat the market. In aggregate, the gross active return is zero. Therefore, on average, the passive asset allocation policy determines 100 percent of returns before costs and somewhat more than 100 percent of the return after costs.

Note that here Ibbotson refers to the level of returns in the aggregate—not for individual investors or managers. Further, he concludes that the asset allocation decision does not explain anywhere near 90 percent of the variability of returns; the variability of returns is primarily driven by market movements.

Perhaps the primary takeaway for wealth managers is Idzorek's conclusion in a Morningstar article referencing the prior study, "For aggregate return levels, asset allocation is king."[8]

Research will likely continue in this area and critics will quibble with what percentage of returns or variability is explained, but the influence and acceptance of the original work of BHB is so pervasive that a wealth manager should not ignore the implications. Even the Russell and subsequent studies do not contradict BHB's conclusion that the policy decision is of paramount importance. In fact, it is clear from these studies taken together that the decision to invest in the market coupled with the asset allocation decision explain the vast majority of both return levels and variability.[9]

Assuming wealth managers incorporate at least an element of managing the asset allocation, they must adopt a process to develop allocations appropriate to the client's needs. For those not yet convinced of the necessity of establishing an asset allocation policy, we next briefly consider the alternative.

THE ALTERNATIVE TO A MANAGED ASSET ALLOCATION POLICY

In the management of an investment portfolio, there are three general categories of decisions that influence the portfolio performance after the initial decision to participate in the market:

- Asset allocation
- Security (manager) selection
- Market timing

All other decisions are subsumed by these. All portfolios have policies regarding each of these decisions. Financial planners frequently tell their clients that everyone has an estate plan. A client's failure to execute a will does not eliminate estate planning; it simply substitutes the state's plan for the client's. An asset allocation policy is analogous to an estate plan; by design or by default, all portfolios have a policy. A portfolio without a managed asset allocation

---

[8]Thomas M. Idzorek, "Asset Allocation Is King," *Morningstar Advisor*, April/May 2010.
[9]The market trauma of the Great Recession resulted in numerous articles questioning the validity of asset allocation. One of the most interesting of recent papers addressing this issue is Fred Dopfel, "The New Policy Portfolio, Navigating through Good and Bad Regimes," Barclays Global Investors, *Investment Insights*, September 2009.

policy still has a policy—a randomly determined policy. The question for the wealth manager, then, is whether to design and manage a policy or to let chance design a policy.

A lack of understanding regarding the unavoidability of an allocation policy has led to unfounded concern over the concept of asset allocation. As an example, Bob Clark, one of our profession's most astute media commentators, discussing asset allocation, asked:

> *But what if we're wrong? What if we're positioning our clients in exactly the wrong assets, setting the stage for another debacle that would make limited partnerships seem like pocket change?*[10]

What If Everything Goes Wrong?

The answer to the question is: "It would be terrible!" But it would be wrong to conclude that wealth managers should not make the effort to design reasonable allocations. Failure to allocate is more likely to lead to the disaster envisioned by Bob Clark. The responsibility of wealth managers is not to guarantee future returns but rather to use their experience and knowledge to maximize the probability of achieving the client's goal.

How might investors have fared in the past during bad times had they invested in individual asset classes versus allocation across multiple asset classes? Exhibit 9.3 examines the worst 5-, 10-, and 20-year average rolling returns over the period 1926 to 2009 for U.S. Treasury bills, long-term government bonds, and large company stocks versus a simply allocated portfolio. The results show that an asset allocation, however simple, has indeed been a very effective strategy.

EXHIBIT 9.3   Worst Rolling Period Return, 1926 to 2009

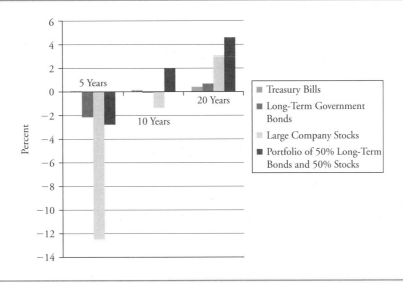

[10]Bob Clark, Editor's Note, *Investment Advisor*, September 1995, 8.

Confusion of the Concept with the Implementation

Some critics of asset allocation confuse the concept with the application. For example, a repeated criticism is that many planners develop asset allocation models based on unsubstantiated input resulting in unrealistic expectations.[11] More specific is the criticism that allocation models are based solely on historical data. As we have discussed and discuss again later, portfolio design should be based on forward-looking expectations, not through the rearview mirror of historical returns. The error is in the selection of the input, not the attempt to manage allocations.

Occasionally, the concept of asset allocation is criticized for ignoring the possibility of global catastrophe. Examples include worldwide nuclear war, a catastrophic virus killing much of the world population, or global economic collapse. Evensky & Katz's implementation of its asset allocation policy does not incorporate these issues, but the fault is the implementation, not the concept of allocation. A wealth manager, haunted by fear of global disaster, can certainly incorporate those nightmares into an allocation policy or manage these risks by other means (e.g., portfolio insurance strategies).

Responding to claims that asset allocation adds no value over equally weighted portfolios, Mark Kritzman in "Defense of Optimization, the Fallacy of 1/N,"[12] Mark Kritzman et al. demonstrate that "optimized portfolios generate superior out-of-sample performance compared with equally weighted portfolios."

Rather obviously, our conclusion is that the only alternative to a managed asset allocation policy is a random asset allocation policy. And as allowing the gods of chance to direct our clients' fiscal lives is not in keeping with professional wealth management, all wealth managers should develop an asset allocation strategy.

ASSET ALLOCATION IMPLEMENTATION STRATEGIES

The balance of this chapter discusses a number of strategies for asset allocation that a wealth manager might consider.

Model Portfolios

Perhaps the simplest solution for the wealth manager is to adopt one of the myriad asset allocation models provided by the purveyors of investment products. One such strategy offers 18 different models ranging from all fixed income to all equity. Reviewed and revised quarterly, the models are clearly delineated by style and asset class allocation. Although the models may have been thoughtfully designed, they still are of limited use for the wealth manager.

Lack of Customization

Wealth managers are professionals, not vendors. They use their expertise and knowledge and make professional judgments. Packaged products will not suffice for their traditional clients. The exception would be the design of model portfolios for employer retirement plans where the wealth manager is providing his expertise for the portfolio design but not providing individualized advice for the investor. Although some models attempt to provide an element

---

[11]Robert Veres, "Apocalypse When," *Investment Advisor*, September 1995, 113–120.
[12]Mark Kritzman, Sebastien Page, and David Turkington, "In Defense of Optimization: The Fallacy of 1/N," *Financial Analysts Journal*, Vol. 66, No. 2 (2010).

of customization by offering many choices, they are still not flexible enough to meet the needs of wealth managers.

Black Box

One of the most frequent criticisms of wealth manager optimization is the use of a complex computer program, frequently referred to as a black box. This pejorative description suggests that the wealth manager is implementing an asset allocation policy without understanding how the allocations were determined. The presumption is that the black box, not the wealth manager, is making the decision. Unfortunately, this is often a valid criticism.

When a wealth manager uses someone else's model, this is often a valid criticism. Instead of using his or her skills to balance the myriad factors necessary to design unique models for clients, the advisor has simply elected to choose from among a limited number of boilerplate products. No matter how sophisticated the thought process that led to the model, from the advisor's perspective, each model is, in effect, the product of a black box. The model developers might briefly describe the global issues influencing their design (i.e., "Bond yields are close to fair value"); however, the advisor has no real feel for the specifics of the model's underlying assumptions (i.e., expected returns, standard deviations, and correlation).

Asset Class Benchmark

Model portfolios are divided into asset classes and, occasionally, styles. If wealth managers elect to use a model portfolio and implement with managers of their own choosing, they must determine how closely their managers match the assumptions of the model. As these assumptions are usually not disclosed, overlaying someone else's model allocation on the wealth management universe of approved managers is as scientific as using the results of the World Cup as a market timing trigger.

Tax Efficiency

In spite of the earlier criticism of many portfolio tax management strategies, there is at least one that always needs to be considered: the use of municipal bonds in a taxable account. Unfortunately, most models do not incorporate even this basic consideration.

Final Thoughts on Third-Party Models

For wealth managers, an asset allocation strategy should be an integral part of their personal wealth management philosophy. Packaged models, no matter how credentialed the creators, are a product. For all of the reasons just noted, they are not an appropriate solution for the wealth manager.

This does not, however, mean that wealth managers should not create their own models. In doing so, they can still address the unique needs of their client base. They will have determined all of the assumptions used in the model's design. They will know what benchmarks were used and they will know when their own models do not meet the needs of a particular client.

Judgmental Intuition

This is an approach that, while acknowledging the necessity of an asset allocation policy, approaches the solution as 100 percent art.

A very well elucidated example was provided by Barry Berlin at a CFA Institute conference on Asset Allocation for Individual Investors.[13] Explaining that his trust company had "toyed" with a black box quantitative approach, they ultimately concluded that the intuition of the experienced staff was a more comfortable and credible strategy.

The company's process is to categorize the U.S. economy into four generic inflation environments—deflation, price stability, disinflation, and rapid inflation. Looking back over the past 100 years, they consider the interaction of inflation and various asset classes during each form of inflation environment.

The investment committee, composed of the most experienced members of the investment staff, meets for several hours twice a year. Based on the belief that the most important decision is to call the "turning points in various asset categories and being in the right place at the right time," the investment committee "simply sift[s] through where we feel the environment will take those assets and arrive at our judgment." As an example, during 1985, the focus was on eight major classes. The target allocations are noted in Exhibit 9.4.

EXHIBIT 9.4   Recommended Asset Allocation

Asset	Possible Range	Current 3- to 5- Year Targets	Prior Targets	
			Jul-85	Jan-85
Reserves	2–30%	6%	4%	3%
Bonds	10–40	24	26	33
Stocks	20–60	45	36	42
Real Estate	5–30	10	14	14
Oil & Gas Partnerships	0–15	1	4	4
Venture Capital	0–10	2	2	2
Precious Metals	0–15	5	4	2
Foreign Securities	0–15	7	10	—

Issues with Judgmental Intuition

While wealth management (and the process known as asset allocation) is part art (i.e., judgment and intuition) and part science, it is important not to discount the science part too much. It is difficult to rationally comment on an approach that rejects academic research and quantitative analysis. Some issues to consider with an active judgmental approach are:

- *Reallocating*. The frequency and magnitude of reallocation can result in significant transaction costs and tax consequences.
- *Heuristics*. Without a well-defined underlying policy, an asset allocation model based on judgment and intuition is likely to be significantly influenced in a negative way by all of the

---

[13]At that time CFA Institute was known as the Association for Investment Management and Research (AIMR).

heuristics discussed earlier. For example, representativeness may result in an inappropriate influence by short-term trends (reflected in significant short-term changes in allocations); availability may result in an inappropriate weighting in hot asset classes; and regret, pride, and shame may result in an unfounded defense of intuitive judgment decisions.

- *Liability.* Intuition may be a weak defense for a failed allocation policy. As Trone, Allbright, and Madden emphasize in their book *Procedural Prudence* (SEI, 1991), the primary defense of an investment fiduciary is procedural prudence, not performance. One hundred percent reliance on judgment and intuition fails the test of procedural prudence.

Multiple Scenario Analysis

Multiple scenario analysis (MSA) is an approach familiar to most financial planners. In its simplest form, it is based on projecting a best case and worse case and, from within that range, selecting a "most probable."[14]

This approach is a disciplined method of applying quantitative analysis to problems of uncertainty. The total process is typically divided into six steps:

1. Define investments.
2. Determine starting points.
3. Create future alternatives (scenarios).
4. Forecast returns for each scenario.
5. Assign scenario probabilities.
6. Choose optional portfolios.

Each scenario is an economic projection defined by expectations for major economic factors, such as real gross domestic product (GDP), consumer price index (CPI), short-term interest, rates, term premiums, and risk premiums. Once a scenario has been defined, estimates are made for returns for each asset class. The time horizon for the scenarios spans an economic cycle.

Only after completing this detailed quantitative procedure does the wealth manager begin a judgmental/intuitive overlay. The first step is for each investment committee member to assign a probability to the various scenarios. The first scenario is the average of these weightings. The next step is for each member, using the consensus scenario as a base, to modify the weightings based on current relative asset class returns, the current yield curve, and investor sentiment. The head of the asset allocation committee uses these optional portfolios to arrive at the firm's recommended policy.

An MSA strategy has its own limitations:

- The process of estimating expected returns for one scenario is difficult; estimating multiple scenarios can seem overwhelming.
- In addition to the compounding effect of multiple scenarios on uncertainty, MSA requires an additional series of estimates regarding the probability of each scenario.

---

[14]David R. Rahn, "Implementing and Managing the Investment Asset Allocation Process for the Individual Part 1," in *Asset Allocation for the Individual Investor*, 99–105 (Charlottesville, VA: Institute of Chartered Financial Analysts, 1987); Peter M. Hill, "Global Asset Allocation," in *Global Asset Allocation*, 264–281 (New York: John Wiley & Sons, 1994).

- Although the final overlay of relative market yields, yield curves, and investor sentiment is intended simply as the fine-tuning of a quantitative process, we fear that it is too susceptible to the heuristic problems associated with the judgmental strategy.
- We believe that the detail of the multiple assumptions and the application of economic probabilities results in an unfounded level of confidence in the results.

Mathematical Optimizers

Depending on your orientation, mathematical optimizers are the solution or the problem. The debate, pro and con, occasionally becomes vituperative and is often silly. In almost all cases, the critics of the black box fall into the trap of wanting to kill the messenger. Optimizers are only tools; they are neither good nor bad. The responsibility of the wealth manager is to have an adequate knowledge base to evaluate their efficacy in his or her practice. If the use of optimizers is rejected by the wealth manager, the decision should be based on a rational and prudent analytical process. The decision should not only consider the absolute benefits and disadvantages of an optimizer, but also the benefits and disadvantages of mathematical optimization relative to other alternatives. The benefits of using an optimizer are many:[15]

- They are exact.
- They provide solutions for an infinite number of efficient portfolios.
- They offer a convenient structure for integrating a client's goals and constraints.
- They provide a mechanism for controlling portfolio exposure to various components of risk.
- They allow the wealth manager to determine the portfolio's sensitivity to changes in expectations of returns, risks, and correlations.
- They assist in the design of a procedurally prudent policy.

Some researchers point out that optimization implies a scientific right and wrong. This arrogance of absolutes is at the core of most objections to optimization:

- Optimizers present a misleading exactness. The inputs are subject to significant statistical errors, and the mathematical process of optimization maximizes the errors.
- The conclusions of optimizers are frequently counterintuitive and occasionally downright stupid.

Other less fundamental and more operational objections include:

- Optimizers are difficult to use and require substantial amounts of quantitative input.
- They require a significant knowledge of quantitative concepts.

Those objecting to the use of optimizers are, for the most part, objecting to a technology that they cannot, do not, or have not bothered to understand. Similar objections were made to the use of the first computers (and probably to the abacus and slide rule). The term GIGO (garbage in, garbage out) predated optimizers, but the concept is the same. Even the best

---

[15]Richard O. Michaud, "The Markowitz Optimization Enigma: Is 'Optimized' Optimal?" *Financial Analysts Journal* (January/February, 1989): 31–40.

technology cannot turn garbage input into good output (with the exception of some recent environmental technology designed to turn refuse into energy). But the villain is the input (and inputter), not the technology. Equally troubling, those objecting to the use of optimizers fail to suggest a better alternative. Because we believe the pros outweigh the cons, we discuss portfolio optimization extensively in the next chapter.

PARTING COMMENTS

The weight of the evidence seems clear: The decision to invest in the market and in which asset classes is a main driver of investment performance. The asset allocation decision cannot be taken lightly. The wealth manager must develop a process by which an asset allocation is fitted to the unique needs (return and risk) of each client. This process is likely to include aspects that are part art and part science.

RESOURCES

Brinson, Gary P., L. Randolph Hood, and Gilbert Beebower. 1995. "Determinants of Portfolio Performance." *Financial Analysts Journal* (July/August 1986; reprinted January/February 1995): 133–138.

Gibson, Roger. 2007. *Asset Allocation*, 4th edition. New York: Irwin.

Hensel, Chris R., D. Don Ezra, and John H. Ilkiw. 1991. "The Importance of the Asset Allocation Decision." *Financial Analysts Journal* (July/August): 65–72.

Ibbotson, Roger G. 2010. "The Importance of Asset Allocation." *Financial Analysts Journal* (March/April): 18–20.

Ibbotson, Roger G., and Paul D. Kaplan. 2000. "Does Asset Allocation Policy Explain 40, 90, or 100 Percent of Performance?" *Financial Analysts Journal* (January/February): 26–33.

Xiong, James X., Roger G. Ibbotson, Thomas M. Idzorek, and Peng Chen. 2010. "The Equal Importance of Asset Allocation and Active Management." *Financial Analysts Journal* (March/April): 22–30.

CHAPTER 10

PORTFOLIO OPTIMIZATION

Any security-specific selection decision is preceded either implicitly or explicitly by an asset allocation decision.

—Scott Lummer and Mark Riepe

Chapter 9, "Asset Allocation," considered a number of strategies that a wealth manager might use to develop an asset allocation model. We believe that an appropriate strategy is the thoughtful and knowledgeable use of mathematical optimizers.

We recognize and agree with much of the criticism directed at the black boxes. The software available for wealth managers generates projections 5, 10, or even 20 years into the future, carried to the fifth decimal place, with probability measures to the tenth decimal place. This illusion of precision is clearly ludicrous. Any wealth manager who unquestioningly accepts the allocations recommended by an optimizer is likely to be a threat to clients' financial well-being.

The solution, however, is not to default to an inferior strategy, but rather to recognize that good optimization is a blend of art and science. By "art," we mean the wealth manager's use of professional judgment, common sense, and intuition. Integrating complexities, such as parametric quadratic programming with the uncertainties of future events, is not an exercise in pure science. In fact, art, not science, may be the predominant factor. However, acknowledging this reality does not excuse a slipshod understanding of the academic and technical aspects of optimization. Instead, it demands a solid grasp of the elements that drive the analysis. It is only by understanding these issues that wealth managers can know when and how to apply their art.

This chapter addresses the optimization topics that are most important to the wealth manager:

- Optimizer inputs
- Asset class constraints
- Sensitivity analysis
- Efficient portfolio selection
- Rebalancing
- Downside risk

OPTIMIZER INPUTS

The wealth manager should remember that we

> *cannot depend on strict mathematical expectations since the basis for making such calculations does not exist; and that it is our innate urge to activity which makes the wheels go round, our rational selves choosing between the alternatives as best we can, but falling back for our motive on whim or sentiment or chance.*[1]

This sobering quote reflects the feelings of many advisors. It is our professional responsibility to concentrate on the "as best we can" while minimizing "whim or sentiment or chance." To ignore all efforts to rationally determine allocations is defaulting 100 percent to chance. To rely solely on judgment and intuition is to rely on whim and sentiment. In doing the "best we can," how do we develop input for our optimizer?

Mean-variance optimization (MVO) requires the wealth manager to make a decision regarding the investment time horizon and estimates for each asset class included in the portfolio:

- Expected return.
- Expected standard deviation.
- Expected correlation with every other asset class.

Time Horizon

The time horizon will affect the wealth manager's estimate of expected returns and risk. Estimates of expected return and standard deviation should match the time horizon outlined in an investor's investment policy statement (IPS). For most wealth manager clients, the investment portfolio is expected to remain largely intact for many, many years (e.g., for the balance of the client's life). Therefore, from a purely academic perspective, a period of 10, 20, 30, or even more years might be appropriate. It is generally difficult to estimate return behavior over short time horizons in any case; and MVO is incompatible theoretically and practically with short time horizons. A common and reasonable approach is to use annual returns—that is, a one-year return interval. The return interval (i.e., the period over which returns are analyzed) should not be confused, however, with the time horizon (i.e., the sum of the return intervals).

Mean-variance optimization assumes long time horizons (i.e., many return intervals), which under certain conditions makes standard deviation a reasonable measure of volatility. For many investors, however, volatility is a schizophrenic concept. When markets are going up, clients have an infinite time horizon. When markets drop, they have a one-day horizon. For example:

- On Black Monday, October 19, 1987, the stock market lost over 20 percent of its value in one day.
- During Black Week, starting October 6, 2008, the stock market lost over 20 percent of its value in a week.

It was the rare investor who looked at his or her portfolio and said, "Looks pretty good compared to 10 years ago!" Most investors lamented, "Oh! What a disaster—I lost 20 percent since Friday!"

---

[1] Frankfurter and Phillips (1994).

The fact is that investors care not only about the value of their portfolio at the end of some time horizon, but also about the path that portfolio takes to its final destination, whatever that might be! As a result, standard deviation is not a complete measure of risk for most clients. It ignores the fact that the portfolio could follow some pretty miserable paths *within* the horizon. Within-horizon risk is the risk that the portfolio might fall in value below some critical level before the end of the time horizon. From a psychological perspective, that critical level almost always changes over time; it grows as the portfolio grows.

Realistically, five years is at the outer limit of a client's psychological commitment to the investment market. It is also long enough to encompass most economic cycles, hence our five-year mantra. As a result, we estimate annual returns that can be expected over a five-year time horizon. It is important to note that we still estimate standard deviation of one-year return intervals to match the interval of the return estimate. One may be tempted to estimate the standard deviation of the average return over five years. Don't do this! The resulting standard deviation will be dramatically lower, and the optimizer will recommend portfolios that are far too aggressive for our behavioral clients. Focusing on annualized measures of standard deviation is theoretically correct, and it works.

EXAMPLE 10.1   The Five-Year Mantra and Stock Market Crashes

Soon after the market debacle in October 1987, Harold met with each of his clients for a session of comfort. He had (and still has) no idea why the market collapsed so precipitously, but he believed that it was a nonevent for his clients. He and his colleagues remained confident that their clients were well invested and, except for rebalancing, they made no changes in their clients' portfolios. The purpose of the meetings was to let their clients know that they were aware of their concern but that their investments remained on course. Clients could ignore the frenetic headlines and could continue with their lives and sleep soundly.

For the first few clients Harold met with, he reminded them of their long time horizon and five-year mantra and said, "Look how much more you have than five years ago." They replied, "Five years ago! Look where I was last Friday!" After that, Harold changed his presentation. He did discuss their long time horizon and the firm's five-year mantra, but added, "Let's put this in a little more perspective than just a few days or months. Look where you were only one year ago." Not one client objected. Although not happy with having seen their portfolios drop, they responded to Harold's framing. Harold also reminded them that AT&T was still in business and tourists were still visiting Disney World and taking pictures with Sony cameras. His clients owned shares of those companies, along with thousands of others, and they were all still in business. The result was that all of his clients recognized that the financial world was not quite as terrible as the headlines trumpeted. One year is an emotionally credible time frame for risk, whereas five years is not. Clients do not think in terms of five-year standard deviations.

Since then, this exercise has become an important part of Harold's presentation in the aftermath of the stock market declines in the early 2000s and in 2008.

Return Inputs

There are innumerable ways of estimating expected returns, from dart boards to Ouija boards; however, the most common are:

- Historical experience.
- Real rates of return.
- Discounted cash flow estimates.
- Risk premium approach.

Historical Experience

Basing expected returns on historical returns is probably the most commonly employed technique. In its simplest form, the assumption made is that future returns will resemble past returns. There are a number of problems with this approach. One must decide what period to include in the historical series. Some practitioners suggest that the longest available series should be used, as it will span the maximum number of different kinds of cycles.[2] Others argue that long series include periods that do not reflect major structuring changes in the economy and thereby include misleading information. This logic, however, can lead to seductive reasoning. For example, prior to the bursting of the technology bubble in the early 2000s, many market pundits eschewed historical measures of earnings growth, arguing that the so-called new economy had rendered old valuation models obsolete and unnecessarily pessimistic. The new economy, however, was subject to the same laws of economics as the old economy. Macroeconomists have also argued that new Federal Reserve structures and policies insulate us against the recurrence of another Great Depression. During the global financial crisis of 2008, though, we experienced severe declines in global equity and real estate markets that triggered the collapse of major financial and industry institutions. It shook the very foundations of our economy and financial system. So although historical aberrations may appear unlikely in more sanguine times, historical returns over long time horizons provide the wealth manager useful perspective.

Historical returns over short time horizons are very sensitive to the choice of starting date. For example, consider a wealth manager on January 1, 2010, using the following historical information from Ibbotson's database of large company stocks in Exhibit 10.1.

EXHIBIT 10.1 Annually Compounded Rates of Return from Large Company Stocks

Period	Average Annual Return
1926–2009	9.8%
1954–2009	10.6
1959–2009	9.5
1964–2009	9.5
1969–2009	9.4
1974–2009	10.5

---

[2]Proponents of "long horizons" take comfort in them and tend to forget that no matter how long the horizon, when using domestic return data they are using a sample of one. As an example, pre–World War II German investors would have felt equally comfortable with their country's long return history.

EXHIBIT 10.1 (Continued)

Period	Average Annual Return
1979–2009	11.5
1984–2009	10.4
1989–2009	9.2
1994–2009	7.6
1999–2009	2.8
2004–2009	2.1
5-Year Rolling Returns (1926–2009)	
High	28.6
Low	−12.5
10-Year Rolling Returns (1926–2009)	
High	20.0
Low	−1.4
20-Year Rolling Returns (1926–2009)	
High	17.9
Low	3.1

Source: Ibbotson SBBI 2010 Classic Yearbook. © Morningstar.

As you can see from Exhibit 10.1, the annually compounded rate of return period depends on the time period chosen, whether looking at annual average returns, five-year rolling returns, 10-year rolling returns, or even 20-year rolling returns. In fact, if you had constructed this chart a year earlier, some of the most recent five-year and 10-year returns would have been negative. These figures demonstrate the difficulty of using MVO for short time horizons. Based on this information, what return should our wealth manager use as an input for large company stocks in an optimizer? You can also see that the range of annualized returns decreases as the time horizon increases. Fortunately, we do not need to limit the backward-looking time frame used to estimate future return. That is, even though our forward-looking time horizon is five years, we are still attempting to estimate annualized compound returns, and we can draw on a longer historical time series to estimate return. Increasing the time horizon decreases the range of annualized returns, which allows us to more realistically estimate our expected return (i.e., determine one that is less sensitive to our starting point).

Overall, Exhibit 10.1 demonstrates the problem of using simple historical projections. Extrapolation of historical returns assumes that return series are stable. Unfortunately, they are not stable. Research to date suggests that simple historical projections do not seem to offer an acceptable solution for return projection. Many wealth managers, however, use long-term averages as a useful frame of reference to establish bounds of reasonableness when implementing other methods. Moreover, historical averages provide a foundation to implement the risk premium approach discussed later.

Real Rates of Return

For long periods, real rate of returns (i.e., nominal returns less inflation) have been more consistent than total returns. However, for short-term projections (e.g., five years), the problems associated with historical returns still apply. Exhibit 10.2 is similar to Exhibit 10.1, but reflects real rates of return—that is, returns adjusted for inflation.

EXHIBIT 10.2 Annually Compounded Real Rates of Return from Large Company Stocks

Period	Average Annual Return
1926–2009	6.6%
1954–2009	6.6
1959–2009	5.3
1964–2009	5.0
1969–2009	4.7
1974–2009	5.8
1979–2009	7.4
1984–2009	7.2
1989–2009	6.2
1994–2009	5.0
1999–2009	0.3
2004–2009	−0.6

Source: Ibbotson SBBI 2010 Classic Yearbook. © Morningstar.

For longer-term projections (e.g., capital needs analysis) where the time horizon may be 20 or 30 years, the use of historical real rates of return might be a viable option.

Discounted Cash Flow Estimates

A frequent method of estimating the expected return for dividend-paying asset classes is the single-stage Gordon growth model (GGM). According to the GGM, the expected return on an asset is equal to its dividend yield plus its long-term expected growth rate, or $E(r) = Div_1/P_0 + g$ where Div_1 is next year's expected dividend, P_0 is the current stock price, and g is the long-term expected growth rate. To be sure, analysts' earnings estimates vary dramatically on an individual stock and by implication the same is true for growth rates.[3] So the single-stage GGM is very crude for estimating expected return for an individual stock.

Much of its noise, however, is canceled out over many stocks. Cornell, Hirshleifer, and James advocate applying this approach to the constituent stocks of the S&P 500 that pay a dividend of at least 3 percent (which is most of them) to estimate an expected return on large-capitalization stocks.[4]

---

[3]See, for example, Dreman and Berry (1995).

[4]Bradford Cornell, John I. Hirshleifer, and Elizabeth P. James, "Estimating the Cost of Equity Capital," *Contemporary Finance Digest*, Vol. 1, No. 1 (1997): 5–26; O. Blanchard, "Movements in the Equity Premium," *Brookings Papers on Economic Activity*, Vol. 75, No. 2 (1993): 75–118.

Risk Premium Approach

Investment theory says that investors demand returns for taking risk. If investors can earn 5 percent from a Treasury bill (T-bill), they are unlikely to invest in a stock with an expected return of only 5 percent. As different assets expose investors to varying levels of risk, the extra returns associated with these investments vary with their risk. These extra returns are referred to as risk premiums. Roger Ibbotson and Rex Sinquefield conducted the original research, and Ibbotson Associates is the primary proponent.[5] Exhibit 10.3 is a graphic description of their "building blocks" approach.

EXHIBIT 10.3   Building Blocks

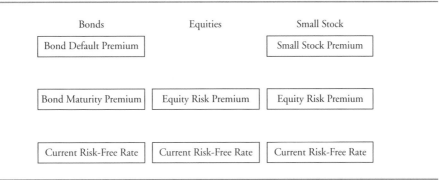

Source: Roger Ibbotson and Rex Sinquefield, "Stocks, Bonds, Bills, and Inflation: Simulations of the Future (1976–2000)," *Journal of Business*, Vol. 49, No. 3 (July 1976); *Ibbotson SBBI 2010 Classic Yearbook.* © Morningstar.

Historical Risk Premium—Theory

The building blocks begin with historical risk premiums. The assumption underlying this strategy is that not only do investors demand incremental return for additional risk, but their expectation of what the incremental return should be is determined by past incremental returns. Therefore, past incremental returns (i.e., the derived risk premiums from the Ibbotson/Sinquefield research) can serve as the basis for estimating future return expectations.

This historical benefit for taking extra risk (i.e., the historical risk premiums) is calculated by subtracting the risk-free return from the asset class return. In a simplified form, the three major risk premiums are calculated as follows (using U.S. Treasury bills as the risk-free rate):

$$\text{Equity Risk Premium} = \text{Equity Returns} - \text{T-Bill Returns}$$

$$\text{Maturity Premium} = \text{T-Bond Returns} - \text{T-Bill Returns}$$

$$\text{Default Premium} = \text{Corporate Bond Returns} - \text{T-Bond Returns}$$

The small stock premium is the difference between small-capitalization and large-capitalization equity returns. Using the building block strategy, future expected returns are determined by adding the historical risk premium to the current risk-free return:

$$\text{Expected Return}_{\text{Asset Class A}} = \text{Historical Risk Premium}_{\text{Asset Class A}} + \text{Current Risk-Free Rate}$$

---

[5]More recently, Dimson, Marsh, and Staunton (2006) have examined the global equity risk premium in 37 different countries over a longer 105-year time horizon that dates back to 1900.

Current Risk-Free Rate

It is important to use current rather than historical yields for the risk-free rate because current yields are market driven and forward looking. The usual default for risk-free returns is the T-bill rate. Although an appropriate standard for determining historical risk premiums, it may not be the factor used in building forecasted expected returns. Instead, the Treasury yield curve serves as the basis for the risk-free rate. The risk-free rate used as the first element of the Ibbotson building block is the return on a zero coupon Treasury bond with a maturity equal to the optimization time horizon. The basis for this choice is quite logical. If the time horizon is five years, it is reasonable to consider a five-year zero coupon T-bond as risk-free because zero coupon Treasury bonds eliminate the credit and reinvestment risk over the defined time horizon. That's the theory.

A caveat is in order, however. Here's some art. Most zero coupon Treasuries (with the exception of three-month T-bills) are significantly less liquid than their coupon-bearing counterparts. As a result, their yields reflect an illiquidity premium and are hence not truly risk-free. Wealth managers need to balance the trade-off between the reinvestment-rate risk of coupon-bearing Treasuries with the illiquidity risk of zero coupon Treasuries. The choice of Treasury (T-bill versus T-bond) also affects our choice of arithmetic versus geometric returns, as we discuss later.

If the wealth manager uses real expected returns in the analysis, like those in Exhibit 10.2, then it is appropriate to use a real risk-free rate. The best measure of the risk-free rate comes from Treasury inflation-protected securities (TIPS) yields. These inflation-protected securities increase the nominal yield paid to investors as inflation increases, thereby protecting their real purchasing power. Because these yields are market-driven and forward-looking, they offer an advantage over historical measures of the real risk-free rate.

Once the risk-free rate has been determined, it would seem that the forecasted expected return can be calculated by simply adding it to the historical risk premium. Not so fast. The earlier discussion was purposefully titled "Historical Risk Premium—*Theory.*" Now we have to address the art.

Historical Risk Premium—Art

Ibbotson's development of the historical risk premiums to be used in building block calculations is an excellent example of the intelligent application of investment art.

In theory, the historical return series would be the longest available with good data. For bonds, this period is over 80 years. However, Ibbotson notes that some asset classes (including bonds) have undergone significant structural changes during the past 80 years. For example, the U.S. fixed income market was subject to an unprecedented structural change in 1979 when the Federal Reserve formally shifted its policy to managing the money supply instead of interest rates. Unfortunately, shortening the series reduces the statistical validity of the analysis. The solution (the art) to balancing the need for a statistically significant series, and yet accounting for the structural change in the bond market, was to begin the analysis in 1970 (a little before the structural shift) and use a monthly rather than an annual series.

Another example of an artful overlay on science is the strategy used to develop an appropriately long historical series for calculating a small company premium. Because the benchmark (the Russell 2000) is relatively new, Ibbotson developed a hypothetical historical return series by applying a size premium to existing large company market data going back to the 1920s. Eugene Fama and Kenneth French followed a different approach and tracked the return of small stocks back to 1963 by separating them from large stocks.[6]

A more recent example supporting our contention that wealth management is 90 percent art is from Ibbotson's 1991 *Forecast Edition*. The following is a description of how the analysts handled the fact that without modification their theoretical model would have resulted in strange results.

> *Historically, the last observation of the annual real riskless rate has been used as the starting value in the . . . equation to generate this forecast. However, applying this method in the unusual interest rate environment of late 1991 achieved nonsensical results for the forecast period. Nominal rates plunged in 1991, reverting to a level near their historical mean of 3.75 percent. Because inflation rates were relatively stable, it is reasonable to assume that real rates plunged in similar fashion, to a level near their historical mean of 0.5 percent. Applying the year-end estimates instead of the actual real rates observed over the course of the year results in a more meaningful forecast.[7]*

Obviously, the selection of specific time series, selection of differing compounding periods, and construction of hypothetical series requires many assumptions based on judgment and intuition. The goal, however, is to reduce the estimation error in the results of the final estimations. It is the responsibility of the wealth manager to understand what these assumptions are and to decide whether to accept the conclusions they lead to.

Finally, it is important to note that the prospective risk premium in the marketplace, although unobservable, likely changes over time. The most recent example of this phenomenon is the financial crisis of 2008. Fearing the collapse of the financial system and the severe economic contraction, investors became highly risk averse and gravitated toward safe investments like U.S. Treasuries. As a result, the yield spread on investment grade corporate bonds (i.e., corporate bond yields less Treasury yields of similar duration) widened to almost 600 basis points by the end of 2008, compared to 200 basis points earlier in that year. As investors' tolerance for risk changes over time, so does the expected risk premium. However, Ibbotson shows that changes in the realized equity risk premium are random from one year to the next, suggesting that changes in the risk premium are difficult to predict.[8] The artful wealth manager may nonetheless choose to adjust the historical risk premium upward during times of financial distress and downward during more halcyon days.

We find both discounted cash flow and risk premium strategies to be credible alternatives to relying exclusively on historical returns to estimate expected return (although historical returns provide a nice reference point for checks of reasonableness). Recognizing that our resources are limited, one may elect to leverage off of the work of Ibbotson Associates and other respected vendors of economic data. Wealth managers can then accumulate estimates from other sources in which they have confidence,[9] and apply art by occasionally adjusting the experts' estimates. If adjustments are in order, we recommend applying only downward adjustments to the building block estimates. It is worth going the extra mile trying to

---

[6]Their seminal work is Fama and French (1993), but subsequent research has substantiated their finding that small stocks exhibit a risk premium in their returns in markets around the world.

[7]Ibbotson Associates, *Stocks, Bonds, Bills, and Inflation, 1991, Quarterly Market Report: Forecast Edition 1992–2011* (Chicago: Ibbotson Associates, 1992), 3–4.

[8]*Ibbotson Stocks, Bonds, Bills, and Inflation Classic Yearbook*, 2009, 100.

[9]For example, Value Line, Wilson, and Callan.

accurately estimate expected return, because William Ziemba estimates that errors in expected return are roughly 10 times more important than errors in standard deviation and 20 times more important than errors in covariances.[10] Michael Best and Robert Grauer demonstrate that a small increase in the expected return of one asset class can force half of the assets from the portfolio.[11] In any case, we recommend a sensitivity analysis to make final adjustments, which we discuss later.

Arithmetic and Geometric Return

The last issue to consider in the building block strategy is the use of arithmetic versus geometric returns. Arithmetic returns are based on simple averages by summing the individual returns over the time horizon and dividing by the number of periods. They ignore the fact that returns compound from one period to the next. Geometric returns, in contrast, take into account that wealth accumulates over time by allowing individual returns to compound. Geometric returns are lower than arithmetic returns whenever returns are not constant.

It would be disingenuous to suggest that the profession speaks with one voice on this issue, and we contrast arithmetic and geometric returns more fully in Chapter 7 ("Mathematics of Investing"). In our review, however, the most convincing case is presented by Hughson, Stutzer, and Yung.[12] They note that compounding returns produces positively skewed distributions of ending wealth (that is, a few very large values combined with many more moderate values). Compounding arithmetic returns exacerbates this skewness and the problem grows worse as the time horizon increases. Median ending values are more realistic representations of actual outcomes and are given by geometric returns. Therefore, using geometric returns is a more conservative and realistic approach.

Summary

The argument in favor of the building block strategy is that, by combining a historical risk premium and the current risk-free rate, it will:

- Account for current market conditions.
- Implicitly include the economic expectations of investors.
- Implicitly include forecasts of economists and financial analysts, as their forecasts are reflected in the building block input.
- Correct for shifts in market fundamentals.
- Correct for market anomalies.

The result will not be a perfect point estimate of future returns but rather a consensus forecast that reflects what the market expects.

---

[10]William Ziemba, *The Stochastic Programming Approach to Asset, Liability, and Wealth Management* (Charlottesville, VA: Research Foundation of CFA Institute, 2003).

[11]Michael Best and Robert Grauer, "On the Sensitivity of Mean-Variance-Efficient Portfolio to Changes in Asset Means: Some Analytical and Computational Results," *Review of Financial Studies*, Vol. 4, No. 2 (1991): 315–342.

[12]Eric Hughson, Michael Stutzer, and Chris Yung, "The Misuse of Expected Returns," *Financial Analysts Journal*, Vol. 62, No. 6 (November/December 2006): 96.

Standard Deviations

The wealth manager must also estimate standard deviations and correlations. Frequently, the estimates of standard deviations are sloughed off based on the belief that, unlike returns, they are generally consistent over time and a wealth manager needs to use only a simple historical projection. This simple assumption is questionable. Exhibit 10.4 shows that the realized rolling 60-month standard deviation for large company stocks, small company stocks, and long-term government bonds is highly variable.

EXHIBIT 10.4   Rolling 60-Month Standard Deviations, 1930–2009

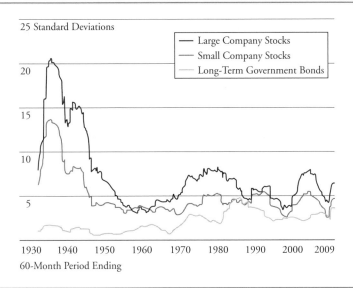

Source: © 2011 Morningstar. All rights reserved. Used with permission.

Studies show that volatility tends to cluster through time.[13] That is, high-volatility periods tend to be followed by other high-volatility periods, and similarly for low-volatility periods. Several methods exist to address this phenomenon. For example, a division at MSCI that is now known as RiskMetrics developed a model that places more weight on recent observations.[14] One can implement a variation of this approach by starting with standard deviations over the past 10 years. These longer-term volatility measures may then be adjusted upward with more recent three-year and five-year standard deviations. When in doubt, it is prudent to assume an asset class will be more volatile as opposed to less.

A more crude, but related, ad hoc approach is to start with the historical time series and eliminate inappropriate periods. The danger of this approach is that the wealth manager may be tempted to delete observations that appear inappropriate but in fact deserve recognition. For example, many analysts at the beginning of 2007 believed that equity markets were structurally more stable than historical returns would suggest. That year, large company stocks fell by almost 19 percent and by 37 percent the following year.

---

[13]See, for example, Drost and Nijman (1993) for a listing of references of studies within various markets.
[14]See Calverley, Meader, Singer, and Staub (2007) for more details.

Other Issues

Another problem with historical series is that they may not accurately measure real volatility. The most obvious example is real estate. Most real estate return indexes are appraisal based. The nature of the appraisal process results in a smoothing of changes in valuations. Volatility between appraisal dates is not incorporated. As a result, the real estate indexes suggest a low volatility that contradicts observable market behavior. In other words, the standard deviation of real estate, based on traditional real estate indexes, seems absurdly low. This phenomenon also applies to other asset classes, such as private equity, venture capital, and some hedge funds that invest in illiquid assets. These investments are subject to a similar appraisal process that artificially deflates their volatility measures.[15]

Renato Staub makes the analogy of a bat flying through a dark tunnel. You may see where the bat enters the tunnel, and you may see where the bat exits the tunnel.[16] Based on those observations, it may appear that the bat's flight path was relatively straight. More likely, however, the bat's flight within the tunnel was characterized by many ups and downs. Andrew Conner shows that ignoring the impact of the appraisal process associated with private equity and hedge funds negatively affects asset allocation recommended by an optimizer.[17] Specifically, much of the perceived diversification benefits associated with these asset classes is attributable to this appraisal process, and the optimizer will overly allocate to these asset classes.

EXAMPLE 10.2   Volatility of Real Estate

Harold attended an Ibbotson seminar many years ago. The second day of the seminar discussed input projections for an optimization program. When considering the asset category of real estate, a long discussion ensued regarding the historical standard deviation of real estate. The gist of the discussion was that, as noted earlier, real estate prices used in developing the historical index data were based on institutional sources. Institutional data is based on appraisals, and appraisals tend to have relatively low variance over time. Further, in bear markets, major holders of institutional real estate, such as insurance companies, tend to hold on to real estate; hence the real variation in market value is unlikely to be reflected in the historical data. At the conclusion of this detailed explanation, Professor Ibbotson recommended that the standard deviation of real estate should "be at least doubled, and possibly tripled!"

Harold was stunned! Until then, he had been careful to refine his projections, frequently to two decimal places, believing that somehow he could generate extremely sound, if not totally accurate, allocation models. Now, here was one of the world's most respected experts telling not only him, but a roomful of world-class investment managers responsible for billions of dollars, that they should take one of the major input criteria for a very major asset class and arbitrarily double or even triple it! From that time on he became a believer in the importance of professional art over science in the implementation of wealth management.

---

[15]See, for example, Andrew Conner, 2007, "Asset Allocation Effects of Adjusting Assets for Stale Pricing," *Journal of Alternative Investments*, Vol. 6, No. 3 (2007): 42–52.
[16]Renato Staub, "Capital Market Expectations," UBS White Paper, February 2005.
[17]Conner, "Asset Allocation Effects."

Correlations

Correlations are no more consistent or easier to project than standard deviations. Exhibit 10.5 shows that the correlation of large company stocks with long-term government bonds can be positive or negative, and significantly so in either direction. Like standard deviations, correlations are unstable, which means that covariances are also unstable.

EXHIBIT 10.5 Rolling 60-Month Correlation between Large Company Stocks and Long-Term Treasuries, 1930–2009

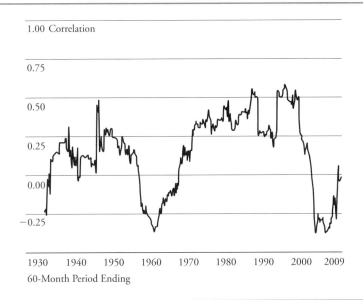

Moreover, correlations are related to the volatility and direction of security markets. As Mark Kritzman points out, when U.S. and non-U.S. equity markets produce returns greater than one standard deviation above the mean, their correlation is a negative 17 percent. By contrast, when these markets produce returns more than one standard deviation below the mean, their correlation is a positive 76 percent.[18] Unfortunately, this phenomenon suggests that diversification fails us when we need it most (i.e., in bear markets).[19]

Harry Markowitz, the father of portfolio theory, recognizes that correlations tend toward one during market crises. He disagrees, however, that diversification fails just when you need it. In his words,

> *If diversification is of little use during crises, then concentrated portfolios should do perfectly well. Consider concentrated portfolios during 2008—their performance clearly depended on the areas in which they were concentrated . . . if a portfolio was*

---

[18]See Kritzman (2009).

[19]Chow, Kritzman, and Lowry (1999) develop a procedure to score historical time periods according to their level of unusualness, which takes into account not just the asset classes' volatilities but also their typical interaction with each other.

concentrated in AIG, Citigroup, General Motors, or the financial or auto industries generally, the result would have been tragic.[20]

So what is the wealth manager to do? One option is to use the correlations that exist in turbulent markets to stress-test our optimized portfolio to see how the portfolio may behave in turbulent times. Alternatively, one can weight volatilities and correlations from turbulent and stable market conditions based on the wealth manager's expectations of turbulence over the time horizon. Because volatility tends to cluster through time, turbulence is something the wealth manager may reasonably be able to estimate.

One can implement a variation of this approach by blending correlations over the past 10 years with emphasis on correlations over the past three and five years. When in doubt, it is prudent to assume that asset classes will be more, rather than less, correlated. For example, because active international managers tend to be more correlated with domestic active managers than historical index correlations would suggest, it is wise to increase the correlations between domestic and international equities. Typically, the adjustment is about a 10 percent increase (e.g., from a correlation of 0.6 to 0.7).[21] On the bright side, errors in estimating correlations are less severe than errors in estimating expected return.[22]

Caveats

Some wealth managers may be tempted to use mutual fund performance data as input for their optimization. Don't! Phil Wilson, who has an excellent database of historical individual fund and manager performance, says,

> *Optimizing among managers of one asset class will generally result in the selection of the manager with the highest return since the managers will all have a very high positive correlation to each other. Reporting the expected returns of a portfolio comprising the actual managers rather than the surrogate indices may result in high expectations and negative surprises. If the benchmark return for a surrogate index is 14 percent and the manager is expected to return 16 percent, the investor may be disappointed if the actual return is 14 percent when in fact that is the more likely return. Remember that the actual performance of the manager is relatively inconsequential when related to the performance of the asset class.* We do not recommend that funds be optimized using the optimization programs. Further, we do not recommend that portfolio returns comprising the managers be used in place of benchmark estimates [*emphasis added*].

ASSET CLASS CONSTRAINTS

Wealth managers have a multitude of tools at their disposal to perform portfolio optimization.[23] However, according to David Swensen, Yale University's chief investment officer,

---

[20]Markowitz (2009, 57).

[21]One interesting possible solution was proposed in a paper by Fred Dopfel, head of Client Advisory Group, Barclays Global Investors, "The New Policy Portfolio," September 2009.

[22]See Ziemba, "Stochastic Programming Approach."

[23]Just a few of the many examples include Zephyr, EnCorr, and Wilson CAM. In addition to these special-purpose software options, Microsoft Excel contains a Solver add-in that is a powerful tool for computing customized efficient frontiers. A number of texts provide guidance on using Excel for financial modeling, including Benninga (2008) and Sengupta (2004).

> *[U]nconstrained mean–variance [optimization] usually provide[s] solutions unrecognizable as reasonable portfolios. . . . Because the process involves material simplifying assumptions, adopting the unconstrained asset allocation point estimates produced by mean–variance optimization makes little sense.[24]*

Despite his criticism, Yale uses mean-variance analysis for its endowment. If run unconstrained, an optimizer will generally assign negative weights to many asset classes that imply the asset class should be sold short, which is either costly or impossible for most investors. An optimizer will also assign asset class weights that are greater than one, implying that investors should borrow money and use leverage to invest more than their available capital in a particular asset class. As a result, portfolio managers most commonly constrain all portfolio weights between zero and one.

Even with these constraints, optimizers typically exclude many asset classes and concentrate the portfolio allocations into a relatively few classes. This concentration is the result of an optimizer's tendency to exaggerate the extremes (i.e., error maximization). The most powerful tool that the wealth manager has to control error maximization and asset class concentration is the ability to set asset class constraints. The wealth manager may find that constraints designed to create a more diversified portfolio than a preliminary, unconstrained portfolio may have only trivial effects on portfolio return. In order to provide some feeling for the process, consider the following example.

EXAMPLE 10.3   Constraints in Four-Asset-Class Portfolio Optimization

Portfolio 1 in Exhibit 10.6 shows the results of a three-asset-class optimization that has been run with only short-selling and borrowing constraints. Adding a fourth asset class (foreign bonds) and optimizing the unconstrained portfolio again results in an increased expected return along with an increased standard deviation. These results were obtained by a total elimination of the allocation to intermediate-term government bonds and the allocation of over one-third of the portfolio to foreign bonds. Suppose we balk at placing all those foreign bonds in the portfolio and we arbitrarily cut the foreign bond allocation by 50 percent. What does that do to the risk-adjusted return (Sharpe ratio)? Incredibly, it reduces it by only 10 basis points. Let's go a step further and constrain the foreign bond allocation to a maximum of 5 percent. In other words, we'll run an optimization, but we'll run it with the restriction that we allow no more than a 5 percent allocation to the foreign bond category. Referring to portfolio 4, this new constraint reduced the optimal portfolio return by only 20 basis points. The point is that the wealth manager needs to investigate the consequences of forcing a more diversified portfolio allocation on a preliminary, unconstrained portfolio.

---

[24]Swenson (2002).

EXHIBIT 10.6   Effect of Constraints on Portfolio Optimization

Portfolio	Treasury Bills	Intermediate Gov't Bonds	S&P 500	Foreign Bonds	Expected Return	Standard Deviation	Sharpe Ratio
1	0.5	45.0	54.5	—	9.4	10.2	0.45
2	8.5	0.0	57.5	34.0	10.1	11.0	0.49
3	6.5	20.5	56.0	17.0	9.7	10.4	0.48
4	2.5	37.5	55.0	5.0	9.5	10.2	0.47

This three- and four-asset-class example illustrates well how constraints can create a more diversified portfolio with little impact on its Sharpe ratio. The following example illustrates the dynamics of placing constraints on a more realistic nine-asset-class portfolio.

EXAMPLE 10.4   Constraints in Nine-Asset-Class Portfolio Optimization

Suppose Delores Wilmott is discussing asset allocation with her client, Cliff Budzynski, and has decided that the universe of investments to be considered will include money market funds, short-/intermediate-term government bonds, intermediate-term municipal bonds, intermediate- to long-term foreign bonds, value funds, growth funds, S&P 500 index stocks, small company funds, and international equity funds. She has also mutually determined with her client a need for a target total return of approximately 9.5 percent and a moderate risk tolerance such that no more than 60 percent of the portfolio is in stock.

Running the optimizer unconstrained, she finds an efficient portfolio C that seems to meet her client's needs. According to the optimizer (Exhibit 10.7), this efficient portfolio requires an investment of 18 percent in money market funds, 28 percent in foreign bonds, 29.5 percent in S&P 500 stock, 19.5 percent in small company stock, and 5 percent in international stock funds. There is no allocation to domestic bonds or growth or value funds. The portfolio has an estimated expected return of 9.8 percent, with a standard deviation of 10 and a fixed income/equity ratio of 46/54 percent.

EXHIBIT 10.7   Nine-Asset-Class Optimization

Asset Class	Portfolio A	Portfolio B	Portfolio C	Portfolio D	Portfolio E
Money market	79.5	49.0	18.0	0.0	0.0
Intermediate gov't	0.0	0.0	0.0	0.0	0.0
Municipal bonds	0.0	0.0	0.0	0.0	0.0
Foreign bonds	9.5	18.0	28.0	27.5	14.5
Equity—growth	0.0	0.0	0.0	0.0	0.0
Equity—value	0.0	0.0	0.0	0.0	0.0

EXHIBIT 10.7 (Continued)

Asset Class	Portfolio A	Portfolio B	Portfolio C	Portfolio D	Portfolio E
Equity—S&P 500	4.0	16.0	29.5	38.0	42.5
Equity—small cap	7.0	13.0	19.5	23.0	21.0
Equity—int'l	0.0	4.0	5.0	11.5	22.0
Expected return	6.8	8.3	9.8	11.0	11.5
Standard deviation	2.5	6.0	10.0	13.0	14.6

Despite the theoretical perfection of the portfolio, Delores is uncomfortable recommending either such a highly concentrated portfolio or such a large allocation to foreign bonds. Also, because she believes in staggered-maturity fixed-income portfolios, the barbell maturity distribution (i.e., money market funds and foreign bonds) is unacceptable.

First, she constrains the foreign bond allocation to 5 percent and optimizes again. The result is presented as constrained portfolio 1 in Exhibit 10.8. It shifts the foreign bond allocation to money market government bonds and S&P 500 equities. That results in an overall balance of 39 percent fixed/61 percent equity. Looking at the new fixed income allocation, Delores realizes that the heavy allocation to money market funds (a low-return asset class) is forcing a greater allocation in equities in order to reach Cliff's target return. She sets a constraint of 7.5 percent on money market funds and reruns the optimizer (constrained portfolio 2). Sure enough, the result is to reduce the allocation to the S&P 500 and increase the government bonds. The overall balance is now 41/59 percent. Delores continually reviews the changes in both expected returns and standard deviations to ensure she is neither significantly reducing expected returns nor significantly increasing volatility. This is the process of sensitivity analysis discussed earlier.

EXHIBIT 10.8   Constrained Nine-Asset-Class Optimization

Asset Class	Constrained Portfolio 1	Constrained Portfolio 2	Constrained Portfolio 3	Recommended Portfolio
Money market	23.0	7.5	7.5	7.5
Intermediate gov't	11.0	28.5	17.5	17.5
Municipal bonds	0.0	0.0	10.0	10.0
Foreign bonds	5.0	5.0	5.0	5.0
Equity—growth	0.0	0.0	0.0	10.0
Equity—value	0.0	0.0	0.0	20.0
Equity—S&P 500	36.5	34.5	34.5	10.0
Equity—small cap	19.5	19.5	19.5	10.0
Equity—int'l	5.0	5.0	5.0	10.0
Expected return				9.7
Standard deviation				10.5

Next, Delores questions that her taxable client should have no allocation to municipal bonds.[25] She sets a minimum allocation of 10 percent for municipals and reruns the optimizer (constrained portfolio 3). It does not change the fixed income/equity allocation. It simply shifts the allocation from government bonds to municipal bonds. Delores is prepared to accept the 41/59 fixed income/equity balance, but that is her equity limit, so she sets a maximum constraint of 59 on equities to prevent future optimizations from recommending an increase in equity allocations. To diversify the equity allocation, she and Cliff agreed to consider small-cap and international stocks as part of the portfolio but to limit them to 10 percent each. She also decides to limit the S&P 500 core holding to 10 percent and to force a split of two-thirds value and one-third growth based on her understanding of the value effect. She arrives at the final recommended portfolio. After making all of the changes, the proposed portfolio provides a return within 10 basis points of the optimum portfolio C, with a standard deviation that is almost the same.

A review of the portfolio indicates that Delores allocated 7.5 percent to money market (to meet Cliff's liquidity requirements), 17.5 percent to short-/intermediate-term government bonds (to provide a second tier of liquidity), 10 percent to intermediate-term municipal bonds (to add longer maturities and provide the tax-free return her client is looking for), and 5 percent to foreign bonds (remember, a small allocation provides significant diversification). She also diversified between growth and value equity by placing 10 percent in growth and 20 percent in value. By agreeing to limit the allocations, Delores has cajoled Cliff to accept an investment of 10 percent each in small-cap and international mutual funds.

Harold's Constraint Recommendations for Traditional Optimization

The previous examples illustrate how one can impose constraints on the portfolio optimization process. For those practitioners using a multi-asset class/style optimization, Harold suggests the following possible constraints (see Exhibit 10.9).

EXHIBIT 10.9   E&K Asset Class Constraint Summary

Asset Class	Constraint	
	Minimum	Maximum
Fixed Income	3% portfolio	100% portfolio
Cash/MMA	3% portfolio	20% portfolio
Short-Term	10% fixed	50% fixed
Short/Intermediate	10% fixed	50% fixed
Intermediate	10% fixed	50% fixed

---

[25]It is important to note that when including a nontaxable asset class such as municipal bonds in a portfolio optimization procedure, its expected return and volatility must be adjusted upward to a taxable equivalent to be comparable with the other taxable asset classes. Otherwise, an optimizer will mistakenly overlook the asset class under the presumption that its return is too low. Horan and Zaman (2008) discuss after-tax portfolio optimization in more detail.

EXHIBIT 10.9 (Continued)

Asset Class	Constraint	
	Minimum	Maximum
Equity	0% portfolio	80% portfolio
Large Cap	30% equity	70% equity
Core	30% equity	60% equity
Value	15% equity	40% equity
Growth	0% equity	20% equity
Small Cap	15% equity	40% equity
Core	15% equity	40% equity
Value	15% equity	40% equity
Growth	0% equity	20% equity
International	20% equity	50% equity
Developed	60% international	100% international
Emerging Market	0% international	40% international
REITs	0% portfolio	10% portfolio

Cash Equivalent/Money Market

To provide flexibility in rebalancing, a reserve for a client's unanticipated emergency cash needs and for billing and a short-term anchor for our duration ladder, consider a fixed 2 to 3 percent allocation to cash equivalents. This allocation is in addition to the cash flow reserve account we discussed in Chapter 3, "Client Goals and Constraints." These combined cash positions should be included as a constraint in the optimization process so that the risky part of the portfolio can be optimized in light of the cash flow reserve account. In this way, the client's overall portfolio is optimized. This depends, however, on how the client's return objectives are defined. If return objectives are defined against an asset base excluding the cash flow reserve account, then the constraint should similarly relate only to the portfolio excluding the cash flow reserve account.

Domestic Fixed Income

Constraining the domestic fixed income allocation is much less structured than the constraint for cash equivalents. The first step is to determine the total fixed income allocation. Once this is set, the total commitment to domestic fixed income is simply the total fixed income allocation less the allocations to cash/money market funds and foreign bonds. For non-sheltered accounts, the next step is to determine the split between municipal and taxable bonds.[26] The final allocation is to maturity ranges.

---

[26]Remember, good tax management is to maximize after-tax returns, not minimize taxes. Depending on the relationship between taxable and municipal yield curves, a combination of taxable and municipal bonds may result in the optimum after-tax returns.

As indicated in Chapter 5, "Data Gathering and Analysis," our asset class taxonomy currently provides for three maturity ranges: one to three years, three to five years, and five to 10 years. As discussed in the following section, the process of setting allocations among these ranges is determined more by projected yield curves than by the optimizer. As we have a strong bias in favor of laddered maturities, we will rarely accept a bullet or barbell allocation.

Our default allocation is one-fourth of the domestic fixed income allocation to the one- to three-year range, one-fourth to the five- to 10-year range, and half to the three- to five-year range. Each of these may be over- or underweighted by half of the default allocation, depending on our evaluation of the yield curves. In a normal yield curve environment, the overall target duration would be five years.

Real Estate Investment Trusts

Studies out of the Wharton School, commissioned by Dimensional Fund Advisors (DFA), indicate that real estate investment trusts (REITs) can serve as an exposure to the real estate market.[27] Based on this research, we elected to cap our initial allocation at 5 percent. In subsequent years we concluded that REITs are in fact too highly correlated with the domestic equity market (specifically midcap value) to provide useful diversification, so we do not currently use a REIT allocation; however, as noted, we continually revisit these decisions, so by the time you read this section, we may once again be using a REIT allocation.

International and Emerging Market Equities

Based on a world portfolio, intellectually, an allocation of half to two-thirds of the equity portfolio to foreign stocks seems a reasonable allocation to international and emerging market equities. For most clients, however, foreign equities (like foreign bonds) are again "foreign." No matter how big the company or how strong its financial statement, if they can't pronounce its name and they don't see its products on TV or in stores, its stock does not feel as safe as General Electric or Coca-Cola. We concluded that 35 to 40 percent was a much more comfortable constraint for a foreign equity commitment.

Domestic Equities

For small-cap domestic equities, we set two constraints. The first is a floor of 15 percent to guarantee at least some allocation to the class. The second is a cap equal to one-third of the large-capitalization allocation. Although we accept the return premium attributable to small companies documented by Fama and French and others, we constrain the allocation to reflect our evaluation of our clients' risk tolerance.

Fama and French (and related research of Dimensional Fund Advisors) also document a return premium for stocks with high book/market ratios (i.e., value stocks).[28] Styles, however, move in and out of favor, so we avoid committing our domestic style allocation 100 percent to value; however, we do apply a significant value and small-cap overlay. In doing so, we may (or may not) be sacrificing an incremental premium, but we also reduce the portfolio's interim volatility.

Harold's Constraint Recommendations for Overlay Optimization

Harold has run innumerable sensitivity and scenario analyses over the years, and the experience has led him to conclude that incorporating numerous asset class and style alternatives in

---

[27]See, for example, Gyourko and Keim (1993). Information regarding this research is available from DFA.
[28]Chapter 16, "Selecting Investment Managers," includes a discussion of the Fama and French research.

the base optimization, as discussed earlier, is often counterproductive. Invariably, the unconstrained higher-risk/return alternative allocations are subsequently constrained significantly below that suggested by an unconstrained optimizer. As a consequence, he now optimizes using a few basic asset classes (e.g., fixed income, domestic large-cap core, international large-cap core). He then overlays more specific equity classes and style allocations (e.g., large-cap value, small-cap growth, emerging markets). The fixed income allocation overlay is determined based on the evaluation of the current fixed income yield curves.

As an example, an unconstrained optimization might result in the following results:

Fixed income[29]

> 0 percent—cash
> 5 percent—short-term bonds
> 35 percent—intermediate-term bonds

Equity

> 0 percent—large-cap growth
> 5 percent—large-cap core
> 10 percent—large-cap value
> 0 percent—small-cap growth
> 0 percent—small-cap core
> 20 percent—small-cap value
> 0 percent—international developed
> 25 percent—emerging markets

An alternative would be to apply an overlay strategy using a broadly optimized portfolio. Based on a forward-looking market view, for the fixed income allocation, the advisor might implement a modified laddered portfolio with a duration target of four years and an average quality of A. If the advisor believes in the Fama/French small-cap and value factors, he or she might allocate about 14 percent of the domestic allocation to large-cap value and 25 percent to small-cap value and, cognizant of clients' lack of appetite for risk, might allocate 15 percent of the international portion to emerging markets. The result would look something like the following.

Initial Optimization

Fixed income

> 40 percent

Equity

> 35 percent—domestic
> 25 percent—international

---

[29]Many years ago we decided that our maximum allocation to equities would be 80 percent. The decision was a result of having lived through numerous boom-and-bust market cycles. With an all-equity allocation we (and our clients) simply had to ride the full cycles up and down. Maintaining a minimum of 20 percent fixed income allocation and establishing rebalance parameters ensures a tactical response in volatile markets; that is, in bull markets our rebalance parameters result in our taking profits, and in bear markets, having some funds in bonds, the rebalancing parameters ensure a tactical move to buy stock. As a consequence, we sell high and buy low.

Overlay Allocation

Fixed income

> 5 percent—cash
> 25 percent—short-term bonds (A or better)
> 10 percent—intermediate-term bonds (A or better)

Equity

> 0 percent—large-cap growth
> 20 percent—large-cap core
> 6 percent—large-cap value
> 0 percent—small-cap growth
> 0 percent—small-cap core
> 9 percent—small-cap value
> 21 percent—international developed
> 4 percent—emerging markets

It's important to note that all of these standards serve as a guide, not a bible. These constraints are moving targets. Over the years we have added, eliminated, and then added again asset classes (e.g., foreign bonds and REITs) and have modified constraints (e.g., growth and value), and we expect to continue doing so. For example, our current allocation model is core and satellite, and we have been gradually adding small allocations to alternatives. These too are added as overlays to the preliminary optimized portfolio.

SENSITIVITY ANALYSIS

Sensitivity analysis is the process of developing a feeling for the influence small changes in input have on the optimization output. The process begins once the wealth manager has selected the asset classes to be considered and has determined the preliminary expected returns, standard deviations, and correlations for each of the asset classes. The wealth manager now has all of the data necessary to run an optimization.

One approach is to change each assumption by 5 percent, holding all other factors constant, and reoptimize. For example, if the return assumption for U.S. equity is 10 percent, change it to 15 percent. Experiment with larger changes, like 10 percent and 20 percent, as well as negative changes, like −5 percent and −10 percent. Apply these changes to returns, standard deviations, and correlations. To be conservative, you might only assume higher volatility and higher correlations. After each run, review the output to see what and how much the allocations had changed, and how the modified assumptions affect the risk/return relationships, perhaps focusing on the Sharpe ratio. This is a long and grueling process but one every wealth manager should probably do at least once with a new optimizer. On a regular basis, the wealth manager can start with minimum constraints in place, rather than an unconstrained model. This process will be equally meaningful, but much quicker.

Sensitivity analysis provides guidance for the final adjustments to input data (subject to the policies discussed earlier) and allows the wealth manager to develop an awareness of the sensitivity for the biases of the optimizer. For example, if two assets are highly correlated, an optimizer will allocate very heavily toward the one with the higher Sharpe ratio, because it views the assets as otherwise indistinguishable. The allocation will remain relatively fixed until your input changes tip the risk/reward trade-off in favor of the other asset, at which time the optimizer will shift quickly and heavily in the other direction.

SELECTING AN EFFICIENT PORTFOLIO

In theory, optimizers create an infinite set of efficient portfolios. The challenge for the wealth manager is choosing the proper efficient portfolios to meet clients' needs. Harold refers to this as "anchoring on the efficient frontier." The logic is that by integrating the conclusions of the capital needs analysis (i.e., what return the clients need in order to accomplish their goals) and the results of the risk tolerance evaluation (i.e., how much risk can the client accept and stay committed to during disastrous market cycles) an advisor can assist clients to determine the most efficient portfolio for their unique needs. This anchoring is highlighted in Exhibit 10.10. In this example, a client's return requirement can theoretically be met by portfolio B.

Unfortunately, the client's risk tolerance suggests that his aversion to risk would restrict him to portfolio A, a combination of investments that would provide a total return less than needed to meet his goals. Depending on the client's willingness to "eat less well or sleep less well," the advisor can help the client anchor on the efficient frontier at a point that best balances his needs (e.g., portfolio C).

EXHIBIT 10.10   Anchoring on the Efficient Frontier

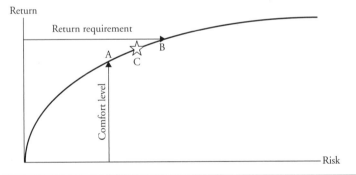

If the results were reversed (i.e., the risk anchor was B and the return A), the practitioner might recommend portfolio B even though the return expectation exceeds the lower targeted return determined by the capital needs analysis. The logic of that recommendation is based on the belief that, as all of the analysis is based on uncertain estimates, planning for the highest acceptable return (within the client's risk tolerance) will provide a potential safety margin.

Another approach, and one practiced by Harold and his firm, is to design based on the return requirement (i.e., portfolio A, one with projected risk no higher than the client's acceptable level). The logic of this approach is that risk tolerance evaluation is uncertain at best and there is a significant risk that clients may overestimate their tolerance. If during a serious bear market clients find that they cannot live with the loss and liquidate the portfolio, the plan would be in shambles. As a consequence, if the planning conclusion is that clients can achieve their goals at a lower level of risk, forgoing the opportunity for higher returns may well be the wise choice. There is no right or wrong in this decision process. Wealth managers will have to determine their own philosophical standard, and then, utilizing this approach, the advisor can assist the client in quantifying two unique anchors and selecting the client's optimal portfolio.[30]

In principle, an investor can often do better than what an optimized portfolio of risky assets suggests by combining the efficient portfolio that has the highest Sharpe ratio with the risk-free asset. The optimized portfolio with the highest Sharpe ratio is called the tangency portfolio (see Exhibit 10.11). By combining it with the risk-free asset through borrowing or lending, the wealth manager can create a portfolio with a higher return (for a given standard deviation) than any of the other efficient portfolios. Alternatively, the manager can create a portfolio with the lower standard deviation (for a given expected return) than any of the other efficient portfolios. The wealth manager then chooses the combined portfolio that best suits the client's needs. If the tangency portfolio is too risky, the manager can combine it with the risk-free asset. If it isn't risky enough, the manager would borrow money or use margin to create a leveraged position in the tangent portfolio. The kink in the line of Exhibit 10.11 reflects the notion that investors cannot typically borrow at the risk-free rate. This higher expense erodes returns.

EXHIBIT 10.11   Beyond the Efficient Frontier

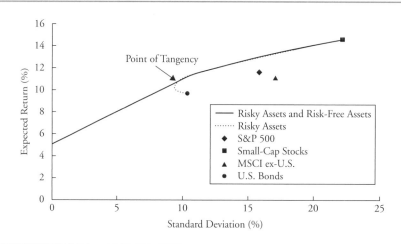

Source: Richard DeFusco, Dennis W. McLeavey, Jerald E. Pinto, and David E. Runkle, *Quantitative Methods for Investment Analysis*, 2nd edition (Charlottesville, VA: CFA Institute, 2004), 614.

---

[30]Karla Curtis and Harold Evensky, "Interactive Capital Needs Analysis: A New Frontier in Client-Driven Consultative Retirement Planning," *Journal of Retirement Planning* (September–October 2001).

Practice varies concerning the use of cash equivalents as an asset class in mean-variance optimization. Risk-free assets, such as U.S. Treasury bills, actually exhibit variability over multiple periods as the short-term rate changes. The common practice, which we adopt here, is to adapt the multiperiod perspective of mean-variance analysis and incorporate cash equivalents as an asset class to be optimized. This approach also allows the wealth manager to place constraints that reflect investors' restrictions against buying risky assets on margin or at the very least liquidity constraints inconsistent with this aggressive strategy.

Risk Tolerance for Optimization

Investors' risk tolerance is critical to selecting the proper portfolio to meet their needs. A perennial problem that has vexed wealth managers has been trying to quantify an investor's risk tolerance and incorporate it into a disciplined and systematic portfolio optimization process. Risk tolerance is a complex, multidimensional concept composed of both qualitative and quantitative factors.

Traditional optimization models would have us find the portfolio that maximizes an investor's expected utility, which is composed of expected return of the portfolio, expected standard deviation of the portfolio, and the investor's risk aversion parameter. In this framework, the risk aversion parameter is a number. Risk aversion of four is considered moderately risk averse. Lower risk aversion parameters are associated with investors having higher risk tolerance, and higher risk aversion parameters are associated with investors having very low risk tolerance.[31] Labeling investors as either a one, a four, or an eight has always been a nebulous process.

Jarrod Wilcox has developed a concept called the discretionary wealth hypothesis, which uses a life balance sheet to take a holistic view of a client's financial and nonfinancial assets as well as financial goals to help determine the client's risk tolerance.[32] As introduced in Chapter 1, "The Wealth Management Process," the life balance sheet is a comprehensive accounting of a client's assets, liabilities, and net worth. The left side of the balance sheet lists a client's assets. It includes traditional financial assets, such as stocks, bonds, alternative assets, and the like, but also includes tangible assets such as real estate, gold, and collectibles. To be comprehensive, the left side of the balance sheet includes implied assets, such as human capital, also known as the after-tax present value of the investor's expected earnings stream.[33]

---

[31]An investor with a risk aversion parameter of zero cares only about return.

[32]See, for example, Wilcox (2000, 2003) and Wilcox, Horvitz, and diBartolomeo (2006).

[33]One question that arises is whether human capital represents the present value of earnings or of savings (e.g., earnings less consumption). Different practitioners have different approaches, but one must be consistent in the choices made. If human capital represents after-tax earnings on the left side of the life balance sheet, then the wealth manager must also include the present value of consumption as a liability on the right-hand side of the life balance sheet. If, however, one chooses to view human capital as the present value of after-tax savings, then consumption should not be included as a liability on the right-hand side because it has already been accounted for in arriving at savings. Moreover, wealth managers' choice of earnings versus savings should affect their choice of discount rate for the present value of human capital. For example, if one views consumption as something of a fixed expense, then savings is a leveraged cash flow compared to wages.

EXHIBIT 10.12   Hypothetical Example of a Life Balance Sheet

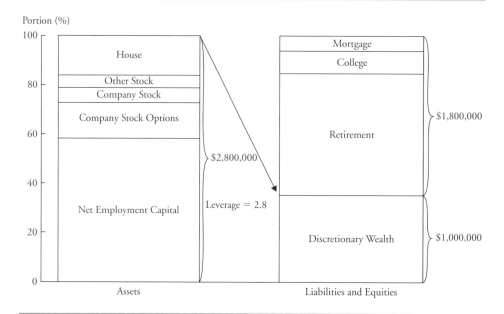

Source: Adapted from Wilcox, Horvitz, and diBartolomeo (2006, 18).

Liabilities on the right-hand side of the balance sheet include mortgages, car loans, margin loans, and other debt secured by tangible or financial property on the left side of the balance sheet. Importantly, however, an investor's high-priority investment goals represent implied liabilities. The nest egg necessary to maintain a certain standard of living through retirement (in today's dollars), for example, is an implied liability that needs to be funded by the assets on the left side of the balance sheet. Aspirations to fund a child's college education, purchase a vacation home, start a business, or fulfill a charitable bequest can represent implied liabilities in a similar fashion.

Exhibit 10.12 presents the simple life balance introduced in Chapter 1. In this example, assets total $2.8 million, and liabilities total $1.8 million, which represents the amount of capital necessary to fund the investor's core requirements as defined by high-priority goals. The assets are sufficient to meet these core obligations, leaving $1 million of excess capital, or discretionary wealth, to meet the investor's low-priority goals, which if not met do not produce devastating consequences. Discretionary wealth is the available economic resources in excess of what's required to fund the high-priority goals.

The key insight is that the relationship between the assets and discretionary wealth dictates a client's implied leverage, which amplifies changes in the value of the assets in terms of the effect on discretionary wealth. In this example the ratio of assets to discretionary wealth is 2.8. By implication, if the assets on the left side drop in value by 10 percent, the value of discretionary wealth drops by 28 percent. High leverage on a client's life balance sheet reduces their tolerance for risk because the available resources are just enough to fund the most important goals. To the extent that goals are considered low-priority or discretionary, the client, by definition, has more tolerance for risk.

The liabilities on the right side should represent those goals that are most important to the investor or have the highest priority—the must haves. Less significant goals are reflected in discretionary wealth. The more significant the high-priority goals are in relation to the assets available to fund them (i.e., the higher the implied leverage), the more risk averse a client is. By contrast, if investors are content to allow a relatively larger proportion of their goals to be subject to the vagaries of the market, they are relatively more risk tolerant and more of their goals would be considered discretionary. In this case, these clients would have relatively few implied liabilities in relation to their assets (i.e., lower implied leverage) and more risk tolerance.

Of course, the natural tendency is for clients to consider everything important. The wealth manager's job is to create and guide the investor through a process that helps prioritize these goals in a meaningful way.

In the discretionary wealth framework, a wealth manager maximizes the following expression:

$$\text{Median Long-Term Wealth} = \bar{r}_p - \frac{1}{2}L\sigma_p^2$$

where $\bar{r}_p$ is the expected return of the portfolio, σ_p is the expected standard deviation of the portfolio, and L is the implied leverage determined by the life balance sheet, or 2.8 in our example. This expression looks daunting! How can the wealth manager use it? Fortunately, this expression is computationally identical to the traditional mean-variance optimization (MVO) performed by almost any optimizer on the market. Happily, however, we have none of the nebulous assumptions about investor utility. There are two noticeable differences, however, between this framework and traditional MVO.

1. The more objective implied leverage from the balance sheet, L, replaces the subjective risk tolerance parameter.
2. We no longer maximize the ethereal utility of the investor but instead maximize median long-term wealth, which is something far more concrete.

What are the implications for the wealth manager? To incorporate the realities of the life balance sheet, the wealth manager can multiply all of the variance inputs by the client's implied leverage, L, from the life balance sheet. Because we have dealt mostly in terms of standard deviation, an equivalent approach is to multiply standard deviations by the square root of L. Even if the wealth manager does not explicitly account for implied leverage in the optimization process, the manager could certainly adjust for it subjectively when selecting from among the array of efficient portfolios by choosing low-risk portfolios when implied leverage is high and higher-return portfolios when implied leverage is low.

Another important implication is to incorporate nonfinancial assets into the recommended asset allocation. For example, suppose your client is an investment banker whose job prospects are highly volatile and move in tandem with the vagaries of the market. The client's human capital, or net employment capital, is equity-like. Therefore, a wealth manager should count the client's human capital as part of the equity allocation recommended by an optimizer that incorporates implied leverage from the life balance sheet. Alternatively, the wealth manager might build a portfolio around the client's preexisting risk exposures. For example, consider a client who is the founder and CEO of a privately held real estate development business. The developer already has a significant exposure to real estate through private holdings and through human capital. The wealth manager may therefore build a portfolio around these exposures by eliminating REITs and deemphasizing other interest-rate-sensitive securities in the financial portfolio.

EXAMPLE 10.5

Sarah Hoffnagle, a single, 50-year-old tenured professor of English at a prestigious university, has come to Richard Erikson for advice on her portfolio allocation. Sarah is well known in her field and has numerous other employment options. Noting the security of Sarah's employment and relative insensitivity to general market movements, Richard considers Sarah's human capital to be predictable and bondlike, and therefore estimates the present value of her earnings stream to be $800,000. In addition, Sarah has accumulated a retirement portfolio and other liquid assets of $500,000 along with a $200,000 home with a $100,000 mortgage remaining.

Richard estimates that securing Sarah's retirement requires $900,000 in today's dollars.[34] Having no children, she has no aspirations to transfer wealth to heirs, nor does she have other philanthropic intent. As a result, Sarah has total assets of $1,500,000 ($800,000 + $500,000 + $200,000) and liabilities of $1,000,000 ($900,000 + $100,000) on her life balance sheet. Her discretionary wealth is therefore $500,000. Richard estimates that Sarah's implied leverage is 3 ($1,500,000/$500,000).

Richard implements a simple three-asset portfolio optimization using cash, intermediate government bonds, and domestic equity using the expected returns in Exhibit 10.13. Noting that Sarah's implied leverage is 3, he multiplies the raw standard deviations for each asset class by the square root of 3, or 1.73.

EXHIBIT 10.13   Sample Leverage-Adjusted Asset Classes

	Expected Return	Standard Deviation	Leverage-Adjusted Standard Deviation
Cash	3%	5%	8.6%
Intermediate bonds	5	10	17.3
Domestic equity	8	20	34.6

Richard's portfolio optimization recommends an asset allocation of cash, bonds, and stock of 5 percent, 65 percent, and 30 percent, respectively. Richard notes that the fixed income allocation seems high, but is consistent with the notion that Sarah has significant implied leverage on her life balance sheet. Because her human capital is bondlike, he plans to incorporate its value as fixed income in the asset allocation process. In other words, Sarah already has 53 percent of her assets ($800,000 of $1,500,000) allocated to an asset class that behaves much like fixed income by virtue of her stable employment. Using her financial assets, he allocates 12 percent of her total assets (including nonfinancial assets) to fixed income to bring her total fixed income allocation to 65 percent.

Notice that the incremental 12 percent fixed income allocation of Sarah's total $1,500,000 in assets equals $180,000. This figure represents 36 percent of her financial assets, which is a typical asset allocation.

---

[34]For methods used to estimate the present value of retirement and other liabilities, see Horan and Robinson (2009).

REBALANCING

In the discussion of portfolio design, the phrase *asset allocation* has been used in a number of ways:

Asset allocation—establishing the normal asset class weights.
Strategic asset allocation—the long-term structure of a portfolio.
Policy asset allocation—the long-term normal asset mix.

Obviously, in all of these uses, the emphasis is on the elements of normality and long term. As asset classes grow at different rates, portfolios do not remain normal without adjustments. Allocations may change radically over time. The wealth manager must decide on a policy regarding the management of market-driven changes in the asset class weightings. There are two general choices: buy-and-hold or systematic rebalancing.

Buy-and-Hold

This term is a euphemism for "Do nothing; allow the market to determine the policy." Advantages of this passive strategy are low management fees, low transaction costs, and greater tax efficiency. The disadvantage is the risk of results significantly different from those projected.

For example, consider a portfolio, originally allocated 40 percent debt/60 percent equity, that had drifted to 20/80 debt/equity after a sustained market run-up, only to be followed by a sharp 20 percent correction (e.g., fourth quarter of 1987). The cost of the allocation drift would be 4 percent.[35] Even with a relatively modest 10 percent drift followed by a 10 percent market correction, the cost would be 1 percent. The flip side is also a risk. An allocation short of its target would suffer an opportunity cost if that asset class were to make a major positive move.

The final risk associated with buy-and-hold is psychological. During volatile markets and after runs (either up or down), passive investors are likely to succumb to fear or greed, ignore their buy-and-hold strategy, and become ill-timed market timers (i.e., buying high and selling low). A much better alternative is to develop a systematic rebalancing strategy.

Systematic Rebalancing

Rebalancing is the action of readjusting a portfolio's asset class allocations from its current weightings, determined by market forces, back to the policy's normal weights. The decision rules for systematic rebalancing fall into either of two categories—calendar or contingent.

Calendar rebalancing calls for rebalancing the portfolio back to its policy asset class weights on a predetermined calendar period. Typically, the trigger is monthly, quarterly, or annually, although it could be measured in years (e.g., every five years). Contingent rebalancing, in contrast, depends on a predefined trigger that is independent of time. For example, rebalancing may be triggered by a 10 percent change in the weighting of any asset class. There are many variations on these themes, some of which are calendar-contingent hybrids.

---

[35]A portfolio balanced according to the policy would have a loss of 12 percent (i.e., $0.6 \times 20\%$). A 20/80 portfolio would have a loss of 16 percent (i.e., $0.8 \times 20\%$)—a 4 percent greater loss.

Research

To date, the research on rebalancing has been limited and inconclusive. One of the earliest articles to address the issue was "Let It Ride" by Kaufman and Goldstone in the December 1988 issue of *Financial Planning*. The authors found that the overall performance of the buy-and-hold portfolio was superior to contingent rebalancing. They concluded that the "fatal flaw in the rebalancing strategy [was]: A portfolio shouldn't be constantly selling out of appreciating assets and increasing its stake in depreciating assets." Viewed differently, selling appreciated assets and buying depreciated assets is a contrarian investment strategy that may be expected to earn a positive liquidity premium over time.

If one believes that, over time, equities will outperform bonds, the Kaufman/Goldstone buy-and-hold conclusion is fairly obvious, as an investor's portfolio will gradually become more and more equity oriented. The fatal flaw in concluding that investors should follow this strategy is that it ignores the critical recognition that, left unconstrained, over time the stock/bond ratio of an investor's portfolio will increase to a point well beyond the investor's risk tolerance.

In fact, subsequent research has not supported the superiority of buy-and-hold. In the April 1992 *Journal of Financial Planning*, Stine and Lewis published "Guidelines for Rebalancing Passive-Investment Portfolios." Based on a comprehensive study of rebalancing strategies for investment horizons of 3, 5, 10, 15, and 20 years, they concluded that a contingent strategy, providing for rebalancing when stock weights varied by $7\frac{1}{2}$ to 10 percent from their policy allocation, was the optimum choice. During that same month, SEI Corporation reported in a position paper titled "Rebalancing" that its research had also concluded that a contingency strategy was optimum. Later SEI research recommended a 6 percent target threshold at the asset class level and a 3 percent target threshold at the style level.

In May 1992, Jeremy Black revisited much of the earlier work and made two significant observations regarding the earlier studies. He noted that the conclusions of the studies were dependent on the asset classes selected and the weights allocated to each. For example, the Kaufman and Goldstone portfolios included a significant allocation to gold during a historical period unique for gold prices. Stine and Lewis's study included only three asset classes and was heavily influenced by estimates of transaction costs.

Most important, Black refocused attention on the wealth manager's financial planning orientation. Money managers measure success by relative performance. For wealth managers, success is measured by their ability to assist clients in meeting their goals. A significant aspect of this success is related to managing the client's expectations.

Black estimates the standard deviation of a portfolio rebalanced to the policy is 7.7 percent compared to 9.7 percent for a buy-and-hold portfolio with a 52 percent commitment to stock. That is a 25 percent higher volatility for the buy-and-hold strategy. Even more sobering is the extreme where a buy-and-hold strategy resulted in an 85 percent commitment to stock. The estimated standard deviation of that portfolio is 14.6 (a 90 percent higher volatility), and the downside risk in any one year is −17 percent. Black's conclusion should serve as a guide to any wealth manager deciding on a rebalancing strategy.

> *If you sold your client on an asset balance with specific risk-reward characteristics and gave the impression that this would not change that much over the years, then not rebalancing could cause some serious misunderstanding and a loss of clients.*

Subsequent studies generally support some form of contingent rebalancing. Art Lutschaunig of Fidelity Investments reported at an AIMR (now known as CFA Institute) conference that after reviewing the empirical studies and based on internal studies, Fidelity uses a contingent trigger of 10 to 12 percent for major asset classes.[36] One interesting addition to the discussion on rebalancing was the observation by Douglas McCalla that percentage rebalancing does not consider that different classes have different volatilities.[37] McCalla suggests using a factor of 1.2 standard deviations as a rebalancing criterion.

More recently, Gobind Daryanani has outlined a variation on the trigger approach in which a 20 percent strategic allocation might have a 10 percent rebalancing band with a 5 percent tolerance.[38] In other words, an asset class can drift between 18 percent and 22 percent allocation before triggering a rebalancing trade, which may rebalance to within 19 percent and 21 percent. Using data from 1992 to 2004, he finds that a 20 percent rebalancing band with a 10 percent tolerance band is optimal.

Still, calendar rebalancing has it proponents. For example, Arnott, Burns, Plaxo, and Moore report the results in Exhibit 10.14 for monthly rebalancing from 1973 to 2003. The rebalanced portfolio experienced an extra 27 basis point annual return over the three decades, but perhaps more significantly experienced less volatility for a high reward-to-risk ratio. To be sure, rebalancing does not necessarily produce a higher return or lower volatility in any given period, but it tends to work on average. Other studies support this conclusion using both historical and simulated data. Tokat and Wicas, for example, show that in light of all the uncertainties regarding mean reversion and investor preferences, annual rebalancing using 5 percent triggers captures most of the rebalancing benefits in a scalable way.[39]

EXHIBIT 10.14   Monthly Rebalancing, 1973–2003

	Rebalancing Return	Drifting Mix Return	Difference
Average annual return	10.22%	9.95%	0.27%
Maximum	35.25	35.75	
Minimum	− 15.71	− 16.57	
Median	12.97	11.96	
Standard deviation	11.38	13.39	
Average/standard deviation	0.90	0.74	

Source: Robert D. Arnott, Terence E. Burns, Lisa Plaxco, and Philip Moore, "Monitoring and Rebalancing," in Maginn, Tuttle, Pinto, and McLeavey (2007).

---

[36]Art Lutschaunig, "Optimal Asset Allocation II," AIMR ICFA Continuing Education, Managing Assets for Individual Investors, February 28–March 1, 1995, 44–49.

[37]Douglas McCalla, "Enhancing Asset Allocation Performance with a Volatility-Based Rebalancing Process," in *Global Asset Allocation*, Jess Lederman and Robert Klein, eds. (New York: John Wiley & Sons, 1994).

[38]Gobind Daryanani, "Opportunistic Rebalancing: A New Paradigm for Wealth Managers," *Journal of Financial Planning*, Vol. 21, No. 1 (2008): 48–61.

[39]Yesim Tokat and Nelson Wicas, "Portfolio Rebalancing in Theory and Practice," *Journal of Investing*, Vol. 16, No. 2 (2007): 52–59.

The Art of Rebalancing

Like most areas of wealth management, the rebalancing decision involves a blend of art and science.[40] Balancing the issues of performance, client risk tolerance,[41] tax consequences, transaction costs, and management costs, a reasonable trigger for rebalancing between the broad asset classes of fixed income and equities is a ±7 to 10 percent absolute drift. The more difficult decision is setting a contingent rebalancing strategy for asset subclasses and styles.[42]

An artful process used to arrive at the solution to this second level of contingent triggers is to heed Jeremy Black's advice and the suggestion of Douglas McCalla to concentrate on the risk factor. Therefore, the rebalancing criteria are influenced by the asset class standard deviation. One might also consider (1) the size of the average commitment to the class, (2) the correlation between the asset classes and styles, and (3) other recommendations for asset subclass rebalancing. Exhibit 10.15 presents a proposed rebalancing policy based on these criteria.

EXHIBIT 10.15   Sample Rebalancing Policy/Allocation Drift

	Style	Subclass	Major Class
Fixed income			±7
Equity			±7
U.S. large cap		±5	
U.S. large cap growth	±3		
U.S. large cap value	±3		
U.S. small cap		±5	
U.S. small cap growth	±3		
U.S. small cap value	±3		
International		±5	
Emerging market		±3	
Real estate		±3	

From a practice management perspective, it is quite practical to overlay a quasi-calendar rebalance trigger. Because client portfolios are unique, it does not make sense to globally rebalance accounts. Each client's portfolio might be scheduled for a formal review on a quarterly basis. A wealth manager can determine the specific quarterly cycle to keep a relatively equal balance of reviews every month. Ideally, the goal may be to have one-third of your reviews on a January, April, July, and October cycle; one-third on a February, May, August, and November cycle; and so on. A sensible rebalancing strategy is to review portfolios quarterly and, during that review, apply the contingent rebalancing policy. With only three months

---

[40]There are a number of software solutions available to wealth managers, including Tamarac Advisor (www.tamaracinc.com/), Redblack Rebalance Express (www.redblacksoftware.com/), iRebal (www.irebal.com/), eAllocator (www.eallocator.net/), Total Rebalance Expert (www.trxpert.com/), and ASI Portfolio Rebalancing Solution (www.advisorsoftware.com/products/ASIportfolioRebalancingSolution.asp).

[41]The less frequent the rebalancing, the further the portfolio is likely to drift from the policy's expected volatility.

[42]See the discussion on the taxonomy of asset classes in Chapter 5, "Data Gathering and Analysis."

between reviews, it is unlikely that a portfolio will ever significantly exceed the rebalance policy. In the event of an exceptional short-term move (e.g., October 1987, March 2001, October 2008), it may make sense to reevaluate all portfolios.

Client-Induced Rebalancing

It is worth noting that the rebalancing we have discussed thus far relates to market-driven changes in the asset allocation weights. The wealth manager may also need to rebalance the portfolio simply because the client's circumstances have evolved in an unexpected fashion such that the portfolio no longer matches the investor's needs or risk tolerance. For example, a client may have unexpectedly taken on the responsibility to care for an older parent or unexpectedly inherited a significant sum. The mix of asset classes may have remained relatively unchanged, but the client's change in circumstance may require revisiting goals.

Tactical Asset Allocation

An investor's investment policy statement lays out a strategic asset allocation, the range of asset class weights appropriate for the investor over the long haul. Some managers may choose to overweight or underweight asset classes within these ranges in an attempt to capitalize on their particular views of the market in processes known as tactical asset allocation.[43] We have a strong belief in strategic allocation. Tactical overlays are more difficult to implement successfully. Our hesitancy is partly due to concerns regarding transaction costs and taxes (for nonsheltered accounts) but is primarily due to our not having found a credible model. Our experience on this point is consistent with the dearth of evidence that active mutual fund managers can successfully time market movements, which we note is different than what is commonly known as tactical asset allocation. Nonetheless, it may be reasonable to occasionally adjust between related classes (e.g., growth and value) or between maturity distributions (e.g., a shift from short- to intermediate-term). However, significant shifts between broad asset classes (e.g., stocks to bonds) are more difficult to justify, because the evidence on successful market timing is not compelling.

DOWNSIDE RISK

The work of Harry Markowitz and the general principles of modern portfolio theory (MPT) are largely accepted by today's investment community. Markowitz's optimization algorithm serves as the basis for most mathematical optimizers; acceptance, however, is not universal. The seeds of discontent can be found in Markowitz's own work.

As discussed in the chapters on theory and math, Markowitz settled on mean variance as a risk measure over other alternatives (including semivariance) as a compromise. He acknowledged that a model based on semivariance might be theoretically better but concluded that, at the time, it was an unrealistic computable alternative. Since then, over 50 years have passed and some commentators argue that making the compromise is no longer valid. They contend that there are two major reasons for revisiting mean variance.

---

[43]We distinguish between market timing and tactical allocation. Classic market timing is often based on technical market factors and suggests either 100 percent in or 100 percent out of an investment allocation. We do not recommend market timing. Tactical allocation is generally based on a belief in mean reversion, and shifts in allocations are modest relative to the total asset class allocation (e.g., a 10 percent tactical variance between bonds and stocks for a portfolio with a strategic 50 percent bond/50 percent stock allocation).

1. A central tenet of MPT is that investors' decisions are guided by a desire to optimize their risk/return trade-off. The Markowitz optimization model equates risk with standard deviation. Modern research in investment theory and cognitive psychology has demonstrated that standard deviation, even for normal distributions, is not necessarily an acceptable measure of risk.
2. Mean variance is an adequate description only for normal distributions. As innumerable studies have demonstrated, return distributions of financial assets are not normally distributed.

Risk Measures

The following illustrations may be useful in demonstrating to your clients the fallacy of simply equating volatility to risk. These are useful concepts to know and to communicate to clients regardless of whether one specifically incorporates downside risk into an asset allocation framework. Exhibit 10.16 compares the performance of manager A and manager B. Manager A has during the past seven years achieved a mean return of 12.8 percent with a standard deviation of 4.8 percent. Manager B has achieved a 6.1 percent return with a standard deviation of 2.0. Although manager A took on more risk, she was the better choice because she always outperformed manager B.[44] Although this example illustrates that manager selection relies on more than standard deviation, it is unfair to cite it as a pure indictment of modern portfolio theory, because MPT would certainly take into account manager A's higher return.

EXHIBIT 10.16   Standard Deviation Does Not Equal Risk, Example 1

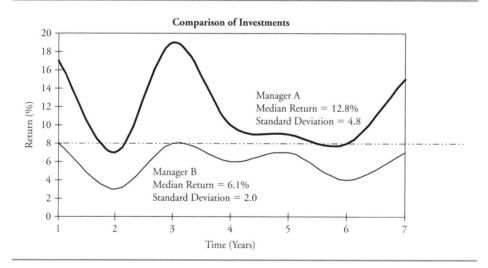

Exhibit 10.17 provides a better example that demonstrates the inadequacy of standard deviation as a measure of risk. In this case, both asset classes have normal distributions. Asset A, with a standard deviation equal to 2, is, by that standard, a much less risky investment than B with a standard deviation of 10. If, however, the investor requires a return of 8 percent (dashed vertical line), in order to meet that goal we had better revisit the definition. Under

---

[44]In mathematical terms, this is stated as manager A stochastically dominating manager B.

this scenario, investment A always fails to meet the investor's needs and, in that sense, it is clearly the riskier of the two choices.

EXHIBIT 10.17   Standard Deviation Does Not Equal Risk, Example 2

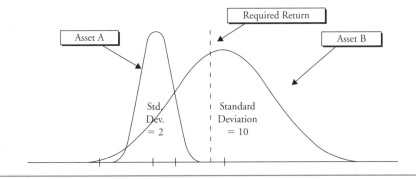

Asymmetric Returns

Consider Exhibit 10.18, a return distribution graph for managers A, B, and C. Manager A's distribution is skewed to the left, and manager B's to the right. Only manager C's returns are normally distributed. If the measure of risk is standard deviation, we would conclude that C is significantly less risky than B. This seems like a strange conclusion given that the returns of C will almost always be less than the average returns for B, and B is never expected to have returns less than C.

EXHIBIT 10.18   Returns for Three Managers

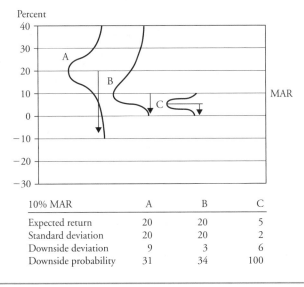

10% MAR	A	B	C
Expected return	20	20	5
Standard deviation	20	20	2
Downside deviation	9	3	6
Downside probability	31	34	100

Source: Sortino and Lee (1994).

To be fair, we are intermingling the concept of risk with return. Mean-variance optimization incorporates mean return as well as variance in its analysis. The point, however, is that two return distributions could have the same mean and standard deviation, but one could be skewed left and the other skewed right. It is important to consider the full description of a return distribution when considering its risk.

A New Risk/Return Paradigm

Instead of equating risk with uncertainty (i.e., the variability of returns around the mean) and using standard deviation as its measure, it is necessary to recognize that risk is not a universal concept. Although there have been a number of earlier articles addressing this issue, Brian Rom and Kathleen Ferguson published the seminal article titled "Post-Modern Portfolio Theory Comes of Age" in the winter 1993 issue of *Journal of Investing*, followed by a series of related articles in the fall 1994 issue[45] and a conference sponsored by the Center for Investment Research in February 1995.

Postmodern Portfolio Theory

The phrase *postmodern portfolio theory* (PMPT) was coined by Rom and Ferguson to describe the new "expanded risk/return paradigm" that could be implemented through sponsor-software (SS) technology. The SS optimizer is based on an algorithm developed by Frank Sortino, the director of the Pension Research Institute and one of the first investment theorists to address practical alternatives to the MV assumption of MPT.

PMPT asserts that investment risk should "be tied to each investor's specific goals and that any outcomes above this goal do not represent economic or financial risk. . . . In PMPT only volatility below the investor's target return means risk." The target return is referred to as the minimum acceptable return (MAR).

Unlike MPT, which is based on the assumption of symmetrical distributions, PMPT can be used to optimize asymmetrical distributions. Downside risk in PMPT is measured by target semideviation, the square root of target semivariance.[46] It also provides for two measures of downside risk:

1. Downside probability (also referred to as shortfall risk) is a measure of the probability of not meeting the MAR.
2. Average downside magnitude measures, in those cases when the MAR is not achieved, is the magnitude of the failure.

Rom and Ferguson compared two "equivalent risk"[47] portfolios, one using traditional MPT optimization (mean variance) and one using PMPT optimization (downside risk). The recommended asset allocation related in similar overall equity positions although the split between domestic and foreign equity differed somewhat. In light of the difficulty and uncertainty associated with estimating expected returns, correlations, skewness, and kurtosis, we are not convinced that the downside risk approach adds that much value.

---

[45]Wealth managers should include a copy of the fall 1994 issue in their reference libraries.

[46]Now you know why Chapter 7 ("Mathematics of Investing") discussed such an esoteric concept.

[47]The two portfolios are designed to have risks equivalent to a globally diversified independent reference portfolio.

Downside Deviation

Included in the fall 1994 *Journal of Investing* is an article by Sortino and Price specifically addressing the measurement of downside risk. Referring back to Exhibit 10.18, we have already demonstrated that manager B is a better choice than manager C. How does manager A compare to manager B?

Referring to the expected returns and standard deviations, they look identical; and if downside probability is used as a criterion, manager A looks better. The authors point out that the downside probability considers only the chance of failure; it ignores the magnitude of failure. They suggest using a measure referred to as downside deviation (i.e., the deviations below the MAR).[48] They conclude that a focus on downside risk is a step in the right direction, but that downside deviation is the only alternative with strong theoretical foundations. It is unfortunately computationally cumbersome and subject to the same estimation problems as standard deviation.

Conclusions Regarding Downside Risk

The work of Rom, Ferguson, Sortino, and others is very persuasive. The question for wealth managers is how to incorporate it in their practices. The following considerations are important:

- The algorithm for PMPT optimization requires estimates regarding asset class skewness in addition to estimates regarding returns, standard deviation, and correlations. According to an earlier paper by Sortino, skewness for an asset class can change dramatically with the methodology of calculation and the economic environment.
- Skewness obviously adds another dimension of estimation error. PMPT recognizes that clients' goals vary, and replaces standard deviation as the risk measure with a more client-dependent measure, the MAR. Unfortunately, capturing a client's goals may require more than a single fixed MAR. For example:
  - Goals are frequently variable (e.g., a minimum return over inflation or a minimum over some benchmark).
  - Goals vary depending on the economic environment (e.g., high returns in good markets and capital preservation in bad markets).
  - Goals are subjective (e.g., to maintain a standard of living).
  - There may be multiple goals (e.g., a MAR as well as a maximum risk of loss).
  - Goals may vary over different economic horizons (e.g., short-run goals may differ from long-term goals).[49]

The analytical process seems to still be in the academic and experimental stage. The clients of wealth managers typically have long investment time horizons. Merriken[50] suggests that downside risk is applicable for investors with short- and intermediate-term horizons. He

---

[48]See Sortino and Price (1994) and Sortino and Forsey (1996).

[49]The question of multiple scenario asset allocation optimization is an interesting related technique discussed by Fong and Fabozzi (1992), and a possible solution has been proposed by Dopfel, "The New Policy Portfolio," *Barclays Global Investors Investment Insights*, September 2009.

[50]Harry E. Merriken, "Analytical Approaches to Limit Downside Risk: Semivariance and the Need for Liquidity," *Journal of Investing* (Fall 1995): 71.

concludes that "whether the semi-variance approach is superior for longer holding periods is not addressed here."

Finally, the decision to use downside variance requires a balancing of its problems (such as those noted earlier) with its benefits. Wealth managers should become familiar with downside risk and incorporate the concept as part of their art, not their science.

PARTING COMMENTS

Developing an asset allocation that manages risk while enabling a client to meet goals is both an art and a science. The mathematics of optimization provides the science. The wealth manager must develop the inputs, manage the optimization process, and ultimately use the results to design an effective asset allocation. This portion is more art than science.

RESOURCES

Arnott, Robert, and Frank Fabozzi, eds. 1992. *Active Asset Allocation*. Chicago: Probus.

Arnott, Robert, and Robert Levell. 1993. "Rebalancing: Why? When? How Often?" *Journal of Investing*, Vol. 2, No. 1: 5–10.

Benninga, Simon. 2008. *Financial Modeling*, 3rd edition. Cambridge, MA: MIT Press.

Beutow, Gerald, Ronald Sellers, Donald Trotter, Elaine Hunt, and Willie Whipple. 2002. "The Benefits of Rebalancing." *Journal of Portfolio Management*, Vol. 28, No. 2.

Black, Jeremy. 1992. "Asset Rebalancing." *Financial Planning Perspectives: Asset Allocation Viewpoint, College for Financial Planning* (May).

Calverley, John P., Alan M. Meader, Brian D. Singer, and Renato Staub. 2007. "Capital Market Expectations." In *Managing Investment Portfolios: A Dynamic Process*, 3rd edition. John L. Maginn, Donald L. Tuttle, Jerald E. Pinto, and Dennis W. McLeavey, eds. CFA Institute Investment Series. Hoboken, NJ: John Wiley & Sons.

Chow, G., E. Jacquier, M. Kritzman, and K. Lowry. 1999. "Optimal Portfolios in Good Times and Bad," *Financial Analysts Journal*, Vol. 55, No. 3 (May/June): 65–73.

DeFusco, Richard, Dennis W. McLeavey, Jerald E. Pinto, and David E. Runkle. 2004. *Quantitative Methods for Investment Analysis*, 2nd edition. Charlottesville, VA: CFA Institute.

Dimson, Elroy, Paul Marsh, and Mike Staunton. 2006. "The Worldwide Equity Premium: A Smaller Puzzle." EFA 2006 Zurich Meetings Paper; AFA 2008 New Orleans Meetings Paper.

Dreman, David, and Michael A. Berry. 1995. "Analyst Forecasting Errors and Their Implications for Security Analysis." *Financial Analysts Journal* (May–June): 30–41.

Drost, Feike, and Theo Nijman. 1993. "Temporal Aggregation of GARCH Processes." *Econometrica*, Vol. 6, No. 4: 909–927.

Fama, Eugene, and Kenneth French. 1993. "Common Risk Factors in the Returns of Stocks and Bonds." *Journal of Financial Economics*, Vol. 33: 3–56.

Fong, Gifford, and Frank J. Fabozzi. 1992. "Asset Allocation Optimization Models" in *Active Asset Allocation*, Robert Arnott and Frank Fabozzi, eds. Chicago: Probus.

Frankfurter, George M., and Herbert E. Phillips. 1994. "A Brief History of MPT: From a Normative Model to Event Studies." *Journal of Investing* (Winter): 18–23.

Gibson, Roger. 2007. *Asset Allocation*, 4th edition. New York: Irwin.

Gyourko, Joseph, and Donald Keim. 1993. "Risk and Return in Real Estate: Evidence from a Real Stock Index." *Financial Analysts Journal* (September/October).

Horan, Stephen M., and Ashraf Al Zaman. 2008. "Tax-Adjusted Portfolio Optimization and Asset Location: Extensions and Synthesis." *Journal of Wealth Management*, Vol. 11, No. 3: 56–73.

Horan, Stephen M., and Thomas R. Robinson. 2009. "Estate Planning in a Global Context." CFA Program Curriculum Level III. Charlottesville, VA: CFA Institute.

Ibbotson, Roger, and Rex Sinquefield. 1976. "Stocks, Bonds, Bills, and Inflation: Simulations of the Future (1976–2000)." *Journal of Business,* Vol. 49, No. 3 (July).

Kritzman, Mark. 2009. "Managing Assets in Turbulent Markets." *CFA Institute Conference Proceedings Quarterly,* Vol. 26, No. 1: 53–61.

Lederman, Jess, and Robert A. Klein, eds. 1994. *Global Asset Allocation.* New York: John Wiley & Sons.

Maginn, John L., Donald L. Tuttle, Jerald E. Pinto, and Dennis W. McLeavey, eds. 2007. *Managing Investment Portfolios: A Dynamic Process,* 3rd edition. *CFA Institute Investment Series.* Hoboken, NJ: John Wiley & Sons.

Markowitz, Harry M. 2009. "Crisis Mode: Modern Portfolio Theory under Pressure." *Investment Professional* (Spring): 55–57.

Merriken, Harry E. 1995. "Analytical Approaches to Limit Downside Risk: Semivariance and the Need for Liquidity." *Journal of Investing* (Fall): 71.

Plaxco, Lisa, and Robert Arnott. 2002. "Rebalancing a Global Policy Benchmark." *Journal of Portfolio Management,* Vol. 28, No. 2.

Rom, Brian, and Kathleen Ferguson. 1993. "Post-Modern Portfolio Theory Comes of Age." *Journal of Investing* (Winter): 27–33.

SEI Corporation. 1996. "Asset Allocation for Taxable Investors: Maximizing After Tax Returns." SEI, March, 27–31.

Sengupta, Chandan. 2004. *Financial Modeling Using Excel and VBA.* Hoboken, NJ: John Wiley & Sons.

Sharpe, William F., Peng Chen, Jerald E. Pinto, and Dennis W. McLeavey. 2007. "Asset Allocation." In *Managing Investment Portfolios: A Dynamic Process,* 3rd edition. John L. Maginn, Donald L. Tuttle, Jerald E. Pinto, and Dennis W. McLeavey, eds. CFA Institute Investment Series. Hoboken, NJ: John Wiley & Sons.

Sortino, Frank A. 1993. "The Look of Uncertainty." *Journal of Investing* (Winter): 30–33.

Sortino, Frank, and Lee N. Price. 1994. "Performance Measurement in a Downside Risk Framework." *Journal of Investing* (Fall): 59–64.

Sortino, Frank, and Hal J. Forsey. 1996. "On the Use and Misuse of Downside Risk." *Journal of Portfolio Management* (Winter): 35–42.

Stine, Bert, and John Lewis. 1992. "Guidelines for Rebalancing Passive-Investment Portfolios." *Journal of Financial Planning* (April): 80–84.

Swenson, David F. 2000. *Pioneering Portfolio Management: An Unconventional Approach to Institutional Management.* New York: Free Press.

Wilcox, Jarrod. 2000. "Better Risk Management." *Journal of Portfolio Management,* Vol. 26, No. 4 (Summer): 53–64.

Wilcox, Jarrod. 2003. "Harry Markowitz and the Discretionary Wealth Hypothesis: A New Focus and a Relatively Simple Framework." *Journal of Portfolio Management,* Vol. 29, No. 3 (Spring): 58–65.

Wilcox, Jarrod W. 2008. "The Impact of Uncertain Commitments." *Journal of Wealth Management.*

Wilcox, Jarrod, Jeffrey E. Horvitz, and Dan diBartolomeo. 2006. *Investment Management for Taxable Private Investors.* Charlottesville, VA: Research Foundation of CFA Institute.

CHAPTER 11

TAXES

Pay tax on your take, not what you make.

—Warren Buffett

Jean Brunel, a leading authority on wealth management issues, says that "The impact of taxes . . . mandate[s] a new investment solution" that focuses on after-tax wealth accumulation rather than periodic returns.[1] Taxes are an expense that creates a drag on wealth accumulation and are therefore worthy of significant attention from wealth managers. However, a number of myths concerning taxes and investments are endemic to modern investment planning. If wealth managers are to provide competent guidance for clients they must eliminate myth-based planning from their repertoires.

This chapter addresses these important issues and presents some strategies to deal with the impact of taxes. Because of the controversial nature of many of these concepts and the ever-changing tax environment, we have included a significant amount of reference material.

TAX REDUCTION VERSUS WEALTH ACCUMULATION

There are a number of issues important to clients' understanding regarding their personal tax constraints, but none is more commonly misunderstood or a source of more bad advice than the myth of tax reduction. The single most common piece of investment advice provided to clients by non–investment professionals is that they should reduce their taxes. Not only is this the most common advice, but it also competes for the title of the dumbest advice. For a wealth manager, clearly the issue is to maximize the after-tax wealth accumulation, not to reduce taxes. Unfortunately, the misunderstanding is rampant.[2]

Because investors generally feel that tax payments are lost dollars, there is naturally an instinctive desire not to pay taxes. This is understandable but myopic, and it results in inefficient investing. The most effective way to clarify this issue is through a simple example:

---

[1]Jean Brunel, *Integrated Wealth Management* (London: Euromoney Institutional Investor, 2002), p. 3.
[2]Many years ago my wise dad told me, "Don't worry about taxes; they are easy to avoid. Just don't make any money."

	Tax-Free Investment A	Taxable Investment B
Return	$10,000	$14,000
Taxes	0	3,900

When asked to choose which of these investment alternatives they might wish for themselves, clients invariably choose the taxable investment. When confronted with the fact that they are choosing an investment that requires them to pay a tax of $3,900 and have rejected the investment that is tax free, they answer that they will have more money left over from the taxable investment after they pay taxes. This is obviously the correct response. Unfortunately, in circumstances any more complex than this, it becomes much more difficult to see the advantage of paying taxes. The wealth manager must keep clients focused on after-tax returns and risk.

GAINS VERSUS INCOME

Frequently a wealth manager must decide between high-dividend and capital-gains-oriented equity investments. A naive solution would always favor low-yielding stocks when the tax rate on dividends is higher than the tax rate on capital gains. Not only is the tax rate on capital gains sometimes lower, but the tax payment can be deferred until the position is liquidated. Although these two factors are important, this simple analysis ignores total return and assumes risk and return are equal between both types of stocks.

Consider Total Return

This naive solution makes several assumptions that may make a singular focus on tax rates and timing incomplete. First, it assumes that the pretax return of high-yielding and low-yielding stocks is the same. There are periods during which this may not be true. For example, a Sanford Bernstein study found that high-yield portfolios had an annualized total return of 14.3 percent (vs. S&P of 11.3 percent) and low-yield portfolios had a return of 9.6 percent over a 23-year period.[3] In any bracket, the excess return of the high-yield portfolio overwhelmed the tax drag of the higher marginal rate on dividends. This example is not to suggest that high-yield portfolios will always have better after-tax performance. It does suggest, however, that the wealth manager should consider that not all returns are necessarily equivalent.

Consider Risk

Another implicit assumption of simply comparing tax rates is that the investment alternatives are equally risky. Using the preceding example, there are good reasons to believe that high-yielding stocks and low-yielding stocks have different risk profiles. Because return and risk are

---

[3]Sanford Bernstein Research (1995). Sanford Bernstein is now known as AllianceBernstein.

inextricably linked, any return differential is likely associated with a risk differential that should also be considered.

Moreover, the mere presence of taxes affects an investor's after-tax risk exposure. By taxing investment returns, the government absorbs some of our investment risk. In the extreme, if the government were to tax 100 percent of your investment income (and give you a deduction on all your losses), you would have no investment risk. You would, of course, have no investment return, either, so the risk absorption is small solace for taxing returns in the first place, but it illustrates the point. We discuss this concept in more detail later in this chapter.

UNSYSTEMATIC RISK VERSUS CAPITAL GAINS TAXES

Consider a client with a large position in a single stock with a low tax basis (cost). This is popularly known as the low-basis dilemma and is a very common situation for wealthy clients. Do you recommend that the client sell the stock, eliminate the risk exposure, and pay the capital gains tax? Or do you recommend that he defer the tax and hold the stock?

The answer to the question depends on a number of factors:

- The relative expected returns of a single position versus that of a diversified portfolio (e.g., the relative returns of IBM vs. the Vanguard S&P 500).
- The subsequent holding period if the stock is not sold immediately.
- The relative volatility of an individual position versus that of a diversified portfolio (e.g., the volatility of IBM vs. the Vanguard S&P 500).

The first two factors are relatively straightforward, but the answer may be unknown. If the security that is being held appears to be fully valued by the market, its expected return may be lower than returns of alternative investments, and this would result in a bias toward selling the investment to eliminate the risk exposure even at the cost of the current tax bill. The longer you intend to hold the stock, the longer any potential taxes would be deferred or in some cases perhaps reduced or eliminated on transfer at death.

Relative Volatility

A great deal of research has been done on the third factor, relative volatility.[4] This research points out a number of concepts that are useful in assisting your client in making a decision.

- Single positions are inherently more volatile than diversified portfolios. The variance due to increased volatility decreases long-term growth, holding the arithmetic mean constant. That explains why the average stock in the market underperforms the stock market. This factor alone is a strong argument for liquidating a single position and diversifying the

---

[4]Messmore (1995); Stein, Siegel, Appeadu, and Narasimhan (2000); and Boyle, Loewy, Reiss, and Weiss (2004).

proceeds. Exhibit 11.1 demonstrates this. Both volatile stock A and the diversified portfolio have the same 10 percent average return, but the more stable diversified portfolio accumulates more wealth.

EXHIBIT 11.1 $100 Original Investment with 10 Percent Average Return

Portfolio	Year 1	Year 2	Ending Value
Volatile stock A	40%	−20%	$112
Diversified portfolio	10%	10%	$121

- The power of diversification can even overcome the initial tax bite from paying capital gains tax. Exhibit 11.2 presents the results of a Monte Carlo simulation that compares the after-tax accumulation of holding a single stock with 40 percent volatility with a strategy of paying a 20 percent capital gains tax and investing the remaining proceeds (80 percent of the pretax liquidation) in a diversified portfolio with 17 percent volatility.
- Although the average after-tax outcome of the single stock position is greater than that of the diversified portfolio, that outcome is highly unlikely because the distribution is so highly skewed. The median outcome is less than half of that for the diversified strategy. Therefore, minimizing our current year's tax bill is not always the best strategy.
- One may want to hold a position and defer the gain in a stock in order to achieve a step-up in basis at death. Although this strategy may be worthwhile for a client with a very high risk of mortality, ultimately the client's mortality, investment fluctuations, and corporate transactions are not within the client's control. In Stein's 2001 study, the concentrated stock strategy had a 39 percent chance of losing nominal principal value over a 20-year horizon compared with only 2 percent for the diversified strategy. In addition, the concentrated strategy has a much greater chance of very bad outcomes.

Based on a 20-year study, Sanford Bernstein found that 35 percent of the companies had failed, liquidated, or merged. In most cases, the activity was precipitated by a severe price decline or caused a taxable event for the stock owner anyway. The subsequent price appreciation of these stocks underperformed a diversified portfolio so much that their poor returns would have eroded any tax savings.

Client Issues

Considering the results of Sanford Bernstein and those of another researcher, Richard Applebach Jr., the following guidelines are useful in assisting clients to make the hold/sell decision.

EXHIBIT 11.2   Probability Distribution of After-Tax Liquidation Value

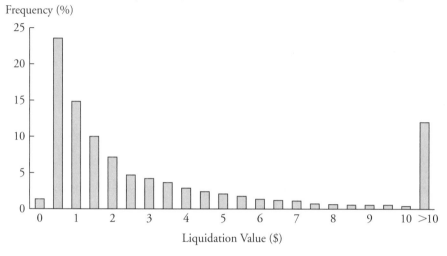

(A) $1.00 in Single Security with Zero Cost Basis and 40 Percent Volatility

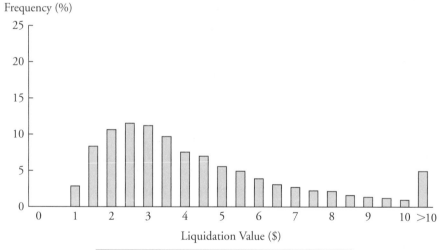

(B) $0.80 in Diversified Portfolio with $0.80 Cost Basis and 17 Percent Volatility

Measure	A	B
Expected Final Value	$5.3	$4.2
Median Value	$1.6	$3.3
Probability of $1 or Less	39%	2%
Probability of $2 or Less	57%	21%

Note: Annual expected return = 10 percent; dividends on stock = 0; dividends on diversified portfolio = 1.2 percent; horizon = 20 years; terminal liquidation.
Source: David M. Stein, "Taxes and Quantitative Portfolio Management," *AIMR Conference Proceedings Quarterly*, CFA Institute, 2001.

For long-term investors,[5] selling 20 percent of the position per year over a five-year period will significantly reduce annualized standard deviations and, in most cases, not reduce returns. The longer the expected time period until step-up, the more favorable the strategy of diversification will be.

Based on these studies, the guidelines in Exhibit 11.3 for determining the maximum percentage of net worth to be held in a single low-basis stock seem appropriate.

EXHIBIT 11.3   Prudent Level of Low-Basis Stock

Life Expectancy	Invested in a Single Stock[a]
10 years	10%
15	6
20	4
25	4
30	3

[a]Assumes cost basis = 10% of market value and that 50% of the portfolio is in equities and a step-up in basis.

An additional technique the wealth manager may find useful to demonstrate to clients the increased volatility of a single stock as compared to a diversified portfolio is to refer to the pricing of put options. For example, in December 2009, the annualized cost of a put option at the market price for blue-chip stocks (Disney, Philip Morris, and Ford) was 50 percent to 300 percent greater than the cost for a similar option on the S&P 500. Intelligent and sophisticated professional investors, voting with their pocketbooks, were willing to pay more than twice as much to protect against the risk of not diversifying. Professionals recognize that there is a real risk to owning a single company, no matter how blue-chip.

TAX-ADJUSTED RETURNS AND ACCUMULATIONS

We have dispelled the myth of tax reduction in favor of risk-adjusted, after-tax return maximization. It is therefore helpful to better understand how we can model after-tax returns.

At the time of this writing in the United States, interest income is taxed annually as ordinary income at relatively high rates. Dividends and capital gains, by contrast, enjoy substantially reduced tax rates, and they are generally taxed at only 15 percent. Moreover, the tax on capital gains may be deferred until the eventual sale of the securities. As a result, an equity portfolio with a relatively low turnover is much more tax efficient than a portfolio of taxable bonds. (See Exhibit 11.4.)

---

[5]Defined as a life expectancy of 15 years.

EXHIBIT 11.4   Proportion of Return Distributed as Ordinary Income and Capital Gains for
Equity Mutual Funds

Fund Style	Ordinary Income (*Poi*)	Realized Capital Gain (*Pcg*)	Unrealized Capital Gain
A. Mean of 10 randomly selected mutual funds[a]			
Aggressive growth	5.2%	63.5%	31.3%
Growth	7.0	44.2	48.8
Growth and Income	20.5	45.4	34.2
Balanced	37.9	30.7	31.4
B. Large mutual funds[b]			
Actively managed	27.3%	50.9%	21.8%
Vanguard Index 500	21.4	11.1	67.5

[a]Mean from 10 randomly selected active and passive funds for 1992–1996 reported in Crain and Austin (1997).
Short-term capital gains are included as realized capital gains.
[b]Median distribution rates from the five largest actively-managed funds with the greatest total assets beginning in
1979, as reported by Shoven and Sialm (2003). Short-term capital gains and dividends are included as ordinary
income distributions because of their tax treatment during the sample period. The distribution rates are the average
rates for each fund for 1979–1998.
Source: Horan (2005).

Exhibit 11.4 shows that management style has an important influence on tax efficiency. Not
surprisingly, aggressive growth mutual funds distribute a relatively small amount of return in
the form of ordinary income but have a relatively high rate of capital gains recognition.
Growth funds recognize fewer gains, and balanced funds have relatively more ordinary
income. Index funds, by contrast, have a relatively large proportion of their return in the form
of unrealized gains, the tax on which is deferred, creating a lighter tax burden.

The impact of these different tax profiles can be illustrated using some simple models of
after-tax accumulation. In general, a portion of a portfolio's investment return is received in
the form of dividends (p_d) and taxed at a rate of t_d; another portion is received in the form of
interest income (p_i) and taxed as such at a rate of t_i; and another portion is taxed as realized
long-term capital gain (p_{cg}) at t_{cg}. The remainder of an investment's return is unrealized
capital gain, the tax on which is deferred until ultimately recognized at the end of the
investment horizon. These return proportions can be computed by simply dividing each
income component by the total dollar return.

EXAMPLE 11.1   Blended Tax Environment

Michael Stephenson has a balanced portfolio of stocks and bonds. At the beginning of
the year, his portfolio had a market value of $100,000. By the end of the year, the
portfolio is worth $108,000 before any annual taxes have been paid, and there have
been no contributions or withdrawals. Interest of $400 and dividends of $2,000 were
reinvested into the portfolio. During the year, Stephenson had $3,600 of realized long-
term capital gains. These proceeds were again reinvested into the portfolio.

1. What percentage of Stephenson's return is in the form of interest?
2. What percentage of Stephenson's return is in the form of dividends?
3. What percentage of Stephenson's return is in the form of realized capital gain?
4. What percentage of Stephenson's return is in the form of deferred capital gain?

Solution to 1: $p_i = \$400/\$8,000 = 0.05$ or 5 percent.
Solution to 2: $p_d = \$2,000/\$8,000 = 0.25$ or 25 percent.
Solution to 3: $p_{cg} = \$3,600/\$8,000 = 0.45$ or 45 percent.
Solution to 4: Unrealized gain = $\$8,000 - \$400 - \$2,000 - \$3,600 =$ a percentage of return, $\$2,000/\$8,000 = 0.25$, or 25 percent. The unrealized gain is the portion of investment appreciation that was not taxed as interest, dividends, or realized capital gain.

The annual return after realized taxes can be expressed as:

$$r^* = r(1 - p_i t_i - p_d t_d - p_{cg} t_{cg})$$

where r represents the pretax overall return on the portfolio. From the preceding example, note that the pretax return was 8 percent [($\$108,000/\$100,000) - 1$]; however, there would be taxes due on the interest, dividends, and realized capital gains. The effective annual after-tax return, r^*, reflects the tax erosion caused by a portion of the return being taxed as ordinary income and other portions being taxed as realized capital gain and dividends. It does not capture tax effects of deferred unrealized capital gains. One can view this expression as being analogous to the simple expression in which after-tax return equals the pretax return times 1 minus the tax rate. The aggregate tax rate has several components in this case, but the intuition is the same.[6]

EXAMPLE 11.2   Blended Tax Environment: After-Tax Return

Continuing with the facts in Example 11.1, assume that dividends and realized capital gains are taxed at 15 percent annually, whereas interest is taxed at 35 percent annually.

1. What is the annual return after realized taxes?
2. Assuming taxes are paid out of the investment account, what is the balance in the account at the end of the first year?

Solution to 1:

$$r^* = r(1 - p_i t_i - p_d t_d - p_{cg} t_{cg})$$
$$= 8\%[1 - (0.05 \times 0.35) - (0.25 \times 0.15) - (0.45 \times 0.15)] = 7.02\%$$

---

[6]This expression could be expanded to incorporate any number of different taxable components, such as a different rate for short-term capital gains or special treatment of certain types of taxable income. The general principle is that a portfolio can generate returns in different forms, each of which may be taxed differently.

Solution to 2: Using the income data from Example 11.1,

Income Type	Income Amount	Tax Rate	Tax Due
Interest	$ 400	35%	$140
Dividends	2,000	15	300
Realized capital gains	3,600	15	540
Total tax due			980

After paying taxes there would be $107,020 in the account ($108,000 − $980). Note that this is consistent with the 7.02 percent return computed for the first question.

We still have not accounted for the entire tax burden. In these examples, 25 percent of the investment return is deferred as an unrealized capital gain. As the tax on this unrealized gain will likely be paid on liquidation of the investment, we should consider the impact on the ultimate after-tax realized gain.

EXAMPLE 11.3 Future Long-Term Accumulation

Continuing with the facts in the previous example, assume there is a five-year investment horizon for the account. Annual accrual taxes will be paid out of the account each year, with the deferred tax on previously unrealized capital gains paid at the end of the five-year horizon when the account is liquidated. For simplicity of exposition, we assume that the account is rebalanced annually and use geometric realized returns, which we assume are the same each period. Consider a $100,000 portfolio with the return and tax profile listed in Panel A of Exhibit 11.5. What is the expected after-tax accumulation in five years?

EXHIBIT 11.5 Hypothetical Tax Profile

	Annual Distribution Rate (p)	Tax Rate (T)
Panel A: Tax Profile		
Ordinary income (i)	5%	35%
Dividends (d)	25	15
Capital gain (cg)	45	15
Investment horizon (n)		5 years
Average return (r)		8%
Panel B: Intermediate Accumulation Calculations		
Annual after-tax return (r^*)		7.02%

In this case, 25 percent of the return is composed of dividends, 5 percent is composed of realized short-term capital gains, and 45 percent is composed of realized long-term gains. These figures imply that the remaining 25 percent (i.e., $1 - 0.05 - 0.25 - 0.45$) of portfolio returns are deferred capital gains and not taxed until the end of the investment horizon. Another way to look at this is that out of the 8 percent annual return, 6 percent is realized each period and 2 percent is deferred. The value of the portfolio at the end of five years before considering the tax on unrealized gains would be $140,386 (future value of $100,000 over five years at 7.02 percent). The tax basis of the account would include any reinvestment of realized gains and income over the five-year period and would be $128,880 (you will need to either trust us on this or create your own Excel spreadsheet—it works!). The accumulated unrealized gain would therefore be $11,506, which would result in a tax of $1,726 upon liquidation, and the after-tax value would therefore be $138,660 ($140,386 less $1,726).

An important question is how much lower these accumulations are as a result of taxes. Knowing that provides a sense of how important an awareness of taxes is. Exhibit 11.6 shows the proportion of investment growth consumed by taxes using the facts in these examples but varying the pretax return and holding period. Several observations are noteworthy. First, the effect of taxes on capital growth is greater than the annual after-tax return would imply, because paying annual taxes decreases the power of compounding. Second, the adverse effects of taxes on capital growth increase over time. That is, the proportional difference between pretax and after-tax gains grows as the investment horizon increases. Third, the tax drag increases as the investment return increases, all else being equal. Fourth, return and investment horizon have a multiplicative effect on the tax drag associated with future accumulations. Specifically, the impact of returns on the tax effect is greater for long investment horizons, and the impact of investment horizon is greater for higher returns because figures in the bottom right corner change more rapidly than figures in the upper left corner.

EXHIBIT 11.6   Proportion of Investment Growth Consumed by Taxes

	Investment Horizon in Years (n)			
r	10	20	30	40
4%	16.9%	18.0%	19.1%	20.3%
6	17.9	20.1	22.6	25.1
8	18.8	22.3	26.1	30.0
10	19.8	24.6	29.7	34.9

Note: The calculations assume the facts in the previous example.

Accrual Equivalent Returns and Tax Rates

A useful way to summarize the impact of taxes on portfolio returns is to calculate an accrual equivalent after-tax return.[7] In the previous example, the $100,000 portfolio has an after-tax accumulation five years hence of $138,660. The accrual equivalent return is found by solving

---

[7]This term is coined by Poterba (2000).

for the return that equates the standard future value formula to the after-tax accumu
solving for the return. The difference between the accrual equivalent return and t
return of 8 percent is a measure of the tax drag imposed on the portfolio.

For example, we can solve for the rate, r_{AE}, that equates the future value of $\$100,000$
with $\$138,660$:

$$\$100,000(1 + r_{AE})^5 = \$138,660$$

The accrual equivalent return, r_{AE}, is 6.76 percent, which is less than the annual return
after realized taxes, r^*, of 7.02 percent because the accrual equivalent return incorporates the
impact of deferred taxes on realized gains as well as taxes that accrue annually. The accrual
equivalent return is always less than the taxable return, r. It approaches the pretax return,
however, as the time horizon increases, which demonstrates the value of tax deferral. The
value of deferral in this example is relatively modest, however, because only 25 percent of
the tax obligation associated with the return is assumed to be deferred. If more of the return is
in the form of deferred gains, the value of the deferral increases.

The accrual equivalent return is similar to the *tax-adjusted return* specified by the
Securities and Exchange Commission (SEC) for calculating a mutual fund's annualized after-
tax return for five- and 10-year periods. Mutual funds are required to disclose in their prospectuses after-tax returns based on the SEC's standardized formulas. The SEC calculation
assumes all income and short-term capital gains are taxed at a maximum federal rate at the
time of distribution and that long-term capital gains are taxed at 20 percent. The main
difference is that the SEC's tax-adjusted return calculation ignores the capital gains tax effect
associated with selling the fund at the end of the period.[8]

Morningstar uses the tax-adjusted return to calculate a tax cost ratio that compares the
pretax return to the after-tax return. Specifically, it estimates the proportion of a mutual fund
investor's assets consumed by taxes. The Morningstar tax cost ratio is calculated as:

$$\text{Tax Cost Ratio} = 1 - \left[\frac{1 + r^*}{1 + r} \right]$$

EXAMPLE 11.4   Tax Cost Ratio

Continuing with the facts in the previous example, the pretax return equals 8 percent.
The tax-adjust return prior to any tax effect from selling the shares, or preliquidation
return, equals 7.02 percent. Therefore, the tax cost ratio equals:

$$\text{Tax Cost Ratio} = 1 - \left[\frac{1.072}{1.08} \right] = 0.0074 = 0.74\%$$

In this case, taxes consume nearly three-quarters of a percent of a mutual fund
investor's assets. In making this calculation over multiple periods, the SEC's tax-
adjusted return is compounded over the five- or 10-year period.

---

[8]This method is also known as the preliquidation method because it estimates after-tax returns prior to
liquidation of the investment.

Calculating Accrual Equivalent Tax Rates

The accrual equivalent tax rate, which is the annual tax rate that would produce the same after-tax accumulation, is another way to express tax drag. It is the hypothetical tax rate, t_{AE}, that produces an after-tax return equivalent to the accrual equivalent return. In our example, it is found by solving for T_{AE} in the following expression:

$$r(1 - t_{AE}) = r_{AE}$$

In our example, $8\%(1 - t_{AE}) = 6.76\%$. Solving for t_{AE}, the accrual equivalent tax rate is therefore 15.5 percent. This rate is much lower than the marginal tax rate on ordinary income and only slightly higher than the favorable rate on dividends and capital gains in this example, because a relatively small portion (i.e., 5 percent) of the portfolio's return is generated from highly taxed income. Most of the return receives preferential tax treatment in either the form of a reduced rate for dividends or a reduced rate on realized capital gains combined with a valuable deferral for unrealized gains. As a result, investments with this tax profile are relatively tax efficient. The accrual equivalent tax rate would increase if either the return had a larger component taxed at ordinary rates or dividends and capital gains received less favorable treatment. In either case, r_{AE} would be smaller, implying a higher value of t_{AE} for a given level of pretax return r in the equation.

The accrual equivalent tax rate can be used in several ways. First, it can be used to measure the tax efficiency of different asset classes or portfolio management styles. Second, it illustrates to clients the tax impact of lengthening the average holding periods of stocks they own. Third, it can be used to assess the impact of future tax law changes. If the client's tax rate is likely to change in the future, the manager can determine the impact of the expected change on the accrual equivalent tax rate. The future tax rate could change for several reasons, such as tax law changes, changes in client circumstances, or the client taking advantage of tax rules designed to encourage certain behaviors, such as charitable contributions, that may be deductible in some tax regimes.

STOCKS, BONDS, AND TAX-DEFERRED ACCOUNTS

Most investors have different types of assets (e.g., stocks and bonds) that can be located in different types of accounts—taxable, tax-deferred, and tax-free (e.g., Roth) accounts. In which account—the tax-free, the tax-deferred, or the taxable—should the investor locate the stocks, and where should she locate the bonds? This choice is called the *asset location* decision and is distinct from the *asset allocation* decision, which determines the mix of stocks and bonds in the aggregate portfolio. Moreover, does the location of assets affect the investor's overall asset allocation? If so, how?

In general, wealth managers should consider placing taxable fixed-income securities in tax-deferred accounts (TDAs) and equities in taxable accounts when income from fixed income securities is taxed at a higher effective rate (ordinary income and currently realized gains). The basic intuition for this approach is that investors can achieve better after-tax results by placing highly taxed assets in tax-deferred accounts, such as traditional and Roth IRAs, or 401(k) plans. Securities with lighter tax burdens (e.g., passively managed equity with unrealized gains) should be placed in taxable accounts where the tax environment is relatively inconsequential.

Recent research shows that high-income investors in the 40 percent tax bracket generally are better off holding stock in taxable accounts and taxable bonds in TDAs if the mutual fund tax burden is relatively light (low dividends and low realized capital gains).[9] If the stock funds are more tax inefficient (distribute more of the return currently as dividends or realized capital gains), the investor should increase his stock holdings in the TDA thereby increasing the investor's pretax exposure to equities. Further, if the tax drag on equities becomes sufficiently onerous such that 68.6 percent or more of the annual returns are distributed, the investor is better off shifting the equities from the taxable account to the TDA and buying municipal bonds in the taxable account. Interestingly, this break point is close to the mean total distribution rates reported in Exhibit 11.4.

For a medium-income individual in the 30 percent tax bracket, the optimal asset location is similar. When distribution rates of the stock fund are low, investors should hold stock in the taxable account and favor taxable bonds in the TDA. But if the stock fund distributes more than 88.5 percent of its return currently (i.e., is highly tax inefficient), stocks are better placed in the TDA, and the taxable account should hold municipal bonds.

TAX EFFICIENCY AND ASSET ALLOCATION

The tendency of governments to change tax rates is familiar to all wealth managers. There have been more than 3,250 changes to the U.S. tax code between 2001 and 2009. If a wealth manager accepts the importance of asset allocation and is interested in the client's real, after-tax return, it is obvious that the impact of tax changes is important. The question is: What changes should the wealth manager make in the portfolio allocations? The solution is counterintuitive.

The most obvious impact of an increase in tax rates is a diminution of after-tax total returns. If a client requires a specific return in order to accomplish goals, the allocation would have to be adjusted in favor of equities to compensate for the increased tax loss. The less obvious impact is the change in the relative desirability of bonds vis-à-vis stock. The counterintuitive influence is the influence a change in tax rates can have on the return/risk relationship of different asset classes. It would seem obvious that if a wealth manager, in response to an increase in taxes, recommends an increase in equities, that the manager will also be recommending a higher-risk portfolio. However, once again common sense fails us.

To demonstrate this, SEI, in its July 1993 *Capital Market Research Report*, developed a "Real Rate of Return to Risk" ratio for stocks and bonds. This ratio, which we will call the SEI ratio, is calculated as:

$$\text{SEI Ratio} = \frac{\text{Portfolio Return} - \text{Inflation}}{\sigma}$$

The ratio can be calculated using both before- and after-tax returns.

SEI then calculates an "Equity Advantage Factor," a measure of real return per unit of risk, as:

$$\text{SEI Factor} = \text{SEI Ratio}_{\text{Equity}} - \text{SEI Ratio}_{\text{Bonds}}$$

---

[9]John B. Shoven and Clemens Sialm, "Asset Location in Tax-Deferred and Conventional Savings Accounts," *Journal of Public Economics*, Vol. 88, No. 1/2 (January 2004): 23–38.

Exhibit 11.7 shows the advantage of equities over bonds. For current taxes, it assumes a 30 percent ordinary and capital gains tax and for new taxes it projects an increase in the ordinary tax rate to 40 percent. Inflation is assumed to be 4 percent.

EXHIBIT 11.7   SEI Factors

	Before Tax		After Tax		After Tax—New	
	Equity	Bonds	Equity	Bonds	Equity	Bonds
Real ROR	6.50%	2.50%	3.35%	0.55%	3.35%	− 0.10%
Risk	21.00	7.00	14.70	4.90	14.70	4.20
SEI ratio	0.31	0.36	0.23	0.11	0.23	− 0.02
SEI factor						

As the table demonstrates, taxes not only reduce returns, but they also reduce the relative risk of equities! This concept is best demonstrated by way of example. Consider a $100,000 investment with an expected return of 10 percent, which is taxed annually at 40 percent. Assume there are three equally likely outcomes, as presented in Exhibit 11.8. The standard deviation of pretax returns is 15 percent. The after-tax accumulations in one year and the after-tax returns are presented in the last two columns.[10]

The standard deviation of after-tax returns equals 9 percent. Taxes absorbed 40 percent of the pretax volatility. As a result, the taxes not only reduce an investor's returns, but also absorb some investment risk. This concept has implications for portfolio optimization discussed next.

EXHIBIT 11.8   Simple Example of Investment Risk and Taxes

Outcome	Probability	After-Tax Accumulation	Pretax Return	After-Tax Market Value	After-Tax Return
Good	1/3	$125,000	25%	$115,000	15%
Average	1/3	110,000	10	106,000	6
Bad	1/3	95,000	− 5	97,000	− 3
Exp. value		$110,000	10%	$106,000	6%
Standard deviation (σ)			15%		9%

Note: Investment returns are assumed to be taxed at a rate of 40% in the year they are earned.

To see how taxes affect after-tax risk in a portfolio context, consider an investor with 50 percent of her wealth invested in equities and 50 percent invested in fixed income, both held in taxable accounts. The equity has a pretax standard deviation of 20 percent and is relatively tax-efficient such that all returns are taxed each year at a 20 percent tax rate. The fixed income is also taxed annually but at a 40 percent rate, with pretax volatility of 5 percent. If the two

---

[10]The astute reader will recognize that this analysis assumes symmetry in the tax system. That is, the $5,000 pretax loss in the bad state is partially offset by a $2,000 tax deduction in the same way a pretax gain is partially offset by a tax liability. In reality, the tax code places restrictions on the amount of losses that can be used to reduce taxes.

asset classes are perfectly correlated, the pretax portfolio volatility is 12.5 percent. On an after-tax basis, however, portfolio volatility would be 9.5 percent. This example illustrates that annually paid taxes reduce portfolio volatility.[11]

Alternatively, suppose that the equity is held in a taxable account and the fixed income is held in a tax-exempt account like those described in the previous section. In this case, the investor absorbs all of the bond volatility in the tax-exempt account, and the new portfolio volatility is 10.5 percent. After-tax volatility has increased from the previous measure of after-tax volatility of 9.5 percent because one of the assets (bonds) became tax sheltered. The government therefore has absorbed less investment risk through taxes, and the investor is left bearing more investment risk.

A final consideration is the influence of inflation on the relative after-tax returns of stocks and bonds. Analogous to the impact of taxes, inflation reduces the real rate of return (ROR) of both asset classes but has a disproportionate influence on bonds. Exhibit 11.9 displays this relationship. The higher the inflation rate, the riskier bonds become relative to stock. This exhibit can be an effective tool in communicating to the client another perspective on the safety of stocks versus bonds.

EXHIBIT 11.9   Impact of Inflation on After-Tax Returns

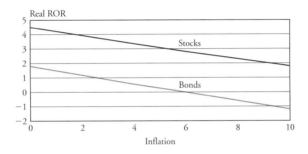

TAX-AWARE INVESTMENT DECISIONS

According to the *Wall Street Journal*, in 1913 the entire federal tax code (including commentary) fit neatly into a single 400-page book. In 2009, Commerce Clearinghouse's tax publications comprised over 67,200 pages, with reportedly 1,638 forms and 3.7 million words.[12] Taxpayers may spend about $370 billion annually just to comply with the requirements of those 67,200 pages. It is therefore not surprising that since the publication of Robert Jeffrey and Robert Arnott's 1993 article *Is Your Alpha Big Enough to Cover Its Taxes?* one of the most popular investment issues has been portfolio tax management.[13]

---

[11]The arithmetic is somewhat more complicated when the two assets are not perfectly correlated, in which case one would use the standard expression for the volatility of a two-security portfolio. The general point that taxes reduce portfolio volatility remains unaffected.

[12]If a person could read 200 words per minute, it would take 308.33 hours of nonstop reading to read the tax code. That's almost two months of full-time work if you read only during business hours.

[13]Other seminal research that has touted the advantages of portfolio tax management includes Dickson and Shoven (1993, 1994); Randolf (1994); Arnott, Berkin, and Ye (2000, 2001); Berkin and Ye (2003); and Horvitz and Wilcox (2003).

Horan and Adler surveyed 322 wealth managers (mostly CFA charterholders), who reported surprisingly widespread adoption of tax management strategies.[14] For example, more than 90 percent of respondents use some measure of tax efficiency in the selection of mutual funds. When selling a security, most investment managers believe the holding period is important and engage in some kind of tax loss harvesting.

Jeffrey and Arnott quote early commentators as observing that "taxes are the biggest expenses that investors face—more than commissions [and] more than investment management fees," and "returns are likely to depend far more on the risk the fund assumes *and more on its tax liability* [emphasis added] than on the accuracy of the analysts' forecasts." Another writer laments, "It has been estimated that over 40 percent of professionally managed balanced portfolios' returns are ultimately taxed away."[15] In a major 1995 study, Goldman Sachs suggested that the investors' growing sensitivity to tax issues might result in major changes for the mutual fund industry, including:

> *A flight of assets from funds that mix both retirement and taxable assets and a cultural upheaval when traditional portfolio managers have to deal with the new management guru—the tax strategist.*

In his excellent text, *Tax-Aware Investment Management*, Doug Rogers (2006) asserts:

> *Some managers are modifying buy-and-sell decisions to incorporate the impact of taxes, and innovative tax-efficient products, such as exchange-traded funds, are rapidly gaining recognition and acceptance . . . tax-aware investing is equally important to investors regardless of the magnitude of wealth. (pp. x–xi)*

Let's sort through the veracity of these claims.

Holding Period Management

Since the first edition of this book (titled *Wealth Management*) in 1997, the tax environment in the United States has changed significantly. One of the most significant changes as it relates to investment management is the preferential tax rate provided for long-term capital gains by the Jobs and Growth Tax Relief Reconciliation Act (JGTRRA) of 2003.[16] As of the time of this writing, long-term capital gains (e.g., those related to holding periods longer than 12 months) are generally taxed at 15 percent, which significantly changes the conclusions in the first edition.

---

[14]Stephen M. Horan and David Adler, "Tax-Aware Investment Management Practice," *Journal of Wealth Management*, Vol. 12, No. 2 (2009): 71–88.

[15]Jacob (1995).

[16]It is worth pointing out that, although the relatively lower tax rate applied to realized long-term capital gains is labeled "preferential," it really only ameliorates (but does not eliminate) the double taxation of equity returns. Unlike interest on bonds, which escapes corporate tax when recorded as interest expense to bondholders, corporations pay tax on retained earnings and dividends paid to investors. When investors receive dividends and realized capital gains, they are taxed once again, leading to the commonly known concept of double taxation.

When short-term capital gains can be taxed at 35 percent and long-term capital gains are taxed at 15 percent, there is a significant economic advantage to favor holding periods greater than 12 months, if possible. To see this point, consider four types of equity investors. The first type is a *trader* who trades frequently and recognizes all portfolio returns in the form of annually taxed short-term gains at a rate of 35 percent. The *active investor* trades less frequently. Active investors realize taxes on all their returns about annually (e.g., with no deferral) but such that gains are considered long-term and are taxed at only 15 percent. The *passive investor* passively buys and holds stock. This investor not only benefits from the preferential tax rate, but also defers the payment of the tax until the end of the investment horizon. The *exempt investor* not only buys and holds stocks, but never pays capital gains tax.

Suppose these four individuals invest $1,000 in non-dividend-paying stocks that earn 8 percent annually for 20 years. The after-tax accumulations and accrual equivalent tax rates are listed in Exhibit 11.10.

EXHIBIT 11.10   Future Accumulations for Different Types of Investors

Investor Type	Future Accumulation	Expression	Accrual Equivalent Return	Accrual Equivalent Tax Rate
Trader	$2,756	$1,000[1 + 0.08(1 - 0.35)]^{20}$	5.2%	40.0%
Active investor	3,728	$1,000[1 + 0.08(1 - 0.15)]^{20}$	6.8	15.0
Passive investor	4,112	$1,000[(1.08)^{20}(1 - 0.15) + 0.15]$	7.3	8.4
Exempt investor	4,661	$1,000(1.08)^{20}$	8.0	0.0

Holding all else constant, the trader accumulates the least amount of wealth, and the tax-exempt investor accumulates the most. The active and passive investors fall in between. This comparison illustrates that trading behavior affects the tax burden on stocks (and other assets that provide capital gain appreciation) when held in taxable accounts.

Notice that the biggest gain associated with portfolio tax management in this simple setting relates to extending investment holding periods beyond 12 months to receive the preferential rate on long-term capital gains. The accrual equivalent return increases 160 basis points annually. By contrast, the incremental benefit from deferring the capital gains tax until the end of the 20-year period is only 50 basis points annually. Moreover, this incremental benefit would decrease dramatically if the investment horizon shortened even to 10 years. The benefit of realizing long-term gains in lieu of short-term gains is substantial in taxable accounts, especially for long investment horizons and higher returns.

Tax Loss Harvesting

Portfolio turnover is often used as a measure of portfolio tax efficiency. Unfortunately, it is a poor proxy for tax efficiency. Not all trading is necessarily tax inefficient. Realizing taxable losses to offset taxable gains, for example, is a common practice called *tax loss harvesting*. It is part of a broader class of tax-motivated trading techniques that can be labeled portfolio tax management.

EXAMPLE 11.5   Tax Loss Harvesting: Current Tax Savings

Eduardo Cappellino has a $1 million portfolio held in a taxable account. The end of the 2010 tax year is approaching, and Cappellino has recognized $100,000 worth of capital gains. His portfolio has securities that have experienced $60,000 of losses. These securities have not yet been sold and their losses are therefore unrecognized. Cappellino could sell these securities and replace them with similar securities expected to earn identical returns.[17] The federal government taxes long-term capital gains at 15 percent.

1. Without making any further transactions, how much tax does Cappellino owe this year?
2. How much tax will Cappellino owe this year if he sells the securities with the $60,000 loss?
3. How much tax will Cappellino save this year if he sells the securities with the $60,000 loss?

Solution to 1: Capital gains tax $= 0.15 \times \$100,000 = \$15,000$.
Solution to 2: If Cappellino realizes $60,000 of losses, the net gain will be reduced to $40,000. New capital gain tax $= 0.15 \times (\$100,000 - \$60,000) = \$6,000$.
Solution to 3: Tax savings $= \$15,000 - \$6,000 = \$9,000$.

It is important to understand that the tax savings realized in a given tax year from tax loss harvesting overstates the true gain. Selling a security at a loss and reinvesting the proceeds in a similar security effectively resets the cost basis to the lower market value, potentially increasing future tax liabilities. In other words, taxes saved now may simply be postponed. The value of tax loss harvesting is largely in deferring the payment of tax liabilities.[18]

EXAMPLE 11.6   Tax Loss Harvesting: Tax Deferral

In the previous example, the securities with an unrealized loss have a current market value of $110,000 and cost basis of $170,000 (an unrealized loss of $60,000). Cappellino could:

Option A: Hold the securities with the unrealized loss.
Option B: Sell the securities in 2010 and replace them with securities offering the same return.

---

[17] Realizing losses by selling and buying similar securities is subject to certain restrictions by the government or taxing authority, which we address shortly.

[18] In cases where securities receive a step-up in basis upon inheritance or are gifted to charity, the government will never recapture the current-year tax savings, greatly increasing the harvesting value to the investor. Furthermore, in the United States the value of a built-in capital loss is lost at death. For example, someone could realize a $1,000 loss before death and save taxes. But the asset sold immediately after death would not benefit from this tax loss.

Next tax year (2011), the securities increase in value to $200,000 and the securities are sold regardless of which option Cappellino chooses.

1. Calculate Cappellino's 2011 tax liability if he holds the securities until year-end 2011.
2. Calculate Cappellino's 2011 tax liability if he recognizes the loss today in 2010, replaces them with securities offering the same return, and realizes the capital gain at year-end 2011.
3. Compare the total two-year tax liability under both options using the 2010 tax liability computed in Example 11.5, in which the 2010 tax liability was $15,000 if the loss was not realized and $6,000 if the loss was realized.

Solution to 1: Capital gains tax = 0.15($200,000 − $170,000) = $4,500.

Solution to 2: If Cappellino recognizes the loss in 2010 and replaces the securities, the basis will be reset to $110,000 from $170,000. Capital gains tax in 2011 = 0.15 ($200,000 − $110,000) = $13,500.

Solution to 3: The two-year tax liability for both options is the same:

	2010	2011	Total
Option A	$20,000	$ 6,000	$26,000
Option B	8,000	18,000	26,000

Although the two-year tax liability does not change, a potential advantage of tax loss harvesting is pushing a portion of the tax liability into subsequent years.

Tax loss harvesting opportunities are most pronounced in portfolios composed of volatile, negatively correlated securities. If the individual securities in a portfolio have stable returns, they will be unlikely to have any significant unrecognized losses to harvest. If individual securities are not negatively correlated (or at least uncorrelated), then there will be no gains against which losses can be offset.

Tax loss harvesting also requires round-trip transaction costs (i.e., to realize the loss on one security and subsequently replace it) and identifying a substitute security with risk and return characteristics similar (but not identical) to the security being sold with the capital loss in the face of wash sale rules (discussed later). The manager must also know the right time to recognize a loss. Ideally, the wealth manager picks the bottom of the market to harvest the loss, but we have little confidence in almost anyone's ability to do that consistently. Of course, being able to time market bottoms is a valuable skill to have in any case, irrespective of tax loss harvesting.[19]

Before harvesting a loss, the wealth manager should have confidence that the current tax savings (which will be repaid later) will be worth the extra transaction costs, the security substitution, the risk that timing could be improved, and the uncertainty of future tax rates.

---

[19]See Horvitz (2005) for a deeper discussion of the difficulties of successfully implementing a systematic tax loss harvesting program.

As we have mentioned, the value of tax deferral associated with systematic tax loss harvesting is far less significant than that associated with having holding periods greater than 12 months to benefit from the substantially lower capital gains tax rate.

Tax Gains Harvesting?

Congress has recently discussed increasing the capital gains tax rate and could do so in the future, which has many investors asking, "Should I recognize or realize gains now while tax rates are still low?" Is it very sensible to violate the truism that taxes should be deferred as long as possible? As is so often the case, the answer is "It depends." Specifically, it depends on the length of your investment horizon and the rate of return you expect to earn on your capital should you not realize the gain and pay the tax immediately.

For example, if the capital gains tax rate is 15 percent at the federal level plus 7 percent at the state level and an investor anticipates the capital gains tax rate increasing to 20 percent at the federal level, the investor could ask the question, "What return would I need to earn on my capital to make it worth deferring the current gain into a higher tax rate environment?" A simple approach would be to sell for the return that equates a $27 (i.e., the federal and state tax payment on a $100 gain in the future), say, 10 years from now to $22 (i.e., the federal and state tax payment on a $100 gain today).

$$\$27 = \$22(1 + r)^{10}$$

In this case, the break-even rate of return equals 2.1 percent. In other words, if the investor anticipates earning more than a 2.1 percent geometric return over 10 years, then it does *not* make sense to harvest the gain in the current low-tax-rate environment. But for shorter time horizons or larger tax increases, it could make sense to harvest a gain. Exhibit 11.11 shows the minimum returns required to make gains harvesting worthwhile.

EXHIBIT 11.11   Minimum Required for Gains Harvesting from a 15 Percent Capital Gains Tax Rate (Plus 7 Percent State Tax Rate)

Years	5	10	15	20
20% capital gain	4.2%	2.1%	1.4%	1.0%
25% capital gain	7.8	3.8	2.5	1.9

Generally, the minimum required returns are quite low for long-term investors. If an investor is likely to recognize a gain shortly anyway or if the tax hike is very significant, it may make sense to harvest a gain in the face of increasing tax rates. Otherwise, a long-term holding period usually favors the avoidance of this technique.

It is also important to keep in mind that tax increases such as this are not typically done on a retroactive basis. That is, investors will have a chance to harvest gains if tax increases do become law. Therefore, we are generally leery of preemptively harvesting a gain until the tax increase is known with some certainty.

Restrictions on Portfolio Tax Management Strategies

A major consideration in the use of tax loss harvesting is constraints set by tax laws, such as the wash sale rules in the United States. These rules prohibit investors from realizing a loss on a security sale unless they refrain from repurchasing the same security (or one substantially identical) for a period of 31 days.

Most of the academic studies make light of the wash sale rules. However, to be sitting on the sidelines for 30 days is a big decision. The simple example we illustrated and the academic research presume that the securities sold for a tax loss can be replaced with economically equivalent securities. In some instances, this can be a heroic assumption, especially for individual securities.

Close substitutions are more viable for some passive index funds, however. Although tax laws are vague on this point, an investor with a loss in an S&P 500 index fund may be able to harvest the loss and replace the fund with the Russell 3000 index fund. The authorities may not recognize this as a wash sale because the funds hold significantly different securities and track different indexes. However, their historical returns are close to 100 percent correlated, making them very reasonable economic substitutes.[20]

Another restriction in the United States, intended for mutual fund managers but impacting individual investors, is the requirement that all realized capital gains be paid annually to the shareholders. If the fund defers the payment of realized gains, it is the fund that will be taxed on the gains. An option in favor of a mutual fund shareholder is the determination of the basis of shares sold. IRC Section 1.1012 provides for the following acceptable methods of determining the basis of shares sold.

- *FIFO (Reg. §§ 1.1.12-1(c))*. FIFO stands for first in, first out. Under this method, when a sale is made, the shares sold are considered to be those first acquired. This is the IRS's assumed default if the investor has not elected one of the other available choices.
- *Identified shares*. This option allows the investor to specify which shares are to be sold. The advantage of this choice is that it allows investors to have some control over the tax consequences of a partial sale by picking and choosing from among their purchases and selecting the highest basis first, thus minimizing the gain and maximizing the tax deferral. This is often referred to as "high in, first out" or HIFO. An investor who has capital losses from another sale can sell particular shares according to basis and offset the losses.

  In order to meet IRS standards, an investor selecting this method must either deliver to the fund the actual certificates for the shares or provide in writing, to the fund, a dated letter specifying the shares to be sold, the number of shares to be sold, and the original purchase date and purchase price. Confirmation of the specifics of the trade should be kept by the investor. Use of specifically identified shares can be difficult, and you should confirm with the brokers whether they permit such identification and what their specific procedures are. You should also confirm with the client's tax advisor.
- *Average cost method (Reg. §1.1012-(3))*. Due to its simplicity, the single category method is the most popular choice. Under this method, the investor merely averages the cost of all of the fund's shares. A somewhat more complex alternative is the double category method, which averages separately the investor's short-term and long-term positions. The latter method may be useful in cases where separating short- and long-term positions works to the benefit of the taxpayer. Once selected, this method can be changed only with permission of the IRS.

Congress has begun implementing legislation requiring brokerage firms to report to the IRS not only the value of securities sold but also the cost basis of securities purchased after January 1, 2011. Investors can still choose the method they prefer for calculating the basis that

---

[20]This discussion does not represent tax advice. Please consult a tax advisor for guidance that applies in any particular situation.

is reported to the IRS, but they need to do it before the trade settles. If they do not specify, the default reporting method is generally FIFO (except for mutual funds, ETFs, and REITs for which brokerage houses can elect to report average costs as the default).

Some Considerations
A number of variables have significant impact on the after-tax returns of an investment portfolio. Not surprisingly, then, the assumptions regarding these variables significantly influence the conclusions. When running models of the potential returns from taxable and tax-deferred accounts, you need to spend some time on these assumptions.

Tax Brackets
The first question that a wealth manager should ask is: "Into which tax bracket are my clients likely to fall?" Few clients fall into either a very low (i.e., 15 percent) or very high (i.e., 35 percent) bracket. Most are in the midbrackets. Having determined appropriate brackets or current marginal rates, the next decision is whether to use historical rates or projected rates. Although it may seem sophisticated to use historical rates, there is little reason to believe that they have any predictive value. You should verify any proposed tax changes or potential changes in the client's income or family status that might affect tax rates in the forecast period. Running scenarios with a range of tax rates may be preferred over a single assumed rate.

Holding Period
The optimum situation would be a buy-and-hold portfolio that does not have any realized gains until the owner's death. In such a case the holding period could well be 30 years and turnover zero percent. This is an unlikely scenario for most clients, money managers, and wealth managers. As a more realistic assumption for low-turnover portfolios, you might consider a passive, low-turnover index fund as a standard for the lowest turnover. The obvious example is the Vanguard S&P 500 with a 5 to 10 percent turnover (i.e., an average holding period of 10 to 20 years).

Any actively managed alternative is likely to range from a very low turnover of 25 percent (an average four-year holding period) to very active at 100+ percent (less than one-year holding period). In addition to the turnover attributed to the portfolio manager, there are extraneous considerations such as turnover resulting from management changes, asset class rebalancing, and modifications attributable to the client's needs. According to industry statistics, the average holding period for mutual fund investors without advisors is less than three years, and for those with advisors, less than four years.

As a result of fund management personnel changes, style drift, or significant and consistent underperformance, it is not unusual to have manager turnover of at least 10 percent. Therefore, one might consider the most optimistic holding period for tax planning to be 10 years.

Portfolio Tax Management Research
In the Jeffrey and Arnott study mentioned earlier, the authors failed to make a case for active tax management beyond managing the holding period to achieve a 15 percent tax rate. Substantively, the before- and after-tax rankings of actual funds remained almost unchanged. In a study of 72 funds, the ranking for the Vanguard S&P 500 before taxes was 16, and the ranking after taxes was 14—less than a 3 percent change![21] Although research has not

---

[21]Before-tax ranking = 16/72 = 22.2%; after-tax ranking = 14/72 = 19.4%.

demonstrated the benefits of active portfolio tax management, it does provide a very powerful argument for the tax efficiency of a passive portfolio and holding periods in excess of one year.

VARIABLE ANNUITIES

According to the Insurance Retirement Institute, variable annuities (VAs) accounted for over $1.19 trillion in assets as of June 2009. Typically, having mutual funds as the underlying asset, they qualify for special tax treatment under U.S. law. Interest, dividends, and capital gains are tax-deferred until the policyholder receives the annuity payments, at which time they are taxed as ordinary income. Often referred to as a "wrapper," variable annuities are more of a product than a strategy. Nonetheless, they are still too important to simply ignore, so we will spend some time on them here.

It is the responsibility of each wealth manager to determine for himself or herself when, if ever, it is appropriate to utilize VAs. Whatever that decision, the wealth manager should be able to defend it. All too often the debate has been couched in marketing terms. This section provides a framework for making decisions about VAs and recommendations for their application.

Positive Attributes

The following are attributes unique to the VA. Attributes associated with the underlying investments (e.g., inflation protection by investing in an equity mutual fund) are available to investors independent of an annuity, so we will not address them here. Rather, the attributes unique to VAs promulgated by proponents include:

- *Tax-deferred growth.* Perhaps the single most important feature of a VA is that U.S. tax law specifically excludes from current taxation all forms of gain in a VA. Not only can an investor defer taxes, but the timing of the deferral is at the option of the investor. Research confirms that taxes play an important role in explaining a household's demand for VAs.[22]
- *Tax-free switching.* For market timers and tactical allocations, the tax shelter advantages of a VA provide a significant benefit by allowing policyholders to switch between investments without triggering a taxable event.
- *Management fees.* Many VA proponents suggest that VA funds are more cost efficient than independent funds. According to the National Association of Variable Annuities (NAVA), management fees average about 77 basis points. The average mutual fund management fee is about 140 basis points. However, this does not factor in the costs of the wrapper (commissions and other fees) that should also be considered.
- *Unlimited contributions.* Unlike individual retirement accounts (IRAs) and qualified plans, there are no limits on the amount that may be invested in VAs.
- *Asset protection.* In a number of jurisdictions, investments in VAs are protected from seizure by creditors.

---

[22]See Jeffrey R. Brown and James M. Poterba, "Household Demand for Variable Annuities," Boston College Center for Retirement Research Working Paper No. 2004-08, March 2004, and William M. Gentry and Joseph Milano, "Taxes and the Increased Investment in Annuities," NBER Working Paper 6525, 1998.

- *Guaranteed minimum death benefit.* In most policies, the beneficiary of a VA is guaranteed to never receive less than the gross amount originally invested upon the policyholder's death.
- *Guaranteed minimum withdrawal benefit (GMWB).* The GMWB is a somewhat recent optional feature that, like the guaranteed death benefit, guarantees to return 100 percent of the contributions (or premiums) paid into the VA. Under the GMWB, however, money is returned to the policyholder in the form of minimum annual withdrawals over a period of years (for example, 14 to 20 years).
- *Guaranteed minimum income benefit (GMIB).* Another optional form of downside protection, the GMIB allows the policyholder to annuitize into a minimum annuity payment.
- *Expense guarantee.* In most policies, the contract guarantees that the insurer cannot increase the charges for operating expenses and mortality costs.
- *Probate avoidance.* As VAs have designated beneficiaries, the proceeds bypass probate upon the annuitant's death. This attribute is actually not unique to VAs, though, because assets in IRAs and trusts can also pass to heirs outside probate.
- *Portfolio insulation.* As a result of various negative tax consequences and possible insurance company penalties for early withdrawal, the portfolios in a VA are less likely to be subject to extraordinary liquidations.
- *Tax-favored distributions.* By utilizing an annuity payment option, the owner can take advantage of the exclusion ratio, which represents the amount of the annuity payment that is not subject to tax. A portion of a VA's value represents the original principal (or cost basis) on which tax was already paid. Therefore, a portion of each annuity payment (i.e., principal/annuity value) is untaxed and called the exclusion ratio. This is also true for any immediate annuity, not just conversion of deferred VAs.

Negative Attributes

- *Mortality and operating expense.* VAs incorporate, in addition to the fund fees, mortality and expense fees to cover the mortality risk and commissions for products sold on a commission basis. According to Morningstar, the average total expense ratio (including management and contract fees) is 2.14 percent.
- *Marketing costs.* Annuities sold on a commission basis include in their expenses a marketing charge. The funding of these charges is through the imposition of mortality and expense fees and/or early withdrawal fees. These charges are analogous to loads (either front-end or back-end) on mutual funds.
- *Surrender (withdrawal) charges.* Some VAs impose surrender charges (sometimes as high as 10 percent) on policyholders who withdraw their funds before a specified period of time ends. These charges typically decline to zero after seven years, but can extend out to 10 years.
- *Tax penalty.* For investors less than 59½ years old, withdrawal of gains from a VA may be subject to a 10 percent tax penalty.
- *Loss of capital gains.* Although the gains in a VA may be deferred at the owner's option, once withdrawn they are taxed as ordinary income, not capital gains.
- *Conversion of capital gains to ordinary income.* All gains in a VA, including long-term capital gains, are ultimately taxed at an investor's marginal ordinary income rate.
- *Loss of step-up.* Upon the annuitant's death, all gains remaining in the annuity are subject to income tax at the ordinary income rate. There is no step-up in basis.
- *Limited choices of investment vehicles.* Although some VAs have as many as 20, 30, or 40+ underlying subaccounts (i.e., manager choices), the variety is insignificant compared

to the thousands in the open-end fund universe. Further, most annuities have only one or two choices in any particular asset class or style.

- *Tax risk.* The more popular VAs become and the more they are marketed as tax shelters, the more likely Congress will eliminate their tax benefits. Given the history of tax legislation, this could include negative retroactive tax law; however, similar legislation has been proposed four times in the past and never passed. Absent such doomsday changes, other tax code changes, such as the increase in income tax rates, can decrease the attractiveness of VAs.
- *Complexity.* VA contracts can be 60 pages long and packed with legalese outlining an investor's rights (and more often obligations). They may or may not include riders for a minimum death benefit, GMWB, GMIB, inflation protection, surrender charges, and so on. The contracts can be so complicated that even the most sophisticated wealth manager has trouble properly evaluating them.

Evaluation

With the pros and cons as a background, wealth managers need to evaluate the viability of VAs based on the nature of their practice.

- *Tax-deferred growth.* Once again, the conclusions of any comparison depend on the assumptions. Analyses supporting the tax benefits of VAs often utilize many of the following aggressive assumptions. You should look at the assumptions used in any variable annuity projections and determine if they are appropriate for your clients:
  - The highest state and federal ordinary income and capital gains rates.
  - Long accumulation periods.
  - Long postretirement withdrawals.
  - Full withdrawals (i.e., no assets left at the owner's death, therefore no penalty for a loss in step-up).

    Alternatively, the analysis compares the after-tax growth of a fund investment to the accumulation value of the VA (i.e., no taxes have been paid on the accumulated gains in the VA).

  - A lower postretirement income tax bracket.
  - Relatively high dividend component of total return.
- *Tax-free switching.* If you do not utilize either market timing or tactical allocation, this is not a benefit for your clients.
- *Costs.* The standard comparison is a generic comparison of apples and oranges. The question is how VA expenses compare to the alternatives. All costs should be considered.
- *Asset protection.* Does the client live in a jurisdiction that provides almost unlimited asset protection for VA investments? If so, you might consider the extra costs and limitations of VAs to be the charges related to insuring your clients' assets against creditor seizure.
- *Guaranteed death benefit (GDB) and expense guarantee (EG).* These seem to have little substantive value. The GDB is the difference between the original investment value and the portfolio value at the time of the annuitant's death, if it is lower than the original investment. Consider the profile of the VA purchaser—a client in his mid-50s with a life expectancy of 30+ years. If the client lives to anywhere near his life expectancy, the probability of the account value at death being less than his investment is statistically zero—exactly equal to

the value of the GDB.[23] If the client lives only 10 years after the purchase and had been so unfortunate as to have purchased at a historic high, his heirs' exposure is likely to be less than 10 percent. Under any rational scenario, the real value of the GDB is negligible.

The value expense guarantee is equally negligible. If our client's alternative is to make a purchase that does not require an expense factor, he is certainly not going to consider the guarantee of no *additional* expense to be of much value.

- *Guaranteed minimum withdrawal benefit (GMWB)*. GMWB riders may sound better than they are. They generally cost between 40 to 75 basis points annually, which adds up substantially over long time periods. Moreover, because the guarantee is paid out over a series of annual withdrawals, the policyholder must live long enough for it to pay off. Nor do GMWB riders typically provide VA holders with inflation protection, which is an important risk exposure in most retirement planning situations.

- *Guaranteed minimum income benefit (GMIB)*. Some contracts provide this protection only if the policyholder chooses a lifetime (rather than fixed) payout period, which can be unfortunate if the policyholder is in poor health at the time of annuitization. The value of this protection also depends on the level of interest rates when it is purchased relative to the level of interest rates when the annuitization decision is made.

- *Unlimited contributions*. By utilizing the term *contribution*, this advantage implies a unique feature of VAs. The option is actually to buy more. This advantage is of little consequence unless the tax savings feature provides significant benefit. After all, an investor can make unlimited contributions to most investments.

- *Probate avoidance*. To the extent the client finds this a useful feature, investing in a VA restricts the advantage to that single investment. The alternative may be to establish a revocable trust, thus providing probate avoidance for all of the client's assets as well as significant additional advantages.

- *Portfolio insulation*. This is a difficult value to measure, and no substantive research has been published on this issue. During a significant market correction, it is quite likely that nervous naive investors in VA equity subaccounts will liquidate and move to cash, while more knowledgeable investors will stay put in the funds we select. If institutional funds are available, they are less likely to face extraordinary liquidations.

- *Tax-favored distribution*. The value of this opportunity is directly related to the same influences as the VA's tax-deferred growth—long periods of withdrawal and significant withdrawals.

We wrap up this stage of the discussion by giving the reader a flavor of the kind of arguments you are likely to encounter in researching the pros and cons of variable annuities:

Con
An independent analysis of variable annuities was prepared by Bob Veres in the February 1996 issue of *Inside Information*.[24] The study was an update of an analysis that ran in the October

---

[23]Although the probability of a shortfall declines with the time horizon, the magnitude of a possible shortfall (should it occur) increases. This phenomenon is why options such as a put provide downside protection: because they become more valuable as the term of the option increases.

[24]A subscription to *Inside Information* is a must for any financial planner. Although I frequently disagree with Bob, he always makes me think. There are a few journalistic stars who write about our profession, and I include Bob in this exclusive list. Bob Veres, Mary Rowland, Bob Clark, and Nick Murray—if they write it, I'll read it.

1994 issue. The original study compared the traditional load variable annuities available at the time to investments in index funds. It concluded that the index investment outperformed the variable annuity every year for a 20-year period. The 1996 article revisited the comparison but compared the index fund investment to the new no-load variable annuities. The index funds beat the variable annuity by a slimmer margin but still won. Bob concluded, "So let's give praise where it is due. Thank you, Vanguard/Skandia/Fortis/Jack White [vendors of no-load annuities] for driving down the costs of a very popular investment. . . . We applaud your character, but we also hope that the planning community will decide, collectively, to pass on your VA offerings." On the basis of tax advantages alone, VAs are rarely appropriate for clients.

More recently, Bill Reichenstein (2009) comes to a similar conclusion about equity-indexed annuities that protect annuitants from market declines. Using 50 years of data, he shows that the various structures of indexed annuities virtually ensure that, in the long run, these contracts will underperform. All the contracts he examined underperformed Treasury bills and had statistically negative alphas, averaging 2.9 percent per year.

Pro

In a review of Bob's article, Michael Lane argues that the analysis neglects two critical variables—state taxes and the type of income distribution. He also points out that less than 1 percent of the variable annuities charge front-end loads and suggests that the assumption of a 4 percent charge "really stacks the analysis" against variable annuities. Not too surprisingly, Michael concludes that such analysis may "lead to misconceptions about an important financial tool and can discourage fee planners from recommending what may be the best long-term investment solution for their clients."

Conclusions Regarding Variable Annuities

Having considered all of the advantages of VAs, we conclude that VAs are most appropriate in those cases when a client is likely to spend down the investment during retirement and has long accumulation and withdrawal expectations or where asset protection is a significant issue, all other things being equal.

Not all things are equal, though. The costs associated with VAs may be significant and the possible tax liquidation penalties may restrict their liquidity in emergencies. If a client does not use the funds, the loss of step-up in basis may be significant.

Finally, in spite of the importance of all of those negatives, they are insignificant compared to the inflexibility of manager selection. Many VAs have poorly defined asset class managers, making it difficult, if not impossible, to control the critical asset allocation balance of a client's portfolio. For those products that offer subaccounts with managers who adhere to a well-defined philosophy and process, there is rarely an alternative within the VA to move to if either the management changes or the existing manager drifts from the original philosophy.

Although VAs may not be suitable for most clients, they are viable strategies for certain clients. The development of no-load and low-cost VAs in recent years has addressed some of our objections. Wealth managers should continue to evaluate the products available.

STRATEGIES FOR DEFERRING GAINS ON LOW-BASIS STOCK

It is common for wealthy clients to have a concentrated holding in a particular stock. Many self-made entrepreneurs have accumulated wealth by building a business that may have been monetized with a stock swap. Corporate executives often accrue large equity positions in the companies they serve. As the old aphorism goes, the rich *get* wealthy by being concentrated in their investments or business, but they need to be diversified to *stay* wealthy.

Many authors have demonstrated the wisdom of reducing the volatility drag and additional downside risk associated with wealth accumulation in concentrated positions even in the face of significant capital gains taxes from liquidating low-basis stock and diversifying. We addressed this in more detail earlier in this chapter.

No matter what a cold, sterile quantitative analysis suggests, there are substantial psychological and behavioral obstacles for clients to liquidate a concentrated position. Investors tend to have unrealistically high expectations for the future performance of their concentrated positions, even when presented with evidence (such as the Sanford Bernstein study discussed earlier in this chapter) and examples of investors going from rags to riches and back to rags again. After all, they have developed an intimate relationship with the firm because it made them rich in the first place, and they have no shortage of reasons why their stock is different.

These unrealistic expectations can be attributed to many of the behavioral biases we discussed in Chapter 4. For example, unrealistic optimism can result from general hubris or hometown bias, in which an investor had excess confidence in a stock simply because they know it. Alternatively, they may succumb to the bias of feeling a stock is on a streak (representativeness), and that they will know when to get out (gambler's fallacy). If the stock is already trading at a loss, they may succumb to regret aversion.

In any case, there are many occasions when a client would like to defer (or avoid) paying capital gains taxes, but nonetheless wishes to eliminate the risk of a concentrated holding. The discussion so far has implicitly assumed that the only techniques available for managing taxes are directly related to the securities held in the portfolio. There are, in fact, numerous strategies that may be implemented for special cases. The following is intended as an introduction. For the most part, these strategies require expertise beyond the realm of the wealth manager and require the assistance of attorneys and accountants.

Consider the problem facing Mr. Brown.

Mr. Brown holds a position in stock A and wishes to reduce his market exposure. The obvious solution is to simply sell shares. Unfortunately, it is a stock that has appreciated significantly. As Mr. Brown has a low basis, an outright sale will result in the realization of significant capital gains and the related obligation to pay capital gains tax.

The problem becomes one of reducing market exposure without triggering a required tax payment.

Prior to the Taxpayer Relief Act of 1997 (TRA), one solution might have been to sell the stock A short in a strategy known as "shorting against the box."[25] The TRA, however, defined this strategy and several others as constructive sales in which the investor effectively divests himself or herself of an economic interest in the position and thereby triggers a capital gain. Other strategies the TRA identifies as constructive sales include equity swaps and forward

---

[25]A short sale is the act of selling shares not owned by the client initiating the sale. Many brokerage firms lend their clients shares for this purpose. This is a trading strategy frequently used by active traders anticipating a future drop in the price of the stock. If correct in their projections, the traders will subsequently repurchase shares (at the then lower price) and return them to the lender (i.e., the brokerage firm that lent them the shares to sell). The trader's profit is the difference between the original sales proceeds and the cost of replacing the lent shares.

or futures contracts that deliver a substantially fixed amount of an asset for a substantially fixed price.[26]

Collars

Somewhat more complex than shorting against the box or an equity swap, collars entail a simultaneous purchase of puts and the sale of calls in an amount equal to the number of shares of the stock the client wishes to protect. In this way, the investor gives up some upside appreciation in exchange for gaining some downside protection.

In theory, a collar constructed with at-the-money puts and at-the-money calls would completely insulate Mr. Brown from exposure to stock A price changes and is not really a collar at all. Any losses in stock A would be offset by gains in the option position and vice versa. Therefore, such a tight collar would be deemed to be a constructive sale under the tax regulations.

Mr. Brown can avoid triggering a capital gain by setting the strike price on the puts sufficiently below the strike price on the calls to retain an economic interest in the net position. How large that range must be is unclear in the tax code, but many commentators believe a 15 percent collar around the stock price is sufficient to avoid a constructive sale.

The puts and calls used to construct the collar may be standard exchange-traded options. Alternatively, a collar may be structured with over-the-counter options, custom derivatives sold by the structuring broker-dealer to investors. The tax treatment between the two structures can differ.

The cost of a collar, not including the structuring firm fee, is the difference between the cost of the puts and the proceeds of the calls. The most common structure, called a zero cost collar, is designed to have these two amounts exactly offset each other.

In addition, Mr. Brown may be able to borrow against this hedged position. How much may depend on the uses of the funds according to Federal Reserve regulations. Historically, Mr. Brown could only borrow 50 cents on the dollar if the proceeds are reinvested in a diversified portfolio. Or Mr. Brown could borrow up to 90 percent of the put strike price for almost any other purpose. New portfolio margining rules have been introduced that allow investors up to 90 percent for any purpose on a collared position. Not all brokers participate in the new margining program, however, so it pays to inquire about it if freeing up capital is important. Yes, it's odd, but it illustrates the complexity and nuances one must consider before embarking on a hedging program.

Specific risks include counterparty default (e.g., failure to meet the put), lack of emergency liquidity, the risk that the structure may not pass tax muster or that tax laws may change, and forced liquidation (e.g., call). Counterparty and liquidity risk are typically ameliorated when a collar is structured with listed options.

Prepaid Variable Forwards

Effectively an over-the-counter variant of the collar, a prepaid variable forward (PVF) is a contract with a bank that would obligate Mr. Brown to sell shares of stock A to the bank at a fixed price at some point in the future. The number of shares depends on the price of stock A.

If stock A's price increases dramatically, Mr. Brown is obligated to sell some or all of his shares at the fixed price (limiting his upside). If stock A's price decreases dramatically,

---

[26]Welch (2002) and Gordon (2001) have excellent discussions of the specific tax treatments of these strategies.

Mr. Brown is obligated to sell enough of his shares at the fixed price so that the proceeds from that sale plus the value of his remaining shares produce a specified floor value (protecting his downside). By adjusting the number of shares within a range of stock prices (rather than adjusting the price), the PVF replicates the pretax outcomes of a collar and avoids violating constructive sale rules, assuming the band through which Mr. Brown retains an economic interest is structured wide enough.

But alas, that is where the similarities end. Gains and losses are treated differently for tax purposes. The collar may force Mr. Brown to recognize gains on the net position as they occur, while losses cannot be recognized for tax purposes until the position is closed. A PVF can overcome this asymmetric and disadvantageous tax treatment if the shares were acquired after 1984. In addition, the PVF may allow Mr. Brown to borrow up to 75 percent of the downside protection for any purpose, even a reinvestment in equities. The rules are dramatically different for shares that were acquired before 1984.[27]

One must be careful in constructing prepaid variable forwards. They have been the subject of several successful challenges by the IRS in 2001, 2006, 2007, 2008, and 2010. The IRS deemed the contracts "common law sales" in these cases because the underlying hedged shares were also lent to the dealer to facilitate the dealer's hedge. To mitigate the significant tax risk associated with these contracts, it is important to not lend the hedged shares to the dealer even in an ostensibly different agreement.

Exchange Funds

Typically formed as a limited partnership, the exchange fund serves as a legal bucket for holders of low-basis stock to pool their positions in a tax-free exchange. Mr. Brown would deposit his shares into the limited partnership along with other investors who similarly deposit their low-basis shares. Each investor now has a prorated interest in the diversified fund without having sold his or her shares. The result is the transfer of risk from a single position to a multiple-security portfolio. In order to meet the IRS requirements, there are numerous restrictions, including a mandatory seven-year investment period, and 20 percent of the portfolio must be invested in "not readily marketable securities" such as real estate, but not hedge funds, private equity, or venture capital.

These structures are more complex than they might appear, and investors do not receive cash that can be used for other purposes as in the case of an outright sale. Specific risks, in addition to the holding period, include the risk of early fund liquidation and what has been called the graveyard effect. The investor has no control over the other securities added to the portfolio, so may end up a partial owner of a portfolio of dogs.

Completion Funds

Completion funds come in different varieties. One variation on a theme is to slowly liquidate stock A over time and use the proceeds to diversify Mr. Brown's portfolio. This is often a more cognitively palatable strategy than an outright sale for many clients.

Another variation is to borrow against stock A shares and use the proceeds to diversify. This strategy, of course, significantly increases Mr. Brown's exposure to market risk, which cannot be taken lightly.

Another approach is to liquidate part of the position or build the nonconcentrated part of Mr. Brown's portfolio around stock A. For example, if stock A were a bank, the wealth

---

[27]Boczar (2007) has a useful tax and nontax comparative analysis of these strategies.

manager may use the nonconcentrated assets to build an index fund that excludes financial stocks. Alternatively, the manager could short a financial ETF in appropriate proportion to hedge the sector risk associated with stock A, if not the firm-specific risk of stock A.

A more technical approach is to construct an optimization algorithm that minimizes tracking error of the concentrated and nonconcentrated positions, using a constraint that the concentrated portion of the portfolio is fixed. The algorithm would then select assets (e.g., sector funds) that complement the concentrated position based on the risk and return inputs used on the optimizer. (See Chapter 10 for a more thorough discussion of optimization.)

The biggest risk of completion portfolios tends to be their incomplete nature. That is, they may hedge only some of the risk associated with concentrated positions. Further, the strategy may reduce the systematic risk but not the unsystematic risk (e.g., Lehman Brothers vs. bank stock).

Conclusions Regarding Strategies for Managing Low-Basis Stock

There are numerous issues to be considered regarding the use of these strategies, with a few that are more important:

- All have a carrying cost, usually in terms of fees paid to the firm assisting in the structuring of the transaction. These costs typically range from 1 to 3 percent per year.
- While clients have reduced their market exposure to the specific equity, they may have eliminated any opportunity of gain (e.g., short against the box) or transferred the risk to a different market exposure (e.g., exchange funds).
- If the position to be deferred is subject to short-term gains (e.g., stock options), there are significant issues regarding extending the holding period for long-term gains. Special supplementary strategies may be necessary (e.g., married put).
- The strategy may disappear with changes in the tax code.

The wealth manager has a legal and fiduciary duty to mitigate undue stock concentration risk and consider the tax and nontax implications of all available strategies to manage a low-basis position. In addition, the manager is obligated to minimize transaction costs, secure good pricing, and have a systematic process by which these decisions are made. Boczar (2007) does an excellent job outlining a best practices framework for fulfilling an adviser's legal duties associated with managing concentrated positions.

PARTING COMMENTS

Taxes can significantly reduce a client's accumulated wealth. It is important for the wealth manager to understand the tax environment facing the client and manage investments with this environment in mind to achieve the best possible risk-adjusted after-tax return.

RESOURCES

Applebach, Richard O. 1995. "The Capital Gains Tax Penalty?" *Journal of Portfolio Management* (Summer): 99–103.

Arnott, Robert D., Andrew Berkin, and Jia Ye. 2000. "How Well Have Taxable Investors Been Served in the 1980s and 1990s?" *Journal of Portfolio Management*, Vol. 20, No. 4 (Summer): 84–93.

Arnott, Robert D., Andrew L. Berkin, and Jia Ye. 2001. "The Management and Mismanagement of Taxable Assets." *Journal of Investing*, Vol. 10, No. 1 (Spring): 15–21.

Berkin, Andrew L., and Jia Ye. 2003. "Tax Management, Loss Harvesting, and HIFO Accounting." *Financial Analysts Journal*, Vol. 59, No. 4 (July/August): 91–102.

Boczar, Thomas J. 2007. "Mitigating the Legal Duties of Fiduciaries and Financial Advisors to Manage Stock Concentration Risk: Conceptualizing and Implementing a 'Best Practices' Framework." *Journal of Wealth Management* (Summer): 16–34.

Boyle, Patrick S., Daniel J. Loewy, Jonathan A. Reiss, and Robert A. Weiss. 2004. "The Enviable Dilemma: Hold, Sell, or Hedge Highly Concentrated Stock." *Journal of Wealth Management*, Vol. 7, No. 2 (Fall): 30–44.

Constantinides, George M. 1983. "Capital Market Equilibrium with Personal Tax." *Econometrica*, Vol. 51, No. 3: 611–637.

Dammon, Robert M., and Chester S. Spatt. 1996. "The Optimal Pricing of Securities with Asymmetric Capital Gains Taxes and Transaction Costs." *Review of Financial Studies*, Vol. 9, No. 3 (Fall): 921–952.

Dammon, Robert M., Chester S. Spatt, and Harold H. Zhang. 2001. "Optimal Consumption and Investment with Capital Gains Taxes." *Review of Financial Studies*, Vol. 14, No. 3 (Fall): 583–616.

Dammon, Robert M., Chester S. Spatt, and Harold H. Zhang. 2004. "Optimal Asset Location and Allocation with Taxable and Tax-Deferred Investing." *Journal of Finance*, Vol. 59, No. 3 (June): 999–1037.

Dickson, Joel M., and John B. Shoven. 1993. "Ranking Mutual Funds on an After-Tax Basis." NBER Working Paper No. 4393.

Dickson, Joel M., and John B. Shoven. 1994. "A Stock Index Mutual Fund without Net Capital Gains Realization." NBER Working Paper No. 5427.

Gordon, Robert N. 2001. "Hedging Low-Cost-Basis Stock." In *Investment Counseling for Private Clients III, AIMR Conference Proceedings*, Vol. 2001, No. 4: 36–44.

Horan, Stephen M. 2005. *Tax-Advantaged Savings Accounts and Tax-Efficient Wealth Accumulation*. Charlottesville, VA: Research Foundation of CFA Institute.

Horan, Stephen M., and Thomas R. Robinson. 2009. "Taxes and Private Wealth Management in a Global Context." *CFA Program Curriculum Level II*, Vol. 6: 495–538.

Horvitz, Jeffrey E. 2005. "Tax Deferral and Tax-Loss Harvesting." *Conference Proceedings Quarterly*, No. 5: 24–30.

Horvitz, Jeffrey E., and Jarrod W. Wilcox. 2003. "Know When to Hold 'Em and When to Fold 'Em." *Journal of Wealth Management*, Vol. 6, No. 2 (Fall): 35–59.

Huang, Jennifer. 2003. "Portfolio Decisions with Taxable and Tax-Deferred Accounts: A Tax-Arbitrage Approach." Unpublished manuscript, Massachusetts Institute of Technology.

Jacob, Nancy L. 1995. "Taxes, Investment Strategy and Diversifying Low-Basis Stock." *Trusts & Estates*, May.

Jeffrey, Robert H., and Robert D. Arnott. 1993. "Is Your Alpha Big Enough to Cover Its Taxes?" *Journal of Portfolio Management* (Spring): 15–25.

Messmore, Tom. 1995. "Variance Drain." *Journal of Portfolio Management*, Vol. 21, No. 4 (Summer): 104–110.

Milevsky, Moshe A., and Steven E. Posner. 2001. "The Titanic Option: Valuation of the Guaranteed Minimum Death Benefit in Variable Annuities and Mutual Funds." *Journal of Risk and Insurance* (March).

Poterba, James M. 2000. "After-Tax Performance Evaluation." *Association of Investment Management and Research Conference Proceedings*. Charlottesville, VA: 57–67.

Purcell, Kylelane. 1995. "VA Investors Gain by Knowing How Clone Funds Differ." *5 Star Investor*, April, 12–13.

Randolf, William. 1994. "The Impact of Mutual Fund Distributions on After-Tax Returns." *Financial Services Review,* Vol. 3, No. 2: 127–141.

Reichtenstein, William. 1998. "Calculating a Family's Asset Mix." *Financial Services Review,* Vol. 7, No. 3 (Fall): 195–206.

Reichtenstein, William. 2001. "Asset Allocation and Asset Location Decisions Revisited." *Journal of Wealth Management,* Vol. 4 (Summer): 16–26.

Reichtenstein, William. 2009. "Financial Analysis of Equity-Indexed Annuities." *Financial Services Review,* Vol. 18, No. 4 (Winter): 291–311.

Reichtenstein, William, and William Jennings. 2003. *Integrating Investments and the Tax Code.* Hoboken, NJ: John Wiley & Sons.

Rogers, Doug. 2006. *Tax-Aware Investment Management: The Essential Guide.* New York: Bloomberg Press.

Sanford Bernstein Research. 1995. "Do I Dare Sell This Stock?" *Taxes and the Private Investor,* 8–16.

Stein, David, Andrew F. Siegel, Charles E. Appeadu, and Premkumar Narasimhan. 2000. "Diversification in the Presence of Taxes." *Journal of Portfolio Management* (Fall): 61–70.

Welch, Scott. 2002. "Comparing Financial and Charitable Techniques for Disposing of Low Basis Stock." *Journal of Wealth Management,* Vol. 4, No. 4 (Spring): 37–46.

CHAPTER 12

RETIREMENT PLANNING

The question isn't at what age I want to retire, it's at what income.

—George Foreman

Prior to retirement the account grows regularly. . . . After retirement the account eventually begins to diminish. Eventually one of two things happens. Either you die (right on schedule) with money in the bank or you run out of money before you die.

—William Sharpe

One baby boomer turns 59½ every seven seconds. The magnitude of the typical investor's retirement liability is usually the single largest liability on his or her life balance sheet. Put differently, cash flow requirements for retirement in a capital needs analysis (CNA) tend to dwarf most other cash outflows. Many wealth managers spend 80 percent of their time planning for and managing their clients' retirements.

To be sure, the investment management principles developed in this book are critical in meeting this client need. This chapter, however, addresses unique issues and challenges in retirement planning. The treatment here will be fairly comprehensive. Author Harold Evensky and his partner Deena Katz edited a book entitled *Retirement Income Redesigned: Master Plans for Distribution* that provides a more robust treatment than what is afforded here. We refer the reader to that text as one of the main references.

The approach we take, broadly speaking, is to organize the issues along two main dimensions—the accumulation phase and the distribution phase. Initially, this approach seems quite intuitive. It is critical to point out, however, that proper planning in the accumulation phase requires one to envision what the world might look like in the distribution phase. Assumptions about the distribution phase inform the accumulation phase, and outcomes in the accumulation phase impact distribution.

ACCUMULATION PHASE

In this section we address methods of estimating how much a client must save during the accumulation phase in order to have sufficient funds for the next phase.

Defining the Problem

The role of defined-benefit (DB) and other retirement plans that were designed to provide income replacement during retirement as well as longevity protection by pooling risks among

267

a large number of retirees is diminishing, as we all know. DB plans also relieve the individual of the burden of making investment management decisions. Moreover, the ability of governmental income programs, such as Social Security in the United States, to predictably provide retirement income is also diminishing. These trends increase the proportion of an individual's retirement liability that must be self-funded, which has implications for savings, investing, and risk management strategies. They also put more of the retirement planning onus on the individual, creating more opportunity for the wealth manager to add value to the client-adviser relationship.

Life expectancy has changed dramatically over the years, as shown in Exhibit 12.1. Not only is the average age of mortality expected to increase from 61.4 years in 1935 to 78.4 years in 2025, but people are remaining healthier throughout their lives. Someone who has survived to age 65 is expected to live another 16 to 18 years, as of the year 2000, compared with only 10 to 13 years in 1900.[1]

EXHIBIT 12.1   Survival Curves for Select Historical Periods

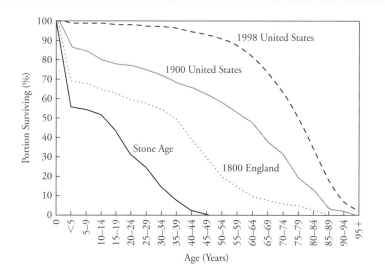

Source: Diamond (2009). Based on data from the Foundation for Infinite Survival.

This phenomenon is even more pronounced for those with higher education and, by extension, higher incomes. Exhibit 12.2 shows that decreases in mortality rates are more pronounced among the more highly educated over the 37 years from 1960 to 1997. Therefore, the impact of changing mortality on retirement planning is even more pronounced for those who are more likely to seek guidance from wealth managers.

---

[1]Peter Diamond, "On the Future of Pensions and Retirements," in *The Future of Lifecycle Saving and Investing: The Retirement Phase* (Charlottesville, VA: Research Foundation of CFA Institute, 2009), 15–30.

EXHIBIT 12.2   Decrease in U.S. Mortality Rate from Least to Most Educated

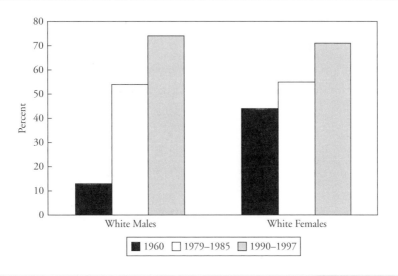

Source: Diamond (2009). Based on Elo and Smith (2003).

Being able to predict improvements in mortality has vexed the DB industry. Although pension plan sponsors are able to pool longevity risk across many individuals, they have consistently underestimated survival rates (overestimated mortality) and have sought ways to transfer the longevity risk to other investors or insurers. Individual investors are faced with the same uncertainty regarding longevity, but do not have the benefits of risk pooling without financial intermediation. So the challenge for them is even greater.

Squaring the Curve

One of the interesting trends in Exhibit 12.1 is the tendency for the survival curve to be pulled to the upper right corner of the graph over time. This trend relates not just to the length of one's life but also the quality of one's life. Whereas an individual's health status may have declined gradually over the course of one's life, the tendency to remain healthy during old age has squared the health status curve. Think back to Harold and his wife on their vacation cruise, mentioned earlier. There were many passengers in their 70s and 80s and a few in their 90s, with canes and walkers, but still having a great time touring the world. The point is, not only are we living longer, but we're also living healthier, and that means we will want to continue to spend. No longer can we assume our clients' living expenses will decrease with age.

As demonstrated in Exhibit 12.3, people's health status deteriorates later in life but more quickly. This phenomenon has implications for how long one is able to work, whether one plans to phase into retirement, and how one plans to spend retirement. Retirees can and do remain more active during the latter end of their life span. Highly skilled and educated workers have more flexibility to decide when and how to retire. Moreover, phased retirement has specific emotional and intellectual benefits for investors in their later working years.[2] Although the phased retirement may alleviate some of the financial burden associated with the

---

[2]Anna M. Rappaport, "The Case for Phased Retirement," in *The Future of Lifecycle Saving and Investing: The Retirement Phase* (Charlottesville, VA: Research Foundation of CFA Institute, 2009), 43–52.

retirement liability, it may fall short of providing financial security later in life and is not guaranteed, which is true of all of our wealth management assumptions.[3]

EXHIBIT 12.3   Health Status by Age over Time

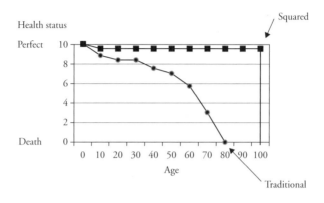

Ironically, although longer and healthier lives give people the option to work longer, few do. According to Exhibit 12.4, labor force participation among older males steadily decreased from 1950 before holding steady in recent years. Labor force participation among women has either increased for ages 55 to 64 or held steady for those over age 65, reflecting the countervailing forces of more career opportunities and earlier retirement. Nonetheless, the trend toward early retirement has slowed, most likely because, as the financial burden of retirement falls on the individual, the economic reality of the retirement decision becomes more apparent.

EXHIBIT 12.4   Annual Labor Force Participation Rate by Age and Sex, 1950–2006

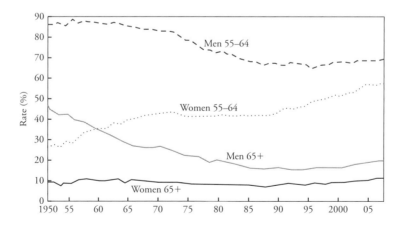

Source: Diamond (2009). Based on data from the Center for Retirement Research.

---

[3]Alicia Munnell, "Phased Retirement Is Not the Path to Retirement Security," in *The Future of Lifecycle Saving and Investing: The Retirement Phase* (Charlottesville, VA: Research Foundation of CFA Institute, 2009), 53–59.

What Is Your Number?

What is your number? This is a question many of us want to know. It is even used in advertising campaigns of some brokerage houses. It is meant to introduce the concept of how large your nest egg needs to be to retire comfortably. It is a complex question with many variables and highlights the challenge of saving for retirement. Perhaps this is why less than half of U.S. workers report that they or their spouses have tried to calculate how much money they will need to save for retirement.[4]

The first step in defining the retirement challenge is to measure the magnitude of the retirement liability, and the wealth manager has several approaches available for this purpose. Regardless of the method chosen, it will likely show that an investor is underprepared for retirement. According to the Retirement Confidence Survey conducted by the Employee Benefit Research Institute, 54 percent of workers report that their household savings and investments are less than $25,000, excluding the value of their primary home and defined-benefit plans.

Capital Needs Analysis

A capital needs analysis (CNA) or capital accumulation planning (CAP) is a comprehensive approach to evaluating the client's retirement goals. The purpose of the analysis is to determine whether the client's current portfolio, preretirement savings, and additional financial resources (e.g., Social Security, inheritances) will satisfy future retirement expectations. The analysis lays out on the time line the timing, magnitude, and priority of seven items:

1. Preretirement income.
2. Preretirement expenses.
3. Preretirement liquidity needs.
4. Preretirement savings (i.e., the first item less the second and third items).
5. Postretirement expenses.
6. Postretirement income.
7. Required retirement distributions.

The wealth manager must also make important assumptions about inflation, taxes and the applicable rate of return on investments, which we discuss elsewhere in this book. We recommend focusing on real returns for the purpose of this analysis because traditional planning based on nominal returns masks the impact of inflation. It is important to emphasize, however, that if one uses a CNA or CAP analysis to estimate the required rate of return necessary to meet one's retirement goals, conservative assumptions about savings and retirement distributions lead to a high required rate of return. The temptation, therefore, will be to meet those return requirements with aggressive investment recommendations that may bear little resemblance to the client's risk tolerance.

A better approach is to incorporate a realistic rate of return assumption in a Monte Carlo analysis that reflects a client's risk tolerance to determine whether the client's resources are sufficient to meet retirement goals. If resources fall short, the most powerful ways to reconcile the two are to increase preretirement savings, decrease postretirement spending, or delay one's anticipated retirement date (which is in some ways a combination of the first two options). These are the factors over which the client has the most control even if they are far less palatable than the illusive allure of capriciously increasing the assumed rate of return on investments and their attenuated risks.

---

[4]Employee Benefit Research Institute, "2010 Retirement Confidence Survey: Confidence Stabilizing, but Preparations Continued to Erode."

Delaying retirement is tough to beat when it comes to trying to make up for a retirement shortfall leak in one's career. It has the dual benefit of adding years of savings to and removing years of spending from the retirement nest egg. The Retirement Confidence Survey shows that the percentage of workers expecting to retire *after* age 65 has increased from 11 percent in 1991 to 33 percent in 2010.[5]

Life Balance Sheet

CNA is an approach based on capital flows. Another method to evaluate the magnitude of the retirement liability is to construct the life balance sheet, a comprehensive accounting of a client's assets and liabilities, which measures capital stock. Assets on the life balance sheet include:

- Financial assets (e.g., stocks and bonds).
- Physical assets (e.g., a residence).
- Implied assets (e.g., the present value a client's earnings stream and Social Security).

Liabilities on the life balance sheet include:

- Personal debts (e.g., mortgage, car loans).
- Implied liabilities or investment goals (e.g., a child's education, retirement).

Retirement is typically chief among these implied liabilities. Exhibit 12.5 presents a hypothetical life balance sheet with assets listed on the left-hand side and on the right-hand side, investment goals, including funding a child's college education, maintaining a current lifestyle, and funding a secure and comfortable retirement.

EXHIBIT 12.5   Hypothetical Life Balance Sheet

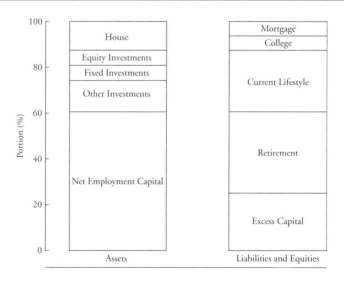

Source: Adapted from Jarrod Wilcox, Jeffrey E. Horvitz, and Dan diBartolomeo, *Investment Management for Taxable Private Investors* (Charlottesville, VA: Research Foundation of CFA Institute, 2006), 18.

---

[5]Ibid.

To contemplate the approximate size of the retirement liability, consider a 60-year-old couple with no specific desire to transfer wealth to their children. Estimates vary about how much they can spend from their portfolio without depleting their resources before the end of their lifetimes, but research places the sustainable spending rate between 3.5 percent and 6 percent of the initial portfolio value, assuming that spending increases by the inflation rate in subsequent years.[6] These figures translate into retirement nest eggs that are approximately 17 times to 29 times the amount of annual spending for retirees. Many people are surprised at how modest spending must be to make a withdrawal program sustainable over many years. Not surprisingly, those who retire later or have shorter life expectancies do not need such a sizable nest egg.

Estimating the Retirement Liability in the Annuity Market

The amount of capital needed to maintain a retiree's lifestyle can be estimated in a number of ways. The simplest way to estimate how much money is required to fund a given level of retirement spending is to use the information provided in the annuity market. Suppose the Smiths, a retired couple, would like to spend $100,000 annually on an inflation-adjusted basis through retirement. If an insured, immediate, inflation-adjusted, fixed annuity were available in the marketplace at a 5 percent interest rate, then the Smiths would need to spend $2 million to fund their retirement.

This is a crude, easy method to determine the amount of capital needed to fund one's retirement. It does not imply that one should use an insured, immediate, inflation-adjusted, fixed annuity to accomplish that goal. It merely takes advantage of all the hard work that the insurance industry put into quantifying a cash flow stream that is free of inflation and longevity risk.

Estimating the Retirement Liability with Mortality Tables

Alternatively, the wealth manager can calculate the present value of anticipated retirement spending over the client's expected life span. By definition, however, every investor has a 50 percent chance of living past the remaining life expectancy.[7] Given that clients of wealth managers are very likely to have had better nutrition and health care than the universe used to develop the mortality table, estimates of the retirement liability based on life expectancy are likely to fall short of what is actually required in a great many cases.[8] It's for this reason that Harold uses in his practice a 30 percent standard as a minimum mortality age (i.e., an age that only 30 percent of individuals the same age and sex as the client will outlive). He also asks about the client's family mortality history (i.e., the age at death of parents, siblings, and/or grandparents who died a natural death). If he finds that the client's grandfather just got married in a shotgun wedding at 85, he might use a 90 or 95 percent mortality standard.

---

[6]We discuss this in more detail later. See, for example, Bengen (1994, 1996, 1997); Guyton (2004); Milevsky and Robinson (2005); Spitzer and Singh (2006); Spitzer, Strieter, and Singh (2007); Stout and Mitchell (2006).

[7]Depending on the methodology used to calculate life expectancy, the probability of living past one's expected life span may be a bit more or less than 50 percent. The point is, however, that there is substantial variation around this estimate.

[8]See Wilcox (2008) for a more thorough discussion about how the skewed distribution of life expectancy impacts the expected value of an individual's surplus ratio.

Another approach is to calculate expected future cash flows by multiplying each future cash flow needed by an investor's survival probability.[9] For example, consider Ernest and Beatrice Webster, ages 79 and 68, respectively. The chance of either one of them surviving is represented in the second column of Exhibit 12.6.

EXHIBIT 12.6   Example of Retirement Liability Calculation for Ernest and Beatrice Webster

Year	Probability of Survival	Annual Spending	Expected Spending	Discounted Value
1	0.9989	$100,000	$ 99,891	$ 97,933
2	0.9954	103,000	102,531	98,549
3	0.9893	106,090	104,960	98,906
4	0.9800	109,273	107,089	98,933
5	0.9677	112,551	108,916	98,649
.	.	.	.	.
.	.	.	.	.
.	.	.	.	.
25	0.1575	203,279	32,009	19,510
26	0.1273	209,378	26,655	15,929
27	0.1009	215,659	21,759	12,748
28	0.0783	222,129	17,387	9,987
29	0.0594	228,793	13,581	7,648
30	0.0439	235,657	10,353	5,716
31	0.0317	242,726	7,690	4,162
32	0.0000	250,008	—	—
			Total	$1,835,391

The Websters' inflation-adjusted annual retirement spending is calculated based on their current spending of $100,000 per year and is increased annually using a 3 percent real growth rate (that is, 3 percent annual spending growth in excess of inflation). The Websters' *expected* retirement spending each year is presented in the column labeled "Expected Spending." It is calculated as the product of their survival probability and their required spending for that year ("Annual Spending" column).[10] Each year's expected spending is discounted back to the present, using a real risk-free discount rate of 2.0 percent. The sum of each year's present value of expected spending represents the investor's core capital. In this case, Ernest and Beatrice Webster have a

---

[9]This section is based heavily on Horan and Robinson (2009).

[10]This approach can be modified by conditioning each year's spending based on each spouse's expected survival. For example, if Ernest were to pass away, Beatrice's independent spending needs may be lower than what would have been required if Ernest were also alive. Alternatively, her spending needs could be higher. Some economists estimate that two people can maintain the same living standard for 1.6 times the cost of one, but estimates vary. Using this estimate, Beatrice could maintain the same lifestyle with 1/1.6 (or 62.5 percent) of the amount of spending if Ernest passed away. Subject to discussion with their clients, Harold's firm suggests a 20 percent reduction.

retirement liability of about \$1,835,391.[11] Ernest and Beatrice's retirement liability is a relatively modest 18 times their annual spending, which is on the low end of the range we cited earlier because both Ernest and Beatrice are already well into their retirement years.

We discount spending needs using the real risk-free rate to match the risk of the cash flows. To be sure, the cash flows are not without risk, but their uncertainty is most likely unrelated to market risk factors that would be priced in a normal asset pricing model, making their beta equal to zero. Although longevity risk in this context is nondiversifiable, it can be hedged with a traditional annuity or longevity insurance, allowing the individual to eliminate the nonsystematic risk even if it is nondiversifiable. Therefore, discounting spending needs with the risk-free rate is appropriate.

It is tempting to discount spending needs using the expected return of the assets used to fund them. The uncertainty associated with retirement spending needs is fundamentally unrelated to the risk of the portfolio used to fund those needs. Robert Merton (2007) draws this distinction in the context of a DB pension plan.[12] He points out that using the expected return of pension fund assets to discount the liabilities they are intended to fund systematically underprices those liabilities, and has contributed to the underfunding and decline of defined-benefit pension plans. The analogy for CNA or CAP is that using the investment portfolio's expected return creates an incentive to use aggressive asset allocation that would ostensibly reduce the retirement liability.

Safety Reserve

This aforementioned approach does not fully account for the risk inherent in capital markets. For example, there is no guarantee that capital markets will produce returns greater than the risk-free rate even over long periods of time. Therefore, the present value of the Websters' spending needs may underestimate the true amount of capital required for retirement. One way to accommodate for this bias is to add a safety reserve designed to incorporate flexibility.[13] Incorporating flexibility in this way can be important for at least two reasons. First, it provides a capital cushion if capital markets produce a sequence of unusually poor returns that jeopardize the sustainability of the planned spending program. Second, it allows the retiree to increase spending beyond that explicitly articulated in the spending program to meet an unanticipated and uninsured need. In this way, the safety reserve addresses not only the uncertainty of capital markets, but the uncertainty associated with a family's future commitments.

These uncertainties once again motivate our five-year mantra—five years, five years, five years. We advocate a safety reserve equal to two years of regular spending for both behavioral and practical reasons. For any lump-sum goals (e.g., college funding, purchase of a second home) we set aside a sum equal to any anticipated need during the next five years. The reserve provides a psychological buffer between an investor and the volatility of capital markets. The investor perceives that spending needs are unaffected by short-term capital market volatility and is better able to adhere to a particular investment strategy during turbulent markets.[14]

---

[11]A more conservative approach is assuming that both Ernest and Beatrice survive throughout the forecast horizon provided, rather than assigning probabilities to their combined survival each year.

[12]Robert Merton, "The Future of Retirement Planning," in *The Future of Life-Cycle Saving and Investing* (Charlottesville, VA: Research Foundation of CFA Institute, 2007).

[13]Wilcox (2008) proposes a more complex solution that accounts for the joint distribution of uncertain life spans and asset returns and that produces even more conservative estimates of core capital.

[14]Harold Evensky, "Withdrawal Strategies: A Cash Flow Reserve Solution," in *Retirement Income Redesigned: Master Plans for Distribution* (New York: Bloomberg Press, 2006).

EXAMPLE 12.1   Retirement Liability with Mortality Probabilities

Chris and Kathy Connor are 64 and 61 years old, respectively. Their survival probabilities based on their current ages are listed in the following table. They would like to maintain annual spending of $100,000 on an inflation-adjusted basis. Inflation is expected to be 3 percent, and the nominal risk-free rate is 5 percent.

	Chris		Kathy	
Year	Age	p(Survival)	Age	p(Survival)
1	65	0.991	62	0.996
2	66	0.981	63	0.986
3	67	0.971	64	0.976

1. What is the probability that either Chris or Kathy will survive in each of the next three years?
2. What is the capitalized value of their retirement spending needs over the next three years?

Solution to 1: The probability that either Chris or Kathy will survive is equal to the sum of their individual probabilities less the product of their individual probabilities.

$$p(\text{Survival}) = p(\text{Chris Survives}) + p(\text{Kathy Survives})$$
$$- p(\text{Chris Survives})p(\text{Kathy Survives})$$

For the next three years, the joint probability of survival is:

Year	Joint p(Survival)
1	0.9999
2	0.9997
3	0.9993

Solution to 2: The capitalized value of their retirement spending needs equals the product of the joint probability of survival and the real spending need for each year discounted using the real risk-free rate. Alternatively, one may discount the nominal expected cash flow at the nominal risk-free rate. Using the first approach, the real cash flows will remain constant in real terms and be discounted at 2 percent real rate of return (or 5 percent less 3 percent).

Year	Annual Spending	Expected Spending	
1	$100,000	$99,996	
2	100,000	99,973	,...1
3	100,000	99,930	94,167
			$288,294

Estimating the Retirement Liability with Monte Carlo Analysis

Another approach to estimating retirement liability uses Monte Carlo analysis, a computer-based simulation technique that allows the analyst to forecast a range of possible outcomes based on, say, 10,000 simulated trials.[15] Rather than discounting future expenses, this approach estimates the size of a portfolio needed to generate sufficient withdrawals to meet expenses, which are assumed to increase with inflation. This approach more fully captures the risk inherent in capital markets than the mortality table approach described earlier. For example, one could forecast a particular path of portfolio values based on a hypothetical sequence of returns that conforms to the statistical properties associated with the portfolio's expected return. That particular path is one of an infinite set of possible outcomes. The wealth manager can then forecast another path based on the same set of statistical properties, which will lead to a different outcome. Repeating this procedure thousands of times provides a range of possible outcomes and an understanding of the risk of the portfolio. Of course, Monte Carlo is only an analytical tool subject to its own problems, so a wealth manager utilizing this technique should use it with care.[16]

---

[15]See Sharpe, Chen, Pinto, and McLeavey (2007) for a more detailed discussion of its applications within the context of a retirement portfolio. In addition, Bernstein (2008) presents Monte Carlo analysis in the larger context of estate planning.

[16]Consider developing an estimate for a simple college funding problem: how much to set aside today to fund four years of college expenses in six years. You estimate college expenses at $40,000 per year, investment earnings at 8 percent, and college inflation at 6 percent. This is a simple time value calculation; unfortunately, the answer is a point estimate that is likely to be too high or too low. In order to apply the power of a Monte Carlo simulation, you must estimate a range for your input. So, for example, you may estimate that expenses will range from $30,000 to $50,000, earnings on investments from 6 to 10 percent, and college inflation from 5 to 7 percent. With those inputs, a Monte Carlo analysis would allow you to provide your client with an answer of how much he or she would need to set aside today in order to fund college with an 80 percent probability of success. Of course in order to reach this conclusion you've had to make an additional nine guesses. Six are obvious, namely the range for college cost, investment returns, and college inflation; the other three, less so. Consider the estimate for inflation. Why 5 to 7 percent? Why not 5 to 9 percent? The point is, we tend to unconsciously default to a normal distribution when we establish ranges, but this is not necessarily a correct assumption. Right or wrong, we have implicitly made three additional estimates (i.e., the distribution for each of our ranges). When presenting Monte Carlo results to a client, a wealth manager needs to consider that the results are based on adding numerous additional estimates (guesses) to the analysis, so

(Continued)

One can incorporate recurring spending needs, irregular liquidity needs, taxes, inflation, and other factors into the analysis. In the context of calculating the amount of capital needed to fund retirement, the wealth manager might estimate the amount of capital required to sustain a pattern of spending over a particular time horizon with, for example, an 80 percent level of confidence. That is, the analyst determines the core capital that sustains spending in at least 80 percent of the simulated trials. A higher required level of confidence leads to larger estimates of capital required for retirement.

A safety reserve may also be added to accommodate spending flexibility. It need not be quite as large as that used in the mortality table method, however, because Monte Carlo analysis already captures the risk of producing a sequence of anomalously poor returns, which we discuss in more detail later.

Milevsky and Robinson developed a method to calculate sustainable spending rates that approximates those based on Monte Carlo simulation but without the need for simulation.[17] Their analysis incorporates life span uncertainty as well as financial market risk. Exhibit 12.7 presents an example of ruin probabilities (i.e., the probability of depleting one's financial assets before death).

This analysis assumes the balanced portfolio has a mean arithmetic return of 5 percent and volatility of 12 percent. It also assumes that the spending rate is determined by the initial portfolio value and increased by the rate of inflation annually thereafter. The wealth manager would look up a client age along the left-hand column and choose a proposed withdrawal rate across the top row (expressed in dollars per $100 of nest egg). The associated ruin probability represents the likelihood that withdrawals will not be sustained for the remainder of the client's life.

EXHIBIT 12.7   Ruin Probability for Balanced Portfolio of 50 Percent Equity and 50 Percent Bonds

Retirement Age	Median Age at Death	Hazard Rate, λ	Real Annual Spending per $100 of Initial Nest Egg								
			$2.00	$3.00	$4.00	$5.00	$6.00	$7.00	$8.00	$9.00	$10.00
Endowment	Infinity	0.00%	6.7%	24.9%	49.0%	70.0%	84.3%	92.5%	96.6%	98.6%	99.4%
50	78.1	2.47	1.8	6.4	14.0	24.0	35.2	46.3	56.8	66.0	73.8
55	83.0	2.48	1.8	6.3	14.0	24.0	35.1	46.2	56.7	65.9	73.7
60	83.4	2.96	1.5	5.2	11.6	20.1	29.9	40.1	50.0	59.1	67.2
65	83.9	3.67	1.1	4.0	9.0	15.8	24.0	32.8	41.8	50.5	58.5
70	84.6	4.75	0.8	2.8	6.3	11.4	17.6	24.7	32.2	39.8	47.2
75	85.7	6.48	0.5	1.7	3.9	7.2	11.4	16.3	21.9	27.8	33.9
80	87.4	9.37	0.3	0.9	2.0	3.8	6.2	9.1	12.5	16.3	20.5

Note: Mean arithmetic portfolio return = 5%; standard deviation of return = 12%; mean geometric portfolio return = 4.28%.
Source: Milevsky and Robinson (2005).

(Continued)
using the results as an educational tool instead of a black-letter answer is probably wise. You can find more detailed discussions of these potential problems in Robert Curtis, "Monte Carlo Mania," in Investment Think Tank (New York: Bloomberg Press), and David Nawrocki, "The Problems with Monte Carlo Simulation," Journal of Financial Planning (November 2001).
[17]Milevsky and Robinson (2005).

It is important to recognize that most Monte Carlo simulations, including this approximation, assume that returns are normally distributed. In fact, historical return distributions are skewed and have more extreme events than a normal distribution would imply (i.e., have fat tails). Both these characteristics diminish the sustainability of a withdrawal program and increase the amount of capital necessary to sustain a particular withdrawal rate.

EXAMPLE 12.2 Estimating the Retirement Liability with Monte Carlo Analysis

Mr. Harper is a single 65-year-old with the same $100,000 annual retirement spending as the Connors in Example 12.1. He is willing to accept a 9 percent chance that his spending pattern may exhaust his retirement nest egg before the end of his life (e.g., 91 percent level of confidence).

1. How long is Mr. Harper expected to survive?
2. How large must Mr. Harper's retirement nest egg be for him to be 91 percent confident that he will not outlive his portfolio?
3. How large must his nest egg be if he wants to be only 84.2 percent confident that he will not outlive his portfolio?
4. How large must his nest egg be if he wants to be 96 percent confident that he will not outlive his portfolio?

Solution to 1: Mr. Harper has a 50 percent chance of dying before age 83.9. He also has a 50 percent chance of living beyond that age.

Solution to 2: Under these conditions, Mr. Harper can spend $4.00 for each $100 of his retirement nest egg, or 4 percent of capital. The capital required for Mr. Harper to spend $100,000 per year is therefore $2,500,000, or $100,000/0.04.

Solution to 3: If he is willing to accept a higher probability of failure, Mr. Harper will need less capital. For example, a 15.8 percent chance of Mr. Harper's spending outlasting his portfolio allows him to spend $5.00 for every $100, which requires only $2,000,000, or $100,000/0.05, of capital.

Solution to 4: If he demands a high level of certainty, Mr. Harper will need more capital. For example, a 3 percent chance of Mr. Harper's spending outlasting his portfolio allows him to spend only $3.00 for every $100, which requires $3,333,333, or $100,000/0.03, of capital.

Choosing the Type of Savings Account—You Say "Tomayto," I Say "Tomahto"

How does an investor implement a savings strategy to meet this goal? Importantly, the government often provides incentives for taxpayers to save for retirement, and choosing the right savings vehicle can dramatically increase the after-tax capital available to investors. There are many different types of tax-advantaged savings accounts. In general, however, they can be classified into those with front-end-loaded tax benefits and those with back-end-loaded tax benefits.[18] We will use several examples that are available under U.S. tax law that cover the many types of accounts. For example, in the United States contributions to traditional IRAs and 401(k) plans are tax deductible. Their earnings grow on a tax-deferred basis, and they are often called tax-deferred accounts (TDAs) as a result. The investor pays tax when the funds are withdrawn, and withdrawals are usually taxed as ordinary income. This is summarized in Exhibit 12.8.

In the simplest of contexts, the traditional IRA will accumulate more wealth when the tax rate applicable to withdrawals is less than the tax rate that applies to contributions to a Roth IRA. The intuition is simple enough. The investment account that taxes capital less heavily is preferred from a tax perspective. It is interesting to note that, although the *amount* of tax paid on the withdrawals from a traditional IRA will be greater than the amount of tax paid on contributions to a Roth IRA (assuming the account grows in value over time), the relevant distinction is the tax rate, not the amount of tax paid. If the tax rate is the same, the value of the deferral associated with the tax on withdrawals exactly offsets the greater amount.

EXHIBIT 12.8   Tax Treatment of Different Savings Accounts

	Traditional IRA, 401(k), 403(b), 457, and Keogh Plans	Roth IRA, Roth 401(k), 529 Plans, and Lifetime Savings Account	Nondeductible IRA	Taxable Account
Initial contribution	Tax deductible	Taxable as ordinary income	Taxable as ordinary income	Taxable as ordinary income
Accumulated earnings	Tax deferred	Tax deferred	Tax exempt	Taxable as either ordinary income, dividend, or capital gain as realized
Withdrawal	Taxable as ordinary income	Tax exempt	Taxable as ordinary income	Previously unrealized gains taxed as capital gain

Source: Horan (2005).

For the sake of clarity and consistency, in the discussion that follows we use the term *traditional IRA* to mean any type of tax-sheltered account with front-end tax benefits on contributions, and *Roth IRA* to mean any type of tax-sheltered account with back-end tax benefits. The analysis generally applies equally to the different varieties of account types.

Although traditional IRAs and 401(k) plans are treated similarly from a tax perspective, contribution limits and income limits are much higher for 401(k) plans, making them a more viable alternative for many investors who have access to them. It is important because the simple comparison of contribution and withdrawal tax rates discussed earlier is applicable only when the contemplated pretax investment is less than or equal to the contribution limit.

---

[18]This section is based heavily on Horan (2005).

Consider a $4,000 contribution limit. An investor in a 20 percent tax bracket can expend $5,000 in pretax funds in the case of a Roth IRA: $4,000 will go into the Roth IRA after $1,000 is spent in taxes. The same investor choosing a traditional IRA can contribute $4,000 into the traditional IRA. But to fairly compare the two alternatives, we need to know what happens to the initial tax savings. The $1,000 of tax savings must be invested in another taxable vehicle, which creates an inherent tax drag associated with the traditional IRA strategy. Therefore, simply having a lower tax rate applied to withdrawals is not sufficient for the traditional IRA to accumulate more wealth if we bump up against contribution limits. The withdrawal tax rate must be sufficiently low to cover the higher taxes paid on the $1,000 tax savings invested in a taxable account. Another way to view the difference between a traditional IRA and a Roth IRA is that, when an investor bumps up against contribution limits, the Roth IRA gives an investor a chance to invest more after-tax dollars than a traditional IRA does.

Exhibit 12.9 shows how low the withdrawal tax rate must be to overcome the inherent tax drag associated with a traditional IRA strategy for various circumstances. Panel A assumes the taxable investment is fully taxed as ordinary income at a 28 percent rate. The curved lines across the surface represent break-even tax rates in five-percentage-point increments. For example, an investor in the 28 percent tax bracket facing a five-year time horizon and an expected return of 9 percent has a 25 percent break-even tax rate, or a drop of one tax bracket. If the withdrawal tax rate is higher than this break-even tax rate, the Roth IRA will produce a better after-tax result. Importantly, the Roth IRA becomes more attractive the longer the investment horizon and the higher the pretax return because both these factors increase the tax drag associated with the non-IRA investment.

Panel B repeats the analysis assuming that the non-IRA investment is taxed as a typical equity mutual fund and is therefore taxed less heavily than what we presumed in Panel A.[19] The slope of the surface is not as steep (meaning the Roth IRA is not quite as attractive) because the tax drag of the non-IRA investment is less severe.

If the non-IRA investment is invested under a buy-and-hold strategy in which the tax is entirely deferred as capital gain until the end of the investment horizon, the traditional IRA strategy becomes relatively more attractive still, as shown in Panel C. In this case, the taxable investment is replicating the tax-deferral features associated with the IRA itself.

There are other nontax differences between traditional IRAs and 401(k) plans, aside from different contribution limits. For example, IRAs typically have a wider menu of investment options than most 401(k) plans have. Many 401(k) plans, however, have provisions that allow an investor to borrow against the assets in the plan, an option not available in IRAs. In fact, the use of margin is not permitted in IRAs. Another nontax difference is that workers can postpone the initiation of the required minimum distributions (RMDs) on funds in 401(k) plans by continuing to work, but not on funds in IRAs. This postponement option can be valuable for those who plan to work past the age of 70½. These differences can sometimes be at least as important as the tax advantages associated with these accounts. The wealth manager should bear them in mind.

---

[19]The model inputs in this case assume that 20 percent of the return is composed of ordinary income, 45 percent of the return is composed of capital gains, and that the tax rates on both are 15 percent.

EXHIBIT 12.9   Break-Even Withdrawal Tax Rates for 28 Percent Tax Bracket Investor

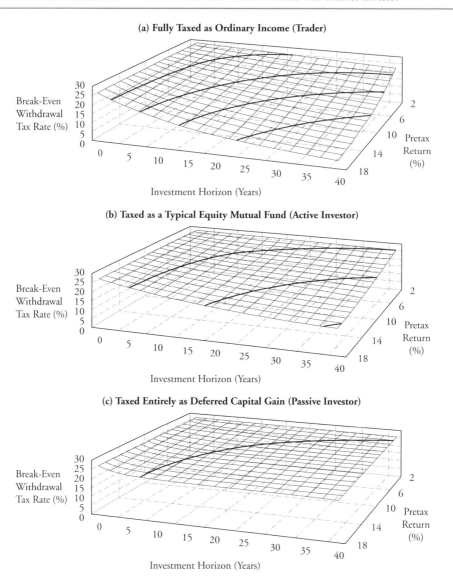

(a) Fully Taxed as Ordinary Income (Trader)

(b) Taxed as a Typical Equity Mutual Fund (Active Investor)

(c) Taxed Entirely as Deferred Capital Gain (Passive Investor)

Source: Horan (2005).

EXAMPLE 12.3   Choosing Among Account Types

Bettye Mims would like to invest for retirement and is willing to reduce this year's spending by $3,000. She will invest $3,000 *after taxes* this year and is in a 25 percent tax bracket. Bettye is choosing between a traditional IRA and a Roth IRA, but regardless of which account she chooses, she would invest in the same portfolio, which is expected to have a pretax return of 6 percent annually and be taxed as ordinary income.

Assuming Bettye will make a single contribution today and withdraw all funds—paying any necessary taxes in 30 years—which type of account will result in the largest after-tax accumulation?

- *Roth IRA.* A tax-exempt account, where a $3,000 contribution is not deductible.
- *Traditional IRA.* A tax-deferred account, where Bettye can make a $4,000 tax-deductible contribution (a $3,000 after-tax cost to her).

Solution:

The Roth IRA would accumulate $17,230 after taxes:

$$FVIF_{Roth} = \$4,000(1 - 0.25)(1 + 0.06)^{30} = \$17,230$$

The traditional IRA would also accumulate $17,230 after taxes:

$$FVIF_{TDA} = \$4,000(1 + 0.06)^{30}(1 - 0.25) = \$17,230$$

Both the traditional IRA and the Roth IRA achieve the same after-tax accumulation, assuming Bettye's tax rates in the contribution year and withdrawal year are the same.

EXAMPLE 12.4   Choosing Among Account Types

Now assume that Bettye is 55 years old and considering maximizing her IRA contribution. The contribution limit (including catch-up contributions for investors age 50 and above) is $6,000.

Assuming she will make a single contribution today and withdraw all funds—paying any necessary taxes in 10 years—which type of account will result in the largest after-tax accumulation?

- *Roth IRA.* An $8,000 pretax contribution results in a $6,000 after-tax contribution, which is the maximum allowed.
- *Traditional IRA.* The same $8,000 pretax contribution is composed of the $6,000 maximum allowable contribution to the traditional IRA and a $2,000 pretax investment in a taxable account. Of the $2,000, $1,500 represents the after-tax investment and $500 represents taxes paid.

Solution:

The Roth IRA would accumulate $17,230 after taxes:

$$FVIF_{Roth} = \$8,000(1 - 0.25)(1 + 0.06)^{30} = \$34,461$$

The traditional IRA would also accumulate $17,230 after taxes:

$$
\begin{aligned}
FVIF_{TDA} &= \$6,000[(1 + 0.06)^{30}(1 - 0.25)] \\
&\quad + \$2,000(1 - 0.25)[(1 + 0.06)(1 - 0.25)]^{30} \\
&= \$31,464
\end{aligned}
$$

The first term is the future value of the maximum allowable $6,000 IRA contribution. The second term represents the future value of the after-tax investment ($1,500) in excess of the contribution limit. The traditional IRA will accumulate less wealth even though the tax rates that apply to the contributions and withdrawals are equal, because a portion of the investment must be invested in a taxable account. Viewed differently, the Roth IRA is the superior alternative because the investor is able to increase the amount of after-tax wealth she is sheltering.

Income Growth, Progressive Tax Rates, and Other Pension Income

This framework for choosing between types of IRAs is somewhat sterile and exists within a limited framework. It assumes that tax rates for contributions and distributions are fixed. In reality, taxpayers face a series of tax brackets with increasing marginal tax rates. Horan and Zaman examined the choice between IRAs in the context of an investor's life cycle during which income grows more quickly than inflation, marginal tax rates change as a result, and investors have access to other pension income.[20]

For aggressive savers enjoying high rates of return, the Roth IRA can be a better choice than a traditional IRA because these conditions create high income-replacement rates, which in turn increase the rate at which traditional IRA distributions are taxed. For similar reasons, retirees with relatively high retirement income from other sources, such as defined-benefit pension plans, may face high tax rates under a progressive regime and therefore favor a Roth IRA.

Less aggressive savers, those with little other retirement income, and those experiencing lower investment returns may prefer the traditional IRA because their withdrawal tax rate is likely to be more modest under a progressive tax rate regime. The moral of the story is that the wealth manager needs to seriously consider the factors that will affect an investor's future tax rate in relation to the current tax rate.

Tax Rate Uncertainty—Crazy Uncle Sam

It bears emphasizing that we are always operating in an environment of uncertainty about future tax rates. The tax code is like that crazy, unpredictable uncle. Standard finance would have us apply a higher discount rate to uncertain cash flows, which, of course, produces a smaller present value. A higher discount rate on a negative future cash flow yields a less negative present value and is therefore a smaller liability than a negative cash flow with a lower discount rate. By this logic, a taxpayer prefers uncertainty about future tax rates because it lowers the present value of his or her tax liability.

Viewed differently, uncertain cash *outflows*, like taxes on investment returns, essentially have negative systematic risk, which hedges the positive systematic risk of investment *inflows*. If the after-tax future value of a traditional IRA as a combination of positive cash flows (i.e., pretax accumulation) and negative cash flows (i.e., taxes), the risk (and hence discount rate) of the combined cash flows is less than the risk of the pretax value alone and thereby increases the present value.[21] In other words, by taxing investment returns, the government shares in

[20]Stephen M. Horan and Ashraf Zaman, "IRAs under Progressive Tax Rate Regimes and Income Growth," *Financial Services Review*, Vol. 18, No. 3 (2009): 195–211.
[21]Lewellen (1977) proffers a more complete version of this argument.

the risk as well as the return of taxable investments. Consequently, the uncertainty surrounding future tax rates can be thought of as a hedge that tends to favor the traditional IRA. That said, with tax rates at historic lows and budget deficits at historic highs, one could make a bet on the direction (rather than the uncertainty itself) of tax rates favoring the Roth IRA. Then again, there's no law of physics that says the Congress can't decide to tax Roth IRA distributions, either.

Tax Diversification—Zig When Uncle Sam Zags

Uncertainty about future tax rates increases the importance of having the option to choose the type of account from which to make withdrawals upon retirement. An investor with only traditional IRAs or only Roth IRAs at retirement is forced to make withdrawals from only one type of account. An investor with both types of accounts may choose the account from which withdrawals are made prior to the mandatory withdrawal age of 70½ years.

This choice has value because, in low-tax-rate regimes, investors can withdraw from the traditional IRA. In high-tax-rate regimes, the Roth IRA can produce tax-free retirement income. Even if an investor is required to make withdrawals from the traditional IRA, the choice can still have value if voluntary withdrawals exceed the mandatory minimums. Having both types of accounts available when making withdrawals creates tax diversification and valuable flexibility for retirees. We discuss the value of this flexibility more later, but the implication for the accumulation phase is that clients may benefit from having a portfolio of account types to diversify their tax risk. This understanding can help guide the choice between a traditional IRA and a Roth IRA, especially when the analytical framework does not clearly suggest one or the other.

Alternative Minimum Tax—One Way or the Other

Established in 1970 to ensure that high-income taxpayers pay some minimum amount of tax, the Alternative Minimum Tax (AMT) has historically affected only a small number of individuals. Over time, an increasing number of taxpayers are being covered by the AMT because it is not indexed for inflation. Four million taxpayers paid AMT in 2007 compared to only 1.1 million taxpayers in 2001.[22] Ironically, the tax cuts of 2001 and 2003 increased AMT coverage because they have not been accompanied by similar cuts in the AMT.

The AMT is a parallel tax system that allows fewer deductions than the standard tax system and has marginal tax rates of 26 percent and 28 percent. Taxpayers calculate their tax liability under both systems and pay the greater of the two tax liabilities. Although the AMT marginal tax rates may be lower than many tax brackets, it often results in a higher tax liability because it disallows certain deductions, such as state tax, property tax, personal exemptions, and dependent exemptions. The first implication of the AMT is that the standard tax brackets used in our analysis may not be an investor's true marginal tax rate. Rather, marginal tax rates for the AMT taxpayer may be 26 percent or 28 percent. If the AMT reduces an investor's marginal tax rate (even if it increases his or her overall tax liability), then the Roth IRA becomes relatively more attractive, holding the withdrawal tax rate constant. Other nuances of the AMT, however, make this implication less straightforward than it initially appears.

---

[22]Tom Herman, "How AMT Confuses Taxpayers," *Wall Street Journal*, August 13, 2008.

The AMT includes an initial exemption that reduces taxable income. For 2011, it is $48,450 for single taxpayers and $74,450 for those who are married and filing jointly. These exemptions are phased out, however, if income exceeds an established base level. For example, a couple filing jointly has their exemption phased out at a rate of 25 cents for every dollar of income over $150,000. This phase out effectively increases the marginal tax rate by 25 percent. Each dollar of income over $150,000 for a married couple filing jointly has two tax effects. On that dollar, the AMT-paying couple pays 26 cents of tax and has 25 cents of their exemption phased out and subject to tax, creating an additional 6½ cents of tax (i.e., 0.26 × 0.25). In this case, the marginal tax rate is 32½ percent, not 26 percent.[23] So an investor's marginal tax rate can be quite high and a bit illusive under AMT. Marginal tax rates this high tend to favor the traditional IRA over the Roth IRA because they increase the effective tax deductibility of contribution.

The AMT can impact the choice between TDAs in other ways, as well. Contributions to TDAs with front-end tax benefits decrease a taxpayer's adjusted gross income (AGI), which decreases the possibility of being covered by the AMT tax and/or reduce the amount of AMT exemption that would otherwise be phased out. Contributions to TDAs with back-end tax benefits, such as Roth IRAs and 529 plans, do not decrease AGI or reduce AMT coverage. Therefore, the threat of AMT coverage can favor the traditional IRA over the Roth IRA. Because taxpayers can contribute up to $16,500 to 401(k) plans and 403(b) plans in 2010, these plans can be significant tools in reducing either AMT coverage or the AMT exemption phase out.

Roth IRA Conversions—Slam Dunk?

As of 2010, Congress removed the income limitations associated with Roth IRA conversions, making it possible for all traditional IRA investors to convert their accounts into Roth IRAs by paying income tax on the amount converted. According to the financial press, everyone should convert to a Roth IRA.

One advantage of a Roth IRA that is not captured in this analysis is that Roth IRAs have no required minimum distributions (RMDs), which require investors to take taxable distributions beginning at age 70½. We discuss RMDs more fully later. Another advantage is that the rules against early withdrawals before age 59½ are somewhat more lax. This section focuses solely on the immediate tax advantages or disadvantages of conversion.

The most important rule to remember is that the value of converting depends largely on whether the conversion tax is paid from a taxable account, thereby avoiding an early withdrawal penalty and leveraging the deferred contribution. This strategy effectively lowers the opportunity cost associated with paying the conversion tax. Under these circumstances, the analysis is identical to that in the previous section. Specifically, we can use Exhibit 12.9 to determine what the break-even withdrawal rate is for traditional IRA withdrawals. In panel A, for example, break-even withdrawal rates drop quickly, indicating that conversion is more attractive when the conversion tax is paid from a highly taxed source. When the conversion taxes are paid from a source with a modest tax drag, such as in panel C, then conversion becomes relatively less attractive. Paying the tax from a taxable account is the equivalent of putting more after-tax dollars into a tax-sheltered account.

---

[23]Income in excess $175,000 for a couple filing jointly is taxed at 28 percent marginal rate. When exemptions are phased out above this amount, the effective marginal rate on income is 35 percent (i.e., 0.28 + 0.28 × 0.25).

When a taxpayer uses the IRA assets to pay the conversion tax, the withdrawal tax rate must be 11 percent higher than his or her current tax rate to make conversion advisable (assuming a 10 percent early withdrawal penalty).[24] Because most retirees have less income in retirement than in their preretirement years, it is unlikely that their withdrawal tax rate during retirement will be higher than what it was in their preretirement years. Therefore, in most cases, conversion is not likely to be advisable unless the conversion tax can be paid from taxable assets.

In sum, the conversion decision rests largely on balancing the likelihood of having a lower tax rate in retirement (which favors sticking with the traditional IRA) against the benefits of putting more after-tax dollars into a tax-sheltered account and being free of RMDs (which favors the Roth IRA).

It must be mentioned that this analysis is predicated on the tax code remaining basically in its current form. If there is a mass conversion of traditional IRAs to Roth IRAs and future Congresses find themselves short of money, it is conceivable that Congress might tax balances in Roth IRAs even though taxes have already been paid. This is not a prediction as much as a recognition that the world can change, especially if Uncle Sam is short of cash.

Do Over! Convert Early and Convert Often

Remember when we were kids and we wanted to take back a bad decision? An important and valuable nuance in deciding whether to convert a traditional IRA to a Roth IRA is that the IRS allows taxpayers to reverse their conversion decision up until the day they file their taxes. This is a valuable option.

Suppose you convert a $100,000 traditional IRA and pay 40 percent tax of $40,000. If the account dropped in value to $70,000, you wouldn't be happy knowing that you paid conversion tax on $100,000. No problem. You can simply recharacterize the conversion as if it had never happened. If the account were to have increased in value to $130,000, you have the good fortune of paying tax on only $100,000. The $30,000 price appreciation is yours tax-free.

This optionlike strategy becomes even more valuable when the time to expiration and volatility on the underlying assets increase. Therefore, converters should convert early and convert often. Conversion is most valuable at the beginning of the tax year to provide as much opportunity for the accounts to go up or down in value before a decision to recharacterize has to be made. If the taxpayer files for an extension, the opportunity to recharacterize (or do over) extends to October following the relevant tax year.

Also, if the IRA has 10 securities, the most extreme strategy would be to convert using 10 different Roth IRAs—one for each security. In this way, the taxpayer can retain the Roth IRAs that increase in value and recharacterize the Roth IRAs that have gone down in value, maximizing the value of the option the government provides. Rather than go to this extreme, a wealth manager might consider recommending at least two Roth IRA accounts—one for the most volatile investments and a second for the least volatile. Or negatively correlated assets can be divided into different accounts.

Nondeductible IRA Contributions

Income limitations may prevent some taxpayers from contributing to tax-advantaged accounts with either front-end tax benefits or back-end tax benefits. These investors can still choose

---

[24]Specifically, the break-even withdrawal tax rate in this situation is equal to $T_n = T_0/(1 - \theta)$ where θ is the early withdrawal penalty.

between a nondeductible IRA contribution and a taxable investment. In general, if returns in a taxable account would be fully taxed as ordinary income, the nondeductible IRA is generally the better choice from a tax perspective, especially as the investment horizon increases if the pretax return increases.[25]

If, however, returns in a taxable account would otherwise be deferred to the end of the investment horizon in the form of a lightly taxed capital gain, a taxable account is generally optimal because the capital gain tax shelter is more valuable than the tax deferral associated with the nondeductible IRA. For taxpayers subject to the AMT, the nondeductible IRA alternative becomes increasingly attractive because the effective marginal tax rates on both investment income and capital gains are relatively high, particularly in income ranges where the standard exemption is phased out.

DISTRIBUTION PHASE

In this section we address techniques for managing the distribution phase of retirement planning, including managing risk, maximizing sustainable withdrawals, and how to handle mandatory distributions.

Risk Management

Retirement carries many unique risks, not all of which are financial. In this section we discuss three of the most important, which relate to longevity, inflation, and medical expenses. The risk of not saving enough is largely a behavioral issue that we addressed in the previous section.[26]

Longevity Risk—How Long Can You Go?

As we noted at the beginning of this chapter, modern medicine and lifestyles have dramatically increased life spans. This is undoubtedly a good thing, but it obviously increases the retirement challenge. Despite improvements in life spans, medical advances have done little to take away the uncertainty of when we might meet our eventual demise.

It is widely known that average American life expectancies are about 75 years and 80 years for males and females, respectively.[27] This commonly cited statistic is based on expectancy at birth. As we advance through our lives, however, our chances of reaching our original life expectancy (i.e., calculated at birth) get better and better. A 79-year-old has a better shot of making it to 80 than a 30-year-old has. So life expectancy depends on one's current age.

According to Exhibit 12.10, 65-year-old males and females have at least a 50 percent chance of living to 85 or 88 years, respectively, or 8 to 10 years longer than their life

---

[25]For a more thorough analysis, see Horan (2005).

[26]Harold reframes this risk by telling the client, "What keeps me awake at night, and ought to keep you awake, is the risk of living, not dying. If you die with money in the bank, that's not so bad, but if you're alive with no money in the bank, that's a problem."

[27]*National Vital Statistics Reports*, Vol. 53, No. 6, November 10, 2004. In comparing means and medians, we are making the simplifying assumption that the distribution of life expectancies is symmetrical. It is not, but the asymmetry does not affect the essence of our discussion here.

expectancy at birth.[28] If our clients are a married couple, then our planning horizon must be based not on their individual life expectancies, but rather on the expectation that either one or the other will survive to a particular age. A married couple has a 50 percent chance that at least one of them will survive until age 91. There is a 25 percent chance that one of them will survive until 96.

EXHIBIT 12.10   Life Span Probabilities of 65-Year-Old Americans

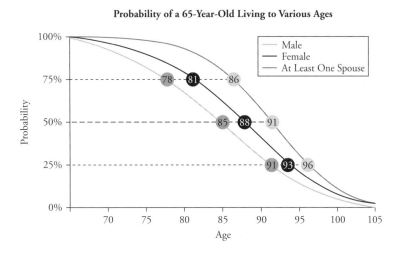

The point here is not to admire our dramatic improvements in life span, but to appreciate the uncertainty of that life span. For example, the difference between the 25th and 75th percentiles is 10 to 13 years, meaning that if we are given the latitude of predicting the *decade* during which a 65-year-old will pass away based on this data, we will still be wrong *half* the time.

Defined-benefit pension funds, like individuals planning for retirement, are charged with generating lifetime income for the participants in the plan. Pension funds, however, have the law of large numbers on their side. A pension fund manager many not know which plan participants will survive or die from one year to the next, but using demographic data the manager can predict with some accuracy how many people will be on the pension roles from one year to the next, on average.[29] Individuals and small families do not have the luxury of being correct *on average*. They need to make decisions that are correct *in their particular case*.

A common technique wealth managers use for planning purposes is to plan an investment and withdrawal strategy that uses the average or median life span. Many years ago, Lynn Hopewell had an experience of working with a client for whom he developed an elaborate

---

[28]Actually, 65 years ago, life expectancy at birth was only 64 and 68 years for men and women, respectively.

[29]Interestingly, even with all their experience and data, pension funds and insurance companies have difficulty precisely forecasting longevity. They have consistently underestimated life span improvements, creating funding problems. Increasingly, many have turned to purchasing longevity insurance or transferring the risk to other investors in an effort to assist their investment planning process, which we will discuss later as it relates to the individual.

financial plan based on the median survival probabilities. After Lynn presented his conclusions with much flourish, the client responded by saying, "This is very impressive. Let me get this straight. You've developed a plan for me that will fail half the time. Is that right?" Unfortunately, the client was right. The initial plan did not properly account for the possibility of outliving one's assets.

Retirement planning would be much easier if we knew our investment time horizon, but we rarely have that luxury. Wealth managers have two basic choices to manage longevity risk in the face of this uncertainty. The first approach is to use precautionary saving to reduce the probability of a plan failing from 50 percent to some acceptable level, say 30 percent or 10 percent.[30] A variant of precautionary saving in the accumulation phase is to adopt a precautionary conservative spending policy during the distribution phase.

Annuities—The Good, the Bad, and the Ugly
The second basic method for managing longevity risk is to transfer longevity risk to a financial institution that can efficiently diversify it across many individuals so it can enjoy the privilege of predicting life spans *on average* rather than in a particular case in much the same way a pension fund does. The most basic means of transferring this risk is through a traditional immediate fixed annuity in which an investor trades a lump sum of, say, $100,000 for a stream of lifetime annual income of, say, $6,000, depending on the level of interest rates and the age of the annuitant. The annuitant can choose to have benefits continue to the last surviving spouse (i.e., survivor option) for a fixed minimum number of years (e.g., a minimum of 10 years) or to have annuity payments increase with inflation over time (more on this in the next section) in exchange for receiving somewhat lower payments.

Insurance companies are able to offer annuity rates that often look attractive compared to AAA-rated fixed income instruments with maturities similar to the annuitant's life expectancy, because the annuity payment incorporates a return of principal and some annuitants in the pool will pass away early—in which case the insurance company wins. The extra return is derived from what is known as "mortality credits." Of course, sometimes the annuitant may live beyond the expectancy, in which case the individual wins.

It important to realize, though, that the decision of whether to annuitize is not about winning; it is about insuring.[31] Most of us carry homeowner, car, and life insurance. We don't hope that our home burns down, our car gets sideswiped, or we die prematurely so we can "win." Just as these risk management tools guard against unlikely events that would have a potentially devastating financial consequence, so too do annuities guard against the prospect of outliving our assets.

Despite the logical appeal and simplicity of using immediate, fixed annuities to provide a safety net of lifetime income to meet our basic living needs, few people annuitize. Jason Scott speculates that individuals don't like to discuss and make decisions about their mortality, and typically like to bequeath assets to their heirs.[32] He also speculates that they view annuities as a gamble. "What if I die tomorrow, next week, or next year? The insurance company will have

---

[30]Reducing the chance of failure to zero would require an exorbitant amount of assets in theory.

[31]See, for example, Roger Ibbotson, Moshe Milevsky, Peng Chen, and Kevin Zhu, *Lifetime Financial Advice: Human Capital, Asset Allocation, and Insurance* (Charlottesville, VA: Research Foundation of CFA Institute, 2007).

[32]Jason Scott, "Behavioral Obstacles in the Annuity Market," *Financial Analysts Journal*, Vol. 63, No. 6 (2007): 71–82.

kept my money." A more generous interpretation is to view annuities as an investment. They are really neither. Fixed annuities are simply a way to manage longevity risk.

A relatively new type of fixed annuity, called a longevity annuity (also known as longevity insurance or a deferred payout annuity) is available that can combat some of these behavioral biases. Rather than beginning payments immediately, as is the case with an immediate fixed annuity, payments of the deferred annuity begin after a period of time, say 20 years. Deferring the initiation of annuity payments has several advantages. First, it significantly reduces the cost of annuitization. Put differently, it significantly increases available retirement spending for each annuitized dollar. Exhibit 12.11 shows how much spending is improved at each year for a 65-year-old who insures each year's worth of retirement income. Not surprisingly, the benefits of annuitization are concentrated near the end of the time horizon. One can significantly reduce the cost of an annuity by insuring only the income later in life when mortality risk is greatest.

EXHIBIT 12.11   Spending Improvement of a Deferred Annuity for a 65-Year-Old

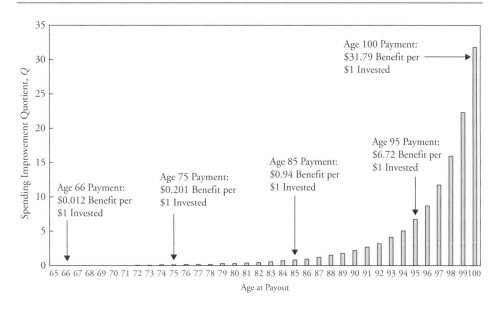

Source: Scott (2008).

This provides an attractive alternative to full annuitization. For example, Exhibit 12.12 shows that an 11.5 percent allocation to an age-85 annuity for a 65-year-old male with $1 million improves guaranteed spending by 33.7 percent over self-insuring with precautionary savings compared to only a 6.5 percent spending improvement for immediate annuitization. This commitment will equalize spending up to and after age 85. Using actual bond and annuity prices, Scott shows that guaranteed spending can be increased by 21 percent with less than an 8 percent commitment to an age-85 annuity. The lower cost can significantly reduce the behavioral obstacle of insuring against the possibility of outliving one's money by decreasing the size of the gamble.[33]

---

[33]In case you missed it the first time, insuring lifetime retirement income is not gambling.

EXHIBIT 12.12   Longevity Annuity Spending versus Immediate Annuity Spending

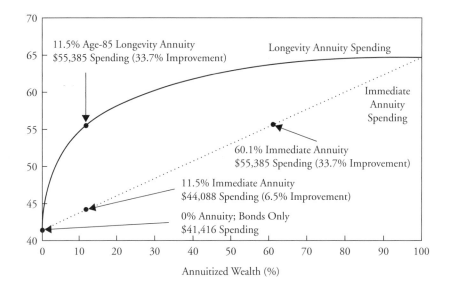

Note: $1 million in assets, age 65, male.
Source: Scott (2008).

A second advantage of the deferred payout annuity is that it transfers to an insurance company the type of risk that it is best suited to manage. In the case of a traditional immediate annuity, an individual gives up a portion of his or her nest egg and immediately begins receiving payments. These initial payments on the front end of the cash flow stream are very easy for individuals to manufacture on their own. There's little longevity risk on the front end. The insurance company adds very little value with respect to these early cash flows. The value of intermediation provided by the insurance company rests in its ability to diversify longevity risk among many people. The value in resolving this uncertainty is in the cash flows near the end of one's life span when the risk of outliving one's assets is the greatest.

The third advantage of the deferred annuity is that it helps to fix the individual's investment horizon. We said earlier that retirement planning would be much easier if we knew how long we would live. A deferred annuity does not guarantee how long we will live (thank God!) but it does allow the wealth manager to devise a spending and investment strategy appropriate for a fixed number of years, after which time the longevity annuity will take over. The core portfolio would need to sustain withdrawals for only, say, 20 years rather than for some conservatively long time horizon.

Many variable annuity products combine longevity insurance with investment products using complicated guaranteed minimum benefits and guaranteed minimum withdrawal benefits that most finance PhD students would have difficulty pricing. In a behavioral sense, they can have substantial appeal, but they tend to be very expensive, with substantial fees and early withdrawal penalties. We discuss them more thoroughly in Exhibit 12.13.

EXHIBIT 12.13   Annuities Defined

Single-Premium Immediate Annuities (SPIAs)

This is an insurance-based product, also known as a payout annuity, designed to insure income for life. As discussed earlier, with increasing life expectancy and the squaring of the curve, planning for lifetime income is a critical aspect of today's retirement planning, and research suggests that SPIAs may play a significant role in meeting this goal.

Immediate Fixed Annuity (IFA)

An IFA provides an investor with a fixed monthly dollar payment for life, providing an element of longevity insurance. However, this benefit is balanced by a number of disadvantages. Because the payments are fixed, the income stream is subject to inflation erosion. In addition, in most cases the purchase of an IFA is an irrevocable decision and the investment traded out of once purchased.

Immediate Variable Annuity (IVA)

An immediate variable annuity (IVA) allows an investor to select from a number of subaccounts (i.e., mutual funds) to design the composition of one's own underlying portfolio. Similar to an IFA, payments are guaranteed for life; however, unlike IFAs, the monthly payment varies depending on the value of the underlying investment portfolio. The uncertainty of the payment stream is offset by the opportunity (expectation) that over long periods an equity-oriented portfolio will provide an increasing income stream. Due to the uncertainty of market returns, at the inception of an IVA the investor selects an assumed investment return (AIR). The AIR determines the initial income payment to the annuitant and the future adjustments to the payment stream. If the underlying investment portfolio has a net return higher or lower than the AIR, the income payments are accordingly adjusted either up or down. A lower AIR results in a smaller initial payment but reduces the likelihood of a future reduction in payments and increases the likelihood that, over time, the income payments will provide an inflation hedge. AIRs typically range from 3½ to 5 percent.

Longevity Insurance (LI)

Although all forms of payout annuities may be considered longevity insurance, as they are designed to pay for one's lifetime, a relatively new product specifically marketed as longevity insurance may well be, in the future, one of the most important investment vehicles in the wealth manager's universe. Basically, LI is an investment a client makes at a relatively young age that does not begin to pay until many years later. When it does begin payments, they last for a lifetime. As an example, a male, age 65, might be entitled to $70,000 per year after age 85 (but nothing if he dies before 85). An insurer can offer such a product because there is a high probability that many policyholders won't live until 85 and will collect nothing, so the mortality credit will inure to the benefit of those who do survive past that age.

Source: R. Carey and Jeffrey Dellinger, "Immediate Annuities: Structure, Mechanics, and Value"; Moshe Milevsky with Anna Abaimova, "Risk Management during Retirement"; Roger Ibbotson, Michael Henkel, and Peng Chen, "Longevity Risk Insurance," in *Retirement Income Redesigned* (New York: Bloomberg Press, 2006).

Whether one uses fixed immediate, longevity, or variable annuities, Exhibit 12.14 offers guidelines to help guide the decision. In general, annuitization is more important for relatively healthy, risk-averse, older investors who are relatively unconcerned about leaving bequests to their heirs. Also, the decision to annuitize affects asset allocation. Investors who have insured much of their retirement income needs have the capacity to accept more risk in their investment portfolios because their basic needs are already largely satisfied.

EXHIBIT 12.14   Annuitization Guidelines

	Fixed Annuity	Variable Annuity
Higher risk aversion	More attractive	Less attractive
Stronger bequest motive	Less attractive	Less attractive
High survival probability	More attractive	More attractive
Older investor	More attractive	Less attractive

It is important to recognize that Social Security and benefits from defined-benefit plans are effectively annuities and can count toward an optimal allocation to control longevity risk. In fact, Social Security and many pension plans offer inflation-adjusted lifetime income that can jointly hedge longevity and inflation risk, making them particularly valuable elements in an overall retirement plan. Moreover, these annuity-like contracts give the investor the option of choosing when to begin annuity payments, which is also valuable. Because they are particularly valuable, they are also particularly expensive for the government and employers to provide to retirees, so they are quickly going by the wayside. In some cases, some companies and municipalities are reducing certain retirement benefits.

One must also be aware of counterparty risk associated with annuity providers—the risk that promised payments will not be made. The U.S. government tends to be a very good credit risk (although the recent financial crisis and its ever-increasing appetite for borrowing and spending has called even that into question). Employers and insurance companies can be different stories. The wealth manager should evaluate the credit risk of these providers, asking questions such as:

• Is the pension fully funded or underfunded?
• What is the likelihood benefits will be eliminated or reduced?
• What is the insurance company's rating?
• Has the rating changed over time?
• Can I diversify counterparty risk by using more than one provider?

When to Take the Plunge

Deciding whether and how much to annuitize is only one problem. Deciding *when* to annuitize is another. We don't have a specific answer to this question, but Ibbotson, Milevsky, Chen, and Zhu argue that annuitizing before age 60 is likely too soon.[34] Milevsky looks at mortality credits from the perspective of required return.[35] Exhibit 12.15 shows that a 65-year-old retiree needs to earn 83 basis points more than the pricing rate available on an annuity to justify not annuitizing and instead managing the money with the systematic withdrawal plan.

---

[34]See, for example, Ibbotson, Milevsky, Chen, and Zhu, *Lifetime Financial Advice.*
[35]Moshe A. Milevsky, "Real Longevity Insurance with a Deductible: Introduction to Advanced-Life Delayed Annuities," *North American Actuarial Journal*, Vol. 9, No. 4 (2005): 109–122.

EXHIBIT 12.15   Value of Unisex Mortality Credits

What must you earn—above the pricing rate—to justify *not* annuitizing?

Age of Annuitant	Spread Above Pricing Interest Rate (*In Basis Points = 1/100%*)	Age of Annuitant	Spread Above Pricing Interest Rate (*In Basis Points = 1/100%*)
55	35	80	414
60	52	85	725
65	83	90	1,256
70	138	95	2,004
75	237	100	2,978

Source: Evensky and Katz (2006). The IFID Centre calculations. Assuming 40m, 60f (static) Annuity 2002 Table at 6% net interest.

The older you get, the more valuable it is to hedge longevity risk and buy an annuity. This phenomenon is illustrated in Exhibit 12.15 as the hurdle rate increases at an increasing rate as the age of the annuitant increases. As we age, our remaining expected life span declines. But the range or variability of our remaining life span relative to that expectation increases. This relative increase in uncertainty grows as we age and increases the value of insuring longevity risk.

As a result, it pays to wait before buying an annuity. It gets cheaper and more valuable as time goes on. The following guidelines offer additional help in timing the annuity decision.

- Annuitizing early eliminates the option for clients to change their bequest preferences. In general, annuitants lose control of their money. Many a widow or widower has married late in life, for example, and developed a desire to leave assets to heirs. Alternatively, retirees often become involved in volunteer and charitable activities that evolve into philanthropic aspirations.
- Annuitizing fixes an investor's fixed income allocation and reduces the ability to rebalance the portfolio. This constraint is more costly at earlier ages and when bond rates are historically low, argues against early annuitization.
- These problems of early annuitization are mitigated with deferred annuities because the financial commitment to them is less onerous. As a result, the constraints imposed by changing bequest preferences and fixing the bond allocation are less severe. Therefore, the use of a deferred payout annuity (e.g., longevity annuity, longevity insurance) would argue for annuitizing relatively early compared to a traditional immediate annuity. In fact, Milevsky argues that the best deal is for investors to purchase deferred payout annuities at a relatively young age (e.g., their mid-40s) that start paying income in their late 70s.[36]

---

[36]Ibid.

There is some value to staggering the purchase of annuities over time from age 65 to age 80, for example. It can overcome some of the behavioral obstacles associated with annuities, provide some flexibility to rebalance during the staggering period, enable the annuitant to reconsider bequest preferences over time, and offer the opportunity to diversify counterparty risk across multiple issuers.

Inflation Risk

Fixed annuities, like other fixed income instruments, decline in real value as inflation rises. Inflation has a pernicious long-term effect on retirement income. Annuities that protect against inflation, sometimes called real annuities, are available.

As of this writing, most real annuities offer fixed annual increases in annuity payments of, say, 3 percent based on expected inflation. Ideally, payments would be adjusted for actual inflation tied to the basket of goods most relevant to the elderly. Future products will likely have this feature. In any case, inflation adjustments are valuable and make real annuities more expensive than plain annuities. The extra cost can be worthwhile in situations where other inflation hedges are not naturally present.

Medical Expense Risk

An annuity is a type of contingent claim investment. It pays a cash flow contingent on the annuitant surviving. This contingency focuses attention on longevity risk and is more economically efficient than precautionary savings. It does not, however, address another important risk in retirement, namely the possibility of large medical costs. Health insurance is designed to manage the risk of acute, unpredictable medical costs. Longer life spans, however, also introduce the specter of large costs associated with long-term care (LTC) in our old age, when we have less ability to do things for ourselves.

According to Finkelstein, two-thirds of 65-year-olds will never enter a nursing home, but for those who do, the expense is significant.[37] Long-term care fits the profile of an ideal insurable event: It is unlikely, but economically significant should it occur. Only about 10 percent of elderly have private long-term care insurance. Many early retirees (ages 65 to 75) are shut out of the long-term care insurance market because of poor health or risky lifestyles. Medicaid provides some coverage, but only after a retiree's personal assets have been depleted.[38] As a result, long-term care insurance is one of the largest uninsured risks faced by the elderly; unfortunately, only wealthy investors are likely to purchase it. Educating less wealthy clients about the benefits of LTC insurance is an important role for the wealth manager.

---

[37] Amy Finkelstein, "The Market for Long Term Care," in *The Future of Life-Cycle Saving and Investing: The Retirement Phase* (Charlottesville, VA: Research Foundation of CFA Institute, 2009).

[38] There are estate planning strategies for those who have bequest motives that can protect personal assets. A primary residence, for example, is sheltered from Medicaid spend-down rules. Many of these techniques require action at least five years before the onset of long-term care, so advance planning is needed. This discussion is well beyond the scope of our investigation here.

Like annuities, investors may not want to think about the unpleasantness of long-term care enough to consider insurance. Alternatively, they may view it as a gamble. Perhaps the biggest barrier is the fact that private insurance will end up paying for at least some long-term care that Medicaid would have paid for. So why buy private insurance? Medicaid pays only after personal assets are depleted and private insurance benefits have been exhausted, which is perhaps why private insurance is more common among the wealthy. In this sense, Medicare crowds out private insurance.

Sustainable Withdrawal Strategies (Spending Policy)

Few retirees annuitize all their assets, which means that they will likely be making periodic withdrawals from their other assets. For retirees, developing a sensible and sustainable retirement withdrawal strategy is at least as important as developing a sensible investment strategy. A simple approach to the problem is to recognize that from 1926 to 2009, large-capitalization stocks have produced an average return of 9.8 percent. Therefore, assuming that return on a consistent basis in the future, retirees could invest 100 percent of their assets into equities, withdraw almost 10 percent of their portfolios, and preserve their principal in the long run. But this would be a terrible mistake! As Milton Friedman says:

Never walk across a river just because its average depth is four feet.[39]

One problem with withdrawing 10 percent is that it ignores the effect of inflation. If one really wants to protect principal in real terms, the portfolio needs to grow by the rate of inflation. To allow for this, annual withdrawals need to be scaled down by the inflation rate to permit withdrawals to grow by inflation over the long term.

Volatility in Planning Retirement Withdrawals—It's Not Just the Destination, It's the Journey

Another reason average return is a bad proxy for a sustainable withdrawal rate is volatility. Obviously, higher return improves sustainability and supports a higher spending rate. With higher return also comes higher volatility, however. Volatility decreases the sustainability of a spending program for at least two reasons. First, even in the absence of a spending rule, volatility decreases future accumulations. This concept can be illustrated by considering a $100 portfolio that experiences sequential returns of +50 percent followed by −50 percent. Although the arithmetic average of those returns is zero, the portfolio's value after two years is only $75. The $25 decline in value is due to the volatility drag.

One can also view this graphically as in Exhibit 12.16. Both lines represent the accumulation from an investment with a 0 percent arithmetic average return. The solid line represents a return with 10 percent variation (i.e., alternating returns of +10 percent and −10 percent), while the dashed line represents a return with 20 percent variation (i.e., alternating returns of +20 percent and −20 percent). In both cases, volatility is a drag on performance. In the 20 percent variation case, however, the drag is much more severe.

---

[39]Bierwirth (1994).

EXHIBIT 12.16   Example of Volatility Drag

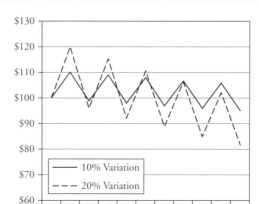

Return Sequence—I'd like My Dessert First, Please

The second reason volatility decreases sustainability relates to the interaction of periodic withdrawals and return sequences. Future accumulations do not depend on the sequence of returns in the absence of periodic spending withdrawals. Put differently, in the example of +50 percent and −50 percent returns, the ending value after two years is the same regardless of whether the portfolio returns are sequenced with the positive return first or last.

This independence disappears when withdrawals are introduced. Specifically, the sustainability of a portfolio is severely compromised when the initial returns are poor because a portion of the portfolio is being liquidated at relatively depressed values, making less capital available for compounding at potentially higher subsequent returns. If the portfolio in our example were to experience a $10 withdrawal at the end of each year, the portfolio would be worth $60 at the end of two years if the positive return occurs first but only $50 if the negative return occurs first. That's a 20 percent difference.

To illustrate these concepts, consider a simple $100 portfolio with no withdrawals over three years in panel A of Exhibit 12.17. The average annual return is 10 percent with volatility of 15 percent. In the absence of withdrawals, the sequence of investment returns does not affect the final outcome. In panel B, however, we introduce a periodic $10 withdrawal. In the first sequence in which good returns precede poor returns, nominal principal is preserved because the portfolio experiences good initial returns. In the second sequence, in which poor returns precede good returns, the investor is left with only $85 of principal after the first year to sustain subsequent withdrawals. As a result, the investor accumulates $6 less wealth and is unable to preserve nominal principal despite the fact that the average returns are the same in both sequences, because poor initial returns combine with the withdrawals at depressed prices to create poor initial conditions that lock in bad outcomes.

We can see the impact of volatility in panel C, which keeps the average return at 10 percent, but increases the volatility from 15 percent to 25 percent. In this case, the impact on the return sequence is nearly twice as great.

EXHIBIT 12.17   Different Return Patterns with and without Withdrawals

Panel A: Without Withdrawals

Year	0	1	2	3
Withdrawal		$0	$0	$0
Return		25%	10%	−5%
Portfolio	$100	$125	$138	$131
Withdrawal		$0	$0	$0
Return		−5%	10%	25%
Portfolio	$100	$95	$105	$131
			Difference	$0

Panel B: With Withdrawals

Year	0	1	2	3
Withdrawal		$10	$10	$10
Return		25%	10%	−5%
Portfolio	$100	$115	$117	$101
Withdrawal		$10	$10	$10
Return		−5%	10%	25%
Portfolio	$100	$85	$84	$94
			Difference	$6

Panel C: Withdrawals and Higher Volatility

Year	0	1	2	3
Withdrawal		$10	$10	$10
Return		35%	10%	−15%
Portfolio	$100	$125	$125	$98
Withdrawal		$10	$10	$10
Return		−15%	10%	35%
Portfolio	$100	$75	$73	$88
			Difference	$11

A useful way to view this phenomenon is to consider periodic withdrawals as the opposite of dollar cost averaging investment. In dollar cost averaging, the investor contributes a fixed dollar amount each period. Conventional wisdom holds that volatility improves the effectiveness of dollar cost averaging because investors are able to purchase more shares when prices are low. The opposite is true in a retirement withdrawal program in which an investor withdraws a fixed amount each period.

Several authors have examined the return/volatility trade-off on portfolio sustainability in the context of asset allocation. Diversification is particularly useful in this context because it reduces volatility without necessarily decreasing return. Not surprisingly, recommendations vary; but equity allocations between 30 percent and 75 percent of total portfolio value seem to maximize portfolio sustainability.

Contrary to conventional wisdom, retirees can often accept more risk as they age because the horizon over which withdrawals must be sustained shortens over time. Several authors have shown that *increasing* equity allocations through retirement can increase sustainability. Put differently, having a heavy cash or fixed income exposure in the early years of withdrawals reduces the chance of suffering catastrophically poor returns early on that create poor initial conditions that are very difficult to overcome with subsequent returns. Grangaard (2002) suggests that a 6.6 percent sustainable withdrawal rate is achievable through a combination of laddering bonds for the early retirement years and having equity for later retirement years.[40]

The 4 Percent Rule

As we mentioned earlier in the chapter, people could estimate how much they could safely spend in retirement by determining how much annuity income their nest egg could buy from an insurance company in a competitive setting. Annuitizing 100 percent of their portfolio is, of course, rare. The pioneer in measuring sustainable withdrawal rates is William Bengen, who began using historical returns to measure withdrawal sustainability for different asset allocations. He uses data that includes the Great Depression (of the 1930s, that is, not the 2000s!), the recession of the early 1970s, as well as bull markets.[41]

Using a 50/50 asset allocation of stocks and bonds, he finds that a 5 percent inflation-adjusted withdrawal program begun in each year from 1926 to 1976 fails to last 30 years approximately a quarter of the time. Withdrawal programs beginning in the late 1960s and early 1970s (periods of poor initial returns and high inflation) performed the worst—worse than the Great Depression because of the persistence of poor real returns between the two asset classes.

This 25 percent failure rate may be too high a margin of error for most clients. A 4 percent inflation-adjusted spending rate would have succeeded 100 percent of the time. This is where the 4 percent rule originated. Interestingly, holding too few stocks substantially reduces the minimum number of years that withdrawals will last. There is little sustainability difference between 50 percent stock and 75 percent stock in terms of minimum number of years, but the 75 percent stock portfolio can generally sustain withdrawals longer and results in a higher probability of a larger estate.

In subsequent studies, Bengen examined whether gradually decreasing stock exposure through retirement helped increase sustainability.[42] It didn't. Introducing small-cap stocks into the asset mix marginally improved the sustainability withdrawal rate to 4.3 percent. Their higher average return combined and modest diversification with large-capitalization stocks slightly outweighed their higher volatility. Introducing Treasury bills had no appreciable effect because returns are so low.

---

[40]Spitzer, Strieter, and Singh (2007) report similar results.
[41]Bengen (1994).
[42]Bengen (1996).

Other authors have used Monte Carlo analysis (discussed earlier) to estimate a sustainable spending rate. It uses the statistical properties of the returns to simulate what might happen to security returns in the future. It recognizes that we can never be 100 percent certain that any particular strategy will succeed. Exhibit 12.7, which we discussed earlier, is an approximation of that method that can help estimate a sustainable spending rate for a given level of confidence.

EXAMPLE 12.5   Estimating a Sustainable Withdrawal Rate with Monte Carlo Analysis

Sophie Collins is a recent widow, 55 years old, living in Stamford, Connecticut. Upon his passing, her husband provided estate and life insurance proceeds of $2 million to maintain her lifestyle. With no children, Sophie has no bequest motives but she has established a charitable remainder trust (CRT) upon which she will rely to maintain her lifestyle in real terms for the rest of her life, with the balance going to her favorite charity upon her death. Assume the trust's asset allocation conforms to the capital market expectations from Exhibit 12.7.

1. How much can Sophie withdraw from the CRT if she wants to be at least 98 percent certain that the portfolio will last for the remainder of her life?
2. How much can Sophie withdraw from the CRT if she is willing to be only 94 percent certain that the portfolio with last for the remainder of her life?

Solution to 1: The 55-year-old retirement age row in Exhibit 12.7 indicates that Sophie's median age at death is approximate 83 years, or 28 years away. However, she is just as likely to live longer than age 83 as she is to die prior to age 83. To be at least 98 percent certain that she does not run out of money, Sophie's maximum probability of exhausting her assets should not exceed 2 percent. A spending rate of $2 per $100 of assets has a ruin probability of 1.8 percent. So Sophie can withdraw approximately $0.02 \times \$2,000,000 = \$40,000$ with 98 percent certainty that the portfolio will last for the remainder of her life.

Solution to 2: If Sophie can tolerate a 6 percent failure rate, then she can withdraw almost 3 percent from the CRT annually on an inflation-adjusted basis, or $0.03 \times \$2,000,000 = \$60,000$, according to Exhibit 12.7. A spending rate of $3 per $100 of assets has a ruin probability of 6.3 percent, which is very close to the stated failure rate of 6 percent.

The 4 percent rule is useful in that it frames our expectations and correctly points out that a 10 percent withdrawal rate is not sustainable for any extended period of time. It should not, however, be taken as gospel. It depends heavily on an investor's time horizon, asset allocation, mortality expectations, and capacity for flexibility as we discuss later. For example, the sustainable withdrawal rate can be increased if part of the portfolio is annuitized.[43]

---

[43]Ameriks, Veres, and Warshawsky (2001).

EXAMPLE 12.6

In December 1999, Joe Tapscott was looking forward to working on his golf game and traveling as he entered retirement. Following advice from the experts, he figured he could safely withdraw $40,000 per year from his $1 million nest egg to supplement his Social Security income and allow for inflation-adjusted increases for the next 30 years or so—the 4 percent rule.

Joe's investment policy was more aggressive than his withdrawal policy. Being entirely invested in broadly diversified equities, he was more than a little disappointed that, after three years, his inflation-adjusted withdrawals and the market's ensuing poor performance had eroded his portfolio to less than $538,000. By that time, his withdrawals represented almost 8 percent of his dwindling portfolio value—a rate that is hardly sustainable.

Strong positive returns over the next five years improved things modestly. But by the end of 2007, Joe's portfolio had grown to less than $670,000, by which time withdrawals were still 7.3 percent of the portfolio.

The stock market declined another 24 percent in 2008 and 2009. Now Joe's retirement nest egg was less than $400,000, and his withdrawals were over 12 percent of his account value, with little prospect of recovery to a sustainable level. These initial returns did not work to Joe's advantage and the 4 percent rule did not serve him well.

Another admonition about all approaches that estimate success with some margin of error is to consider not just the probability of failure but the magnitude of failure. What would failure actually look like? To be sure, certainty is necessarily illusive. As Helen Keller once said, "Security is mostly a superstition: it doesn't exist in nature."

Although we cannot be sure of anything, we can contemplate what failure in a retirement withdrawal plan context looks like. It may not look too bad or it might look awful. Failure may just mean playing golf on your second favorite course, dining at three-star instead of five-star restaurants, or traveling to less exotic places. Or the consequences of retirement withdrawal failure may be severe. It may mean financial destitution, perhaps being subject to the inflexibility, bureaucracy, and vagaries of social safety nets or being dependent on family. The consequences of retirement withdrawal failure may be severe. Harold uses the concept of "ideal" and "acceptable" goals for his clients. He finds that in most cases failure to achieve the ideal is not catastrophic, but this needs to be determined on a case-by-case basis.

Viewed in this context, the risk appears to be one that is ideally managed from an insurance perspective, which we have already addressed. The point here is that one should weigh the probability of failure against the magnitude of failure so that you and your client can make a fully informed decision.

Mortality Comes to the Rescue?

Longevity risk actually improves the chances of success—if you consider success to be not outliving your assets by way of not living too long. Wealth managers who do not annuitize typically assume a conservatively long time horizon (e.g., maximum life span with 95 percent confidence) for planning purposes. Because a retiree may die before the end of a conservative time horizon of, say, 30 years, the chance of sustaining withdrawals for only their lifetime (rather than the full 30 years) increases.

For example, a 4.5 percent inflation-adjusted withdrawal rate has a 13.4 percent chance of depleting a portfolio before the end of a 30-year horizon, but the probability of ruin before death (using assumptions in standard mortality tables) is only 7.16 percent, according to Stout and Mitchell.[44]

Being Flexible Is Good for Fiscal Health

The biggest improvement in sustainable withdrawal rates comes from incorporating flexibility into a withdrawal program. These dynamic withdrawal strategies come in many forms, but a simple one is forgoing the annual inflation adjustment in years following negative returns. This ad hoc strategy increases the sustainable withdrawal rate from 4.0 to 4.3 percent to 5.8 to 6.3 percent, depending on the equity allocation.[45] This kind of flexibility avoids locking in losses in bear markets. A flexible spending strategy essentially mitigates the extent to which volatility and withdrawals interact to erode the corpus of a portfolio over time. Of course, this strategy can result in some dramatic consequences during extended periods of hyperinflation and poor investment performance, but it illustrates the cost of rigidity in a withdrawal plan.

Other more complicated, dynamic withdrawal strategies tie withdrawals to an account's value over time but constrain them from becoming too high in strong bull markets or too low in strong bear markets.[46] More simply, if client circumstances allow, one can begin a with-drawal program using a reduced withdrawal rate percentage to lessen the possibility that large withdrawals will exacerbate initial poor returns and create poor initial conditions for portfolio sustainability.[47]

A key phrase in the preceding paragraph is "if client circumstances allow." Many, if not most retirees, live on the margin, so that a small decrease in retirement withdrawals may have a relatively large impact on lifestyle. For example, a "modest" reduction of income from $100,000 to $90,000 may mean no going out to dinner for the year or canceling that long-planned vacation. The wealth manager should be careful not to overemphasize flexibility in situations that do not allow for it.

As an alternative, one can use asset allocation, hedging strategies (e.g., protective puts), or our cash flow reserve strategy to protect portfolio value during the critical red zone period surrounding the initiation of retirement withdrawals.

Climbing the Retirement Ladder

Incorporating flexibility into retirement withdrawals can be difficult for retirees who place a very high value on the predictability of their withdrawals. Regarding the issue of flexibility, it's important to keep in mind that the quality of a client's life is often determined at the margin. To tell clients that they may "only have to cut their expenses for the year by 10 or 15 percent" may not sound very intimidating, but consider that in terms of their daily living experience. After all of their core expenses have been covered (e.g., mortgage, taxes, insurance, basic living expenses) the supposedly modest reduction might mean no dinners out, no vacations, no

---

[44]R. Gene Stout and John B. Mitchell, "Dynamic Retirement Planning," *Financial Services Review*, Vol. 15, No. 2 (Summer 2006): 117–131.

[45]Guyton (2004) and Guyton and Klinger (2006).

[46]See, for example, Stout and Mitchell (2006), Spitzer (2008), Spitzer and Singh (2006), and Spitzer, Strieter, and Singh (2007).

[47]Frank and Blanchett (2010).

extras of any kind. That is far more than a modest impact on the quality of someone's daily life. The point is that most clients, if the consequences of adjustments are explained, will probably place a high value on predictability.

For those clients for whom withdrawal flexibility is not desirable and annuities are unpalatable, another viable alternative is to develop a laddered investment strategy based on the safety reserve (remember the five-year mantra!) philosophy.

Bucket Planning

The combination of the baby boomer generation approaching retirement age and the market volatility in recent years led to a search for new cash flow distribution strategies. One of the more popular has been the concept of bucket planning, also referred to as bucketing or time-segmented asset allocation. The strategy incorporates Richard Thaler's seminal work on mental accounting.[48] Mental accounting refers to an individual's tendency to mentally divide one's money into separate mental buckets: "my checking account, my risky stock account, my conservative retirement account, my son's college savings account."

The application of this concept to retirement cash flow has been developed in a number of forms. One strategy divides investments into mental buckets based on goals—"pay the rent" and "spoil the grandkids" accounts[49]—and another is based on the expected timing of the cash flow need (e.g., income segment 1: years 1 to 5; income segment 2: years 6 to 10, etc.), "each targeting financial objectives that apply at different times in the future."[50] The argument in favor of these bucketing strategies is that they take advantage of investors' behavioral mental accounting by making it easier to determine if funding of goals is on track, and they may be more efficient.[51] As Reinhard, Richard, and Ye argue, "the transparency afforded by this approach not only helps temper any emotionally driven decision making but, according to our analysis, also results in a higher success rate—in terms of not running out of income or principal through a target date—than a single-portfolio approach."

Unfortunately, to date there has been no substantive academic work evaluating the long-term efficacy of this approach; however, there are a number of factors a practitioner should consider before implementing such a strategy:

- Although at the initial implementation stage the total portfolio can be invested in a manner that meets a client's risk tolerance (e.g., in a time-segmented strategy, 40 percent fixed income allocated over buckets 1, 2, and 3, and 60 percent equities allocated to buckets 3, 4, and 5), at the end of time segment 1, as a significant portion of the fixed income allocation will have been liquidated, the total portfolio allocation would no longer be appropriately allocated for the client's risk tolerance. As a consequence, if a consistent risk level is to be maintained, the strategy requires continual rebalancing of assets with the attendant tax and transaction friction, a reality generally ignored in the evaluation of bucketing strategies.

---

[48]Richard Thaler, "Mental Accounting and Consumer Choice," *Marketing Science*, 1985.
[49]G. Loewenstein, "Tangible Mental Accounts: Bucketing Assets into Specific Subaccounts Can Increase Retirees' Ability to Meet Their Financial Needs," distillation of an interview with Shlomo Benertzi, 2010.
[50]Charles Reinhard, Nicolas Richard, and Zi Ye, "Putting Investors' Eggs in Separate Time Baskets," Morgan Stanley Smith Barney, 2010.
[51]Jason S. Scott, William F. Sharpe, and John G. Watson, "The 4 percent Rule—At What Price?" April 2008, http://ssrn.com/abstract=1115023.

- Alternatively, if the market exposure is not managed, then over time, as the client grows older, the allocation to equities may increase significantly. Although this increasing hidden risk may be acceptable to a rational investor, it may not be acceptable to the behavioral investor most advisors deal with.
- Multiple buckets may require multiple, redundant investment positions. For example, buckets 1, 2, and 3 might have positions in the same fixed income mutual fund, and buckets 3, 4, 5, and 6 might have investments in the same equity fund. If the investments are made in individual accounts, there will be additional transaction costs associated with the multiple purchases. If not, the managing and reporting of bucket allocations for investments held in a single account will be potentially complex and time consuming.
- Bucketing by goals ignores the issue of importance. For example, if a client has a wedding bucket (a moderate importance goal due in 2013) and a college funding bucket (a high importance goal due in 2016), there is the possibility that if the wedding is fully funded in 2013 there may be a shortfall for college in 2016. Or consider a goal for a special trip in 2013 and another for a major gift in 2016. If the 2013 bucket fails to grow at the rate anticipated, the trip may have to be scaled back or even eliminated. It will be of little value if, in 2016, the investor discovers that the gift bucket is significantly overfunded. The investor has no time machine and can't go back and take that 2013 trip.

As with most issues facing today's wealth manager, there are no absolute answers as to the right or wrong solution; however, a practitioner should carefully consider and evaluate the alternatives before deciding what strategy to implement. Harold suggests that the cash flow reserve strategy (actually a form of bucketing) may be an optimal alternative. Rather than bucketing by goals or multiple time horizons, the bucketing is simply divided into two components—short-term liquidity needs and long-term investment goals. In doing so, the advisor can manage the risk of short-term portfolio volatility while at the same time managing a total return investment portfolio in an efficient tax and transaction-cost manner that also takes into account the goal importance and priorities.

Importance Scale and Acceptable Level—Beyond Priority Order

The concept of priority order for goals is far superior to a forced chronological ordering, but it too has limitations. Prioritization ranks goals from 1 to n, where n is decreasing order of importance. Goals are then funded in that order, with goal 1 being fully funded before goals 2 through n get any money. This is better than the prior method of funding based on time sequence, but it is not an accurate representation of what people do in real life. Integrating the concepts of an importance scale and acceptable goals provides a much more realistic solution.

A simple example is with two goals, retirement living expense and a car. While the living expense is priority 1, the client also needs a car (even if it is used and older). Clients generally try to spread their money over a number of goals to gain maximum overall value. The replacement of priority order for goals with ideal and acceptable amounts more realistically reflects how clients make spending decisions. Importance is a rating scale, not a ranking order like priority. Each goal is rated individually, with 10 being highest and 1 being lowest on the scale. Multiple goals can have the same rating. The importance rating can then be used to optimize the use of available funds across all goals simultaneously.

In the prior example, the living expense goal (with an importance of 10) might be funded at an amount greater than acceptable (but less than ideal), whereas the car (importance of 6) received only the acceptable amount. The use of the importance ranking scale and the ideal and acceptable goal amounts allows the practitioner to create a recommendation that maximizes the value provided by whatever total amount of money the client will have available over the rest of his or her life.

Variable Annuities

Another method of preserving the portfolio from poor initial returns is to use variable annuities with embedded financial guarantees. Guaranteed minimum income benefit riders give the variable annuity holder the ability to annuitize a guaranteed amount of principal at a specified rate at some future date. If the underlying portfolio suffers from negative returns in early retirement years, the annuitant can still choose to receive a stream of fixed income.

This protection sounds great in theory, but we don't always like it in practice. This kind of variable annuity protection is like a put option on an equity portfolio and typically costs an extra 50 to 80 basis points of extra management fees each year. Unlike a standard put option, its cost is uncertain and spread out over a number of years, rather than set at a fixed price today—an arrangement that obscures the price.

Equity-linked annuities are similar in this regard. Most of the annuity premium is invested in a fixed annuity, and the remainder is invested in a series of equity index call options. Like a variable annuity with a guaranteed minimum income rider, they are designed to provide potential upside return in exchange for a slightly reduced fixed income. Because equity-linked annuity returns are generally based on returns that exclude dividends and have annual return caps, the returns may be far less than the equity market returns investors are led to expect. Reichenstein (2009) shows that many equity-linked annuities are doomed to fail.

Investors can construct similar results themselves by combining a diversified equity portfolio with an index long-term equity anticipation security (LEAPS) put option. With expirations up to three years, LEAPS put options can protect investors during the critical early years of retirement. This do-it-yourself strategy is often far less costly but still not cheap.

Knowing the costs of a retirement strategy is vital. The protections offered by a variable annuity can sometimes be overwhelmed by the cost of acquiring them.

Required Minimum Distributions

Required minimum distributions (RMDs) relate to traditional IRAs and 401(k) plans, but not the Roth variety. Uncle Sam would not want you to sock away money into a traditional IRA, get a tax break for it, and never take the money out and subject it to taxation. He therefore requires you to begin pulling it out no later than April 1 in the calendar year after you turn 70½, called the required beginning date.

The amount that must be withdrawn is equal to the account balance divided by the taxpayer's remaining life expectancy, which is determined by the Uniform Life Table published by the Treasury Department.[52] Subsequent annual RMDs are calculated in the same manner but must be taken by December 31 of the relevant tax year. The penalty for not doing so is equal to 50 percent of the amount that should have been taken. So these rules are important to know and abide by.

The rules are riddled with nuances and become complicated quickly. They are also different when they are applied to annuity contracts, and Caudill has an excellent discussion that provides more detail.[53] Because RMDs relate to traditional IRAs but not Roth IRAs, they can be an important factor in choosing between the two types of accounts.

---

[52]www.irs.gov/publications/p590/ar02.html.

[53]April K. Caudill, "Understanding Required Minimum Distributions," in *Retirement Income Redesigned: Master Plans for Distribution* (New York: Bloomberg Press, 2006).

Stretching IRA Distributions

Stretching IRA distributions is an estate planning technique. Designated beneficiaries who receive traditional IRA assets as an inheritance are allowed to take RMDs based on their own life expectancies, rather than the life expectancy of the original IRA owner. For younger beneficiaries, this can substantially reduce the amount of money that must be withdrawn, because their life expectancies are longer and allow the assets to accrue returns in the tax-sheltered manner for a much longer period of time.

Stretching distributions from 401(k) plans and 403(b) plans is generally not an option. Although plan sponsors are permitted to allow stretches from the plans of deceased employees, most sponsors require beneficiaries to cash out of the plan within five years of the participant's death. Because the stretch option is valuable to one's heirs, it may make sense to roll a 401(k) plan over into a traditional IRA.

As we discussed earlier, Roth IRAs have no RMDs. If, however, the original account holder passes away and designates someone other than his or her spouse as the beneficiary, that beneficiary becomes subject to RMDs. These withdrawals will almost always be tax-free. And if the beneficiary is young, withdrawals will be modest, at least in the early years, and allow the opportunity for the account to continue to grow tax-free.

Tax-Efficient Withdrawal Strategies

Determining how much one can withdraw each year during retirement is only part of the distribution strategy. Another decision relates to the order in which different types of accounts should be tapped. Because different types of accounts (e.g., taxable, traditional IRA, Roth IRA) have different tax treatments, the order in which these accounts are tapped can impact an investor's tax bill over time.

In general, it makes sense to deplete taxable accounts first to the extent that RMDs allow. The rule of thumb is to exhaust accounts that have the highest effective tax rates first. An effective tax rate should take into account all methods of taxation (e.g., ordinary income, dividends, realized capital gains, unrealized capital gains) and the timing of their payment.

There are some notable exceptions to the taxable-account-first rule. For example, many entrepreneurs or C-level executives have accumulated wealth with stock in the companies that they have founded or managed. These stock positions often have a very low tax basis. As such, liquidating a portion for retirement withdrawals triggers a significant tax liability. In this case, a taxable account composed of low-basis stock is more like a tax-sheltered account. Preserving the low-basis stock position could be particularly valuable for older investors who are likely soon to receive a step-up in basis at death, but one must always consider the dangers of not diversifying one's assets.

Investors who have depleted the bulk of their taxable savings or decided to preserve them (e.g., low-basis stock) must decide whether to withdraw from traditional IRAs before Roth IRAs, or the reverse. As it turns out, if taxable distributions will be subject to a single tax rate that doesn't change over time, taking withdrawals from one type of IRA account or the other doesn't really matter. These circumstances are rare, however.

If withdrawals are subject to a series of progressively higher tax brackets, then it becomes disadvantageous to take large taxable distributions that would push a taxpayer into a relatively high tax bracket. However, it is advantageous to take taxable distributions that fill up relatively low tax brackets. In this way, investors are able to get money out of traditional IRA accounts with a relatively light tax burden.

For example, consider an investor with $1 million in a traditional IRA and $666,667 in a Roth IRA. If the investor makes 5 percent inflation-adjusted withdrawals annually by depleting the traditional IRA first, then depleting the Roth IRA (naive strategy 1 in panel A of Exhibit 12.18), the investor will have $2,704,153 left over at the end of 25 years (assuming no volatility in the returns). If the accounts are tapped in the reverse sequence (Roth IRA first, then traditional IRA), then the investor will have $2,250,068 left over at the end of 25 years—a difference of almost $450,000. Tapping the traditional IRA first takes advantage of relatively low tax brackets.

We can improve the end result further by modifying our strategy. If we take taxable distributions from the traditional IRA up to the point where we exhaust the 15 percent tax bracket and take the remainder of our retirement withdrawals from the Roth IRA in the tax-free fashion, then the accounts will have $2,950,321 left over. That's $700,000 more than tapping the Roth IRA first!

You may be asking yourself: "What about RMDs? Don't we need to take a certain amount of money from the traditional IRA first, anyway?" You are absolutely correct. The amount of the RMD depends on the taxpayer's age, of course. Interestingly, however, RMDs are not likely to disrupt this strategy much, if at all. You may be surprised to learn that, according to the 2010 tax code, a married couple filing jointly and taking advantage of the standard exemptions and deductions can report taxable income up to $86,700 and still remain in the 15 percent tax bracket. That represents a lot of RMDs! In fact, assuming that amount represents a 5 percent withdrawal, that implies an account value of $1,734,000.

Of course, what is considered a low tax rate to one investor may not be a low tax rate to another. For example, if one repeats the preceding analysis assuming the investor has $2 million in a traditional IRA and $1.33 million in a Roth IRA, it would be optimal to take taxable distributions from the traditional IRA up to the 25 percent tax bracket, which corresponds to $156,000 according to the 2010 tax code for a married couple filing jointly and taking advantage of the standard exemptions and deductions. This strategy can more than double final accumulations after 25 years for aggressive withdrawal rates. For wealthier investors with $3 million in a traditional IRA and $2 million in a Roth IRA, it is optimal to fill up the 28 percent tax bracket taxable distributions.

A variation on this theme is to take taxable distributions in years you enjoy a relatively low tax rate, perhaps due to extraordinary deductions. For example, a year in which a retiree has many deductions, such as large medical expenses, may be a good time to load up on taxable distributions from a traditional IRA if the taxpayer is in an unusually low tax bracket, even if this means forgoing distributions from a taxable account. The goal is not to minimize your tax bill in any given year, but manage your after-tax proceeds over time.

Reverse Mortgages

Reverse mortgages can be an effective way for retirees to tap into the value of what may be their most valuable asset—their home. Like a traditional mortgage, a reverse mortgage is borrowing against residential real estate. The borrowing can take the form of a lump sum, a line of credit, or periodic monthly payments made to the property owner. The reverse mortgage gets its name because, under the last option, borrowers *receive* monthly payments that increase the outstanding mortgage balance, rather than *make* monthly payments that decrease the mortgage balance.

The accrued balance on a reverse mortgage does not need to be repaid until the last surviving homeowner either voluntarily and permanently moves out of the house or passes away, at which time the homeowner's estate can choose to repay the reverse mortgage or sell the property, using the proceeds to pay off the mortgage. Any excess passes on to the property

EXHIBIT 12.18 Residual Accumulations after 25 Years and Withdrawal Sustainability for Various Strategies and Withdrawal Rates

Strategy	Withdrawal Rate, w								
	4.0%	4.5%	5.0%	5.5%	6.0%	6.5%	7.0%	7.5%	8.0%
A. Residual accumulations and withdrawal sustainability									
Naïve 1: Trad., then Roth	4,612,749	3,648,393	2,704,153	1,772,786	869,832	[24]	[21]	[19]	[17]
Naïve 2: Roth, then trad.	3,735,164	3,000,054	2,250,068	1,491,069	722,091	[24]	[21]	[18]	[16]
Withdrawal from trad.									
Up to exemption	3,878,717	3,142,400	2,389,500	1,622,084	846,444	61,375	[21]	[19]	[17]
Up to 10% bracket	4,087,292	3,237,748	2,468,517	1,697,960	921,667	131,395	[22]	[19]	[17]
Up to 15% bracket	4,649,409	3,799,865	2,950,321	2,100,777	1,251,233	401,689	[23]	[20]	[18]
Up to 25% bracket	4,612,749	3,648,393	2,704,153	1,772,786	869,832	[24]	[21]	[19]	[17]
Up to 28% bracket	4,612,749	3,648,393	2,704,153	1,772,786	869,832	[24]	[21]	[19]	[17]
Up to 33% bracket	4,612,749	3,648,393	2,704,153	1,772,786	869,832	[24]	[21]	[19]	[17]
B. Incremental residual accumulations and withdrawal sustainability over Naïve 1									
Naïve 2: Roth, then trad.	−877,585	−648,339	−454,085	−281,717	−147,741	[0]	[0]	[1]	[1]
Withdrawal from trad.									
Up to exemption	−734,033	−505,993	−314,653	−150,702	−23,388	nmf	[0]	[0]	[0]
Up to 10% bracket	−525,457	−410,644	−235,635	−74,826	51,835	nmf	[1]	[0]	[0]
Up to 15% bracket	36,660	151,472	246,168	327,991	381,400	nmf	[2]	[1]	[1]
Up to 25% bracket	0	0	0	0	0	[0]	[0]	[0]	[0]
Up to 28% bracket	0	0	0	0	0	[0]	[0]	[0]	[0]
Up to 33% bracket	0	0	0	0	0	[0]	[0]	[0]	[0]

Notes: For an investor with $1 million in a traditional IRA and $666,667 in a Roth IRA. The amounts in brackets represent the number of years over which withdrawals are fully sustained.

nmf = not a meaningful figure.

Source: Horan (2006).

owner's estate. If the sale proceeds are insufficient to cover the outstanding mortgage balance, the reverse mortgage lender will absorb the loss (not the estate).[54]

These two features are perhaps the most important advantages of reverse mortgages because they provide both longevity protection and a valuable put option for heirs on the value of the home. If one of the two spouses who have taken out a reverse mortgage with monthly payments lives longer than expected and their home declines in value or does not appreciate as expected, neither the retirees nor their beneficiaries are devastated. The retirees continue to receive monthly income for the remainder of their lives, and their heirs are not obligated to repay the debt beyond the value of the home.

Like variable annuities, reverse mortgages have some conceptual appeal. That appeal comes at a cost, however. The direct costs of a reverse mortgage vary depending on the financial intermediary, but they can be sizable. For example, a Federal Housing Administration (FHA) home equity conversion mortgage (HECM) requires an up-front mortgage insurance premium of 2 percent of the loan value, an annual service fee of 0.5 percent of the loan amount, and typically an origination fee of no more than $2,000. There are also likely to be other fees typically associated with the traditional mortgage, such as closing costs, attorney and title fees, appraisal fees, and so on.

Reverse mortgages are certainly not for everyone, and to get one a borrower needs to meet certain eligibility requirements. Homeowners must own the property being mortgaged, be at least 62 years old, occupy the mortgaged property as their primary residence, and receive reverse mortgage counseling. Alexander and Anderson provide a more detailed discussion about the difference among various reverse mortgage products and the intermediaries that provide them, but we list some of the disadvantages here.[55]

One feature of all reverse mortgages is that the interest rate is variable. It may be based on the Treasury bill rate, London Interbank Offered Rate (LIBOR), or variable certificate of deposit (CD) rate, and may leave the borrower exposed to interest rate risk. On the one hand, this interest rate risk does not represent a natural hedge to the assets or liabilities of most retirees. Most retirees are already exposed to negative consequences of interest rate increases in their investment portfolios by being long stocks or fixed interest rate bonds. On the other hand, if the reverse mortgage borrowers are convinced that they will live in the home until they die, then interest rate increases will only decrease the size of their estate. Even so, the downside risk for the heirs is limited because they will not be responsible for repaying the loan if its balance exceeds the value of the property when the homeowner passes away.

This possibility of leaving one's home before death highlights another disadvantage of reverse mortgages. In general, they are inflexible financing tools. Only if retirees are nearly 100 percent convinced that they will be in their home until they die, and they have few other resources to fund their retirement, is the reverse mortgage a viable option.

Another disadvantage is that the interest on a reverse mortgage is not tax deductible in the year it is accrued like it is for a traditional mortgage. The tax deduction on accrued interest is deferred until the mortgage is repaid, oftentimes when the homeowner passes away. Deferring tax deductions is typically not advantageous. It is possible that a large deduction in the year of death may lower the estate's marginal tax rate, which can offset the cost of the

---

[54]If the reverse mortgage is insured as a home equity conversion mortgage (HECM), then the lender can request reimbursement from the FHA.

[55]Roxanne Alexander and Michael J. Anderson, "Reverse Mortgages and Distribution Planning," in *Retirement Income Redesigned: Master Plans for Distribution* (New York: Bloomberg Press, 2006).

deduction's deferral. But it is impossible to know the timing of one's passing, and how valuable a large tax deduction at the end of one's life might be.

In general, a reverse mortgage is more suitable for retirees with few assets from which to fund their retirement other than the equity in their home, or for whom passing assets on to their heirs is relatively unimportant. For retirees with sufficient nonresidential assets to fund their retirement and for whom making bequests to their heirs is important, the benefits of a reverse mortgage are less valuable.

Estate Planning

We have made some passing references to estate planning as we discussed issues such as IRA accounts, annuities, and reverse mortgages. It should be clear that the wealth manager cannot ignore these issues. Clients' wealth transfer and philanthropic goals are an integral part of their financial plans. That said, a detailed or complete discussion of estate planning is far beyond the scope of this book.

A wealth manager should have enough awareness of estate planning goals to properly incorporate them into an investment policy statement and investment strategy, and enough sense to know when to refer the client to an allied professional, such as an accountant or an estate attorney.

PARTING COMMENTS

Retirement planning neither begins nor ends with retirement. It requires careful planning and diligent saving during the accumulation phase, and a rigorous understanding of the unique risks retirees face in the distribution phase.

It should be clear by now that retirement planning is a comprehensive and complex part of wealth management. It often consumes the bulk of the wealth manager's time and energy. But developing a sensible accumulation and distribution strategy can be among the most valuable services a wealth manager provides to clients.

RESOURCES

Ameriks, John, Robert Veres, and Mark J. Warshawsky. 2001. "Making Retirement Income Last a Lifetime." *Journal of Financial Planning*, Vol. 14, No. 12 (December): 60–76.

Bengen, William P. 1994. "Determining Withdrawal Rates Using Historical Data." *Journal of Financial Planning*, Vol. 7, No. 1 (January): 14–24.

Bengen, William P. 1996. "Asset Allocation for a Lifetime." *Journal of Financial Planning*, Vol. 9, No. 4 (August): 58–67.

Bengen, William P. 1997. "Conserving Client Portfolios during Retirement Part III." *Journal of Financial Planning*, Vol. 10, No. 6 (December): 84–97.

Bernstein. 2008. *Multigenerational Wealth Management: Getting a Legacy Up*. Global Wealth Management Research Series. New York: AllianceBernstein L.P.

Bierwirth, Larry. 1994. "Investing for Retirement: Using the Past to Model the Future." *Journal of Financial Planning*, Vol. 7, No. 1 (January).

Bodie, Zvi, Laurence B. Siegel, and Rodney N. Sullivan. 2009. *The Future of Lifecycle Saving and Investing: The Retirement Phase*. Charlottesville, VA: Research Foundation of CFA Institute.

Elo, Irma, and Kirsten P. Smith. 2003. "Trends in Educational Differentials in Mortality in the United States." Paper presented at the annual meeting of the Population Association of America, Minneapolis (May).

Evensky, Harold, and Deena B. Katz. 2004. *Investment Think Tank: Theory, Strategy, and Practice for Advisers*. New York: Bloomberg Press.

Evensky, Harold, and Deena B. Katz, eds. 2006. *Retirement Income Redesigned: Master Plans for Distribution*. New York: Bloomberg Press.

Ezra, Don, Bob Collie, and Matthew X. Smith. 2009. *The Retirement Plan Solution: The Reinvention of Defined Contribution*. Wiley Finance. Hoboken, NJ: John Wiley & Sons.

Frank, Larry R., and David M. Blanchett. 2010. "The Dynamic Implications of Sequence Risk on a Distribution Portfolio." *Journal of Financial Planning*, Vol. 23, No. 6: 52–61.

Grangaard, Paul. 2002. *The Grangaard Strategy: Invest Right during Retirement*. New York: Perigee Trade.

Guyton, Jonathan T. 2004. "Decision Rules and Portfolio Management for Retirees: Is the 'Safe' Initial Withdrawal Rate Too Safe?" *Journal of Financial Planning*, Vol. 17, No. 10 (October): 54–62.

Guyton, Jonathan T., and William J. Klinger. 2006. "Decision Rules and Maximum Initial Withdrawal Rates." *Journal of Financial Planning*, Vol. 19, No. 3 (March): 48–58.

Horan, Stephen M. 2005. *Tax-Advantaged Savings Accounts and Tax-Efficient Wealth Accumulation*. Charlottesville, VA: Research Foundation of the CFA Institute.

Horan, Stephen M. 2006. "Withdrawal Location with Progressive Tax Rates." *Financial Analysts Journal*, Vol. 62, No. 6: 77–87.

Horan, Stephen M., and Thomas R. Robinson. 2009. "Estate Planning in a Global Context." *CFA Program Curriculum Level III*.

Lewellen, Wilbur G. 1977. "Some Observations on Risk-Adjusted Discount Rates." *Journal of Finance*, Vol. 31, No. 4 (September): 1331–1337.

Milevsky, Moshe A., and Chris Robinson. 2005. "A Sustainable Spending Rate with Simulation." *Financial Analysts Journal*, Vol. 61, No. 6 (November/December): 89–100.

Reichtenstein, William. 2009. "Financial Analysis of Equity-Indexed Annuities." *Financial Services Review*, Vol. 18, No. 4 (Winter): 291–311.

Scott, Jason. 2008. "The Deferred Annuity: Annuity for Everyone?" *Financial Analysts Journal*, Vol. 64, No. 1: 40–48.

Spitzer, John J. 2008. "Retirement Withdrawals: An Analysis of the Benefits of Periodic 'Midcourse' Adjustments." *Financial Services Review*, Vol. 17, No. 7 (Spring): 17–29.

Spitzer, John J., and Sandeep Singh. 2006. "Extending Retirement Payouts by Optimizing the Sequence of Withdrawals." *Journal of Financial Planning*, Vol. 19, No. 3 (April).

Spitzer, John J., Jeffrey C. Strieter, and Sandeep Singh. 2007. "Guidelines for Withdrawal Rates and Portfolio Safety during Retirement." *Journal of Financial Planning*, Vol. 20, No. 10 (October): 52–59.

Sharpe, William F., Peng Chen, Jerald E. Pinto, and Dennis W. McLeavey. 2007. "Asset Allocation." In *Managing Investment Portfolios: A Dynamic Process*, 3rd edition. John L. Maginn, Donald L. Tuttle, Jerald E. Pinto, and Dennis W. McLeavey, eds. CFA Institute Investment Series. Hoboken, NJ: John Wiley & Sons.

Stout, R. Gene, and John B. Mitchell. 2006. "Dynamic Retirement Withdrawal Planning," *Financial Services Review*, Vol. 15, No. 2 (Summer): 117–131.

Wilcox, Jarrod. 2008. "The Impact of Uncertain Commitments," *Journal of Wealth Management* (Winter).

Wilcox, Jarrod, and Frank J. Fabozzi. 2009. "A Discretionary Wealth Approach for Investment Policy." *Journal of Portfolio Management*, Vol. 40, No. 2: 45–59.

CHAPTER 13

INVESTMENT POLICY STATEMENT

Plan the plan, play the plan.

—Anonymous

In the framework of wealth management, an investment policy statement (IPS) is, in effect, a focused financial plan (i.e., an investment plan). It is a highly customized, client-centric strategic guide to the planning and implementation of any investment program. As a strategic document, the IPS should be relatively stable. Constant changes in investment policy erode the efficacy of a long-term investment plan and dilute the other benefits of an IPS. However, it should not reflect a "hold-and-forget" strategy. As a living document, it should be reviewed on a periodic basis (e.g., annually) and updated as markets and client circumstances change.

We use the term *policy* rather than *plan* to avoid misunderstanding by the client regarding the scope of our work. Still, wealth management is a financial planning process, and the steps leading to the development of the investment policy should follow that process.

Historically, the excellent guides regarding the development of an investment policy have focused on the institutional client (e.g., pension plans).[1] More recently, CFA Institute has developed IPS guides specifically for the individual investor.[2] This chapter draws from these resources and provides an example of an IPS designed for an individual (i.e., noninstitutional) client to discuss the rationale behind the wording and structure of the policy.

As Donald Trone mentions in his book, *The Management of Investment Decisions*, the IPS "is a virtually indispensable tool for investment management and communication that should be used by every investor."[3] CFA Institute describes it as the "cornerstone of the portfolio management process."[4] Among its many functions, an effective IPS:

- Provides a road map for making future investment decisions as the investment environment and client circumstances change.

---

[1]Trone (1996) and Guy (1994).
[2]Bronson, Scanlan, and Squires (2007) and Schacht, Allen, and Dannhauser (2010).
[3]Trone (1996).
[4]Maginn, Tuttle, McLeavey, and Pinto (2007).

- Helps avoid overreacting to both bull and bear markets because investors' emotional tolerance for risk increases in the former and decreases in the latter, especially during turbulent markets.
- Enhances client communication and provides a useful point of reference to remind both client and manager about first principles of the long-term investment philosophy.

The earlier chapters of this book discussed many of the activities and decisions that must occur before developing an IPS. To recap, the wealth manager must:

- Work with and educate the client in order to determine investment goals (including the hidden goals), their relative prioritization, and their time and dollar specificity.
- Evaluate existing investment assets and other assets on the life balance sheet.
- Determine the client's risk tolerance.
- Determine projected cash flow needs (or surplus).
- Determine the constraints (e.g., asset class limitations, nonrepositionable assets, taxes, legal issues).
- Develop an asset allocation.

INVESTMENT POLICY STATEMENT

The basic IPS can be organized into five main parts, around which this chapter is organized. They include:

1. Client Description and Goals

   Preface
   Overview and Client Goals
   Context
   Scope of the Client and Assets
   Scope of Advisement

2. Investment Objectives

   Return Requirements
   Risk Tolerance and Risk Capacity

3. Investment Constraints

   Liquidity Needs
   Time Horizon
   Tax Considerations
   Legal and Regulatory Considerations
   Unique Circumstances

4. Strategic Asset Allocation

   Investment Philosophy and Strategies
   Capital Market Assumptions
   Asset Allocation
   Investment Constraints
   Hiring, Firing, and Monitoring Managers
   Risk Management

5. Implementation, Monitoring, and Review

   Responsibilities and Governance
   Performance Measurement
   Performance Evaluation/Benchmarks
   Review Process
   Rebalancing

We address each in turn with commentary and the use of examples. Some of the samples come from Harold's firm; some are taken from *Elements of an Investment Policy Statement for Individual Investors* by Schacht, Allen, and Dannhauser[5]; others are contrived. Because the IPS is a highly customized document uniquely tailored to an individual client, templates that offer one-size-fits-all convenience necessarily fall short of an effective IPS. What follows, therefore, is not a template but a listing of common IPS elements using excerpts from different client policies as examples.

Client Description and Goals

The first section of an investment policy statement typically describes the client, the client's goals, and the scope of the engagement.

Preface

This is a first warning that a policy is a guide, not a guarantee. It also draws the client's attention to the assumptions that form the basis for recommendations.

EXAMPLE 13.1   Preface

Many of the illustrations in this plan involve the use of numbers because they are the most effective means of presenting a financial picture. These figures can lend an aura of false precision. Sets of numbers dealing with financial issues five years (and longer) down the road are not intended to be viewed as predictive but rather represent projections, based on a certain set of assumptions. While real-life events can rarely be predicted with accuracy (e.g., your decision to retire at age 50; if and when you will sell your boat and second condo; your part-time work and the anticipated inheritance; the return on your land development; or the return on your currency hedge program), these projections are useful in comparing the likely results of different approaches and plans of action. If, upon reviewing this plan, you have any questions regarding the data or assumptions, please bring them to our attention.

Overview and Client Goals

This section is customized to reflect and reference clients' needs. It is not intended to be a full description of their investment objectives that come later. Nonetheless, the description needs

---

[5]Schacht, Allen, and Dannhauser (2010).

to be accurate. For example, many of Harold's clients do not need current income. In that case the first sentence of Example 13.2 would exclude the reference to current income. He also begins the investment policy statement with a strong statement reflecting a commitment to diversification and a reminder that the client's goals direct the recommendation.

EXAMPLE 13.2   Sample IPS Excerpts for Overview and General Goals

- Building capital to generate current and future income is a primary objective of your investment policy. Our strategy for accomplishing this objective is based on the concept of diversification, which we call asset allocation. It is a long-term strategy, designed to suit your individual aspirations and circumstances, that provides a durable framework within which to make specific investment decisions.
- In designing your personal investment strategy, we began by reviewing your objectives and constraints. We then develop recommendations appropriate for you.
- Peter and Hilda Inger own and operate IngerMarine, a producer of luxury pleasure boats sold worldwide. The Ingers are eager to convert their equity stake in Inger-Marine to cash and have received bids indicating probable proceeds to Peter and Hilda of $52 million, net of taxes. They consider everyone in their family to be financially secure and wish to preserve that security.
- Roger and Crista Hemmingway are both young working professionals with no children or plans to have children. With relatively few financial assets and high-salaried positions, their primary objective is to balance current consumption with savings and prudent investing to fund an early and comfortable retirement consisting of part-time consulting, golfing, sailing, and international travel.
- Provide for a portfolio that will be diversified and managed such that you can take an extended sailing trip through the Pacific and Australia without having to be concerned about your investments.

Context

The context of an individual's or family's wealth is often the motivating force behind investment objectives and constraints. As such, they warrant referencing in the preamble of an IPS to provide context and reminder for both managers and investors.

EXAMPLE 13.3   Sample IPS Context

- The assets of the Leveaux Family Trusts trace back to the establishment of Leveaux Vintners in 1902 by Claude Leveaux. Over the course of the next 77 years, three generations of the Leveaux family worked to build the family business, LVX Industries, to include distilled spirits, gourmet snack foods, and the LVX chain of cafes in Europe and Canada. Each business line was grounded in the philosophy of delivering outstanding quality and value to consumers as well as investing in the communities in which Leveaux did business. In 1979, LVX Industries was purchased by the British conglomerate FoodCo for the equivalent of US$272 million. Michelle Leveaux established the Leveaux Foundation with $100 million of the sale proceeds, and much of the remainder constituted the Leveaux Family Trusts, which are the subject of this Investment Policy Statement.

Scope of the Client and Assets

Because clients come in all shapes and sizes, it is important to define who the client is. For example, suppose that Mr. Elkamedes comes to your office seeking your investment council. He is married with three children. Who is your client? It depends. Although rare, Mr. and Mrs. Elkamedes may have separate savings accounts, checking accounts, investor portfolios, and financial plans. She may have her own investment advisor. If that's the case, then your client is a single individual, Mr. Elkamedes.

More commonly, husband and wife engage in financial planning and investment management jointly, in which case your "client" is both of them. What is more typical in many high-net-worth and ultrahigh-net-worth situations is for the client to be defined as a multigenerational family. Even here, there is need for definition. Is your client Mr. and Mrs. Elkamedes and their children (i.e., first and second generation)? Or does the client include the third generation and beyond? The scale of the client tends to grow with the wealth of the first generation.

In addition to identifying the relevant clients, it is important to identify the relevant assets belonging to those clients that the IPS governs. Clients may hold assets with another advisor or broker over which the wealth manager has no control. Alternatively, the client may have a separate investment account for play money.[6] Even when assets are held outside the manager's control, it is important for effective communication, a functional client-manager relationship, and a truly comprehensive investment policy for the wealth manager to be aware of not only the existence of those outside assets but their composition, as well.

EXAMPLE 13.4 Sample IPS Excerpts for Scope of the Client and Assets

- This Investment Policy Statement governs the personal investment portfolios of Mr. Chen Guangping.
- This Investment Policy Statement governs all the investment portfolios of Mr. and Mrs. Chen Guangping and the trusts for their five children.
- The Inger family consists of Peter and Hilda Inger, son Hans, daughter Krista, and grandson Jürgen.
- Although this policy does not cover your retirement funds, we recommend the following. Your TIAA is invested in fixed income. We suggest that you move this to

---

[6]A separate account for a client to exercise unfettered discretion is oftentimes a useful tool for insulating a core investment portfolio from being sabotaged by an impetuous client's impulses.

the CREF, which is invested in equities. The time horizon for these funds is at least 20 years. Your current IRA investments are also fixed income. We suggest that you place these funds in a U.S. large-cap index fund (e.g., the Schwab 1000 or the Vanguard S&P 500). Again, the time horizon for these funds is at least 20 years.

Scope of Advisement

Although wealth management is holistic and comprehensive, that does not mean the wealth manager is necessarily accepting responsibility for updating the homeowner and life insurance coverage or developing and implementing the estate plan. Some may; others may not. That is why we mentioned in the opening of this chapter that it is important that the client not misunderstand the scope of our work.

EXAMPLE 13.5   Sample IPS Excerpts for Scope of Advisement

- Janice Jones, as financial advisor to Sam and Mary Smith, is responsible for coordinating updates to the investment policy, including soliciting input (with the clients' permission) from the designated tax and legal advisors to Sam and Mary Smith. Ms. Jones is also responsible for monitoring application of the Investment Policy Statement and shall promptly notify Sam and Mary Smith of the need for updates to the Policy and/or violations of the Policy in implementation. Sam and Mary Smith shall be responsible for approving the Investment Policy Statement and all subsequent revisions to it.
- Fuji Advisors acts as a fiduciary in its capacity as advisor to the Takesumi Family Accounts and acknowledges that all advice and decisions rendered must reflect, first and foremost, the best interests of its clients. Fuji Advisors also affirms its compliance as a firm with the CFA Institute Asset Manager Code of Professional Conduct.

This section may also include a capital needs analysis (CNA). It spells out the basic assumptions made in the analysis and a brief summary of the conclusions.

EXAMPLE 13.6   Capital Needs Analysis

- In conjunction with your investment policy, you have asked us to address the issues of capital needs planning to plan, with a high probability that each income source is utilized in proper balance to create an adequate stream of income, including adjustments for inflation, throughout the balance of your life. Your investment policy is driven by this analysis and we incorporate projections based on our investment recommendations. However, the total return assumptions may vary from the investment policy as noted in our assumptions for retirement.

Capital Needs Assumptions

Inflation Projection	4.0%
Social Security Annual Increase	3.0%
Taxes—Marginal	28.0%

Capital Accumulation
There are no projected savings.

Income Sources (In Addition to Capital)

Social Security while both boys are in school	$24,800
Social Security when William is 16, until he is 18	$ 8,200
Pension from Exxon (no COLA)	$40,056
Insurance Annuity (after tax)	$14,800
Social Security after the blackout period	$10,000

Income Needs
Your expenses are classified, as necessary, into two categories:

1. Inflatable Basic—Nondiscretionary living expense
2. Fixed Terminable—Home mortgage

Capital Needs Planning Conclusions
The capital needs projections we've prepared are, at best, a very rough projection of the future. Your life expectancy and uncertainty regarding future income, growth of investments, and expenses are major question marks in the analytical process.

Based on the assumptions noted, we believe you that you will fall short of your stated goals. However, you should keep in mind that these are long-term projections and incorporate many variables. We believe that the more short- and intermediate-term volatility you can tolerate, the more likely you are to improve your overall financial picture. We also note that returning to work and moving to a less expensive home will also add favorably to your financial future. We will discuss this with you, in detail, during our meeting.

Investment Objectives

The clients' investment objectives come from an analysis of their financial position and their life balance sheet. Investment objectives consist of both return requirements and risk tolerance. The two are inherently linked and cannot be discussed without reference to the other.

As the examples (from many different client policies) that follow illustrate, we attempt to describe our understanding of their goals with as much specificity as possible.

Return Requirements

Articulating a useful return requirement means the IPS must address a number of different issues. First, the IPS should articulate the terms in which returns are denominated—nominal or real, absolute or relative, pretax or posttax. We have argued that the appropriate measure for return is the portfolio's total real return. Whatever standard is decided on, it should be specified.

The return requirements section should also distinguish between a client's desired return and the return necessary to achieve a particular investment goal, such as accumulating a sufficient nest egg to fund retirement.

EXAMPLE 13.7   Sample IPS Excerpts for Return Requirements

- Prior to retirement, provide for supplemental income during your preretirement years in the amount of approximately $7,200 per year, in real after-tax dollars.
- You wish to retire in three years and maintain your standard of living during your retirement. You estimate this to be $62,000 (after tax and in today's dollars) and $16,400 annually for 13 years for your fixed mortgage payment. In addition, your families are long lived and you believe that it is appropriate to plan for an income need for approximately 30 years.
- Factor in part-time income of $50,000 per year until Harriet reaches 70.
- Preserve principal. Reasonable efforts should be made to preserve principal, but preservation of principal shall not be imposed on each individual investment.
- The investment program governed by the IPS is intended to supplement the earned income of Marcel Perrold in satisfying ongoing living expenses and to provide funds upon his retirement in 2016.
- The financial plan developed for Margarita Mendez in 2007 indicates a required real growth rate of 4 percent to satisfy her future obligations and allow her to retire in 2017 as planned.
- Based on the overall expected portfolio return of 7.5 percent, fees of 1.2 percent, inflation of 2.8 percent, and an effective tax rate of 32 percent of total appreciation, the Linzer Trust Portfolio may support an annual spending rate of 1.2 percent of the portfolio market value while retaining potential for capital preservation or nominal growth.

Risk Tolerance and Risk Capacity

An investor's return objective should be consistent with his or her risk objective. Like the return objective, the risk objective should specify the method by which risk is measured. The most appropriate method is often determined by the client's return objectives. For example, standard deviation may not be the best measure of risk for a client whose primary return objective is to preserve wealth—a measure of downside risk might be more appropriate even if expressed nonquantitatively. Similarly, tracking error risk, the standard deviation of the differences between a portfolio's return and the benchmark return, would be consistent with a relative return requirement but not with an absolute return requirement.

A client's risk tolerance and risk capacity must also be specified. In establishing these it is useful to state relevant facts that give rise to each, as we illustrate in the examples that follow. For example, the degree of flexibility clients have in their financial position can influence their ability to accept risk. A risk objective is more specific than a general statement, such as a person having a "lower than average risk tolerance." It has an operational relevance, such as "minimize the probability that the loss in any one year should not exceed x percent of the portfolio value" or "minimize the probability that the annual volatility of the portfolio should not exceed y percent."[7]

EXAMPLE 13.8   Sample IPS Excerpts for Risk Tolerance

- James and Jennifer Jensen understand that the very nature of risk is uncertainty about the future—specifically, uncertainty as to future investment returns. The Jensens seek to generate investment returns that are proportional to the risks assumed in the Family Trust portfolios. Tower Capital, as investment advisor, seeks to implement an investment strategy that balances the need to build the Family Trust assets as stated in the objectives identified in the 2009 Financial Plan with the risks associated with that strategy.
- In establishing your risk tolerance, we have considered your ability to withstand short- and intermediate-term volatility. Based on our discussions and your answers to our risk tolerance questionnaire, we understand that you can accept a moderate volatility portfolio. However, based on your current portfolio and our capital needs analysis, we believe that you can comfortably accomplish your goals with a low-volatility portfolio and our recommendations are governed by your retirement goals. Note, however, that due to the significant nonrepositionable Life Annuity, our recommendation for your repositionable assets (referred to as the "managed portfolio") is growth oriented.
- Your personal income prior to retirement cannot be projected with any degree of certainty. However, your expectations are that your new consulting venture will provide you with adequate income to cover your living expenses. In addition, between your personal cash reserves and your personal stock and bond holdings, you have adequate emergency reserves. Based on these assumptions, the policy for your 401(k) assets does not include any emergency reserve.
- In establishing your risk tolerance, we have considered your ability to withstand short- and intermediate-term volatility. The results of our analysis of your risk tolerance questionnaire and your current portfolio were somewhat contradictory. The answers to a number of our questions suggest that you have a very low tolerance for short-term volatility. Other answers, however, indicated a willingness to accept moderate volatility, and your current portfolio is allocated almost 75 percent in the equity market. Finally, our analysis indicates that in order to approach your retirement goals, you must invest for growth. We have balanced these issues in our recommendations.

---

[7]Maginn, Tuttle, McLeavey, and Pinto (2007, 13).

Here are some sample excerpts related to risk capacity.

EXAMPLE 13.9   Sample IPS Excerpts for Risk Capacity

- Your savings are substantial compared to your modest financial goals; consequently, you have the financial capacity for a portfolio allocation with a much higher stock allocation than is reflected in your risk tolerance.
- Your modest financial goals coupled with your significant savings and pension income suggest that your financial capacity to take market risks is significantly higher than your risk tolerance.
- Although you have indicated a significant risk tolerance, your spending needs relative to your investment portfolio suggest that your financial capacity to take market risk is significantly less than your risk tolerance; consequently, our recommendations are based on your more limited risk capacity.
- In establishing your risk tolerance, we have considered your financial (as opposed to emotional) ability to withstand short- and intermediate-term volatility. Based on our discussions and the composition of your current portfolio, we believe that your portfolio can withstand, in the intermediate term, a moderate-volatility portfolio without risking your long-term financial success. Your strategic asset allocation is based on this long-term perspective. Short-term liquidity requirements are anticipated to be nonexistent, or at least should be covered by your earnings prior to retirement.

Finally, it is helpful to include text to educate clients regarding risk. It serves to remind them that markets are volatile and uncertain. It also reminds them that they have living-standard goals that may not be achievable by short-term safe investing (e.g., CDs). The concluding paragraph, based on a question in Harold's risk tolerance questionnaire, is a reminder that they are loss averse, not risk averse. They do not wish to take risks to get rich, but they are prepared to take a risk (i.e., volatility) in order to avoid the loss of their standard of living. The following are examples.

EXAMPLE 13.10   Sample IPS Excerpts for Reminders of Risk Aversion and Loss Aversion

- Building capital to generate future income is a primary objective of your investment policy. Our strategy for accomplishing this objective is based on the concept of diversification, which we call asset allocation. It is a long-term strategy, designed to suit your individual aspirations and circumstances and to provide a durable framework within which to make specific investment decisions. I know that you said you didn't want to hear "You have to be patient; you're in it for the long haul," but unfortunately it's true. Building your capital in order to protect your purchasing

> power from the erosion of inflation requires investments in the equity markets. Equity markets rise and fall with the business cycle. In simple terms, that means you need to have substantial investments in the stock market, and those investments *will* lose money when the whole market goes down and it *will*! The good news is that your current allocation to stock is very likely to be more than adequate!

Investment Constraints

Satisfying an investor's return objectives and risk objectives must be done within the context of internal and external constraints, including liquidity needs, time horizon, tax considerations, legal and regulatory issues, and unique circumstances. Oftentimes, these constraints help determine, in part, the risk and return objectives.

Liquidity Needs

Liquidity needs can be either anticipated or unanticipated. A client may anticipate needing $50,000 per year over a four-year period to pay for college tuition, the amount and timing of which are fairly predictable. Moving down the continuum, a client may anticipate needing $40,000 to pay for a daughter's wedding, although we may not know when or even if this will actually be necessary. In the extreme, a client's lifestyle or business ventures may lend themselves toward a series of unanticipated liquidity needs that are unpredictable in both timing and amount. Such unpredictability calls for a larger liquidity reserve, all else being equal.

Alternatively, the retiree whose primary objective is to play golf may have few if any liquidity needs other than the stable retirement income the portfolio is intended to generate. Exhibit 13.1 presents some examples of liquidity needs with predictability characteristics that vary according to both size and timing.

EXHIBIT 13.1   Example of Liquidity Needs

		Timing	
		Predictable	Unpredictable
Size	Predictable	College tuition	Daughter's wedding
	Unpredictable	Overseas travel	Business opportunities

Liquidity events need not be negative. A young couple, for example, may receive an inheritance from a family member—something that is likely unpredictable with respect to both size and timing. It is possible, of course, that the size of an inheritance is predictable because the terms of a will or trust are known. The important thing is to incorporate what is known and what is not known into the IPS.

Ongoing expenses, such as those required for daily living, are sometimes listed as a return objective. Other times they are listed as liquidity need. The categorization is less important than its proper articulation and incorporation into investment policy.

Clients' liquidity needs should not be confused with the liquidity characteristics of their investments or portfolios, although the latter should be consistent with the former.

EXAMPLE 13.11 Sample IPS Excerpts for Liquidity Needs

- Provide for a wedding in two years. You estimate this to require approximately $30,000. You have reserved funds for this purpose.
- Provide for the purchase of a second home in Maine in approximately two-plus years. You estimate this goal to require $200,000 (in today's dollars).
- Provide for at least half of the cost of a four-year college education at a major private university for your two grandchildren, ages 4 and 7. We estimate this to require approximately $20,000 per year, per child, in today's dollars.
- Provide for gifting of approximately $30,000 per year for the balance of your life.
- For the next three years, plan for the investing of future savings, particularly your $52,000 annual pension contributions.
- As we have discussed, the recommended cash flow reserves are far in excess of any recommendation we might make solely for emergency reserves; however, we believe that maintaining a liquid cash reserve for your supplementary cash flow needs over the next few years is an effective way to manage your short-term needs.
- All dividend and interest income will be transferred to the James Jensen checking account at the end of each month. In addition, up to 15 percent of the market value of the portfolio should be invested in such a way that it can be liquidated upon five days' notice without suffering significant capital depreciation.

Time Horizon

The time horizon is usually a direct function of the investment objectives and liquidity needs. Significant short-term liquidity needs lead to a shorter time horizon. It is rarely the case that an investor has a single time horizon. Rather, multiple investment goals lead to a series of intermittent time horizons, each with its own investment implications. Time horizon is often informed, but not determined, by an investor's stage of life. In this regard, an understanding and description of the investor earlier in the IPS helps to articulate an appropriate time horizon.

In general, the longer an investor's time horizon, the greater the risk capacity. This relationship is not because risky investments become any less risky over long time periods. Rather, in most situations long time horizons give investors the ability to recover investment losses from other sources, such as delaying retirement (although that is not always the case).

This section of the IPS is also an opportunity to formally reiterate the five-year mantra. The time horizon in the plan is always at least five years and usually 10 years or more.

EXAMPLE 13.12 Sample IPS Excerpts for Time Horizon

- The investment guidelines are based on an investment horizon of greater than five years, so that interim fluctuations should be viewed with appropriate perspective. Similarly, your strategic asset allocation is based on this long-term perspective.

- John and Kathy Smith are both 45 years old and intend to retire at the age of 60. They anticipate having long retirements funded by their portfolio, because their families have a history of significant longevity.
- Ron and Cynthia Donaldson have two boys ages 6 and 8. They intend to provide them with a private college education when each reaches the age of 18.

Tax Considerations

The taxes of greatest consequence to the investor in the United States include the income tax (which applies to interest income and income from some alternative investments), capital gains tax (which applies to price appreciation on securities held for 12 months or more), and wealth transfer tax (which applies to both lifetime gifts and bequests at death).

It is important to articulate the salient features of a client's tax position, because they affect investment strategy, security selection, asset location, rebalancing strategies, and estate planning.

EXAMPLE 13.13   Sample IPS Excerpts for Tax Considerations

- Sam Walker is in the prime of his career and nearing his peak earnings capacity. As such, it is expected that he and his wife Dorothy will be in the highest marginal tax bracket of 35 percent during the remainder of their accumulation phase. Taxable income is expected to be more modest after retirement, when the Walkers are expected to be in the 28 percent tax bracket.
- Mr. and Mrs. Lewiston have high annual income, live in a state with high income tax, and have several dependents for income tax purposes. Consequently, we expect their annual income tax obligations to be covered under the Alternative Minimum Tax (AMT) for the foreseeable future. Their ostensible marginal tax rate is expected to be 26 percent or 28 percent, but deduction phaseouts are expected to increase their effective marginal tax rate to 32 percent. For this reason, the investment recommendations do not include allocation to AMT municipal bonds.
- In general, the investment policy will be for the Wen portfolios to invest for appreciation in the taxable individual accounts and invest for dividend and interest income in the individual retirement accounts. In addition, the investment advisor shall consider tax loss harvesting of existing high-basis holdings as transactions in similar industries or sectors are considered, secondary to the primary investment objective of the purchase/sale decision.
- The income from your pension and annuity and the taxes generated by your significant investment portfolio are likely to keep you in the 28 percent marginal bracket. Our investment recommendations reflect this. If, after reviewing your taxes with your accountant, we find that your marginal bracket drops to 15 percent, we will work with you to adjust the investment portfolio accordingly.
- As we have discussed, we recommend the sale of the Exxon stock in spite of the significant capital gains that will be due upon sale. As we noted, the only ways to

ultimately avoid the taxes are to die holding the stock, to wait until the market price drops to the basis price, or to gift the stock to charity. The first two choices are clearly unacceptable, and, with the exception of minor gifting to Big Brothers/Big Sisters, charitable strategies are not a viable alternative. By delaying the sale, taxes are not avoided but merely deferred except in the case of a step-up in basis at death. The savings are the present value of the possible earnings on the deferred taxes. This is not an adequate reward for accepting the unsystematic risk associated with holding one unmanaged stock position.

- The Greenwich Family Trust is a revocable, discretionary grantor trust. Consequently, investment returns are treated as income for Mr. and Mrs. Greenwich and subject to their marginal tax rates.
- We recognize the value of designing and implementing wealth transfer strategies prior to death. For example, initiating an annual gifting strategy for excess capital well before the end of one's life expectancy allows Mr. and Mrs. Wellington to take advantage of annual gift tax exclusions and reduces the taxable value of their estate by the amount of the appreciation that would have taken place between the time of the gift and the time of the eventual bequest were the gift not made.

Legal and Regulatory Considerations

One of the more ubiquitous and regulatory constraints in investment management is the Prudent Investor Rule. This rule certainly applies to the management of trust assets or to those acting as a trustee for an estate. Although it has been updated to reflect modern portfolio theory and recognizes that diversification is a concept that applies to the whole portfolio and cannot be evaluated on a security-by-security basis, some trusts and other governing documents contain language that specifically distinguishes between income and capital gains and does not recognize the concept of total return. It is, therefore, important to document these constraints on investment behavior.

EXAMPLE 13.14   Sample IPS Excerpts for Legal and Regulatory Constraints

- Management of the Aquilla Family Foundation account is subject to the provisions of the Uniform Prudent Investor Act.
- Although we recognize the superficial distinction between income and capital gains in pretax investment management, the Caesar Family Trust document specifically calls for investment income to be distributed for the benefit of the Caesar children and capital gains for the benefit of the Caesar Charitable Foundation. As a result, assets within the Caesar Family Trust will be managed with that distinction in mind.
- Clyde Smith has 100,000 shares of restricted company stock that cannot be sold until July 31, 2013.

Unique Circumstances

This section is where customization can become most apparent. It is where clients may express a preference for investment strategies that adhere to certain environmental, social, or governance agendas. Alternatively, clients may express these preferences in the investment constraints section that follows. This section may also list assets that are legally restricted from being sold, such as a concentrated position in a low-basis stock. Alternatively, it may stipulate any privacy concerns, health concerns, or contingency plans.

EXAMPLE 13.15   Sample IPS Excerpts for Unique Circumstances

- Mr. Parimore is chronically ill and likely to pass away prematurely in the next five years. His health condition increases the importance of deferring capital gains until securities can receive a step-up in basis.
- As we have discussed, your emergency reserves are far in excess of any recommendation we might make for this purpose; however, we understand your desire to maintain a substantial cash reserve for your personal comfort, and the investment recommendations reflect this.
- Mr. and Mrs. Blakeman share a passion for wine. They have an inventory of over 1,000 bottles of high-quality wine worth over $100,000 cellared at their residence. Their intention is to continue consuming and adding to the inventory, likely making it a significant part of their estate. As a passion investment, it may or may not grow in value but may contribute to their ultimate estate value.

Strategic Asset Allocation

The strategic asset allocation section is the heart of the IPS. It is the place where the information in the previous sections culminates in the form of recommendations.

Investment Philosophy and Strategies

This section lays out the philosophical basis for investment recommendations. A wealth manager who is committed to the concept of market efficiency would state so and likely gravitate toward passive investments as a result. A manager seeing alpha opportunities would state this as a rationale for a more active portfolio management approach.

EXAMPLE 13.16   Sample IPS Excerpts for Investment Philosophy

- James and Jennifer Jensen have as a philosophical basis for investment the conviction that many segments of domestic equity markets are efficient, and thus active management of such assets is unlikely to add value net of investment costs beyond the short term. James and Jennifer Jensen believe that some equity market segments (including global equity markets of stocks with market capitalizations of less than US $250 million) are relatively inefficient and that active management strategies may be applied profitably in these segments. Furthermore, James and Jennifer Jensen believe in a long-term orientation for their investment program and do not intend to seek to exploit investment opportunities that may exist in the very short term, because they believe they cannot profitably do so consistently.

- Although we believe markets are generally efficient, we also believe that tactical asset allocation decisions based on relative market movements of asset classes provide opportunities to exploit temporary inefficiencies within the context of the strategic asset allocation parameters.

Capital Market Assumptions

Although Harold quantifies the market expectations in terms of real rate of return (ROR), he continually reminds clients not to expect these returns to be achieved in a smooth pattern. He continually invites them to consider the underlying assumptions regarding financial markets. During the delivery of the policy to the client, a process we refer to as plan presentation, Harold discusses the assumptions and relates them to both long-term and recent-term historical real returns. He warns clients that if they do not find the underlying assumptions credible, they should not accept the policy recommendations. If a client has radically different market expectations, Harold will revise the policy to reflect the client's assumptions. However, the revised policy will include a caveat noting that the conclusions are based on the client's assumptions. Also, Harold will not assume the responsibility of implementing a modified policy, as he does not feel competent to manage what he believes to be unrealistic expectations.

EXAMPLE 13.17 Sample IPS Excerpt for Capital Market Assumptions

- Our recommended portfolio allocation is for a moderate-growth portfolio of 45 percent fixed income securities and 55 percent equities. A reasonable expectation for the long-term rate of return of the recommended portfolio is 4.5 percent greater than the rate of inflation as measured by the consumer price index (CPI). This expectation is based on the forward-looking real return assumptions of the firm as reflected in the capital needs analysis. You realize that market performance varies and that a 4.5 percent rate of return may not be meaningful during some periods. The financial assumptions that provided the basis for our analysis may be found in the Appendix.

Asset Allocation

This section sets forth the bias of Harold's firm. As a standard policy, he considers only six major asset classes. One element of his investment selection criteria is measured by how well an investment helps his clients sleep during bad markets. For this reason, we do not consider short sales or margin trades. Metals and natural resources were once generally eliminated from consideration due to the inability to find appropriate investment vehicles. Now, with the proliferation of commodity exchange-traded funds (ETFs), this is no longer the case. So although they now pass the availability criterion, they may still fail the "sleep" criterion.

EXAMPLE 13.18   Sample IPS Excerpts for Asset Allocation

- We believe that your portfolio's risk and liquidity are, in large part, a function of asset class mix. We have reviewed the long-term performance characteristics of various asset classes, focusing on balancing the risks and rewards of market behavior. The asset classes selected reflect your risk tolerance and the unique circumstances of your current investments. Six major asset classes were considered:

  1. Cash equivalents
  2. Domestic equities
  3. Domestic bonds
  4. International equities
  5. International bonds
  6. Real estate

  The following securities and transactions were not considered: metals, commodity contracts, short sales, and margin trades.

- At least annually, Tower Capital shall review the asset allocation of the Family Investment Accounts and, if appropriate, suggest revisions for final approval by James and Jennifer Jensen. The asset allocation plan is incorporated as Appendix A to this Investment Policy Statement. It shall consider the proportions of investments in cash equivalents, municipal securities, U.S. fixed income obligations, U.S. large-capitalization equities, U.S. small-capitalization equities, and American depositary receipts (ADRs). Tower Capital shall consider expected returns and correlations of returns for a broad representation of asset classes in the U.S. capital markets and consider anticipated changes in the rate of inflation and changes in marginal tax rates.

The asset allocation table is a detailed numerical description of the client's existing portfolio and our recommended reallocation. Harold refers to his recommendations as "generic but specific." They are generic in that he does not recommend the purchase of named investments (e.g., IBM or American Mutual Fund). They are specific in that he makes allocations to very narrow investment classes and styles.

Exhibit 13.2 is a simplified example. Column 1 describes the broad asset classes, while column 3 further divides these classes into subclasses and styles. Column 4 identifies the client's current investments in terms of these subclasses and styles, column 2 is used if there are multiple accounts (e.g., IRAs, individual and joint accounts, etc.). The entire portfolio is treated as a single unit. Column 5 quantifies the current investment in terms of both dollar and asset class percentages. Column 6 is the quantification of the policy recommendation. Because a client rarely comes with all cash, the recommended reallocation may be constrained by existing investments. Column 7 is the recommendation for reallocation reflecting these constraints.

EXHIBIT 13.2   Investment Policy Asset Allocation Table

Policy	Owner	Style	Description	Current		Policy		Proposed	
MMA	**Joint**		MMA	$ 30,000	3.0%	$ 30,000	3.0%	$ 30,000	3.0%
	MRIRA		MMA	$ 40,000	4.0%			$ 0	
U.S. fixed income	**Joint**	SH Corp/Govt	T-Bills and Notes	$ 60,000	6.0%	$ 60,000	6.0%	$ 60,000	6.0%
	MRIRA		CD (6 month maturity)	$ 30,000	3.0%	$ 30,000	3.0%	$ 30,000	3.0%
	MSIRA	S/I Corp/Govt	"ABC" Short term gov't fund	$ 170,000	17.0%	$ 70,000	7.0%	$ 70,000	7.0%
		SH Muni				$ 30,000	3.0%	$ 0	
	Joint	S/I Muni	"DEF" Short/Inter muni fund	$ 110,000	11.0%	$ 110,000	11.0%	$ 110,000	11.0%
	Joint	Inter. Muni	"GHI" Intermediate muni fund	$ 150,000	15.0%	$ 100,000	10.0%	$ 100,000	10.0%
International bond	**MSIRA**	International	New international bonds			$ 50,000	5.0%	$ 50,000	5.0%
			Fixed Income	**$ 590,000**	**59.0%**	**$ 450,000**	**45.0%**	**$ 450,000**	**45.0%**
U.S. large cap	**Joint**	Core	New index fund			$ 50,000	5.0%	$ 50,000	5.0%
	Joint	Tactical	New tactical			$ 40,000	4.0%	$ 40,000	4.0%
	MS	Value	New L.C. value			$ 90,000	9.0%	$ 90,000	9.0%
	Joint	Growth	"JKL" L.C. growth fund	$ 130,000	13.0%	$ 60,000	6.0%	$ 60,000	6.0%
	MS		IBM (recently inherited)	$ 90,000	9.0%			$ 0	
	Joint		"MNO" L.C. growth fund	$ 120,000	12.0%			$ 0	

Asset class	Account	Style	Fund	$	%	$	%	$	%
U.S. small cap	Joint	Value	New S.C. value	$ 0		$ 70,000	7.0%	$ 70,000	7.0%
	Joint	Growth	"PQR" S.C. growth fund	30,000	3.0%	40,000	4.0%	40,000	4.0%
International	Joint	Developed	New international			$ 110,000	11.0%	$ 110,000	11.0%
	Joint		"STU" international fund	$ 40,000	4.0%			$ 0	0
	MRIRA	Emerging	New emerging market			40,000	4.0%	$ 40,000	4.0%
Real estate	MSIRA		New REITs			$ 50,000	5.0%	$ 50,000	5.0%
			Equity	**$ 410,000**	**41.0%**	**$ 550,000**	**55.0%**	**$ 550,000**	**55.0%**
			Total	**$1,000,000**	**100.0%**	**$1,000,000**	**100%**	**$1,000,000**	**100%**

Some observations pertaining to Exhibit 13.2:

- *Short corporate/government.* Although the policy calls for a 6 percent allocation, the recommendation is to maintain the client's current 9 percent. The transaction cost of selling the short-term Treasuries and moving to short-term municipals does not justify making the change. The 3 percent excess allocation will be moved to the short-term municipal allocation as the T-bills and CDs mature.
- *Short/intermediate corporate/government.* Having analyzed the ABC fund, we concluded that it was well managed and had an appropriately low expense ratio. The recommendation is to sell $100,000 of the fund to bring the investment in line with the policy.
- *Short municipals.* The recommendation is to gradually fund this allocation with the proceeds of maturing Treasuries and CDs.
- *Short/intermediate and intermediate municipals.* We determined that both funds were acceptable. The $50,000 recommended sale of GHI is simply to bring the allocation down to meet the policy.
- *International bonds.* Using the proceeds from GHI, purchase $50,000 of foreign bonds (or funds).
- *Index, tactical large-capitalization value, small-cap value, emerging markets, and REITs.* Invest in diversified portfolios of stocks or appropriate mutual funds or ETFs to match the policy allocations.
- *Growth.* JKL is well managed and style consistent. The sale of a portion is simply to bring the fund allocation into alignment with the policy. The liquidation of IBM is recommended due to lack of diversification. The liquidation of MNO fund is recommended due to excessive expenses, style drift, and new management.
- *International developed.* STU fund is inconsistently managed and, as a consequence, exhibits significant style drift. It should be sold and replaced with new stocks or funds.
- *Ownership.* To the extent possible, we use sheltered accounts to improve after-tax returns. In this case the short-term fixed income and municipal bond investments are concentrated in the joint account for liquidity and tax reasons, respectively. Due to the relative tax efficiency, the market index and tactical equity funds have also been placed in the joint account.

Unfortunately, many clients find this level of detail overwhelming. In an effort to simplify the recommendations and convey a feeling for the broad allocation changes, we include the two pie charts in Exhibit 13.3 and Exhibit 13.4.

EXHIBIT 13.3   Current Portfolio

EXHIBIT 13.4   Proposed Portfolio

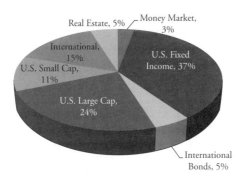

Harold also presents the pie chart information in a simplified tabular form (Exhibit 13.5). It is just an alternate way of communicating the same information. He has learned by experience to err on the side of redundancy when presenting information to clients. Throughout his continuing client relationship, he presents data and concepts in repetitive but differing formats.

EXHIBIT 13.5   Investment Policy in Tabular Form

Establishing the Fixed Income Category—Proposed Allocation

Invest in the following fixed income investments:

Money market funds	$ 30,000
Short-term government/corporate bonds	60,000
Short-/intermediate-term government/corporate bonds	70,000
Short-term municipal bonds	30,000
Short-/intermediate-term municipal bonds	110,000
Intermediate-term municipal bonds	100,000
International bonds	50,000

Establishing the Equity Category—Proposed Allocation

Invest in the following equity investments:

Large-capitalization U.S. core	$ 50,000
Large-cap U.S. tactical	40,000
Large-cap U.S. value	90,000
Large-cap U.S. growth	60,000
Small-cap U.S. value	70,000
Small-cap U.S. growth	40,000
International developed equities	110,000
International emerging equities	40,000
Real estate index	50,000

Investment Constraints

Investment constraints are sometimes derived from a client's unique circumstances. For example, a client may have accrued a large concentrated position in a low-basis stock over time. If it should not be sold, it should be listed in this section. Islamic clients may choose to invest in only sharia-compliant securities. There is a nearly infinite number of possible constraints. Oftentimes they are listed in the unique circumstances section of the IPS.

EXAMPLE 13.19   Sample IPS Excerpts for Investment Constraints

- Consistent with her personal beliefs, Jennifer Jensen requires that no investments be made for her account in companies that derive revenue from products or services that are contrary to the teachings of the Catholic Church. The advisor will work with the client to monitor portfolio positions in an effort to maintain a portfolio consistent with the client's personal beliefs.
- Shares of Exxon held in Mr. Houlihan's taxable account have been acquired over an extended period of time and have an extraordinarily low cost basis. The client understands the unsystematic risk; however, he has requested that the position not be sold, in the expectation that it will receive a step-up in basis upon Mr. Houlihan's death.
- Except for the margin account established at GGG Securities, no charitable remainder trust securities shall be lent or otherwise hypothecated or pledged as collateral.

Hiring, Firing, and Monitoring Managers

Some wealth managers engage in security selection, whereas others do not. If the wealth manager is selecting investment managers rather than securities, the IPS should state in broad terms the selection criteria that will be used and the process by which managers will be selected. This is an example of the specific guidelines we recommend for each broad asset class.

EXAMPLE 13.20   Sample IPS Excerpts for External Managers

Domestic Equities
- Core equity holdings in any one company should not usually exceed more than 5 percent of the market value of the manager's portfolio. The industry sector weightings should not generally exceed 3 times that of the S&P 500.
- Equity managers shall have the discretion to invest a portion of the assets in cash reserves when they deem appropriate. However, the managers should, in accordance with Global Investment Performance Standards, be evaluated against their peers on the performance of the total funds under their direct management.
- Equity mutual funds, if well diversified, should generally have moderate betas and a higher R-squared relative to their benchmark for passive styles, and long-term

positive alphas for active styles. Less well diversified funds should have favorable Sharpe ratios compared to comparable style managers. Funds should have no loads and expense ratios should be less than their peer average. The managers should have at least a five-year operating history and a consistent management record.

- Marcel Perrold delegates exclusive authority to his financial advisor, Francois Finault, to retain and dismiss individuals and/or firms to manage Mr. Perrold's investment assets. Francois Finault shall, prior to hiring any external investment manager, disclose in writing to Mr. Perrold any compensation or other consideration received or due to be received from the external investment manager.

Risk Management

Risk management may or may not be included in the wealth manager's scope of advisement. A risk management section of the IPS obviously takes on greater importance if it is within the manager's scope of advisement. Even if it is not part of the scope of advisement, however, risk concerns and other financial planning observations will likely arise in the advisory process, and these issues deserve to be documented in the IPS. Example 13.21 has some samples.

EXAMPLE 13.21   Sample IPS Excerpts for Risk Management

- We suggest that you review your disability coverage, as well as property/casualty (renter's) insurance. You do not have an umbrella liability policy. We suggest that you discuss these issues with Mr. Brown, your insurance agent.
- Given the substantial size of your estate, have your property and casualty insurance professionally reviewed, especially your liability coverage on your real estate, auto, and boat, as well as your personal umbrella coverage.
- We also believe that you should consider the purchase of individual long-term care policies that meet the guidelines outlined in the attached.

Implementation, Monitoring, and Review

This section of the IPS is the most recursive in that it relates to many of the sections that precede it. In fact, many of the individual components relate to each other, creating potential overlap between one area and the next. For example, the IPS should establish a review process that will include the frequency with which the portfolio and client circumstances will be reviewed. Rebalancing, however, also requires a certain portfolio review frequency, which overlaps with the review process. Nonetheless, we review the individual components here.

Responsibilities and Governance

The IPS should establish accountability for determining and implementing the investment policy and monitoring the results. It will lay out the responsibilities of the advisor, the client, and related parties who are expected to provide information or counsel into the planning and/ or investment process.

EXAMPLE 13.22   Sample IPS Excerpts for Responsibilities and Governance

- As trustee for the charitable remainder trust, Nigel Brown is responsible for approval of the investment policy and any subsequent changes to it. In its capacity as counselor to the trust, Tower Capital shall counsel the trustee as to development of the investment policy, suggest appropriate revisions to the policy on an ongoing basis, and monitor and report results achieved through implementation of the policy on no less than a monthly basis.
- At least annually, Tower Capital shall review the asset allocation of the Family Investment Accounts and, if appropriate, suggest revisions for final approval by James and Jennifer Jensen. The asset allocation plan is incorporated as Appendix A to this Investment Policy Statement. It shall consider the proportions of investments in cash equivalents, municipal securities, U.S. fixed income obligations, U.S. large-capitalization equities, U.S. small-capitalization equities, and American depositary receipts (ADRs). Tower Capital shall consider expected returns, risks, and correlations of returns for a broad representation of asset classes in the U.S. capital markets and consider anticipated changes in the rate of inflation and changes in marginal tax rates.
- As investment advisor, Tower Capital is responsible for using the statements prepared by CCC Brokerage as a basis for evaluating that the risk profile of the Jorge Luiz account is consistent with the risk management policies approved and adopted by Jorge Luiz (see Appendix ZZZ). Tower Capital shall be responsible for identifying variances in risk positions that exceed tolerable limits as specified in the risk management policies and shall take prompt corrective action. No less than quarterly, Tower Capital shall provide to Jorge Luiz a reporting of all such variances in the prior quarter.
- The HHH Trust Company will provide custody services and is responsible for rendering a monthly financial report for the Devereaux Trust. The HHH Trust Company report shall be considered to be the official record for the Trust accounts and shall be the basis for the risk review to be performed by Judith Jones as advisor to the Trust.

Performance Measurement

The IPS should state the method by which investment returns will be calculated. For example, if clients will be making contributions to and taking withdrawals from the investment portfolio at their discretion, then an appropriate return methodology is to use the time-weighted rate of return. However, if the wealth manager has control over when more or less money will be invested as a means to implement a market timing strategy, then the money-weighted rate of return may be more appropriate. In many instances it may be appropriate to report both, as the dollar-weighted return will provide the client with the actual performance of the portfolio and the time-weighted return will serve as a reasonable basis for the measurement of the impact of those decisions under the control of the advisor. The IPS should also state the intervals over which these calculations were made and any relevant valuations that need to be made.

EXAMPLE 13.23 Sample IPS Excerpt for Performance Measurement

- Portfolio performance will be calculated and presented quarterly, which will be calculated by linking together monthly time-weighted rates of return. If the portfolio receives a contribution or experiences a withdrawal representing over 5 percent of the portfolio value, the portfolio will be revalued as of the date of the cash flow. The next valuation date will be the coming month's end or the next significant cash flow date, whichever comes first.

Performance Evaluation/Benchmarks

Evaluating performance requires more than performance measurement. It requires a benchmark against which returns will be compared. A valid investment benchmark must be unambiguous, investable, measurable, appropriate, reflective of current investment options, and specified in advance. We often think of benchmarks as market indexes, an approach that leads to evaluation based on relative performance. Although appropriate for an individual manager, if a client's investment objectives are stated in absolute terms, a market index benchmark for the total portfolio is likely to be inappropriate. A more appropriate benchmark might be some fixed amount above the inflation rate if the investment objective is to provide for a fixed real return or some other fixed rate of return.

EXAMPLE 13.24 Sample IPS Excerpts for Performance Evaluation/Benchmarks

- In light of the strategic asset allocation ranges specified in Appendix A, the benchmarks for the fixed income portion of the portfolio will consist of the Lehman Aggregate Government Index and the Value Line Short Muni Index in equal proportion. Benchmarks for the equity portfolio will consist of the Standard & Poor's 500, the Russell 2000, and the Russell 1000 Value index in equal proportion.
- In addition to performance reporting, Tower Capital shall report to the Marcel Family Trust trustees on a quarterly basis the following risk metrics: (1) risk calculated as the annualized standard deviation of portfolio returns relative to each portfolio's specified benchmark and (2) the information ratio [excess return divided by risk in (1)] for each portfolio based on annualized returns for the portfolio and benchmark as of the end of each quarter.
- Because Mr. and Mrs. Connor have as their primary investment objective to preserve their purchasing power for retirement, the return target is a 3 percent real return, on average. The benchmark for portfolio performance will be the consumer price index.
- Review Process

The review process relates to both the investment portfolio as well as a review of client goals and circumstances. Significant changes in the portfolio may trigger rebalancing activities. Significant changes in client goals or circumstances may trigger changes in the investment policy or the strategic asset allocation itself.

EXAMPLE 13.25   Sample IPS Excerpts for Review Process

- Susan Smith, as investment advisor to Russell Roberts, is responsible for monitoring investment risks and reporting them to Russell Roberts in the reporting format that has been agreed to, a sample of which is presented in Appendix XX.
- Wanda Wood is responsible for monitoring the investing requirements of Sam and Susan Smith, as well as monitoring investment and economic issues, and Ms. Wood is responsible for suggesting changes to the IPS as necessary. Ms. Wood shall offer to review the IPS with Sam and Susan Smith no less frequently than annually.
- After the first 12 months, the investment advisor will provide the Wood Family Trust trustees with a quarterly report that summarizes the performance of each investment manager, each asset class, and the Family Trust in its entirety. Although such quarterly reports are essential for monitoring purposes, in order to focus on long-term performance evaluation, relative success in achieving investment objectives will be evaluated on a rolling 12-quarter basis (most recent three-year period).

Rebalancing

An investment manager can employ any number of rebalancing techniques. The IPS document should articulate the process by which this is done. It should include the intervals or dates at which the portfolio will be reviewed, whether trigger points are a function of time or valuation, and the target to which the portfolio will be rebalanced should rebalancing become necessary.

EXAMPLE 13.26   Sample IPS Excerpts for Rebalancing

- On the first business day of each new quarter, the investment advisor for the Jensen personal accounts shall propose rebalancing transactions to return the accounts to their target allocations and shall execute these transactions within two business days of receiving authorization from the Jensen Family Investment Committee, except that if the principal value of a proposed rebalancing transaction is less than $50,000, that rebalancing transaction shall be deferred indefinitely.
- Capitol Hill Advisers will review the portfolio at least on a quarterly basis to detect variations from our strategic asset allocation parameters. Deviations beyond five percentage points of the strategic allocation range will be rebalanced to the middle of the range.

PARTING COMMENTS

A well-constructed IPS can be a lengthy document. Unfortunately, lengthy documents can intimidate and confuse clients. It may even make them suspicious that an important clause is buried in the fine print. A useful strategy is to cull down the full IPS into a summary, like Exhibit 13.6. It is a concise, easy-to-understand reminder of the important elements of the IPS. It may seem repetitive, but Harold has discovered that presenting information in multiple ways is an important element to good communication and client education.[8]

EXHIBIT 13.6   Investment Policy Summary

	Sample Client, January 2011	
Type of Assets	Personal & IRA Assets	
Current Assets	Approximately $1,275,000	
Investment Time Horizon	Greater than 10 years	
Expected Return	4.5% over CPI	
Risk Tolerance	Moderate—Intermediate-Term	
	Low—Long-Term	
	Losses not to exceed 11%/year with a 90% confidence level	
Asset Allocation	Cash Equivalents	3%
	U.S. Fixed	37%
	International Fixed	5%
	U.S. Large Cap	24%
	U.S. Small Cap	11%
	International	15%
	Real Estate	5%
Allocation Variance Limit	Quarterly	10%
Broad Classes	Yearly	5%
Representative Evaluation Benchmarks	Cash Equivalent –Barcap 6 month Treasury Bill –Donoghue Tax MMA	
	Fixed Income –Muni Bond 3yr –Barcap Intermediate Credit –Aggregate Bond	

(Continued)

---

[8]Sources for IPS development include: Morningstar, "Creating Your Investment Policy Statement," http://news.morningstar.com/classroom2/course.asp?docId = 4439&page = 1&CN = ;   Norman   M. Boone and Linda S. Lubitz, *Creating an Investment Policy Statement* (FPA Press, 2004); Jack Gardner, *How to Write an Investment Policy Statement* (Marketplace Books, 2004); Donald Trone, William Allbright, and Philip Taylor, *The Management of Investment Decisions* (New York: McGraw-Hill, 1996).

EXHIBIT 13.6   (Continued)

Sample Client, January 2011

Equity
–S&P 500 & 500 Growth & Value
–S&P 400 & 400 Growth & Value
–S&P 600 & 600 Growth & Value
–Russell 3000 & 3000 Growth & Value
–MSCI EAFE
–MSCI EM

Although the IPS framework is consistent from one client to the next, the IPS is not a template or a perfunctory questionnaire. Each IPS is unique because it is client-centric. The IPS is a critical governing document in the advisory relationship. In addition to being a tool that helps investors find the discipline to stick to a well-conceived investment policy over time, especially in turbulent markets, the structure of the IPS provides a framework to facilitate communication between the wealth manager and the client.

RESOURCES

Bronson, James W., Matthew H. Scanlan, and Jan R. Squires. 2007. "Managing Individual Investor Portfolios." Chapter 2 in *Managing Investment Portfolios: A Dynamic Process*, 3rd edition. John L. Maginn, Donald L. Tuttle, Jerald E. Pinto, and Dennis W. McLeavey, eds. CFA Institute Investment Series. Hoboken, NJ: John Wiley & Sons.

Guy, John. 1994. *How to Invest Someone Else's Money*. Burr Ridge, IL: Irwin Professional Publishing.

Maginn, John L., Donald L. Tuttle, Dennis W. McLeavey, and Jerald E. Pinto. 2007. "The Portfolio Management Process and the Investment Policy Statement." Chapter 1 in *Managing Investment Portfolios: A Dynamic Process*, 3rd edition. John L. Maginn, Donald L. Tuttle, Jerald E. Pinto, and Dennis W. McLeavey, eds. CFA Institute Investment Series. Hoboken, NJ: John Wiley & Sons.

Schacht, Kurt N., James C. Allen, and Robert W. Dannhauser. 2010. "Elements of an Investment Policy Statement for Individual Investors." Standards in Financial Market Integrity Division, CFA Institute, Charlottesville, VA. www.cfapubs.org/doi/pdf/10.2469/ccb.v2010.n12.1.

Trone, Donald, William Allbright, and Philip Taylor. 1996. *The Management of Investment Decisions*. New York: McGraw-Hill.

CHAPTER 14

PORTFOLIO MANAGEMENT

Asset allocation policy should be long-term but not rigid.

—Ng Kok Song, Group Chief Investment Officer,
Government of Singapore Investment Corporation,
and Chairman, Wealth Management Institute

Earlier chapters discussed the importance of asset allocation and investment policy, as well as the use of techniques such as optimization to select an appropriate asset allocation, given a client's risk tolerance and assumptions about capital market expectations. This resulting asset allocation is referred to as strategic asset allocation or policy allocation. A strategic asset allocation is designed to meet long-term goals using long-term risk and return expectations. After a client's strategic asset allocation is selected, the wealth manager must implement the policy, which requires a number of additional decisions, including selecting appropriate investments within each asset class and managing the resulting portfolio. Questions to be answered include:

- Should the short-term asset allocation differ from the strategic asset allocation?
- Within asset classes, what strategies or styles will be selected?
- Will the wealth manager choose money managers to manage investments within each asset class?
- Will the wealth manager use pooled investment vehicles, separate accounts, and/or direct investments in securities?

SHORT-TERM ASSET ALLOCATION

The strategic asset allocation is intended to be long-term in nature. Some wealth managers maintain this asset allocation without adjustment other than rebalancing until changes in a client's situation or market expectations warrant revisiting the strategic asset allocation. Some wealth managers perform a new strategic asset allocation at specified intervals, such as every five years. Other wealth managers make short-term adjustments to the strategic asset allocation, such as tactical asset allocation or dynamic asset allocation.

Tactical Asset Allocation

Tactical asset allocation (TAA) involves making short-run adjustments tilting the current asset allocation away from the strategic asset allocation. Often the strategic asset allocation specifies ranges rather than fixed percentages for each asset class, such as 50 to 60 percent equities. Tactical asset allocation is typically a tilt within these permissible ranges based on expected relative short-term performance of the asset classes used in the strategic asset allocation. TAA proactively rebalances in order to enhance returns by shifting from relatively overvalued asset classes to relatively undervalued classes. As tactical allocations typically involve moving assets from areas perceived to be overvalued (i.e., hot investment classes) to those areas perceived to be undervalued (i.e., underperforming), the strategy is inherently contrarian. However, in a typical tactical asset allocation a portfolio is never completely in or out of a single asset class, and adjustments are made infrequently.

Most TAA is based on the theoretical assumption that asset class returns are mean-reverting (i.e., their returns will fluctuate around equilibrium values). As a result, TAA requires only the limited forecasting ability that enables an allocator to determine if the current pricing is above or below equilibrium. Mean reversion will then generate the profits. Research on the efficacy of tactical asset allocation is mixed. Most research shows that, on average across investors, tactical asset allocation does not add much value over and above the strategic asset allocation decisions. However, some managers do add alpha through their tactical decisions. This should not be unexpected; outperforming the broad markets is a zero-sum game—while individual managers will outperform based on their tactical allocation, others will underperform.

Market Timing

Market timing is an extreme form of tactical asset allocation that involves frequent shifts into and out of asset classes in an attempt to time the peaks and troughs of the markets. For example, a market timing strategy might involve moving the portfolio allocation between equities and cash equivalents (e.g., Treasury bills) based on technical indicators. Market timing can involve being totally in or out of individual asset classes. There have been innumerable studies of market timing, and the vast majority concludes that the strategy cannot add value. We have mentioned on numerous occasions our belief that market timing does not work.

Dynamic Asset Allocation

Dynamic asset allocation (DAA)[1] is a term that evolved from the work on portfolio insurance by Professors Hayne E. Leland and Mark Rubinstein in 1976. The term itself was introduced as a service mark in 1981 for a firm they established, along with John W. O'Brien, to market the strategy. Based on arbitrage concepts, DAA is a mechanistic strategy designed to respond to market movements. The portfolio asset mix is constantly shifted between risky (e.g., stocks) and riskless (e.g., T-bills) assets. In a dynamic strategy, if stocks are declining in value you would reduce exposure to stocks and increase exposure to T-bills. Unlike other active

---

[1]Mark Kritzman, *Asset Allocation for Institutional Portfolios* (Business One Irwin, 1990), 92–104; Robert Arnott and Frank Fabozzi, editors, *Asset Allocation: A Handbook of Portfolio Policies, Strategies and Tactics* (Probus, 1988); J. S. Parsons, "Incorporating Options Technology into Asset Allocation," in *Global Asset Allocation* (New York: John Wiley & Sons, 1994), 97–100; Scott L. Lummer, PhD, CFA, and Mark W. Riepe, "Introduction: The Role of Asset Allocation in Portfolio Management," in *Global Asset Allocation* (New York: John Wiley & Sons., 1994), 3; Charles DuBois, "Tactical A.A.: A Review of Current Techniques," *Citicorp Investment Management*, 283–336.

management strategies that attempt to increase returns, the value added by DAA is to insure the portfolio against declines below a floor value. A later version, known as constant proportion portfolio insurance (CPPI), was developed in 1986. CPPI has the advantage, compared to traditional portfolio insurance, of being simpler to implement and non-time-dependent.

In a CPPI approach, some floor is set below which the portfolio should not be allowed to fall. The amount to be invested in stocks is:

$$\text{Dollars in Stocks} = m(\text{Assets} - \text{Floor})$$

where m is a multiplier set by the portfolio manager. For example, with a portfolio of $1 million, a desired floor of $750,000, and a multiplier of 2, the portfolio manager would initially allocate $500,000 to equities and $500,000 to a riskless asset. If the value of the equities falls to $400,000 ($900,000 total portfolio) the new desired allocation to equities would be $300,000; $100,000 of equities would be sold to rebalance to $300,000 in equities and $600,000 in the riskless asset. Conversely, if equity values rise, equities exposure would be increased. It should be apparent that this is not a contrarian approach. Equities are purchased in a rising market and sold in a falling market. This approach does well when the trend continues, but poorly in markets that are not trending (i.e., that revert to some mean level).[2]

The optimization framework that incorporates investors' implied leverage as a measure of their risk tolerance that we introduced in Chapter 10 ("Portfolio Optimization") is version of CPPI. As equity markets fall, investors' implied leverage on their life balance sheets will increase, thereby decreasing their risk tolerance. As a result, the leverage-adjusted optimization will allocate less to equity (all else being equal) during falling markets and more during rising markets.

Core-Satellite Approach

Another approach is to maintain the bulk of client assets in a core portfolio with a strategic asset allocation often managed passively, with the balance of assets in a satellite portfolio with a tactical overlay that is managed more actively. Effectively, the core portfolio provides beta exposure (if it is passively managed), while the satellite portfolio seeks to add alpha. Harold's firm uses a core-satellite approach for the equity portion of client portfolios with about 80 percent allocated to the core portfolio and 20 percent allocated to the satellite portfolio. His firm's motivation for the implementation of a core-satellite portfolio is to manage the friction of taxes and expenses in a low-return environment.[3]

DIRECT VERSUS INDIRECT INVESTMENTS

Once the amounts to be invested in each asset class are determined, the wealth manager selects investments within each asset class. Implementation could be made by selecting individual securities such as stocks and bonds, separately managed accounts, or pooled investment

---

[2]For more information on dynamic strategies such as CPPI, see Andre Perold and William Sharpe, "Dynamic Strategies for Asset Allocation," *Financial Analysts Journal* (January/February 1995): 149–160, and Robert Arnott, Terence Burns, Lisa Plaxco, and Philip Moore, "Monitoring and Rebalancing," in Maginn, Tuttle, Pinto, and McLeavey (2007, 682–716).

[3]Harold Evensky, "Changing Equity Premium Implications for Wealth Management Portfolio Design and Implementation," *Journal of Financial Planning* (June 2002).

vehicles such as mutual funds or exchange-traded funds (ETFs). The wealth manager may also use combinations of these different approaches.

Selecting and managing portfolios of individual securities requires the wealth manager to have expertise not only in wealth planning and asset allocation but also in evaluating all types of individual securities that will be included in the portfolio. Managing individual securities normally involves having members of the wealth manager's team who can manage the individual securities. Such accounts normally require large minimum balances to achieve adequate diversification and to justify the additional time and effort necessary to manage such accounts. However, individually managed accounts can have advantages in terms of being able to tailor the portfolio to client needs (such as using bond immunization techniques described later), potential greater flexibility in managing the taxes, and eliminating the middlemen.

Alternatively, the wealth manager can select individual money managers who manage portions of the portfolio in which they have expertise—for example, a large-cap value equity manager or fixed income manager. These are known as separately managed accounts (SMAs). Separate accounts are maintained for each client and each asset type. For a client with five asset classes, there would likely be five separate accounts, each managed by a different money manager. Each account is titled in the customer's name, but all such accounts are typically managed to the money manager's model portfolio, with trades being allocated to the individual client accounts.

A unified managed account (UMA) is similar to an SMA except that it involves a single account with assets from the different asset classes commingled and with the account managed by multiple money managers.

The wealth manager may utilize pooled investment vehicles, such as open- or closed-end mutual funds, exchange-traded funds (ETFs), or exchange-traded notes (ETNs). Open-end mutual funds are pooled investment vehicles managed by a professional money manager to some specified objective. Open-end funds issue new shares continuously and can normally be purchased at net asset value at the end of the trading day. Closed-end funds are similar to open-end funds but have a set number of shares issued. A prospective buyer must purchase existing shares on the market from an existing shareholder. Closed-end funds can trade at a premium or discount to net asset value. An ETF is a fund that trades on an organized exchange much like stock. It can be purchased or sold at any time during the trading day. An ETN is a similar instrument except that rather than being backed by the individual securities underlying the fund, it is a debt instrument subject to the creditworthiness of the issuer. ETNs are typically used to gain exposure to alternative asset classes, such as commodities. Chapter 16 addresses selection of funds in more detail.

STRATEGY: ACTIVE VERSUS PASSIVE

The debate between proponents of active and passive management has a long and acrimonious history. Some of the conflict results from a confusing use of terminology. In order to remove one element of confusion from the discussion, let's first define our use of a few terms.

Active management is the art and science of security selection based on a belief in a manager's ability to consistently and accurately evaluate current valuations and/or future events better than other investors. The core philosophical basis is that by brains, hard work, and/or technology the active manager can, over time and net of costs, beat the system. Note that selecting one asset class in lieu of another is also an active decision, so tactical asset allocation is an example of active management.

Passive management is the antithesis of active management. Its core philosophical tenet is that by brains, hard work, and/or technology, a manager cannot, over time and net of costs, beat the system; the passive manager can, however, beat most active managers. Passive management is often assumed to be the equivalent of index management. It is not. Index management is a special subset of passive management. Passive managers may make active trading decisions (e.g., rebalancing). Their decisions, however, are based on information currently available to all investors, not on an ability to read between the lines or predict future trends and events. Index management is passive management with the added constraint that the manager does not make active trading decisions.

The efficient market hypothesis (EMH) is a subject covered in some depth in Chapter 8, "Investment Theory." For purposes of this discussion, we use the version of the concept accepted by most proponents of passive management. They do not argue that markets are perfectly efficient. In fact, most readily acknowledge market inefficiencies and anomalies. Efficient market proponents do argue, however, that net of transaction costs and management fees, markets are functionally efficient, on average. In other words, active management proponents win no points arguing that markets are obviously inefficient. Many passive managers agree.

As measured by investment dollars, active managers are currently winning the debate. Approximately a quarter of pension assets are passively managed, according to a survey of pension funds.[4] Interestingly, however, almost half of the domestic equity assets are indexed. However, passive investing is a relatively new concept (only about 35 years old) and its growth has been extraordinary. In 1973, only $50 million was passively managed. Today, it is estimated that more than 90 percent of the nation's largest pension plans passively manage at least a portion of their investments. It is estimated that about $1.1 trillion is indexed to the S&P 500 alone.[5] That said, Yan (2006) estimates that less than 6 percent of mutual funds (not necessarily assets under management) are index funds.

Passive investing received a boost in the 1990s with the introduction of ETFs. Dominated primarily by index strategies, ETF popularity has increased rapidly. There are now more than 2,600 ETFs or similar products that trade on more than 40 exchanges around the world, and ETF assets under management increased 500 percent from 2002 to 2007. Most of the larger ETFs track broad-based indexes, such as the S&P 500 or the FTSE All-World Index. A growing number of these products track more focused indexes, such as a particular industry or sector. Recently, a growing number of ETFs that are being introduced follow actively managed strategies. Nonetheless, this part of the market is still dominated by passive strategies, whether they are indexed or not.

In Favor of Active Management

History doesn't repeat itself but it rhymes.

—Mark Twain

It would seem unnecessary to defend active management. As almost all investment management is active, it seems the value added must be obvious. Given that, we will simply recap a couple of ways in which active managers may add value.

---

[4]The Council of Institutional Investors Asset Allocation Survey 2010 surveyed 59 of its general members whose assets represent over 10 percent of the pension assets (defined contribution and defined benefit) in the United States.

[5]Standard & Poor's Annual Survey of Index Assets 2010.

Fundamental Research

Graham and Dodd subscribed to this philosophy. They advised the intelligent investor to "devote his attention to the field of undervalued securities . . . which are selling well below the levels apparently justified by a careful analysis of the relevant facts." Another famous proponent of this form of value added is Warren Buffett, who, as a disciple of Graham, has made many long-term investors in Berkshire Hathaway quite wealthy.

Other managers attempt to add value through fundamental research, but rather than focus on current financials, such as assets and capital structure, these growth managers make educated guesses about the future. They attempt to add value by purchasing securities they believe to be undervalued as a result of other investors underestimating the company's future prospects. By any standards, adding value is a tough hurdle. Whenever the debate over passive and active management is encountered, the active proponents martial the same few names: Buffett and Peter Lynch (and occasionally John Neff and John Templeton).

Active Asset Allocation

This is a strategy that adds value by managing the weights of investments relative to the normal policy—for example, tactical asset allocation discussed earlier. This can also be implemented within an asset class (depending on how asset classes are defined). This is referred to as a policy tilt. It is a strategy designed to add value by overweighing an investment class or style in order to take advantage of a perceived market anomaly. An example would be the overweighting of small-cap stocks in January to take advantage of the January effect. A more general example would be the permanent overweighting of the portfolio with low price-to-book stocks. At this stage, strategies get fuzzy, as passive managers also use similar portfolio tilts. The difference is that active managers see themselves as taking advantage of a market anomaly overlooked by others whereas passive managers see themselves as accepting additional risk in order to take advantage of a different factor of market returns.

One quasi-strategy that straddles market timing and portfolio tilt is sector rotation, the technique of tilting the portfolio in favor of market sectors that are expected to benefit most from the next economic wave.

Potential Advantages of Active Management

The potential advantages of active management are:

- *Adding returns and minimizing downside risks.* These are the most frequently offered reasons for selecting active management. In a thoughtful article titled "Devising an Investment Philosophy," Lou Stanosolouvich (a fine wealth manager, a good friend of Harold's, and one of the most passionate defenders of active management) wrote that he rejects passive management because "passive management lacks the potential downside protection offered by active management and the ability to invest in the best portfolio managers who have outperformed their corresponding indices over time."[6]
- *Psychological rewards.* Active management offers a number of psychological benefits:
  - The investor is a player. For example, an understated boast to a friend: "Oh yeah, I made a little on my technology play."
  - The investor can get rich. For example: "Look at our 10-year record. If you invest now and compound at that rate, you will have a zillion dollars by the time you retire."

---

[6]However, Harold argues that existing research does not support this argument.

- The investor is likely to feel brilliant or abused but never stupid. For example: "I have quite a record of selecting successful money managers," or "I lost a bundle. That manager was a disappointment, but I've replaced him with a real winner."

In Favor of Passive Management

Proponents of passive management have no quarrel with the benefits proposed by active management. They simply do not believe that active management can consistently deliver these benefits. Unquestionably, the most passionate (and most fun) critic of active management and defender of passive management is Rex Sinquefield, one of the founders of Dimensional Fund Advisors (DFA). In his well-known, understated way, he staked out his position in an address to participants at the 1995 Schwab National Conference.

> *Active management does not make sense theoretically, isn't justified empirically, and doesn't work for your clients. Passive management stands on solid theoretical ground, has enormous empirical support, and works very well for your client.*

Lest that seem a little strong, we will add the observation of Charles Ellis, a less fiery commentator, but no less eloquent.

> *The investment management business . . . is built upon a simple and basic belief: professional money managers can beat the market. The premise appears to be false.*[7]

The argument in support of passive management is based on three premises:

1. Active management can best be described as "that dog don't hunt."[8]
2. Passive management works.[9] It does not result in average results; it is analogous to shooting par in golf.[10]
3. Investing is second only to health where you want life to be boring.

Efficient Markets

As noted earlier, passive management supporters point out that the question is not whether the market is totally efficient but whether there is a systematic way to find, after costs, a better security and/or portfolio. Their answer is no. On average, Eugene Fama suggests, information moves so fast that the market knows more than any individual.[11]

---

[7]Charles D. Ellis, "The Loser's Game," in *Classics: An Investor's Anthology* (Homewood, IL: Dow Jones–Irwin, 1989), 524–535.

[8]My thanks to Cy Hornsby for this useful colloquialism.

[9]Goldman Sachs reported in its October 1995 "The Coming Evolution of the Investment Management Industry" that for one-, three-, and five-year periods, equity managers outperformed the S&P 500 index only 28.3 percent of the time (based on Plan Sponsor data).

[10]And our golfing friends tell me that par is *very* good. The reason for suggesting that par is a better analogy is that passive managers, due to the low implementation costs, are mathematically guaranteed to consistently be in the top 50 percent and, as some active managers in the top 50 percent fall into lower quartiles in subsequent periods, over time passive managers often move to rank in the top one-third, one-fourth, or higher. Given the uncertainty of consistently selecting active managers who will perform better than average in the future, Harold argues that a portfolio consisting of a universe of managers guaranteed to be in the top half and frequently in the top quartile or higher is definitely not average.

[11]Peter Bernstein, *Capital Ideas* (New York: Free Press, 1992), 136.

Historical Returns

The active manager's use of historical returns and market anomalies assumes that unusual behavior will repeat. Research suggests it does not. As many observers have suggested, active management based on historical returns is akin to driving forward by looking in a rearview mirror.

Gurus

Basic economics suggests that profitable quantitative investment analysis will not be commercialized. Successful research requires consistent detection of opportunities that others do not see. It is more profitable to take advantage of the research than to market the results.[12] Paul Samuelson acknowledges that some market gurus may exist, but they are hard to find and expensive to rent.[13] And, if they exist, it's unlikely they will hire out to manage wrap accounts, or small (even multimillion-dollar) portfolios. Active management supporters always reply with their mantra of Buffett and Lynch. Passive management defenders point out that there are tens of thousands of managers, and the laws of probability predict that some will demonstrate outstanding performance due to chance. Statistically, no manager has a long enough track record to rule out luck as the basis for his success. Even if one was proven to be exceptional, how does the investor find the next Buffett or Lynch (in each asset class)?

Costs

The major hurdle active managers must leap is not beating a benchmark return but beating the cost of getting there. Charles Ellis provides a simple formula for calculating this threshold:[14]

Required Break-Even Return Relative to the Benchmark for Active Management

$$= [(\text{Turnover} \times \text{Cost}) + \text{Management Fee} + \text{Target Return}]/\text{Market Return}$$

Using his example, assume:

Equities earn a historical rate of 10 percent.
Target return equals market return.
Turnover equals a modest 30 percent.
The average cost of turnover (commission and spread) equals 3 percent.
There is a modest management fee of 0.5 percent.

Break-Even Return $= [(0.3 \times 3\%) + 0.5\% + 10\%]/10\% = 1.14 = 114\%$ of Benchmark

This is a useful calculation for the wealth manager to use when comparing active and passive management. However, keep in mind that the formula ignores taxes, so it is biased in favor of active management. An appropriate tax adjustment would be to add 25 to 75 basis points to the numerator.

---

[12]H. Russell Fogler, "Investment Analysis and New Quantitative Tools," *Journal of Portfolio Management* (Summer 1995): 39–47.
[13]Bernstein, *Capital Ideas*, 143.
[14]Ellis, "Loser's Game."

Policy Drift

Actively managed funds often exhibit style, asset class, and/or size drift and active asset allocation can result in asset class drift. The result of either form of drift is a portfolio that does not maintain a strategic balance.

In a paper titled "Diversification Returns and Asset Contributions" published in the May/June 1992 issue of *Financial Analysts Journal*, David G. Booth and Eugene Fama investigated the value of a passive, strategically balanced portfolio. Their conclusion should be considered by the wealth manager when making decisions regarding the use of active management (particularly active asset allocation) and when making decisions regarding a rebalancing policy.

> *Investors need a large premium to be willing to incur the additional uncertainty of active management. Recent studies indicate that investors cannot expect such a premium.*
>
> *Active management introduces so much uncertainty that we cannot document a premium return over benchmark returns. By contrast, fully diversified portfolios reliably increase portfolio compound returns through the diversification process and eliminate "benchmark risk."*

Loser's Game

Charles Ellis subtitled his book *Investment Policy "How to Win the Loser's Game."*[15] He argues that investing, once a winner's game, has now become a loser's game. In a winner's game, victory goes to the participant winning more than others. In a loser's game, the outcome is determined by the actions of the losers. A participant wins a loser's game not by winning more; the system makes that impossible. He or she wins by avoiding mistakes and letting other participants blunder. For example, in tennis the way to win is by making fewer bad shots. Investing has become a loser's game because money managers are no longer competing with amateurs; they are competing with themselves—they are the market. Since the old commonsense rules do not apply, Ellis recommends the following guidelines for wealth managers.

Stop searching for winners. "Only a sucker backs a 'winner' in the loser's game. . . . the real opportunity to achieve superior results is not in scrambling to outperform the market, but in establishing and adhering to appropriate investment policies over the long term."

Research: Active versus Passive

So much for the debate; what does the research on this issue conclude? The research concludes that both sides of the debate are right, that both sides are wrong, and that "it depends" or "it's impossible to reach a conclusion." In other words, there is a research study with a conclusion that will match any bias you may have.

A useful summary of academic research was included in "Does Historical Performance Predict Future Performance?" by Ronald Kahn and Andrew Rudd, published in 1995.[16] An update was provided by William Droms in 2006.[17]

---

[15]Remember, this is not only a "must read"; it is a "must read frequently." The second edition was published by Irwin in 1993.

[16]Ronald Kahn and Andrew Rudd, "Does Historical Performance Predict Future Performance?" BARRA Newsletter and the *Financial Analysts Journal* (November/December 1995).

[17]William Droms, "Hot Hands, Cold Hands: Does Past Performance Predict Future Returns?" *Journal of Financial Planning* (May 2006): 60–66.

Studies in favor of the persistence of winners (i.e., the efficacy of active management) included:

- Greenblatt and Titman (1992)—based on 157 mutual funds during the period 1975–1984.
- Lehman and Modest (1987)—130 funds from 1968 to 1982.
- Brown and Draper (United Kingdom)—530 pension managers from 1981 to 1990.
- Hendricks, Patel, and Zeckhauser (1993)—165 funds from 1974 to 1988.
- Goetzmann and Ibbotson (1994)—728 funds from 1976 to 1988. This study concluded that performance ranking was important and that winners repeated with frequency when analyzed for three-year periods. However, the authors' caveats noted that superior performance was relative to other active managers. The superior performers might not beat the market. Also, the study did not consider risk (volatility).
- Droms and Walker (1994, 2001a and b)—multiple studies covering 1971–1996. Short-term performance persists.
- Jan and Hung (2004)—3,316 funds from 1961 to 2000. Short-run and long-run persistence.

It is important to note that most of these studies use databases that are plagued with survivorship bias, which statistically increases the likelihood that an investigator will find performance persistence when none exists.[18]

Studies demonstrating that performance does not persist or can be explained by other factors included:

- Jensen (1968)—115 funds from 1945 to 1964. This was the seminal study that led to the familiar disclaimer "Past performance is no guarantee of future performance" that every prospectus includes but few practitioners believe. Ibbotson and Goetzmann referred to this as "the most influential article on the topic."[19]
- Kirtzman (1983)—10-year study of 32 fixed income managers employed by the AT&T pension plan.
- Dunn and Theisen (1983)—201 institutional portfolios from 1973 to 1982.
- Elton, Gruber, and Rentzler (1990)—51 commodity funds from 1980 to 1987.
- Carhart (1997)—1,892 funds across various categories from 1962 to 1993 in a survivorship bias-free database. Carhart shows that the "hot hands" effect is mostly driven by a one-year momentum effect that can be captured passively.
- Carhart, Carpenter, Lynch, and Musto (2002)—over 2,000 funds from 1962 to 1995. Persistence is driven by expenses and impacted by survivorship bias.
- Bollen and Busse (2004)—230 funds from 1985 to 1995. Short-term persistence, but not economically significant.
- Pfeiffer (2010)—A study using data from the most recent decade suggests that investors do not benefit from active management due to the cost of active management, poor persistence, and the low probability of identifying superior managers in advance. In aggregate; however, the findings suggest active managers have just enough skill to offset their fees.

---

[18]Survivorship bias is the phenomenon that databases include only managers who survive over an evaluation period and not managers who failed to survive mostly likely because of poor performance. Selection bias, a different but related phenomenon, is the notion that a manager database preselects for good-performing managers by virtue of a selection filter.

[19]Ibbotson and Goetzmann, "History," *Financial Planning*, 95–96.

Kahn and Rudd found many potential problems with the earlier research: incomplete accounting for fund expenses and fees, survivorship bias, period-specific conclusions, and style variations. More recent research has addressed some of these factors. Kahn and Rudd also adjusted their analysis for each of these factors. Their conclusions were encouraging for the passive camp. They wrote:

> *For equity funds, the implications are simple. With no persistence of selection returns, unless you have another basis for choosing future winners (i.e., your selection criteria include information other than historical performance), the solution is to index perhaps to a set of style indexes weighted to match your investment objectives.*

For fixed income funds they found significant evidence of persistence. The appropriate use of historical performance information provided strong odds for beating the median. Unfortunately, fear and transaction costs reared their ugly heads, and the median had a negative selection return. They concluded that "the investment implications for fixed income funds, surprisingly, are similar to those for equity funds. Once again, index funds are a very attractive strategy."

Not referenced by Kahn and Rudd but frequently reported was a study by Lakonishok, Schleifer, and Vishny (LSV) titled "The Structure and Performance of the Money Management Industry."[20] Their results generally supported Kahn and Rudd. After almost 30 years, the research comes back to echo Jensen's conclusion: Past performance is no guarantee of future performance.

Just like their academic brethren, the practitioners' results seem to support any conclusion one could wish. In the fall of 1995, the Mobius Group revisited LSV and after adjusting for "problems" they found with the earlier study, reevaluated the data and concluded that, on both a risk-adjusted and a style basis, superior performance persisted.[21] Callan concluded that active management added a 135 basis point risk-adjusted premium for non-U.S. equity managers versus the Morgan Stanley Capital International Europe, Australasia, Far East (MSCI EAFE) index. However, Callan did acknowledge a significant variation among managers.[22] Frank Russell, however, reported, "Given the wide range of previous statistical attempts to find persistence, it should come as no surprise that our data, likewise, support no such hypothesis."

John Bogel developed a number of tables demonstrating over various holding periods the failure of funds to maintain their superior rankings.[23] One of his more fun (and marketing-oriented) comparisons was "Bogel tests the *Forbes* Honor Roll." He found the following:

For the Period 1973–1990	
Honor Roll	12.2%[24]
S&P 500	12.2%
Wilshire	12.4%

---

[20]Josef Lakonishok, Andrei Shleifer, and Robert W. Vishny, "The Structure and Performance of the Money Management Industry," *Brookings Papers on Economic Activity*, 1992, 339–391.

[21]Mobius Group, Inc., *Mobius Strip*, Vol. 2, No. 5 (Fall 1995): 1–12.

[22]Callan Letter (Spring 1995), 4–9, 13–14.

[23]These tables are included in John Bogle, *Bogle on Mutual Funds: New Perspectives for the Intelligent Investor* (New York: Random House, 1994).

[24]This assumed a purchase of an equal amount of each Honor Roll fund each year with no fees or transaction costs.

Dimensional Fund Advisors, having a bit of similar fun with its active manager competitors, published the following comparisons at the end of 1995.

Worth Magazine's "Best Mutual Funds," Selected November 1994

	Performance 12/31/94–12/31/95	Value Added
"Best Global Equity Fund"		
Worth: Warburg Pincus Int'l Equity	9.85%	–2.42%
DFA Large Cap International	13.05	
DFA International Value	11.49	
"Best Large Cap Growth Fund"		
Worth: Fidelity Disciplined Equity	29.01	–8.07
DFA U.S. Large Cap	37.03	
"Best Large Cap Value Fund"		
Worth: Mutual Beacon	25.89	–12.47
DFA U.S. Large Cap Value	38.36	
"Best Small Cap Growth Fund"		
Worth: Wasatch Aggressive Equity	28.12	–6.34
DFA U.S. 9–10	34.46	
"Best Small Cap Value Fund"		
Worth: Heartland Value	29.80	+ 0.51
DFA U.S. Small Cap Value	29.27	

An updated analysis through October 2010 provided to us by DFA using a broader group of actively-managed funds reaffirms the conclusion that active mutual fund managers on average do not outperform passively-managed portfolios.

Out of all of the practical research, the most interesting is from SEI Corporation,[25] which notes that many of the studies, when adjusted for style, reached not one but two conclusions. First, when using the S&P 500 as a benchmark, selection ability was statistically insignificant. Second, when performance was measured relative to each manager's appropriate style, selection ability was both positive and statistically significant. SEI's independent research confirmed these findings.

What to Do?

Okay, once again, what's a poor, confused wealth manager to do? On one hand, the arguments in favor of passive management seem far too compelling to ignore. On the other hand,

---

[25]SEI Corporation, *SEI Equity Portfolio Structure: Large Capitalization Value*, 1994, 1–19.

there are a number of problems associated with passive management (at least from the perspective of the wealth manager) that academic and institutional research does not address.

Passive funds are designed to track a specific benchmark. The selection and management of that benchmark may be based on the vendor's intuition and may change (e.g., DFA Real Estate Index originally included land development companies but was subsequently changed to include only REITs). Passive funds are not all science; there is plenty of room for art.

Similar benchmark descriptions may mask fundamental differences in composition (e.g., whose definition of value).

Many passive funds have moderate to high turnover and may not be especially tax efficient.

Wealth managers deal with real retail clients. One of our responsibilities is to make our clients comfortable with their investment portfolios. At least today, many clients are incapable of being comfortable with an all-passive portfolio.

Wealth managers are human. The research in favor of passive management is compelling but not overwhelming. Many of us are as attached to passionate money managers. We are unprepared to reject their possible contribution to our clients' well-being.

Financial theory is not the only academic input of interest to the wealth manager. The contributions of behavioral psychology are important to us. For example, risk-adjusted performance is certainly important, but for some of our clients, so are bragging rights. We may be able to provide our clients' performance with passive management, but it will not provide bragging rights. As an early commentator noted, "Each investment professional is responsible for his or her client's expectations."[26] Roger Gibson constantly reminds us—first we manage our clients' expectations and then their portfolios.

Balancing these conflicting issues is more of the art of wealth management. Too often the choice is presented as either/or. In fact, there is a third choice. Harold's firm uses both active and passive managers. In those asset classes and styles where they believe the passive manager has an advantage, they select him. In cases where the advantage is less clear or where they find an active manager with a persuasive philosophy and a passion, they select him.

Currently, Harold's portfolios are approximately one-half passive and one-half active. In fixed income, they are currently 100 percent active. In equity allocations his firm uses passive management for the core domestic equity position, a significant portion of the international allocation, and all of the value style allocations (more on that in the next section). The satellite allocations are frequently to active managers.

EQUITY ANALYSIS AND STRATEGIES

This section addresses techniques used to analyze and select equity securities for inclusion in a portfolio that are relevant whether the wealth manager is analyzing and selecting the securities himself or evaluating the process and strategy of an outside money manager.

Top-Down versus Bottom-Up Process

There are two basic approaches for the equity analysis process. In a top-down approach, the manager takes a high-level macroeconomic approach initially and then works downward

---

[26]Fred Spence at the 1988 Institute of Chartered Financial Analysts seminar, "Serving the Individual Investor."

toward the individual equities that would be expected to do well given overall macroeconomic expectations. A high-level example of such an approach is depicted in Exhibit 14.1.

EXHIBIT 14.1   Top-Down Analysis

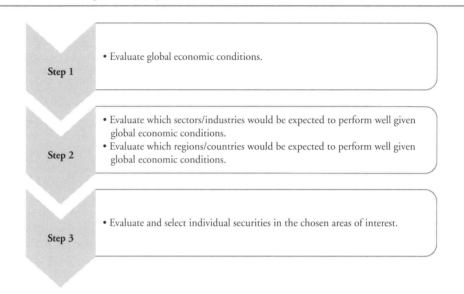

Step 1
- Evaluate global economic conditions.

Step 2
- Evaluate which sectors/industries would be expected to perform well given global economic conditions.
- Evaluate which regions/countries would be expected to perform well given global economic conditions.

Step 3
- Evaluate and select individual securities in the chosen areas of interest.

In a bottom-up approach the manager focuses on company-specific factors of interest and searches for companies that exhibit those factors. A high-level example of this approach is depicted in Exhibit 14.2.

EXHIBIT 14.2   Bottom-Up Analysis

Step 1
- Identify factors of interest to use in screening the universe of potential equity investments (such as revenue growth, low price-earnings ratios, or strong cash flow).

Step 2
- Screen universe of potential investments and collect additional information on those companies passing the screens.

Step 3
- Evaluate and select individual securities from those passing the screens.

These two approaches are not mutually exclusive, and some aspects of each are often included in a manager's process. Regardless of the approach, an understanding of macroeconomic factors is necessary when evaluating individual securities in order to forecast future expected performance and cash flows, and in order to narrow down the securities of interest some form of screening on fundamental factors is likely to be necessary.

Fundamental versus Technical Analysis

There are also two main approaches to evaluating individual equity securities: fundamental analysis and technical analysis. Fundamental analysis involves an examination of factors of interest such as profitability, financial strength, cash flows, and business prospects of the company of interest. Technical analysis involves examination of price and volume charts of the company's stock in order to identify attractive investment opportunities.

Fundamental Analysis

Fundamental analysis[27] typically involves a detailed examination of a company's past performance, current situation, and forecasted future performance, including:

- An analysis of the company's financial reports to assess its profitability (income statement), financial position (balance sheet), and cash flows (cash flow statement). Since accounting rules permit some discretion in financial reporting, this should include an analysis of the company's accounting methods and other available information to determine whether any adjustments to historical data are necessary for a proper assessment of trends over time or performance relative to peers.
- Ratio analysis to assess profitability (e.g., profit margin or return on equity); efficiency (e.g., how quickly it collects on its receivables); liquidity (ability to meet short-term obligations); solvency (ability to meet all obligations); and valuation (e.g. price-to-earnings or price-to-book ratios). Ratios are assessed over time and relative to peer companies.
- An evaluation of business prospects in light of expected economic conditions.
- A forecast of future earnings, cash flow, and financial position.
- A formal valuation of the company, which might be performed using discounted future expected cash flows or a relative valuation method (such as price-to-earnings).

Academic research has found that fundamental factors such as ratios can be effectively used to select securities for inclusion in portfolios.[28]

Technical Analysis

Proponents of technical analysis[29] generally argue that fundamental information is reflected in stock price and volume information and therefore the analyst can focus on charts of price and volume. Common technical analysis techniques involve:

- Examination of stock price patterns in combination with volume information (e.g., a rising stock price on rising volume or a head-and-shoulders topping formation).
- Stock prices crossing over or under a moving average line or lines.

---

[27]Detailed fundamental analysis is beyond the scope of this book or even a single book. For more information see *International Financial Statement Analysis* by Robinson, van Greuning, Henry, and Broihahn and *Equity Asset Valuation* by Pinto, Henry, Robinson, and Stowe.

[28]See J. Ou and S. Penman, "Financial Statement Analysis and the Prediction of Stock Returns," *Journal of Accounting and Economics*, Vol. 11 (1989): 295–329; J. Abarbanell and B. Bushee, "Fundamental Analysis, Future Earnings, and Stock Prices," *Journal of Accounting Research*, Vol. 35 (1997): 1–24; J. Piotroski, "Value Investing: The Use of Historical Financial Statement Information to Separate Winners from Losers," *Journal of Accounting Research*, Vol. 38 (2000): 1–41.

[29]A primer on technical analysis by John Murphy (1999) provides insight into the market behavior behind many technical indicators.

- A stock price pattern that indicates that the price has risen to a resistance level or fallen to a support level.

Technical analysis can be viewed as studying the behavior of participants in the market, and psychological/behavioral effects can explain why some patterns may exist. Support and resistance lines are a good example. If an investor likes a stock that has been trading at $20 for some time but decides not to buy and the stock then increases above $20, that investor may be inclined to buy the next time the stock hits $20. Similarly, if an investor holds a stock that rises in value to $30 but chooses not to sell it and it subsequently falls in value, the investor may indeed step in and sell the next time the stock reaches $30. Aggregate behavior of investors can create support and resistance areas.

The research on the effectiveness of technical analysis is less favorable than that on fundamental analysis. Most studies have found that technical strategies are not profitable after considering transaction costs. However, in one of the most comprehensive recent studies, Andrew Lo, Harry Mamaysky, and Jiang Wang examined a large sample of stocks over the period 1962 to 1996 and found that several technical indicators (out of 10 indicators studied) may have some value in selecting securities.[30]

Fundamental analysis and technical analysis are often viewed as polar opposites, but they need not be mutually exclusive. Some fundamentalists use technical analysis to examine stock patterns for entry or exit points for securities they have decided to purchase based on fundamental analysis.

Styles

Wealth managers generally classify equity investments based on size (relative market capitalization); geography (domestic, international, emerging market, frontier market); and relative valuation (value versus growth). Portfolios are often diversified across these classifications or tilted toward one or more categories. The classifications are also used to subdivide the equity asset class and treat the different subdivisions as different asset classes (e.g., small-capitalization growth, large-capitalization growth, small-capitalization value, and large-capitalization value).

Research has shown that over time and on average smaller-capitalization stocks have generated higher returns than large-capitalization stocks but with higher variability. This is consistent with the expectation that investors must be compensated for taking on additional risk. The higher the risk, the higher the return required to compensate the investor for that risk. Research has also shown that adding international stocks to a portfolio is an effective diversification strategy, except in times of market stress when securities globally can become more highly correlated.

Growth versus Value—Fama and French

One of the classifications receiving the most attention and controversy is the classification of stocks into growth stocks or value stocks. On the surface, the issue of a growth versus value style seems simple. Until recently, it was not much of a discussion. The client who wanted growth was advised to look for high-growth managers and close his or her eyes to short-term

---

[30]Andrew Lo, Harry Mamaysky, and Jiang Wang, "Foundations of Technical Analysis: Computational Algorithms, Statistical Inference, and Empirical Implementation," *Journal of Finance*, Vol. 55, No. 4 (August 2000).

volatility. The client who couldn't sleep with volatility should seek out stodgy value managers and accept lower returns.

The investment world has changed, and the old paradigm has been shattered. In order to understand how and why, it is important to know investment history. Graham and Dodd's *Security Analysis,* published in 1934, was the seminal event regarding the concept of intrinsic value in security pricing and had a strong focus on dividends and the balance sheet. Subsequently, researchers have investigated variations based on earnings projections rather than dividends, and the price-to-earnings (P/E) ratio has become a measure of prominence. Investment research, once a field only for academic dilettantes,[31] became a legitimate calling. One of the areas of interest to this new crop of investment-theory academics was the study of market returns. Gene Fama and Ken French were two academics who joined forces to consider this question. These two University of Chicago professors posed the following questions:

- Which of the many variables, claimed to have some value in explaining market return, really did have value?
- Of the variables that had value, what subset provided the most information if they were all combined?

Their research was first released as a white paper titled "Size and Book-to-Market Equity: Returns and Economic Fundamentals."[32] It was finalized and published as "Cross Section of Variation in Expected Stock Returns" in the *Journal of Finance* in June 1992. Their conclusions, summarized in Exhibit 14.3, stimulated a debate that continues today.

EXHIBIT 14.3   Summary of Fama and French Results, July 1963 to December 1990

Factor	Result
Beta	Not meaningful.
Size	Size is significant. Small stocks have higher standard deviations than large stocks.
Beta and size	Size is significant. Not only is beta not meaningful, but it works in the wrong direction although not statistically significantly so. Adjusted for size, low-beta stocks have higher returns than high-beta stocks.
Book value	Book value is significant. Stocks with high book-to-market ratios have higher returns than stocks with low book-to-market ratios.
Leverage	Adjusted for book value of assets, the smaller the company and the greater the book value of equity assets, the greater the stock return. Leverage is significant.
Earnings	Earnings are significant. Stocks with high earnings yields (E/P) have higher returns than stocks with low earnings yields.
Size and book-to-market	Both factors are significant, and in the same way as when each factor is considered separately.

(Continued)

---

[31]Remember Milton Friedman's comments regarding Markowitz's dissertation quoted in Chapter 7, "It's not math, it's not economics, it's not even business administration."

[32]Eugene F. Fama and Kenneth R. French, "Size and Book-to-Market Equity: Returns and Economic Fundamentals," draft paper (June 1992), 1–33.

EXHIBIT 14.3. (Continued)

Factor	Result
Size, book-to-market, and earnings yield	Only size and book-to-market are significant when the three factors are taken together; earnings yield is not meaningful.

Source: Dimensional Fund Advisors, Inc., "The Dimensions of Stock Returns," February 1992.

The Fama/French research has became known as the three-factor model after the three factors (market risk, company size, and book-to-market ratio) that collectively explain 95 percent of the variability of expected market returns. By now you may be wondering what all of this has to do with the subject at hand—growth versus value. The first two factors, market risk and company size, are easy to accept. The market factor simply suggests that the higher a security's covariance relative to market, the higher the returns. The second factor suggests that the higher the small company allocation in the equity portfolio, the higher the returns.

The third factor suggests that the wealth manager who wishes to invest clients' money for higher returns should seek value managers, not growth managers. Although the original research was based on domestic equities, subsequent research suggests that the value factor is universal.[33] Morningstar/Ibbotson provides updated Fama-French data each year in the *Ibbotson SBBI Classic Yearbook*. The 2010 yearbook provides cumulative compound average returns and standard deviation of annual returns from 1928 to 2009, summarized in Exhibit 14.4.

EXHIBIT 14.4   Fama-French-Based Data, 1928–2009

	Compound Average Return	Standard Deviation
FF large growth stocks	8.7%	20.4%
FF large value stocks	11.0	28.0
FF small growth stocks	9.0	33.5
FF small value stocks	13.9	33.0

Also, as shown in Exhibit 14.4, higher returns for the size factor are associated with higher standard deviations. This is consistent with the tenet of the capital asset pricing model that higher returns are associated with higher systematic risk. The surprise in the Fama-French research was the third return factor—higher book-to-market. This is a measure with value—a high book-to-market ratio (or conversely a low price-to-book ratio) indicates a low market price relative to the underlying assets of the company. Results also indicated that the higher returns associated with the book-to-market factor were not necessarily associated with higher levels of systematic risk. Notice that small value stocks exhibited a higher return than small growth stocks but not a higher standard deviation.

---

[33]For example, a number of articles in the *Financial Analysts Journal*, including "Can Fundamentals Predict Japanese Stock Returns?" by Louis K. C. Chan, Yasushi Hamao, and Josef Lakonishok, Vol. 49, No. 4 (July/August 1993): 63–69; "International Value and Growth Stock Returns" by Cario Capaul, Ian Rowley, and William F. Sharpe, Vol. 49, No. 1 (January/February 1993): 27–36; and "Value versus Growth Stocks: Book-to-Market-Growth and Beta" by Robert S. Harris and Felicia C. Marston, Vol. 50, No. 5 (September/October 1994): 18–24. See also "Value versus Growth: The International Evidence," by Eugene F. Fama and Kenneth R. French in *Journal of Finance*, Vol. 53, No. 6 (December 1998): 1975–99.

Much of the debate regarding this high book-to-market factor (i.e., the value factor) centers on its lack of a theoretical underpinning.[34] Fama and French readily admit that the fundamentals driving the book-to-market effect are not well understood. Many academics argue that without a definite theory, the empirical results are interesting but may simply be a chance blip in the data. Fischer Black, famous for the Black-Scholes option pricing formula, warns that the availability of market data provides a false sense of security and a temptation to data mine (i.e., search historical data for a period during which the data will confirm the researchers' conclusions). Black suggests that "Fama and French do not seem to believe much in theory."

Although the Fama-French-based research makes a strong case for investing solely in value securities, agreement on this conclusion is not unanimous, either in academia or in practice.

Growth versus Value—Practical Issues

Even if a wealth manager accepts the concept of a value factor, there remains the problem of describing value. Value seems to be a classic case of "in the eyes of the beholder." Fama and French used the simple book-to-market ratio as their measure. However, it is not the only choice. SEI research suggests a number of subclassifications of value:

- Relative dividend yield (i.e., yield > historical average).
- Low expectations—multifactors (e.g., price-to-book, price-to-earnings, dividends, so-called fallen angels).

Morningstar/Ibbotson uses the following criteria to create the Morningstar Style Indices based on market capitalization and value versus growth:

- Large cap is defined as the top 70 percent of market capitalization among U.S. publicly traded securities.
- Mid cap is defined as the next 20 percent of market capitalization.
- Small cap is defined as the next 7 percent of market capitalization (the last 3 percent is excluded from classification).
- Value stocks are classified based on five value factors—forward price-to-earnings ratio, price to book, price to sales, price to cash flow, and dividend yield. The greatest weight is allocated to the forward price-to-earnings ratio. Value stocks represent about one-third of the available stocks in each capitalization category.

---

[34]Fama and French argue that the higher returns must be related to either rewards for taking risks (perhaps from leverage) or inefficient pricing (perhaps from behavioral biases). In their initial inquiry into the matter in their 1992 study, they find that simple tests are inconsistent with long-term market overreaction, and state, "The systematic patterns in fundamentals give us some hope that size and book-to-market proxy for risk factors." They eschewed behavioral explanations in a 1995 paper that showed that higher returns from value and small stocks are related to improvements in subsequent profitability and cash flow of the next four years; see Eugene Fama and Kenneth French, "Size and Book-to-Market Factors in Earnings and Returns," *Journal of Finance*, Vol. 50, No. 1 (March 1995): 131–155. They remain similarly unconvinced of behavioral explanations in their recent work, saying that "proxies for expected net cash flows will identify differences in expected returns whether they are due to irrational pricing or rational risks. Thus, evidence that variables that predict future cash flows also predict returns does not, by itself, help us determine how much variation in expected returns is caused by risk and how much is caused by mispricing." See Eugene Fama and Kenneth French, "Dissecting Anomalies," *Journal of Finance*, Vol. 63, No. 4 (August 2008): 1653–1678. In the journals, the debate continues.

- Growth stocks are classified based on five growth factors—forward long-term earnings growth rate, book value growth, sales growth, cash flow growth, and trailing earnings growth. The greatest weight is allocated to the forward long-term earnings growth rate. Growth stocks represent about one-third of the available stocks in each capitalization category.
- Core stocks are those not classified as value or growth. They represent the remaining one-third of the available stocks in each capitalization category.

Data on these indexes are available from June 1997 through December 2009 and are summarized in Exhibit 14.5.

EXHIBIT 14.5   Morningstar Style Index Family Compound Annual Total Return

U.S. Market Index	U.S. Value Index	U.S. Core Index	U.S. Growth Index
4.02%	5.00%	5.09%	1.14%
Large-Cap Index	Large Value Index	Large Core Index	Large Growth Index
3.07%	3.88%	4.26%	0.06%
Mid-Cap Index	Mid Value Index	Mid Core Index	Mid Growth Index
6.25%	7.71%	6.74%	3.71%
Small-Cap Index	Small Value Index	Small Core Index	Small Growth Index
6.14%	8.57%	8.57%	1.69%

Source: Ibbotson SBBI 2010 Classic Yearbook, p. 99. © Morningstar.

These differences in definition can result in significantly different portfolio structures, however, as shown by the data in Exhibit 14.5. Similar results have been shown under different definitions.

Another issue related to the definition of value is distinguishing between valuable companies and valuable securities. It is the stock that is priced by the market. Thus, the stock of a valuable company may be priced so high relative to the company's value that there is no value in the stock (i.e., it is overpriced). Or a lousy company's stock may be so underpriced that even relative to its poor prospects the stock may have value. Relating a stock's price to the company's fundamentals (e.g., book value, historical earnings, forward earnings, sales, cash flow) is intended to accommodate this issue, but does not do so completely. Additionally, selecting securities solely with a value criterion might result in a portfolio overweighted in a few industries and underweighted in others.

Value stocks are not very pretty. Don Phillips quotes value managers, recalling that "the stocks that made a difference were the ones that make you want to hold your nose."[35] Gene Fama says that a value manager does not manage a portfolio but instead manages a kennel, a kennel of "dogs." Hence, value investing runs afoul of the client's heuristics (e.g., fear of regret). If the client buys a value stock and it goes down: what a dummy. If, however, the client buys a stock in a good company that all the experts like (i.e., a growth stock) and it declines in value, it's either bad management or bad luck: no blame on the client.

An important study concerning the failure of value managers to live up to the promise of extra returns attributable to the Fama-French value factor was John Rekenthaler's article, "Where Have All the Top Value Funds Gone?"[36] in the April 1995 *5-Star Investor* newsletter.

---

[35]Evan Simonoff, "Value: Why Funds Can't Find It," *Financial Planning*, July 1995, 38–44.

[36]The *5-Star Investor* is one of the few newsletters I regularly read. Although I consider the tables and fund statistics of little value, the commentary alone is worth the price of admission.

In the article, he notes that many academics and practitioners claim that the way to great returns is to buy value. He adds:

There's only one catch: It doesn't work that way in the mutual-fund industry. Value investing may dominate the academic studies, but it sure doesn't dominate the fund performance charts.

Based on 5-, 10-, and 15-year periods, Morningstar studies concluded that growth funds outperformed value funds. Rekenthaler then asks,

Who is to blame? . . . if growth funds have performed unexpectedly well relative to value funds, given the academic evidence, then either growth funds have been especially well-run or value fund managers have failed in some fashion.

Morningstar addressed this question by preparing the two simple exhibits reproduced here as Exhibits 14.6 and 14.7. The tables compare the performance of growth and value style funds with the performance of similarly labeled Wilshire stock indexes for various periods through February 28, 1995. A negative number indicates that the funds trailed the indexes by that amount.

EXHIBIT 14.6   Growth-Style Funds versus the Indexes: A Draw?

	5-Year Excess Total Return	10-Year Excess Total Return	15-Year Excess Total Return
Large growth	−1.31%	−1.37%	−0.54%
Mid growth	−2.73	−0.78	−0.44
Small growth	−1.26	−1.10	−1.19

EXHIBIT 14.7   Value versus the Indexes: Not Even Close

	5-Year Excess Total Return	10-Year Excess Total Return	15-Year Excess Total Return
Large value	−0.30%	−2.87%	−3.75%
Mid value	−3.90	−3.26	−4.99
Small value	−2.41	−4.19	−7.86

The failure of growth managers, in most cases, to match their index benchmarks is in line with what one might expect for average, after expense, performance. The magnitude of the failure of value managers is staggering. Rekenthaler concludes by suggesting that the exhibits demonstrate:

that investors seeking the most profitable funds over the long haul may need to attempt something more complex than simply seeking those funds with the cheapest, ugliest portfolios.

To supplement his conclusion, Rekenthaler includes examples of underperforming value managers he assumes managed based on the academic research related to the value factor—specifically the American Association of Individual Investors (AAII)'s shadow stock and

DFA's 9–10 Small Cap. The assumption, however, is incorrect. These funds were not designed to be value funds as defined by Fama, French, and others. The AAII shadow stock uses criteria other than book-to-market (e.g., institutional holdings) and the DFA 9–10 is based solely on a size criterion. We found the statistics in the Morningstar article compelling, but the conclusions misleading.

We believe that the underperformance of the active value managers is due to two factors:

1. Their efforts to add value by eliminating the dogs in fact subtracts value by eliminating the real value stocks.
2. By their very nature, value stocks, particularly small-cap value stocks, have relatively large trading spreads; therefore, active management of a value portfolio generates significant trading costs.

Contrary to Rekenthaler's conclusion, the solution to participating in the benefits of value investing is not to search for more complexity. It is just the opposite. Search for greater simplicity. Eliminate the active management, thereby avoiding the errors of active value management as well as saving the management fee and the transaction costs. We should repeat another important point used in an earlier chapter and earlier in this chapter. Wealth managers are dealing with individuals. While value may have been shown to outperform growth in the long run, performance from year to year varies. Exhibit 14.8 shows the returns from large growth and large value from 1980 to 2009. This table shows returns based on Fama-French's classification of growth versus value stocks, with the winner highlighted each period. Note the constant flip-flopping of value and growth style returns. If an investor's portfolio is invested in only one style, it will have periods of underperformance relative to the overall market or other styles. This could lead the investor to lose a long-term focus and to want to sell or switch styles at precisely the wrong time.

Harold's firm finds the argument in favor of value so compelling that they consciously overweight their core allocations with a significant tilt to value.

Regarding the implementation of value investing, the wealth manager should consider passive management. After reading Rekenthaler's Morningstar 5-Star article on the value fund performance/underperformance mystery, Harold wondered how the managers used by his firm would fare in a similar comparison. However, instead of comparing DFA value funds to the Ibbotson recommendations, he compared DFA value funds' performance to the performance of the active value managers he had previously selected for his clients' portfolios. DFA won hands down and across the board. Add to DFA's performance premium the inherent tax advantage of passive management and the elimination of style drift risk, and it was an easy decision for our investment committee to conclude that our value allocations would largely be passive. Needless to say, Harold is a big fan of DFA. We recommend that all wealth managers make a similar analysis of their value allocations and compare the performance of their active value managers to passive value managers.

FIXED INCOME ANALYSIS AND STRATEGIES

Fixed income securities, such as bonds, are generally perceived as less risky than equity securities, and the long-term return and standard deviation of return data support this perception. However, fixed income securities typically have offered a lower average return than

EXHIBIT 14.8   Comparison of Investment Styles

	1980	1981	1982	1983	1984	1985	1986	1987	1988	1989
Large Growth	35.2%	−7.1%	21.5%	14.7%	−0.7%	32.6%	14.4%	7.4%	12.5%	36.1%
Large Value	16.5%	12.8%	27.7%	26.9%	16.2%	31.8%	21.8%	−2.8%	26.0%	29.7%

	1990	1991	1992	1993	1994	1995	1996	1997	1998	1999
Large Growth	1.1%	43.3%	6.4%	2.4%	2.0%	37.2%	21.3%	31.6%	34.6%	29.4%
Large Value	−12.8%	27.4%	23.6%	19.5%	−5.8%	37.7%	13.4%	31.9%	16.2%	−0.2%

	2000	2001	2002	2003	2004	2005	2006	2007	2008	2009
Large Growth	−13.6%	−15.6%	−21.5%	26.3%	6.5%	2.8%	8.9%	14.1%	−33.7%	27.9%
Large Value	5.8%	−1.2%	−32.5%	35.1%	18.9%	12.2%	22.6%	−6.5%	−49.0%	39.2%

Source: Ibbotson SBBI 2010 Classic Yearbook. © Morningstar.

equities, appropriate for the lower risk involved. Fixed income securities, as with any investment, are still subject to risks such as:

- Credit risk/default risk
- Liquidity risk
- Inflation risk
- Interest rate risk
- Reinvestment rate risk

A fixed income security is a credit arrangement where the investor (creditor) is lending money to the issuing entity (such as company or government body). Credit risk includes the risk that the issuer will default on its obligation, missing interest and/or principal payments. It can also include a decline in the creditworthiness of the issuer (e.g., a ratings downgrade), which causes the current market value of the bond to decline. In order to consider credit risk, investors can either perform their own credit analysis of the issuer and the particular bond issue or can rely on the work of others such as credit rating agencies. Credit analysis is much like fundamental analysis of equity securities—the financial statements, ratios, collateral, and business of the issuer are examined to assess the level of risk involved and whether the promised yield to maturity is sufficient to compensate for that risk.

The market for individual bonds is less liquid than that for publicly traded equities and hence bonds have a higher level of liquidity risk—the risk that the bond cannot be sold quickly at a desired price. Liquidity risk also increases in times of crisis.

Inflation risk is the risk that inflation will be higher than expected when a fixed income security was issued and the real return received will be less than expected. Inflation risk and credit risk are also a component of interest rate risk. For example, say an investor purchases a $1,000 bond offering to pay 5 percent a year when interest rates on other securities of similar risk and maturity are also paying 5 percent. Recall our discussion of bond math and risk in Chapter 7. The fair price would be $1,000. If the required interest rate for this investment rises (because inflation increases, credit risk increases for this particular bond, or general market risk for similar securities rises), then the current value of this bond will decline. If the investor holds the bonds until maturity and the bond makes all promised payments, the investor's return is still expected to be 5 percent; however, if the investor desires to liquidate the bond earlier than maturity, the realized return will be less. Conversely, when required interest rates fall, current bond values increase. Note from Chapter 7 that duration and modified duration, measures of the weighted average time to maturity of a bond, are indicators as to how sensitive a bond's price is relative to changes in required interest rates.

Reinvestment risk moves in the opposite direction. The expected realized return on a bond assumes that any interest payments received can be reinvested at the expected yield to maturity on the bond. If interest rates decline after the bond is purchased, the investor will not be able to reinvest the payments received at the expected rate and the ultimate realized return will be less than expected, even though held to maturity. Conversely, if interest rates rise after purchase, the investor can reinvest interest payments received at a higher rate and the realized yield will be higher than expected. It should be apparent that since interest rate risk and reinvestment risk move in opposite directions, they can mitigate or offset each other,[37] but interest rate risk tends be the more dominant effect.

An Immunization Strategy

If investors need cash at a particular point in time, they might be inclined to purchase a portfolio of bonds with a maturity equal to their time horizon. However, they are subject to reinvestment rate risk, as noted earlier, and do not have an offset for interest rate risk since they are not planning on selling the securities prior to maturity. It turns out that duration is the point in time when the impact of interest rate risk is expected to offset the impact of reinvestment rate risk. If the investor purchases a portfolio of bonds with a duration equal to the investment time horizon, then these two risks are mitigated (at least for relatively small parallel shifts in the yields). Immunization can also be performed when there are multiple time horizons to satisfy multiple expected obligations, although the process is more complicated.

A Cash Flow Matching Strategy

In a cash flow matching strategy, bonds are selected for the portfolio such that the expected principal and interest payments to be received match the cash flow needs. This process involves first purchasing a bond to satisfy the final expected cash flow and working backwards to the present time such that each needed cash flow is satisfied with the sum of future interest and principal payments.

---

[37]Assuming the investor is not using the income for living expenses.

Yield Curve Risk—Ladders, Bullets, and Barbells

The yield curve measures the current level of yields to maturity of bonds of different levels of maturity. Exhibit 14.9 presents a recent yield curve on U.S. Treasury fixed income securities.

EXHIBIT 14.9   Yield Curve at October 15, 2010

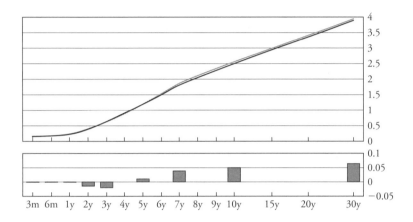

The yield curve in Exhibit 14.9 is upward sloping, which is its normal shape. The longer the time to maturity, the higher the required yield to maturity. On occasion the yield curve can be flat, inverted, or humped. As would be expected, the shape of the yield curve changes over time. The curve can shift in a parallel fashion (similar change in yield for all maturities) or nonparallel fashion where the curve flattens, becomes steeper, or becomes humped. Thus, there is another risk of investing in a portfolio of bonds—the risk that the yield curve shifts in a manner adverse to the bond holdings.

A laddered bond portfolio would have bonds of varying maturity along a range of the yield curve and is often used as a simple version of cash flow matching and to have exposure across the yield curve. As bonds mature, the cash flow is used for client needs or reinvested at the long end of the ladder. As an alternative to a ladder, the investor may prefer a bullet strategy to invest only in either the long end of the yield curve (higher duration and volatility) or the short end of the yield curve (lower duration and volatility). Another alternative would be to have a portfolio with a similar aggregate duration to a laddered portfolio but investing at both the long and short ends (a barbell strategy) or investing at some midpoint (an alternative bullet strategy). The choice of strategy would depend on expected future shifts in the yield curve.

Assuming that three portfolios (ladder, barbell, and bullet) have the same duration equal to the investment time horizon and similar convexity, then they will be immunized and behave similarly for parallel shifts in the yield curve. However, for nonparallel shifts, the barbell strategy would be the riskiest. A barbell strategy could pay off if there is a nonparallel shift in the yield curve such that long-term interest rates decline more than short-term rates. The long-term bonds increase in value while a high yield is maintained on short-term bonds. However, a nonparallel shift, where long-term rates increase but short-term rates decrease, would be costly for a barbell strategy.

ALTERNATIVE INVESTMENTS

Investments in alternatives are often viewed as an asset class separate from other asset classes such as equity and fixed income investments, and treated as such in an optimization. In reality, alternative investments are not a separate asset class. An investment in private equity or a long-only hedge fund is just another type of equity investment. Some have argued that a long-only hedge fund is simply a private pooled vehicle or money manager's compensation scheme as opposed to an alternative asset. As noted by Anson, "Alternative assets . . . are just alternative investments within an existing asset class."[38] As with classifying equities into capitalization ranges or value versus growth investments, alternative investments can be treated as separate asset classes or categories for purposes of optimization and allocation since they tend to have low correlation with traditional investments in public securities (other than long-only hedge funds).

We subscribe to Anson's view. Alternative investments can include alternative assets or alternative investment strategies that can either hedge other investments or expand the investment opportunity set. They can include investments other than those in traditional long-only equities and fixed income. As with others, we include real estate in the alternatives definition, recognizing full well that real estate investments have been traditional investments for many investors (including many of our clients, whose families accumulated their wealth through real estate) for centuries. We will discuss the following typical alternative investments:

- Real estate
- Private equity/venture capital
- Commodities/managed futures
- Hedge funds
- Structured products (including credit derivatives)

Real Estate

There are a variety of ways of investing in real estate. The most common form for most individuals is a direct investment in individual properties, in most cases leveraged. Other means include real estate limited partnerships (RELPs), real estate investment trusts (REITs), mutual funds, and exchange-trade funds (ETFs).

Direct investments in real estate provide the investor with the opportunity to select key properties and control decision making regarding the investment, such as the timing of disposition. However, there are a number of drawbacks to direct investments. Unless the client's investable assets are substantial, it is difficult to achieve adequate diversification. Further, real estate is by its nature illiquid, and it is likely to be difficult to sell in a timely manner at a desired price. As demonstrated in the recent financial crisis, it may be necessary to hold the property for many years before liquidation unless the investor is willing to sell at a distressed price. The lack of current objective market prices for properties also makes it difficult to evaluate periodic returns on this portion of the portfolio and to compute correlations with other investments.

Real estate limited partnerships (RELPs) are a means of investing in a diversified portfolio of real estate managed by a professional manager while maintaining limited liability for

---

[38]Anson (2009, 3).

losses. In exchange, the investor gives up a portion of the income through fees paid the managers and organizers of the partnership as well as potentially a portion of any gains upon disposition of property. RELPs are not much more liquid (and can be less liquid) than direct investments in real estate as there is a limited secondary market for limited partnership interests. As with direct investments, RELPs also lack objective periodic prices for evaluating returns.

Real estate investment trusts (REITs) can be publicly traded or nontraded. Effectively, a REIT is treated much like a mutual fund and has favorable tax provisions in jurisdictions where they are available. Generally, a REIT must annually distribute most of its income to shareholders and in exchange is not taxed on its income at the trust level. REITs provide for diversification and in the case of publicly traded REITs, have better liquidity than other real estate investments. Publicly traded REITs also provide market prices for return and correlation computations. Since they trade like stocks, they often behave like stocks. The correlation from 2000 to 2010 was about 0.84 with large-cap stocks and 0.90 with mid- and small-cap stocks.[39] REITs that are not publicly traded lack both price information and liquidity. Oddly, we have heard distributors of these products tout them at financial planning conferences as a low-volatility investment. Low volatility derived from a lack of current objective pricing is not an advantage!

There are many funds (open-end mutual funds, closed-end funds, and ETFs) that invest in REITs. Through these indirect investments, additional diversification can be achieved, but that is in exchange for an additional layer of expenses. In a matter of bad timing, a major financial services fund attempted to launch a closed-end fund invested in high-quality real estate properties in 2008, but withdrew registration of the fund in early 2009. We would expect more vehicles for diversified investments in real estate properties to become available once the industry is past the recent crisis.

Private Equity/Venture Capital

Similar to real estate investments, private equity investments are made through limited partnerships, limited liability companies, or similar entities in which the general partner is a private equity firm managing the fund. The fund is typically invested in a portfolio of private companies. The general partner may also be actively involved in managing portfolio companies. Venture capital is a subset of private equity that involves investments in new ventures. Types of private equity firms include:

- Venture capital firms
- Buyout firms (including leveraged buyouts)
- Mezzanine financing
- Growth equity/private investments in public equity
- Distressed investments

Some private equity funds do not stick to one strategy and may use multiple types of investments. In fact, in recent years there has been some blurring between private equity funds and hedge funds.

Venture capital firms can be investments at various stages of a new venture's life such as seed financing, start-up financing, or later stage (expansion) financing. Buyouts involve taking

---

[39]Morningstar Principia Database at December 2010.

an existing company private using a highly leveraged transaction that may involve the retention of existing management.

Mezzanine financing includes debt and equity (often hybrid) financing to firms requiring capital for expansion or operations beyond what they can obtain in traditional borrowing arrangements. This financing is subordinate to the company's traditional debt but has a preference over the company's equity investments—hence the term *mezzanine*.

Firms, including public firms, sometimes require equity capital but do not want to go through the time and expense of a public offering. A private offering of securities is often used as an alternative. The newly issued shares are restricted as to the type of investor and when they can subsequently be sold. As a result they are sold at a discount to the firm's previously issued equity.

Distressed investments are typically investments in debt securities of companies that are in trouble. Debt is purchased at a substantial discount. If the company's situation improves, the price of the debt recovers. Alternatively, the company may go through a recapitalization, reorganization, or bankruptcy where the distressed debt investor ends up as an equity owner.

Private equity investments provide access to types of investments and returns that may not be available in traditional debt and equity markets. The fee structure for private equity investments is high, including management fees of about 2 percent of capital and performance fees of 20 percent. In spite of high fees, Anson reports that venture capital firms have generated returns 400 to 800 basis points higher than large-capitalization public equities, while buyout firms have had excess returns of 100 to 200 basis points relative to public equities.[40] Correlations with large-capitalization equities range from 0.39 for venture capital to 0.79 for buyout firms.[41] There are of course offsets to the higher expected returns and lower correlations:[42]

- Private equity investments are illiquid.
- Large long-term continuing capital commitments are generally required.
- Information on the performance and valuation of underlying portfolio companies can be limited. Reported periodic returns of private equity funds therefore exhibit stale pricing.

A key to investing in private equities is performing due diligence on the general partner. It is especially critical to examine the performance of prior funds managed by the general partner. Private equity funds are complicated, with a waterfall structure that determines how distributions are apportioned between limited and general partners, and distributions may be delayed for many years—particularly for venture capital firms. The capital commitment, fee structure, and distribution structure for any private equity investment should be carefully examined.

Commodities/Managed Futures

Commodities are often proposed as an inflation hedge and strong diversification vehicle for adding to portfolios. Empirical evidence does support both propositions over the long term.

---

[40]Anson (2009, 417, 448).

[41]Ibid., 522.

[42]Jot K. Yau, Thomas Schneeweis, Thomas R. Robinson, and Lisa R. Weiss, "Alternative Investments Portfolio Management" in John L. Maginn, Donald L. Tuttle, Jerald E. Pinto, and Dennis W. McLeavey, eds. *Managing Investment Portfolios: A Dynamic Process*, 3rd edition. CFA Institute Investment Series (Hoboken, NJ: John Wiley & Sons, 2007): 509–510.

Correlations of commodities in the aggregate and energy commodities in particular with unexpected inflation are moderate—about 0.50. Correlations of commodities with large-capitalization stocks over the long term are near zero. We should note, however, that as with international investments, correlations of stock and commodities can increase in times of crisis and they did so very strongly in the recent crisis.

Investing in commodities in the past was difficult—limited to investing in physical commodities or commodities futures. Investing in physical commodities is not practical for most investors. Investing in commodities futures is complicated, involves leverage, and requires constant attention. This should be done only by someone with expertise in both the commodities and futures contracts. Evaluating commodities is also difficult. Unlike a stock or a bond, there are no expected cash flows from the investment to forecast. The prices of commodities are driven by supply and demand forces.

Today commodities can be included in a portfolio through the use of a managed futures account or through an exchange-traded fund (ETF) or exchange-traded note (ETN). Managed futures accounts for commodities are managed by commodity trading advisors, who can go long or short individual commodities. They often employ a trend-following strategy. ETFs or ETNs, in contrast, hold a basket of commodities or commodity futures that are long only and are designed to mimic some commodity index such as the S&P Goldman Sachs Commodity Index (GSCI) or Dow Jones–UBS Commodity index. There are a limited number of commodity ETFs; most of the exchange-traded commodities securities are structured as ETNs. Because ETNs are structured notes, they have the added complication of being subject to the credit risk of the issuer. Further, while their tax treatment is currently favorable, it is uncertain as to whether this will remain the case.

When investing in a commodity fund, it is important to understand the investment strategy, which commodities are involved, and which index, if any, the commodity fund is designed to mimic. Returns on different commodity indexes can be drastically different. For example, the GSCI is weighted by the world production (as well as liquidity) of the included commodities without limitation and is heavily weighted toward energy commodities, while the Dow Jones–UBS index has limits on the aggregate weighting per commodity group (33 percent maximum).

Some suggest that investments in commodity-related companies can be used as a substitute for commodities in a portfolio. As might be expected, correlations of commodity-related stocks with other stocks are quite high and much of the diversification benefit is lost.

Managed futures accounts can also be used for futures contracts other than commodities, such as financial futures and currency futures. Additionally, some mutual funds and ETFs have recently become available whereby the investor can get access to long and short managed futures without having to open a managed futures account.

Hedge Funds

Hedge funds are essentially private investment vehicles that can invest in a variety of markets and strategies.[43] The name implies the use of hedging strategies, such as derivatives and short selling; however, many hedge funds do not use these techniques. There are many ways to classify hedge fund strategies. Common classifications include:

---

[43]For more information, see Anson (2009) and Mark Hurley, "Alternative Investments," in *The Investment Think Tank*, Harold Evensky and Deena B. Katz, eds. (New York: Bloomberg/Wiley, 2004).

- Directional
- Event-driven
- Relative value
- Global macro/multistrategy
- Fund of funds

Directional funds include those that invest in long-only strategies, short-only strategies, or long/short strategies, such as 130/30. These funds are making a directional wager on the markets in which they invest. Event-driven funds invest in strategies such as merger arbitrage, distressed securities, credit arbitrage, and private investments in public entities. Relative value funds typically go long and short in related securities, purchasing the relatively inexpensive securities and selling the relatively expensive securities in an attempt to arbitrage the difference. Global macro and multistrategy funds invest in a variety of strategies, often based on expected global macroeconomic trends. Funds of funds create diversified portfolios of other hedge funds, but do so with an additional layer of fees.

As with private equity funds, the fee structure of hedge funds is high. The typical fund has had a management fee of 2 percent and performance fee of 20 percent; however, with the proliferation of funds some fee structures have come down from this level. Hedge funds are also illiquid and require a great deal of due diligence. Historical returns for hedge funds are difficult to evaluate due to the variety of fund strategies and biases in reported data. Since these are private investment vehicles, funds with poor performance have an incentive to not report their data to data aggregators. There are also problems with databases containing survivorship bias (only the strong funds survive) and backfill bias (only strong funds enter the database and their data is often backfilled in the index). Correlations with traditional asset classes can vary considerably, depending on the type of fund. Anson reports average correlations of hedge fund indexes with large-capitalization equities of about 0.60. As with private equity, funds' correlations are higher with small-capitalization equities.

Structured Products

Structured products can include a variety of investment instruments and products. They typically involve the use of derivatives or other contractual arrangements linked to other types of assets. Unfortunately, this category of alternative investments includes many of the products involved in the recent financial crisis—namely, credit derivatives and collateralized debt obligations. These toxic securities made their way into the unlikeliest of places, including many money market funds.

This alternative investment category also includes so-called principal-protected securities, which are structured products typically linked to an equity index but offering a floor value or minimum return. The offering documents of these instruments are complex and often obscure important information.[44] For example, it is not uncommon for a promotional brochure to state that the instrument will capture a large percentage increase in the S&P 500 index but fail to mention that the investor in this instrument is missing out on the dividend yield of the S&P 500 or that the annual return caps may significantly truncate the compounded return over the life of the investment.

---

[44]For a review of how to evaluate offering documents of these types of securities, see Howard Marmorstein, Thomas Robinson, David Schulte, and William Trent, "Evaluating the Offering Documents of Principal Protected Securities," *Journal of Financial Planning* (December 2006).

If structured products are to be used in part of a portfolio, they should be used cautiously. They require a thorough understanding of the assets underlying the instrument and how the instrument will vary in comparison with changes in the underlying asset. As a wealth manager, you also need to understand the embedded fees and expenses as well as the potential credit exposure. Do not invest in any product that both you and the client do not completely understand.

PARTING COMMENTS

This chapter has provided a framework for managing portfolios for individual investors, from the asset allocation decision to techniques for selecting and managing the individual investments within the portfolio. As noted at the inception, many wealth managers perform the asset allocation and overall management of the portfolio but use other money managers or funds to manage investments within specific asset classes. The following two chapters discuss the selection and evaluation of managers and funds.

RESOURCES

Anson, Mark J. P. 2009. *CAIA Level I: An Introduction to Core Topics in Alternative Investments.* Chartered Alternative Investment Analyst Series. Hoboken, NJ: John Wiley & Sons.

Bollen, Nicholas P., and Jeffrey A. Busse. 2004. "Short-Term Persistence in Mutual Fund Performance." *The Review of Financial Studies*, Vol. 18, No. 2 (Summer): 569–597.

Brown, Gavin, and Paul Draper. 1992. "Consistency of U.K. Pension Fund Investment Performance." Working paper 13-86. Anderson Graduate School of Management University of California at Los Angeles.

Carhart, Mark M. 1997. "On Persistence in Mutual Fund Performance." *Journal of Finance*, Vol. 52, No. 1 (March): 57–82.

Carhart, Mark M., Jennifer N. Carpenter, Anthony W. Lynch, and David K. Musto. 2002. "Mutual Fund Survivorship." *The Review of Financial Studies*, Vol. 15, No. 5: 1439–63.

Droms, William G., and David A. Walker. 1994. "Investment Performance of International Mutual Funds." *Journal of Financial Research*, Vol 17: 1–14.

Droms, William G., and David A. Walker. 2001a. "Persistence of Mutual Fund Operating Characteristics." *Applied Financial Economics*, Vol 11: 457–466.

Droms, William G., and David A. Walker. 2001b. "Performance Persistence of International Mutual Funds." *Global Finance Journal*, Vol. 12: 1–13.

Dunn, Patricia C., and Rolf D. Theisen. 1983. "How Consistently Do Active Managers Win?" *The Journal of Portfolio Management*, Vol. 9, No. 4 (Summer): 47–50.

Elton, E., M. Gruber, and J. Rentzler. 1990. "The Performance of Publicly Offered Commodity Funds," *Financial Analysts Journal*, Vol. 46, No. 4 (July/August): 23–30.

Fabozzi, Frank J. 2007. *Fixed Income Analysis*, 2nd edition. CFA Institute Investment Series. Hoboken, NJ: John Wiley & Sons.

Goetzmann, William N., and Roger G. Ibbotson. 1994. "Do Winners Repeat? Patterns in Mutual Fund Performance." *Journal of Portfolio Management*, Vol. 20 (Winter): 9–18.

Grinblatt, Mark, and Sheridan Titman. 1992. "The Persistence of Mutual Fund Performance." *Journal of Finance*, Vol. 47, No. 5: 1977–84.

Hendricks, Darryll, Jayendu Patel, and Richard Zeckhauser. 1993. "Hot Hands in Mutual Funds: Short-Run Persistence of Relative Performance, 1974–88." *Journal of Finance*, Vol 48, No. 1: 93–130.

Jan, Yin-Ching, and Mao-Wei Hung. 2004. "Short-Run and Long-Run Persistence in Mutual Funds." *Journal of Investing*, Vol 13 (Spring): 67–71.

Jensen, M. 1968. "The Performance of Mutual Funds in the Period 1945–1964." *Journal of Finance*, Vol. 23, No. 2 (May): 389–416.

Kahn, Ronald N., and Andrew Rudd. 1995. "Does Historical Performance Predict Future Performance?" *Financial Analysts Journal*, Vol. 51, No. 6 (November/December): 43–52.

Kirtzman, Mark. 1983. "Can Bond Managers Perform Consistently?" *The Journal of Portfolio Management*, Vol 9, No. 4 (Summer): 54–56.

Lehmann, Bruce N., and David M. Modest. 1987. "Mutual Fund Performance Evaluation: A Comparison of Benchmarks and Benchmark Comparisons." *Journal of Finance*, Vol. 42, No. 2 (June): 233–65.

Maginn, John L., Donald L. Tuttle, Jerald E. Pinto, and Dennis W. McLeavey, eds. 2007. *Managing Investment Portfolios: A Dynamic Process*, 3rd edition. CFA Institute Investment Series. Hoboken, NJ: John Wiley & Sons.

Murphy, John J. 1999. *Technical Analysis of the Financial Markets: A Comprehensive Guide to Trading Methods and Applications*. New York: New York Institute of Finance.

Pinto, Jerald E., Elaine Henry, Thomas R. Robinson, and John D. Stowe. 2010. *Equity Asset Valuation*, 2nd edition. CFA Institute Investment Series. Hoboken, NJ: John Wiley & Sons.

Pfeiffer, Shaun. 2010. Unpublished Texas Tech PhD Research Paper. Texas Tech University, Lubbock, Texas.

Robinson, Thomas R., Hennie van Greuning, Elaine Henry, and Michael A. Broihahn. 2009. *International Financial Statement Analysis*. CFA Institute Investment Series. Hoboken, NJ: John Wiley & Sons.

Yan, Xuemin. 2006. "The Determinants and Implications of Mutual Fund Cash Holdings: Theory and Evidence." *Financial Management*, Vol. 35, No. 2 (Summer): 67–91.

CHAPTER 15

PERFORMANCE APPRAISAL AND EVALUATION

An ounce of performance is worth pounds of promises.

—Mae West

In the previous chapter, we discussed the idea of portfolio management in terms of equity, fixed income, and alternative investment strategies. The next chapter discusses the process of selecting investment managers. Whether the wealth manager constructs portfolios with individual securities, selects managers for separately managed accounts, or constructs portfolios with mutual funds, being able to measure, evaluate, and appraise portfolio performance is a critical component of portfolio construction monitoring described in the wealth management process in Chapter 1. Performance is ultimately measured by clients' ability to meet their goals in a wealth management context, and sound portfolio management is a crucial step toward that end goal. Therefore, this chapter focuses on principles of portfolio performance measurement in the traditional sense.

MEASURING RETURN

The notion of measuring return seems straightforward. It is simply a portfolio's change in value over a given period divided by its initial value in the period.

$$r_t = \frac{MV_t - MV_0}{MV_0}$$

MV_t is the market value at the end of the evaluation period, while MV_0 is the market value at the beginning of the evaluation period.[1] The market value of the account should include all realized and unrealized capital gains, dividends and interest received, as well as any accrued fixed income interest that has been earned but not yet received.

---

[1]An equivalent expression is $r_t = MV_1/MV_0 - 1$.

Interim Portfolio Cash Flows

The situation is a bit more complicated when the portfolio experiences either cash inflows or outflows during the evaluation period. An investment manager should obviously not be credited with an increase in portfolio value due to a discretionary deposit by the client. Likewise, the portfolio manager should not be penalized for a decline in market value due to a discretionary client withdrawal from the portfolio. An accommodation must be made.

Suppose Michael Conner is managing Kate Dean's portfolio. At the beginning of 2011, the portfolio has a market value of $1 million. At the end of December 2011, the portfolio's market value is $1,300,000. If there are no interim cash flows, then the portfolio experienced an impressive 30 percent return during the year.

$$ r_t = \frac{\$1,300,000 - \$1,000,000}{\$1,000,000} = 30.0\% $$

Let's suppose more realistically only part of the account's impressive increase in market value was attributable to Michael's investment prowess because Kate actually deposited $200,000 into the portfolio on May 1, 2011. Obviously, Michael was responsible for only $100,000 of the increase in portfolio value, which is still more than respectable.[2] He informs Kate that the portfolio return for the year was 10 percent—the $100,000 investment gain divided by $1 million initial value.

Kate's not so sure. She readily concedes that Michael earned $100,000 worth of investment returns. She points out, however, that Michael had $1,200,000 of capital to work with to earn those returns—the original $1 million account value plus the $200,000 deposit. She believes the correct calculation is $100,000/$1,200,000 = 8.33%.

Who's right?

They're both wrong. This situation is tricky because the cash flow occurred during the evaluation period. Although the portfolio started out with $1 million of invested capital at the beginning of the year, it had $1,200,000 of invested capital for two-thirds of the year.

If the cash flow had occurred at the end of the year, Michael would have been right. If it had occurred at the beginning of the year, Kate would have been right. Since the cash flow occurred closer to the beginning of the year, Kate is "less wrong" than Michael.

Time-Weighted Return

Kate suggests breaking this Gordian knot by splitting the annual evaluation period into two periods defined by the timing of the deposit on May 1 and calculating a return for each subperiod. Notice that the two subperiods have different lengths. This will not matter for our purposes here, but will come into play in the next section.

We will need to know, however, the account's value on the cash flow date to calculate the two subperiod returns. Suppose the market value of the account on May 1 was $1,100,000, including the deposit, as in Exhibit 15.1. The account actually lost $100,000 after taking into account the deposit!

---

[2] We are ignoring for the time being how the performance compares to a relevant benchmark index.

	1-Jan	1-May	31-Dec
Market value	$1,000,000	$1,100,000	$1,300,000
Cash flow		$ 200,000	

EXHIBIT 15.1   Hypothetical Example of an Account with Interim Cash Flows

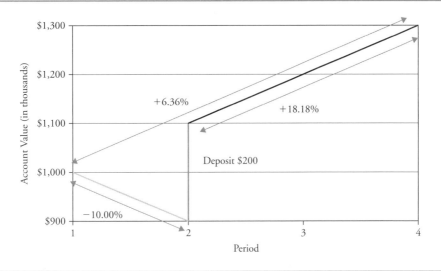

The returns for each subperiod are calculated by adjusting the ending market value of our simple return equation for any cash flows into or out of the account. In this case, the $200,000 deposit at the end of the first subperiod is subtracted from $1,100,000 end-of-period market value because that amount of the account's growth was not attributable to investment returns.[3] No adjustment is required for the second subperiod because there was no cash flow.

The returns for the two periods are:

$$r_{\text{Jan-Apr}} = \frac{(\$1,100,000 - \$200,000) - \$1,000,000}{\$1,000,000} = -10.00\%$$

$$r_{\text{May-Dec}} = \frac{(\$1,300,000 - 0) - \$1,100,000}{\$1,100,000} = 18.18\%$$

The portfolio began the year with $1 million of invested capital and lost 10 percent during the first third of the year (i.e., four months). It began the second two-thirds of the year (i.e., 8 months) with $1,100,000 of invested capital having accounted for the deposit and earned 18.18 percent for the remaining eight months. We've displayed this graphically in Exhibit 15.1.

---

[3]If the cash flow were a withdrawal rather than a deposit, we would have added the amount of the withdrawal.

So how much did the portfolio return over the entire year? Kate says that the portfolio earned 6.36 percent, calculated as:

$$(1 + r_{\text{Jan-Apr}})(1 + r_{\text{May-Dec}}) - 1 = (1 + -0.10)(1 + 0.1818) - 1 = 6.36\%$$

The process of multiplying 1 plus each subperiod's return with another is called geometrically linking subperiod returns. This calculation is referred to as the time-weighted return.

Internal Rate of Return

Michael disagrees. He suggests calculating the portfolio's internal rate of return (IRR)[4]—the return that, when applied to the beginning market value (including the interim cash flows) for the amount of time each was available for investment, yields the portfolio's ending market value. In other words, Michael sets the future value of beginning market value and interim cash flows (using the amount of time each was in the portfolio as the compounding period) equal to the ending market value. Specifically, in this case, the annual return is:

$$\$1,000,000(1 + \text{IRR})^{1/3} + \$200,000(1 + \text{IRR})^{2/3} = \$1,300,000$$

Notice that the exponents associated with the beginning value and interim cash flow on the left-hand side correspond to the amount of time (i.e., the proportion of the year) those funds were in the portfolio and available for investment. Solving by trial-and-error for IRR, Michael figures the portfolio experienced an 8.84 percent return, which is quite different from (and far more flattering than) Kate's result. Why is Michael's figure higher?

Kate calculated the time-weighted return (TWR), whereas Michael calculated the internal rate of return (IRR). Michael's IRR is greater than Kate's TWR in this case because Kate deposited money into the account just prior to a period of strong performance. Had the second subperiod performance been poor relative to the first, the IRR would have been less than the TWR. In other words, Michael's IRR calculation benefited from Kate timing her deposit well.

In general, money managers should be neither credited nor penalized for the timing of client-initiated deposits or withdrawals. The TWR neutralizes the impact of client-initiative deposits and withdrawals into an account and is therefore viewed as a better measure of evaluating the manager's performance. The Global Investment Performance Standards (GIPS)[5] established by CFA Institute generally require that the TWR be used when presenting performance data to prospective clients.[6]

The differences between the two methods are generally modest if the cash flows are relatively small or interim return volatility is low. Differences are quite significant if the cash flows are large relative to the account value or if volatility during the evaluation period is high.

In certain alternative investment asset classes, such as private equity and real estate, the IRR might be the recommended return calculation because the manager rather than the client

---

[4]Also known as a money-weighted return.

[5]The GIPS are a set of standardized, industry-wide ethical principles that provide investment firms with guidance on how to calculate and report their investment results to prospective clients.

[6]However, the wealth manager's role is broader than that of a traditional money manager; the wealth manager is concerned with both the unique return achieved by the client (i.e., the IRR) and the return attributable to the portfolio investment policy (TWR). Therefore, the wealth manager should consider providing and explaining the meanings of both returns to the client.

may take cash flows into and out of the investment portfolio through the use of capital calls and liquidations. This is generally the exception rather than the rule, however.

In addition, the IRR might be appropriate for wealth managers to measure their own performance if they are advising their clients on when to deposit and withdraw cash from their portfolios.

As you can see, having an agreed-upon calculation methodology among investment managers is an important step in achieving comparability among managers. The GIPS are designed to facilitate comparability. Providing clients with both calculations provides information for the client regarding how their portfolio performed (i.e., the IRR) and how the advisor's allocation advice contributed to that performance (TWR).

Modified Dietz Method

You may have noticed from the previous example that the TWR requires the portfolio to be valued on the date of all large cash flows. In fact, the GIPS require firms to value portfolios at least monthly as well as on the date of large cash flows to support the TWR calculation. For publicly traded and highly liquid asset classes, this is generally not difficult aside from the administrative obligations. It can be more problematic for less liquid assets, however. This was particularly so before technological advances automated much of our data gathering processes.

There are, therefore, approximations to the TWR process of geometrically linking subperiod returns called the Deitz and modifed Dietz methods. Basically, the modified Dietz method accounts for interim cash flows within subperiods by adjusting the denominator for the amount of capital invested in the account in accordance with the proportion of the period that interim cash flow is available for investment. For example, applying the modified Dietz method over the year in our example would produce the following return:

$$r_{\text{Modified Dietz}} = \frac{\$1,300,000 - \$1,000,000 - \$200,000}{\$1,000,000 + \$200,000 \left(\dfrac{2}{3}\right)} = 8.82\%$$

There are several things to notice with this calculation. First, notice that the 8.82 percent result falls between both the calculation assuming the cash flow occurs at the beginning of the year and the calculation assuming the cash flow occurs at the end of the year. Because the modified Dietz method does not know the account value on the date of the large cash flow, it implicitly assumes that the account's return accrues evenly over the evaluation period. In this case, the result is much closer to the IRR than the TWR because the valuation on the cash flow date is very important.

Second, notice that the numerator is identical in form to the subperiod return calculations for TWR. That is, the amount of appreciation in dollars due to investment performance is unrelated to the timing of the interim cash flow. The timing of the interim cash flow affects the amount of capital effectively invested in the account in the denominator, which brings us to our third point.

Third, notice that the $200,000 deposit is multiplied by two-thirds in the denominator because it was available for investment for two-thirds of the year. If the cash flow had occurred very early on in the year, the weight would be very close to one. However, if the cash flow had occurred very late in the year, the weight would be very close to zero.

If the timing of the cash flow cannot be determined with precision to calculate the appropriate weight, an even more crude approximation, called the Dietz method, is available.

It assumes that the cash flow occurs in the middle of the evaluation period and is calculated as:

$$r_{\text{Dietz}} = \frac{\$1,300,000 - \$1,000,000 - \$200,000}{\$1,000,000 + \$200,000(0.50)} = 9.09\%$$

If the evaluation period is short, cash flows are relatively small, and the account's return during the evaluation period has relatively low volatility, the Dietz and modified Deitz methods provide similar results to each other and similar results to the TWR and IRR. As we can see from this example, however, if any of those conditions are violated, the calculated returns can vary dramatically. As a result, the Dietz and modified Dietz approximations should be treated with suspicion unless used for short subperiods.

What does all this mean for the wealth manager? It means that there are "lies, damn lies, and statistics." More seriously, like most data and statistics, it would be inadvisable to take an investment manager's investment performance data at face value. The circumspect wealth manager might ask the following questions.

- Is the firm GIPS-compliant?
- If prepared for prospective clients, are the return calculation and composite construction methods consistent with GIPS? If not, why not?
- Are returns calculated using a time-weighted return or a money-weighted return methodology?
- Were there significant cash flows into and/or out of the accounts during the evaluation period? If so, who initiated them and how were they handled?
- Was the portfolio marked to market when significant cash flows occurred?
- If subperiod returns are geometrically linked, what is the length of the subperiod?

COMPOSITE CONSTRUCTION

Another way investment managers could mislead potential investors is to manipulate the way a composite on which returns are calculated is constructed. A composite is a group of client portfolios from which returns are calculated and aggregated. A firm may have several or many composites (e.g., high-yield fixed income, small-cap value, international equity). There is an obvious incentive for managers of individually managed accounts to exclude poorly performing portfolios from the composite portfolios and include portfolios that have performed well.

The construction of a composite should be fair and valid along several dimensions, including defining portfolios that qualify for inclusion in the particular composite, composite investment strategies, criteria for including and excluding portfolios, and criteria for carve-outs.

Qualifying Portfolios

In the interest of promoting a fair representation of an investment manager's performance, a composite should include only "actual fee-paying, discretionary" portfolios, and all actual fee-paying portfolios should be included in at least one composite.[7] The term *actual* simply means that a composite must not include hypothetical portfolios.

---

[7]GIPS allow non-fee-paying portfolios to be included with the proper disclosure.

The term *discretionary* relates to the manager's ability to implement the intended investment strategy. If a mid-cap manager focusing on the energy sector is managing a portfolio with an environmental responsibility investment constraint against investing in companies with petroleum-based businesses, it is reasonable to conclude that this restriction inhibits the ability of the manager to implement the intended strategy. This account might reasonably be judged to not qualify for the composite.

Determining whether a portfolio qualifies can certainly be a matter of judgment. It is important, however, that this judgment be made prior to the beginning of an evaluation period to prevent a manager from exercising this judgment in an opportunistic fashion after its relative performance is already known.

Investment Strategies

A guiding principle for composite construction is that composites should include only portfolios with the same investment mandates, objectives, or strategies as the composite. For example, an "equity" composite should not include some portfolios that have a large-cap mandate, other portfolios that have the mid-cap mandate, and other portfolios that have a small-cap mandate. An "equity" composite would be a fair representation if the manager offered only a single, generic equity product to clients without regard to investment style.

Portfolio Inclusion/Exclusion

New portfolios that meet the fee-paying, discretionary criteria should be included in a composite in a timely manner after the portfolio comes under the manager's discretion (e.g., beginning of the next full performance measurement period) subject to the manager's ability to invest the assets according to the desired investment strategy. In a similar way, when a manager loses discretion over a portfolio determination or some other cause, it should be included in a composite through the last full measurement period prior to the loss of discretionary authority.

At least as important as the criteria for inclusion and exclusion is for the manager to have documented policies, to implement decisions prior to knowing the outcome of investment performance (if possible), and to implement the policies consistently.

Carve-Outs

Investment managers who manage balanced accounts (e.g., stocks, bonds, cash) may wish to carve out the equity portion of the portfolio to include it in an equity composite. This practice carries with it the potential for abuse because it violates the principle of having an actual portfolio with its associated cash balance. Cash balances are required to be included in the performance calculation of any portfolio in a composite. If, however, the equity portion of a balanced portfolio were managed in a separate discretionary stand-alone account so that any associated cash balances can be included in the return calculation, the manager could carve out the equity portion and maintain a fair representation of investment performance.

When evaluating investment performance, the diligent wealth manager might ask the investment manager:

- Is your performance reporting for prospective clients GIPS-compliant?
- If not, do your composites include hypothetical portfolios?

- What is your level of investment discretion over the accounts included in the composite?
- Are non-fee-paying accounts included in the composite? If so, why?
- Do you have documented policies and procedures for including and excluding portfolios from your composites?
- Are decisions about including portfolios in a composite made prior to the beginning of a performance evaluation period?
- How do the investment strategies of your investment products relate to the definition of your composites?
- Do you carve out asset class segments from multiple strategy portfolios? If so, on what basis do you make these decisions? Are carve-out portfolios managed in separate, discretionary, and stand-alone accounts?

AFTER-TAX PERFORMANCE MEASUREMENT

Investors cannot eat pretax returns. As we mentioned in the beginning of our chapter on tax-efficient investing, the investment goal of the wealth manager ought not to be to maximize returns. Nor should it be to minimize taxes. It ought to be maximizing risk-adjusted, after-tax returns.

If a wealth manager incorporates tax considerations into investment decision making, it follows that his or her performance should also be measured on a tax-adjusted basis. Interestingly, however, Horan and Adler (2009) find, in a survey of U.S.-based wealth managers, that very few report their performance on a tax-adjusted basis, even though the survey respondents show a high degree of tax sensitivity in their investment management practices. Peterson, Pietranico, Riepe, and Xu show that a mutual fund's after-tax performance is related to its investment style, redemptions and cash inflows, and past tax efficiency.[8]

Tax-adjusted performance can be measured in three basic ways. The preliquidation method accounts for taxes realized during the measurement period but does not recognize any tax liability (benefit) associated with unrealized gains (losses) embedded in the portfolio's ending market value.[9] The postliquidation method, by contrast, assumes that unrealized gains are recognized at the end of the measurement period.

The preliquidation method can understate a portfolio's tax liability, whereas the postliquidation method can overstate it. Ideally, after-tax performance measurement should recognize some tax burden related to unrecognized gains. The Global Investment Performance Standards (GIPS) *Guidance Statement for Country-Specific Taxation Issues* (2005) requires U.S. after-tax rates of return to be calculated based on portfolio values using a preliquidation method. Postliquidation returns may be presented as supplemental information. The 2010 GIPS have since removed country-specific guidance on taxation and delegated their development to country committees.

A third method, which conforms to neither of these extremes, measures tax-adjusted performance as the change in a portfolio's tax-adjusted value. It considers the impact of future tax liabilities arising from embedded unrealized capital gains without assuming they are recognized immediately. These methods tend to be more computationally intensive than either the preliquidation or postliquidation approach and require some forecast assumption

[8]James D. Peterson, Paul A. Pietranico, Mark Riepe, and Fran Xu, "Explaining After-Tax Mutual Fund Performance," *Financial Analysts Journal*, Vol. 58, No. 1 (January/February 2002): 75–86.
[9]See Lawton and Remington (2007).

about how and when gains are likely to be recognized in the future.[10] For these reasons, they have not been adopted by GIPS or country sponsor committees. And you can be pretty certain that most investment managers will not report after-tax returns in that fashion.

Developing an after-tax benchmark index is at least as difficult.[11] As a result, precious few after-tax benchmarks exist,[12] so it is difficult for the wealth manager to make much use of them. Most managers revert to using after-tax returns on an exchange-traded fund (ETF) having an appropriate style as reported by Morningstar.

All in all, as important as taxes are to a client's economic welfare, the industry has simply not evolved enough to address this important issue from a reporting perspective.

BENCHMARKS

Of course, measuring returns is only part of the performance evaluation story. Wealth managers need a point of reference to properly interpret them. In other words, they need a benchmark. A 4 percent annual return reported by a small-cap growth manager might seem lackluster. But what if the manager earned that return in the year 2000 when similar securities *fell* by 22.6 percent according to Ibbotson Associates?[13]

Similarly, suppose a small-cap value manager reported the same 4 percent return for the same year? By similar logic, this performance would look relatively good, too, right? Not really! The Ibbotson Associates small-cap value index was *up* 22.7 percent that year.

As you can see, it is important to identify and develop a valid benchmark against which returns can be evaluated. According to Bailey, Richards, and Tierney (2007),

[A] valid benchmark is:

- Unambiguous. *The identities and weights of securities or factor exposures constituting the benchmark are clearly defined.*
- Investable. *It is possible to forgo active investment and simply hold the benchmark.*
- Measurable. *The benchmark's return is readily calculable on a reasonably frequent basis.*
- Appropriate. *The benchmark is consistent with the manager's investment style or area of expertise.*

---

[10]See, for example, Stephen M. Horan, Philip N. Lawton, and Robert R. Johnson, "After-Tax Performance Measurement," *Journal of Wealth Management*, Vol. 11, No. 1 (2008): 69–83; David M. Stein, "Measuring and Evaluating Portfolio Performance After Taxes," *Journal of Portfolio Management*, Vol. 24, No. 2 (Winter 1998): 117–124.

[11]Despite its lack of acceptance in the industry, some authors have made significant advances in the field. Some of the more pertinent references include: Horan, Lawton, and Johnson, "After-Tax Performance Measurement"; Jean L. P. Brunel, "An Approach to After-Tax Performance Benchmarking," *Journal of Private Portfolio Management*, Vol. 3, No. 3 (Winter 2000): 61–67; David M. Stein, Brian Langstraat, and Premkumar Narasimhan, "Reporting After-Tax Returns: A Pragmatic Approach," *Journal of Private Portfolio Management*, Vol. 1, No. 4 (Spring 1999): 10–21; Jeffrey L. Minck, "Tax-Adjusted Equity Benchmarks," *Journal of Private Portfolio Management*, Vol. 1, No. 2 (Summer 1998): 41–50.

[12]One notable exception is a series of Australian after-tax indexes based on franking credits. But even these indexes may include only partial after-tax adjustments.

[13]According to the *Ibbotson Stock, Bonds, Bills, and Inflation 2007 Yearbook*, © Morningstar.

- Reflective of current investment opinions. *The manager has current investment knowledge (be it positive, negative, or neutral) of the securities or factor exposures within the benchmark.*
- Specified in advance. *The benchmark is specified prior to the start of an evaluation period and known to all interested parties.*
- Owned. *The investment manager should be aware of and accept accountability for their constituents and performance of the benchmark. It is encouraged that the benchmark be embedded in and integral to the investment process and procedures of the investment manager. (pp. 733–734)*

Not all benchmarks possess these characteristics. One of the most common benchmarks used by manager search and selection consultants is the median manager from a broad investment manager universe or peer group. Unfortunately, it fails to meet many of these qualities. Most notably, the identity of the manager with the median level of performance in a particular period cannot be known in advance. As a result, the median manager is ambiguous and is not investable. In addition, like any benchmark based on a manager universe, the median manager is subject to survivorship bias, which is the phenomenon that manager databases tend to be populated with managers who have survived through the performance period because of good performance but tend to exclude managers who have been dropped from the database because of poor performance.[14]

Broad market indexes are often perfectly acceptable benchmarks because they are unambiguous, generally investable (with the exception of transaction costs), measurable, and may be specified in advance. They have the additional advantages of being well-known and well understood. A broad market index may be inappropriate, however, if the manager's style deviates significantly from what is reflected in the broad market index. It would make little sense, for example, for a small-cap value manager to be evaluated against the S&P 500 Index.

As a result, wealth managers often use style indexes that closely parallel a given investment manager's investment philosophy. As we discussed in Chapter 14, style is often defined based on market capitalization (small-cap versus large) or relative valuation (value versus growth). This approach can present difficulties in some instances, however. Style definitions can be ambiguous or inconsistent. For example, is a value manager someone who invests in stocks with low price-earnings (P/E) ratios, stocks with low price-to-book ratios, stocks that have experienced extended periods of historically poor performance, or some combination of these? Such ambiguities can result in large performance differences in seemingly similar benchmarks. For example, in 1999, the S&P Large Value Index had a return of 12.72 percent, while the Russell Large Value Index had returned 7.35 percent.[15]

Thus, it is important to carefully evaluate the underlying fundamentals of potential benchmarks to ensure that the one selected reflects the characteristics of the manager's portfolio. With the growth of the ETF universe, there are investable indexes in almost every style, sector, and size available, so in many cases an ETF may serve as an appropriate benchmark.

---

[14]In addition, "manager universe" is really a misnomer. The term *universe* implies something that is all-inclusive. By contrast, a manager universe includes only those managers in a particular database, only those meeting particular criteria (such as a style definition), and only those who have survived an evaluation period. A better label might be "manager galaxies" or "manager solar systems"!

[15]This example was derived from Bailey, Richards, and Tierney (2007).

RISK MEASURES

We hope it goes without saying at this point that a manager's performance record must be viewed in light of the risk the manager took to achieve it. A manager who assumes a higher level of risk *should* earn higher returns. If the manager did not, the investor would be taking a degree of risk for which he or she is not fully compensated. An advisor who recommends a manager operating at a higher risk level because that manager has attractive returns must realize that the client is more vulnerable to losing money in the future.

We discussed risk measures more fully in Chapters 7 and 8. The following, however, is a recap of some of those measures.

Standard Deviation

Standard deviation measures total portfolio risk, which includes both market- and security-specific risk. The most recent GIPS require complying firms to report the three-year annualized standard deviations (using monthly returns) for all their composites and the benchmarks. One can debate whether standard deviation is the best measure of risk to use in a performance evaluation context. But this development sends a very strong message that it is imprudent to evaluate investment manager performance based only on return.

Standard deviation is often provided on a monthly rather than an annualized basis. Monthly standard deviation can be converted to annualized standard deviation by multiplying by the square root of 12, or 3.464.

It is worth noting that standard deviation as a risk measure is questionable in settings when the wealth manager anticipates a skewed distribution of returns. This is often the case in options-based investment strategies and in many hedge fund strategies. It should, therefore, be applied and interpreted with caution in these situations.

Beta

Beta is a measure of the systematic and undiversifiable risk in a portfolio. Beta measures the relationship between a fund's excess return over Treasury bills compared to the excess return of the benchmark index over Treasury bills.[16] Accordingly, a fund with a 1.10 beta is expected to perform 10 percent better, after deducting the T-bill rate, than the index in up markets and 10 percent worse in down markets.

Importantly, a low beta does not imply that the fund has a low level of volatility. It could imply that the fund's market-related risk is low because its correlation with the market is low. It would be very easy for a fund or investment manager to have returns that are highly volatile, but the volatility is unrelated to direction movements in the market. A good example would be the returns to an individual, undeveloped oil field. The returns to the field will depend highly on whether oil is actually discovered in the field, how much oil is discovered, the quality of the oil, and the price at which it can be sold. If the oil field beta were calculated compared to the S&P 500, it might be exceptionally low; however, it would also be meaningless, as all of these factors can vary greatly but are not directly related to the performance of the overall stock market.

---

[16]It is important to note the caveat "of the benchmark index." All too often it is erroneously assumed that beta always refers to the broad stock market (i.e., the S&P 500); however, a correct beta calculation is based on an index appropriate to the manager's style.

R^2

Although R^2 is not a risk measure per se, it is an indicator of how reliably beta measures risk and the reliability of Jensen's alpha risk-adjusted performance measure. Technically, it measures the proportion of variation in the fund's or manager's returns that are explained by market movements. There is no objective rule for what level of R^2 is considered significant for a diversified portfolio, but you will want to develop some threshold with which you are comfortable. Harold, for example, uses a threshold of 75 percent in his work; that is, unless the R^2 is at least 75, he places no value in the information provided by alpha or beta.

Tracking Error

Tracking error is the degree to which an investment manager's performance differs from the agreed-upon benchmark. By definition, it does not measure risk in an objective sense. It measures risk in relation to the performance of a benchmark. For the wealth manager, this may have little bearing on a client's reaction, as the behavioral evaluation is based on relative return in a positive market but absolute return in a bear market. For example, if a benchmark is up 22 percent and the manager is up 25 percent, the client is likely to be pleased. However, if the benchmark index is down 25 percent and the investment manager produced a –22 percent return (i.e., the investment manager outperformed the benchmark index by 3 percent), don't expect the client to be impressed by the manager's prowess.

Tracking error has several different definitions depending on the context in which it is used and the preference of the person doing the analysis.

Raw Differences

The simplest definition of tracking error is the raw difference between the portfolio return and the benchmark return, $R_P - R_B$. This measure of tracking error blends not just risk relative to a benchmark but also the manager's investment performance. It can, therefore, be misleading. For example, consider the returns in Exhibit 15.2.

EXHIBIT 15.2   Examples of Tracking Error

	2007	2008	2009	2010	Average Return	Standard Deviation	Cumulative $R_P - R_B$	$\lvert R_P - R_B \rvert$	Std. Dev. $(R_P - R_B)$
Benchmark Index	5%	3%	–2%	8%	3.5%	4.2%	0.0%	0.0%	0.0%
Calamity Capital	8%	0%	1%	5%	3.5%	3.7%	0.0%	20.0%	6.2%
Innocuous Investments	6	2	–1	7	3.5	3.7	0.0	4.0	1.2
Persistent Partners	7	5	0	10	5.5	4.2	8.0	8.0	0.0

Source: Fictitious data, for illustration purposes only.

Calamity Capital and Innocuous Investments have the same average return (3.5 percent), standard deviation (3.7 percent), and average tracking error over the four years measured in terms of raw differences (0.0 percent). But a casual inspection reveals that Innocuous Investments has tracked the benchmark index much more closely than Calamity Capital has. Innocuous Investments deviated from the benchmark by only 1 percent each year whereas Calamity Capital deviated by 3 percent each year. The average in each case is zero because the year-to-year differences cancel each other out over time.

Absolute Differences

Because the variations of raw differences cancel each other out over time, another definition of tracking error is the absolute value of the difference between the portfolio return and the benchmark return, or $|R_P - R_B|$. The total absolute difference over the four years for Calamity Capital is 12 percent versus 4 percent for Innocuous Investments. That is, 5 percent versus 1 percent on an average annualized basis.

One of the drawbacks of using absolute differences is that consistently outperforming the benchmark will increase the absolute difference and make the manager look relatively risky according to this measure of risk. For example, consider Persistent Partners, which has consistently outperformed the index by two percentage points each year. Its average return is higher than the benchmark and the standard deviation is the same. However, according to both the raw and absolute difference measure of tracking error, it looks more risky than its competitors and the benchmark index.

Volatility of Differences

The volatility, or standard deviation, of the difference between the portfolio return in the benchmark return overcomes some of these difficulties. Following the example in Exhibit 15.2, we can see that the standard deviation of the raw differences between the portfolio return in the benchmark return for Persistent Partners is zero, which does not penalize Persistent Partners for persistently outperforming the benchmark index year after year.

Downside Risk Measures

When measuring performance of an investment manager relative to some level of required return, it should not come as a surprise that the investor would not be concerned with deviations above the required return. The investor is really concerned with unwanted deviations—those below the required or expected return. As a result, it is useful to take a close look at downside deviations. Chapter 7 presented two such related measures; semivariance and semideviation. Semivariance and semideviation are computed in the same manner as variance and standard deviation except that only deviations below the mean are used in the computation. If some minimum acceptable return is used rather than the mean, the result is generally referred to as downside deviation.

Another downside risk measure is drawdown—commonly used in the evaluation of hedge funds or managed future strategies. Drawdown is a decline in value from a high historical point and can be computed over different periods. A maximum drawdown measures the maximum loss that an investor would have received over some prior time period measured from the highest point to the subsequent lowest point during that period.[17]

---

[17]Lhabitant (2008, 55). However, it is important to keep in mind that drawdown is calculated on historical performance. As many hedge fund investors learned to their sorrow during the great recession, historical data is no guarantee of future performance.

PERFORMANCE APPRAISAL MEASURES

A key element in evaluating performance is evaluating return in relation to the appropriate measure of risk. Chapter 7 discusses these measures of risk-adjusted performance in more detail, but we review them here in the context of manager search and selection. An important point to realize is that there is no best, single measure of risk or performance that applies in all situations.

Sharpe Ratio

The Sharpe ratio relates manager's return in excess of T-bills to the portfolio's standard deviation.

$$\text{Sharpe Ratio}_p = \frac{r_p - r_f}{\sigma_p}$$

Notice that this performance measure does not measure the manager's performance in relation to the benchmark index. The wealth manager can interpret the Sharpe ratio by comparing it to the Sharpe ratio for the benchmark index. This exercise can help assess the value of active management. In addition, the Sharpe ratio can be compared to other investment managers having a similar investment style.

Because the Sharpe ratio uses a measure of total risk (both systematic and unsystematic), it is appropriate in many situations when a manager's mandate includes managing total risk, not just systematic risk. It would be inappropriate for a sub-asset-class manager focusing on a particular market sector or niche because, by design, that manager's investment mandate is not intended to eliminate unsystematic risk.

Again, because the standard deviation is an incomplete description of return dispersion when returns are skewed or have fat tails, the Sharpe ratio may be inappropriate for options-based investment strategies and many hedge fund strategies.

Graphically, the Sharpe ratio measures the slope of the line connecting the risk-free asset and the manager's portfolio in a graph plotting return against standard deviation. In Exhibit 15.3, for example, Safety Steve Asset Manager is represented by the square, which had a 6.5 percent return for a 10 percent standard deviation. The slope of the dashed line is the Safety Steve's Sharpe ratio and is equal to (6.5% − 3.0%)/10% = 0.35. At this relatively low level of volatility, Safety Steve plots one percentage point above the capital market line (CML), which connects the risk-free asset with a return of 3.0 percent and the market index represented by the circle. The CML would normally predict a 5.5 percent return for portfolio with a 10 percent standard deviation similar to Safety Steve.

Normal Nelly Capital Management, represented by the triangle, also plots one percentage point above the CML. It outperformed the market index because it had a 9 percent return and a more normal standard deviation of 20 percent, whereas the market index had only an 8 percent return for the same level of risk. The CML would have predicted only an 8 percent return for such a portfolio. Although it plots one percentage point above the CML, its Sharpe ratio is only (9.0% − 3.0%)/20% = 0.30. So, it underperformed Safety Steve with a Sharpe ratio of 0.35. As a result, the slope of the line (not shown in the graph) connecting the risk-free asset and Normal Nelly is flatter than the slope of the line for Safety Steve.

M^2

Modigliani and Modigliani propose a variation of the Sharpe ratio that accounts for the ability to scale risk upward or downward by borrowing or lending and measures performance

EXHIBIT 15.3   Sharpe Ratios for Two Portfolios with Different Standard Deviations

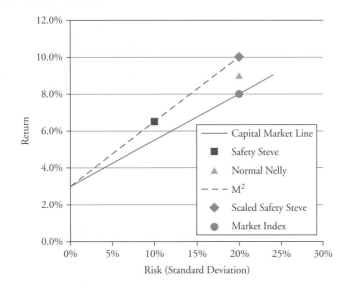

at a standardized level of risk. They create a benchmark called M^2 that represents what a portfolio would have returned if it had taken on the same total risk as the market index, just like the dashed line does in Exhibit 15.3.[18]

The Sharpe ratio and M^2 measure will always agree on whether a skillful manager plots above or below the CML. The M^2 measure also allows advisors to compare performance from one manager to the next controlling for their different levels of risk.

Treynor Ratio

The Treynor ratio is potentially useful in situations where the Sharpe ratio or M^2 do not naturally apply, specifically in situations where total risk is not relevant to the manager being evaluated. Like the Sharpe ratio, it evaluates a manager's return over and above T-bills relative to risk. The Treynor ratio, however, uses beta to measure risk.

$$\text{Treynor Ratio}_p = \frac{r_p - r_f}{\beta_p}$$

Because beta is used as a measure of risk, the Treynor ratio is subject to the same pitfalls as beta. It is subject to significant statistical error. For example, portfolio return might have a relatively low beta simply because the R^2 is low and unreliable. In such cases, the Treynor ratio looks very good but is unreliable, as well.

Like the Sharpe ratio, the Treynor ratio measures the slope of the line connecting the risk-free rate and portfolio in risk/return space. The difference is that risk is measured according to beta as in Exhibit 15.4. The Treynor ratio for Safety Steve with a beta of 0.5

[18]Franco Modigliani and Leah Modigliani, "Risk-Adjusted Performance," *Journal of Portfolio Management*, Vol. 23, No. 2 (1997): 45–54.

equals (6.5% − 3.0%)/0.50 = 0.07, which is greater than the slope of the security market line (SML) equal to (8.0% − 3.0%)/1 = 0.05.

EXHIBIT 15.4   Treynor Ratios and Jensen's Alphas for Two Portfolios with Different Betas

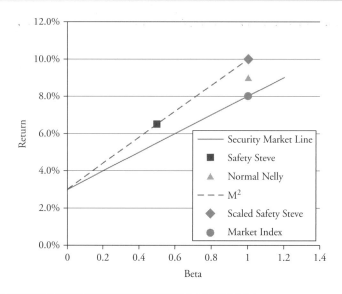

Similarly, Normal Nelly with a beta of 1 has a Treynor ratio equal to (9.0% − 3.0%)/ 1.0 = 0.06, which is less than the Treynor ratio for Safety Steve but greater than the Treynor ratio for market index [(8.0% − 3.0%)/1.0 = 0.05].

Jensen's Alpha

Jensen's alpha is another risk-adjusted measure of performance. Like the Treynor ratio, it captures only systematic risk and is subject to significant statistical error.

$$\text{Alpha} = \alpha = (r_p - r_f) - \beta_p(r_m - r_f) - \varepsilon$$

Rather than measuring the slope in Exhibit 15.4, Jensen's alpha measures how far above or below the CML the manager plots.

Jensen's alpha holds high-beta managers and low-beta managers to the same standard. For example, in Exhibit 15.4, Safety Steve Asset Manager has produced a positive 1 percent Jensen's alpha over the past five years with a beta of 0.5. The 1 percent alpha is represented by the vertical distance between the square and the security market line.

Normal Nelly Capital Management also produced a positive 1 percent alpha over the past five years, represented by the vertical distance between the triangle and the SML, but the beta was 1.0.

Both Safety Steve and Normal Nelly had better risk-adjusted performance than the market index. But did one outperform the other?

According to the Jensen's alpha, they performed equally well. An investor, however, could have scaled Safety Steve's performance by borrowing money to double the investment.

This levered investment represents a portfolio with the same beta as Normal Nelly. By leveraging investment in Safety Steve, the investor would have experienced a 10 percent return for the same level risk, in contrast to Normal Nelly's 9 percent return.

It seems we have a difference of opinion.

In this sense, Safety Steve outperformed Normal Nelly after adjusting for the different risk levels. One advantage of the Treynor ratio is that it overcomes this shortcoming of Jensen's alpha. Specifically, it looks at performance per unit of systematic risk.

The reliability of Jensen's alpha is also dependent on how consistently the manager outperforms or underperforms the benchmark index over time. One manager may produce positive risk-adjusted returns on a fairly consistent basis over time. Another manager may have more erratic risk-adjusted returns in which the superior performance is concentrated in one or two periods. Both managers can produce the same Jensen's alpha, but the former manager's performance may be more reliable.

The wealth manager therefore needs to examine other statistical measures such as the R^2 and the alpha's standard error to properly interpret its meaning.

Alpha Star

An interesting performance measure for evaluating consultants and advisors is something called Alpha Star, developed by Dick Marston from the Wharton School of Business.[19] Dr. Marston's Alpha Star is similar to Jensen's alpha but is based on standard deviation as a measure of risk rather than beta. Specifically, in equation form it is equal to:

$$\text{Alpha} = \alpha = (r_p - r_f) - \left(\frac{\sigma_p}{\sigma_m}\right)(r_m - r_f) - \varepsilon$$

The difference between the two expressions is that Jensen's alpha measures the portfolio risk in relation to comovements with the market—that is, correlation as well as volatility. Alpha Star, by contrast, measures risk only in terms of the portfolio's volatility, or total risk, in relation to the market.

Graphically, Alpha Star is represented by the vertical distance between the manager and the CML in Exhibit 15.3. Both Safety Steve and Normal Nelly have Alpha Star measures of 1 percent, but they have different standard deviations. It is subject to the same scaling criticism as Jensen's alpha.

Alpha Star can be appropriate for advisors (as opposed to individual money managers) because it examines a portfolio's total risk rather than just its systematic risk. While it may be appropriate to evaluate an individual investment manager in terms of systematic risk, the advisor (or manager of managers) may more appropriately be charged with managing total risk across the entire portfolio. This fundamental difference may imply that tools used to evaluate money managers may not be appropriate to evaluate advisors.

Information Ratio

The information ratio relates a portfolio's return differential from its benchmark to the volatility of that differential, otherwise known as its tracking error. The numerator is commonly called active return. The denominator is commonly called active risk, which is essentially a variation of tracking error discussed earlier.

---

[19]Richard Marston, "Risk-Adjusted Performance of Portfolios," *Journal of Investment Consulting* (February 2004).

$$\text{Information Ratio} = \frac{r_p - r_B}{TE_p}$$

The tracking error of the portfolio in the denominator is the standard deviation of the return differential between the portfolio and the benchmark.

Sortino Ratio

The Sortino ratio is similar to the Sharpe ratio and information ratio in that it computes excess return relative to risk. In the Sortino ratio, the excess return is computed relative to some minimum acceptable return, and risk is measured based on downside deviation (DD). It is therefore appropriate when evaluating the performance of a manager and the investor is primarily concerned with downside risk.[20]

$$\text{Sortino ratio} = \frac{r_p - MAR}{DD_p}$$

Sterling Ratio

A similar measure, which can be used for investments for which drawdowns are an important measure of downside risk, is the Sterling ratio. The Sterling ratio measures excess return relative to the average maximum drawdown during some specified period.

$$\text{Sterling ratio} = \frac{r_p - r_f}{\text{Average Drawdown}}$$

PERFORMANCE ATTRIBUTION

Measuring performance is one thing. Knowing whether to attribute it to skill, randomness, or some other cause is another. Being able to attribute performance to the correct drivers is a critical component in an advisor's manager search and selection process.

We focus here on performance attribution for a particular investment manager with an appropriate benchmark, such as the S&P 500. The value added by a manager is his or her tracking error expressed in terms of raw differences, $r_P - r_B$. This is sometimes called active risk.

Any manager will add (or destroy) value by constructing a portfolio with weights that are different from the benchmark. Overweighting individual securities that outperform the benchmark as a whole has a positive performance impact, while overweighting individual securities that underperform have a negative performance impact. This is summarized in the first row of Exhibit 15.5 where w_{pi} is the portfolio's weight in security i, and w_{Bi} is the benchmark's weight in security i.

---

[20]Of course, this requires estimates regarding asset-class skewness in addition to estimates regarding returns, standard deviations, and correlations. According to an earlier paper in the *Journal of Portfolio Management* by Frank Sortino titled "Downside Risk" (Vol. 17, No. 4 [Summer 1991]: 27-31), skewness for an asset class can change dramatically with the methodology of calculation and the economic environment.

EXHIBIT 15.5   Performance Impact for Relative Weighting and Relative Return Combinations

	Outperforming Security $(r_i > r_B)$	Underperforming Security $(r_p < r_B)$
Overweight $(w_{pi} > w_{Bi})$	Positive	Negative
Underweight $(w_{pi} < w_{Bi})$	Negative	Positive

Similarly, underweighting securities that outperform the benchmark index has a negative performance impact, while underweighting securities that underperform the benchmark index has a positive performance impact.

Therefore, the portion of portfolio performance that can be attributed to each individual security is equal to its over- or underweighting relative to the benchmark weighting times the security's return relative to the benchmark, or:

$$\text{Individual Security Contribution} = (w_{pi} - w_{Bi})(r_i - r_B)$$

The total valued added by the manager is simply the total of each security's individual contribution.

Performing attribution analysis on a security-by-security basis is often unwieldy in diversified portfolios with a large number of securities. Some insight, however, can be derived by organizing the performance impact of individual securities according to some sensible categorization such as industry, sector, market capitalization, or relative value so that patterns can be detected.

PARTING COMMENTS

Performance measurement, evaluation, and appraisal can be a complex and nuanced process. In fact, it is a recognized field of study. CFA Institute administers the Certificate in Performance Measurement (CIPM) and is dedicated to promoting the highest professional and educational standards in this area.

Wealth managers should view performance figures with caution, especially if they are not compiled in a manner consistent with the GIPS, and know the right questions to ask to interpret them properly. They might also inquire whether the firm employs performance specialists with the CIPM designation and whether return calculations are verified.

In addition, wealth managers should choose evaluation criteria (e.g., Sharpe ratio, Treynor ratio) that best suit the particular circumstance (e.g., whether total risk or systematic risk is more relevant). However, it is important to remember that the most important decision is the selection of the appropriate benchmark, for no matter the quality of the analytics, the results will be meaningless or misleading if based on an inappropriate benchmark.

RESOURCES

Bailey, Jeffery V., Thomas M. Richards, and David E. Tierney. 2007. "Evaluating Portfolio Performance." In *Managing Investment Portfolios: A Dynamic Process*, 3rd edition. John L. Maginn, Donald L. Tuttle, Jerald E. Pinto, and Dennis W. McLeavey, eds. CFA Institute Investment Series. Hoboken, NJ: John Wiley & Sons.

Horan, Stephen M., and David Adler. 2009. "Tax-Aware Investment Management Practice." *Journal of Wealth Management*, Vol. 12, No. 2: 71–88.

Lawton, Philip, and Todd Jankowski. 2007. *Investment Performance Measurement: Evaluating and Presenting Results*. CFA Institute Investment Perspectives. Hoboken, NJ: John Wiley & Sons.

Lawton, Philip, and W. Bruce Remington. 2007. "Global Investment Performance Standards." In *Managing Investment Portfolios: A Dynamic Process*, 3rd edition. John L. Maginn, Donald L. Tuttle, Jerald E. Pinto, and Dennis W. McLeavey, eds. CFA Institute Investment Series. Hoboken, NJ: John Wiley & Sons.

Lhabitant, Francois-Serge. 2008. *Hedge Funds: Quantitative Insights*. Reprint. West Sussex, England: John Wiley & Sons.

CHAPTER 16

SELECTING INVESTMENT MANAGERS

You can have many different selection systems, but the bottom line has to be a system that, once the judge takes office that judge will feel that he or she is to decide the case without reference to the popular thing or the popular will of the moment.

—Stephen Breyer

Chapter 14 addressed critical issues in portfolio construction related to equity, fixed income, and alternative assets, including the processes for the selection of individual securities within an asset class chosen by the wealth manager and client. Chapter 15 discussed how we measure, appraise, and attribute performance in these various asset classes. This chapter builds on those principles to define a process and structure around which a wealth manager can select investment managers from the vast universe of mutual funds and independent asset managers to manage investments within each asset class.

One of the reasons for separating this chapter from the preceding one on performance evaluation is to emphasize the point that the manager search and selection process is much more involved and nuanced than simply finding managers with the best historical performance. The practice of performance chasing has led many a wealth manager down the same path as the frenzied individual investor whose investment behavior tends to be one of the strongest contraindicators in investment management. According to the Investment Company Institute, fund flows into equity mutual funds and technology funds reached their peak in early 2000, just before the collapse of the tech bubble, while they reached their bottom in the first quarter of 2003, just as the equities market embarked on a four-year bull market. A similar pattern occurred during the 2008 bear market and the 2010 recovery.

The wealth manager has two broad options for implementing the investments in each asset class—individual management and pooled (or commingled) management. The second option, pooled management, is the universe of mutual funds, ETFs, hedge funds, and similar vehicles. Individual management may be further divided into three forms: individually, separately, and unified managed accounts.

INDIVIDUAL ASSET MANAGERS

Before turning attention to the external money managers, let's consider the special case of the wealth manager implementing investment strategy by personally making security-specific buy and sell decisions. In this form of individual asset management, the wealth manager changes hats and becomes a money manager. Wealth managers considering this alternative should apply the same standards of evaluation to their role as money manager as they would to an independent money manager. This would include an unbiased evaluation of their investment management experience and credentials (e.g., CFA charter); their performance record (Global Investment Performance Standards [GIPS]); and their benchmark performance, trading costs, technology, research facilities, time devoted to money management, and so on. Setting aside the inherent conflict of interest in judging oneself, a competent wealth manager is unlikely to pass the screen as a money manager, if for no other reason than both wealth management and money management are full-time professions. It is difficult (if not impossible) for a single individual to maintain competence in both. The wealth manager's firm will need to have adequate and well-educated staff in order to perform both functions. It is not uncommon for a wealth management firm to have a team of wealth managers and a team of money managers to manage individual asset classes. Even in such cases, the firm may not have expertise in all asset classes and will likely select external managers for some asset classes.

Individually Managed Accounts (IMAs)

This form of management is uniquely customized and professionally managed for the client. From the client's perspective, primary attributes of this form of management are:

- The account(s) is/are in the client's name.
- The securities are in the client's name.
- The process is based on a relationship between the client and the manager.
- The portfolio is specifically tailored and managed for the unique requirements of the client.
- The portfolio goals can be changed significantly without changing managers.

    From the manager's perspective, individually managed accounts:

- Require substantial minimum investments, typically ranging from $10 million to $50 million or more.[1]
- Require the attention of the most experienced, successful, and most highly compensated of the management team.
- Limit the number of clients the firm can accept.
- Require individual attention to each security in each portfolio.
- Require a direct relationship between the client and the manager.

Separately Managed Accounts (SMAs)

This is a packaged form of private money management. Its name, *separately managed*, is derived from its similarity with an individually managed account. The characteristics from the client's perspective are:

- The account is in the client's name.
- The securities are in the client's name (i.e., separate from others).

---

[1]In their October 1995 study, "The Coming Evolution of the Investment Management Industry," Goldman Sachs developed a profile for a small investment management company. For even this small firm, over 15 years ago, the average account size was over $12 million.

Unlike IMAs, customization of a separate account might be based on computer screening and arbitrary reallocation. A separate account is often based on a model portfolio. Each separate account will own a pro rata share of the model portfolio's securities. As a result, separate accounts often have odd lot positions. For example, consider Ms. Boone with $100,000 placed with Manager Hot in Exhibit 16.1.

EXHIBIT 16.1   Example of Standard Separately Managed Account

	Manager Hot's Model		Ms. Boone's Portfolio		
Stock	Share Price	Allocation	Allocation	Value	Shares
A	$20	25%	25%	$25,000	1,250
B	30	25	25	25,000	833
C	40	25	25	25,000	625
D	50	25	25	25,000	500

Ms. Boone discovers that stock A is in a company that she believes is harming the environment. Unlike a mutual fund, the account allows her to request that stock A be eliminated from the portfolio. In an IMA, the manager might search for a replacement for stock A. In an SMA, the customization simply requires a programmer to instruct the computer to reallocate the client's funds against the model while setting the allocation to stock A equal to zero (see Exhibit 16.2).

EXHIBIT 16.2   Example of Customized Separately Managed Account

	Manager Hot's Model		Ms. Boone's Portfolio		
Stock	Share Price	Allocation	Allocation	Value	Shares
A	$20	25%	0%	$0	0
B	30	25	33	33,333	1,111
C	40	25	33	33,333	833
D	50	25	33	33,333	667

From the manager's perspective, separate accounts:

- Provide for significant leveraging of management talent. Senior management can design model portfolios, and junior managers, following the model and using computer allocations, can manage hundreds of accounts.
- Allow client contact to be managed by sales staff and third-party representatives (e.g., brokers or Registered Investment Advisors).

Unified Managed Accounts (UMAs)

Unified managed accounts (UMAs) are a kind of hybrid between individually managed accounts and separately managed accounts. If a wealth manager determines that the best managers for various asset classes and investment styles are in the form of SMAs rather than mutual funds or other pooled vehicles, the manager can combine their collective buy and sell decisions into a single centrally managed account. It combines all of the assets into one account with a single registration.

The advantage of this approach is that the UMA allows the wealth manager to control and manage interactions among the investment decisions of the various submanagers. For example, consider a UMA with separate value and growth managers. The value manager may purchase a particular stock because it has a low price-earnings (P/E) ratio. As the wisdom of this investment decision is borne out in the financial markets, the low-P/E stock may become a high-P/E stock. As a result, the value manager may sell the investment to realize the strategy's success at the same time that the growth manager purchases the same stock.

The simultaneous purchase and sale of the same security by different managers has several negative implications. First, it unnecessarily increases trading costs. Second, it can impose unnecessary tax obligations on the client. In the example, the client unnecessarily or at least prematurely pays a capital gains tax despite continuing to hold the security. In other situations, one manager may sell a security to cut losses or because the security no longer fits the mandated investment style while another manager purchases the same security, creating a wash sale that excludes the client from realizing the tax loss.

These are just a few of the many interactions that a UMA can manage. Like the IMA, however, it requires substantial assets for proper diversification and economic feasibility, so it is not a viable option for many clients. A variation of the UMA can be implemented with mutual funds and other pooled vehicles, in which case the wealth manager functions effectively as the UMA manager.

Putting the Pieces Together

For the wealth manager, the only form of private money management realistically available is the SMA. Even if the minimum for truly customized private management were as low as $500,000 or $1 million, it would be impossible to adequately diversify most portfolios. A wealth manager using minimal asset class allocations would still need five or more managers (e.g., large-cap growth and value, small-cap growth and value, international, short- and intermediate-term bonds, taxable and municipal bonds).[2]

In considering separate account management, the wealth manager must determine the pros and cons vis-à-vis a pooled management alternative. The issues most frequently considered are listed next.

Customization

Separate accounts offer limited and mechanical customization. However, on the rare occasion that a client has a very specific need (e.g., "I refuse to own any company whose name begins with the letter C"), a separate account may be the only choice. Such unique needs are rare.

Of course, the ability to restrict certain positions from a portfolio is only one form of customization. For the wealth manager, the ability to customize by diversification is far more important. With thousands of managers from which to choose in every conceivable asset class and style, the ability to customize with funds dwarfs the limited choices available in separate accounts.

---

[2]The nation's largest pension plans use an average of 33 managers per plan.

Tax Advantages

One argument in favor of separate account management is that the account can be managed tax efficiently. We have noted in a prior chapter that the seminal study by Jeffery and Arnott demonstrates a modest value of separate account tax management of 10 basis points. However, subsequent research by Berkin and Ye (2003) under a different tax regime suggests that benefits of tax loss harvesting are initially quite high and level out to about 50 basis points annually after about three years.[3] In fact, related research suggests that these techniques can be particularly well suited to advanced portfolio management strategies, such as active extended 130/30 strategies.[4]

Another tax-related argument is that long-term investors in funds will suffer when less patient fund investors sell in a panic during a bear market. This argument assumes that well-managed mutual funds have a significant percentage of naive investors; that the funds selected by wealth managers will not have adequate liquidity to meet redemptions; and that in a bear market, the forced sales, if any, will generate gains, not losses. None of these assumptions have been substantiated.

Mutual fund investors are often cautioned against buying shares of a fund with large unrealized capital gains because the new mutual fund shareholder will be responsible for paying capital gains tax on those gains if and when they are realized even if it is shortly after the investor purchases the shares and did not receive the benefit of the gains. This can happen if the manager decides the shares are overvalued or if a sale is triggered by liquidity needs of other shareholders redeeming shares.

Although paying a capital gains tax on returns one has not enjoyed is undoubtedly a bad thing, what is rarely mentioned is that investors can increase the cost basis on their mutual fund shares by the amount of the distributed capital gains. In other words, the gain they must realize on the sale of their mutual fund shares is reduced by the amount of the gains that were distributed by the mutual fund on the underlying investments. As a result, the tax disadvantage is really a timing mismatch (paying taxes sooner rather than later) rather than paying taxes on investment returns that are never realized.

The wealth manager needs to weigh the possible tax advantages of an SMA against the efficiencies of mutual funds and exchange-traded funds (ETFs). We note that it depends, at least in part, on the investment strategies. For example, passive investment strategies are often better suited for mutual funds because the potential SMA tax advantages are significantly reduced.

Access to Exceptional Managers

Managers of SMAs are rarely the most experienced or talented of a firm's management team. Extraordinary talent is drawn to larger portfolios that provide more challenge and more compensation. Mutual fund portfolios are commonly multibillion-dollar portfolios. In addition, their performance commands significant, immediate, and continual public scrutiny. Basic economic logic suggests that large and visible portfolios are where firms are going to devote their top resources. In addition, it is the rare separate account manager that a wealth manager cannot access either through a public or an institutional mutual fund.

---

[3]See Andrew L. Berkin and Jia Ye, "Tax Management, Loss Harvesting, and HIFO Accounting," *Financial Analysts Journal*, Vol. 59, No. 4 (2010): 91–102.

[4]See Andrew L. Berkin and Christopher Luck, "Having Your Cake and Eating It Too: The Before- and After-Tax Efficient Seas of an Extended Equity Mandate," *Financial Analysts Journal*, Vol. 66, No. 4 (2003): 33–45.

Costs

Occasionally the argument is made that separate account management is more cost effective. Traditionally, pooled accounts have had the advantage of institutional commissions, but separate accounts have tended to have less market impact. Because commission rates have dropped so dramatically since the 1990s, the difference in commissions is not as great.

So where is the cost-benefit of the separate account? Usually, the argument for cost efficiency relates to a strategy of implementing separate account management known as the *wrap account*, which derives its name from the packaging of the fees, commissions, and other expenses. In effect, they are wrapped into a single one-charge-covers-all account. Wrap accounts offer the advantage of eliminating any concerns regarding excess trading and other potentially excessive fees. Typically, a wrap account also includes the advice of an independent advisor who assists the client in selecting and maintaining the specific money manager.

The cost advantage projected when marketing wrap accounts is usually based on adding average independent advisor fees to average mutual fund fees. Unfortunately, the fee comparisons are grossly misleading. As an example, the average mutual fund fee is typically based only on equity funds and includes funds with 12b-1 fees (as shown in Exhibit 16.3). The average of the expense ratio for funds used by a wealth manager is likely to be half (or less) of the fees shown in wrap account marketing material.

However, the independent fee advisor, marketing against wrap accounts, tends to present equally misleading information. The standard wrap account fee is sometimes represented as 3 percent, although the average actually is much lower. The independent advisor also sometimes ignores the expense ratio of the funds used to implement the policy and almost always ignores the fund manager's commission costs. A fair comparison is likely to find that the total costs for separate account, wrap account, and wealth manager "mutual fund management" are fairly close.

Exhibit 16.3 breaks down costs into explicit and implicit costs. Direct costs are wrap fees, management fees, and commissions—all of which vary by the type of financial intermediation. Implicit costs are composed of the bid-ask spread, market impact, and the opportunity cost of cash for liquidity purposes. Cost of cash refers to forgone returns and missed investment opportunities because a mutual fund or portfolio must hold a certain amount of cash to meet liquidity needs. One of the things to consider is that the implicit costs of equity portfolio management can easily be half of the total cost.

Exhibit 16.4 takes a closer look at the source data by summarizing the results of the studies used to construct Exhibit 16.3. Unlike commissions, mutual fund management fees have been remarkably stable over the years.

Reporting

Separate account proponents argue that ownership of individual securities results in greater accountability by the manager. To some extent, that is true. Fund managers frequently drift in their management style and, as they only have to report positions semiannually, there are potential gaps in accountability. The danger, however, is that small and mutual fund accountability is increasing.

Wealth managers' primary insurance against this risk is their original due diligence—hire managers who are prepared to be accountable. In addition, new technology, including factor analysis, provides additional tools to warn of drift. Finally, as the presence, prestige, and economic clout of wealth managers grow, fund companies will find it to their advantage to become more accountable. Many already voluntarily provide positions on a quarterly basis, and a few are beginning to provide information monthly, on a 30-day delayed basis.

EXHIBIT 16.3   Costs of Financial Intermediation for Equity Portfolio Management

	Hypothetical Index	Index Mutual Fund or ETF	Actively Managed Mutual Fund	Full-Service Retail Brokerage (Commission)	Full-Service Retail Brokerage (Wrap Fee)
Explicit Costs					
Wrap fee	0.0%	—	—	—	1.00% to 2.00%[a]
Expense ratio[b]	0.0%	0.20% to 0.50%[c]	~1.42%[d]	—	—
Commissions[e]	0.0%	0.07%	0.39%	~2.5%[f]	—
Implicit Costs					
Bid-ask spread[g]	0.0%	0.17%	0.60%	0.60%	0.60%
Market impact[h]	0.0%	~0.25%	~1.00%	~0.25%	~0.25%
Cost of cash[i]	0.0%	—	~0.74%	0.74%	0.74%
Total	0.00%	0.44% to 0.74%	4.15%	4.09%	2.59% to 3.59%

[a]Based on industry experience and informal survey.

[b]Includes 12b-1 fees for mutual funds, but excludes sales charges, such as front-end and back-end loads. Bergstresser, Chalmers, and Tufano (2006) report that, on average, total sales charges annuitized over a five-year holding period is 1.07%.

[c]From Swedroe (2000) and industry experience. According to Bergstresser, Chalmers, and Tufano (2006) domestic equity index funds represent 4.1% of mutual funds. Yan (2006) reports index funds represent 5.33% of mutual funds.

[d]The average expense ratio for actively managed funds in the meta-analysis in Exhibit 16.4 is 1.41%. These expense ratios exclude loads, however, and therefore underestimate the true annual expense ratio. The average expense ratio for large-capitalization growth funds is 1.47%, according to Yahoo! Finance. As of this writing, the average expense ratio for all domestic equity funds according to Morningstar is 1.37%. The average expense ratio for all taxable bond funds according to Morningstar is 1.03%.

[e]Commission estimates for mutual funds come from Karceski, Livingston, and O'Neal (2004), whose figures are conservative in relation to estimates from Swedroe (2000).

[f]No known studies exist, but the anecdotal experience of the authors suggests annual commissions for commission-based full-service brokerages are about 2.5%.

[g]Estimates are based on Karceski, Livingston, and O'Neal (2004).

[h]Conservatively estimated using figures from Barra Inc. as reported in Swedroe (2000). The Barra study indicates that the typical small-cap or mid-cap stock fund could incur market impact costs of 3% to 5%. Using the most conservative estimates, market impact costs are at least 1%. Market impact costs for index funds are likely much lower than for actively managed funds because of their low turnover. Barra has since combined with Morgan Stanley Capital International to form MSCI Barra. Full-service brokerages would normally include some amount of market impact, but its magnitude in relation to mutual funds is uncertain. This figure is therefore conservatively extrapolated from index mutual fund data.

[i]Actively managed funds are assumed to hold a 9.3% cash balance as reported by Mohatra and McLeod (1997) and Lipper Analytical Services. The cost of cash assumes an 8% return differential between stock and cash. Swedroe (2000) estimates the differential at 12%. The cost of cash can be estimated as the product of 8% and 9.3%. Index funds typically carry de minimis cash balances.

With little lost regarding accountability, a great deal is gained regarding independent performance and portfolio data. With resources such as Morningstar, Value Line, and others, there is an almost endless stream of independent, substantive data available to the wealth manager to use in monitoring selected fund managers. By comparison, the independent reporting on separate accounts is virtually nonexistent.

EXHIBIT 16.4   Summary of Mutual Fund Studies

	Expense Ratio[a]	Turnover	Commission	Implicit	Market Impact
Bergstresser, Chalmers, and Tufano (2007)[b]	1.60%				
Yan (2006)[c]	1.45%	88.9%			
Karceski, Livingston, and O'Neal (2004)	1.12% active 0.25% passive		0.393% active 0.071% passive	0.601% active 0.172% passive	
Swedroe (2000)	1.53% active 0.20% to 0.50% passive	80% active 15% passive	1.60% active 0.30% passive		~1.00%
Fortin and Michelson (1999)	~1.45%	~80%			
Jayaraman, Khorana, and Nelling (2002)	~1.45%	~65%			
Dowen and Mann (2004)	1.06%	107.4%			
Dellva and Olson (1998)	1.46%				
Bers and Madura (2000)	1.49%	73%			
Molhatra and McLeod (1997)	1.57%[d]				
Bogle (2005)	1.56%	112%			
Chalmers, Edelen, and Kadlec (2001)	1.09%	79%	0.28%	0.46%	
Ennis (2005)	1.56%				
Yahoo! Finance	1.47%				
Morningstar	1.37%	95%			

[a]Excluding loads.
[b]Bergstresser, Chalmers, and Tufano (2007) report that, on average, total annuitized fees over a five-year holding period including sales charges is 2.16%.
[c]Yan (2006) also reports average front-end loads of 1.34%, average back-end loads of 0.51%, and average cash holdings of 5.33%.
[d]Quoting Lipper Analytical Services. They also report a cash ratio of 9.3%.

POOLED INVESTMENT VEHICLES

Today there are more mutual funds than there are stocks on the New York Stock Exchange. According to the Investment Company Institute, there is over $11 trillion invested in 7,554 mutual funds, almost twice the amount invested at the turn of the millennium (which was more than twice the amount invested five years before that).[5] There is another $800 billion invested in 900 different exchange-traded funds (ETFs). As a result, a fund exists to meet almost every investment objective. However, with thousands of funds it is difficult to select the appropriate funds to meet individual needs. An initial step in the selection process is to classify funds by objective, style, strategy, and asset class.

Types of Pooled Investment Vehicles

Many wealth managers use these pooled investment vehicles rather than direct investments to manage client portfolios. These vehicles include open-end mutual funds, closed-end funds, exchange-traded funds and notes, and private vehicles such as hedge funds.

Open-End Funds

Once upon at time there were only two primary types of widely available pooled investment vehicles in the form of mutual funds—open-end funds and closed-end funds. Open-end mutual funds are pooled investment vehicles in which investors make purchases and sales directly from the mutual fund company. When an investor purchases shares, the mutual fund company creates more shares and expands the size of the fund (thus the name "open"). Likewise, the fund company must draw on its cash reserves or liquidate securities to meet redemptions. Share purchases and redemptions are transacted at the fund's net asset value (NAV), or the per-share value based on the market value of the underlying securities.

Closed-End Funds

By contrast, closed-end funds represent shares of a pooled investment fund that trades on an exchange. Investors purchase shares from existing shareholders rather than the fund company. Similarly, investors selling shares must find a willing buyer in the open market rather than from the fund company. In this way shares of closed-end mutual funds trade at prevailing market price based on supply and demand rather than at NAV. In general, closed-end mutual funds trade at a discount to NAV, although that is not always the case, and there is a robust body of research investigating why that is so. Interestingly, there is some evidence to suggest that the premium or discount is positively related to realized future performance.

Exchange-Traded Funds

A more recent financial innovation that has done much to change the mutual fund landscape is the exchange-traded fund (ETF). Like a closed-end mutual fund, ETFs trade on an exchange, as their name implies. Like an open-end mutual fund, the sponsoring fund company can create or redeem shares based on market demand. Unlike either a closed-end mutual fund or an open-end mutual fund, the share creation and redemption process can be done in kind. For example, a fund company for an S&P 500 Index ETF can infuse the ETF with shares of the constituent stocks underlying the S&P 500 Index to create more shares rather than using cash. Similarly, to redeem shares the fund company can receive the underlying S&P 500 stocks without triggering a taxable event. This in-kind creation and redemption process adds another layer of tax efficiency on an already potentially tax-efficient passive investment strategy.[6]

---

[5]As of August 2010.
[6]The tax efficiency of in-kind distribution is related to the ability of the ETF fund manager to redeem with low-basis positions.

The market for ETFs has grown rapidly since their introduction in 1997 in terms of assets under management, the number of funds, and the variety of underlying assets. ETFs can be found for nearly all equity and fixed income management styles, as well as many alternative assets, including commodities, real estate, and even hedge funds.

Most ETFs track a particular broad market or style-based index, or are at least managed passively. In recent years, however, a growing number of newly introduced ETFs are actively managed, so it is no longer accurate to equate ETFs with passive asset management.

Exchange-Traded Notes

Exchange-traded notes (ETNs) are similar to ETFs in that they trade on an exchange. Unlike an ETF in which the investor owns a pro rata share of the underlying securities, an ETN is simply a senior unsecured debt security issued by an underwriting bank. The security may promise to pay an amount equal to the return on a particular index. Alternatively, it may promise payment that limits the upside potential in exchange for providing some downside protection, similar to a payoff of a structured product.

As senior unsecured debt, ETNs have counterparty risk not present in ETFs. As we saw in the recent financial crisis, counterparty risk is a very real and significant issue. So what are the possible advantages?

Because ETNs do not have any underlying securities, there are no interest payments, dividend payments, or capital gains on underlying securities. Rather, ETNs are often treated like forward contracts for tax purposes. Unlike mutual funds, the entire gain is determined by when and if the investor sells the security and not by either the investment behavior of other fund shareholders or the tax characteristics of the underlying investments. This tax treatment, however, has not escaped the attention of tax authorities and may be revisited.

ETNs also have the advantage of having no tracking error with the indexes they are intended to mimic because each has a contractual obligation based on that index. Aside from their additional credit risk, ETNs also enjoy less liquidity than do many ETFs. Wealth managers need to weigh carefully the advantages and disadvantages and compare them to the situation at hand to determine which vehicle is best suited for portfolio construction.

Hedge Funds

Much can and has been said about hedge funds. Unlike their name implies, they may or may not implement an investment strategy related to hedging. Their primary distinguishing feature is the fact that they are not subject to the same regulatory and reporting requirements as traditional mutual funds under the theory that they are reserved for sophisticated high-net-worth investors. As a result, they are not an asset class as some would have us believe. This more lax regulatory oversight allows hedge fund managers to implement investment strategies that mutual funds cannot. For example, hedge funds often use leverage and short sales in their investment strategies.

An exhaustive discussion of hedge funds is beyond the scope of this chapter.[7] We would like to focus, however, on two fundamental characteristics of many (if not most) hedge funds that in our opinion significantly limit their value. First, a typical fee structure is the 2/20 arrangement in which a hedge fund manager receives as compensation 2 percent of assets under management on an annual basis plus 20 percent of any investment gains. By itself, 2 percent is a very hefty management fee that is extremely difficult for most investment managers to

---

[7]For additional detail see Mark Hurley, "Alternative Investments," in *The Investment Think Tank* (New York: Bloomberg Press).

consistently overcome. Adding the 20 percent incentive fee raises their hurdle even further. As a result, hedge fund managers must add substantial value to overcome the fees they charge.

Consider the unusual hedge fund manager who can consistently produce 14 percent returns annually. (Keep in mind that Bernie Madoff lured the investors that he swindled by fallaciously reporting a consistent annual return of 12 percent annually.) The 2 percent management fee reduces this investment return to 12 percent. The 20 percent incentive fee reduces it by another 2.8 percent (that is, $0.20 \times 14\%$), leaving only a 9.2 percent return for the investor. That doesn't sound too bad, but consider that the average geometric return for the stock market from 1926 to 2009 was 9.8 percent. But wait! There's more.

That 9.8 percent return could have been earned using a tax-efficient passive investment strategy. Many, if not most, hedge fund strategies are highly tax-inefficient because they either are based on high-turnover investment strategies or use relatively heavily taxed investment vehicles, such as options. This tax inefficiency can easily consume another 20 percent of the fund's pretax investment returns, reducing the investor's after-tax return to 7.36 percent.

Hedge fund fees have come under pressure in the aftermath of the most recent financial crisis, but they remain high. We are not categorically opposed to hedge funds and believe that they can be a useful investment vehicle in certain situations, but these concerns as well as others (such as the strong survival bias associated with hedge fund returns, limited retail access to institutional quality funds, and sometimes limited liquidity and strict lockup periods) lead us to believe that for retail investors, hedge funds are useful in the special case rather than the usual case.

MUTUAL FUND CLASSIFICATIONS

The most common classification system, and the one most familiar to the public, is the mutual fund's objective as reflected in its prospectus. Ostensibly, this is a statement of the objective the fund is trying to achieve. For many funds today, that objective may be to mimic a particular index, so one common classification that applies to both equity and fixed income mutual funds are index funds.

Equity Mutual Funds Classifications

In addition to equity index funds, a variety of other fund styles are available.

Balanced Funds

A balanced fund invests in a combination of stocks and bonds. In general, many balanced funds will keep at least 25 percent of the portfolio's assets in stocks and bonds at all times. Balanced funds can be flexible in response to economic change by shifting their mix of stocks and fixed income securities.

Growth and Income Funds

Growth and income funds seek both long-term capital growth and current income by investing primarily in equity securities. Growth and income are usually considered near equal objectives, although many funds classified as growth and income specifically state that income is secondary. These funds tend to invest in well-established companies that have a stable and reliable dividend history. When compared to growth and aggressive growth funds, these funds tend to have less volatility, lower expenses, lower turnover, and lower market value (price-earnings and price-book) ratios.

Equity Income Funds

Equity income funds have as their prime objective current income, with capital appreciation being secondary. As a result, these funds emphasize companies that pay above-average dividends. Since dividend yield is the less volatile component of total return (compared to price appreciation), these funds are generally less volatile than growth funds and growth and income funds.

Growth Funds

Growth funds invest for capital appreciation rather than current income. Their focus is on companies whose long-term earnings growth may exceed that of the market. Current income is either a secondary objective or not an objective at all.

Aggressive Growth Funds

Aggressive growth funds seek maximum capital gains. Toward this objective they may take high risks, buy volatile stocks, and trade them actively. They may employ techniques such as options, short selling, and leverage.

Fixed Income Mutual Funds Classifications

Unfortunately, the fund's stated objective is often misleading, particularly for fixed income funds. For example, some funds may say they are invested in government securities but allow a certain percentage of the fund to be invested in lower-rated securities or futures contracts. A few money market funds were found to have pieces of toxic asset-backed securities in them, causing their sponsors to "break the buck" during the financial crisis.

The wealth manager must be familiar with the various fund objectives, as they are the classifications clients will normally use (at least until they have been reeducated by the wealth manager). However, the wealth manager must also examine the underlying holdings of each fund to determine whether some other classification should be considered.

Corporate Bond (General)

Corporate bond funds seek income by investing in fixed income securities, particularly investment-grade bonds. They may be further defined by the quality of bonds in the portfolio. Subclasses include:

- *Corporate bond (high-quality)*—Primarily invested in bonds with ratings of A or better. Generally maintain an average rating of AA.
- *Corporate bond (high-yield)*—Primarily invested in bond with ratings below BBB.
- *Convertible bond*—Invested in convertible bonds and preferred stock.

Government Bond (General)

Funds that seek income by investing in Treasuries, agencies, and government-guaranteed mortgage-backed securities. Subclasses include:

- *Government (Treasury)*—Largely restricted to Treasury issues.
- *Government (mortgage)*—Primarily invested in GNMAs, FNMAs, and FHLMCs.

Municipal Bond

Funds that seek income in fixed income securities exempt from federal income taxes.

Money Market

Money market funds are designed to be short-term in nature and cash equivalents. As a result, they offer a low rate of return at low risk.

Market Capitalization

As noted in Chapter 14, returns and risk vary by company size. Equity mutual funds are further classified based on the market capitalization of the underlying holdings.

Small-Cap

Mutual funds that invest in companies with low market capitalizations are considered small-cap mutual funds. While there is no precise definition of small-cap, evaluation services such as Morningstar often define a small company as one with a market capitalization of below \$1 billion.

Mid-Cap

Mutual funds that emphasize medium-size companies are considered mid-cap. A mid-cap company usually has a market capitalization ranging from \$1 billion to \$8 billion.

Large-Cap

Mutual funds that emphasize companies with market capitalizations above \$8 billion are considered large-cap funds.

Geography

Mutual funds are also classified based on the geographic location of their underlying holdings.

International or Global

International mutual funds are typically defined as those that invest in markets outside of the United States. Global funds mix asset classes and generally invest in any country in the world, including the United States. Most international managers focus on the 20 major markets that represent the majority of the developed world.

Emerging Markets

Emerging market funds focus on smaller, less efficient markets (not necessarily smaller companies), which, despite the diminutive size of the individual markets, in aggregate are estimated to account for between one-quarter and one-half of the world's total economic output. While investments in these funds tend to be very volatile, they offer the potential for high returns.

Frontier Markets

Frontier markets are actually a segment of the emerging markets category representing the less economically developed markets within the emerging market classification.

Styles

As noted in Chapter 14, equity mutual funds are also typically classified by investment style: value, growth, and core (or blend). Morningstar/Ibbotson uses the following criteria to create the Morningstar Style Indices and Style Boxes based on underlying equity holdings:

- Value stocks are classified based on five value factors—forward price-to-earnings ratio, price to book, price to sales, price-to-cash flow, and dividend yield. The greatest weight is allocated to the forward price-to-earnings ratio.
- Growth stocks are classified based on five growth factors—forward long-term earnings growth rate, book value growth, sales growth, cash flow growth, and trailing earnings growth. The greatest weight is allocated to the forward long-term earnings growth rate.
- Core stocks are those not classified as value or growth.

Other Classifications

A variety of other classifications are available, particularly since the advent of ETFs and ETNs.

Sector

Not true asset classes, specialty or sector funds represent various undiversified funds that emphasize a specific market sector. This could include financial services, health care, technology, and utilities. Many specialty funds have high expenses, high portfolio turnover, and high manager turnover.

Commodities

This category can include aggregate commodity index funds or subsets invested in individual commodities, including precious metals. As discussed in Chapter 14, these funds add diversification to a portfolio due to their low correlation with other asset classes, other than during times of crisis.

Real Estate

Real estate funds direct their investment dollars to companies that derive the majority of their profits from real estate (primarily REITs). As with commodities funds, it is important to verify the correlation of the selected fund(s) with the asset class assumptions.

INFORMATION SOURCES

Information on mutual funds is widely available both directly from the funds and from independent sources.

The Fund

All too frequently, when evaluating managers, the wealth manager turns to independent data providers only. Although the independent provider is an indispensable source, the wealth manager must also carefully analyze the information available from the fund itself.

Fund Prospectus and Other Related Offering Documents

These documents should be scrutinized carefully so that the wealth manager fully understands the risks, opportunities, and fees of the offering.[8]

Summary of Expenses

The summary includes the various types of expenses that the fund will incur, such as management fees, 12b-1 fees, audit, legal, shareholders' services, transfer agent, and custodian expenditures. It will also provide information regarding items such as sales charges and deferred sales charges.

One common technique used by fund companies is to absorb a portion of the expenses for a limited period of time. If so, the agreement will be described in this portion of the prospectus. The agreement to absorb expenses is at the option of the fund and may be terminated without shareholder action. The wealth manager needs to carefully monitor such funds. If he or she does not monitor, a wealth manager may naively maintain a fund that subsequently eliminates its subsidy, effectively raising the expenses to the investor beyond an acceptable level.

Financial Highlights

This section includes information regarding income and capital charges. In addition, the ratio/supplemental data table includes historical data on the fund's net assets, expense ratio, and portfolio turnover.

Objective, Policy, and Risk Considerations

These sections detail how the fund will be invested and specify limitations regarding the types of securities it can invest in. They also detail such things as the ratings on bonds, the various countries the fund is allowed to invest in, as well as limitations regarding the investments in any one security or type of securities. Another section may stipulate its limitation on investing in restricted securities. Requested changes in a prospectus should be a caution flag for an advisor. For example, the request of a domestic equity manager to increase foreign holdings or a fixed income manager's request to increase its holdings in illiquid private placement securities should be a trigger for further investigation.

These sections also discuss to what extent a fund may borrow or lend its portfolio securities; whether it can write options on securities, indexes, or currencies; to what degree the fund will use futures; and its hedging ability if it invests in foreign securities. Other areas that may be covered are the ability of the fund to invest in closed-end funds or utilize repurchase agreements. Unfortunately, the trend has been for funds to request, from their shareholders, the authority to do practically anything they wish; hence, there is less value in relying on prospectus restrictions and a greater necessity for active monitoring.

Purchasing and Sale of Shares of the Fund

This section covers the sales charge break points and minimums. Also, there may be provisions in this section by which an advisor can acquire a load fund as a net asset value purchase.

---

[8]See also Robinson, Schulte, Marmorstein, Trent, and Gervais (2010).

Management of the Fund
This section discusses the management of the fund. Unfortunately there is likely to be limited information here. Rarely will the name of the individual(s) be disclosed. At most this section will alert the advisor to the existence of a submanager. The advisor must use other sources to adequately evaluate the management.

Investment Limitations
Included in this section are the restrictions imposed on the fund manager, and the types of securities, and investment techniques the manager is allowed to use.

Trustees and/or Board Members and 5 Percent Shareholders
If a single shareholder owns too much of the fund and decides to liquidate his or her ownership, it may adversely affect the market value of the fund. This is a particular risk in funds that invest in limited-market securities, such as small stocks, real estate investment trusts (REITs), municipal bonds, or any other low-trading-volume security.

Detailed Financials
In addition to a detailed listing of investment positions, the payables section under "Liabilities" provides information regarding the dollars being redeemed versus the amount being invested. This allows the advisor to review the degree of inflows and outflows of funds under management on a net basis that occur over a period of time. If too much cash in relation to the fund's asset base is flowing into or out of the fund, it may have too much cash, which may cause the fund manager to deviate from the specified management style. Too much cash outflow may force the manager to sell illiquid securities.

The next items to review are the fund's investment income and expenses. In the case of some high-expense funds, the investment income may actually be negative.

Footnotes
The next and last section to review is the statement footnotes. The footnotes many times provide substantial detail on what occurred in the fund, as well as the history behind its operations.

Annual and Semiannual Reports

Included in the semiannual or annual report, of course, are the financial statements. These statements provide the same type of financial data discussed earlier. Semiannually, the funds are required to provide their current holdings. As many of the independent data providers have agreements with many funds to receive more current updates, the independent data provider is a better source for position information.

A significant section is the letter written by the fund management. The letter may provide valuable insight as to the ongoing business and investment philosophy that the fund will utilize over time. A management that writes a letter providing little insight may in fact be providing important information regarding management's concern for the fund's investors.

Independent Publishers, Analysts, and Databases

There are a number of independent firms that provide data services to the practitioner regarding fund managers. As the major players are so well known and heavily marketed, here we simply share with the reader Harold's biases and recommendations.

Primary Independent Sources

We use the expression "primary independent" to describe those firms that are in the business of obtaining and distributing information regarding funds. These firms often provide their own proprietary rating systems; however, the rating systems are relatively simplistic and irrelevant for the wealth manager.

It is the responsibility of the wealth manager to evaluate a fund's style, performance, and risk in a far more detailed, sophisticated, and professional manner. A useful list of criteria for selecting data providers includes the following:

- *Extent of coverage.* How many funds are covered by the service?
- *Frequency of updates.* How frequently is the data updated, and how current is the data in the updates?
- *Search capabilities.* What fields are available for screening? Can specific search criteria be saved for future reference? Can the results be ranked?
- *Customization.* Does the database allow customized comparisons (e.g., one fund vs. another) or tracking of customized portfolios? Does it allow you to display only those data fields of interest?
- *Hypotheticals.* Does the program allow you to design hypothetical portfolios? Does it provide for comparisons between benchmarks and funds? Will it handle variable cash flows? Taxes?
- *Graphics.* Can the data be graphically displayed? In color? Printed? Printed in color?
- *Technical support.* What kind of technical support is available?

SCREENS AND THE SELECTION PROCESS

As noted earlier, fund descriptions such as "aggressive growth" and "growth and income" may have little meaning when selecting managers to implement an optimized portfolio. Once the wealth manager has determined which asset class and strategies will be used in the practice, he can begin the manager selection process. The following discusses the process Harold uses in determining those managers to include in his approved list.

Manager Sieve Overview

The process or sieve is designed to screen out inappropriate and unsuitable managers. Because there are thousands of managers to select from, the Manager Sieve requires multiple screens. We offer brief descriptions of these four screens followed by recommendations for specific criteria to be used in each screen.[9]

Screen #1—Asset Classes

This first pass eliminates thousands of inappropriate managers. The process requires that the wealth manager screen the available list of managers against the selected asset classes. For example, if he restricts the choice of managers to those participating in the Charles Schwab One Source Select list, he would overlay the One Source list with the selected asset classes. The funds passing that screen would include only One Source funds that matched the asset

---

[9]The following screens are general guidelines. If exceptional managers come to our attention and they do not pass screens #1 and #2, we will still pass them on to be tested by screen #3.

classes used in the firm's allocations. If, for example, he did not use load funds, their past performances, risk profiles, and expense structures would be irrelevant and they would not pass a no-load screen.

Screen #2—Fatal Flaws

Like screen #1, this is a global screen (i.e., it is applied across the board to all of the managers remaining in the selection pool after having passed screen #1). The criteria in screen #2 are what Harold calls fatal flaws. While screen #1 eliminated inappropriate but possibly good funds, screen #2 is intended to eliminate generically bad funds. Naturally, the criteria for generically bad are the responsibility of the wealth manager. An example of such a criterion is a maximum expense ratio or the existence of sales charges.

Screen #3—Philosophy, Process, and People

This screen is applied to each group of funds, asset class by asset class. It is based on a manager selection model suggested by Robert Ludwig of SEI that we call "Ludwig's Three Ps."[10] The premise of the model is that manager performance is an output. Initial manager evaluation should not focus on performance but on the three critical input factors that result in the performance output:

1. Philosophy
2. Process
3. People

    Screen #3 filters out managers based on these three Ps.

Screen #4—Performance

Now, after the universe of available managers has been whittled down to the relatively few remaining after passing through screens #1 through #3, we apply the test of performance. It is applied asset class by asset class.

Manager Sieve—The Specifics

Now let's take a look at the specifics of each screen within the manager sieve.

Screen #1—Asset Classes

As noted earlier, the screening process begins with the universe of available funds. In our case we generally begin with the no-load funds available through Charles Schwab, Fidelity, or TD Ameritrade. This includes ETFs, retail and institutional no-load funds, as well as those load funds offered to the clients of advisors at net asset value.

Selecting Funds by Asset Class

This is the first filter. Using our asset class taxonomy as detailed in Chapter 5, "Data Gathering and Analysis," we eliminate thousands of managers from consideration. For example, our criteria for core allocations eliminate all long-term and low-quality fixed

---

[10]Robert Ludwig, "The Role of Performance in the Mutual Fund Selection Process," *SEI Research*; Robert Ludwig, "Mutual Fund Performance: Predictive or Deceptive," IAFP 1994 Convention & Exposition, September 1994.

income funds, global fixed income funds, specialty funds, convertible funds, and aggressive growth funds.

Selecting Funds by Capitalization Class

This criterion narrows down the pool of appropriate managers by eliminating those funds that do not meet our required capitalization criterion. A significant decision required of the wealth manager is to determine whether the criterion chosen to select a manager's capitalization class will be average capitalization or median capitalization.[11] For example, Morningstar uses the median and Value Line uses the average. Harold recommends that the wealth manager use the median. At this stage, we eliminate from consideration any manager who purported to be a small-cap manager but had a portfolio median capitalization in excess of $2 billion.

Selecting Funds by Style

At this stage of the process, we use a style screen based on the portfolio style analysis used by Morningstar. Even though this standard will pass a number of managers who have a weak style orientation and managers who do not remain consistent to their style, we are not concerned, as screen #3 will later eliminate any managers considered wishy-washy. In the early stage of the analysis, the preference is to err on the side of passing an unacceptable manager through the screen rather than inadvertently rejecting a good manager.

Screen #2—Fatal Flaws

These are the criteria that a wealth manager considers mandatory. For example, we apply the following criteria.

Concentration

We do not believe in the use of sector funds in our core allocations. We are also concerned with excessive sector concentration. In order to avoid such managers, we screen out funds with sector weightings in excess of three times that of the S&P 500. For international equity funds we screen for weightings in excess of 35 percent for any country ex-Japan. The fund is eliminated in screen #2 if the allocation to Japan exceeds 150 percent of Japan's weighting in the EAFE index.

Quality

In keeping with our focus on high-quality fixed income investments, screen #2 eliminates those funds with less than an average bond quality rating of A.

Foreign Equities

As we believe that the asset class allocation is a critical factor in the long-term performance of the portfolio, we are hypersensitive regarding managers who drift from their style. At the stage of screen #2 we eliminate domestic equity managers who have allocations in excess of 20 percent in foreign equities.

---

[11]The median for the companies in the NYSE Composite is about $1.5 billion; the average is closer to $8 billion.

Expenses

If future returns revert to (or go even lower than) the mean of long-term historical returns, as we believe likely, then a fund's expenses will be one of the primary determinants of its performance for the next decade. Funds that are able to control costs and manage expenses will, all else being equal, outperform their peers that are burdened by higher expenses. A 1.5 percent expense ratio on an equity fund that earns 10 percent means that 15 percent of the return is lost.

Based on our belief that even the best of managers cannot overcome the hurdle of excessive expenses, we generally eliminate all fixed income funds with expense ratios in excess of 0.8 percent, domestic equity funds with expense ratios in excess of 1.2 percent, international equity (developed countries) funds with expense ratios in excess of 1.5 percent, and emerging market funds in excess of 2 percent.[12]

Performance Record

In spite of all of the research and the traditional warning that "past performance is no guarantee of future performance," most investors begin the manager selection process by starting with the manager's past performance. Evensky's Manager Sieve, with one exception, does not seriously consider performance until after screen #3. The exception is the elimination of poor performers at this stage. The traditional warning actually misstates the results of many studies.

A more accurate statement describing the results of the research would be that past superior performance does not guarantee future superior performance; however, past poor performance may predict future poor performance.[13] As a result, we screen out those funds that have performed in the bottom half of their asset class for the prior five years or the bottom one-third for the prior three years.

Soft Sieves

The following criteria do not automatically eliminate funds in screen #2. They are applied to each of the funds passing the screen. The decision to eliminate a fund based on these soft criteria is made by the investment committee case by case.

Fund Capitalization. There are different schools of thought about the ideal size of a mutual fund. On the one hand, one says that bigger is better—the more assets, the more a fund can benefit from economies of scale in administration and other expenses, brokerage costs, and so on. Also, a small fund may lack the buying power necessary to command a large enough share of the choicest stock issues, especially initial public offerings (IPOs). (This has occurred among real estate mutual funds, where the smaller funds may not be able to obtain positions in new REITs.)

On the other hand, some studies have indicated that the promised economies of scale often never materialize. As funds increase assets, the manager may find it difficult to find stocks meeting his investment criteria. This may cause the manager to purchase equities outside his guidelines, or to hold large sums of cash. Both problems can negatively impact performance.

In addition to the absolute size of the fund capitalization, it is important to study the history of a fund's growth in assets. Has the fund lost assets over the past few years? If so, why?

---

[12]We consider these generous standards; however, at this stage we would still rather err on the side of passing through a manager we might later reject than reject a manager we should have considered.

[13]The consistency of poor performance seems to primarily be related to excessive fund expenses, not incompetent management skills, and research bears this out.

Has the fund grown too rapidly over the past few years? Many funds solve the problem of rapid growth and large influxes of cash by closing to new investors. Part of the art of fund selection is to evaluate the credibility (or lack thereof)[14] of fund closings. We rarely eliminate funds from consideration solely due to the size of assets; however, we frequently eliminate funds at this stage due to rapid growth.

Manager Tenure. When analyzing a fund's historical performance, it is obviously important to determine whether the person(s) (or at least the philosophy and process) responsible for the past performance is still there. At screen #2, we typically eliminate funds with new managers if their management style seems to be significantly different from the prior managers. In effect, hiring such a manager would be to accept the famous pig in a poke. As funds rarely report this information, we rely on our manager interviews and the observations of Morningstar and Value Line analysts to alert us to these changes.

Turnover. A fund's total expenses are not completely revealed by an examination of its expense ratio. Brokerage commissions and trading costs, including bid-ask spreads, *are on top of* the disclosed expense ratio (see Exhibit 16.3). A fund's turnover rate is often the best indicator of trading costs. Hence, we will occasionally eliminate a fund due to what we consider excessive turnover.

Screen #3—Philosophy, Process, and People

We consider screen #3 the heart of our selection process. By the time we have completed screens #1 and #2, there are relatively few funds in each asset class remaining. With a reasonable number of candidates to consider, we can devote significant resources to evaluating each manager.

Philosophy

We ask managers why we should give them some of our clients' funds to manage. We expect a clearly defined, credible, and consistent statement of their strategic view of their investment markets. We agree with Charles Ellis that this is a competition of professionals. We want to know how managers will provide our clients excess risk-adjusted returns on the funds under their care, given that the market for alpha is a zero-sum game.

In order to evaluate a fund's philosophy (and process and people), we employ the following steps.

We review the fund's prospectus, most recent semiannual and annual reports, and marketing materials.

With that as background, we then review the comments of the Value Line and Morningstar analysts.

We then query our Alpha Group[15] friends for any information or thoughts they may have regarding the manager.

Finally, with all of this information at our disposal, we interview the manager. On occasion the meeting is in person, but it is usually by phone. The interview allows the manager to elaborate on his or her philosophy. It is also an opportunity for us to obtain a gut feeling as to the manager's competency and a comfort level with his or her style and

---

[14]For example, was the closing enacted well in advance of the effective date as a marketing strategy to generate new investments?

[15]The Alpha Group is an informal study group of 17 financial professionals founded over a decade ago.

personality. Although it may not be scientifically sound, we have rejected managers based on our interview. We hire commitment, brains, and passion, and we reject pomposity, simplicity, and marketing hype.

Process

Process is the manager's daily implementation of his or her philosophy. As with the philosophy, we are looking for a clearly defined, consistent, and verifiable process. Examples of process would include:

- Who makes the decisions (e.g., research, allocations, purchases, and sales)?
- How are new investment ideas generated?
- What resources are devoted to research?
- What is the manager's trading discipline?
- What is the manager's buy and sell discipline?
- What is the firm's compensation policy?

We are not concerned with the amount anyone is paid. We want to know if the manager is paid based on long-term or short-term performance. We want to know if the compensation structure encourages teamwork or star performance.

People

Generally, we are concerned with the background and experience of all of the members of the fund's management team. Also important are the capabilities of the staff support and the process for managing professional growth. Naturally, we are particularly concerned with the lead decision maker(s). It may be of little value to know that the fund passed the philosophy and process test if the manager is new and plans on implementing a new philosophy and a new process. A new manager may have a fabulous track record, but if the new investment style is different from that of the predecessor, the portfolio repositioning may generate portfolio turnover. This could mean increased trading costs and increased capital gains distributions, as well as style drift. However, just because a fund has a new manager does not automatically eliminate a fund from consideration. If the new manager's investment philosophy and discipline can be determined from an examination of his or her prior record, either at the fund (if the new manager was a member of the investment team) or the record of a fund previously managed and it is consistent with the past manager, the fund may still be an acceptable choice. As Don Phillips of Morningstar recommends, we are looking for managers who have a passion for their work.

Philosophy, Process, and People—An Example

Many years ago I received a marketing piece from a fund that so impressed me that I saved it for future reference. When writing this section I realized that although the Three Ps describe the core of our selection process, they may not be meaningful without an example. The following excerpts from a few sections provide an excellent example of a marketing piece that reflects the substance of the Three Ps instead of marketing hype.

Our Investment Philosophy

Over the years we have been guided by the philosophy that the most profitable investment opportunities are found in companies experiencing periods of rapid change. We believe these dynamic companies fall into one of two categories:

1. *High Unit Volume Growth: This includes both established and emerging firms, offering new or improved products.*
2. *Positive Life Cycles: These companies experiencing major change . . . change as varied as new management, products, or technologies.*

The Research Staff
Most analysts have gone through our in-house training process. As a further aid to staffing, we established a program to track the careers of thousands of practicing securities analysts.

Streamlined Decision Making
Purchase Decisions—Our "bottom up" approach to stock selection places primary emphasis on individual security selection . . . analysts present investment ideas directly to senior management . . . if senior management agrees with the case made for a stock, a buy program is implemented immediately. For optimum liquidity, we never own more than eight days' average trading volume of any stock across all accounts (four days for NASDAQ stocks).

Portfolio Management
A performance run is performed twice daily to give us a sense of overall performance. Additional computer tabulations show how each stock is performing in absolute terms and relative to the market for 5, 10, 15, and 20 days, and for the year-to-date.

The top-down component links the firm's database to each portfolio. Portfolio managers can evaluate overall portfolio characteristics such as weighted growth of earnings per share . . . as well as each portfolio's reaction to different stimuli from the economy.

Only after a fund has passed through screen #3 do we begin to seriously consider its performance record.

Screen #4—Performance

> If the only reason you give someone to buy your fund is because you are No. 1, then you should expect people to sell when you are No. 2.
> —*William Guilfoyle, President of G.T. Global*

As this screen is performance based, it is worthwhile to once again place the importance of performance in perspective having already discussed the technical details of measuring and evaluating performance in the previous chapter. As we have already mentioned numerous studies that suggest how worthless past performance is as a predictor of future performance, Harold thought it would be more interesting to hear from the real world. The following are the comments of three friends he considers among the best of wealth managers:[16]

- Ross Levin[17]—"Past performance has been a very poor indicator of future performance."
- Roger Gibson—"Trying to identify funds that will beat the market represents a triumph of hope over experience."

---

[16]Robert N. Veres, "Rest in Peace?" *Investment Advisor*, September 1994, 54–67.
[17]This is a surprise for Ross. He didn't think Harold would ever publicly admit that he's "among the best."

• Lynn Hopewell—"Picking individual mutual funds is the last thing a financial advisor should get paid to do."

Wrapping it all up, Harold's favorite curmudgeon-journalist, Bob Veres, wrote, "Put another way, all of the time and research spent evaluating track records may be just as ineffective as consulting an astrologer, relying on a Ouija board, or using Tarot cards to select mutual funds."

With those sobering reminders regarding the importance of performance (and the admission that I keep a Ouija board and crystal ball in my office), let's continue our description of the Evensky & Katz performance screen.

Total Return—Relative
Historical returns should not be viewed in a vacuum but must be viewed *relative* to appropriate benchmarks. The selection of appropriate benchmarks is another piece of the wealth manager's art. Until the advent of ETFs, we used the manager's peer universe as our benchmarks. However, now that ETFs exist in almost every conceivable market flavor, we consider an investable index a far superior benchmark alternative. Once the benchmarks have been selected, it is necessary to compare the fund's performance over a wide variety of periods.

By Market Cycles. According to Standard & Poor's (S&P) there have been about 10 completed bear markets and bull markets since 1950. S&P defined bear markets as a drop of 20 percent or more from the market's previous high. Returns on the subject fund can be compared to returns on appropriate benchmarks for the same periods. In comparing relative returns during bear markets, you can assess how well the fund manages downside risk. S&P reports the following dates for bear market periods:[18]

August 3, 1956, to October 22, 1957
December 12, 1961, to June 26, 1962
February 9, 1966, to October 7, 1966
November 29, 1968, to May 26, 1970
January 11, 1973, to October 3, 1974
November 28, 1980, to August 12, 1982
August 25, 1987, to December 4, 1987
July 16, 1990, to October 11, 1990
March 24, 2000, to October 9, 2002
October 9, 2007, to March 9, 2009

By Year, Quarter, and Month. An examination of a fund's total return on a rolling year-by-year and even on a quarter-to-quarter and monthly basis is advisable. Did a fund get lucky in only one year, which has boosted its historical three-year or five-year returns, but has never duplicated that superior performance before or since?

Exceptional Returns. Did the fund achieve returns that were too good? That is, did the fund's performance far exceed the returns of other funds in its asset class? Such exceptional returns can be a warning that the manager is either investing outside of the asset class and/or

---

[18]"Surviving a Bear Market," Standard & Poor's, www.standardandpoors.com.

implementing aggressive strategies. How about the *bad* returns? If a fund had a quarter or an entire year where it showed a substantial loss relative to its benchmark, can your clients stand a similar loss in the future? Morningstar provides monthly return tables that can be quickly scanned for exceptional returns.

Risk Matters.   It is, of course, unwise to examine performance without also considering risk. Therefore, it is helpful to examine risk-adjusted performance using the performance appraisal measures (Sharpe ratio, Treynor ratio, etc.) discussed in Chapter 15.

MONITORING THE MANAGER—EVENSKY & KATZ POLICY

What gets measured gets managed.

—Anonymous

Once the wealth manager has selected a universe of approved managers, he or she must constantly monitor their performance. The primary focus of the process should be to monitor the approved managers' adherence to their stated philosophy and process; presumably that's why they were hired. We are very patient with poor performance and very impatient with changes in philosophy or process.

Performance

In evaluating performance, it is important to examine the returns generated by the manager relative to the risk undertaken as well as relative to other investment alternatives.

Relative to the S&P 500

Unless the manager is a core domestic manager, we consider performance relative to the broad domestic market irrelevant. This seems like an obvious policy. Unfortunately, the media loudly and consistently trumpets "market" returns (i.e., the Dow or S&P 500) as if they represent the only real measure of performance. The framing of this policy is part of our continuing effort to manage our clients' expectations. By discussing our policy early on with new clients, we reduce their discomfort during those periods when our asset class managers underperform the broad market.

Relative to Other Peer Group Managers

Although we track our managers' performance compared to other managers with similar asset class/style orientations, we do not use a divergence in performance as a specific criterion for manager evaluation. As we discussed in Chapter 15, peer groups make poor benchmarks because they lack several qualities of a valid benchmark.

We use the comparison of a manager's performance to a peer group as an early warning signal for style drift. For example, extraordinary short-term performance vis-à-vis a peer group raises a red flag. We then investigate the cause of the superior performance. If it is attributable to the successful implementation of the stated philosophy, we smile and call the manager to say, "Great job!" If it is attributable to a successful but out-of-style bet, we frown and call and ask, "What's up?" Our primary standard for relative performance is comparison to an appropriate benchmark (i.e., an investable index).

Relative to Their Benchmark

If managers have remained consistent to their philosophy and process, we are patient with underperformance. For approximately two to three quarters, we take no action. If the underperformance continues through the fourth quarter, we place the manager under review.

Under Review

At this stage, we neither fire the manager nor do we remove him or her from the approved list. We do, however, significantly increase our monitoring efforts. This includes a personal interview with the manager to discuss the underperformance, contact with the Morningstar analyst who monitors the manager, and queries of Alpha Group friends for any observations they may have. We also carefully review the changes in the fund's portfolio positions as well as a detailed historical review of its modern portfolio theory (MPT) statistics.

The goal of this process is to confirm our preliminary conclusion that the manager has remained consistent to the philosophy and process and is just suffering from the endemic market malady of being in the wrong place at the wrong time. If we are comfortable with the manager's response to our concerns and we believe that he is remaining consistent in his philosophy, we make no changes. However, we notify our clients that the fund is under review and, as a precaution, we also begin the process of searching for a possible replacement manager.

If the manager's performance continues to be subpar for an additional three to four quarters, we either place him on the watch list or replace him with a new manager.

Watch List

This describes a list of funds that are no longer on our approved list but in which we maintain positions. Although we are patient, there comes a time that the pain of underperformance becomes so intense as to require action. For our practice, that is about two years. By then, even if we cannot account for the underperformance, we consider firing the manager.

The problem we frequently face is that firing a manager may generate a significant taxable event for our taxable clients. We do not let taxes dominate our investment management, but we do not ignore their potential impact. Once again, relying on our intelligent application of the art of wealth management, we attempt to balance the tax consequences of firing the manager with the market risk of keeping the manager. If the manager has remained consistent to his style, if his underperformance is relatively modest, if we believe that his performance is likely to improve, and if our clients have significant capital gains exposure, we will keep our positions in the fund for our taxable clients. For sheltered accounts and new clients, we will use a new manager in that asset class. The old manager is placed on our watch list.

Consistency

> Someone might ask, "Did they turn stupid overnight?" The answer is no. We under-performed, but we stuck to our philosophy.
> —*David Minella, President, LST Asset Management*

For managers on our approved list, our monitoring of consistency is based on fundamental qualitative portfolio analysis and mathematical fundamental factor analysis, not statistical factor analysis. That's a fancy way of saying we look at the portfolio and talk to the manager. We look at, but do not rely on, the style analysis charts.

Portfolio

In spite of his belief in the value of return analysis, fundamentally Harold agrees with Don Phillips. When it all shakes out, it's what's in the portfolio that counts. What is the manager doing with our client's money? We review the positions, name by name, to see if they seem consistent with the manager's philosophy. We do not expect to see go-go firms in our value manager's portfolio or dogs in our growth manager's portfolio. The process is unquestionably subjective, but we consider it our first line of defense.

Fundamental Factors—Primary

The four primary factors we track are management, book-to-market ratio, capitalization, and standard deviation. If there are any significant changes in any of these factors, the result is an immediate and detailed review of the portfolio.

Fundamental Factors—Secondary

These factors are secondary in that variations do not necessarily trigger an immediate full-scale review but often trigger a call to the manager for an explanation. The secondary factors include:

- *Cash positions.* We look for variations from the manager's normal cash allocation range.
- *Turnover.* A significant increase in turnover. For example, if the normal turnover is 40 percent, we become concerned if it exceeds 60 percent; if the normal turnover is 90 percent, we are unlikely to become concerned unless it exceeds 135 percent.
- *Maturity/duration.* We look for movements toward either end of the fund's policy range.
- *Quality.* We watch for any change in the average quality rating.
- *Expenses.* Any change in excess of 5 basis points gets our attention.
- *Sector allocations.* Any changes that result in the portfolio's allocations exceeding the standards described in the Investment Policy Statement (see Chapter 13) prompt a call to the fund.

Statistical Factors

Although our primary criteria for monitoring our approved managers are fundamental factors, we see little reason to ignore the possible benefits of statistical factors, so we review the funds' style analysis charts.

External Factors

External factors include any source of independent information. Examples include:

- Morningstar and Value Line Analysis.
- *No-Load Fund* newsletter—Ken Gregory and Craig Litman's manager interview and comments are always worth reading.
- Information provided directly from the fund, including the fund's marketing material.

We cannot count on information being available on every manager. We use what we can find, including:

- Interviews.
- Commentary and analysis in the media (e.g., *Forbes*, *Barron's*, *AAII Journal*).

- Manager interviews.
- Conference calls (e.g., Schwab, fund sponsor, Alpha Group).
- Meetings: Morningstar, Financial Planning Association, The National Association of Personal Financial Advisors, CFA Institute.
- Networking (e.g., Alpha Group).
- Professional conferences.

PARTING COMMENTS

Once managers have been approved, it is critical to continually evaluate whether they adhere to their investment philosophy and how consistently they follow their investment process. Fund managers should not change their stripes as market cycles come and go. Otherwise, all of the effort expended in the selection process will be worthless. Although we may not be able to guarantee the managers' performance, we should be able to guarantee our diligence.

RESOURCES

Bergstresser, Daniel, John Chalmers, and Peter Tufano. 2007. "Assessing the Costs and Benefits of Brokers in the Mutual Fund Industry." SSRN Working Paper #616981, October.

Bers, Martina, and Jeff Madura. 2000. "Why Does Performance Persistence Vary among Closed-End Funds?" *Journal of Financial Services Research*, Vol. 17, No. 2 (August): 127–147.

Bogle, John C. 2005. "The Mutual Fund Industry 60 Years Later: For Better or Worse?" *Financial Analysts Journal*, Vol. 61, No. 1 (January/February): 15–24.

Chalmers, John M. R., Roger M. Edelen, and Gregory B. Kadlec. 2001. "Fund Return and Trading Expenses: Evidence on the Value of Active Management." Working paper.

Dellva, Wilfred L., and Gerard T. Olson. 1998. "The Relationship between Mutual Fund Fees and Expenses and Their Effects on Performance." *Financial Review*, Vol. 33: 85–104.

Dowen, Richard J., and Thomas Mann. 2004. "Mutual Fund Performance, Management Behavior, and Investor Costs." *Financial Services Review*, Vol. 13, No. 1 (Spring): 79–91.

Fortin, Rich, and Stuart Michelson. 1999. "Fund Indexing versus Active Management: The Results Are . . ." *Journal of Financial Planning* (February): 74–81.

Jayaraman, Narayanan, Ajay Khorana, and Edward Nelling. 2002. "An Analysis of the Determinants and Shareholder Wealth Effects of Mutual Fund Mergers." *Journal of Finance*, Vol. 83, No. 3 (June): 1521–1550.

Karceski, Jason, Miles Livingston, and Edward S. O'Neal. 2004. "Portfolio Transactions Costs at U.S. Equity Mutual Funds." Working paper.

Malhotra, D. K., and Robert W. McLeod. 1997. "Any Empirical Analysis of Mutual Fund Expenses." *Journal of Financial Research*, Vol. 20, No. 2 (Summer): 175–190.

Robinson, Thomas, David Schulte, Howard Marmorstein, William Trent, and Eric Gervais. 2010. "Reading the Fine Print: Helping Clients Evaluate Mutual Fund Prospectuses." *Journal of Financial Planning* (April): 54–63.

Swedroe, Larry. 2000. "Is It a Search for the Holy Grail?" *Journal of Accountancy* (January): 32–39.

Yan, Xuemin. 2006. "The Determinants and Implications of Mutual Fund Cash Holdings: Theory and Evidence." *Financial Management*, Vol. 35, No. 2 (Summer): 67–91.

CHAPTER 17

PHILOSOPHY, PROCESS, AND PEOPLE

Find your niche; listen closely; reward substance; insist on value; recognize quality; demand quality; question basic assumptions; encourage simplicity; question certainties; imagine the future; become better informed; give the most.

—Harold Evensky

Our previous chapter, "Selecting Investment Managers," suggested that the criteria for selecting a money manager should be philosophy, process, and people. We believe that wealth managers should be judged by the same standards. This concluding chapter is about these three Ps: philosophy, process, and people. The following section describes the practice philosophy at Evensky & Katz (E&K). The astute reader may view it as a summary of much the book. This would be correct, but should not be a surprise. Any wealth manager's practice philosophy should reflect his or her core investment management style.

PHILOSOPHY

Without a clearly defined philosophy, the process is irrelevant and the people rudderless. The following is the philosophy of Evensky & Katz. As with all of the opinion pieces in this book, it is not intended as a recommendation or model for everyone's practice. It is offered as a framework for readers, to stimulate them to develop their own philosophy. It is important that wealth managers have a philosophy, not that they adopt the E&K model.

Having set the scene for this chapter, the following is a formal statement of the philosophy that defines E&K's practice. The entire staff participates, at different levels, in the development of the firm's philosophy. All members of the firm are committed to its consistent implementation.

Financial Planning

We believe that ours is a financial planning practice, albeit one specializing in what we call wealth management. We are solely concerned with assisting our clients in meeting their life goals through the proper management of their financial resources. Our success is not measured by performance statistics but rather by our clients' success in achieving their goals.

Our practice begins and ends with the needs of the client. It is process driven. Solutions can be developed only after appropriate data (both quantitative and qualitative) have been gathered and evaluated. Related issues may be identified, and clients should be directed to other appropriate professionals for their resolution. Implementation, continuous monitoring, and, as necessary, modification are integral parts of the process.

The firm's advisors are expected to become CFP licensees and are supported in earning additional professional designations (e.g., CFA, AIF). All of the advisors are expected to be active participants in professional organizations such as the Financial Planning Association (FPA), CFA Institute, The National Association of Personal Financial Advisors (NAPFA), and other professional organizations.

Continuing education is mandatory, and the expectation is that the hours earned will far exceed the minimum required. Advisors are expected to maintain basic competence in all areas of comprehensive planning as well as particular expertise in the specialties of estate, retirement, and investment planning.

Goal Setting

We believe that our clients must set their own goals. It is our responsibility to educate them in the process and to assist them to define, quantify, and prioritize their goals. It is also our responsibility to assist them to recognize that there may be hidden goals (e.g., risk management issues) that may take priority over investment issues. Our ultimate task is to empower our clients to achieve their goals.

Rule of Thumb Planning

We believe that planning according to rules of thumb is an incompetent and unprofessional way for a wealth manager to plan for a client's financial independence. Examples of rule of thumb planning include simplifying assumptions for capital needs analysis, life cycle investing, packaged asset allocation models, and black box optimization.

Cash Flow

We believe that clients need total, after tax and expense, real return, not dividends and interest. The traditional concept of an income portfolio is archaic and places unnecessary and inappropriate restrictions on portfolio design. Plans structured to match dividends and interest with cash flow, in the long run, are likely to fail to meet the client's inflation-adjusted cash flow needs.

Capital Needs Analysis Assumptions

We believe that conservative assumptions are a dangerous myth. A conservative assumption (e.g., ignoring Social Security) will result in a need for a higher-return, greater-volatility portfolio. Capital needs analysis return requirements should be based on real rate of return estimates. Retirement planning time horizon (i.e., mortality) should be based on the client's unique family health history, not standard mortality tables. Plans should not be prepared based on a client's unrealistic expectations; if necessary, we will refuse the engagement.

The Client

As noted earlier, we believe that wealth management is a specialty of financial planning and, as such, the wealth manager's primary concern and allegiance is to the client. However, we cannot successfully assist clients without their full cooperation. The planning process must be at least as important to the client as it is to us. If this commitment on the part of the client is not forthcoming, we will not agree to an engagement.

The client need not be an individual. It might be a trust, endowment, or pension plan. However, as financial planners, we will treat the client as we would an individual, following the financial planning process as it applies to that client. For example, with a trust client, we will not simply focus on the investment portfolio. We will carefully balance the unique needs of each of the income and remainderman beneficiaries (e.g., current cash flow requirements, inflation, taxes, risk tolerance, and legal constraints).

Risk Tolerance

We believe that a client's risk tolerance is the maximum emotional pain a client can sustain while remaining fully invested. It is a significant constraint in the wealth management process. Our success can be measured by our clients' ability to sleep during turbulent markets. Clients have a fuzzy understanding of risk. It is our responsibility to ensure, as much as possible, before proceeding with the development of recommendations, that we share with the client the same concept of risk. This can be accomplished by client education and appropriate risk tolerance questionnaires. We believe that we must make an effort to continually improve our knowledge of cognitive psychology as it applies to these issues.

Tax Constraints

We believe that taxes must be considered, much like the need for liquidity. However, the goal of tax planning should be to maximize after-tax returns, not to minimize taxes. Investment issues (e.g., risk exposure) should take priority over taxes. For example, non-diversified low-basis stock should be sold. Neither reported turnover nor holding period calculated from reported turnover is a useful measure of tax efficiency. Variable annuities should be considered only when asset protection is an issue (in those states where the law protects annuity assets) or when the tax savings can demonstrably overcome the costs associated with the annuity and provide a premium adequate to offset the annuity's relative inflexibility.

Behavioral Clients

We believe behavioral theory is a far better descriptor of our clients' behavior than the "rational man." As a consequence, we incorporate the lessons of behavioral theory into our practice (e.g., risk coaching, report design).

Investment Theory

We began this chapter with the observation that "Without a clearly defined philosophy, the process is irrelevant and the people rudderless." For the wealth manager there can be no more important "rudder" than the firm's basic investment philosophy. The following is the underlying investment philosophy that guides Harold's firm.

Risk and Return Measures

We believe in the use of appropriate mathematical measures of risk and return. The primary measure of risk should be standard deviation. The concept of semivariance is intellectually appealing but not yet a useful measure for the wealth manager. Total return should be the basic criterion for the measurement of return. This includes real, time-weighted, and dollar-weighted returns. Our primary measure of risk-adjusted return is the Sharpe ratio. We no longer use alpha and beta as measures. Duration, not maturity, is the appropriate measure of a bond's exposure to interest rate risk (within narrow rate changes). Convexity is an important measure of a bond's sensitivity to large changes in rates.

Mathematical Tools and Techniques

We believe that wealth managers should stay abreast of current investment research and mathematical tools and techniques and incorporate them in their practices as they become useful. Current examples of useful tools include Monte Carlo simulation and regression analysis (e.g., factor analysis). Examples of techniques that wealth managers should be following include advances in concepts such as semivariance and neural networks.

Efficient Market Hypothesis

We believe in the weak form of the efficient market hypothesis (EMH). We reject the use of classic technical analysis and market timing.

Growth versus Value

We believe in the conclusions of the Fama-French research that, over time, value portfolios will provide superior returns. However, we also believe that a sole allocation to value will result in interim divergence from the broad markets that our behavioral clients would find unacceptable.

Active versus Passive

We believe that the choice between active and passive management is not either-or. We use both. Passive management offers lower transaction costs and minimal asset class drift; the portfolio is frequently more tax efficient; and there is significant academic research suggesting long-term superior investment performance. Active management offers the opportunity for superior returns, controlled volatility, and bragging rights.

Asset Allocation

We believe that for retail investors, the portfolio policy is the primary determinant of long-term portfolio performance. Implementation of concentrated portfolios, either in economic sectors or with specific managers, is risky and inappropriate for wealth management clients. The major asset classes are cash equivalents, fixed income, and equity. We consider taxable and tax-free domestic and foreign bonds all to be important potential fixed income classes. We do not consider long-term or low-quality fixed income for our fixed income allocations. Equity allocations are divided between domestic and foreign. Domestic stock allocations are divided between large-cap and small-cap. We further divide the domestic allocations between growth and value styles. We believe that international equity allocations belong in all portfolios.

We believe that reasonable expectations for real equity market returns over the next decade are in the range of 3 percent to 6 percent. In such a low return environment, for retail investors, the expense and tax drag on net-net real portfolio returns overwhelm the enhanced return benefits associated with traditional multi–asset class, multistyle portfolio design. Very simply, for retail clients the old way will not work in the future. As a consequence, we believe that advisors must revisit and revise their investment policy design and that an appropriate viable alternative is core and satellite.

We believe in maintaining a strategic allocation and only infrequently revise that allocation. Although we believe in rebalancing to the strategic allocation, the influence of taxes and transaction costs leads us to conclude that contingent rebalancing with fairly wide bands is the most appropriate solution. Although we do not currently implement a broad portfolio tactical allocation overlay, we do allocate between 10 percent and 30 percent of the equity allocation to satellite investments that are managed with a tactical overlay.[1]

Optimization

We believe that mathematical optimization is the appropriate method for designing a strategic asset allocation model. However, we also believe that an optimizer is simply a tool to be used by a knowledgeable wealth manager. The primary controls over the optimizer are the development of logical forward-looking input data (input should not be historical projections) and an awareness of the optimizer's sensitivities to the input and appropriate constraints. The final recommendations should not be based on the optimizer's unconstrained optimal solutions but rather the optimal suboptimal solution.

Arithmetic versus Geometric Returns

We believe in using geometric returns for historical analysis and future estimates. Arithmetic returns do not appropriately incorporate the drain that investment volatility has in the wealth accumulation process.

Time Diversification

We believe that the concept of time diversification is appropriate for retirement planning. As a related issue, we do not believe that any investment should be made for a goal with less than a five-year time horizon. Generally, funds required in less than five years should be placed in money market funds or fixed income securities (e.g., CDs, Treasures) with maturity dates equal to or less than the goals' time horizons.

Implementation

As critical as it is for a practitioner to have a clearly defined investment philosophy, it remains an academic concept until it's translated into action. Here are some of the critical implementation steps at Evensky & Katz.

Policy

We believe that an investment policy should be written and should be customized to the needs of the client. It should describe the client's goals and discuss the client's risk tolerance. The policy should describe the strategic model and the parameters for rebalancing. Any special constraints should be specified. Criteria for manager selection and evaluation should be included.

The policy should include a measure of expected real return and a discussion of expected volatility. It should include pertinent assumptions used in the development of the strategic allocation.

Managers

We believe that professional money managers will provide results far superior to a client's or wealth manager's direct security selection and management. With rare exceptions, for most

---

[1] "Tactical asset allocation (TAA) is a dynamic strategy that actively adjusts a portfolio's strategic asset allocation (SAA) based on short-term market forecasts. Its objective is to systematically exploit inefficiencies or temporary imbalances in equilibrium values among different assert asset or subasset classes." (From a primer on tactical asset allocation strategy evaluation, Vanguard Research, July 2010.)

retail investors individual security wrap account management is inefficient and expensive. The universe of public and institutional funds and exchange-traded funds (ETFs) offers the best alternative for superior management.

We believe that managers should be selected and evaluated based on their philosophies, processes, and people. Once selected, an active manager should be allowed periods of poor performance if the manager remains consistent to the philosophy and process but should be replaced immediately if he strays significantly from the stated philosophy or process.

Evaluation of managers should entail a detailed review of all available pertinent information, including both fundamental qualitative and return factor analysis. However, the ultimate decision to hire or fire should be based on fundamental data. Performance measurement should be against appropriate benchmarks, not broad market indexes.

Ongoing Management

We believe that there should be a regular review of a client's situation to determine if the client is continuing to move in the direction of achieving stated goals. This includes revisions in strategic allocations as a result of revised assumptions or changing client circumstances or goals. We should continue to educate our clients, always remaining sensitive to the volatility of each one's expectations. Our responsibility is to ensure that our client stays the course and does so with a minimum of emotional pain. The focus should always be the client and the achievement of the client's goals, not the performance of the portfolio.

Cash Flow

We believe in a two-bucket approach, as reflected in the Evensky & Katz cash flow strategy that bifurcates a client's assets between a liquidity bucket and an investment bucket. Further bucketing the investment portfolio is expensive and tax inefficient.

The Practice of Wealth Managers

We believe that we are uniquely qualified to integrate the skills and talents of financial planning with investment skills, knowledge, and technology previously available only to large institutional clients, and to do so for the benefit of the retail client. In effect, we are the institutional advisor for the retail client.

The primary market for our services is clients (including trusts, pensions, and other fiduciary accounts) with investment portfolios between $500,000 and $10 million.

We believe that we serve in a fiduciary capacity and that we are particularly qualified to serve as advisor to investment fiduciaries (e.g., pension trustees).

Our philosophy is the description of how we put the prior chapters into practice. Now it's your turn to determine and define what sets you apart.

PROCESS AND PEOPLE

For the balance of this chapter we invited Deena Katz,[2] one of the profession's leading experts on practice management, to address the last two Ps, process and people.

---

[2]Dr. Katz is an Associate Professor in the Personal Financial Planning Division at Texas Tech University, where she brings over 20 years of practice and consulting experience to the education of the next generation of financial planning practitioners. She is also a principal with Evensky & Katz. The material in this section is based on her guidebook (Katz 2009).

The Killer Process

Practitioners have long dreamed of the "killer software," the fully integrated program that would solve all our back-office problems and take out the garbage too. A few years ago, Moss Adams completed an operational study of the industry for Pershing, called *Mission Possible* (you can get this from a Pershing representative—start with www.pershing.com) that discussed advisor operational issues, including software needs. Pershing discovered that most advisors don't use much of the capability of any of their software programs. Most learn enough to get the job done and that's it. The learning curve for most software programs is high, and advisors just don't allocate enough time to get the most out of each one. Pershing's conclusions? What advisors need is the "killer process."

That process begins with software. I think every good practice should have to operate efficiently. I won't make specific suggestions because new software is made available all the time, but I will give you a contact to stay current with the brightest and best: www.Virtual OfficeNews.com. It's the brainchild of David Drucker and Joel Bruckenstein, who track new software, test it, and then report how or whether you should give it a spin.

There are three types of software I believe are essential to every planning practice:

1. *Client relationship management (CRM) software* with the capability to track and store information about your client and handle client systems and processes, as well as interoffice and external communications.
2. *Financial planning software*—Software with the ability to assist you in making planning recommendations for clients, including retirement calculations, life insurance needs, college funding, and tax and estate planning strategies.
3. *Portfolio management software*—Software specifically designed to download client positions and pricing and generate reports with time-weighted and dollar-weighted performance at intervals you set.

While there are other resource software programs that you will find useful, these few are essential to your smooth operations.

Beginning the Process

Once you have your software in place, focus on your processes. An easy way to begin is to build a flowchart of the major activities you have in your practice. The idea is to track how each job is handled and who handles it so you can assess where you might make improvements to reduce time and energy. If you have never tracked your processes, or if you are starting from scratch, try creating a flowchart of where information flows. Exhibit 17.1 presents a sample prospect process.

The point here is that in order for you to see how information flows, you are going to have to document it. Once this is done, review it with your staff to see how you can manipulate the flow to become more efficient. Try to automate as much as possible. Ask these questions:

- What functions must I perform?
- What functions can someone with lesser skills do?
- What functions can a machine accomplish?
- What functions are redundant?
- Are there any systems of checks and balances we need to incorporate?

EXHIBIT 17.1   Prospect Process

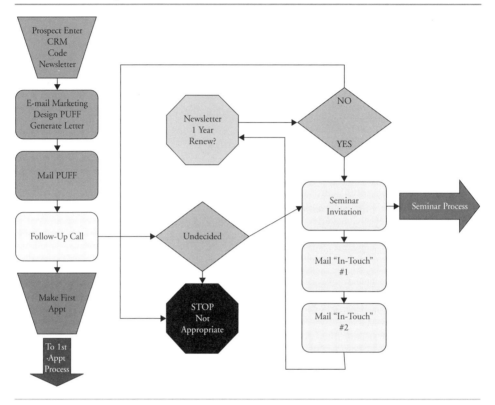

- Does the information flow logically and efficiently?
- Can or should any of these functions be outsourced?

Once you have visually reviewed your systems, you can begin to document how each function is being accomplished. Look at the chart in Exhibit 17.1. The first shape indicates that someone is entering a prospect into the client relationship management software and coding it for a newsletter. If we were to break this job down, we would document how to start the software, how to enter potential clients, and how to code them as prospects. We would indicate that they are to receive a number of mailings from us, including our newsletter, and enter a decision date that will require them to actively ask for a continuation of the mailings.

Each job that must be accomplished within your process should be documented. It sounds daunting, I know, but think of how much easier it will be to train new people when you have training manuals ready to assist. The summary of each of these functions helps you to formulate job descriptions. And having well-constructed job descriptions will assist you in hiring the best people for the positions you need to fill.

Outsourcing

Years ago most advisors were absolutely opposed to outsourcing, particularly anything that involved client information. The fact is that many third-party vendors have a much better chance at protecting your data than you do. It's very costly to put technology and firewalls in place to protect data.

One of the questions to ask while reviewing your processes is whether any of the functions should be outsourced. Outsourcing can help you focus on core competencies, become more profitable, and streamline your processes. Look at each of the processes you've developed and consider them in terms of outsourcing. Use the guide in Exhibit 17.2 to help you.

EXHIBIT 17.2   Outsourcing Guide

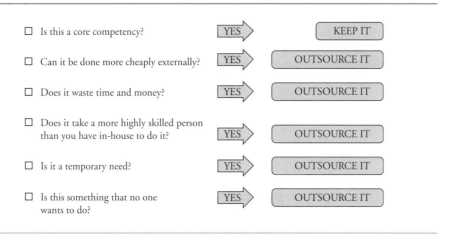

Almost anything can be outsourced, and many advisors have found areas where outsourcing improves profits and morale. Here are seven activities you might consider:

1. Data management
2. Portfolio management
3. Accounting, payables, and receivables
4. Payroll and benefits
5. Human resources
6. Training
7. Compliance

Of all these items, compliance is the one thing where you can outsource the activities, but you can never outsource the responsibility. I will talk about compliance later.

Sequencing

Devising sequencing steps to track work flow is one process that helps immensely. Utilizing client relationship management software allows practitioners to build a sequence profile to alert you to jobs that need to be done. Let me tell you how this works.

Whether you do a job once a week or once a year, it is efficient to document the steps needed to perform that task from beginning to end. Once that is complete, you are assured you will never forget a step, nor do you have to rethink it each time the task occurs. If you do the task infrequently, a sequencing document is a real time-saver. If more than one person works on the task, it's essential. I am a private pilot. Each time I step into the cockpit, I pull out my checklist that is permanently affixed to the visor. Even though I have many hours in the air, I always refer to my checklist for takeoff procedures. Just one time, relying on memory alone could mean disaster for me. I'm not sure you would crash if you forgot a step in preparation for your reviews or a client meeting, but you get the idea.

Our sequences are then loaded into Junxure (our CRM of choice). Then, when it's time to perform a task, Junxure sends out e-mails to all people involved. Each e-mail sets a time frame in which the work needs to be done. The e-mail keeps popping up until the task is completed. (That can be very irritating if you are behind, but it works just the same.) If delayed a set time beyond the due date, it also alerts a supervisor of the delay.

Back-Office Models

As you think about operations, it is wise to review your current structure. Moss Adams has identified three basic back-office models:

1. *Advisor-centric*—Designed for one advisor. If there are more advisors, each process is replicated with each advisor.
2. *Client-centric*—Clients direct activities, either choosing from a service/option menu or asking for one-offs, and advisors and staff accommodate.
3. *Process-centric*—Standardized process with few or no exceptions.

Moss Adams discovered in their survey of advisors that the most efficient and most profitable arrangement is process-centric, allowing for the most standardization and least duplication of efforts. Process-centric offices, depicted in Exhibit 17.3, are centralized, with support areas servicing many advisors.

EXHIBIT 17.3   Centralized Back Office

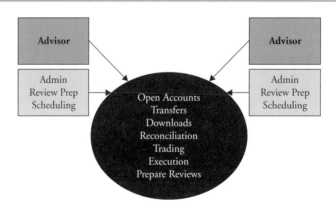

Naturally, if you are a sole practitioner, you will need to use your back-office resources differently. But you will want to be as highly processed as possible. Whatever the size, highly processed firms are more profitable.

Process and Communication

There is no question that e-mail has improved intra-office communication drastically. Yet as valuable as we find e-mail to be, it is important to use it properly. It is never a replacement for face-to-face communication. When we first got our e-mail system running, I would leave long directives to my new secretary each evening. She would answer these directives each morning. I would answer, then she would ask for clarification. This went on for three days until I realized I hadn't seen her during all that time. I walked into her office and remarked that she hadn't been in to see me yet that week. "Oh," she replied, "I thought you felt more comfortable communicating from a distance, you know, the *Wizard of Oz* management style."

Even Bill Gates, at a Microsoft CEO summit, acknowledged a problem with the emphasis we often place on e-mail today. "Sometimes people must meet face-to-face. If they are going back and forth more than three or four times on e-mail and are disagreeing, the wise thing is to get together and discuss the matter, because it's very hard to come to an agreement in an electronic mail exchange."

Clarity begins at home, inside the office, by promoting face-to-face conversation among staff. All our office systems are based on checks, balances, and cross-training. No one person is totally responsible for the completion of any single project. For small companies or work groups, this is important. If someone is absent, the work can still be completed.

Time Management and Processes

Julie Littlechild of Advisor Impact produced a time management report (www.Advisor impact.com—Practice Update 2007, "Time Management and Personal Productivity") based on the surveys done with U.S. advisors. The study concluded that many time management problems would be solved through better systems and processes.

As part of the report, Advisor Impact provided a self-assessment in time management. The 30 questions in the report are reprinted here for your use by permission.

1. I have clearly established goals for my own retirement.
2. I have clearly established goals for my business, which link directly to my personal retirement goals.
3. I have a clear definition of my ideal client and this links to my client selection criteria.
4. My clients are segmented based on the value they bring to the business, and service levels are clearly defined for each segment.
5. I have clearly defined processes within my business for routine activities (e.g., welcoming a new client or updating a financial plan).
6. I set specific time aside in my schedule to plan the upcoming:
   a. Year.
   b. Quarter.
   c. Month.
   d. Week.
   e. Day.
7. I spend at least 30 minutes in planning activities each week.
8. The roles and responsibilities on my team are clearly defined and documented.
9. I delegate all or most activities that I am not uniquely qualified to do.
10. The majority of my time is invested in activities that I believe will actively support my business management and growth goals.
11. My clients are educated as to how we work together as a team to manage the relationship.
12. I hold regular meetings with my team to review priorities for the week or day.
13. My team members all have sufficient training to do their jobs very well.
14. If a client calls and asks me to do something that is not part of my role description, I pass him or her over to the appropriate team member.

15. I have invested time into tracking how I spend my time now in order to identify inefficiencies.
16. I have a set schedule of meetings and tasks for each workday.
17. I deviate from my schedule only if there is some urgency with an important client.
18. I have a manageable number of to-do items on my list each day and can reasonably expect to complete all items on that list.
19. The tasks on my to-do list are clearly prioritized.
20. I have defined and measurable goals for the number of client and prospect meetings I will hold each week.
21. I schedule all or most of my activities, including personal activities, so that I know what needs to be accomplished each day.
22. I schedule my meetings back-to-back or with a defined amount of time between meetings.
23. I schedule all or most of my activities using an electronic calendar.
24. We preschedule client meetings well in advance so that nothing falls through the cracks with our clients.
25. I set specific time aside to respond to phone calls and e-mails, rather than dealing with them as they come in.
26. I have defined time blocks for core activities, such as meetings, business planning, or research.
27. I hold my client meetings at defined times each week (either specific days of the week or in defined time blocks throughout the week).
28. My office and desk are clean and well organized.
29. I do not need to work on evenings and weekends just to keep up with my workload.
30. I schedule enough time to recharge my batteries and be with my family.

This list may help you assess where you could use improvement.

The moral of this section? SYSTEMATIZING YOUR PRACTICE is essential for client retention, for saving money, for efficiency, for consistency, and ultimately, for transfer or sale. I've provided some ideas about systematizing your own practice. As you review what you're doing now, keep the following hints in mind:

- Any activity that has multiple steps should have a checklist so that no steps are forgotten.
- To the extent possible, important tasks should employ a system of checks and balances, necessitating more than one pair of eyes to review.
- For critical tasks, have a designated backup person and complete documentation.
- Consider outsourcing activities that are time-consuming and not productive. In the long run, buying these services may save you money.

People Make It Happen

It is virtually impossible for you to meet all your clients' needs without the help of a good support staff. As your practice grows, delegating to key people is crucial to your growth and success. Yet, nearly every advisor I know has experienced difficulty finding the right people, hiring them, and keeping them. The larger the practice, the more difficult that job gets.

There are many proven ways to attract good personnel, but the only way to keep them is through quality training; good compensation and benefits; and a nurturing, stimulating, challenging work environment. The success of your practice depends on the people who interact with your clients every day. Long-term clients are comfortable and secure with long-term employees.

You've probably spent significant time figuring out how to manage your clients' expectations. It's worth the effort to figure out how to manage your staff's expectations as well. Just remember, where clients are concerned, there is no way to compensate for lousy support staff.

Mentoring and Internships

A good source for new staff is through internships. Internships provide a free look at potential employees, and many interns are offered positions with the same firm when they graduate. On the downside, this requires a two- to three-year training period, and a considerable corporate investment of time and money. This method of promoting from within does not necessarily mean that you are hiring someone who cannot hit the ground running. There are currently hundreds of academic degree programs at colleges and universities globally that offer financial planning or investment management programs affiliated with the CFP Board of Standards or CFA Institute. Programs may be delivered at the undergraduate or graduate level, and many may include practice management classes, as well as specialized courses such as charitable gifting and behavioral finance.

Interns are young, eager to learn, enthusiastic, grateful for the work, and always able to teach you something.[3]

Selecting and Retaining Good Staff

Before you hire, be sure that you have a complete job description written so that you can search for the exact position that you require. Be specific about the responsibilities and career path. New entrants in today's financial profession want to know what their future opportunities will be.

Next, you will want to advertise your position to get the best possible responses. CFA Institute (www.cfainstitute.org), the Financial Planning Association (www.fpanet.org), NAPFA (www.napfa.org), and Schwab Institutional (www.schwabinstitutional.com) have employment opportunities on their web sites. Many universities, such as Texas Tech (www.pfp.ttu.edu), also have employment opportunity programs for current students and graduates.

Invest a few dollars in testing your potential candidates. There are some great tests available that will help you make good choices. It is far too expensive in time and money to bring on someone just because you think it might work. It is far better to get some help with your decision making. I recommend the following:

- Myers & Briggs (www.myersbriggs.org) offers a personality test to help you understand the personality characteristics that will best fit with your current practice and your future plans.
- Kolbe Indexes (www.kolbe.com) are work-style assessments, to help you gain knowledge about how a candidate will work with you, other staff, and clients. Kolbe tests help uncover natural instincts and innate abilities.

---

[3]Texas Tech in Lubbock, Texas, where Deena teaches, requires all undergraduates to complete an internship in financial services prior to graduation. The semester prior to their internship experience, the students take a professional practices course to prepare a business plan and a marketing plan so they can assist in some practical ways when they serve as interns. Universities such as Texas Tech also provide extensive software training in financial planning, portfolio management, and client relationship management, as well as portfolio software such as Morningstar/Ibbotson, MoneyGuidePro, NaviPlan, Portfolio Center, Junxure, Sunguard, Moneytree, and iRebal.

- Wonderlic Personnel Test (www.wonderlic.com) measures general intelligence or cognitive ability to help you determine if your candidate has the ability to perform well on the job.
- Financial DNA Profiles (www.financialdna.com) will determine how your staff makes financial decisions at their most basic, visceral level. It will also provide communication keys to facilitate the best communication among you, staff, and clients.

Interviewing

Tests alone will not give you the comfort of bringing the best people into your firm. Develop some situational questions for young, new hires that will test critical thinking skills, leadership, or management capabilities. Try some of these:

- You are a first-year financial planner. You have been asked to sit in on a planning meeting with clients. Before the meeting, you have familiarized yourself with the client's situation by reading the client diary, and you have also worked on the update of the client's financial plan. In the meeting, the senior planner makes a statement that is clearly not factual. You assume that this is unintentional. What do you do, and why?
- You have been working for the same fee-based firm for two years. One of the firm's clients asks if you will take their children (ages 23 and 27) as clients. The children's assets do not meet the firm's minimums. How do you handle this situation?
- You have a well-qualified prospect who says that she is prepared to take reasonable risk, but that she is expecting a return in the 12 to 15 percent range annually. What do you tell this prospect, and why?

Don't ask belt-roller questions!

"If I go into any drawer in your house, what will I find?" If they tell you they roll their belts, you'll conclude they are well organized. Any idiot can figure out what you'd like them to answer. Well, let's put it this way: If they can't figure it out, you wouldn't want them anyway.

"Are you organized?" Realistically, how do you think a smart person would answer this? Stick to Socratic questions (open-ended) that will allow your prospective candidate to think and talk.

Here are 10 questions you might consider:

1. What kinds of projects have you worked on?
2. What is your personal definition of success?
3. What motivates you?
4. Tell me about yourself.
5. What do you think you can contribute to our practice?
6. What are your strengths and struggles?
7. What goals have you set for yourself in the next five years? Ten years?
8. Have you ever had a conflict with someone at work? How was that resolved?
9. Do you have plans for further education?
10. Would you rather work with information or with people?

Some questions are taboo under any circumstances, so don't ask a woman if she is pregnant or plans to be. Don't ask if someone has ever declared bankruptcy, has served in the military, or is gay. Stay away from questions of nationality, sex, weight, or religion.

It's a good idea to interview your prospective employees more than once, giving them different opportunities to impress you. It is also a good idea to have your key personnel interview them as well. Prospective employees will often become more relaxed around your other staff and will make a different impression with them.

Be prepared to discuss salary and benefits with serious prospects. To see if you are in the ballpark, you might ask, "What are your salary requirements?" Your compensation structure should be well-defined, industry-competitive, and incorporated in your career path structure. I discuss compensation and career path structures shortly.

Last, don't spend your interview time talking about what you want. You won't gain any new information by listening to yourself. Let your prospective hire ask you about the job and responsibilities.

Taking Care of Your Most Valuable Asset: Your Staff

Let's assume that you find a candidate you really want to hire. First, I suggest that you provide the candidate an offer letter, stating that you are formally offering a position, what the position is, and what salary and benefits you are providing. Extending your offer in writing formalizes your intention and guards against any misunderstanding.

Your staff members are the people who make the very first impression on your prospects and can enhance or destroy relationships with existing clients. If you want to attract great clients, you must hire great staff, train them, and then empower them. You must give them a sense of self-worth beyond their value as employees, and then compensate them accordingly. Just as you would with your best clients, find out what they expect from this relationship and manage their expectations. We want our staff to know how important they are to our business, so we spend significant time demonstrating how much we value them.

But employee bonding and creating the right environment make up only one aspect of your relationship with your employees. The career path and the compensation you provide will keep your employees happy and satisfied. Rebecca Pomering of Moss Adams explains the compensation issues this way: "Your employee should be able to say, 'If I do more of X, then I will get Y.' That includes salary, incentive compensation, and career paths."

Compensation

Design your compensation based on the career path the individual has chosen. If you want to ensure that your new hires remain successful, satisfied members of the staff, provide flexibility; career paths should not be written in stone. One of our advisors began working in back-office operations. Each year for several years, we met and discussed his plans for the future. Every year, he told us he was happy in operations and had no plans to do anything else. Then one year, because of personnel changes, we asked him to sit in on some client meetings until we hired someone new. Within the month, he declared an intention to take Certified Financial Planner (CFP) courses and accept the responsibilities of an advisor. He has subsequently earned both the CFP and CFA designations, is an owner in the firm, and is our chief investment officer.

Compensation is composed of base salary, benefits, and incentive compensation. Base compensation and benefits are relatively straightforward; where you need to give special consideration is to the incentives you put in place. The key is to align your incentive compensation to encourage the behavior that you want to reinforce (e.g., retention, new business, increased technical skills). In addition, consider issues such as achievement of professional designations, professional development, and public recognition.

Frankly, most new advisors want to see some equity in their future, while many founders are reluctant to structure equity ownership plans and reject even the smallest percentage of equity ownership in their firms. A misunderstanding seems to exist on both sides. On the one hand, older advisors need young, enthusiastic, well-educated people to join us in our efforts, particularly if we are thinking about management succession and exit strategies. On the other hand, those who want to succeed us will need to demonstrate leadership abilities and entrepreneurial qualities to earn the right to purchase equity. As I see it, equity is not a gift for working five years. Plenty of business models, including law and accounting, seem to have successful models for integrating new people into practices and providing equity. In any case, advisors, young and old, need each other.

Recently, I needed to see a doctor, but I was in my Texas home, where I have not established new medical relationships. My old family doctor is in Florida, where I also have a home, but this wouldn't wait. I took myself to a local clinic that immediately allowed me to see the doctor, a young man in his mid-30s. He greeted me warmly, then turned to the computer terminal attached to the wall in the examining room. After unsuccessfully connecting to the system, he opened the door to the hall and yelled, "Katie! Is there something wrong with the computer system? I can't connect and I can't do anything in here without it. Get John on it right now!" Despite the pain I was in, I cracked up. My old doctor would have been poking and prodding by now and probably already formulating a diagnosis. The truth is, this young doctor was very good, and from the half-dozen questions he asked, ordered tests that confirmed my condition.

This incident only confirmed what I suspected; it takes an old doctor and a new physician to provide good patient care. Think about it; the old doctor:

- Has taken care of some patients for decades, developing tight, loyal relationships.
- Has learned from an older set of principles.
- Prefers paper charts, prescriptions, and textbooks.
- Is an excellent diagnostician, using tests to confirm.
- Relies on standard medications.

The new physician, in contrast:

- Has not had long-term patients.
- Is well versed in the newest tests and drugs.
- Was trained with computerized medical records and cyber-literature.
- Uses tests to diagnose.
- Explores newer medications and tests frequently.

Now think of this analogy in terms of a financial planning practice. Together older and newer advisors can bring the newest thinking and the best relationships together to benefit all clients. The ability for more experienced advisors to mentor and guide newer planners, and the ability for younger planners to bring new, fresh ideas and techniques to the table are both invaluable.

Bringing your new hires on board is as important as their selection. Develop operational policies around each position in your firm to ensure that your new hires understand their responsibilities. Review your staff frequently to hand out warm fuzzies, as well as help them focus or change behavior that is unacceptable. Help your staff develop benchmarks so they can see their own progress. Finally, empower your staff to make critical decisions as necessary. Back them up if they have used poor judgment, but guide them to better choices in the future.

Have them complete a self-assessment form each year. You will be surprised how honest your people will be with their own strengths and struggles.

PARTING COMMENTS

The information in this chapter is how Harold and Deena run their practice. We hope it helps you in shaping your own philosophy and practice. Regardless of how you run your practice, remember the importance of the three Ps: having a philosophy, establishing processes that support that philosophy, and developing a strong team of people to deliver on helping your clients meet their goals.

RESOURCES

Evensky, Harold, and Deena Katz. 2004. *The Investment Think Tank: Theory, Strategy and Practice for Advisors*. Hoboken, NJ: Bloomberg Press/John Wiley & Sons.

Katz, Deena. 2009. *Deena Katz's Complete Guide to Practice Management: Tips, Tools, and Templates for the Financial Advisor*. Hoboken, NJ: Bloomberg Press/John Wiley & Sons.

ABOUT THE AUTHORS

Harold Evensky, CFP®, AIF®, President, Evensky & Katz

Mr. Evensky is the President of Evensky & Katz. Prior to forming his own company, he served as a Vice President of Investments with major investment banking firms. Mr. Evensky received his bachelor's and master's degrees from Cornell University. He has been a featured speaker on investment topics at numerous national and international conventions, including the AICPA, the American College, the American Society CLU and ChFC.

He has served as Chair of the TIAA-CREF Institute Investment Advisor Advisory Board and is a member of the Financial Planning Association, the Academy of Financial Services, and CFA Institute, and is an associate member of the American Bar Association. He is the past Chair of the International CFP® Council, the CFP® Board of Governors, the Board of Examiners, and the Board of Appeals. He has served on the Editorial Advisory Board of the *Asia Financial Planning Journal*, a columnist for Worth.com, and a member of the Editorial Advisory Board of the *Journal of Financial Planning*, and he is currently the research columnist for *Financial Planning* magazine. He has also served on the National Board of the IAFP and the Charles Schwab Institutional Advisory Board and Council.

Stephen M. Horan, PhD, CFA, Head, Professional Education Content and Private Wealth, CFA Institute

As head of professional education content for CFA Institute, Dr. Horan is responsible for leading a team of content specialists who develop lifelong educational opportunities for CFA Institute members and other serious investment professionals. Dr. Horan joined CFA Institute as Head of Private Wealth Management in 2007. Previously, he was a professor of finance at St. Bonaventure University, principal of Alesco Advisors LLC, and a financial analyst and forensic economist in private practice, providing expert witness testimony and preparing economic impact studies. Dr. Horan has published dozens of articles in finance and economics journals, including the *Financial Analysts Journal* and the *Journal of Wealth Management*. He has been the author or coauthor of several books, has received numerous research awards, and is frequently cited in the press. Dr. Horan earned a BBA in finance with a minor in mathematics from St. Bonaventure University and a PhD in finance with a minor in economics from the State University of New York at Buffalo.

Thomas R. Robinson, PhD, CFA, CFP®, Managing Director, Educational Division, CFA Institute

As managing director of the Education Division at CFA Institute, Dr. Robinson leads and develops the teams responsible for the production and delivery of educational content and examinations for CFA Program and CIPM candidates, and the educational content for CFA Institute members and other investment professionals. Dr. Robinson joined CFA Institute as Head, Educational Content in 2007. Previously, he was an accounting faculty member at the

University of Miami, serving as director of the master of professional accounting and personal financial planning programs. Concurrently, he was managing director of a private wealth investment advisory firm and served as a consultant in valuation and financial statement analysis. Prior to working in academia, he worked in public accounting, performing tax and financial planning services. Dr. Robinson is a CFA charterholder, a Certified Public Accountant (CPA) (Ohio), a Certified Financial Planner (CFP®), and a Chartered Alternative Investment Analyst (CAIA). He holds a bachelor's degree in economics from the University of Pennsylvania, and a master's and doctorate from Case Western Reserve University. He was active both locally and nationally as a volunteer for CFA Institute and CFA Miami prior to joining the CFA Institute staff.

ABOUT THE CFA INSTITUTE INVESTMENT SERIES

CFA Institute is pleased to provide you with the CFA Institute Investment Series, which covers major areas in the field of investments. We provide this best-in-class series for the same reason we have been chartering investment professionals for more than 45 years: to lead the investment profession globally by setting the highest standards of ethics, education, and professional excellence.

The books in the CFA Institute Investment Series contain practical, globally relevant material. They are intended both for those contemplating entry into the extremely competitive field of investment management as well as for those seeking a means of keeping their knowledge fresh and up to date. This series was designed to be user friendly and highly relevant. Each book in the series includes extensive references for those who would like to probe a given concept.

We hope you find this series helpful in your efforts to grow your investment knowledge, whether you are a relatively new entrant or an experienced veteran ethically bound to keep up to date in the ever-changing market environment. As a long-term, committed participant in the investment profession and a not-for-profit global membership association, CFA Institute is pleased to provide you with this opportunity.

THE TEXTS

One of the most prominent texts over the years in the investment management industry has been Maginn and Tuttle's *Managing Investment Portfolios: A Dynamic Process*. The third edition updates key concepts from the 1990 second edition. Some of the more experienced members of our community own the prior two editions and will add the third edition to their libraries. Not only does this seminal work take the concepts from the other readings and put them in a portfolio context, but it also updates the concepts of alternative investments, performance presentation standards, portfolio execution, and, very importantly, managing individual investor portfolios. Focusing attention away from institutional portfolios and toward the individual investor makes this edition an important and timely work.

Quantitative Investment Analysis focuses on some key tools that are needed by today's professional investor. In addition to classic time value of money, discounted cash flow applications, and probability material, there are two aspects that can be of value over traditional thinking.

The first involves the chapters dealing with correlation and regression that ultimately figure into the formation of hypotheses for purposes of testing. This gets to a critical skill that challenges many professionals: the ability to distinguish useful information from the over-whelming quantity of available data. For most investment researchers and managers, their analysis is not solely the result of newly created data and tests that they perform. Rather, they synthesize and analyze primary research done by others. Without a rigorous manner by which to understand quality research, you cannot understand good research, nor do you have a basis on which to evaluate less rigorous research.

Second, the last chapter of *Quantitative Investment Analysis* covers portfolio concepts and takes the reader beyond the traditional capital asset pricing model (CAPM) type of tools and into the more practical world of multifactor models and arbitrage pricing theory.

Equity Asset Valuation is a particularly cogent and important resource for anyone involved in estimating the value of securities and understanding security pricing. A well-informed professional knows that the common forms of equity valuation—dividend discount model-ing, free cash flow modeling, price-earnings models, and residual income models—can all be reconciled with one another under certain assumptions. With a deep understanding of the underlying assumptions, the professional investor can better understand what other investors assume when calculating their valuation estimates. This text has a global orientation, including emerging markets. The second edition provides new coverage of private company valuation and expanded coverage of required rate of return estimation.

Fixed Income Analysis has been at the forefront of new concepts in recent years, and this particular text offers some of the most recent material for the seasoned professional who is not a fixed-income specialist. The application of option and derivative technology to the once-staid province of fixed income has helped contribute to an explosion of thought in this area. Not only have professionals been challenged to stay up to speed with credit derivatives, swaptions, collateralized mortgage securities, mortgage-backed securities, and other vehicles, but this explosion of products strained the world's financial markets and tested central banks to provide sufficient oversight. Armed with a thorough grasp of the new exposures, the professional investor is much better able to anticipate and understand the challenges our central bankers and markets face.

Corporate Finance: A Practical Approach is a solid foundation for those looking to achieve lasting business growth. In today's competitive business environment, companies must find innovative ways to enable rapid and sustainable growth. This text equips readers with the foundational knowledge and tools for making smart business decisions and formulating strategies to maximize company value. It covers everything from managing relationships between stakeholders to evaluating mergers and acquisitions bids, as well as the companies behind them.

Through extensive use of real-world examples, readers will gain critical perspective into interpreting corporate financial data, evaluating projects, and allocating funds in ways that increase corporate value. Readers will gain insights into the tools and strategies used in modern corporate financial management.

International Financial Statement Analysis is designed to address the ever-increasing need for investment professionals and students to think about financial statement analysis from a global perspective. The text is a practically oriented introduction to financial statement analysis that is distinguished by its combination of a true international orientation, a struc-tured presentation style, and abundant illustrations and tools covering concepts as they are introduced in the text. The authors cover this discipline comprehensively and with an eye to ensuring the reader's success at all levels in the complex world of financial statement analysis.

Investments: Principles of Portfolio and Equity Analysis provides an accessible yet rigorous introduction to portfolio and equity analysis. Portfolio planning and portfolio management are presented within a context of up-to-date, global coverage of security markets, trading, and market-related concepts and products. The essentials of equity analysis and valuation are explained in detail and profusely illustrated. The book includes coverage of practitioner-important but often neglected topics, such as industry analysis. Throughout, the focus is on the practical application of key concepts with examples drawn from both emerging and developed markets. Each chapter affords the reader many opportunities to self-check his or her understanding of topics. In contrast to other texts, the chapters are collaborations of respected senior investment practitioners and leading business school teachers from around the globe. By virtue of its well-rounded, expert, and global perspectives, the book should be of interest to anyone who is looking for an introduction to portfolio and equity analysis.

The New Wealth Management: The Financial Advisor's Guide to Managing and Investing Client Assets is an updated version of Harold Evensky's mainstay reference guide for wealth managers. Harold Evensky, Stephen Horan, and Thomas Robinson updated the core text of the 1997 first edition and added an abundance of new material to fully reflect today's investment challenges. The text provides authoritative coverage across the full spectrum of wealth management and serves as a comprehensive guide for financial advisors. The book expertly blends investment theory and real-world applications and is written in the same thorough but highly accessible style as the first edition.

ABOUT THE
CFA PROGRAM

The Chartered Financial Analyst® designation (CFA®) is a globally recognized standard of excellence for measuring the competence and integrity of investment professionals. To earn the CFA charter, candidates must successfully pass through the CFA Program, a global graduate-level self-study program that combines a broad curriculum with professional conduct requirements as preparation for a wide range of investment specialties.

Anchored by a practice-based curriculum, the CFA Program is focused on the knowledge identified by professionals as essential to the investment decision-making process. This body of knowledge maintains current relevance through a regular, extensive survey of practicing CFA charterholders across the globe. The curriculum covers 10 general topic areas, ranging from equity and fixed-income analysis to portfolio management to corporate finance, all with a heavy emphasis on the application of ethics in professional practice. Known for its rigor and breadth, the CFA Program curriculum highlights principles common to every market so that professionals who earn the CFA designation have a thoroughly global investment perspective and a profound understanding of the global marketplace.

www.cfainstitute.org

INDEX

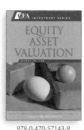